Buddhism and Peace:
Theory and Practice

Edited by Chanju Mun

Honolulu, USA

Blue Pine
**Honolulu, Hawaii

I wish to dedicate this humble book to Ven. Daewon Ki, with whose deep insights and ideas it is originated. I am also publishing it in order to commemorate his 30th anniversary for propagating Buddhism to his newly adopted nation, the United States of America since 1975.

Contents

Part 1. *Individual Peace*

Part 2. *Society / Conflict Resolution*

Part 3. *Environment*

Part 4. *Health*

Part 5. *East Asian Buddhism*

Notes

1. The Pinyin system is used for Chinese terms, the Korean Government Romanization System revised in 2000 for Korean ones, and the Hepburn system for Japanese ones.
2. Diacritics are used on most of Sanskrit and Pali terms.
3. Foreign terms, those not included in the Webster English Dictionary, appear in italics.
4. Where authors have romanized their names in ways contrary to East Asian Standard Romanization Systems have i adapted their spellings.
5. Where names have not previously been romanized, the editors have done so using East Asian Standard Romanization Systems.
6. Standard PTS abbreviations are used for Pali texts.
7. This book is edited based on the 15th edition of *The Chicago Manual of Style* (Chicago: University of Chicago Press, 2003).
8. Each contributor's academic affiliation and title reflects their status as of the year 1995.

Abbreviations

BG	*Bhagavād-gīta*
GVC	*Gaṇḍavyūha-sūtra*
NB	*Dai Nihon bukkyō zenshō*
ND	*Nihon daizōkyō*
PTS	The Pali Text Society
T	*Taishō shinshū daizōkyō*
UPS	*Upāsaka Precept Sūtra*

Pali Text Abbreviations

A	*Aṅguttara*
Abhp	*Abhidhānappadīpikā*
Ap	*Apadāna*
Av.Ś.	*Avadāna-śataka*
Bdhd	*Buddhadatta*
Bu	*Buddha-vaṃsa*
Cp	*Cariyā-piṭaka*
D	*Dīgha*
Dāvs	*Dāṭhā- vaṃsa*
Dh	*Dhammapada*
Dhs	*Dhammasangaṇi*
Dhs trsl	*Atthasālinī*
Divy	*Divyāvadana*
Dpvs	*Dīpa-vaṃsa*
It	*Itivuttaka*
J	*Jātaka*
Jtm	*Jātakamālā*
Kacc	*Kaccāyana*
Kh	*Khuddakapāṭha*
Kvu	*Kathāvatthu*
Lal.V.	*Lalita Vistara*
M	*Majjhima*
Mhbv	*Mahābodhi- vaṃsa*

Abbreviations

Miln	*Milinda-pañha*
M Vastu	*Mahā-vastu*
Mvyut	*Mahāvyutpatti*
Nd¹	*Mahāniddesa*
Nd²	*Cullaniddesa*
Nett	*Netti-pakaraṇa*
Pgdp	*Pañcagati-dīpana*
Ps	*Paṭisambhidā-magga*
Pug	*Puggala-paññatti*
Pv	*Petavatthu*
S	*Saṃyutta*
Sdhp	*Saddhammopāyana*
Śikṣ	*Śikṣāsamuccaya*
Sn	*Sutta-nipāta*
Th 1	*Theragāthā*
Th 2	*Therigāthā*
Ud	*Udāna*
Vbh	*Vibhanga*
Vin	*Vinaya*
Vism	*Visuddhi-magga*
Vv	*Vimānavatthu*

Preface

This humble book, edited by me, originated completely from my personal and precious encounter with my spiritual guide and the religious advisor, Ven. Daewon Ki, founder of Korean Buddhist Dae Won Sa Temple of Hawaii, the biggest Korean Buddhist Temple in North America, in the end of 1995 in Honolulu, the United States of America.

The following brief explanation on my relation with him might help readers understand how this book has been published. In late 1995, I was able to come to the United States through his invitation and began to have a deep relation with him. Since then, he has remained a spiritual advisor and a major financial patron to me.

In mid-1995, I was discharged from the Korean Army as a Buddhist chaplain officer after serving around three and half a years. Afterwards, I traveled several nations with deep connections with Buddhism, such as India, Nepal, China, Thailand and so on, for half a year. While in travel, I recognized how important English was as a communication medium in the international context.

In late 1995, Ven. Daewon Ki invited me to come to the United States where I naturally had to have opportunity to learn English. I cannot forget how much he helped me become accustomed to the new world during my stay in Hawaii between December 1995 and August 1997. For instance, he took me to the Social Security Administration Office to let me apply for a Social Security Number, arranged for me to take the driver license exam and helped me to open a bank account.

He gave opportunities for me to work and lead religious services in his temple. He trained me how to organize lay Buddhist groups and how to consult lay Buddhists in trouble to adjust in their adopted nation. In addition to temple works, I could learn English in an ESL program at the University of Hawaii – Manoa via his financial support.

He was my closest senior and religious advisor until my departure in August 1997 to study Buddhism academically in the Buddhist Studies program in the Department of Languages and Cultures of Asia at the University of Wisconsin – Madison, where I received a Ph.D. in Buddhist Studies in 2002. To this day, he remains the most important advisor and the most reliable senior monk for me to consult and to solve difficult problems. Whenever I need his help, advice and suggestions, he is very kind and considerate to answer my requests.

This book is composed of the thirty-one articles presented in the Seventh International Seminar on Buddhism and Leadership for Peace in Honolulu during June 3-8, 1995. I want to generally introduce the background of the International Seminars on Buddhism and Leadership for Peace, 1983-1995. To make readers understand the seminars more concretively, I will briefly explain the Korean Buddhist Dae Won Sa Temple of Hawaii.

The temple complex of Dae Won Sa originated from Ven. Daewon, who arrived in the United States in 1975. On a mountainside in Honolulu's Palolo Valley, he began the first structure in 1980 and finished it in 1982. The plans for the larger complex were first drawn in 1983 and construction began in 1984. The work has been long and arduous and is still going on. It is the only traditionally structured Korean Buddhist temple and the largest cluster of Korean traditional architectural works outside the boundaries of Korea. It is composed of the Four Heavenly Kings Gate, the World Peace Pagoda, the Bell Tower, the Hall of Memorial to the Departed, Donor's Tablets, the Main Hall, the Statue of Maitreya Bodhisattva, Buddhist Cultural Center Building, several residential houses and other structures.

Since 1983, seven international seminars on Buddhism and Leadership for Peace have been convened. They originated from the vision of Ven. Daewon Ki. The concept underlying the seminar is to bring Buddhist thinkers, peace leaders and peace scholars together from several countries on themes of common interest for mutual benefit. Although Buddhism provides the convening inspiration, all participants need not be Buddhist in any formal sense. So he, leading these seminars, has opened the seminar to all scholars who want to participate in regardless of their religion or belief. Thus participants have included Christians, Gandhians, Hindus, Jains, Muslims, Marxists, Secular Humanists and others.

The first seminar was held in Honolulu, Hawaii during October 22-28, 1983 on the theme of "Buddhism and Leadership for Peace." It was held under the auspice of the Dae Won Sa Temple of Hawaii and was co-sponsored by the Department of Political Science, University of Hawaii at Manoa. Professor Glenn Paige from the Political Science Department served as the Director of the Seminar. There were three discussion papers on Buddhism by Wimal Dissanayake, leadership by Chaiwat Satha-Anand and peace by Johan Galtung. Participants came from China, South Korea, Sri Lanka, Soviet Union, Thailand and the USA. The seminar is contained in Glenn D. Paige, ed., *Buddhism and Leadership for Peace* (Honolulu: Dae Won Sa Buddhist Temple of Hawaii, 1984).

The second seminar was held in Tokyo, Japan, during December 2-7, 1985 on the theme of "Buddhism in the Context of Various Countries." The seminar was held under the joint auspices of the Dae Won Sa Temple of Hawaii and the Peace Research Institute of Soka University. Professor Glenn Paige from the Political Science Department of the University of Hawaii – Manoa served as the

Director of the Seminar. Context papers included those on Bali by Gedong Bagoes Oka, China by Zhao Baoxu, India by N. Radhakrishnan, Japan by Nakano Tsuyoshi and Takamura Tadashige, Mongolia by I. Ochirbal, the Soviet Union by V. Baykov and V. Hlynov, Thailand by Chaiwat Satha-Anand and the United States by Ryo Imamura. Bali, India and Mongalia were added to the nations represented in the first seminar. The proceedings are included in Soka University, Peace Research Institute, ed., *Buddhism and Leadership for Peace* (Tokyo: Soka University, Peace Research Institute, 1986).

The third seminar was held in Honolulu, Hawaii during May 23-28, 1987, on a theme suggested by Chaiwat Satha-Anand from Thailand, "Peace Making in Buddhist Contexts." It was co-sponsored by the Dae Won Sa Temple of Hawaii and the Peace Institute of the University of Hawaii. Participants included those from China, India, Japan, South Korea, Mongolia, the Soviet Union, Thailand, and the USA. Principal discussion papers concentrated on Sri Lanka by A. T. Ariyaratne, Thailand by Chaiwat Satha-Anand and Vietnam by Thich Nhat Hanh. Professor Glenn Paige from the Political Science Department served as the Director of the Seminar. I am planning to publish selected papers from this seminar together with those from other sources in a general volume on *Buddhism and Nonviolence.*

The fourth seminar was held in Ulan Bator, Mongolia during August 16-24, 1989 on theme of "Buddhism and Nonviolent Global Solving." It was held under the joint sponsorship of the Dae Won Sa Temple of Hawaii, the Asian Buddhist Conference for Peace (ABCP) and the Center for Global Nonviolence Planning Project of the Institute for Peace, University of Hawaii. Professor Glenn Paige from the Political Science Department served as the Director of the Seminar. Theme of papers included Buddhism by Sulak Sivaraksa, leadership for global problem solving by Mushakoji Kinhide, and the context for peaceful global transformation by Johan Galtung. Discussions focused on the relevance of Buddhism for solving the interrelated problems of disarmament, economic justice, human rights, environmental preservation, and transnational problem-solving cooperation. Participants came from China, India, Japan, two Koreas, Mongolia, the Soviet Union, Sri Lanka, Thailand, Vietnam and the USA. Some seminar papers have been published in the journal of the Asia Buddhist Conference for Peace, *Buddhists for Peace*, Vol. 11, No. 4 (1989).

The fifth seminar was held in Seoul, Korea during November 18-21, 1991 on theme of "Exploration of Ways to Put Buddhist Thought into Social Practice for Peace and Justice." It was held under the joint sponsorship of Dae Won Sa Temple of Hawaii and Korean Buddhist Research Institute of Dongguk University, cosponsored by Korean Buddhist Federation and Korean Buddhism Promotion Foundation. Prof. Jung Il Doh from the Department of English Literature of the Kyung Hee University served as the Director of the Seminar. More than 60 participants came from Canada, China, Germany, India, Japan, Korea, Mongolia, Sri Lanka, Sweden, Thailand, Vietnam and the USA. I am planning to publish selected papers from this seminar as one of serial volumes on *Buddhism and Leadership for Peace.*

The sixth seminar was held in Honolulu during November 24-28, 1993 on the theme "A Buddhist World View and Concept of Peace." The seminar was held under the joint auspices of the Dae Won Sa Buddhist Cultural Institute of Hawaii and the Department of Philosophy at the University of Hawaii. Ten participants presented papers related to early Buddhism, Mahāyāna, East Asian Buddhism as well as modern Buddhist movements in Asia and the West. Participants included those from Korea, Sri Lanka and the USA. Professor David Kalupahana of the Department of Philosophy served as the Director of the Seminar. I am planning to publish the seminar's papers under the title "Buddhist World Views and Concept of Peace" as one of serial volumes on *Buddhism and Leadership for Peace*.

The seventh seminar was held in Honolulu during June 3-8, 1995 on the theme of "Buddhism and Peace: Theory and Practice." The seminar was held under the joint sponsorship of the Dae Won Sa Buddhist Cultural Institute of Hawaii and the Department of Philosophy, University of Hawaii at Manoa. More than 40 scholars and religious leaders from Asia, Europe and the USA participated in the seminar. Papers deal with five themes: (1) Individual and Peace, (2) Society and Conflict Resolution, (3) Environment, (4) Health and (5) East Asian Buddhism. Professor Kalupahana directed the Seminar. I am currently working on this book under the title of the same theme *Buddhism and Peace: Theory and Practice* and plan to publish it.

As you have seen in the above passages, the articles presented in the first, second and fourth international seminars on Buddhism and Leadership for Peace, held in 1983, 1985 and1989 respectively were selected and published. This book that I am working on for now is totally the outcome of the seventh international seminar on the same topic in 1995.

In the near future, I am planning to publish remaining three books by selecting and editing the articles submitted in the third, fifth and sixth international seminars held in 1987, 1991 and 1993 respectively as the serial volumes. However, unfortunately, the international seminar has not been continued until to now after 1995. I really hope to revitalize the international seminar in order to promote the peace in this struggling society domestically and internationally by succeeding the original vision of Ven. Daewon Ki in Hawaii or in any place as soon as possible.

Chanju Mun
Los Angeles, California
January 2006

Acknowledgements

First of all, I want to express my sincere appreciation to Ven. Daewon. He provided me an invaluable opportunity for me to edit and to publish the precious articles that were presented in the Seventh International Seminar on Buddhism and Leadership for Peace held in 1995 on the theme of "Buddhism and Peace: Theory and Practice." He convened seven international seminars from 1983 to 1995 biannually, each of which has its own theme under his profound vision to promote the peace in this problematic human society.

I wish to extend my thanks to Ven. Dawon's religious followers without whose financial supports and various activities the seven successive seminars could not be held. They enthusiastically supported for Ven. Daewon in constructing the huge temple complex in the Palolo valley in Honolulu, Hawaii and in making a peace bridge between two Koreas in particular and two political antagonist blocs in general during the cold war period.

I am very appreciative of the more than forty participants and particularly the contributors of the thirty one articles. I am also honored to include the precious articles by the worldwide well-known eminent scholars in this humble book. Especially, I thank the seminar director Prof. David Kalupahana and his seminar assistants Mr. In-sub Hur and Mr. John T. Smith. I am tremendously sharing with their organization frame that they had in the seminar when I make the table of contents in this book.

I cannot omit my heartfelt thanks to my close colleague Dr. Ronald S. Green who edited this book English and offered invaluable ideas and suggestions on it. Dr. Green also created the index and made the camera-ready preparations necessary for publishing this humble book. My student Ms. Ling Yu Chang also provided much help with the countless miscellaneous items needing editing in order to produce this final version.

Finally, I attribute my humble book to my religious master Ven. Jeongwoo who has been guiding me for two decades. He has also provided me precious opportunities to study Buddhism at various education and monastic institutions in Korea and overseas with his financial support. He introduced to me his close senior monk Ven. Hyunho, the spiritual leader of Korea-sah Buddhist Temple in Los Angeles. Ven. Hyunho and his religious followers have sincerely helped me to settle down in Southern California.

Introduction

Ronald S. Green
Chanju Mun

This book is composed of the thirty-one articles presented at the Seventh International Seminar on Buddhism and Leadership for Peace in Honolulu. The seminar was held from June 3rd through the 8th of 1995, on the theme: "Buddhism and Peace: Theory and Practice." We can now see that the ideas contained in the papers presented at that time were and continue to be particularly momentous in the advancement of perhaps the most significant development in Buddhist philosophy and practice in our time: socially engaged Buddhism.

Looking at its more than two thousand years of history, Buddhism is often characterized by historians as highly adaptable to time and place. In keeping with this, the emergence of socially engaged Buddhism is seen as a significant feature in the evolution of Buddhism over the past century. In terms of the world today, the last twenty years in particular has been a time of great growth in the area of socially engaged Buddhism, owning in no small part to the activities of some of the authors of these articles. In pace with recent eruptions of war and political aggression throughout the world, these Buddhists and theorists are increasingly emerging as advocates of peace and nonviolence. Characterized by a reorientation of Buddhist soteriology and ethics, engaged Buddhism identifies and addresses sources of human suffering beyond individual cravings and ignorance, expanding such classical concepts to include social, political and economic injustices, warfare and violence, and environmental issues. Today, engaged Buddhism is manifested in a wide range of popular movements, development projects and service organizations in Asia and the West. As such, it emerges as a potentially potent force for social betterment in many parts of the world. Like Dr. Martin Luther King Jr., some of the writers in this volume have become international symbols of struggle against repression and brutality.

The Seventh Seminar on Buddhism and Leadership for Peace was held under the joint sponsorship of the Dae Won Sa Buddhist Cultural Institute of Hawaii and the Department of Philosophy of the University of Hawaii at Monoa. Professor David Kalupahana served as director of the seminar and is a contributor to this book. More than forty participants, including some of the foremost scholars and religious leaders from Asia, Europe and the USA discuss five themes: (1) the Individual and Peace, (2) Society and Conflict Resolution, (3) the Environment, (4) Health and (5) East Asian Buddhism. From these points of reference, the authors directly address and contribute to the theory and practices of socially engaged Buddhism.

Among the presenters at the conference, four were professors from the University of Hawaii: Professor Emeritus Alfred Bloom of the Department of Religion; Dr. Daniel E. Ponce of the Department of Psychiatry, School of Medicine; Professor David Chappell of the Department of Religion; and Professor David Kalupahana of the Department of Philosophy.[1]

There were many participants from the mainland of North America. These include: Professor George Bond, Chair, Department of Religious Studies, Northwestern University; Professor Ronald Burr, Department of Philosophy and Religion, University of Southern Mississippi; Professor Steve Heine, Department of Religion, Pennsylvania State University; Professor Arthur Herman, Department of Philosophy, University of Wisconsin - Stevens Point; Professor Sallie B. King, Department of Philosophy and Religion, James Madison University; Professor Sung-bae Park, Director, Department of Comparative Studies; Professor Donald Swearer, Department of Religion, Swarthmore College; Professor Robert Zeuschner, Department of Philosophy, Pasadena City College; Professor Nona R. Bolin, Department of Art and Sciences, Memphis College of Art; and Professor David Putney, Department of Philosophy, Old Dominion University. Professor Leslie Kawamura, Department of Religious Studies, University of Calgary came from Canada.

Some participants came from British Kingdom as follows: Dr. Stewart McFarlane, Department of Religious Studies, Lancaster University, United Kingdom; Dr. Ian Charles Harris, Senior Lecturer, S. Martin's College, United Kingdom; Dr. Peter Harvey, Reader in Buddhist Studies, School of Social and International Studies, University of Sunderland, United Kingdom; Professor Padmal De Silva, Institute of Psychiatry, United Kingdom; and Dr. Lance Cousins, formerly Senior Lecturer in Comparative Religion, University of Manchester, United Kingdom.

Several scholars attended the seminar from South and South East Asia as follows: Professor S. N. Dube, Department of History and Indian Culture, University of Rajasthan, India; Professor K. N. Upadhyaya, Forensic Science Laboratory, Government of Vihar, India; Meenakshi Gopinath, Principal, Lady Shri Ram College, University of Delhi, India; Dr. A. T. Ariyanatne, President of Sarvodaya Shramadana Movement, Sri Lanka; Professor P. D. Premasiri, Department of Philosophy, University of Peradeniya; Dr. Sanath Nanayakkara, Deputy Editor, Encyclopedia of Buddhism, Sri Lanka; Professor Lily de Silva, Department of Buddhist Studies, University of Peradeniya, Sri Lanka; Dr.

---

[1] The titles and academic institutions listed in association with the contributors represent the positions they held in 1995, that is, at the time of the seventh seminar.

Suwanna Satha-Anad, Lecturer, Department of Philosophy, Chulalongkorn University, Thailand and Dr. Kwan Kah Yee, Vice President, Singapore Buddha Yana Organization, Singapore.

Some scholars participated from East Asia as follows: Professor Fumihiko Sueki, Department of Indian Philosophy, University of Tokyo, Japan; Professor Hajime Nakamura, Director, the Eastern Institute, Japan; Byung-Jo Chung, Department of Ethics, College of Liberal Art, Dongguk University, Korea; Jae-Ryong Shim, Department of Philosophy, Seoul National University, Korea; and Woo-Sung Huh, Department of Philosophy, Kyung Hee University, Korea.

The original five themes devised by the seminar organizers are presented as the five headings of this book. Six articles are included in Part One, under the heading "Individual Peace." First, to see the applications of Buddhist ethics to social conditions of today, Dr. Cousins examines Buddhist canonical sources. The article focuses particularly on the important ideas of *kusala* and *puñña*, sometimes translated as 'good' or 'virtuous.' Titled, "Going Beyond Good and Evil? Kusala and Punna in Canon and Commentary," it contributes to our understanding to Buddhist ethics and how they will be taught today. In the second article, "Buddhism as a Principle of Tolerance," Professor Byung-jo Chung explores the question of whether peace is possible and, if so, how. The third article is "Personal Peace and Philosophical Conflict: Ho-tse Shen-hui and His Attack Upon Northern Chan." In it, Dr. Robert B. Zeuschner looks at the case of the Seventh Patriarch of Chan (the Chinese version of Zen), suggesting how in China and Japan, Buddhist masters have curried favor from those in power. In the fourth article, "Arhat Ideal in Early Buddhism," Dr. S. N. Dube treats the earliest Buddhist writings in order to discover the origins of the ethical ideas applicable today. The fifth article is by Professor P. D. Premasiri and is titled, "Can Peace in the Larger Society be Promoted without Inner Peace within the Individual? A Response in terms of Early Buddhism." The sixth is Mr. Sanath Nanayakkara's "The Noble Eightfold Path as a Way to Harmoniously Blend Material Progress with Spiritual Progress."

Nine articles are included in Part Two, "Society / Conflict Resolution." First is Professor K. N. Upadhyaya's contribution, "Early Buddhist Attitude to War and Peace." This article is particularly interesting in relation to the previously mentioned contributions on early Buddhism by Dr. Dube and Professor Premasiri. Second in this section is a very important article by Dr. Sallie B. King, titled, "Towards a Buddhist Theory of Social Ethics." In terms of socially engaged Buddhism, Dr. King examines the Four Noble Truths, addressing their relevance to Western ethical theory: the individual and society; human rights and social responsibilities; utilitarian and deontological ethical theory. Her study reveals the heart of the issues addressed in this book. The third article in this section is by Professor A. L. Herman, entitled, "Community: Violence, Peace and the Ways of Community." Fourth is Professor David W. Chappell's "Searching for a Mahāyāna Social Ethics." This article by Professor Chappell is a particularly significant contribution to the presently changing orientation of

Buddhist soteriology. In it, he looks specifically at the ethical foundations of Buddhism, such as the famous Six Perfections, to see how those teachings are adaptable in the changing world. The fifth article is by Professor George D. Bond, "The *Sarvodaya* Movement's Quest for Peace and Social Awakening." This article begins an important examination of the history of the *Sarvodaya Shramadana* movement in Sri Lanka. The movement represents one of the earliest examples of socially engaged Buddhism. Through Professor Bond's article, we also come to understand the place of the leader of the *Sarvodaya* moment, Dr. A. T. Ariyaratne, who is a contributor to this volume. The sixth article in this section is by Dr. Stewart McFarlane, entitled, "Skilful Means, Moral Crises and Conflict Resolution." In it, Dr. McFarlane argues that skilful means are fundamental to understanding Buddhism as a soteriology. He also shows how Mahāyāna skilful means, as articulated in texts and historical cases, challenge conventional understandings of Buddhist ethics and potentially provides guidelines for today's Buddhist leaders. In the seventh article, Professor Ron Burr returns to the theme of the *Sarvodaya* movement of Sri Lanka. In his article, "Buddhist Conflict Management," Dr. Burr takes the reader through a seminar on engaged Buddhism given by members of the *Sarvodaya* movement. The eighth article in this section is by Dr. A. T. Ariyaratne, the internationally acclaimed leader of the *Sarvodaya* movement. His article, "Buddhist Thought in *Sarvodaya* Practice," explains the goals and practices of the moment as well as the challenges he has personally faced.

The third part of the book addresses the "Environment" and includes nine articles. The first is by Professor Nona R. Bolin and is entitled, "From Nature to Buddha Nature: Towards A Buddhist Environmental Ethics." The second is by Professor Lily de Silva, "Environmental Crisis and Survival." The third is Professor Donald K. Swearer's "Two Perspectives on Buddhist Ecology." Fourth is Dr. Suwanna Satha-Anand's "Ethics of Wealth: Buddhist Economics for Peace." Fifth is "The Lotus and the Wheel by Dr. Meenakshi Gopinath. Sixth is Professor Peter Harvey's "Buddhist Attitudes To and Treatment Of Non-Human Nature." Seventh is "Varieties of Religious Ecology: A Typology of Buddhist Environmentalism" by Dr. Ian Charles Harris. Dr. Jae-ryong Shim presents a particularly important article for English readers, "Korean Buddhist Land-Wisdom in Theory and Practice: The Case of Pine Broad Temple Against Modern Development." Currently, there are few articles on the specifics of the history of Korean Buddhism or socially engaged Buddhism of East Asia. The ninth article is by Professor Rebecca Clare, "Some Women of the *Gaṇḍavyūha-sūtra.*"

Four articles are included in the fourth part of this book under the heading "Health." First is an article by Professor Daniel E. Ponce, "Is Buddhism Psycho-therapy?" Dr. Ponce draws upon his extensive knowledge of psychiatry in pointing to possibilities of applying Buddhist thought to that field. Second is Professor Padmal de Silva's "The Role of Buddhism in Mental Health in the Modern World." Third is "Psychological Transformation of Mind: the Foundation for Overcoming Disease," by Dr. Leslie S. Kawamura. The fourth article in this section is by Dr. Kwan Kah Yee and is entitled, "Buddhist Meditation and Mental Health."

Part Five of this book is of itself a distinct contribution to our understanding of socially engaged Buddhism: "East Asian Buddhism." The few English language sources appearing on socially engaged Buddhism are typically focused on the activities of Tibetan and Southeast Asian Buddhists: the Dalai Lama of Tibet, Aung San Suu Kyi of Burma and Thich Nhat Hanh of Vietnam. The articles in this section clearly contribute in that they expand the exploration of socially engaged Buddhism to the essential area of East Asia. The first article in the section is by Professor Steve Heine, "The Role of Repentance – Or Lack of it – in Zen Monasticism." The second article addresses a topic immediately recognizable as important in the development of Japanese Buddhism: "How Can Grasses and Trees Attain Buddhahood? An Aspect of the Japanization of Buddhism," by Professor Fumihiko Sueki. The third article is Professor Woo-sung Huh's "Beyond Manhae (1869-1944) and Songch'ol (1912-1993)." Professor Huh examines the lives and works of central Korean Buddhist activists to find ways of addressing social problems today. The fourth article in this section is by Professor Alfred Bloom, "The Shin Buddhist Approach to Spiritual Discipline and Peace." Professor Bloom considers Japanese Shin Buddhism, finding relevance in its historic teachings for addressing oppressive conditions in the world today.

This book is likely the most comprehensive treatment of our topic to date. Of the seven international seminars on Buddhism and Leadership for Peace, which have had worldwide reputation in leading discussions on Buddhism and peace, the seventh and latest seminar is considered the most successful. The thirty-one scholars and Buddhist activists contributing to this book equally represent the two major Buddhist traditions, the Theravāda and the Mahāyāna. Likewise, a balance is struck in this book in terms of the number of articles dealing with theory and those concentrating on practice.

Since the conference convened in 1995, escalating acts of terrorism and cruelty, as well as the outbreak of wars have shocked the world. At no time has this issue been more important than today. The seven conferences held thus far, originated from the vision of the venerable master Daewon Ki of Dae Won Sa Buddhist Cultural Institute of Hawaii. His motivation was to bring Buddhist thinkers, peace leaders and scholars together from around the world in order to discuss themes of common interest. The articles in this book address issues of Buddhist philosophy, particularly ethics and the role of Buddhism in dealing with political and economic injustices. While this book will have wide appeal to scholars and students of Religious Studies, we hope it will also be attractive to a broader audience of sociologists and political scientists. Peace activists, Buddhists and non-Buddhists, might find ways to apply this information for building peace in the world. Thus, activists, social scientists, Buddhist scholars, engaged Buddhists and others can incorporate the Buddhist wisdom contained in these pages to broaden their understanding of peace and to find ways to bring it to this troubled world.

Part 1

Individual Peace

CHAPTER 1

GOING BEYOND GOOD AND EVIL?:
Kusala and *Puñña* in Canon and Commentary

L. S. Cousins

It has sometimes been argued that the highest levels of Buddhist practice in some sense transcend both the morally good and the bad. More recently this view has come under attack both on philosophical and on historical or textual grounds. This paper seeks to assess the traditional Buddhist view on this matter, at least as far as the Pali sources are concerned and then to evaluate some of the arguments put forward.

Probably the two most frequently used terms which can be taken to correspond to the use in English of such words as 'good' or 'virtuous' are the variously translated *kusala* and *puñña,* generally rendered as meritorious or merit. It seems helpful then to begin with an examination of the use of these two words in the Pali sources.

1. *Kusala*

Damien Keown comments as follows:

> The most natural translation for *kusala* when used in a moral context is 'virtue' or 'goodness'. It is very common for *kusala* to be rendered as 'skilful', but it should be recognized that this translation carries with it a specific implication for the nature of Buddhist ethics, namely that it is utilitarian.[1]

In fact, as we shall see, I am not convinced that a utilitarian implication does in fact necessarily follow. Keown then distinguishes what he calls the moral and the technical senses of the word *kusala* and argues strongly against translating it as 'skilful':

---

[1] Damien Keown, *The Nature of Buddhist Ethics* (London: Macmillan, 1992), 119.

Although I have no statistics to back this up there can be little doubt that in the *Nikāya*s the occurrences of *kusala* in a technical context are massively outnumbered by those in a moral context. So why, when translating the term into English, is the tail allowed to wag the dog and the moral sense suppressed in favor of the technical one?

He goes on to point out as follows:

> The problem with using 'skilful' as a translation of *kusala is* that whereas both 'good' and '*kusala*' extend in their respective languages to both moral and technical commendation, the English word 'skilful' does not. 'Skilful' denotes approval in the technical sense only and does not figure at all in the vocabulary of moral discourse in English.

As Keown indicates, the use of 'skilful' is stylistically slightly unnatural here in terms of English usage. Perhaps, however, this only shows that Buddhist concepts are themselves unfamiliar to ordinary English usage and we should be cautious about adopting concepts with many hidden implications, deriving from a long history of European theological and philosophical use. Indeed I think that the use in the Buddhist literature is rather more complex than Keown allows and deserves to be investigated more fully. Here I shall look first at the commentarial account and then turn to the earlier sources.

2. *Kusala* in the Commentarial Sources

In the commentary to the *Dīgha-nikāya* Buddhaghosa gives five senses of the word *kusala*:[2]

1. *ārogya:* absence of illness, health
2. *anavajia:* (originally) not reprehensible, blameless; (later) faultless
3. *kosalla-sambhūta:* produced by skill
4. *niddaratha:* freedom from distress
5. *sukha-vipāka:* bringing pleasant results

The first of these he attributes to the *Jātaka* method of exposition (*pariyaya*) and in fact it is clear that this represents a popular Indian usage, rather than a technical sense of Buddhist thought.[3] What is referred to is such expressions as *kacci nu kusalam*, meaning 'Are you well?' or something similar, usually found in verse texts. This usage is indeed particularly common in the

---

2 *Sv.*, III.883.
3 *Sv.*, III.883.

Jātakas.[4] The second meaning Buddhaghosa refers to as the *suttanta* method of exposition; it is extremely often applied by him in the exegesis of particular *sutta* passages.[5] Sometimes this is referred to as the *Bāhitika-sutta(nta)* method of exposition.[6]

The remaining three senses are all attributed by Buddhaghosa to the *Abhidhamma* method of exposition. In fact the fourth: 'freedom from distress' is rather unusual and seems to be dropped by the later commentarial tradition[7]. Indeed I have not so far been able to find a context where Buddhaghosa himself uses it and the *ṭīkā* writer cannot offer a source passage to illustrate it. For present purposes we can disregard this meaning. The fifth we can also put on one side. The notion that skilful actions bring pleasant results is of course well-established, but it is noticeable that the commentators do not in fact often explain the word *kusala* as having this sense.[8] It is clear that Buddhaghosa has placed it in an *Abhidhamma* context because of the importance of this idea to understanding the first triplet of the *Abhidhamma-mātikā*.

The *ṭīkā* writer's first comment on Buddhaghosa's explanation of *kusala* is to ask why the sense of *cheka* 'skilled' is not given as a sixth meaning. This is at first sight surprising; for this explanation is given by Buddhaghosa and other commentators in a number of contexts, including some cases where the word is used in what Keown calls its technical sense.[9] However, the *ṭīkā* writer answers his own question by pointing out that this sense is included in the third meaning given by Buddhaghosa: 'produced by skill' and hence is not taken separately. Skill of course is listed in the *Abhidhamma* register for understanding (*paññā*) and so the intended meaning is 'produced by wisdom'. The *ṭīkā* writer explains this as equivalent to 'caused by appropriate bringing to mind' (*yoniso-manasikāra-hetuka*).

In fact this explanation is used in non-*Abhidhamma* contexts also, as well as in explanations of *akusala* 'unskillful'.[10] Moreover, there are also contexts where the sense of expert (*paṇḍita*) *is* given, but seems to converge on the sense

---

[4] E.g., *J.*, IV. 427*f;* V. 323; 348; 377; VI. 418; 515; 532; 542; 569; but see also: *Sn.*, 981; *Nidd.*, II.1; *Vv.*, 25; 45; Cp. 93. Also unrelated to the specifically Buddhist senses is the expression *icc' etaṁ kusalaṁ*, common in the *Vinaya*, but occurring a few times elsewhere, e.g., *M.*, III.129.

[5] *Sp.*, II.436; *Sv.*, I. 286; *Ps.*, III.443; *Mp.*, III.203; IV. 123; V. 1; 30. Compare *JA.*, 1275; cf. III. 411; IV. 223; VI. 175; *Nidd-a.*, II. 373; *It-a.*, I.173; *Th-a.*, III.77.

[6] Buddhaghosa has *Bāhiya-suttanta*, but this is probably an error in view of the *ṭīkās*. The *Mūlaṭīkā* (C. 1938) 21, however, interprets the *Bāhitika-sutta* in relation to the sense of health.

[7] At *Dhs-a.*, 63 it is subsumed in *anavajja*..

[8] But cf. *Spk.*, III.141.

[9] *Sp.*, VII. 1360; 1377; *Ps.*, III.323; *Mp.*, III.132; *Vibh-a.*, 290; *Pj.* II.433; *Nidd-a.*, I.199; 240; II.292; *Patis-a.*, I. 77; *JA.*, II. 298; V. 326; VI. 260; *Th-a.*, III.160; *Bv-a.*, 49; *Ap-a.*, 283; 286.

[10] *Spk.*,III.141; *Mp.*,III.161; *Vibh-a.*, 289; *Nidd-a.*, I .219; 306; 439 and in relation to *akusala: Sp.*, I .135; II.404; *Ps.*,III.346; *Nidd-a.*,165; *Ud-a.*,220.

12   L. S. Cousins

of 'Wise' or 'knowledgeable'.[11] Closely related to this are passages where the
expression 'skilful *dhammas*' *is* explained as referring to the *dhammas* which
contribute to awakening (*bodhipakkhiya*).[12]

The author of the *Abhidhamma* commentary, probably a senior
contemporary of Buddhaghosa,[13] takes a slightly different approach.[14] He offers
just three senses: 1. Health; 2. Faultless; and 3. Produced by skill. He too relates
the first to the *Jātaka* method of exposition and the second to the *Bāhitika-sutta*
method of exposition. (He cannot relate it to the *suttanta* method, as he wishes
to argue that it is found in *Abhidhamma*.) Again like Buddhaghosa, he links the
third to the *Abhidhamma* method of exposition and then addresses the obvious
problem that this creates; for wisdom would be expected to lead to
consciousness connected with knowledge (*ñāṇasampayutta*), but not to that
which lacks knowledge. Yet the term 'skilful' in *Abhidhamma is* also applied to
two-rooted consciousness which is without knowledge.

The commentator argues that even this can be called skilful by convention.
He gives the example of a palm-leaf fan which is still given that name even
when made out of other materials. He agrees, however, that in terms of strict
Abhidhamma (*nippayiyāyena*) only consciousness with knowledge can be called
skilful in a three senses. In the case of consciousness without knowledge only
the two senses of health and faultless strictly apply. The inclusion of the sense of
'health' here is of course good hermeneutics; in fact, however, its inclusion as a
sense of *kusala* must be a later development, derived from the kind of
expression mentioned above.

Surprisingly, however, this is the *Abhidhamma* commentator's second
discussion of the meanings of the word *kusala*. In an earlier passage he gives
four senses:[15]

   1. *ārogya:* absence of illness, health
   2. *anavajja:* not reprehensible, blameless; faultless
   3. *cheka:* skilled
   4. *sukha-vipāka:* bringing pleasant results

---

[11] *Sp.*, V. 1391; VII. 1360 (ñāṇapāramippatta); *Pj.*, II. 574; *Nidd-a.*, II.284;
Patis-a.,III. 549 (ñāṇa); *JA.*, III.210; Cp. V. 66.

[12] E.g., *Ps.*, III. 244*ff*, *Mp.*, II.45*ff*, Dhs-a., 405*f*, *Vibh-a.*, 289*ff*, *Pj.*, II.503; cf.
JA.,I.275; II.22; *Mūlaṭīkā* (C. 1938), 21; cf. Gethin (1992), 75.

[13] In the introduction to the first two volumes the author states that he was
asked to write the commentary by the bhikkhu Buddhaghosa. It seems very unlikely that
if the author's name was Buddhaghosa, he would have referred to another Buddhaghosa
without some designation to indicate the difference. If there were two Buddhaghosas in
the same monastery, then a distinguishing name would have been in use. The same
applies in case this Buddhaghosa was not the famous Buddhaghosa. Most probably then
it was Buddhaghosa himself who requested the author to compose this commentary.

[14] *Dhs-a.*, 62-63; cf. Moh., 6.

[15] *Dhs-a.*, 38*ff*.

Exactly this list is given also by Buddhadatta and by Mahanama.[16] It seems to be standard for later writers.[17] For most sources the third meaning is excluded for the main *Abhidhamma* contexts[18] and this view is adopted by many modern commentators.[19] Budbhadatta, however, allows only the two senses of 'faultless' and 'bringing wished for results' (*iṭṭha-vipāka*).

Why then does the *Abhidhamma* commentary offer two different explanations? This must be because in the earlier passage he is commenting on *kusalā dhammā* in the first triplet of the *Mātikā*, whereas the later passage refers to *kusalaṁ cittaṁ* in the *Dhammuddesa* of the first type of consciousness, i.e., that connected with knowledge. This will in part account for the inclusion of 'produced by skill' as a meaning of *kusala*. However, it must also have been embedded in his source material[20]; here, as elsewhere, the *Abhidhamma* commentary preserves material for us in a less digested form as against the more carefully styled writings of Buddhaghosa.

There is perhaps more to it than this. The Pali *Abhidhamma* system is unusual in allowing skilful consciousness without knowledge. In the *Sarvāstivādin* system, for example, knowledge is a universal and so there cannot be skilful consciousness without it. It may be that at an earlier stage the connection between the skilful and wisdom was felt more strongly. That said, the commentaries do preserve the link. In the mnemonic exegesis of the word *kusala,* the first two syllables are sometimes taken as a word *kusa,* meaning 'wisdom' (cp. Skt. *kuśāgra*?).[21] No doubt too the question of how far even skilful consciousness can be entirely unrelated to wisdom is closely connected to the issue as to whether faith (*saddhā*) that is not based on wisdom can occur.

In summary then, it seems that the commentators (except perhaps Buddhaghosa) would probably not have disagreed with Damien Keown's remarks:

> No one would describe a simple act of generosity as a 'skilful deed', and who has ever heard of a boy scout doing his 'skilful deed for the day'? Instead, one naturally speaks of 'good' or 'virtuous' deeds.[22]

---

[16] *Abhidh-av.*, v. 11; *Patis-a.*, I.129; 205-106; *Bv-a.*, 49. At *Pj.*, II.503 we have the same number of senses, but with *iṭṭha-phala* in place of *sukhavipāka* and *kosalla-sambhūta* instead of *cheka*.

[17] But Dhammapāla occasionally explains *kusala* in terms of *khema* or *khemin*, e.g., *Th-a* I.100; *It-a* I.93.

[18] E.g., *Dhs-a.*, 38.

[19] See for example U. Narada's discussion: *Conditional Relations*, pp. cviii-cix.

[20] That this is so is perhaps also suggested by the need of Mahanama, in his second treatment of the subject, to refer also to the threefold definition of *kusala*: *Patis-a.*, I.206.

[21] *Dhs-a.*, 39; *Abhidh-av.*, v. 9 (pt and t).

[22] *Ibid.*

Yet there are suggestive hints of an underlying connection to wisdom and it may be wondered whether in fact this is a later development. Edgerton defines the word *kuśala* (BHSD s.v.) as "good in a moral sense (not so in Sanskrit literature), merit, righteous action." So the question arises as to whether in fact the earlier texts already have this meaning or is it, largely or partially, something which only arises at a later date.

3. *Kusala* in the Canonical Literature

The use which Keown describes as the technical meaning of the word *kusala* occurs more than thirty times in the Canon[23]. In many of the passages in which it occurs it is simply a case of mentioning proficiency in some art or craft. However, in some places there is a little more to it than that; for the mention of such proficiency is directly linked to some further point. So when in the *Mahāvagga* Sona's proficiency in getting the right sound from the strings of a harp (*vīṇā*) is mentioned, it is in order to emphasize the necessity to control vigor and balance the faculties (*indriya*).[24] In other words there is an underlying implication that meditation is an activity requiring a kind of skill.

When the simile of the skilled elephant tracker is given, it is to emphasize the qualities of wisdom which can recognize a tathāgata and to compare the *jhānas* and higher knowledges to the footprints of an elephant.[25] Again Prince Abhaya's knowledge of chariotry is adduced in order to compare it with the Buddha's penetration of the *dhammadhātu,* i.e., his wisdom.[26] Or Prince Bodhi's proficiency in chariotry is compared to the Buddha's ability to teach.[27] Or the skilled cook is likened to the monk who develops the four establishings of mindfulness in the right way.[28] The chariot-maker, skilled in the crookedness of wood, is compared the Buddha as an arahat skilled in crookedness of body, mind and speech.[29]

Around twice as frequent as passages where *kusala* is used in the sense of proficient are places where it has such meanings as expert, clever or wise[30]. In fact there is no clear dividing line between the two, just as there is no very

---

[23] *Vin.,* II.201; V. 64 = 158; *D.,* II.183; *A.,* I. 116*f;* II.185; *Sn.* 321; *Dhp.,* 44*f;* *Th.,* 1139; *Pp.* 42; *J.,* II.162; 298; III.477; IV. 469; V. 148; 157; 326; 490; VI.25; 77; 85; 87; 213; 260; 475 and next six notes.

[24] *Vin.,* I. 182 =*A.,* III.375.

[25] *M.,* I. 178*ff.*

[26] *M.,* I. 395*f.*

[27] *M.,* II. 94*f.*

[28] *S.,* V. 149-152.

[29] *A.,* I. 112*f.*

[30] *Vin.,* V. 130; 197; 216;216; *D.,*II. 136; *M.,*I. 226*f,* II.144; III.5; *S.,*I. 35; 169; *A.,* II.46; 138; III.201; 431; V. 96; 98; *Kh.,* 8 = *Sn.,* 143; *Sn.,* 48; 591; 881; 1039; 1078; *Nidd.,* I. 69; 71-72; 105; 325; 177; 450; II.9; 127; 128; *Th.,* 251; *Pv.,* 4; 44; *Bv.,* 62; *J.,* III. 210; 348; V.65; VI. 356; *Ap.,* I.26; 29; 43; *Ii.,* 499; 518; 570; *Vibh.,* 3 10; *Kv.,* 170*ff,* 176*ff,* 180*ff,* 190*ff.*

definite distinction to be made between mundane cleverness and various kinds of superior understanding, whether in terms of understanding Buddhist theory or that involved in developing insight. A few passages concerned with mastery of *jhāna* or *iddhi* can also be mentioned at this point[31]. The notion of skill in theory or practice develops further both in the Pali commentarial literature and in the Mahāyāna.[32]

This brings me to the very large number of passages in which *kusala* is linked with *dhamma,* either in the singular or more often in the plural. It is important to note that many of the passages here are meditational in their orientation. So in the *Mahāvagga* (*Vin.,* I. 104) the Buddha declares that if a monk does not make known a *Vinaya* offence when the *Pātimokkha* is recited, this would be a deliberate lie and a deliberate lie is an obstacle. The text defines an obstacle (*antarāyiko dhammo*), first of all as an obstacle to achieving the first *jhāna*, then successively to the remaining *jhāna*s up to the fourth, then various kinds of meditational experience are mentioned, ending (summarizing) with 'to the achieving of skilful *dhamma*s. Similarly, in the discussion of the fourth *pārājika* (at *Vin.,* III. 191), in the list of higher states which must not be falsely claimed by the monk these meditational attainments (*jhāna, vimokkha, samādhi,* etc.) are referred to as skilful *dhamma*s.

This kind of direct linkage between higher states and skillfulness is found in a number of contexts.[33] So in the *Saṃyutta-nikāya* we find the ascetic who wishes to attain a skillful *dhamma* and realize higher states (*uttari-manussa-dhamma; alam-ariya-ñāṇa-dassana*). In the *Lohicca-sutta* we meet the idea that if someone attains a skilful *dhamma,* he should not tell anyone else. Or the Buddha is asked if he has achieved this skilful *dhamma* for a long while. Again in the *Aṅguttara-nikāya* we learn of the six factors which make a monk fit (or unfit) to attain a skilful *dhamma:* he is skilful in coming, skilful in going, skilful as to means (*upāyakusala*), he arouses the purpose (*chanda*) of attaining a skilful *dhamma* which has not been attained, he guards skilful *dhamma*s which have been attained and is successful in constant action. Compare too passages in which are found the expression: (he succeeds in) the method, the *dhamma* that is skilful (*ñāyaṃ dhammaṃ kusalaṃ*).[34] Usually this makes the point that, whether householder or renunciant, he can succeed if he follows the right way, i.e., the eightfold path.

---

[31] *S.,* III. 264-277; *A.,* III.311; IV. 34; *Th.,* 1183; *Patis.,* I.48*f.*

[32] See Ulrich Pagel, *The Bodhisattvapitaka. Its Doctrines, Practices and their Position in Mahāyāna Literature*, Buddhica Britannica, Series Continua V (Tadeusz Skorupski, ed.) (Tring: The Institute of Buddhist Studies, 1995), Index s.v. skill and p. 258*ff*; Peter Skilling, "*Vimuttimagga* and *Abhayagiri*: The Form Aggregate, according to the *Saṃskṛtāsaṃskṛtaviniścaya,*" *JPTS* 20 (1994):171-210.

[33] *S.,* IV. 337-339; *D.,* I.224-229; *M.,* I.318; *A.,* I. 115*f;* III.431; cp. *Vin.,* 148.

[34] *M.,* I.514-522; II.181-184; 197*ff; S.,* V. 19; *A.,* I.69; cf. *M.,* I.502.

16   L. S. Cousins

Similar usages occur in the plural too.[35] So in the *Majjhima-nikāya*, when the Jains admit to not knowing: 'the arousing of skilful *dhamma*s, the reference must be to the absence of the higher *jhāna*s in the Jain system. Or, in the *Aṅguttara-nikāya*, when skilful *dhamma*s explicitly refer to mental peace (*cetosamatha*) within and insight into *dhamma*s from the standpoint of wisdom (*adhipaññādhammavipassanā*). In the *Paṭisambhidā-magga* we are even told that all skilful *dhamma*s lead in the direction of the liberations (*vimokkhānuloma*).

There are a great many places in which skilful *dhamma*s are referred to briefly or without much qualification, where it is not possible to be sure whether the intention is to refer specifically to meditational states. Nevertheless, this is probably the meaning which should be assumed in the majority of cases. I do not wish to argue that a broader usage which includes other desirable states is entirely excluded, only that in such cases the expression points primarily to meditational practice. This makes translation by such expressions as 'good states' misleading; for such renderings point first and foremost to the ordinary ethical dimension and only secondarily to meditational experience. By contrast I believe the intention of the Pali texts in these passages is to point first to the *jhāna*s and the states later known as the *dhamma*s contributing to awakening. In other words the use of *kusala* in these contexts is concerned with the fact that these are special states which are, directly or indirectly, produced by wisdom. That, I think, is why they are called 'skilful'.

There are equally a great many passages where the meditional context is beyond real dispute. One example of this is the occurrence of skilful *dhammas* in the formula of the four right efforts and in related formulae concerned with vigor (*viriya*), such as descriptions of effort (*vāyāma*) in the eightfold path.[36] This of course is simply a specific case of the bodhipakkhiyas in general and indeed the seven sets are sometimes cited in relation to *kusala:*

> But, Venerable sir, there is another incomparable quality (*anuttariyā*): how the Lord teaches *dhamma* as regards skillful *dhammas*. As to that, the skilful *dhammas* are as follows: four establishings of mindfulness, four right efforts, four bases of success, five faculties, five powers, seven factors of awakening, the noble

---

[35] *M.*, I.93; II.215; 217; *A.*, V. 17-21; 26-29; 96-98; 99*ff*; 123-138; *Patis.*, II.70; note too passages where *sīla* or *adhisīla* is defined as *the mukhaṁ pamukhaṁ kusalānaṁ dhammānaṁ samāpattiyā*: *Vin.*, I.103; *Nidd.*, I. 39; 148; 270; 348; cf. 365; *Vibh.*, 246 and compare *D.*, V. 143; 165; 167; 188.

[36] *D.*, II.312; III.221; 237; 268; 285; *M.*, I.124?; 356; II.11; 95; 128; *S.*, III. 364; V. 9; 197*f*, 225; 244-247; 268; *A.*, I.39; 117; 153; 244*ff*; 296; II.15; 74; 93; 95; 250*f*; 256; III.2; 11; 65; 135; 152-155; 310; IV. 3; 153*f*; 234; 291; 352; 357*f*; 462-643 (expand); V. 15; 24; 27; 90*f*, 339; *Ud.*, 36*f*, *Nidd.*, I.477; II. 96*f*, 104; *Patis.*, I.41; 103*f*; II.15; 17; *Vibh.*, 105; 208-214; 216-219; 235. To these could probably be added some passages related to *appamāda*: *D.*, III.272; *S.*, I.89; V. 45; 91; *A.*, I. 11; *Nid.*, II. 90; compare also with *chanda*: *A.*, V. 99-100; 104-105; *Nidd.*, II.90.

> eightfold path ... That, Venerable Sir, is an incomparable quality as
> regards skilful *dhammas* ... there is nothing further to be known by
> higher knowledge, such that another mendicant or brahmin, knowing
> by higher knowledge, would know more deeply i.e. as regards skilful
> *dhammas*.[37]

Sometimes the link is made directly to the first of the seven sets: the four establishings of mindfulness.[38] So for example in the *Janavasabha-suttanta* we are told by Brahma Sanamkumara that the four establishings of mindfulness were made known for the purpose of attaining the skilful - here the reference must be to the remaining six sets. Some at least of the discourses where things *kusala* are mentioned, while leading up to a culmination with the eightfold or the tenfold path probably belong here.[39] Compare also the *Kāya-gatā-sati-sutta* where we are told, in relation to the person who has brought into being, made much of and immersed himself in mindfulness of the body, that whatever skilful *dhamma*s he has are connected with the knowledges (*vijjā-bhāgiya*), i.e., lead to the three knowledges.[40]

When in the *Mahā-hatthi-padopama-sutta* Sāriputta tells (*M.* I. 184) us that all skilful *dhamma*s are included in the four noble truths, we should again interpret skilful *dhamma*s here as referring to meditational. states. Indeed, this is made clear later in the *sutta* by the references to equipoise connected with the skilful. More generally, there are many passages in which skilful *dhamma*s are spoken of in association with *bhāvanā*

'bringing into being' or some form of the verb *bhāveti*[41]. In most of these what is implied is the technical sense of these words, as referring to the bringing into being of the eightfold path in particular or the *dhamma*s which contribute to awakening in general i.e., the fourth noble truth. This is even more likely to be the case when the skilful to be brought into being is contrasted with the unskillful 'to be abandoned', i.e., the corresponding function of the second noble truth.[42] No doubt closely related to this is the idea of achieving a stage of fixity in relation to skilful *dhamma*s, an idea closely related to some interpretations of what is meant by stream-entry.[43]

---

[37] *D.*, III.102; compare *Nidd.*, I.13-14; 361*f*;468*f*; 486; II.200; cf. *Th.*, 900.

[38] *D.*, II.216; cp. *S.*, V. 171*f*, 186 *f*, 187; 188.

[39] E.g., *M.*, II. 24-29; cf. *A.*, V. 215*f*; 241.

[40] *M.*, III.94; cp. *A.*, I. 43*f*.

[41] *M.*, III. 76*f*; 94; *S.*, V. 402; *A.*, I.58; II.40; 182; IV. 109-111; 120-122; 353; V. 215-216; *Sn.*, 66; *It.*, 9; 10; 21; *Th.*, 83; *Thi.*, 9; *J.*, I.275; 278; II.22.

[42] Of course, whether a usage is to be taken as technical or not, may depend in part on the age of the text concerned. Many scholars believe that some of the later technical usages only develop at a later stage. This may of course be so, but there is as yet no real consensus as to the course of development of early Buddhist literature. For present purposes this problem will not in any case greatly affect the overall picture, as many of the passages are probably somewhat later.

[43] Usually something like: *okkamati niyāmaṁ kusalesu dhammesu sammattaṁ*, cf. *A.*, I. 121*f*; III.174*f*; 435*f*; *Patis.*, I.124; *Vibh.*, 341-342; *Kv.*, 94; 309; *Pp.*, 13; 28.

There are a number of passages which refer to someone who is (not) applying insight (*vipassaka*) to skilful *dhamma*s.[44] Sometimes this probably refers to a type of insight meditation.[45] However, it also merges into contexts where skilful *dhamma*s or the skilful is simply the object of doubt or wisdom.[46] We also have the idea of the monk who abides in the measureless mental concentration (*ceto-samādhi*) even as he enjoys the four requisites. It is not easy to measure the amount of *puñña,* of the skilful, of pleasant results, etc. which will flow from this.[47] The same comment is made in relation to, for example, *dāna* to a noble disciple. So this brings us to the other major cluster of concepts associated with the skilful i.e. those concerned with future results.

Naturally there are a considerable number of contexts in which *kusala* is, explicitly or implicitly, associated with *kamma* and many more which could be interpreted in such terms. There are some too where it is related to *puñña* in some way (see below) and others where it is connected with good conduct (*sucarita*) or precepts (*sīla*). Since there is no real doubt that, whatever *kusala* is, it can be explained as bringing pleasant results, I will not attempt to explore these here. But we should bear in mind that even the *kamma* which arises from non-greed, non-hate and non-delusion: "that *kamma* is skilful, blameless and bringing pleasant results, that *kamma* conduces to the cesssation of *kamma,* that *kamma* does not conduce to the origination of *kamma.*"[48]

Many passages are, as previously suggested, ambiguous. If the *kusala* is simply recommended or spoken of in terms of something which can increase or decline, we cannot really tell what exactly is meant. Even the *Abhidhamma* references to the triplet of the skilful, unskillful and the undeclared (*avyākata*) or to *kusala-citta* can refer either to a context of *kamma* and result or to a meditational frame. This is most obvious in the *Dhamma-saṅgaṇi* which, like others of the canonical *Abhidhamma* works, uses a framework which is strongly meditation-orientated. The list of the fifty-five *dhamma*s present in the first kind of skilful consciousness with knowledge is quite sufficient to establish that: nearly all of them are either the classic subjects of insight meditation (aggregates, etc.) or connected with the *bodhi-pakkhiya dhamma*s.[49]

Of greater interest for the present purpose are those passages in which *kusala is* linked with groups of apparent synonyms. So we have the context

---

[44] In association with the term *bodhi-pakkhiya / -ika*: *Vin.,* III.23; *A.,* III.70*f;* 300*f.* In other contexts: *It.,* 41; *Patis.,* I.58; 60; 70; II.27-29.

[45] Note the link to the word *bodhi-pakkhiya*, etc. For a full discussion of the eighteen or so canonical contexts in which this term is found, see Gethin, *op.cit.,* 289-298.

[46] This is common in the standard formula for the five hindrances: *D.,* I 71, etc; *M.,* I.181; 269; 275; 347; III.3; 136; 251; *A.,* II. 211; III.93; IV. 437; V. 207; *Vibh.,* 245; 256; *Pp.,* 59, but also in relation to wisdom or questioning: *D.,* I. 24*f;* II.214-216; 222*f;* 228; III.61; 157; *Pp.,* 30*f;* cf. 65.

[47] *A.,* II. 54*f;* 56*f;* cf. III.51*f;* IV. 245-247; *S.,* V. 391-392; 399-402; *Kv.,* 346.

[48] *A.,* I.263.

[49] It must be noted that the six pairs, unique to the Pali system as far as we know, are simply an expansion of the fifth *bojihaṅga*: tranquility.

where (e.g., in the *Mahāvagga*) someone has "done the auspicious (*kalyāṇa*), done the skilful, done what protects from fear (*bhīru-ttāṇa*), not done what is ill-fortuned (*pāpa*), not done things dreadful (*ludda*), not done things which are filthy (*kibbisa*)."[50] This seems usually to be in a situation where death is envisaged as nearby. It is in any case obvious that in this context the *kusala* is very much to do with future consequences.

There is also a passage which occurs in the famous story of the Buddha-to-be Vipassin (and traditionally all Buddhas) seeing the four sights which motivated him to renounce the confines of the household life. The fourth sight is of course 'a shaven-headed man, wearing brown, who has gone forth', i.e., a religious mendicant. In the story Vipassin who has presumably never seen such an individual, asks who and what he is. He is given as the explanation for such a mendicant the comment: "good (*sādhu*) is the practice of *dhamma*, good is the practice of tranquillity (*sama*), good is the doing of the skilful, good is the doing of *puñña*, good is, absence of harming (*avihiṃsā*), good is sympathy for beings."[51]

In the great majority of cases, however, whatever other terms are associated with *kusala,* the term which is always present, usually immediately next to *kusala,* is blameless (*anavajja*).[52] It is then not surprising that Buddhaghosa preserves for us the tradition that this is precisely the *suttanta* method of exposition. The commentaries clearly understand this to be in principle distinct from the sense of 'having pleasant results' which often occurs in conjunction with 'blameless'. It is doubtful whether the explanation of this was ever meant to imply that this is only found in *suttanta* works, as opposed to *Abhidhamma.* Conversely, the description of 'produced by skill' as the *Abhidhamma* method of exposition does not mean that it is found only in the *Abhidhamma-piṭaka.* Rather, it is intended to suggest that this is in some way a higher or more profound explanation of *kusala,* or at least one which is more strictly correct.

This is perhaps born out by analysis of the terms associated with *kusala* and *anavajja* in the passages I have cited. In fact they are not synonyms - just as *kusala* here means 'skilful' and *anavajja* means 'blameless', but these are not the same thing. Of course, a skilful action i.e. one produced by wisdom is indeed likely to be one which could not be criticized by a knowledgeable person. Similarly, both are indeed likely to bring pleasant results (*sukha-vipāka; sukhudraya; kalyāṇa*), both in terms of commonsense and in the light of the

---

[50] *Vin.*, III.72; *M.*, III.164; *A.*, II. 174*f*; *It.* 23. Note that the two halves of this follow the rule of 'waxing syllables.' On this see now: Mark Allon, "Some stylistic features of the prose portions of Pali canonical sutta texts and their mnemonic function," Ph.D., Cambridge, 1995.

[51] *D.*, II. 28*f*; cp. (without the last two items) *S.*, I. 101*f*; V.456. Note that by the rule of 'waxing syllables' *puñña-kiriya* is out of place.

[52] *D.*, I.163-165; II.83*f*; *M.*, II. 115*f*; *S.*, V.104;106; *A.*, I.97*f*; 104;129;189-191; 194*f*; 263; 293*f*; III.165; IV. 363*f*; V. 240-245; *Patis.*, I.80; II.79; *Pp.*, 65; *Kv.*, 344*f*; 439*f*; 442*f*; 481*f*; 484; 577. Note, however, *M.*, I.416-419; *A.*, II.36*f*.

theory of *kamma-vipāka*. They are also 'appropriate to the saint' (*alaṁ-ariya*), refined (*paṇīta*) and 'do not cause harm' (*avyāpajjha*, cf. *avihiṁsā* above). Naturally, they are also 'to be followed' (*sevitabba*) and are 'praised by the wise.'

4. *Puñña*

Space does not permit a detailed discussion of *puñña* here. I would like to suggest, however, that what is often translated 'merit' refers to the fortune-bringing or auspicious quality of an action, not, as Keown would have it, to the 'felt consequences' of the act.

The etymology of the word *puṇya* from which the Pali *puñña* derives is not entirely clear. It probably derives from a form *pṛṇya*, but it is uncertain precisely which root it is related to. Senses such as 'protecting' or 'satisfying' may be implied. The Indian grammatical tradition usually links it either to a root *puṇ* in the sense of '(performing) subhakarman'[53] or to the root *pu* 'cleanse, purify.' Dhammapāla gives the second explanation and also, apparently, one which relates *puñña* to *pūjā* or *pujja*.[54] In the earliest (pre-Buddhist) literature (*Ṛg-veda* and *Atharva-veda*) it appears first with the senses of 'happiness' or 'good fortune' as a noun and 'pleasant' or 'happy' as an adjective.[55] Initially, there seems to have been no suggestion that this was necessarily the result of anything done by the individual. Such a wider sense of the word remains current in later Sanskrit literature, although the meaning which associates the term more closely with acts and their results tends to become predominant.

Already in the pre-Buddhist period the word had developed in its usage and become part of the brahmanical cults, both sacrificial and more general. So what was earlier probably simply 'good fortune' came to refer to whatever brings fortune and hence to the rites and practices intended to assure good fortune. The sacrifice is precisely an act intended to provide protection and happiness in the future. Naturally then with the process of ethicization that occurs in Buddhism and other contemporary religious traditions, just as the true sacrifice is now the act of generosity, so the true fortune-bringing action is no longer seen in terms of ritual action. Instead it is precisely the skilful actions of the precepts and the meditative process which bring good fortune.

The *PTS Dictionary* gives only the sense of 'merit, meritorious action, virtue' for Pali, but this may not be correct in all of the oldest passages. Indeed, Dhammapāla (*It-a.,* I.73*f*) gives the following meanings for *puñña*:

---

[53] Cp. *Dhatup*, 19: *puṇa kammani subhe*; and *Dhatum*, 41: *puṇo suhhakriye*. Also *Amg-D.*, Vol. 5, 661*ff.*

[54] *It-a.*, I.78; II.23; *Vv-a.*, 19 (for the reading *pujja-*, see Trsl., p.38.n.143; C.1925, p. 15, also reads this.) Compare also *Bv-a.*, 67.

[55] See Jean Filliozat, "Sur le domaine semantique de Punya," in *Indianisme et Bouddhisme, Melanges offerts a Mgr Etienne Lamotte* (Louvain-La-Neuve: Institut Orientaliste, 1980), 101-116.

1. *puñña-phale* 'in the sense of result of meritorious action';
2. *kāma-rūpāvacara-sucatito* 'in the sense of *kāmāvacara* and *rūpāvacara* good conduct';
3. *sugati-visesa-bhūte upapatti-bhave* 'in the sense of rebirth existence which consists of a specific good destiny'; and
4. *kusala-cetanāyaṁ* 'in the sense of skilful volition'

Buddhaghosa too seems to extend the meaning of *puñña* to results of *kamma.*

What is clear, if one examines the canonical use of the word *puñña,* is that it occurs both much less frequently than *kusala* and, on the whole, in a more restricted context. Especially in the earlier texts, it occurs in mainly in connection with *dāna* and other activities of the lay life. Indeed it quite commonly occurs in an expression that is used in relation to a motive for a monk to backslide: he can enjoy life's pleasures and still perform acts which bring good fortune (*puññāni*).[56] It also occurs quite often in direct connection with heavenly or other future lives.

P. D. Premasiri has sought to differentiate the usage of *puñña* and *kusala.*[57] Essentially I agree with him that, although there is some overlapping, *puñña* is most often used in regard to actions intended to bring about results of a pleasant kind in the future. It is almost exclusively *kusala* which is used in relation to the Buddha's path. Indeed one may go further and suggest that *puñña* was almost certainly not a technical term in the thought of the Buddha and his early disciples. It was no doubt a part of the background understanding of the time, but there is certainly no reason to suppose that they objected to the notion as such. Of course their understanding as to what constitutes *puñña* would not be the same as that of all their contemporaries.

What I am less happy with is the use by many scholars of the translation 'merit' or 'meritorious', at least for the earlier literature. The notion of merit seems to imply the notions of 'deserving' or 'being entitled'. To the extent that this is so, it seems inappropriate for *puñña,* which simply means fortunate or happy. As a noun it is applied either to an act which brings good fortune or to the happy result in the future of such an act. Of course the early Buddhists certainly taught that the kind of act which brings good fortune is precisely one which is blameless and praiseworthy, one which is skilful in the sense that it is produced by wisdom or at all events because it is the kind of thing that a wise person would do or approve. As we read in the *Cakkavatti-sīha-nāda-suttanta:*[58]

---

[56] E.g., *Vin.,* I.182.

[57] P. D. Premasiri, "Interpretation of Two Principal Ethical Terms in Early Buddhism," *Sri Lanka Journal of the Humanities* 2.1 (1976): 63-74.

[58] *D.,* III.58; 79; co. 73*f.* Here, for the layfolk, the skilful dhammas which are undertaken are the kammapatha, beginning with not killing and so on, and the good fortune is longer life and better looks, by implication also children and enjoyable things, even the power of the universal monarch. For the monks the skilful dhammas are the four

22   L. S. Cousins

By reason of the undertaking of skilful *dhammas, monks,* in this way this good fortune increases. (*Kusalānaṁ bhikkhave dhammānaṁ samādāna-hetu evaṁ idaṁ puññaṁ pavaḍḍhatī ti*).

5. Beyond Good and Evil?

A number of scholars have discussed the issue as to whether the highest goal in Buddhism somehow transcends good and evil.[59] I will not recap their views here, but the issue seems to break down into three main areas: *kamma*, the activity of the *arahat* and *nibbāna*.

As regards *kamma,* most scholars have accepted that the texts clearly state that the highest kind of *kamma* transcends both *puñña* and *pāpa*; it is no longer concerned with good or bad fortune. This view is prominent in the *Sabhiya-sutta* of the *Mahā-vagga* in the *Sutta-nipāta*, where the alternative terminology which speaks of *kamma* which is neither white nor black is also found.[60] Various sources can be cited for this, but the general idea is perhaps most clearly set out in a *sutta* in the *Aṅguttara-nikāya* (III. 383-87). In response to the *Ajīvaka* theory of six classes, put forward by Purana Kassapa but not accepted by others, the Buddha puts forward a more generally acceptable set of six alternatives. Whether or not one is born in inferior conditions (the black class), one can produce after death a black or a white *dhamma*, i.e., a hellish or a heavenly existence. Or one can produce *nibbāna* which is neither white nor black, by abandoning the hindrances and developing the factors of awakening, while well-established in the four establishings of mindfulness. The same three possibilities apply in the case of the white class. (Note that the term 'white' (*sukka*) occurs quite frequently in association with *kusala*.)

---

foundations of mindfulness, while the good fortune is the *iddhi-pādas* (long life), the observance of the training rules of the *Pātimokkha* (good looks), the four *jhānas* (happiness), loving-kindness and the other three immeasurables (enjoyable things) and arahatship (power). So for the laity the *puñña* is fortunate results, while for the monks it is new, fortunate actions.

[59] See Premasiri, *op. cit.*, 1976; Carter, John Ross, "Beyond Good and Evil," in *Buddhist Studies in Honour of Hammalava Saddhatissa*, eds. G. Dhammapāla, Richard Gombrich and K. R. Norman (Nugegoda, Sri Lanka: Hammalava Saddhatissa Felicitation Volume Committee, 1984), 41-55; a revised version in John Ross Carter, *On Understanding Buddhists. Essays on the Theravāda Tradition in Sri Lanka*, Matthew Kapstein, ed. (Albany, NY: SUNY Series in Buddhist Studies, 1993), 89-103; Keown, *op. cit.*, e.g., 124-126.

[60] Sn., 520; 526; 547. It is noteworthy that whereas *puñña* is mainly used in the *Mahāvagga*, kusala is more frequent in the *Aṭṭhakathā-vagga*. Indeed in its only occurrence in the *Aṭṭhakathā-vagga* (Sn., 790), *puñña* and its opposite are referred to as something which is not clung to, rather than as something which is abandoned, as also in the concluding verse of the *Sabhiya-sutta*.

What is particularly interesting about the above *sutta* is that it is put forward in a context which implies that it is generally accepted. Yet it is clear that such an acceptance was bound to prove a problem when Buddhist thought was set in a more systematic form. For the *Abhidhamma* literature, *puñña* and *kusala* tend to become identified. In the *Vibhajjavadin Abhidhamma* tradition preserved for us in Pali these terms are therefore not applied to the *arahat*. That this solution was not necessarily accepted by other schools is indicated by the *Katha-vatthu* debate, precisely on the issue as to whether an *arahat* accumulates *puñña*. The commentary attributes the view that he does to the *Andhaka*s, i.e., the *Mahāsāṅghika* schools of the Deccan. This may well be correct for the precise statement made. More generally, however, we know from surviving literature in Sanskrit that other schools too did not share this *Vibhajjavadin* position.

The *Katha-vatthu* seeks to refute the opposing position by referring to the *arahat* as one who 'neither accumulates nor disperses; having dispersed, he abides' (*Kv.*, 543), i.e., the skilful *citta* of the path of arahatship has dispersed defilements and he simply abides (*ṭhita*). It is notable that the term *kiriya,* which would probably not have been part of the opponent's terminology, is not used. Yet this is fundamental to the Pali *Abhidhamma* tradition: all the canonical *Abhidhamma* texts (except *Pp?*) apply the term *kiriya* (or *kiriyāvyākata*) to the consciousness of the *arahat.* For all later *Theravadin* writers the *arahat* has *kiriya* consciousness, where others have *kusala* or its opposite. This necessarily creates a problem; for there are sutta passages in which the term *kusala* is applied to the Buddha. It seems that in part this is the reason why the commentators prefer to explain *kusala* in such passages as 'blameless', i.e., to exclude the sense of 'having pleasant results'.[61]

We may then say that the Buddhist saint has gone 'beyond good and evil'. I think the problem here is, largely but not completely, a verbal one. A Buddhist *arahat* has indeed gone beyond the *kusala* and the fortunate, but this only means to say that he has a new type of *sīla* called *kiriya* - his love and compassion, etc. are no longer *kusala* (seen as ultimately self-serving) but *kiriya*, i.e., wholly appropriate to the situation and without any biasing effect on the mind. So the Buddhist arahat has certainly gone beyond 'good and evil' if by 'good' is meant an inferior kind of goodness, but not in the usual understanding of the term in English. He is precisely conceived of as an individual, all of whose actions are informed by great wisdom, inner peacefulness and wholesomeness. Yet his actions are in some important way more than merely good; his wisdom, compasssion, etc., are different in kind from those of lesser beings.

What then of *nibbāna*? Of *nibbāna* in the *Abhidhamma* we can certainly say that it is 'not declared' (*avyākata*) to be either skilful or unskillful. Yet it cannot be apprehended by or recollected with an unskillful *citta;* so it is at any rate firmly disassociated from that. As to *nibbāna* in the *sutta*s, i.e., that which follows the death of the *arahat* - there, for sure, we have transcendence: the transcendence of silence.

---

[61] *Pṭ* to *Sv.*, I. 286.

CHAPTER 2

BUDDHISM AS A PRINCIPLE OF TOLERANCE

Byung-Jo Chung

1. Is a Peaceful World Possible?

The history of humanity is a trail of blood. There has never been a time on this planet when there was no conflict of one degree or another. According to some statistics, there have been about 2, 000 armed conflicts of varying scale on the Korean Peninsula, almost one per year in its written history.

Is peaceful co-existence an impossibility? Bertrand Russell defined war as a necessary evil, an unwanted but sometimes inevitable phenomenon. Kṛṣṇa emphasizes the significance of a holy war against evil in the *Bhagavād-gīta.* Why does the peaceful co-existence of the members of humanity, of humanity with nature, and of one universe with another tend to beak all too often?

I can think of three reasons. The first is economic inequality. Humans attain economic gains according to their ability. Complete equality of all people is not possible even in the most ideal communist society. A worker in a collective farm cannot wine and dine the same way as the party secretary or other party officials. Every person is born with a capitalistic drive, and it is absurd to advocate uniform equality without regard for this inherent human attribute.[1]

The economic inequality of modern industrial societies inevitably results in relative poverty and the buildup of invisible barriers and caste systems among people. Eternal peace is not attainable as long as a person's worth is measured with a materialistic and mammonistic gauge.

The second reason is the collapse of ethical values. As Arnold Toynbee pointed out, morality is the basic value of the middle class. It is difficult to expect mature moral consciousness from a society's privileged class or its lowest class. The most serious malady of an industrial society is the inability to feel morally indignant. The intellectual, in particular, is very adept in criticizing

---

[1] The great monk Hyeshim (1178-1234) of the Goryeo period (918-1392) said: "Equality is not to cut off the leg of a crane and fit it to a duck or to flatten a mountain and fill a pond. The principle of equality is to acknowledge the differences and appreciate a long leg as it is and a short leg as it is." *Sayings of National Preceptor Jingak,* 15-16.

others but very inept in self-criticism. The values of young people are deteriorating due to the rampant decadence and hypocrisy of the established generation that condones the pleasure-seeking industry and the merchandising of sex. As Lewis Mumford accurately pointed out, humans are becoming Philistines engrossed in adventure, sex and gamble.[2]

The third reason is selfishness. Self-indulgence and egoism are rampant in the society. Competition and struggles are justified in the name of the survival of the fittest. Too often the importance of the means is neglected because society places more importance on the end. It is all too easy to justify the ways and means, whatever they are, once the goal is achieved. The doctrine of power that advocates the rule by the strongest has long dominated human life, convincing a great many people that humans by nature are fundamentally evil.[3]

It is very difficult to attain peace because of these three reasons. Difficult but not impossible. For there is a deep chasm between these two concepts. If the causes of the present situation originate with humans, humans should be able to determine the means to overcome them.

Buddhism attributes this to *avidyā*, ignorance coming from a failure to see the true nature of things in the universe. It thus teaches that peace can be attained through one's restoration of one's natural self, the elemental mind. In this sense, Buddhism is an optimistic philosophy, a creed that constantly reaffirms humanity's unlimited spiritual freedom and possibility.

2. The Order of the Universe and Life

Buddhists call the universal order *dharma*, a generative term which implies nature, providence, order, truth, and many others. It is a concept that sets order among humans and in their relationship with nature. The term also implies the circulation of seasons and the unswerving rules of nature. In basic Buddhism, it is explained with the following formula called dependent origination (*paṭicca-samuppāda*), or the law of co-existence.

That being thus this comes to be; from the coming to be of that, this arises; that being absent, this does not come to be; from the cessation of that, this ceases.[4]

---

[2] *Cf.* Karl Jaspers, *Die Geistige Situation der Zeit* (Berlin: W. De Gruyter, 1955) and Lewis Mumford, *The Transformation of Man* (New York: Harper & Row, 1956)

[3] Y. S. Hakeda, *Dacheng qixin lun* (*The Awakening of Faith*) (New York: Columbia University Press, 1967), 37-38. Man is a being of Original Awakening but becomes a Non-Awakening being because of spiritual darkness. He can enjoy happiness by recovering his original nature. Awakening means the recovery of man's original self. Monk Uisang (625-702) said: "Wherever we go, we go to the origin; wherever we arrive, we arrive at the starting point."

[4] *S.*, 65: "*imasmin sad nadi hoti, imassā uppada idam uppajjati, imasmin asati idam hoti, imassā nirodhā idam nirujjati.*"

In other words, when we understand the interrelations between lives, we can attain the universal principle of non-violence. We can surmise the philosophical development of *dharma* as follows:

First, from the point of basic Buddhism, it is the "three-clearness mind," a realization of "great compassion," or the theory of co-dependence, coming from the understanding of the dependent origination, or the law of co-existence.

Second, it is the Emptiness (*śūnyatā*), the awareness of no permanency, referred to in Prajñā Buddhism. Because the origin of every entity is dependent on its antecedent, it has no self and is thus empty. However, the emptiness does not necessarily mean futility. Being a transient existence, changing from one phenomenon to the next, it is also pregnant with the possibility of creation.

Third, it is the consciousness of the mind, or what the Vijñāna Buddhists call the "fundamental unconsciousness." All phenomena are illusions born of the mind, which alone exists and is the all-embracing fountainhead of life. The mind in the 8th *ālaya-vijñāna* (fundamental unconsciousness) being a sea of infinite possibility, the Buddha-nature can be manifested by means of discipline.

Fourth, in Huayan Buddhism, it is a "perfect freedom" from obstacles posed by the "six forms" of life, which are the whole, the partial, the universal, the diverse, the perfect, and the disintegrating. The whole, the universal and the perfect are collective and comprehensive forms, whereas the partial, the diverse and the disintegrating are individual and characterizing forms. The two sets are paired to complement each other in forming an entity.

Fifth, it is the seeing-nature of Son Buddhism. The agony of life and death disappears when the selfish ego is surmounted and universal self replaces it. When a person realizes the truth that death and life are one through historical development, he or she embraces a farsighted view, freedom from all obstacles, and transcendency as the canons of behavior and thus attains Buddhahood.

The *bodhisattva* is the embodiment of those five philosophies. The *bodhisattva* is the ideal of the Buddhist persona and the basis of tolerance we are discussing here.

I am going to tell you of the spirit of boundless compassion and tolerance by quoting the teachings in the *Aṅgulimāla-sūtra*. Aṅgulimāla was a brutal bandit who murdered people without remorse but later became a disciple of Buddha. He led a thoroughly ascetic life and underwent exceptionally hard discipline to redeem his past evil deeds, but people harassed him when they learned he was Aṅgulimāla. One day, he came to Buddha badly beaten and bleeding and asked: "What is the most difficult thing in the world? I find it the most difficult not to hate someone when he is wielding his sword to kill me." Buddha replied with a smile, "Good, Aṅgulimāla! But there is a more difficult thing than that. Not to hate the person who is going to kill you is not enough. The most difficult thing in the world is to be able to say 'You are the Buddha' to him."[5]

---

[5] PTS, ed., *Anguttara-nikaya*, Vol.2, 66-68.

This shows us how far Buddhist tolerance should extend. A simple reverence for life is not enough. This teaching cannot be understood without first understanding that oneself and others are one. We believe everyone has the innate potential for this much tolerance, for this is how life was originally created. The multitudes, however, have forgotten their fundamental selves and lead a life of estrangement.

The dharma, which penetrates all things of this universe, is none other than the rule of cause of effect. Individuals or objects, which appear to be of no relation to each other, actually exist through this circle of cause and effect. We might replace the upper three forms of the Six Forms of the *Huayan Sutra,* i.e., the whole, the universal and the perfect, with the concept of the world and the lower three forms, i.e., the partial, the diverse and the disintegrating, with the concept of humanity. We can also equate the upper three with the Buddha and the lower three with the multitude.

Here we can conclude that the universal self and the individual self are but one. The self in me is thus a universal self I am a living entity. The universe is filled with innumerable living entities and I am but a tiny speck in the enormous stream of lives in the universe. If I died, it would be a devastating event for me, my family and friends, but it would not make any difference to the great stream of life. For the universal life is an endless repetition of birth and death. Right at this moment, a life is born and a life is dying, neither making a difference to the entire flow. If we can identify the individual self with the universal self, the life and the death will no longer make a difference. The Son masters realized this truth and led their lives based on their realization.

The grand motto World Peace should in truth be based on this philosophical introspection. The Western concept of peace seems to be as an antonym of war. Peace, however, is not a world without war. We should understand the importance of inner peace, a world inhabited by people who have freed themselves from the chain of Three Poisons, i.e., greed, anger, folly. I believe the fundamental value of peace is an all-embracing world where the universal and the individual are identified with each other.

The *Huayan-sūtra* emphasizes that the natural tendency to destroy dharma stems from the ignorance of the sentient multitude. It can be explained with the example of a house in relation to the timber of which it is built. A thick, sturdy timber is used as a ridge beam and a slender timber is used as a rafter. Good quality wood is made into a living room door and lower quality wood is made into a kitchen or toilet door. If all of the wood insisted to become a ridge beam, the house would never get completed. It is only through the dedication and sacrifice of each part that order is achieved in the form of a completed house. Nature observes this order completely. Laozu says in his *Way of Dao* that it is the law of nature to fill what is lacking and remove what is superfluous .[6] Hence

---

[6] Floyd H. Ross, *Questions that Matter Most, Asked by the Worlds' Religions* (Boston: Beacon Press, 1956), 76-86. "Nature" is the key to all the Taoist's answers to the questions life makes us ask.. A person's highest good and his sincere happiness are to

the dialectic of the enacting nature, or nature perfect without the interference of humans.

This order is not observed in human society, however. Every human wants to play the role of the hero or heroine on the stage called the universe. Imagine a movie full of heroes and heroines with no supporting actors or extras. The Buddhist tolerance comes from its compassion for other people. It evokes thoughts that the Chinese character meaning "deception" comprises two characters which, when individually used, mean a "human deed." A Son Buddhist's expression here, however, would be "I am satisfied with what I am." We can interpret it as knowing one's own limitations.

Human prejudices destructive of the universal order can be summarized as the following two points. The first is a dichotomous way of dividing the world in relation to oneself. The black or white logic which is prominent in biased thinking is steeped in analytic knowledge, often at the risk of missing the comprehensive understanding. As the proverb goes, one can't see the forest for the trees.

The second is the lack of determination to realize dharma. As Vijñāna Buddhism points out, it is a disease caused by justifying the progress of the selfish mind.[7]

I believe it is necessary for us to understand ourselves in relation to the universal order and to endeavor to live an altruistic life. Such terms as mutual interrelation and mutual equality in the structural logic of Buddhism come to mind. Mutual interrelationship means that subjectivity and objectivity influence each other. Mutual equality thus means that both becomes one.

Monk Uisang (620-702) summed it up in *Hwaeom ilseung beopgye-do,* his commentary on the *Huayan-sūtra (Hwaeom gyeong),* that "a thought of an instant is for eternity." The ideal of Buddhism then is the realization of togetherness in Great Compassion.

3. Harmony through Perfect Freedom from All Obstacles

For a long time, humans have lived in the midst of conflicts and confrontations. In ancient societies, the cause of confrontations was differences in religious ideologies. A religious belief is a system of absolute conviction which offers absolute justification for one's own beliefs and condemns the beliefs of the other as utterly worthless. A good example is the Crusades in the

---

be found through conforming with the way of all nature, the Dao. When one is natural, he is relaxed within and able to accept what life offers. When one is ambitious or aggressive, he contradicts his true nature. In the ensuing civil war within himself, he strikes his possible happiness a fatal blow.

[7] Oda Kyuki, *Depth Psychology of Buddhism,* trans. by Jung Byong-Jo (Seoul: Hyeoneumsa, 1985), 211-214. An outstanding feature of the seventh *manovijñāna* is selfishness. However, we can expect a positive consequence when it is converted into the good energy. In other words, it can become a tonic that converts despair into hope and the impossible possible.

Middle Ages. The bigotry of denouncing others' religion in adherence to one's own in the belief it is the one and only religion is a sad legacy born of prejudices. And this unfortunate malady is rampant in Seoul at this moment.

On the other hand, the conflicts in the Middle Ages derived mostly from a desire for conquest. The competition of the so-called great men to acquire and expand their territories reduced the populace to perpetual anxiety and fear. Their vainglory was responsible for the colonization of the Orient by the Western countries and the adventurism of the imperialists, which resulted in the two World Wars. In the modern era, the mode of confrontation gradually took on the shape of proxy wars incited by ideologies, their most convincing examples being the tragedies of the Korean Peninsula and Vietnam. The misadventures of the 20th century summed up as the Cold War, however, seem to have come to an end. It appears the confrontations of the future will take the form of economic conflicts. The protectionism of advanced nations and the Uruguay Round are their harbingers. Futurists are already describing the economic confrontations as wars without swords and guns.

What will be the end of these confrontations going to be? Is it impossible after all to have a truly quarrel-less world?

Here we need to remember again what motivated the Buddha to leave his home and enter the monkhood. Witnessing senseless killings in the secular world, Prince Siddhartha lamented: "What makes living things harass and kill one another? Is it truly impossible for them to co-exist peacefully?" (*Chulyo-gyeong-sūtra*). Later in his life, after achieving Enlightenment, he experienced numerous personal sorrows such as the rebellion of Devadatta, the death of Śāriputra and Maudgalyāyana, the downfall of his Gautama tribe, and the endless condemning of Buddhism as a religion that ends family lines. He says: "I fight not with the world, ye monks. The world fights with me. He who proclaims the truth, ye monks, fights with no one in the world."[8] The end of confrontations pursued by Prince Siddhartha remains the quest of all humanity.

I have already summarized the Buddhist position in the matter in five points. What we need here is the determination and institutional support to put them into practice. Some complain Buddhist ideals are too unrealistic, much like the babbling of a dreamer, but we should endeavor to thwart such self-doubt and self-derogation. From the Fourfold Principles of Bringing Together[9] to the Four

---

[8] Karl Jaspers, *Buddha*, 24-25. But for Buddha it was a matter of principle to offer no resistance. The struggle was carried on with spiritual weapons. Buddha did not confront a united spiritual power. Also see *Diamond Sutra*, trans. by Edward Conze (London: Allen & Unwin, 1958). "Subhūti is the best of the persons who acquired the purest Samādhi."

[9] The Fourfold Principles of Bringing Together: (1) Benevolence (*danā*); (2) Loving Words (*priya-vadita-saṁgraha*); (3) Welfare Promotion (*artha-carya-saṁgraha*); and (4) Participation (*samanārthāta-saṁgraha*).

Immeasurable Minds[10] and Six Pāramitā,[11] there is nothing that is not idealistic in the path of a bodhisattva. And there are many real examples of people who willingly and successfully took that harsh path of life.

We must, therefore, increase companions in faith who appreciate this way to the truth. Some people suggest that a constitutional government is what we need most to bring an end to the combativeness in our lives. However, the ideal way is to enlighten the entire populace. This is the justification of Buddhism. The propagation of Buddhism is the spreading of a mode of life ideal for humankind.

Obviously future society is going to be multi-religious. We cannot say a religion is superior to another because it has a greater number of believers, sanctums and clergy. The important point is how close it is to the world of truth it professes to strive to reach.

Buddhists should question constantly how close they are to the *bodhisattva* mind they strive to attain. If we take pride in being the followers of Buddha, we should live his teachings. As proclaimed in the *Lotus Sūtra*, we should be able "to reside in Buddha's room, wear Buddha's clothes and speak in Buddha's voice."

After all, the true nature of all living things is the Buddha. I firmly believe it is our spiritual assignment to enlighten our unfortunate neighbors of their Buddha nature of which they are unaware.

---

[10] The Four Enormous Mind: (1) *Maitrī:* Compassion; (2) *Karuṇā:* Remove sorrow from beings; (3) *Muditā:* Enjoying oneself over the other's delight; and (4) *Upekṣā:* Acquiring the peaceful mind.

[11] The Six Pāramitās are (1) *Dāna:* Offering materials, dharma and fearlessness; (2) *Śīla:* Observing the precepts; (3) *Kṣānti:* Fortitude against persecutions; (4) *Vrīya:* Practicing the truth continuously; (5) *Dhyāna:* Concentrating the spirit and stabilizing it; and (6) *Prajñā:* Getting the wisdom of truth.

CHAPTER 3

PERSONAL PEACE AND PHILOSOPHICAL CONFLICT: HEZE SHENHUI AND HIS ATTACK UPON NORTHERN CHAN

Robert B. Zeuschner

1. Introduction

Anyone even mildly knowledgeable about Chinese Buddhism knows about the 8th century division of the Chan school into two lines, the Northern gradualistic line of Shenxiu and the Southern sudden line of Huineng. In fact, one of the most important persons in the Chan tradition in China and the Zen tradition of Japan is Huineng (Enō), the Sixth Patriarch of the Chan school. The Chan legends proclaim him to be the person who single-handedly put Chan on the track of non-conceptual sudden enlightenment. What is not so well known is that Huineng had an official successor, the Seventh Patriarch of Chan, Heze Shenhui.[1] Shenhui's dates are usually given as 670-762 but newer findings place the dates as 684-758.[2]

Why don't we hear more about Heze Shenhui, the Seventh Patriarch? One reason is because none of the existing lineages of present-day Chinese Chan or Japanese Zen trace their link to the pivotal Huineng through him or his students. Another reason is that he typified the earlier intellectual style of Chan, rather

---

[1] In 796, thirty-eight years after the death of Heze Shenhui, the designated heir of Emperor Dezong (d. 805) called a meeting of Chan masters in order to determine which of the two lines of Chan, Northern or Southern, should be accepted as orthodox. At this meeting, the Southern line was officially declared to be the orthodox school, Huineng was declared the Sixth Patriarch of Chan (not the Northern master Shenxiu, as was claimed by his followers), and Heze Shenhui was declared to be the Seventh Patriarch. Historically speaking, by this time the Northern line had been eclipsed by the Southern lineages. This is recounted in Zongmi's *Yuanjue jing dashu chao*, found in the *Dai-Nihon Zokuzōkyō* 14.277b.

[2] A Japanese summary of recent Chinese discoveries can be found in Takeuchi Kōdō, "Shinshutsu no Kataku Jinne tomei ni tsuite," *Shigaku kenkyū* 27 (March 1985).

than the more modern emerging *kongan* style perfected by Southern Chan. But, it is likely that there is another reason that he is not so well known. He is somewhat of an embarrassment to the tradition, because he seems to have been a crusty, cantankerous personality who did not suffer those whom he felt did not deeply comprehend the dharma, and he carried on a lengthy attack upon the Northern tradition of Chan.

The *Lidai fabao ji* describes this:

> The chief priest Shenhui of the Eastern capital temple of Heze, every month erected a platform, and for the sake of the people, preached the Dharma. He attacked the "Chan of purity" and [instead] established "Tathāgata Chan".[3]

The text provides an example of this where, in a dialogue with a monk, Heze Shenhui asks for a summary of his teacher's doctrine, and after hearing the teaching described, Shenhui responds:

> The Chan master Shen of Jiannan is a Dharma-master, and does not preach the highest doctrine. The Chan master Tang is a disciple of Shen, and does not preach the highest doctrine. The Chan master Tang's disciple, Chao of the state of Zi is a Dharma-master. Wang of the state of Ling is a teacher of the rules (*vinaya*). Xi Biao is a Dharma-master. Jian of the state of Yi is a Chan master and preaches the profound doctrine, but you have not grasped it. Although these [others] do not preach the highest teaching, the Buddha's Dharma is found only in his place.[4]

In theory, an established Chan teacher ought to have a profound experience of awakening, and as a result, should be experiencing tranquility, equanimity, great compassion and a deep personal peace.[5] One would think that this should preclude outbursts of condemnation or unjustified and undeserved denunciation that causes conflict and dissention in the *sangha*. Yet, Heze Shenhui did cause conflict in the *sangha*. Chan master Heze Shenhui, the formally recognized student of and successor to the Sixth Patriarch (Huineng), seems to have engaged in a thirty-year vendetta against the philosophical concepts of and the leaders of the Northern tradition of Chan, and it has been suggested that his motives were egocentric and self-serving. This paper will explore the nature of the disagreement and explore the question of whether self-serving behavior precludes authentic enlightenment in a teacher.

---

[3] See *Lida fabao ji* (A Record of Successive Generations of the Dharma Treasure), T.51.2075.185b. The phrase "Chan of purity" is a reference to the Northern Chan meditative practice, "arousing the mind and regarding purity."

[4] *Ibid.*

[5] These are counted among the seven factors of enlightenment (*bojjhaṅga*).

There has been one book written on the subject of the conflicts in Northern Chan (by Professor John McRae). This paper will argue that, despite the excellence of his work, his treatment is insufficient and incorrect in many important ways.

2. Sources

One of the most difficult problems facing the philosophical and historical study of the Chinese Chan tradition is the task of separating legends and propaganda from historical fact. The Chan school itself is responsible for creating numerous legends about itself and its history, [6] and, in the West, the majority of these legends were accepted as fact until as recently as the 1960s. [7]

However, sixty years ago, Japanese scholarship was way ahead of Western and Chinese scholars on the issue of the early history of the Chinese Chan patriarchs. Important historical analyses include the three-volume *Zenshūshi kenkyū* by Ui Hakuju [8] which was instrumental in putting a new historically accurate perspective on Chan history, and this was followed up by the extremely important writings of Yanagida Seizan. Yanagida's widely varied works provide the foundation for two of the most important Western books about Northern and Southern Chan. One book is Philip Yampolsky's valuable 1967 *Platform Sūtra of the Sixth Patriarch*. [9] The other one is the 1987 *The Northern School and the Formation of Early Ch'an Buddhism* by Professor John McRae. [10] Among other topics, Dr. McRae discusses the political and power agenda behind Chan in those early centuries [11] and, following Yanagida and Ui, makes clear that there

---

[6] It is very likely that a good many of these were created by Heze Shenhui himself, including the fiction of the transmission of the robe from Bodhidharma to Huineng.

[7] The first English edition of Dumoulin's *A History of Zen Buddhism* (London: Farber & Farber, 1963) was little more than a careful and accurate compendium of the legends which Chan had constructed for itself, treating these as historical fact.

[8] Ui Hakuju, *Zenshūshi kenkyū* (Studies in the History of the Zen School), published in Tokyo during 1939-1943. Chapter five of volume one dealt with the rise and fall of the Heze lineage.

[9] Philip B. Yampolsky, *The Platform Sūtra of the Sixth Patriarch* (New York: Columbia University Press), 1967.

[10] John McRae, *The Northern School and the Formation of Early Ch'an Buddhism* (Kuroda Institute, Studies in East Asian Buddhism, no. 3) (Honolulu: University of Hawaii Press, 1987).

[11] McRae's book is divided into two parts. The first part is historical and biographical. Part Two focuses upon philosophical doctrine: (1) earliest teachings of Chan (especially Bodhidharma's *Eru sixing lun*); (2) doctrines of East Mountain teaching of Hongren (including a superb translation and analysis of the teachings of the Fifth Patriarch, the *Xiuxin yaolun*, "Treatise on Essentials of Cultivating Mind", 121-132); (3) Shenxiu and the religious philosophy of the Northern School (including translations of the *Yuanming lun* and a combination of several of the *Wu fangbian* texts on pp. 171-196). In addition, he translates the *Yuanming lun*, which *might* be a Northern Chan text (more

really is NO evidence of any connection between Bodhidharma and the later
Chan patriarchs. Bodhidharma was not the first Chan patriarch, and there was
never any line linking Bodhidharma to the Sixth Patriarch, Huineng.[12]

3. *The Platform Sūtra of the Sixth Patriarch*

In the past, the primary source for the division of Chan into gradual-North
and sudden-South has been the *Platform Sūtra of the Sixth Patriarch* (Liuzu
Tanjing). The *Platform Sūtra* portrays itself as a record of a sermon or series of
talks given by the Sixth Patriarch, Huineng and has been treated as historically
accurate by most Western scholars until the late 1960s. It tells the tale of
Huineng (638-713) and his contest of poetry with Shenxiu (605?-706).
Essentially, this text stresses how the Southern school became the official
teaching of Chan, and it minimized or ignored the Northern line of Shenxiu. As
has often been pointed out, the *Platform Sūtra* does not furnish us with an
unbiased picture of Northern Chan. Indeed, recent research has questioned the
very authenticity of the *Platform Sūtra*.

According to Yanagida Seizan's hypothesis, one of the best ways to account
for the contents of this text is that the earliest version of what we know as the
Platform Sūtra of the Sixth Patriarch has nothing to do with the Sixth Patriarch,
and was not a record of the sermon of Huineng. It was actually a text composed

---

on this later). In part two, McRae struggles mightily to find some continuity between the
earliest teachings and the later Northern doctrines.

The back of the book includes a careful translation of the *Chuan fabao ji*
("Annals of the Transmission of the Dharma-treasure," a history text composed around
712 stressing Northern Chan), plus collated and edited Chinese texts of the *Xiuxin yaolun*
(a record of the teachings of Hongren) and the *Yuanming lun*. McRae's translations are
scholarly, very useful and valuable. It is curious that so many translations come from pre-
Northern sources, such as texts attributed to Bodhidharma, Dao Xin, and Hongren.
Considering the title and focus, one cannot but wonder why he didn't put more emphasis
upon the texts attributed to Shenxiu, the pivotal Northern Chan patriarch (such as the
Guanxin lun, the *Poxiang lun* and the *Miaoli yuancheng guan*).

[12] One major problem for those who explore Chan history is the connection
between the putative founder, Bodhidharma, and the later East Mountain Teaching of
Tao-hsin and Hungjen. McRae shows that the connection is tenuous at best, and admits
that no early evidence connects the East Mountain Teaching with the tradition of
Bodhidharma (p. 31), doctrinally or historically. Given that, it is strange that he goes on
to spend so much time trying to show that it is possible to interpret Bodhidharma's text in
a way that is consonant with Northern Chan ideas. What is the point? McRae seems
unwilling to accept the results of his own research, i.e., that there really wasn't any
connection between Bodhidharma and East Mountain. Instead, McRae is concerned with
showing that, by following one less-than-obvious interpretation of the text, we can
conclude that Bodhidharma might have influenced Northern Chan, or at least that there
was no fundamental disagreement between the two.

by a member of the independent Ox-Head school,[13] a line which has little relationship to what we consider the mainline Southern lineage. Yanagida suggests that this Ox-Head text was later consciously falsely attributed to Huineng in order to put an end to existing divisiveness between North and South. How? By accepting Heze Shenhui's philosophical position but avoiding any significant reference to Heze Shenhui himself; by putting Shenhui's ideas into Huineng's mouth. Thus Heze Shenhui's ideas win out because they are correct, but people who were upset by his approach can still accept the ideas, because now they are put in the mouth of the revered Huineng.

Why avoid reference to Heze Shenhui? Because of his embarrassingly belligerent criticisms and not-very-enlightened attitudes towards the Northern line.

4. The Criticisms of Heze Shenhui

What did Heze Shenhui say that was so embarrassing? Heze Shenhui criticized the North with several different allegations:

(1) Northern Chan espoused a form of quietistic seated meditation, whereas the genuine meditation of the patriarchs had nothing to do with sitting quietly; Heze Shenhui stresses their practice of seated meditation "inspecting purity," which he seems to believe is dualistic and "an obstacle to *bodhi*."[14]

(2) Northern Chan had a tendency to interpret the Buddhist path as a gradual path, rather than seeing that enlightenment occurs suddenly; he characterizes the North as "gradual" and his own Southern line as "sudden," and says "No one considers Sudden and Gradual to be the same ... All six generations of great teachers of my lineage spoke of chopping through like a knife and directly realizing and seeing your own true nature, and did not speak of [the path being] gradual or in steps. Students of the way, you must suddenly see your Buddha-nature, and then gradually cultivate causal conditions; without leaving this life yet you will achieve liberation."[15]

(3) The writings of Northern Chan were clearly dualistic stressing pairs of concepts, instead of seeing the ultimacy of non-dual insight which was in consonance with the fundamental Prajñāpāramitā literature; he criticizes their dualistic position found in their lack of understanding of the fundamental identity of *dhyāna* and *prajñā,* of meditation and wisdom (attributed to Huineng and stressed in the *Platform Sūtra of the Sixth Patriarch*).

(4) Shenxiu, the Northern patriarch, did not receive the robe and bowl of Bodhidharma from the Fifth Patriarch (but Huineng of the South did), and therefore Shenxiu could not be the real Sixth Patriarch (and thus it was a serious

---

[13] The *locus classicus* for this appears in Yanagida's classic work, *Shoki Zenshū shisō no kenkyū* (Studies in the Historical Writings of the Zen Sect) (Kyoto: Hōzōkan, 1966), 100-213.

[14] *Ibid.,* 287-88; 175.

[15] *Ibid,* 286-87; 175.

falsification of history when the disciples of Shenxiu incorrectly called their teacher the "Sixth Patriarch").

It should be noted that the Northern master Shenxiu and his disciples were powerful in the court of Empress Wu, and certainly had much more political power and influence than the relatively unimportant side-line of Chan disciples who followed the obscure Huineng and his disciple, Heze Shenhui.

What was wrong with Heze Shenhui and his stance? Summarizing Professor McRae's criticisms, we find: (1) Heze Shenhui is self-serving because he minimized the discipline of the meditative life[16] and wanted for himself the fame and glory which accrues from the life-style which results from governmental or imperial patronage; (2) he wanted to establish his own Southern line of Chan as the official Buddhist teaching, replacing the position of the Northern line; (3) Heze Shenhui's criticisms can be ignored because they were merely restatements of ideas first asserted by the Northern Chan authors (i.e., there wasn't much difference between Heze Shenhui's criticisms and Northern Chan's own analyses of deficiencies in teaching approaches); (4) Heze Shenhui was simply wrong when he criticized Northern Chan as gradualistic; (5) also, according to Professor McRae, Heze Shenhui "dangled the lure of the enlightenment experience in before the noses of his students," but the Northern Chan masters bravely refrained from doing so.

How many of these criticisms apply? Did Heze Shenhui have an ego problem? He seems to have felt that he was the only one who genuinely and deeply understood the "Tathāgata Chan" of Bodhidharma. One reason he provides for calling his meetings is this:

> There is no longer anyone in the world who understands the single entrance of the Southern school of Bodhidharma. If there were anyone else, I would no longer teach. Today's address is for the sake of students of the way to distinguish the true and the false [teachings], and for the sake of students of the way to realize the essential meaning.[17]

In. another place in the same text, after a dialogue with a Dharma-master, Heze Shenhui says that he could easily be like the Dharma-master, but

---

[16] There is a famous quote from the Huayan master Zongmi about Huineng. "When Caoji [Huineng] saw someone seated in cross-legged meditation, he took his staff and beat the person until he got up." Quoted from Zongmi's *Chanyuan zhu chuanji duxu* (General Preface to the Fountainheads of Chan), in Kamata Shigeo, *Zengen shosenshō tojo*, Vol. 9 of *Zen no gōroku* series (Tokyo: Chikuma Shobō, 1971).

[17] "Treatise Establishing the True and False According to the Southern School of Bodhidharma," in Hu Shi, *Shenhui heshang yiji* (The Surviving Works of the Master Shenhui), text #1, 162; also 263-64.

> However, if the Dharma-master were to study Shenhui [try to imitate
> Shenhui], you would go through three incalculable *kalpa*s and still
> not be able to accomplish it.[18]

However, was Heze Shenhui really so contentious? The audience wants an argument, but on the next page we find him declining to argue:

> The master Shenhui sat quietly in meditation and did not dispute with
> the others; although he wanted to engage in the dispute he declined to
> do so for a long while.[19]

Yet, does Heze Shenhui really disparage the Northern patriarch? Actually, he acknowledges the understanding of Shenxiu. When asked why Shenxiu is not in the sixth generation of patriarchs, Heze Shenhui replies, "It is because Chan master Hung-jen [the fifth patriarch and teacher of Huineng and Shenxiu] did not transmit the mandate [of the robe] to Chan master Shenxiu, although later he did attain the fruits of the Way."[20] Heze Shenhui says the reason Shenxiu is not the sixth generation patriarch is that Shenxiu does not possess the robe which symbolized the successive transmission of the dharma from the time of Bodhidharma.

Is this self-serving? Well, perhaps yes. In this passage he objects to the position of prominence that the Northern line has attained by labeling itself in the sixth generation, and in the seventh generation. Does Heze Shenhui want himself to occupy that position of prominence? Very probably. Of course, depending on how one counts generations, the Northern line was in the sixth or seventh generation. What Heze Shenhui has done is argue that only one teacher per generation can have the robe of Bodhidharma, and just as a country can have only one king, so Chan generations should be counted as just one person per generation.

How does he criticize the Northern masters was for utilizing a fundamentally dualistic way of describing the Buddhist path? In Huineng's *Platform Sūtra* we find:

> Students, be careful not to say that meditation gives rise to wisdom,
> or that wisdom gives rise to meditation, or that meditation and
> wisdom are different from each other. To hold this view implies that
> things have duality - if good is spoken while the mind is not good,
> meditation and wisdom will not be alike.[21]

Heze Shenhui echoes this same criticism (or, following Yanagida, perhaps the above quote is from Heze Shenhui himself). He attacks "the view that

---

[18] Hu Shi, *ibid.*, 267.
[19] *Ibid.*, 268.
[20] *Ibid.*, 283.
[21] Yampolsky, *ibid.*, 132.

concentration is to be practiced first and it is only after its attainment that *prajñā*-wisdom is awakened." He goes on to say,

> But, according to my view, the very moment I am conversing with you, there is *dhyāna,* there is *prajñā,* and they are the same. ... when *dhyāna* and *prajñā* are the same, this is called "seeing Buddha-nature.[22]

Northern Chan writings constantly analyze things into pairs, sometimes contraries, sometimes contradictories, and sometimes sequentially related pairs such as concentration leading to insight. In particular, Northern Chan had an unfortunate scholastic and dualistic tendency to divide two-character technical terms, providing two complementary explanations for the single term. Is this tendency unique to the North, or were Northern teachers merely following a tendency which ran through Chinese Buddhism at the time? Dr. McRae points out that this dualistic dividing can be found in one other commentary of the period but admits that it is not clear if this commentary is a Chan text or not (p. 204). Even if this text were not a Northern text, the fact that other texts do it too does not absolve Northern Chan of the charge that they have a tendency to dualize central terms and concepts. At best it shows that other texts were equally dualistic and scholastic. Further attempting to justify the dualizing proclivity of the North, McRae notes what appears to be an archetypical Chinese tendency to make "arbitrary correlations" in an attempt to understand Buddhism (p. 206). But, even if this tendency were demonstrated to be equally strong in Southern Chan texts, it doesn't absolve the North of responsibility for dualizing key concepts. Northern Chan may have not understood these dualistically, but they use pairs and they do not explicitly stress their fundamental non-dualism (which the Southern Chan line constantly stresses). Heze Shenhui's criticism still seems to apply: how can dualistic explanations lead to non-dualistic insight? How can dualistic meditative practices lead to non-dualistic realization?

However, Heze Shenhui's criticisms are not just philosophical; it is worse than this. In the same text,[23] Heze Shenhui accuses Puji of sending a thief to steal the head from the body of Huineng, Shenhui's teacher. He also accuses Puji of twice sending someone to deface and rub out the memorial monument for Huineng. Heze Shenhui accuses Puji of trying to eliminate Huineng from Chan history and trying to substitute his own teacher, Shenxiu of the North as the sixth patriarch in the sixth generation, and thereby making himself the seventh patriarch. Although Heze Shenhui doesn't say so explicitly, he is saying

---

[22] Hu Shi, *ibid.,* 138.

[23] Yanagida Seizan considers this story slander, and believes that Heze Shenhui made it up. Yanagida says that people in those days were not concerned with ethics. See Yanagida Seizan, *Shoki zenshū shisō no kenkyū* (Studies in the Historical Texts of the Earliest Period of Zen") (Kyoto: Hōzōkan, 1966), 116-117, fn. 14.

that the title of seventh patriarch of the seventh generation belongs to himself, and not to the Northern teachers.

Professor McRae's book on Northern Chan takes a curious position on some of these issues. First, he castigates Heze Shenhui for taking a genuinely ego-centric and self-serving attitude towards the Northern line, arguing that Heze Shenhui is criticizing the North merely for personal and political gain. Heze Shenhui wanted his own line established as the dominant line, because political influence and fame would accrue. Of course, this is reprehensible in a Chan Buddhist teacher. To the extent that Heze Shenhui was self-serving, he deserves censure. But Professor McRae doesn't utter a word of criticism for those Northern Chan masters who had been equally self-serving: Dr. McRae admits that Shenxiu and Puji wanted political power, and wanted to establish their Northern line of Chan as the official Buddhist teaching. He writes that one of the tasks of Northern Chan was "to establish Chan as legitimate--in its own eyes, the legitimate--school of Chinese Buddhism (p. 75)." Wasn't this exactly Heze Shenhui's agenda? If it is venal of Heze Shenhui to want this, then it would seem equally venal of the Northern Chan leaders.

In fact, concerning the political entanglements of the Northern patriarch, Shenxiu, Dr. McRae utters nary a critical word about his closeness to the patronage of the Imperial court and association with Empress Wu and court intrigue. Historical evidence supports the picture of Northern Chan temples supported by wealthy people who wanted to be associated with anything approved of by the throne, people who go with what's popular.[24] The best Dr. McRae can say in defense of Northern Chan is that it did not clearly see that the meditative life and governmental life-styles are incompatible[25] (if Shenhui is to be criticized for not seeing that, we must ask why couldn't Northern Chan see that, and ask why we shouldn't tar them both with the same brush?).

In addition, when it comes to explication of Buddhist doctrine, Professor McRae admits that Shenxiu of the North tried to surround himself with an aura of supernaturalism,[26] but McRae doesn't think that this is negative. In order to strike the fancy of the Empress, "Teachings would have had to be conventional yet original, orthodox yet iconoclastic, inspired yet flawed ... mutually contradictory." (p. 197). But McRae doesn't ask why a Chan master would want to distort and make alluring the fundamental insights of Buddhism in order to strike the fancy of the Empress. In fact, McRae is describing how one has to teach in order to curry favor with the court.

At this point, the only conclusion is that if Heze Shenhui had the motives we ascribe to him, then he was wrong, and it follows that when the same motives can be ascribed to the Northern line, and they too deserve censure. If Heze Shenhui of the South was not behaving in a way which we associate with an enlightened Chan master, then too the supposedly enlightened Northern Chan

---

[24] McRae, *op. cit.*, 242.
[25] McRae, *ibid.*, 243.
[26] McRae, *ibid.*, 197.

followers were not behaving in a way we associate with an enlightened teacher. Two wrongs don't make a right; the conclusion is that neither side acquits itself very well in this debate (although Professor McRae censures only Heze Shenhui and absolves the North).

Heze Shenhui, who offered such effective and biting criticisms of the Northern line, was ultimately banished by a government official, most likely a follower of the government-supported Northern school of Shenxiu. If the North couldn't make Heze Shenhui quiet down, rather than answer his objections, they invoke political power and banish him. However, Dr. McRae claims that the North was not responsible for his banishment; but instead of any evidence, he offers alternative "may have" interpretations of Shenhui's banishment (p. 241). What can we conclude about this incident? Only that there is not enough information available to settle for sure whether it was Northern political retribution.

An interesting question arises. Why didn't the Northern teachers respond philosophically to Heze Shenhui's criticisms? Professor McRae argues that the reason Northern Chan followers did not bother to respond philosophically to the various criticisms is because those criticisms were merely restatements of ideas first asserted by Northern Chan School authors (i.e., there wasn't much difference between Heze Shenhui's criticisms and Northern Chan's own analyses of deficiencies in teaching approaches).

However, if Northern Chan followers made these same criticisms, then *it follows that the content of Heze Shenhui's criticisms were justified and correct,* it is only their application to the North which is in doubt. In support of his statement that there really wasn't so much difference between Northern Chan authors (who based their position on the *Laṅkāvatāra* and the *Awakening of Faith*) and Heze Shenhui's position (based more upon the *Diamond* and other *Prajñāpāramitā* sūtras), Dr. McRae mentions that the Huayan patriarch Chengguan (738-840) was unable to see any significant differences between the Northern Chan masters and Southern Chan teachers. However McRae doesn't mention Chengguan's successor, Zongmi (780-841), who, in his detailed study of Chan, finds many important differences between the two. However, we must point out that Zongmi considered himself as belonging to the lineage of Heze Shenhui but never knew Heze Shenhui personally (Heze Shenhui died in 758, twenty-two years before Zongmi was born).

Professor McRae considers Heze Shenhui's criticism that Northern Chan was gradualistic, but misinterprets the criticism, setting up a straw man argument. That is, Heze Shenhui's criticism is distorted to make it easier to refute. Specifically, Heze Shenhui argued that gradualism is found in Northern Chan doctrine and practice; Dr. McRae exaggerates this into the much stronger claim that Northern Chan was consciously "defending gradualism." By treating Heze Shenhui's criticism as the stronger claim that Northern Chan was "defending gradualism," it is easy to show that Northern Chan was not consciously defending gradualism. But, he has still not dealt with Heze

Shenhui's original criticism; Dr. McRae has merely knocked down the "straw man" which McRae set up.

In fact, earlier, Professor McRae admitted that it is fair to label the meditation teaching of the Northern patriarch, Shenxiu, as gradualistic, yet Dr. McRae argued that this label, although accurate, is mitigated by other considerations (p. 217). Heze Shenhui argued that in the North, we find an error of gradualism, of duality and an error advocating progressive attainment. Heze Shenhui claims that Northern Chan practiced a meditative technique of gradually removing the impediments to full awakening, which include both the affective (removed by the practice of morality) and the conceptual (eliminated by the attainment of *prajñā* wisdom.

In fact, something like Heze Shenhui's claims is clearly seen in the writings of the North. The path is gradual, and the steps are achieved "one after another." In Shenxiu's *Guanxin lun,* we find:

> There are innumerable dharma-gateways and one after another you will attain and understand them. You will transcend the ordinary and awaken sagehood. Enlightenment takes place in a moment.[27]

Another phrase is repeated over and over in the Northern Chan text *Wu fangbian,* "... emancipation of the mind and then the body."[28] In fact, Dr. McRae acknowledges this. But then he explains why Northern Chan was mistakenly seen as gradualistic and philosophically incorrect:

> This [factor that allowed it to be philosophically caricatured as backward] is the absence of any obvious difference between the school's doctrines of [a] constant practice and the perfect teaching and the much more elementary notion of [b] gradual self-perfection.[29]

In other words, Professor McRae argues that "constancy of application" is a correct description of an essential religious practice of Northern Chan, but when taken out of context, it can be mistaken for simple gradualism.

> This mistaken impression was no doubt rendered more likely by the tendency of Northern School texts to use apparently sequential or progressive forms of expression [I think McRae is admitting that Shenhui had some basis for his criticisms], even though the doctrines themselves were essentially non-sequential, i.e., either perfect or sudden.[30]

---

[27] T.48.2009.369c10.

[28] This phrase is quoted in McRae, *op. cit.*, fn. 173, 331.

[29] Page 245.

[30] Page 245; emphasis mine.

As I read it, McRae is saying that the Northern Chan authors used wording which is clearly sequential and which suggests gradual attainment, but this is merely an unfortunate and careless matter of wording, which continued for another fifty years after the initial criticisms of Heze Shenhui.[31]

As to the charge of gradualism, McRae admits that there is justification in the writings of the North for someone to mistakenly conclude that their teachings were gradualistic. So, does the charge of gradualism leveled by Heze Shenhui then reflect a character flaw on his part? I think not; not if the appearance of gradualism is found in Northern writings. It would be a character flaw only if Heze Shenhui knew that he was mistaken, and yet continued to make the charge simply for political gain. No evidence whatsoever has been offered to support the claim that Heze Shenhui knowingly mis-described the North as gradualistic.[32] It seems awkward to even assert this, because Heze Shenhui was putting this charge forth in the capital beginning around 732, and the actual teachings of the Northern line of Chan had been promulgated for the past twenty years in the capital and were well-known; if you simply tell lies to those who know better, they are not taken in by falsehoods. How is it that Heze Shenhui's criticisms were effective at all? Yet McRae admits the effectiveness of Heze Shenhui's attacks: on page 71 he explains that he believes that Heze Shenhui and the *Platform Sūtra* actually did "tarnish the image" of Northern Chan, but that Northern Chan remained important for a long time.[33]

There was a difference between North and South on this point of sudden enlightenment. Heze Shenhui stresses a sudden breakthrough experience, which is then followed by continual cultivation to deepen that insight. It seems to me that the phrase that best describes Northern Chan would be "gradual cultivation

---

[31] And, if Heze Shenhui were merely repeated earlier Northern Chan admonitions, then it becomes more difficult to understand why the apparently gradualism continued for so long.

[32] Admittedly, it would be virtually impossible to establish what Heze Shenhui knew and what he did not know. Without his personal diary or the statement of someone with whom he had a conversation, we have only silence. But, no conclusion at all can follow from silence. Ignorance, or silence simply tells us that we do not know. It is no more probable that Heze Shenhui knew than that he did not know. The fallacy of drawing a conclusion from the absence of information is called the Fallacy of Ignorance. It becomes a fallacy if we reason the fact that "We don't know what he really thought because we have no information about it; therefore we may conclude that we know something about what he thought."

[33] Dr. McRae points out that there is no mention of any Northern master in the 740 epitaph of Faxian -- then Dr. McRae says that apart from this, there is no evidence of the impact of Shenhui's campaign negatively affecting Northern Chan. Yet this is rather strong evidence, isn't it? (p. 59) John admits Northern Chan was NOT the most creative Chan sect when he says after *755*, the most creative factions (Mazu and Ox-head) operated in the provincial centers of south-central China (p. 243). But in what respect were they the most creative? Does this reflect a flaw in Northern Chan doctrines, methods, or techniques? John is silent. If the *Platform Sūtra* tarnished their images, it must have been many years after 780, not as early as 755.

followed by sudden enlightenment." There is a progression of steps, followed by the experience of sudden enlightenment. Heze Shenhui stresses the abrupt moment of insight as the true beginning of the path; the North took a much more gentle approach, stressing the awkward steps of the beginning student which lead finally to a sudden illumination.

On page 245, McRae asserts that Northern Chan masters bravely refrained from "dangling the lure of the enlightenment experience in front of their student's nose." However, earlier he writes, "enlightenment is clearly considered something to be energetically sought for and achieved..." (p. 136). Perhaps there is a difference between these two, but it does call for further explication. McRae then says that Heze Shenhui was the first and most obvious violator of this convention (where and when was this convention established?), and thus was wrong in doing so.[34]

The major problem with Professor McRae's book, excellent as it is, is that it reads as an unabashed apology for Northern Chan. Indeed, there may be some justification for this stance because most Western scholars blindly accepted traditional accounts and, until the late 1970s, almost no one had a good thing to say about Northern Chan. Some correction was needed, but not only does Dr. McRae absolve Northern Chan of every possible negative charge, he seems to want to make Northern Chan responsible for everything good about later Chan. For example, Professor McRae does not utter a word of criticism concerning the Northern Chan leadership's love of the limelight, their passion for political influence, their tight involvement with imperial privileges and entanglements;[35] nor a word of praise for the Southern Chan people who avoided them[36] ... yet this factor may be as important as any other event in the history of the development of later Chan, certainly more important than the completely

---

[34] I point out in my 1977 dissertation, and more fully worked out in a paper presented at the 1981 conference on Sudden and Gradual Enlightenment, that the Southern Chan masters of Shenhui's time seem to have considered the Buddhist path to have begun with the experience of Sudden Enlightenment, and the Northern masters seem to emphasize the beginning student's gradual attainment of the skills necessary to cross this hurdle.

[35] In another article by Professor McRae, we find a description of an Ox-head master, Fachin, who is summoned to the court amid much pomp and circumstance. John writes: "Fachin's entry into court is somewhat reminiscent of the treatment accorded the great Shenxiu some two-thirds of a century before: After the master was carried into the palace on a palanquin ... [But], Taking no pleasure in the lavish gifts bestowed upon him, Fachin requested and received permission to return to his temple." Someone less sympathetic to Northern Chan might note that the Northern Chan masters took a lot of pleasure in the lavish gifts, the adulation, the pomp and circumstance--perhaps no less than Shenhui. The quotation is from John R. McRae, "The Ox-Head School of Chinese Chan Buddhism" in Gimello and Gregory, eds., *Studies in Ch'an and Hua-yen* (Honolulu: University of Hawaii Press, 1983), 192.

[36] Yet Dr. McRae does criticize the Southern Chan Seventh Patriarch, Heze Shenhui for attempting to gain some of that political patronage for himself when he offers criticisms of the Northern line of Chan.

apocryphal verses from the *Platform Sūtra* which he feels compelled to discuss at length (i.e., the "from the very beginning, not a single thing...").

Dr. McRae offers excellent advice to fellow scholars, and I wish it had been followed a little more closely by the author himself, i.e., "Doctrinal pronouncements cannot be immediately accepted at face value, but must be analyzed in terms of any polemical or propagandistic intent. We should pay close attention to our own presuppositions and examine where we are unconsciously adopting the originally propagandistic positions of the orthodox tradition. ... We must recognize when the available data is either not sufficient or not conducive to historical analysis and refrain from misrepresenting our sources to satisfy a desire for completeness." (p. 252). I could not agree more. That such advice is difficult to follow is clear.

Is this problem of less-than-perfect attainment in a Chan teacher unique to the 8th century battle between Northern and Southern Chan? I think not. If we knew more of the daily details of the life of Linji (Rinzai) or Mazu (Baso), what might that reveal? Sometimes we have a great deal of information about the personal life of a teacher, and we can find similar flaws. For example, consider one of the greatest and most highly regarded of all the Japanese Zen teachers, Dōgen Kigen, the grand patriarch of Japanese Soto Zen. In his second volume of *Zen Buddhism: A History*,[37] Dumoulin freely discusses Dōgen's depressions[38] and his rather bitter criticism of Linji[39] which developed in his later life, perhaps reflecting the success of the Rinzai school in Japan and the lack of success of his own Soto Zen. Dumoulin also notes Dōgen's outbursts of emotion directed against the non-Caodong lineages of China, and mentions evidence of a weakness of leadership when Dōgen was older.[40]

5. Conclusion

So, can we conclude that Heze Shenhui was correct in his objections? No, we cannot; some seem appropriate and others inappropriate. Northern Chan documents do say that enlightenment is attained suddenly; it never advocated gradual enlightenment. But it did stress *upāya*, devices or techniques which deepen one's gradual progress along the path. Heze Shenhui and the Southern line place great stress on sudden enlightenment, and seem to consider the genuine beginning of the Buddhist path to start here. And, at least with Heze Shenhui, seated meditation is downplayed. Northern Chan stresses techniques which gradually lead to sudden enlightenment, which is followed by constant practice, and seated meditation is stressed.

---

[37] Heinrich Dumoulin, *Zen Buddhism: A History* (Volume 2: Japan), tr. by James W. Heisig and Paul Knitter (New York: Macmillan, 1990).

[38] If, at this point, one wonders, "How can a Zen master be depressed?" then it is clear that the stereotype of "Zen master" needs to be reevaluated.

[39] *Ibid.*, 65-69.

[40] *Ibid.*, 104.

Northern Chan did have an unfortunate tendency to stress dualisms, pairs of concepts, and it did not stress that all dualities are incorrect (although Northern Chan texts reveal that these pairs are not understood as ultimate).

We are seeing a difference in styles, a difference in how the Buddhist path is conceptualized, and a difference in how it is described. Do these differences justify the conflict between the two lines in the 8th century? Not from the perspective of the 20th century.

Was Heze Shenhui self-serving? Very possibly, even probably. However, were the Northern teachers self-serving? Equally probable.

Were the actions of both sides incompatible with our understanding of the enlightened state of a Chan teacher? Most certainly.

However, the problem that we started out with was: how can a supposedly enlightened Chan master behave in a self-serving manner, in a way that is not indicative of the highest peace?

There are two strategies available to us. One way to preserve the status of Chan master; we simply reduce the status of those who do not fit into our schema. These Chan and Zen teachers are not really enlightened. However, this won't do. The various Chan and Zen teachers have been recognized as enlightened *roshi* by their own traditions, and by people who knew them. Therefore I cannot advocate devaluating their insight.

I would argue for a different conclusion, namely that we have elevated the status of a Chan or Zen master to much too high a level. The Chan master is not at the tenth level (or the 52nd level) of the Bodhisattva path. These people have gained insight, but it is not perfect. Not only did some Chan and Zen teachers have some troubling flaws, we find the pattern continued in the contemporary teachers, many of whom have come to the United States to teach; their students have imbued them with an aura of sainthood, and these people are not perfect. They have engaged in sexual relationships with their students, and sometimes they have not even recognized that this is a problem (yet every psychotherapist is taught to beware of transference, and taught to be careful of potential sexual involvement with patients). Such behavior does NOT correspond to what we think of as "enlightened."

In summary, master Heze Shenhui wasn't as bad as Professor McRae makes him out to be, and the Northern line of Chan masters were not much better than Heze Shenhui, despite Dr. McRae's protestations to the contrary. I am not arguing that "two wrongs make a right." Rather, two wrongs make both sides wrong. Actions which cause us to doubt the depth of enlightenment of Heze Shenhui equally cast doubt upon the Northern Chan teachers.

In China and in Japan, Chan and Zen masters have curried favor from those in power, have modified Buddhist doctrine to accommodate political shifting winds (especially in Japan where Buddhist doctrine had a distressing tendency to become subservient to the Emperor). This is clear evidence that the Chan / Zen experience of being a *roshi* is not the same as "complete unexcelled Buddhahood." In fact, I suspect that whatever "complete unexcelled

Buddhahood" (*samyaksaṃbodhi*) may be, it is much rarer than any Buddhist current tradition has allowed.

CHAPTER 4

ARHAT IDEAL IN EARLY BUDDIUSM

S. N. Dube

Disgusted with the ills of life, Buddha renounced the world to seek what is good, the excellent station of peace.[1] He finally attained to Enlightenment by discovering the relatedness and contingency of all things and the ineffable peace which lies beyond.[2] These twin principles of *pratītyasamutpāda* (*paṭiccasamuppāda*)[3] and *nirvāṇa* (*nibbāna*)[4] are the core of Buddha's philosophy. It is through their divergent interpretations that subsequent Buddhist philosophical systems have arisen. The Buddha does not seem to announce a categorically defined system. Instead he gave expression only to the need of the occasion. The Buddha, in fact, allowed his words to be remembered by everyone in his own dialect,[5] the meaning being important, not the word.[6] Consequently, after the passing away of the Buddha, his collected words gave rise to diverse attempts at systematizing them, and, thus, many different schools and sects came into existence.

---

[1] *kiṁkusalagavesī anuttaraṁ santivarapradaṁ pariyesamāno*, cf. *Majjhima Nikāya, Pāsarāsi-sutta*; cf, *Buddhacarita*, V. 14.

[2] *S.*, II, 105-106. (For citations from Pali texts *vide* Nalanda edition except where otherwise specified).

[3] On *Pratītyasamutpāda* see David J. Kalupahana, *Causality: The Central Philosophy of Buddhism* (Honolulu:University of Hawaii Press, 1975), 54 *ff*; see also G. C. Pande, *Studies in the Origins of Buddhism* (3rd ed., Delhi: University of Allahabad, 1983), 406*ff*.

[4] On Nirvāṇa, see T. I. Stcherbatsky, *The Conception of Buddhist Nirvāṇa* (Delhi: Motilal Banarsidass, 1996); see also G. C. Pande, *Studies in the Origins of Buddhism*, 443 *ff*.

[5] *Cullavagga*, 228-229: *anujānāmi, bhikkhave, sakāya niruttiyā buddhavacanaṁ pariyāpuṇituṁ*.

[6] *Arthaḥ pratiśaraṇam na vyañjanaṁ*.

In the course of its history, Buddhist missionaries have traversed for the 'happiness and welfare of mankind'[7] the far corners of the earth. As the Buddhist Order (*Sangha*) expanded, Councils claiming to be ecumenical have been held from time to time. Alongside this expansion the spirit of Buddhism has been liberal and democratic and its organization highly decentralized. This has given the widest possible latitude to thought and has led to the proliferation of numerous sects and schools. Traditionally by the time of Aśoka their number had reached eighteen. There is a common ground in the traditions of the different sects in holding that the differentiation of sects had arisen early, mostly within the first two centuries of the Nirvāṇa era.[8] In the evolution of the Buddhist sects and schools it is noticed that the 'great schism' in the *Sangha* resulting in the rise of two sects, i.e., Theravāda and Mahāsaṃghika at the time of the Second Buddhist Council, was followed by a series of schisms leading to the formation of various new sects. C. A. F. Rhys Davids calls the non-Theravāda schools dummies and observes that the ancient treatises on them by Vasumitra, Bhavya and Vinītadeva offer us only the dry disintegrated bones of doctrines.[9] Yet the dummies appear to have been once alive and the dry bones clothed with flesh and blood. The records, doubtless, present a dry conspectus because they are the products of scholastic activity.

The schism between Sthaviras (Theravāda) and Mahāsaṃghikas was occasioned by the question of the status of Arhat (Arhant). The concept of Arhatship, thus, forms a significant issue of debate amongst the early Buddhist sects. Arhat is the title given to the perfect man in Buddhism. The Buddhists seem to derive the term from *ari,* i.e., 'enemy' and *han,* i.e., 'to kill', and thus the term stands for a 'slayer of enemy', the term obviously being passions. Some modern scholars, however, prefer to derive this term from *arhati,* i.e., 'to be worthy of' or 'deserving' and 'worthy of worship and gifts.'[10] It seems that originally Arhat was a popular appellation given to ascetics. In Buddhism, however, it assumed a technical significance as denoting only the fully and finally emancipated saints. The Buddha is generally called an Arhat. In the

---

[7] *Mahāvagga,* 23: *caratha, bhikkhave, cārikaṃ bahujanahitāya bahujanasukhāya lokānukaṃpāya atthāya hitāya sukhāya deva-manussānaṃ.*

[8] Cf. *Dpvs.,,* V. 39 *ff, Mhvs.,* V. 3 *ff,* J. Masuda, "Origin and Doctrines of Early Indian Buddhist Schools," *Asia Major* II (1925): 14-18; A. Bareau, "Trois Traites sur les Sectes Bouddhiques du Petit Vehicule," *Journal Asiatique,* Fomme CCLIV (1956), II Partie, 167*f,* 172*f,* 192.

[9] Cf. *Points of Controversy* (London: Hurst and Blackett, 1960), Prefatory Notes, XXXII *ff.*; see also S. N. Dube, *Cross Currents in Early Buddhism* (Delhi: Manohar, 1980), 37*ff.*

[10] Rhys Davids and Stede, *Pali English Dictionary,* Pt. I , 76, S.V. Arhati; see also Ed Conze, *Buddhism, Its Essence and Development* (New York: Harper & Row, 1965), 93.

earliest Buddhist usage, Buddhahood and Arhatship are so closely allied that it is difficult to draw any significant distinction between the two.[11]

The Pali canonical texts lay down in various formulae the qualities which go to make Arhatship. An Arhat is described as one who is in possession of the excellent goal, free from attachment, hatred, delusion, in short, all impurities, relieved of the burden of 'five constituents' (*skandhas*), accomplished in all that is to be accomplished and devoid of any future existence.[12] The Arhat is one in whom the 'intoxicants' or 'outflows', i.e., sense desire, becoming, ignorance, wrong views, are destroyed, who has lived the life, who has done his task, who has laid down his burden, who has attained salvation, etc.[13] Similarly it is said that an Arhat is alone, secluded, earnest, zealous, master of himself.[14] He exerted himself and realized that the circle of 'birth-and-death' (*jarā-maraṇa*) with its 'five constituents' (*skandhas*) is in constant flux. He abandoned all the defilements and won Arhatship. On becoming an Arhat he lost all his attachment to the world. He has obtained 'gnosis', the 'super-knowledge' and 'the powers of analytical insight'.[15] Thus, he is supposed to be possessed of both *kṣayajñāna*, i.e., the knowledge that tie has no more *kleśas* and *anutpādajñāna*, i.e., the knowledge that he will have no more rebirth.[16] An Arhat has, thus, acquired the clear vision of the origin and destruction of things, got rid of all doubts (*kaṅkhā*) about the Buddha, *dhamma* and *saṅgha,* non-existence of soul and the theory of causation. He has seen things for himself unaided by others.[17] This, in short, is the image of an Arhat as preserved in the Pali canonical texts. It is this image of the Arhat which the early Buddhists, especially the Theravādins, cherished and commended.

The ideal of early Buddhism may, in fact, be described aptly as consisting of the attainment of *arhattva* and Nirvāṇa. With the attainment of Arhatship one reaches the climax of his career. The Buddha himself was described as an Arhat and so were his early disciples who became Arhat within a short time.[18] One might say that early Buddhism was a process and system of training in perfectibility of which the culmination was a spiritual status technically termed Arhatship, exemplified by the personality of the Buddha himself. The doctrine that leads to Arhatship is designated as the 'doctrine of Arhat'.[19] The earliest

---

[11] *Dialogues of the Buddha*, Pt. III, *Pāṭhika-sutta*, introduction, 6.

[12] *D.*, III, 66, 76; *M.*, I , 7, 94; *S.*, I , 70, IV, 142-3, 258; *A.*, I , 133; *It.*, 208.

[13] Cf. *Cullavagga*, 18, 34-35, 202; *D.*, I, 149, 168; *M.*, I , 184; *S.*, I , 141, II, 44, 70, 81-82, 103, 204, III, 20, 41, 52; *A.*, I , 152, II , 225.

[14] *D.*, I , 149, II, 118; cf. *S.*, I , 141, 16 1; *A.*, I, 263.

[15] *Av. Ś.*, II (ed. J. S. Speyer, St. Petersburg: Commissionnaires de l'Académie Impériale des Sciences, 1919), 348.

[16] N. Dutt, *Early Monastic Buddhism*, Vol. II (Calcutta: Firma K. L. Mukhopadhyay, 1945), 204; cf. J. Masuda, *op. cit.*, 42.

[17] See *Kvu.*, 174 *ff.*

[18] *Cullavagga*, 18.

[19] See *Sn.*, 296.

usage does not distinguish Arhat from Buddha just as the Jains did not distinguish Arhat from Jina. This earliest usage is not distinctively Buddhist either. Within Buddhism, however, a distinction between mere Arhat and a Buddha emerged quite early.[20]

Gradually the ideal of Arhatship was diluted and delimited. During a century or so of the passing away of Lord Buddha, there emerged several significant disputes over the concept of Arhatship and the quality of perfection attained in it. It is borne out by the account of *Kathāvatthu*[21] that a variety of such views, which came to be held by a section of early Buddhists, postulated clear possibilities of imperfections in the state of Arhatship. It is interesting to note that some of these so-called heterodox views are also recorded in the accounts of Vasumitra,[22] Bhavya[23] and Vinītadeva,[24] and Mentioned as the five points of Mahādeva finally leading to the great schism in the Buddhist Order and its division into the first two sects, viz., Theravāda and Mahāsaṃghika[25]. Occasionally the *Abhidharmakośa* provides valuable insight into them[26]. At least four of the five points of Mahādeva appear to render a direct blow to the orthodox conception of Arhatship as it appears in the *Nikāyas* and other Pali texts.

Vasumitra's treatise enumerates the failings thus:

(1) The Arhat can be tempted by others.
(2) He still has ignorance.
(3) He still has doubt.
(4) He gains knowledge through the help of others. [27]

The corresponding heterodox views on Arhatship as enumerated in the *Kathāvatthu-Aṭṭhakathā* are:

(1) Arhat has impure discharge, i.e. he may be subject to unconscious temptations[28].
(2) He may lack knowledge, i.e. one may be an Arhat and not know it[29].

---

[20] Cf. David J. Kalupahana, *op. cit*, 155.

[21] Cf. S. N. Dube, "The Date of Kathāvatthu," *East and West* (New Series, Vol. 22 - Nos. 1-2, March June, 1972), 79-86.

[22] J. Masuda, *op. cit.*, 24, 36, 38, 52.

[23] A. Bareau, *"Trois Traites sur les Sectes Bouddhiques du Petit Vehicule,"* J.A., Tomme CCLIV (1956): 174,179.

[24] *Ibid.* 194.

[25] Cf. Louis de la Vallee Poussin, "The Five Points of *Mahādeva*", *JRAS* (1910): 414 *ff*; and E. Lamotte, "Buddhist Controversy Over the Five Propositions," *Indian Historical Quarterly* 32.2-3 (1956): 148-162.

[26] Cf. *Abhidharmakośa*, II. 210.

[27] A. Bareau, *"Trois Traites sur les Sectes Bouddhique du Petit Vehicule,"* J.A., Tomme CCLIV (1956): 172.

[28] Cf. *Kvu.*, II.1.

(3) He may have doubt on matters of doctrine[30].
(4) Arhat is excelled by others[31].

While the *Kathāvatthu-Aṭṭhakathā* attributes these new assertions to the Pūrvaśailas (Pubbaseliyas) and Aparaśailas (Aparaseliyas),[32] Vasumitra, Bhavya and Vinītadeva attribute some of these to the Mahāsaṃghikas in general and their sub-sects, i.e., Ekavyavahārikas, Lokottaravādins, and Kaukkuṭikas in particular, as also to some of the Theravāda sects[33]. It is interesting that even the *Kathāvatthu-Aṭṭhakathā* attributes some of these assertions to certain offshoots of the Theravāda sect. For example, the thesis 'that an Arhat can fall away from Arhatship'[34] was held, according to Buddhaghoṣa, by the Sammatīyas, Vajjiputtīyas, Sabbatthīvādins and some of the Mahāsaṃghikas.[35]

The so-called heterodox movement against the ideal of Arhatship was disputed and criticized at length by the Theravādins. They defended the status of Arhat and his attainments with equal vehemence. The *Kathāvatthu-Aṭṭhakathā* picks up the above four points, along with various other assertions denigrating Arhatship, discusses them in considerable detail, and finally claims: to establish their untenability. For example, on the alleged fallibility of Arhat, the Theravādins observe that the thesis must also imply: (a) that he may fall away everywhere, (b) at all times, (c) that all Arhats are liable to fall away, and (d) that an Arhat is liable to fall away not only from Arhatship, but from all the four 'Path-fruitions'.[36] The proponents of the thesis do not, however, admit the possibility of universal retrogression. They concede that the Arhat retrogresses only up to the *sotāpattiphala,* and that the retrogression occurs only in the sphere of *kāmaloka* and not in the two higher spheres, viz., *rūpa* and *arūpa.* And this retrogression too is confined only to the *mudindriya* or *samaya-vimutta* Arhats.[37]

It is in this strain that the Theravādins categorically reject the thesis about the possibility of falling away of an emancipated one, even such, who attained this only occasionally in meditation. Still less can he fall away from Arhatship, because, as suggested by some, he might have calumniated a saint in some previous birth. They also deny that the gods of the *Māra* group can impose physical impurities upon an Arhat. He has acquired complete knowledge and hence cannot have any doubt or be surpassed by others in knowledge. He has

---

[29] *Ibid,* II .2.

[30] *Ibid,* II .3.

[31] *Ibid,* II . 4.

[32] See *Kathāvatthu-Aṭṭhakathā, 24 ff.*

[33] J. Masuda, *op.cit.,* 24, 36, 38, 52; A. Bareau, "Trois Traites sur les Sectes Bouddhiques du Petit Vehicule," *J.A.,* Tomme CCLIV (1956): 174, 179, 194.

[34] *Kvu.,* I .2.

[35] *Kathāvatthu-Aṭṭhakathā,* 35.

[36] See *Kvu.,* 71 *ff.*

[37] *Kathāvatthu-Aṭṭhakathā,* 36-37.

cast aside every fetter of ignorance and doubt in attaining his end. Nevertheless, he is human and hence the thesis that he is entirely free in every regard from any association with the four 'intoxicants' (*āsavas*) cannot be sustained for the simple reason that his body and sense organs cannot be considered absolutely uncontaminated by these 'intoxicants'. The only things which are really free from any connection with the 'intoxicants' are the 'Paths', their 'Fruits', 'Nirvāṇa' and 'the factors leading to insight'. Similarly, though an Arhat is indifferent to sense impressions, his indifference is manifested under human conditions; he cannot attend to more than one sense impression or idea at the same time, for his consciousness is essentially momentary. Moreover, the progress to Arhatship must be carried out in strict accordance with the stages laid down. It is, therefore, wrong to assume that the attainment of Arhatship means the simultaneous destruction of all fetters. In the first three stages, five of the fetters are cast away; in the last, the aspirant rids himself of the desire for rebirth either in the *rūpa-loka* or *arūpa-loka,* conceit, distraction and ignorance. It is also wrong to associate an Arhat's insight to a learner. Similarly no one can attain to Arhatship unless he has laid aside the life of a layman. It is also impossible for an embryo to become an Arhat at the moment of rebirth. Nor by offering gifts, paying homage to the shrines, and so on, does an Arhat become subject to a process of accumulating merit. If he could win merit he could also win demerit, which is absurd. Nor is it true to say that he cannot have an untimely death, for he has to experience the results of all his former actions as was opined by some, since the liability to accidents cannot be wholly ruled out. It is also denied that he possesses consciousness subject to moral distinctions at the time of his death. Nor is it right to say that an Arhat attains the completion of existence while in the imperturbable absorption of meditation.[38]

An analysis of the unpalatable new assertions about Arhatship might suggest that some of the theses may have their genesis in observed failings, e.g., (1) the ideal of Arhat may not be so attractive as that of the Buddha. A comparison between the two would highlight the limitations of the former. (2) There is some reason to postulate a psychological hostility arising from institutional and historical reasons. (3) Some of the theses suggest actually observed failings and limitations. (4) There is also room for divergent interpretation in the canonical statements on Arhatship.

---

[38] For discussions on these points, see S. N. Dube, *Cross Currents in Early Buddhism,* 97*ff.*

According to the Pali tradition, the Second Buddhist Council[39] was held at Vaiśālī to discuss the ten practices of the Vajjian monks for which not only recognition was categorically refused but these acts were unanimously declared to be un-Vinayic. From the metaphysical point of view, the acts of the Vajjians hardly appear significant. But they do indicate a more liberal attitude on the part of eastern monks in general and Vajjians in particular. A people thoroughly immersed in democratic traditions, they were unlikely to submit to the exclusive powers and privileges claimed by the Arhats and thus 'the real point at issue was the rights of the individual, as well as those of the provincial communities as against the prescriptions of a centralized hierarchy.'[40] Undoubted as the Vajjian monks' liberal views were not acceptable to the orthodox elders, they must have been severely impeached by the latter as indicated by the details of the Second Council. Discomforted thus in the Council, the eastern monks seem to have started as a reaction, their campaign against the very same Arhats by calling in question their claims and authority, and seeking to propound their fallibility. In order to uphold their views and innovations with regard to the Vinaya and Dhamma, they organized at Pāṭaliputra a separate council called *Mahāsaṅgha* or *Mahāsaṅgīti* without making any discrimination of Arhat or non-Arhat. In view of the high number of attendance at the *Mahāsaṅgīti*, which is given as 10,000,[41] it seems likely that no such discrimination was really made. In this council the Vajjian monks are supposed to have carried out things according to their own wishes. They altered the course of the sūtras in the Vinaya and the five Nikāyas, removed some of them and interpolated new ones. It is also added that they refused to accept the authenticity of *Parivāra, Paṭisambidāmagga, Niddesa*, certain *Jātaka*s and six texts of the Abhidhamma.[42] It is difficult to assume, however, that all these texts had really been compiled by that time. Nevertheless, the *Mahāsaṅgīti* of Pāṭaliputra seems to have formalized the division of the original order into two sects. On the one hand was the large bulk of eastern monks with its strongholds at Vaiśālī and Pāṭaliputra, and, on the other, was the section of western monks with their chief centers at Kausambi, Avanti and Mathura, a group in which the influence of the old Sthaviras was predominant.

---

[39] On the Second Buddhist Council see G. C. Pande, *Bauddha Dharma Ke Vikas Ka Itihasa*, Third Edition (Lucknow: Uttara Pradeśa Hindi Saṃsthana, Hindi Samiti Prabhaga,1990), 169-175; N. Dutt, *Early Monastic Buddhism*, Vol. II, 31-46; Rockhill, *Life of the Buddha and the Early History of His Order* (Boston: J.R.Osgood, 1885), 171-180; E. Obermiller, *Bu-ston: History of Buddhism in India and Tibet*, Pt. II (Heidelberg: In Kommission bei O. Harrassowitz, 1932), 96 *ff*; J. Masuda, op. *cit.*, 14 *ff*, A. Bareau, "Les Sectes Bouddhiques du Petit Vehicule," *Bulletin de l'Ecole Francaise d'Extreme Orient*, Saigon (1955); Louis de la Vallee Poussin, *Encyclopaedia of Religion and Ethics*, Vol. IV, s.v., Councils; *Indian Antiquary*, Vol. XXXVII, 86 *ff.*

[40] C.A.F. Rhys Davids, *Sakya* (London: K. Paul, Trench, Trubner, 1931), 355; G. C. Pande, *Studies in the Origins of Buddhism*, 559-560.

[41] *Dpvs.*, V.30.

[42] *Ibid*, V. 37-38.

The other tradition on the Second Buddhist Council, preserved by Vasumitra and followed by Bhavya and Vinītadeva, in fact, clearly asserts that the first breach in the *Sangha* resulted from the 'Five Points of Mahādeva'.[43] The first four propositions of Mahādeva, as noted above, relate to Arhat of whom a startling conception is put forth. It is gathered from the *Abhidharma-mahā-vibhāṣā-śāstra* (chapter 99)[44] that Mahādeva was a Brahmin from Mathura and he received his ordination at Kukkuṭārāma in Pāṭaliputra. His zeal and abilities crowned him with the headship of the *Sangha* there. With the help of the ruling king, who was his friend and patron, Mahādeva succeeded in ousting the senior monks from that monastery. Thereupon he started propagating his five propositions. These points clearly indicated that the Arhats were not all fully perfect persons as was the view of orthodox Theravādins, and that the Arhats had a few limitations. Such stipulations naturally gave rise to a serious dispute leading ultimately to the first schism in the Buddhist *Sangha* and the emergence of the two sects, Mahāsaṃghika and Theravāda. The points raised by Mahādeva are evidently suggestive of a critical attitude of the emerging sect towards the elders who claimed Arhatship to be the highest attainment. It is likely, therefore, that the Vajjians, having suffered a defeat in the Second Council, launched a counter-attack against the conservatives and the prevalence of 'bogus Arhats' among the latter provided them a favorable issue of criticism. Mainayeff has observed that the Buddhist *Sangha* was undergoing a state of demoralization about the time of the Second Council.[45]

Thus, it appears that within a century of the passing away of Lord Buddha, the Arhat ideal of the original teaching tended to give rise, within a monastic system, to a kind of soteriological individualism. At the hands of some orthodox sects, especially the Theravādins, the ideal received an individualistic twist. They strenuously emphasized on Arhatship to be the only goal of salvation and freedom from suffering. One might say that the Theravādins tried to faithfully adhere to the moral, monastic and disciplinary life of early Buddhism. It does not, however, mean that the Theravāda standpoint thoroughly represents the spirit of original Buddhism or that the entire Buddhism is comprised in the Pali canon as was the accepted belief of the older generation of Buddhist scholars. Thus, the purely individualistic attempts of the Theravādins to pursue the threefold development of *śīla, samādhi* and *prajñā* (*paññā*) with the consequent attainment of Arhatship could well be deemed inadequate from the point of view of the average mass of mankind. On the other hand, for the spiritually more ambitious the ideal of Arhatship would appear pale beside the glory of the Buddha and may well lead them, through this comparison, to look at Arhatship with critical eyes. The individualistic tendency of the Theravāda, therefore,

---

[43] A. Bareau, "Trois Traites sur les Sectes Bouddhique du Petit Vehicule," *J.A.*, Tomme CCLIV (1956): 192.

[44] Cf. Thomas Watters, *On Yuan Chwang's Travels in India* (London: Royal Asiatic Society, 1905), I , 267-268.

[45] J. F. Minayeff, *Recherches sur le Bouddhisme* (Paris: E. Leroux, 1894), 207.

provoked protests from others in the Buddhist community and contributed by way of a reaction in a significant measure towards the growth of heretical and unwholesome notions about the ideal.

From the debates on the issue, as recorded in the *Kathāvatthu,* it seems that there was something inherent in the oldest tradition itself which underlies the growth of heterodox views and subsequent controversies on Arhatship. Taking, for example, the relationship between the conceptions of Buddhahood and Arhatship, there are some enigmatic passages in the canonical literature the testimony of which makes it difficult to draw any distinction between the two. For example, it was asserted that 'Every Buddha was an Arhat. Every Arhat was Buddha.'[46] The Buddha himself is habitually called an Arhat. At one place it is said: 'Let us ask Gotama, the awakened one, who has passed beyond anger and fear....'[47] But the same adjectives, as we find here, are used elsewhere for an Arhat.[48] Similarly, in a long description of the Buddha,[49] all the epithets used for him are generally found applied to one or other of his disciples. Arhat is, in fact, one of the oft-used titles for the Buddha, but it was not an exclusive title, and all those who as a result of his teaching came to realize the Truth are said to have become Arhats, the number amounting to as many as sixty-one.[50] In the third *dhyāna,* which denotes the final stage of I worldly' wisdom just before the 'Path' is reached, the equanimity of the Arhat, who 'never abandons his natural state of purity' when presented with desirable or undesirable objects, is similar to the equanimity of a Buddha which is often lauded in the scriptures. It is said that the equanimity of Buddhas and Arhats is unaffected by the reception their teachings may receive, and they feel no joy when it is accepted, no displeasure when it is rejected,[51] but remain unmoved and fully mindful. The teacher never called himself a Buddha as distinct from an Arhat. When addressed as Buddha or spoken of as such by his disciples, it is always doubtful whether anything more is meant than an enlightened Arhat. In the oldest documents the two conceptions seem to be still in a state of fusion. In fact, the word Arhat has been used in early texts without any great precision. It may be an epithet of the Buddha, or a name for the eighth of the 'hold persons', the one who has won final sanctification. At other times, however, the Arhat is either a disciple (*śrāvaka*) who must 'hear' from a Tathāgata, or a Pratyekabuddha.[52]

However, it is doubtful to maintain that the ideal of Arhat was synonymous with Buddhahood and that no distinction was made between the two in early canonical works. The view inevitably implies equality between the teacher and

---

[46] Cf. *S.,* Ⅱ, 309 *ff.*

[47] *Sn.,* 309.

[48] Cf. *It.,* 228.

[49] Cf. *Sn.,* 353 *ff.*

[50] *Mahāvagga,* 18-23.

[51] *Abhidharmakośa,* VII, 76-77.

[52] E. Conze, *Buddhist Thought in India* (Ann Arbor: University of Michigan Press, 1967), 89.

58   S. N. Dube

his disciples which would have been difficult to sustain for the Buddhist
community with such an exalted figure as the Buddha being their teacher. We
come across such passages in the early texts where the difference between the
two concepts may be brought out clearly. Attention may be drawn to a dialogue
between Sāriputta and the Buddha.[53] here confesses that he has no knowledge
about the able and 'awakened ones' that have been and are to come, as also, of
the present times. Sāriputta was one of the greatest direct disciples of the
Buddha and yet his figure, as compared to the Buddha, is completely dwarfed by
his confession. It was logical to assume that a Buddha would possess a number
of additional qualities of perfection as compared to an Arhat.[54] There is an
illuminating incident referred to in the *Spuṭārthā* on the *Abhidharmakośa* where
it is shown that the Buddha surpasses all his disciples which enables him to
become the universal teacher or savior.[55] Further, the theory of a number of
successive Buddhas[56] presupposes the conception of a Buddha as a different and
more exalted personage than an Arhat. In a famous dialogue, Lord Buddha is
reported to have said that he is neither a man (*manussā*), nor a *gandharva*
(*gandhabba*) nor a *yakṣa* (*yakka*) nor even a *deva* or *brahma*, but a Buddha.[57] In
fact, the Buddhist Theravāda tradition itself speaks of three kinds of saints (*ārya*,
i.e., persons having won the Path) as being 'adepts', or 'enlightened', or as
'having' Nirvāṇa. They are the Arhats, Pratyekabuddhas and Buddhas.
Vasubandu points out[58] that the Lord Buddha alone has destroyed ignorance in
its entirely and is wholly free from that which prevents us from seeing things as
they are. The Arhats and Pratyekabuddhas have freed themselves from the
delusion which is soiled by defilements; but in them the ignorance which is
unsoiled by the defilements continues to operate. They do not know the special
attributes of a Buddha, nor objects which are very distant in time or space, not
the infinite complexity of things. The Arhat is content to know everything which
concerns him personally, the Pratyekabuddha in addition knows conditioned co-
production, but still the bulk of the universe lies beyond him. The distinction
between an Arhat and a Buddha is made evidently clear in the works of
Mahāyāna where it is said that Arhats who are perfect *śrāvakas* get Ad of only
kleśāvaraṇa, i.e., the veil of impurities consisting of *rāga*, *doṣa*,
sīlabbataparāmāsa, and *vicikicchā*, but not of *jñeyāvaraṇa*, i.e., the veil which
conceals the Truth, the veil which can only be removed by realizing the *dharma-
śūnyatā* or *tathatā*. It is the Buddha alone who, as perfectly emancipated, has

---

[53] *D.*, II, 65 ff.

[54] *Ibid,* , 8 ff.

[55] *Spuṭārthābhidharmakośa-vyākhyā*, ed. U. Wogihara (Tokyo: The Tōyō
bunko, 1930-36), 5.

[56] Cf. *D.*, II , *Mahāpadāna-sutta; Khuddaka Nikāya, Buddhavaṃsa.*

[57] *A.*, 41.

[58] *Abhidharmakośa,* I .2; cf. E. Conze, *Buddhist Thought in India*, 166-173.

both *kleśāvaraṇa* and *jñeyāvaraṇa* removed. [59] It is interesting that the Theravādins, though they desperately try to defend the cherished status and image of Arhatship, themselves have to grant ultimately that the *bodhi* attained by an Arhat is characterized by the knowledge of the four paths (*catumaggañāṇa*) and not omniscience (*sabbaññutañāṇa*) which is the *bodhi* of the Buddhas. [60] It is plausible, therefore, that the basic difference in the two conceptions inherent in the *Nikāya*s was brought to the fore in course of time, and led to two parallel developments in a new direction in the history of Buddhism. One led to the gradual decline in the ideal of Arhatship and the other towards eventual deification of the Buddha.

There appears to have been a close inter-relationship between the two tendencies. Generally, the same group of sects which carried on the anti-Arhat campaign led *pari passu* a movement seeking to establish the transcendentality of the Buddha. [61] A process was, thus, set moving under which the life of the Master formed the edifice, and the rival sects provided the material for the superstructure. Consequently, while the orthodox Theravādins adhered strictly to the realistic view of the person of their Teacher, the heterodox radicals proceeded boldly to idealize and eventually deify Him.

---

[59] See N. Dutt, *Aspects of Mahāyāna Buddhism and its Relations to Hīnayāna* (London: Luzac & Co., 1930), 35 *ff*, T.R.V. Murti, *The Central Philosophy of Buddhism*, 2nd Ed. (London: George Allen and Unwin, 1960), 380 *ff*.

[60] See *Kathāvatthu- Aṭṭhakathā*, 76.

[61] See S. N. Dube, *Cross Currents in Early Buddhism*, 90*ff*.

CHAPTER 5

CAN PEACE IN THE LARGER SOCIETY BE PROMOTEDWITHOUT INNER PEACE WITHIN THE INDIVIDUAL?: A RESPONSE IN TERMS OF EARLY BUDDHISM

P.D. Premasiri

The lesson that mankind should have learnt from Hiroshima and Nagasaki in the year 1945 is that the survival of mankind on this planet depends on creating the conditions necessary for lasting peace. But unfortunately, this lesson does not seem to have been learnt. For how many wars which could have escalated into similar or even more disastrous consequences have been fought all over the world since then? Despite the break down of the Soviet Union, wars, violent conflicts and tensions seem to be widespread in the contemporary world, displacing innocent civilians from their homelands, causing bereavements of loved ones in families, and killing or maiming people for life and producing immense misery and woe. Is all this evil necessary is an appropriate question to raise in such circumstances. It may be thought by some that it is necessary as a means of social transformation. But today the question is whether society would survive at all if the current trend continues. It is now a question of survival or extinction. For in a third world war no party would survive to celebrate victory. Today the need for a serious search for the causes of war and effective means to preserve peace and harmony in society has become extremely urgent. The attempt in this paper is to examine what contribution the philosophy of the Buddha can make in this direction.

There are a number of ways in which the ultimate goal of Buddhism could be conceived. It is sometimes conceived as the ending of misery (*dukkha*), the eradication of the cankers (*āsavakkhaya*), the destruction of the three roots of evil or unwholesome behavior (*akusalamūla*), namely, greed (*lobha*), hatred (*dosa*) and delusion (*moha*) and the attainment of enlightenment (*sambodhi*). The ultimate goal is also characterized as the attainment of peace (*santi, upasama*). We are more accustomed to think of war and conflict, peace and harmony as conditions that apply to the larger society. The conflicts and wars that occur in society are seen in Buddhism as an unavoidable part of saṃsāric misery (*dukkha*). The Buddhist emphasis is primarily on the psychological roots of war, conflicts and violence. Buddhism considers the conflicts in society as an outward manifestation of the lack of peace in the minds of individuals constituting society. War and conflict are largely symptoms of diseased minds. Treating the external causes of war cannot be as effective, according to Buddhism, as treating its deeper inner roots.

Buddhism was aware of the sufferings inflicted on human beings due to wars, conflicts and all forms of violence even during the time of the Buddha when technology of war was extremely primitive compared to what is witnessable today. The weapons of war during those days were sticks, swords, pikes, bows and arrows. The damage done to innocent civilian populations was largely restricted due to the limited efficacy of the weapons of war used during that time. The situation today is vastly different due to the presence of large nuclear arsenals. Weapons of war today are so destructive that in the event of a third world war this planet is likely to become uninhabitable, for, the destruction caused by such a war will extend even to animals and plants and even the physical environment which sustains life in any form. Hence the urgency of understanding the dynamics of war, the root causes of it, and adopting all possible means of preventing war and establishing conditions conducive to social harmony and peace.

The minor conflicts that occur within small and isolated social groups are not negligible from the Buddhist standpoint for the understanding of the dynamics of war. For they reflect the same symptoms of the larger disease. One might be inclined to think that the insights of the Buddha, the Enlightened One, are irrelevant today, for the world has changed to such a degree that the problems of contemporary man have to be seen as new problems which require new solutions. But the truth is that it is only the nature of the content of the problems that has changed; the form of the problems remains essentially the same. Therefore, it is not altogether irrelevant to attempt to benefit from the sagacity and wisdom of the great spiritual men of the past whose ideologies have been instrumental in historically determining the cultures and life-styles of millions of people through many centuries of the civilized history of mankind. The realization of the practical usefulness and the potency of the insights of these spiritual innovators is specially relevant in the context of the contemporary world in which conflict, violence and strife are so rampant.

In attempting to identify Buddhist notions of the dynamics of war, it may be relevant to study the contexts in which Buddhism discusses conflicts. Buddhism discusses conflicts mainly because it associates conflict with evil, with the process of misery (*dukkha*), the deliverance from which is the goal of the Buddhist. The characteristic of the Buddhist *Nibbāna,* the ultimate goal is peace and tranquility (*santi, upasama*). In this respect, it is conceived entirely as inner peace and tranquility (*ajhattasanti*), which is attainable by each individual by himself or herself. The spiritual path of the Buddha is supposed to lead one to this noble and incomparable goal of peace. There is no doubt that the emphasis here is on the peace of the individual. An individual who has attained the goal of peace in this sense is one who has overcome all conflicts, put an end to misery, and lives unaffected by all the vicissitudes of nature. The mind of such a person is forever at peace; it is unruffled by what happens in the outside world. Such a person can live at peace even in an environment in which peace is absent. Buddhism speaks of the possibility of such inner transformation enabling a person to live at ease amidst people who are hateful, malicious, vicious and intent on harm. The *Dhammapada*, for instance, presents the ideal of the life of the Buddhist in the following terms:

> Let us live happily indeed without hate among those who are hateful.
> Among those who are hateful, let us live free from hate.[1]

This is a reference to the lotus-like life of the Buddhist saint. Explaining the Buddha's relationship to society in general, he makes it clear that his life is comparable to that of a lotus which arises in water, grows in water, but stays yet in water rising above the level of the water without being sullied by its impurities.[2] This is the ideal way of life to be emulated by the Buddhist.

There is no doubt that Buddhism has no reservations about the practical possibility of reaching such a state of peace, however difficult and challenging it may be to accomplish it. The Buddha has certainly considered this to be the main purpose of his teaching. For, when he is once questioned what his teaching is, he answers that he professes a teaching which enables a person to live without entering into conflict with any one in the world.[3]

Here, the Buddha is not referring to the attainment of peace and harmony in society, but the possibility for the individual to live at peace without coming into conflict with others in society. Some of those who are struck by this characteristic of Buddhism are often inclined to interpret Buddhist pacifism as promoting an escapist attitude. They hold that this is to ignore one's social responsibility, to withdraw from genuine social commitment and to adhere to the self-centered ideal of the life of the cloistered hermit. Furthermore, they may link this to the familiar characterization of Buddhism by some critics as offering a pessimistic view of life. They might argue that from the Buddhist point of view, wars and conflicts are part of the miserable order of *saṁsāric* existence that nothing could be done to stop them. The only solution is to develop peace and harmony within oneself so that one could live without feeling the pains of such conflict that is inevitable in one's social environment and finally escape such misery altogether by putting an end to *saṁsāra*. There is no need to doubt that Buddhism aims at the deliverance of the individual from suffering in the aforesaid sense, and even that this is the principal aim of Buddhism.

---

[1] *Dh.,* 197.
[2] *A.,* II. 38-39.
[3] *M.,* I. 109.

But if this is the only contribution that Buddhism can make to the promotion of peace its vision regarding the possibility of social change and the possibility of promoting harmonious and satisfactory living in society can be said to be totally pessimistic. It would follow that Buddhism is indifferent or apathetic to the necessity of improving society and identifying and removing social ills and injustices that lead to violations of peace. It would be a formidable task indeed to make every member of the society enlightened in the Buddhist sense. Buddhism is aware of this, and if the expression of this awareness amounts to pessimism, Buddhism finds it difficult to escape the charge of pessimism. But while recognizing the difficulty of bringing about a society totally free of conflicts, Buddhism admits the possibility of contributing in a considerable way to conflict reduction by calling upon people to think and act reasonably. It offers a realistic account of the psychological origins of conflict and shows how conflict could be reduced in society by changing the way people think and behave. The influence that Buddhism seeks to exercise is primarily educational.

The Buddha speaks of conflict in the form of quarrels (*kalaha*), disputes (*viggaha*) and contentions (*vivāda*) at different levels of social interaction. They occur between nations or states as large scale wars when one head of state disputes with another. They also occur between religious ethnic or other groups within the same nation. They occur also between members of the same family, between people who are in the closest social relationship like between the father and son, between siblings and so forth[4]. According to the *Sakkapañha Sutta* conflict is a common and inevitable occurrence among all classes of sentient beings. Despite the desire of the higher sentient beings to live in unity harmony and concord conflict frequently occurs.

> Devas, men, Asuras, Nāgas, Gandhabbas and whatever other different types of communities are there, it occurs to them that they ought to live without mutual hatred, violence, enmity and malice; yet for all they live with mutual hatred, violence, enmity and malice.[5]

In the *Mahādukkhakkhanda Sutta* the Buddha describes how conflict finds expression in war involving death and destruction to those who participate in it.

> ... having taken sword and shield, having girded on bow and quiver, both sides mass for battle and arrows are hurled and knives are hurled and swords are flashing. Those who wound with arrows and wound with knives and decapitate with their swords, these suffer dying then and pain like unto dying.[6]

---

[4] *Ibid.*, 86.

[5] *D.*, II . 276.

[6] *M.*, I .86, translated by I.B. Homer, *Middle Length Sayings* (London: PTS, 1954), I. 114.

Thus the early Buddhist scriptural sources express the Buddhist awareness of the frequent occurrence and the widespread nature of war, conflict and violence in society.

Buddhism does not consider conflict as having a positive value. It is viewed necessarily as an evil. A situation of conflict apart from the innumerable miseries associated with it, produces a large part of the modes of behavior that Buddhism considers to be evil. In a conflict the Buddhist virtue of abstaining from the destruction of life is violated. The Buddhist principle of non-injury and non-violence and the ideal of a life full of mercy and compassion towards all living beings are violated. Lying, slander and mutual accusations with abusive language take place. Situations of conflict generate numerous unwholesome and unskilled states (*pāpaka akusala dhamma*). Therefore, their causes are to be properly understood and measures taken to remove the real causes. Since Buddhism does not attach a positive value to conflict it differs from those doctrines which look upon conflict as the vehicle of social change. Conflict is not advocated as the means whereby the "good society" is to be brought into existence. Instead, Buddhism sees conflict and its associated evils as morally debasing, dehumanizing and brutalizing man. No social change brought about by the brutal force of violence which has the tendency of strengthening and nourishing the ill-will, malice and unwholesome traits of character in those who perpetrate such violence, is thought in Buddhism to be desirable. Seeking solutions to social problems through war merely results in a chain reaction of further wars and conflicts. Unsatisfactory social arrangements are therefore not to be done away with through means that involve conflict, war and violence, but through peaceful means. The Buddhist preference of peaceful means to war and violence for bringing about social change seems more relevant to the contemporary world rather than to the time in which the Buddha lived. For, solutions in terms of promoting the psychology of war does not seem to suit the level of technological progress that mankind has now achieved.

In order to see the relevance of the teaching of the Buddha to the promotion of peace in the larger society it is important to examine the Buddha's analysis of the causes that lead to wars and conflicts. The Buddha utilizes the principle of Dependent Arising (*paṭiccasamuppāda*) to analyze such issues. The Buddhist concept of Dependent Arising explains events in the universe without resorting to explanation in terms of abstract metaphysical concepts. It is a principle which takes into account the variety of conditions that are related to a single event, depending on which such an event is produced. In the application of this principle to the problem of social conflict there are two sets of causes which the Buddha has identified. First there are the external socio-economic causes such as unjust social and economic arrangements and institutions. Secondly, there are the internal moral and psychological causes. Both types of causes have to be removed if lasting peace is to be achieved in society.

These two types of causes themselves exist in mutual dependence. It is when society is morally corrupt that unwholesome psychological traits become the motivational roots of human behavior. When human behavior is determined by unwholesome motives institutional structures such as political and economic systems also get adversely affected. This leads to a vicious circle involving a corrupt social, political and economic order and a society consisting of morally debased individuals.

In the *Kūṭādanta Sutta* and the *Cakkavattisīhanāda Suttanta* the Buddha draws attention to the external causes of social conflict. It is shown that violations of peace could occur in a society when a section of the people is deprived of the basic material needs to lead a decent life. People arm themselves and resort to criminal behavior, rebellion and insurgency if equal opportunity is not given to them to lead a comfortable life with dignity. Buddhism seems to consider economic deprivation of any section of the community as the most serious cause for the disturbance of peace. It is, therefore, the foremost duty of the state to create the necessary conditions for the elimination of poverty. In the *Kūṭādanta Sutta* it is pointed out that under circumstances in which criminal behavior and violence in society are the consequence of the existence of poverty side by side with affluence, those who wield political authority cannot succeed in quelling criminal and rebellious behavior by resorting to the force of arms and state punitive measures. It becomes necessary to eliminate the root causes of the problem. The same point is made even more forcefully in the *Cakkavattisīhanāda Sutta*. It is pointed out that when there is poverty in a society, neither occasional acts of charity nor punitive measures can stop the people from turning to armed uprising. The *Sutta* points out that the process of moral deterioration originating with economic deprivation reaches its climax in a catastrophic war in which human beings become totally brutalized.

The above-mentioned explanation of the Buddha is applicable to many instances of social unrest in the contemporary world. This is an explanation in terms of die mechanistic causal processes that operate between the material conditions of human life and human consciousness and behavior. The Buddha does not seem to disregard this aspect of die causal process. However, it would be erroneous to reduce the causes of all instances of social unrest to economic disparities or other external factors in the social or material environment. At the same time consider-able importance has to be given, even where social tensions are due to religious, ethnic and other differences to the predominance of the economic factor. For it is central to the provision of equal opportunities in society.

It was already noted that the Buddhist goal of *Nibbāna* is a personal attainment reached as a consequence of inner transformation and moral and mental culture. A person who reaches this goal has completely eradicated the psychological motives prompting a person to become a participant in any form of conflict or controversy involving the expression of unwholesome emotions and evil modes of behavior. However, this attainment is a practical possibility only in the case of a very minute proportion of the larger society. Therefore, we posed the question as to how Buddhism can contribute to peace if it only prescribes such an arduous way which would ensure peace of mind to only a fortunate few who have the capacity to transform themselves. It may be argued that what this achieves in promoting peace in the larger society is negligible. A few individuals staying away from conflict and not participating in it, it may be argued do not make much of a practical difference to peace. Subsequently, it was noted that Buddhism sees a causal relationship between poverty and social unrest. Then, can we conclude that the solution to the establishment of peace in the larger society lies in the elimination of poverty? The answer is partly an affirmative one. But the problem is not as simple as that. For, we are now left with the question of appropriate means and measures to achieve this goal of eliminating economic disparities. To the extent that these means and measures are to be adopted and implemented through the agency and instrumentality of human actors whose behavior is determined by their motives we are compelled to divert our attention to the inner roots of human behavior.

In the *Suttanipāta* the question is raised, "How do conflicts arise?"[7] The same question is posed to the Buddha in the *Sakkapañha Sutta*.[8] In the *Mahādukkhakkhandha Sutta* conflicts at all levels of society are said to be caused by and grounded in sense desire.[9] In the *Madhupiṇḍika Sutta* the analysis goes much deeper to trace its psychological origins. The analysis offered in the *Madhupiṇḍika Sutta* begins with the sensory process and identifies *papañca* as the most noteworthy psychological cause of social conflict.

> Depending on the eye and material objects arises visual consciousness. The coming together of these three is sense contact. Depending on sense contact arises sensation. What one senses one recognizes (or conceptualizes). What one recognizes one thinks about. One gets obsessed with (*papañceti*) what one thinks about. As a result of this, thoughts of conceptual obsession (*papañcasaññāsankha*) assail the person with respect to material objects cognizable by the eye, belonging to the past, present and future.[10]

The same process is repeated with reference to all the senses.

> As long as the sensory process leads to the psychological consequences outlined in the above passage certain latent tendencies of the mind remain deeply entrenched. They are the latent tendency to lust or attachment (*rāgānusaya*), hatred (*paṭighānusaya*), dogmatic views (*diṭṭhānusaya*), doubt (*vicikicchānusaya*), conceit (*mānānusaya*), lust for becoming (*bhavarāgānusaya*) and delusion (*avijjānusaya*). They co-exist with *papañca* which is characterized by craving (*taṇhā*), conceit (*māna*) and dogmatic views (*diṭṭhi*).

---

[7] *Sn.*, 168*f.*
[8] *D.*, II. 276*f.*
[9] *M.*, I. 86*f.*
[10] *Ibid.*, I. 111.

The reference to *diṭṭhi* as a form of *papañca* is very significant. Buddhism invariably includes *diṭṭhi* among the unwholesome aspects of the human mind that create sufferings and tensions. *Diṭṭhi* is a mental canker as well as a latent unwholesome tendency of the mind (*anusaya*). It is also one form of grasping (*upādāna*). Clinging to a view is characterized by the thought "This alone is the truth and everything else is false". This is considered by the Buddha as a great hindrance to understanding the real nature of things. It becomes a major source of disputes and contentions. In a number of *Sutta*s of the *Aṭṭhakavagga* of the *Suttanipāta*, the Buddha draws attention to the undesirability of clinging to views. Dogmatism breeds intolerance. The consequence of it is hatred against those who do not agree with one's own views. There are enough instances in which people quarrel due to ideological differences or the incompatibility of their belief systems. Dogmas are explained in Buddhism as consequences of craving. Hence dogmatism is a major source of social conflict.

What follows from the above is that one becomes a victim of one's own erroneous thinking. Buddhism analyses the process of perception without the preconception of a personal entity called the self or soul. The perceptual process is seen merely as a transient and causally conditioned process. The contact between the senses and the appropriate stimuli give rise to pleasurable or painful sensation. The world of sense experience has the characteristic of being either attractive or repulsive. The psychological response of attachment to what is attractive and aversion to what is repulsive is associated with the notion of the ego. With the sense of the ego an erroneous attempt is made to claim ownership where in reality there is neither anything to be owned nor anyone to own. The *Madhupiṇḍika Sutta* points out:

> If one neither delights in nor asserts, nor clings to that which makes one a victim of thoughts of conceptual obsession then that itself is the end of the latent tendencies of lust, hatred, dogmatism, doubt ... That itself is the end of taking the stick, of taking weapons, of quarrels, disputes, contentions, accusations, slander and lying speech.[11]

In the *Sakkapañha Sutta* the Buddha considers envy and miserliness (*issamacchariya*) as the proximate psychological cause of all quarrels. *Issa* (envy) is defined in Buddhism as a person's displeasure at, or the inability to endure the gain of another. Miserliness (*macchariya*) is defined as a person's tendency to hide and protect one's own possessions. In the *Mahānidāna sutta* miserliness (*macchariya*) is connected to craving (*taṇhā*) in the causal process. The causal process which is usually presented to explain the causal links in the production of saṁsāric suffering is here presented with a view to show the link with social interaction. It is said that craving causes searching for objects of enjoyment (*pariyesana*), searching for objects of enjoyment causes acquisition

---

[11] *Ibid.*, 109.

of goods (*lābha*), acquisition of goods causes judgment about them, judgment causes desire and attachment, desire and attachment causes cleaving to things, cleaving to things causes grasping and grasping causes miserliness. Miserliness results in protective behavior. When one seeks to protect something with great attachment if there is a threat to what is protected from any other persons the reaction is force and violence.[12] This conflict becomes really intense when those who threaten the possessions that are protected act from the motive of envy (*issa*).

The sensory process presents human beings with stimuli that are attractive as well as repulsive (*sata asata*). The *papañca* activity of the mind responds to the sensory environment with the sense of an ego. The sense of the ego creates attachment (*piya*) or greed (*lobha*) and desire (*chanda*). The consequence is *issamacchariya*, for mankind is placed in a world consisting of limited resources. In a world of unlimited resources where people could effortlessly obtain whatever they desired, the problem of competing for limited resources would not arise. If mankind were endowed with unlimited sympathies even in a world of limited resources conflicts are not likely to arise. But the reality of the situation is that mankind is found to have limited sympathies in a world of limited resources. Some are deprived of what others possess by nature itself (for instance beauty, intelligence or other desirable talents and aptitudes). When others possess things that one desires to possess, but for some reason or other, one does not possess, the sense of the ego produces *issa*. Those who cling to what they possess due to their own sense of the ego are not willing to part with what they possess. They feel constantly threatened by the possible encroachment of others upon their possessions. This is the feeling of *macchariya*. The existence of two parties afflicted with either or both of these states of mind over something commonly desired by both parties is sufficient to produce social conflict. The hatred of those who wish to acquire the good things that they are deprived of, especially if they are deprived of them unjustly or unreasonably gets intensified and assumes the form of collective anger. On the other hand the fear of those who want to greedily cling to the good things that they enjoy, even if they enjoy them as unreasonable and unjustified privileges is sufficient for them to collectively poise themselves to meet the threats to their possessions. The result is a clash of interests which develops into quarrels, conflicts and wars.

Now, the question is whether this situation could be averted by altering the external conditions that generate *issa-macchariya*, that is by eliminating all inequalities with respect to all the good things that people desire to possess. Theoretically, this might be possible in the case of economic goods although the possibility of practically realizing it may be open to doubt. But there are things other than economic goods which people desire to possess (for instance, power). Given the nature of the human condition equality in respect of all the good things that people desire to possess is not a possible goal to achieve. Mankind has necessarily got to live in the midst of inequality. If they are destined to live

---

[12] *D.*, II. 58-59.

amidst inequality the only way to live satisfactorily is by making an inner spiritual adjustment. Satisfaction can never be reached by adjusting the external factors in keeping with one's own interest and - frame of mind. For the external factors involved are so numerous.

Even where tensions could be reduced by eliminating unjust patterns of distribution of goods, the failure of mankind could be attributed to the lack of inner discipline. Social injustices and inequalities which create tensions cannot be eliminated by making use of the very traits that generate and perpetrate such injustices and inequalities. When collectivized anger, hatred, jealousy, ill will etc. are used as psychological instruments to motivate people for social change the usual consequence is reversal or interchange of people's fates, but not a stable and lasting solution to the problems of injustice and inequality. A lasting solution could be found only through a spiritual reorientation, a transformation of the emotive and cognitive roots of human behavior. According to the Buddha all unwholesome behavior proceeds from the three psychological roots greed (*loha*), hatred (*dosa*) and delusion (*moha*). A transformation of attitudes based on wisdom is required to overcome the internal causes of conflict. The Buddhist path to *Nibbāna* is one which has the consequence of gradually reducing and finally eradicating the internal causes of conflict. It is a part of psychological adjustment which recognizes the human potential to understand the sensory process and prevent the person from becoming a victim of *papañca*. From the Buddhist point of view, social unrest is a consequence of psychological maladjustment. Deluded or confused thinking and unwise reflection produces craving, greed, envy, jealousy, hatred, violence and aggression. Such character traits are very noticeably contagious. The sense of group identity is used to give collective and organized expression to such unwholesome emotions. The consequence is a generalized and collectivized psychology of war and violence. The solution to it lies in wise reflection and a genuine attempt to abandon those cankers of the mind (*āsava*) which disturb inner peace. This needs to be undertaken individually as well as socially. Collectivized anger, ill-will, malice, envy and the like have to be replaced by collectivized loving kindness (*mettā*), compassion (*karuṇā*), sympathetic joy (*muditā*) and equanimity (*upekkhā*). These wholesome attitudes need to find practical expression in the willingness to give and share (*dāna*), in pleasant ways of verbal communication with one's fellow beings (*piyavacana*), in personal commitment to the welfare of all beings including oneself (*aṭṭhacariya*) and in equal treatment of all (*samānattatā*).

The inner change which Buddhism insists upon may be brought about through a process of moral education. The Buddhist scheme of mental culture can meaningfully be expressed in terms of educational psychology. Education for peace is undoubtedly an urgent requirement of the contemporary world. Buddhism is extremely resourceful for the development of a theory of education on such lines. Interest in moral education has noticeably declined due to preoccupation with learning associated with science and technology during the last two centuries. Such preoccupation appears to have promoted a mechanistic approach to the solution of all problems including those ones in which human thinking and behavior play a principal role.

The psychology that has dominated the Western world during this century is the behaviorist or the stimulus response psychology. This conforms to the mechanistic worldview which is derived from modern science. In terms of this worldview, the human potential to bring about a cognitive and emotive transformation by dealing with the inner activity of the mind has been totally overlooked. Human behavior is thought to be modifiable only mechanistically by dealing with the external conditions. This from the Buddhist point of view is the source of the failure.

Implicit in the eightfold path of Buddhism is a practical scheme which could be adopted as a basis for evolving a viable program of moral education or education for peace. Methods of Buddhist mental culture (*bhāvanā*) have great psychological significance. But they have been misconceived due to ignorance, prejudice, or preconceptions as mere sectarian practices of religious ritual. They can be extremely resourceful in developing an applied psychology for desirable forms of behavior modification, the education of human emotions, and for purposes of moral education. Buddhism is a system of thought which attaches great value and significance to human effort (*viriya*), the potency of the human will (*adhiṭṭhāna*) and human endeavor (*padhāna*). Buddhism does not believe in mysterious forces that mechanically bring about desirable changes either in ourselves or in the outside world. Human beings can escape numerous existential ills if the proper effort is made (*samāvāyāma*) with the proper understanding (*sammā-diṭṭhi*). *A* mechanistic view of life is a hindrance to this, for it expects problems that involve human interaction to be solved merely by making adjustments in things external to the human mind. The crisis of the contemporary world is essentially a moral crisis, which has to be remedied through wise reflection (*yoniso manasikāra*) and a novel approach to education.

No one seriously doubts that education makes a difference to the way in which people conduct their thinking or the way in which people behave. If education has not achieved considerable progress in the promotion of peace either education has not seriously been applied in this connection or the way in which it has been applied is likely to have been defective. The Buddhist path of spiritual training can be conceived as an educational path which takes human beings from ignorance to understanding, from delusion to enlightenment. It is a path of cultivating wisdom or self-transforming understanding. It has no sectarian application, because the factors in the path are psychological factors testable in the common human experience of mankind. It does not involve any special relationship with a sectarian God. Therefore the principles involved in it are universally applicable. If we realize that external adjustments are ineffective in bringing about peace and that the only possible alternative is an inner spiritual adjustment, it may be worthwhile to make sufficient educative use of the psychological insights of Buddhism to bring about a change in the way people think and behave. If sectarian identity is a hindrance to this, at least the principles involved could be usefully adopted as universally valid principles in formulating practically efficient schemes of education.

An obvious objection to this is that even in societies where Buddhism is found to be the dominant religious influence, there does not seem to be any difference with regard to the social proneness to conflict and violence. Buddhism itself provides an answer to such a criticism. The Buddha warned that his teaching could have completely the opposite effect if it is handled in the way that a man handles a cobra by its tail. The Buddhist path is no mechanistic devise to solve individual or social problems. It is one to be freely adopted by those individuals or communities whose aim is the reduction or elimination of suffering. It has to be adopted as the primary educational influence in the life of the community. If there is no substantial evidence that it is so, there does not seem to be any validity to the above objection.

CHAPTER 6

THE NOBLE EIGHTFOLD PATH AS A WAY TO HARMONIOUSLY BLEND MATERIAL PROGRESS WITH SPIRITUAL PROGRESS

Sanath Nanayakkara

The scope of the present paper is limited to show how the Noble Eightfold Path (*ariya-aṭṭhaṅgika magga*) which first used to achieve inner peace of the individual was later also adopted as a way to attain progress, both material and spiritual, of the individual and consequentially to have peace and prosperity in society. In showing this it is, however, not intended here to discuss in detail how each Path-factor contributes to achieve these objectives. Instead, it is attempted to explain the historical context in which the Path that was originally meant for a "limited circle" and purely for "ending of *dukkha*" was later adopted for a much "wider circle" of followers and for achieving well-being in this life and lives to come.

According to the Buddha's own summing up, his teaching pertains to two things: namely, the predicament of man, that is, the *dukkha* he is subject to, and to the possibility of its cessation, that is, *nirodha,* which means realization of *nibbāna.*[1] This teaching on *dukkha* and *nirodha* are embodied in his teaching on the Four Noble Truths, which also presents, in a nutshell, the Buddhist world-view. The importance of this teaching is such that it forms the theme of the Buddha's first public discourse, namely, the.[2] The concept of *dukkha* is explained in the First Noble Truth. The complexity of this concept *Dhammacakka-pavattana Sutta* is made obvious by a remark made by the Buddha elsewhere. He says: "In this Noble Truth of *dukkha* described by me, immeasurable are the shades and details, immeasurable are the implications.[3] This complexity of the concept of *dukkha* has led to much misunderstanding and

---

[1] *M.,* I , 140.

[2] *Vin.,* I , 10; *S.,* V, 420.

[3] *S.,* V, 430.

misrepresentation of the Buddha's teaching, then as well as now, and specially now by modern scholars on Buddhism.[4]

When considered in its philosophical and psychological contexts, the word *dukkha* generally denotes an agonizing, tormenting mental experience of varying intensity, caused by conflicting emotions in the individual. These conflicting emotions cause psychological disturbance, leading to inner conflict. It is in this sense of inner conflict that the term *dukkha is* generally used in the First Noble Truth. But, as mentioned before, in this term are also capsuled many other shades of meaning, and these include various forms of conflicts and quarrels that occur at different levels in human life and society. And that the Buddha's teaching is meant also to appease such conflicts is seen from another utterance of the Buddha. When he was asked as to what his doctrine is, what he proclaims, the Buddha replied that "by teaching which there would be no dispute, quarrel or contending with anyone in this world, such is my teaching, such is the doctrine I proclaim."[5] However, according to Buddhism, in the final analysis these social conflicts also are nothing but external manifestations of inner conflicts of the individual.[6]

The one and only goal of Buddhism is the complete extinction (*khaya*) or cessation (*nirodha*) of *dukkha* or all forms of conflict, both inner conflict and outer conflict.[7] This goal, the *summum bonum* of Buddhism which is *nibbāna*, is defined variously as extinction of craving (*ragakkhaya*), hatred (*dosakkhaya*) and confusion (*mohakkhaya*),[8] release from all *dukkha*,[9] or end of *dukkha* (*dukkhassa-anta*).[10] Positively it is referred to as Supreme Bliss (*parama-sukka*),[11] for it is devoid of all *dukkha*; or as a state of tranquility or peace.[12] This cessation of inner conflict caused by craving (*raga*), etc., brings about inner peace (*ajjhatta-santi*).[13] Taking the term *dukkha* strictly in this sense of inner conflict, the Buddha has explained it is in this fathom long body which is endowed with perception and mind that *dukkha* as well as its cessation lie.[14] The final solution presented by Buddhism to this problem of *dukkha* is the ethical perfection of the individual, which in other words means his realization of

---

[4] On this see Walpola Rahula, *What the Buddha Taught* (London: Gordon Fraser, 1959), 16*ff*; *Encyclopedia of Buddhism* (=*EB*) (Colombo: The Government of Sri Lanka, 1990), V, 696-702.

[5] *M.*, I , 108.

[6] See P. D. Premasiri, "The Buddhist Analysis of the Nature of Social Conflict," in *Essays in Honor of Ananda* (Colombo: W.P. Guruge, 1990), 103*ff*.

[7] *M.*, I , 93, 191, II , 10.

[8] *S.*, V, 8.

[9] *Sabbadukkhapamocana*, in *S.*, II , 278.

[10] *Ud.*, 80.

[11] *Dh.*, 204.

[12] *A.*, II , 18.

[13] *Sn.*, 837; *Suttanipāta-aṭṭhakathā*, 545.

[14] *A.*, II , 50.

nibbāna. As Buddhism is an ethical religion, this goal of ethical perfection as its *summum bonum is* quite in keeping with it.

At the inception of Buddhism the only goal of religious life (*brahmacariya*) was cessation of this *dukkha*.[15] And the only means of realizing this was the ethical perfection of the individual. This explains the Buddha's concern, from the outset, to guide and encourage his followers to revolutionize their characters and attitudes. His intention was to build a community of followers totally free from conflict and who, therefore, could live at peace with themselves and others. The *Saṅgha* formed that community.

The Buddha presented a Path which helped to achieve this end, and this is the Noble Eightfold Path. The successful practice of this Path was not a simple task. It is similar to an attempt to swim against the current, for it called for the complete change of the usual behavioral pattern of an individual.[16] This clearly shows that such an attempt called for complete dedication and indefatigable effort. Therefore, total commitment was considered very necessary.

Household life with its endless encumbrances was considered not only as being not conducive, but also an obstacle to such a commitment. The alternative suggested was recluseship (*pabbajjā*), giving up the household life and taking up the life of a homeless recluse, for such a life was viewed as the open space, free of all encumbrances.[17] Hence, it is not surprising to find the Buddha encouraging and inspiring the new converts to enter recluseship so that they could devote themselves completely to the practice of the Path,[18] nor is it surprising to find all the converts who firmly decided to follow the Path giving up the household life. Premasiri on this point observes that *pabbajjā* (going forth from the life of the household) was considered in the early Buddhist tradition to be both a symbolic and an actual break away from the life of sense pleasures. One was expected to shave off the hair and beard, don yellow robes, leave all household ties and possessions, and enter into the life of a *bhikkhu* The Buddhist scriptures often mention the conviction expressed by the listener to the Buddha's message that it is difficult to lead the higher life prescribed in Buddhism in its complete purity while living in the household. If immediate progress is intended, one is expected to join the *bhikkhusaṅgha*.[19] However, as Premasiri himself rightly observes: "Buddhism never held that the fruits of the Buddhist path

---

[15] *M.,* I , 197.

[16] The usual lifestyle led by an individual is compared to swimming with the current; any attempt to change this lifestyle through ethical progress is compared to attempting to swim against the current. *S.* I , 136; *A.* II , 6.

[17] *Vin.,* II , 180; *M.,* I , 179, 240, 267, 344.

[18] As the *Bodhisattva,* he himself found the household life an obstacle to such an undertaking. Therefore, he gave it up. So it is through his personal experience that he encouraged the followers to do so if they really desired to free themselves from *dukkha.*

[19] See P. D. Premasiri's article on "Ethics" in *EB.,* V, 151.

cannot be reaped by the people who lived a household life."[20] But this is more the exception than the rule.

Thus, it is seen that if one undertook to follow the Path shown by the Buddha with the genuine intention of eradicating *dukkha,* such a one necessarily had to enter recluseship. Therefore, it could be reasonably surmised that at the beginning, the practice of the Path was meant for no other purpose than the eradication of *dukkha* and realizing inner peace, and hence it was meant for those who opted to give up the household life and become "full-timers" in the religious life (*brahmacariya*). Y. Karunadasa, explaining the practice of the Path, observes: "As a moral teaching it is the ideal that Buddhism upholds for all the laymen and the monks."[21] True, it is the ideal presented by Buddhism to all Buddhists. But whether Buddhism held or even holds that this ideal could be equally and successfully pursued by laymen and monks is open to question. As shown earlier it was not held so at the beginning, nor is there any reason to believe that it is held so now. The impression one gets by reading Karunadasa's article is that from the beginning this Path was meant for both the monks and the laity alike, to be followed "as far as possible."

Explaining his position, Karunadasa writes: "Since the path is often defined as the path that leads to *nibbāna,* this has given rise to a misconception that it is not meant for laymen who lead a worldly life."[22] But he holds the contrary view, and to substantiate this view of his, he gives three reasons:

> (1) Firstly, ". . . all Buddhist moral teachings, whether they concern the clergy or the laity, are ultimately traceable to the Noble Eightfold Path. It therefore follows that the Buddhist teachings pertaining to happiness in this world (*diṭṭhadhammasukha*) and well-being in future existence (*samparāyahita*) are all based on it."
>
> (2) Secondly, ". . . [that] laymen too were taken into consideration in defining; the path factors is shown by the definition given to *sammā-ajīva* or right livelihood." According to him the definition of *sammā-ajīva* as abstention from five kinds of harmful profession means that the Path was meant for the laity, also.
>
> (3) Thirdly, the Buddha equally dissuades both laymen and monks from following the *micchā-paṭipadā* (wrong path). This wrong path is the direct opposite of the Noble Eightfold Path. This Karunadasa considers the most important reason that substantiates his view, and he adds: "This clearly shows that the Middle Path which, according to Buddhism is this Right Path, is meant for both laymen as well as monks."[23]

---

[20] Premasiri, *ibid.*

[21] Y. Karunadasa, "The Moral Life, Both as a Means and an End", *Middle Way* 69-1 (May 1994): 20.

[22] Karunadasa, *ibid.*

[23] Karunadasa, *ibid.*

There is no doubt that this is the ideal presented by Buddhism for both laymen and monks. But there is reasonable doubt as to whether Buddhism holds that both lay-life and monk-life are equally conducive to the successful pursuit of this path. The preponderance of evidence is to the contrary. The history of the growth and spread of Buddhism, too, makes this point clear.

Premasiri observes: "Buddhism started as a movement of liberation seekers. It was a spiritual movement of those who were already disenchanted with the ordinary pleasures of the world and were seeking for something believed to be higher. A life of renunciation of the ordinary sensuous pleasures was considered to be a primary requirement if one's immediate goal was to attain moral perfection."[24]

It is also clear that at the beginning the Path had only one goal and that was *nibbāna*. Hence, originally it was not meant for any purpose other than this, not even for the "well-being in future existence." Such a purpose contradicts the sole objective of the Path. To say that the Path was "originally" meant also for such a purpose, appears to be an attempt to throw back to an earlier stage a feature that got appended at a later stage. Whether *sammā-ajīva* (the 5th Path-factor) was defined originally as abstention from five harmful professions, namely trading in arms, living beings, flesh, intoxicating drinks, and poison, is very doubtful.

Karunadasa himself admits a possible objection to such a view. He says: "One objection that could be raised here is that some who have given up the household life in order to practice the higher life (*brahmacariya*) could also engage in this kind of activity." This objection could also be supported by reference to some of the rules laid down in the Buddhist *Vinaya*. In spite of such supportive reference, he rejects the objection, saying: "However, we wish to submit that the likelihood is otherwise."[25]

This objection cannot hold ground in the context of the early stage of the *bhikkhusangha* when such recalcitrant monks were conspicuous by their absence, yet the Path was known to have been followed in its pristine purity. There is yet a more plausible objection. These Path-factors are more descriptive than prescriptive, and it is reasonable to accept that *sammā-ajīva* meant activities which were in keeping with the life of a recluse who was following the Path as taught by the Buddha.

The *Brahmajāla-sutta*[26] is full of reference to *samanas* and *brāhmanas* who, while living on the food provided by the faithful lay devotees, engaged in numerous activities which were not by any standard in keeping with their vocation. It is possible that this Path-factor was meant to give a clear idea of what monks should do and should not do to eke out their existence. That this reference to these five professions is not related to the life of monks is seen from

---

[24] P. D. Premasiri, "Ethics," *op. cit.,* 151.
[25] Karudasa, "The Moral Life," *loc. sit.*
[26] *D.,* 1*ff.*

the *Aṅguttaranikāya* which lists them as five activities that should not be done by a lay devotee.[27]

As Karunadasa considers the Path to be equally meant for both monks and laymen, he concludes that "it could be followed on different levels or in varying degrees of intensity." He thinks that the implication of all this is that if the Noble Eightfold Path cannot be followed fully, it is better to follow it as far as possible. Such an implication is not at all possible when one takes into consideration the total commitment of the early liberation seekers. Those early converts never entertained any idea of postponing the realization of *nibbāna.* Their aim was an immediate one, the attainment of freedom from *dukkha* here and now. That is why they opted for recluseship and committed themselves totally. The Buddha also always encouraged them to strive hard without relaxing their effort.

Another distinct feature is that the Path had to be followed each by himself. It was not considered the outcome of a collective effort. Even the Buddha can contribute only as a Guide, a Pathfinder, and each one has to do what has to be done.[28] One could practice successfully irrespective of external influences, even if they happened to be adverse, though congenial external influence could facilitate the practice.

All these suggest that at the beginning the Path had only one goal, and that the serious followers of the Path were required to enter into recluseship and totally commit themselves to the practice without depending on any external contribution.

It is seen that not long after its inception, Buddhism spread rapidly to all sections of society. Of these new converts among the laity, only a very small minority entered into recluseship. The majority, for various reasons, could not afford to leave the household life. But they did not want to be left out of the Buddhist fold because of this inability of theirs. They admired the Path and were convinced about it. But they found it to be too exacting, for it demanded total commitment and entering into recluseship. Their household responsibilities did not permit this. As more and more lay converts came in, there arose a sort of popular request for some kind of relaxation of the Path. There is an instance recorded in the *Aṅguttaranikāya* (IV, 281 *ff*) where such a request is made to the Buddha openly. Herein, a Koliyan layman Dīghajānu approaches the Buddha and pleads with the Buddha about his plight as a layman which does not permit him to follow the Path as laid down the Buddha. He says that he is a layman given to enjoyment of pleasures and that he has family encumbrances. And as such he requests the Buddha to teach a doctrine in keeping with his vocation in life and which would be conducive to his well-being in this life as well as in future existence. The implication of his request was that Buddhism as practiced at that time was too exacting and hence average laymen like him were unable to follow it.

---

[27] *pañc 'imā bhikkhave vaṇijjā upāsakena akaraṇiyā satthavaṇijjā. A.,* III, 208.
[28] *Dh.,* 276.

The Buddha readily granted his request and made known such a teaching within the framework of the Path. Premasiri explains this evolution of a kind of 'secondary path' as follows: "The layman is also considered to be capable of attaining the highest goal of Buddhism if he cultivated the threefold training or the eightfold path to its fullest perfection. But the household life and its responsibilities are considered as an encumbrance to fulfill the requirements of the higher spiritual life. Therefore, depending on the aims and interests of the layperson who does not intend to give up the pleasures of sense altogether, the Buddha gives valuable moral guidance to make that kind of life a success to the higher stages of spiritual training. If the lay person's life is not properly guided, Buddhism maintained that there is a possibility of regression into states of existence from which liberation would be very difficult."[29]

Thus, one clearly notices a change in the kind of followers of the Path as well as a shift in the immediate goal. The interest of the new lay converts pertained more to happiness in this world and in the next; the ideal of attaining total emancipation from *dukkha* was gradually becoming a remote one. As lay converts increased and became an important component of the Buddhist society, it became incumbent on Buddhism to address itself to key social problems of the time which needed immediate analysis and solution. In the earlier analyses, all conflicts were explained as manifestations of an individual's inner conflicts. Such analyses could have appeared too idealistic to laymen and the solution presented may have seemed impracticable within the social context to which they belonged. Thus, to analyze these actually prevalent social conflicts and anomalies, the Buddha adopted a sociologically oriented approach instead of his psychologically oriented earlier approach. In doing this, the Buddha took into consideration two important spheres of lay society. These are: (1) material life, and (2) spiritual life. He pointed out how these two spheres mutually influence each other and how life here as well as future existences could be made well and happy by the balanced development of these two spheres.

The Buddha identified a number of sources that produced social conflict and disharmony. Social discrimination, inequality of opportunities, dogmatic clinging to views and ideologies, mal-distribution of national wealth and resulting unemployment and poverty, misrule, and a host of such other factors were pinpointed as immediate causes of contention, strife, wars and endless misery. To make the life of laymen in this world happy, these conflicts had to be resolved. Unless this was done, the Buddha found that it would not be possible to stop the regression of laymen both materially and spiritually. So, with regard to laymen, the Buddha was not attempting to lead them directly towards the attainment of inner peace, which they found hard to follow. Instead, he presented to them a graduated course.[30] The Four Noble Truths including the Path was considered far too advanced for average laymen. This teaching came to

---

[29] P. D. Premasiri, "Ethics", 162.

[30] It appears that as time passed even monks wanted their practice formulated in a graduated method. *M.*, III, 1*ff.*

be considered as the totally elevating teaching (*sāmukkaṁsikā desanā*) as against the simplified graduated discourse (*ānupubbīkathā*) dealing with elementary virtues such as charity and their beneficial consequences.[31]

The Path came to be divided into two levels as supra-mundane (*lokottara*) and mundane (*lokiya*).[32] The former was intended for the dedicated "full-timers" who gave up the household life and strove towards the realization of *nibbāna*. The latter was for the pleasure-enjoying layman, encumbered with household responsibilities. They followed the same Noble Eightfold Path but "on different levels or in varying degrees of intensity."[33] They were expected to follow the Path to the best of their ability, for if they did not do so, at least as far as possible, it was felt that it could lead to individual as well as social regression in all aspects.

Thus, it is seen that the Path, which was originally meant to realize *nibbāna*, subsequently, due to the demands of the laymen, was adjusted to use as a means to make the individual personally happy and contented, and also to make him socially relevant and useful. So, the Path meant for the laymen is more or less a practical guide to character building, and its immediate aim is to help individuals become members of a peaceful, prosperous, harmonious community. Individual effort and dedication is necessary in the practice of this Path. But that is not enough to the successful accomplishment of the Path. The effort needed to build such a society is a collective one. The individuals as well as the society with its numerous social institutions have to collaborate if success is to be assured.[34]

It was pointed out earlier that the Buddha intended to mold a community of followers totally free from inner conflict. The laymen's immediate goal was of a lesser order, namely peace, harmony, and prosperity in a secular sense. To achieve this everyone in the society had to contribute by discharging the responsibilities expected of him. Buddhism elaborately lays down guidelines for this. And these guidelines are all ethical; and as Karunadasa has pointed out, all such guidelines are ultimately traceable to the Noble Eightfold Path[35]. These guidelines are based on the Buddha's teaching on avoidance of bad (*akusala, pāpa*) and doing good (*kusala, puñña*).[36] The first Path-factor, namely *sammā-diṭṭhi* (right view) in its mundane level, provides the means of distinguishing right and wrong, and thus helps to keep individuals away from the wrong path. What is right and what is wrong? Whatever is right is *kusala or puñña*, that is, whatever that is conducive to one's well-being and the well-being of others.

---

[31] *D.*, I, 110; II, 41f.

[32] See Ven. Piyadassi, *The Buddha's Ancient Path* (London: Rider, 1964), 91 *ff.*

[33] Y. Karunadasa, "The Moral Life," *loc.sit.*

[34] W.S. Karunaratne, *Buddhism, Its Religion and Philosophy* (Singapore: Buddhist Research Society, 1988), 11 *ff.*

[35] Y, Karunadasa, *ibid.*, 20.

[36] *Dh.*, 183. This ethical norm is largely influenced by the belief in *kamma* and rebirth.

What is wrong is the opposite. To know what is right and wrong is to be equipped with a suitable ideology to regulate one's behavior. What is meant by one's behavior is the responsibility one owes to oneself as well as to others in the society. It is a virtue to discharge these responsibilities in the proper way, hence all those who do so are considered virtuous people. All members have to be virtuous if the society is to become peaceful and prosperous.

Virtue, or *sīla*, forms the first item in the scheme of Threefold Training (*ti-sikkhā*), based on the Noble Eightfold Path, and it is the cultivation of *sīla* that is specially emphasized with regard to laymen. It is considered the foundation on which this spiritual life is built. It is said that an intelligent man first establishes himself in virtue and then begins to cultivate his mind and wisdom.[37] This cultivation of *sīla* also marks the beginning of character and attitude revolution of a man which is so indispensable for mutual understanding, harmony and peace in all social units and institutions.

The ideational basis formed through Right View pave the way for Right Intention, that is intention free from excessive selfishness, ill-will and violence. Such intention promotes good verbal and physical actions and also makes one pursue harmless professions. One who cultivates *sīla* regulates all his verbal[38] and physical actions,[39] and engages in professions which are not harmful to the society.[40] Thus it is seen that the Path is here primarily employed to socialize the individual. These same ethical norms are introduced also as the five precepts (*pañcasīla*). This on the personal level makes everyone respect the other's basic right to safe living and private property. It also makes one respect the sanctity of family life, and induces everyone to maintain integrity, trustworthiness[41] as well as personal dignity.

When established in virtue, one behaves in a way that is benevolent to oneself and others. This makes every member of the society discharge his responsibility properly. In a lay society that follows the Path for the purpose of cultivating *sīla*, this ethical norm regarding the proper discharge of responsibility applies equally to all. Some are professional responsibilities and some belong to the sphere of family and social relations. Whatever the responsibility one owes to others, one has to discharge it properly. The kings have to be just, the rich have to be considerate and compassionate to the poor by practicing charity, the masters have to look after the servants well, the employers have to be considerate to employees, and so on. In fact, this discharge of duty is mutual; the subjects, the poor, the employees, etc., have to reciprocate in the appropriate manner as well. The same is expected in the sphere of family

---

[37] *S.,* I ,13.

[38] Avoids false speech, slanderous speech, harsh speech and frivolous speech.

[39] Avoids killing, stealing and sexual misconduct.

[40] These include the five kinds of harmful professions as well as all forms of cheating, exploitation, etc.

[41] Lily de Silva, "The Privilege and the Problem of Man," in *Essays, op. cit.,* 56-62.

and other social relations, from husbands and wives, parents and children, and so on.

This practice of the Path by laymen calls for a collective effort without which it is not possible to achieve the objective aimed at. If all cooperate and collaborate to achieve the objective aimed at, they will be able to pave the way for both material progress and spiritual progress, for the Buddhist concept of progress means a fine blend of both these aspects. The *Dvicakkkhu-sutta*[42] clearly enunciates this Buddhist concept of progress which consists of a fine balance of both material and spiritual progress. The cultivation of *sīla* lays the necessary foundation for the total development of the individual. This 'total development' of the individual is attainable by paving the way to prosperity the laymen so much wish for, but tempering it with virtue.

The Path practiced in this manner will, while laying a firm foundation for gradual spiritual progress, enable laymen to make the world a better place to live in, with peace, harmony and prosperity, each being pleased with the other, having complete trust and confidence in each other, and as the *Kūṭadanta-sutta*[43] puts it very sufficiently, "dancing their children in their arms, dwelling with open doors."

---

[42] *A.*, I , 128*f.*

[43] See *Dialogues of the Buddha*, part I, 175*f.*

Part 2

Society / Conflict Resolution

CHAPTER 7

EARLY BUDDHIST ATTITUDE TO WAR AND PEACE

K.N. Upadhyaya

Indian tradition as a whole, whether Hindu or Buddhist, condemns violence and commends non-violence and peace as the controlling concepts of human conduct and normal modes of conflict-resolution. But in some special situations when one has to deal with notorious aggressors and heinous criminals, one is hard-pressed to decide if a deviation from the standard code of conduct and normal mode of conflict-resolution is morally justified. The early Buddhist position, as embodied in early Buddhist texts, is almost antithetical to what is recommended under such situations in Hinduism, as depicted in its classical text, the *BG*. This paper seeks to demonstrate on the basis of textual evidences how the early Buddhist attitude to the problem of war and peace and its mode of conflict-resolution are diametrically opposed to those of the *Gīta* and how it stands unequivocally committed to non-violence or peace as a universal principle of moral conduct and the uniform mode of conflict resolution, whether in personal or public affairs.

In order to understand and appreciate fully the subtlety and cogency of the early Buddhist position, it is useful to refer briefly to the arguments of the *Gīta* which provide traditional justification for war or violence in exceptional situations.

The *Gīta*'s advocacy of war is principally based upon the dual concepts of one's prescribed duty (*svadharma*) and the disinterested performance of actions enjoined by such a duty. Every individual is required to perform his own duty relentlessly and dispassionately irrespective of the consequences, for man is to attain perfection by discharging his own duty (*BG*, XVIII.45) with a detached view (*BG*, XVIII.49). Now, to fight gallantly in the battle and not to run away from it is one of the prescribed duties of a Kṣatriya. The *Gīta* enumerates the duties of a Kṣatriya as follows: "Heroism, valor, fortitude, skillfulness, as well as not running away from the battle, charity and lordship...are the natural duties of a Kṣatriya."[1] Thus Arjuna, as a Kṣatriya, is exhorted to remain firm and detached in performing his duty of fighting.

This dispassionate discharge of the duty of fighting is reinforced by the *Gītā* from its metaphysical and theological standpoints. From the metaphysical point of view, Arjuna is reminded of the eternal and indestructible nature of his soul and asked not to be perturbed by the physical destruction of the destructible body.[2] The true self is not slain when the body is slain (*BG*, II.20). Thus by pointing out the inevitability of the destruction of the physical body, on the one hand, and the impossibility of the destruction of the eternal metaphysical self, on the other, Arjuna is asked to remain firm and unflinching in his duty of fighting. Kṛṣṇa says: "These bodies of eternal, imperishable and incomprehensible soul are said to be perishable. Therefore, fight, 0, Arjuna."[3] From the theological point of view, it is said: "Man attains perfection by worshipping Him (God) through his own duty."[4] Disinterested work is considered as the best worship, for in so doing a man dedicates his whole being to God. In that case, he is said to remain absolutely free form the bonds of actions bearing good and bad results.[5] It is said: "He who works having given up attachment, resigning his actions to God is not contaminated by sin even as a lotus leaf (is untouched) by water."[6] Arjuna is therefore, advised: "Dedicating all actions to me through your spiritualized mind, being disinterested and free from egoism, fight dispassionately."[7] It is said: "He who is not self-conceited, whose intellect is not attached, though he slays these worlds, he (really) neither slays not is he bound." (*BG*, XVIII. 17). In light of this attitude, Arjuna is given the following explicit advice: "Treating alike pleasure and pain, gain and loss, victory and defeat, get ready for battle. Thus you shall not incur sin."[8]

Lest Arjuna may still desist form fighting on the ground that the ideal state of mind, viz., the utter detachment, required for remaining unsullied in the battle, is not possible for him to attain, Kṛṣṇa further adds that "even a little of this discipline saves one from great fear."[9]

Kṛṣṇa further points out to Arjuna that to follow his prescribed duty (*svadharma*) of fighting is in keeping with the noble tradition of the royal sages, virtuous enough to lead to heaven and glorious enough to establish fame on the earth. Thus it is emphasized that this line of action has come down through tradition (*BG,* IV.2) of the royal sages (*loc. cit.*). It is said that "for a Kṣatriya

---

[1] *BG,* XVIII. 11-30.
[2] *Ibid,* II. 11 30.
[3] *Ibid.,* II. 18.
[4] *Ibid,* XVIII.46.
[5] *Ibid.,* IX.26.
[6] *Ibid.,* V. 10.
[7] *Ibid.,* III.30.
[8] *Ibid,* II.38.
[9] *Ibid,* II. 40.

there is no good higher than a righteous fight,"[10] and for him it is like "an open door to heaven" (*BG,* II.32). On the other hand, to fall from this duty is to incur ill-fame or dishonor and "for a man of repute, ill-fame is worse than death" (*BG,* II. 34). In short, desisting from fighting" is neither trodden by noble ones, nor is it conducive to heaven nor can it give rise to fame."[11] Arjuna is therefore clearly told: "If you do not fight this righteous battle you shall fall from duty and fame, and incur sin."[12] But his participation in war would do good in any case: "If slain, you shall go to heaven and if victorious, you shall enjoy the earth" (*BG,* II. 37).

It must, however, be borne in mind that the war which Arjuna is exhorted to plunge in is not a reckless aggression but a righteous war (*BG,* II. 31; *BG.* II. 33) aimed at fighting against evil-doers (*BG,* I. 36). Kṛṣṇa (the incarnate God) Himself is said to "assume birth for the protection of righteous ones, the destruction of evil-doers and the establishment of righteousness."[13] Thus the *Gīta* considers it morally right to kill or destroy evil-doers for the establishment of righteousness, if no other way is left open to restore righteousness. This is how the *Gīta* vindicates its concept of righteous war.

In light of this justification of what the *Gīta* calls the 'righteous war', we can now clearly see how the early Buddhist attitude to war and peace is diametrically opposed to what the *Gīta* prescribes.

In the first place early Buddhism does not accept the validity of the concept of prescribed duty. Secondly, it rules out the very possibility of disinterested warfare. Regarding the concept of prescribed duty taught by the Brahminical priesthood (and upheld by the *Gīta*) Buddha points out that he, in contradistinction to Brahmins who teach the fourfold duty (M. II. 180), teaches the supra-mundane Noble Doctrine as the only duty of man (*M.,* II. 181). This practice of holy life is alike meant for all without distinction. The idea of adopting unrighteous profession or ignoble means of livelihood, such as fighting, under the guise of a prescribed duty is utterly unacceptable to early Buddhism.

Repudiating the concept of prescribed duties based on caste, Buddha points out that *Brahmins* have acted unwarrantedly in laying down specified duties for different castes. Addressing Esukari Brahmin, he says: "Just as, O Brahmin, they might separate a morsel (of meat) for a poor needy destitute man without his desire, saying: 'you must eat this meat, my good man, and must also pay a price for it'--- even so do the *Brahmins* lay down the fourfold virtue or conduct without the assent of recluses and true Brahmins."[14]

In fact, the incompatibility of the *Gīta*'s ideal with that of the Buddhist is evident from the very fact that Buddha, in spite of being born as a Kṣatriya, renounces his royal duties and becomes a recluse. Not only does he himself lead the life of a recluse but he also ordains many other Kṣatriyas and royal princes

---

[10] *Ibid.,* II. 31.
[11] *Ibid.,* II. 2.
[12] *Ibid.,* II. 33.
[13] *Ibid.,* IV.8.
[14] *M.,* II. 181.

to the Order. He does not entertain the theory of prescribed duty as a cloak for covering the immorality of certain professions. Wrong means of livelihood must be abandoned and immoral acts must not be performed even though it is deemed as part of one's duty to the king (*M.,* II. 191).

According to the Buddha, it is impossible for a disinterested and enlightened man to take recourse to immoral acts. In no circumstance can a truly detached and disinterested man resort to violence. Of the nine moral vices which a truly detached person is considered incapable of doing (*D.,* III. 133), the deliberate destruction of life of a living creature (*loc. cit.*) *is* reckoned as the first. The enlightened one is said to be incapable of doing such a bodily, verbal or mental action, which is morally wrong or deprecated by recluses, brahmins and the wise. [15] Buddha altogether precludes the possibility of war without attachment, passion or desire.

The *Gita*'s advocacy for the doctrine of action without concern for the fruit is clearly found faulty by early Buddhism. According to Buddha, it is immaterial whether an action is performed with an expectation, without an expectation, with and without an expectation or neither with nor without an expectation (M. III. 138, 139). What really matters is whether the action is performed properly (*yoniso*) or improperly (*ayoniso*). If one makes due efforts, the fire is bound to be kindled out of the dry wood whether one does or does not desire it.[16]

Since the Buddha's attitude is anti-metaphysical and there is no place for God in his system, the entire metaphysical and theological arguments of the *Gita* lose their seriousness for the Buddha. From the metaphysical standpoint, Arjuna is exhorted to fight in view of the indestructibility and eternity of the soul. But the very existence of it is questioned by the Buddha. Even if the existence of the supra-mundane or transcendental soul is admitted for argument's sake, it cannot be said to have bearing on mundane acts prompted by passion and emotion. How then can it be invoked for either justifying or condemning a mundane act? Indeed, in so doing one is led to an absurd position of moral anarchism. Professors Ranade and Belvalkar have noticed the absurdity involved in this absolutistic concept of the self. They observe: "To say that *Atman* dies not is legitimate. To say that weapons cannot cut Him nor fire burn Him is also a legitimate varying of the phrase. But to argue that therefore the murderer is no murderer and there is nobody really responsible for his action is to carry this '*sasvata*' or '*akriya*' doctrine to a point, which if seriously preached would be subversive of all established social institutions and religious sacraments."[17] The theological argument also fares no better in the Buddhist context. Early Buddhism clearly rejects the divine-origin theory of social orders and the divinely ordained duties of men, thus cutting the very root of the *Gita*'s doctrine that perfection can be attained through disinterested discharge of prescribed

---

[15] *M.,* II. 113-114.

[16] *M.,* III. 143-144.

[17] S.K. Belvalkar and R. D. Ranade, *History of Indian Philosophy,* Vol. II (Poona: Bilvakuñja Pub. House, 1927), 399.

duties.[18] Unlike the *Gīta* which approves of even defective professions (*Gīta,* XVIII. 47-48), early Buddhism recommends only righteous professions. Selling arms is the first and foremost among the five trades considered mean and forbidden in early Buddhism.[19]

As regards the *Gīta*'s exhortation to Arjuna to follow his prescribed duty even before attaining the ideal state of detachment on the ground that even a little of the discipline of detachment will save him from great fear, the Buddha is found to take an opposite stand by saying that one must fear even a little bit of vice (*D.,* I . 63; III. 78), because even that much of defect may prove detrimental and dangerous. The Buddha gives the simile of a man pierced by a poisoned arrow, who, only because the arrow has been taken out, moves about carelessly, not protecting his still unhealed wound and, as a result, comes to grief once again.[20] The Buddha, therefore, emphatically urges us to maintain utmost care and vigilance till the goal is fully realized, lest the consequences may be grave. He does not permit any slackness or complacency in the course of following the discipline.

Regarding the considerations of the noble tradition, the attainment of heaven and the establishment of fame, also, early Buddhism takes an opposite stand. A warrior chief telling Buddha that he had heard from his ancestral teachers in the martial arts that the spirited soldier who fights energetically and kills his enemies in the battle is born in heaven, wants to know whether it is correct.[21] Buddha, to the utter disappointment and dismay of the warrior chief, says that such a soldier "at the dissolution of body after death is born in a hell named, *Parajita*" (*S.,* IV. 309). So far as the question of fame about gallantry and bravery is concerned, it is pointed out that the real gallantry consists in achieving victory over one's own passions and in meting out love or non-anger to the angry. The display of brutal force is considered merely foolish and this can win applause and fame only from fools. The truly enlightened one should not care for such fame and try to acquire true virtue and real fame. Thus Buddha observes: "One may conquer a thousand of a thousand men in the battlefield, yet he, indeed, is the noblest victor who conquers his own single self."[22] It is again stated: "One expressing no anger to the angry (really) wins a war difficult to win" (*S.,* I. 222).

The *Gīta*'s concept of righteous war, according to which it is deemed morally right to fight against evil-doers, is also incompatible with the Buddhist ideal. In fact, according to the true Buddhist ideal, the phrase 'righteous war' cannot but be a contradiction in terms, since righteousness and war can hardly go hand in hand. In no circumstance is a true Buddhist to resort to violence. The instruction of the Buddha is to meet anger with love and not with anger; evil

---

[18] *Ibid.,* XVIII.45.
[19] *A.,* III. 208.
[20] *M.,* III. 256-257.
[21] *S.,* IV.308-309.
[22] *Dh.,* 103.

with good and not with evil. He says: "Conquer anger with non-anger (love), evil with good; conquer the miser with generosity and the liar with truth."[23] This is the Buddhist ideal.

The Buddha makes it clear that people resort to violence and war on account of their selfish desire or passion and reap the consequences of their evil deeds both here as well as hereafter. Thus he observes: "It is on account of passion or desire that kings dispute with kings, Kṣatriyas dispute with Kṣatriyas.... They entering into quarrel, conflict and dispute, attack one another with hands, stones, rods and weapons.... It is on account of passion or desire that they wage war having taken sword and shield, having girded on bow and quiver and being drawn out in battle-array on both sides. Hurling arrows, hurling daggers, flashing swords, they pierce with arrows, pierce with daggers and cut off heads with swords. They thereby suffer death or death-like pain. This, monks, is the visible worldly consequence of passion or desire. Having performed evil deeds by body, speech and mind they at the destruction of body after death are born in lowly and evil state of downward hell. This, monks, is the otherworldly (saṃparāyika) consequence of passion or desire."[24] Thus the Buddha discards not only the traditional view of war being the prescribed duty of a Kṣatriya and the possibility of its being fought dispassionately or disinterestedly, but he also speaks of its dreadful consequences both from a worldly as well as an otherworldly point of view, a position diametrically opposed to that of the Gītā.[25]

A sharp contrast between the attitude of the Gītā and that of early Buddhism is evident from the two different approaches taken by Kṛṣṇa and the Buddha in virtually similar situations. When the armies of the two cousin brothers, the Kauravas and the Paṇḍavas, were facing each other on the battlefield, Kṛṣṇa is found to encourage Arjuna, the hero of the Paṇḍavas, to fight the battle. But when the Buddha finds that the Śākya and their blood brothers, the Kolivas, have their armies assembled and they are ready to fight over the issue of the flowage of the waters of the river Rohini between their territories, he promptly intervenes and stops them from fighting by pointing out the futility of the cause of dispute and disastrous consequences of the fight. Making a fervent appeal to both parties, he impresses upon them how foolish it is for them to destroy invaluable human lives for a matter so trivial. He says: "Why on account of some water of little worth would you destroy invaluable lives of these soldiers?"[26]

Through his own personal example, the Buddha clearly demonstrates how a virtuous person should conduct himself and behave with utter dignity and calmness even in the most provocative situations. He remains calm and unperturbed when the notorious robber and murderer Aṅgulimāla, threatening to

---

²³ *Ibid.*, 223.
²⁴ *M.*, 186-187.
²⁵ Contrast the *Gītā*'s view, *BG*, II. 37.
²⁶ *J.*, V. 412-4.

kill the Buddha, rushes towards him with his sword drawn out. The *Mahāsīlava Jātaka* narrates the story of the Buddha's previous life when he, as the King of Benares, was attacked by the then King of Kosala. It is said that while the Buddha was reigning righteously under the title of Mahāsīlava (the king of great virtue), one of his ministers treacherously broke out from him and joined the ministry of the King of Kosala. In the course of time, he gained the confidence of the King of Kosala and prompted him to conquer the kingdom of Benares ruled by a feeble king. The King of Kosala, in order to have an idea of the attitude and strength of the King of Benares, sent some ruffians to plunder some villages of the kingdom of Benares and massacre the people. The ruffians were captured and brought before the King of Benares, but the latter, instead of punishing them, gave them enough wealth and asked them not to repeat the offence in the future. Thrice such incursions were made, and each time the offenders were treated in the same way. The King of Kosala, being emboldened by the utter goodness of the King of Benares, ultimately marched his troops against the latter's kingdom. But the latter would not allow his brave warriors to offer resistance to the invading king, saying: "None shall suffer because of me. Let those who covet kingdom seize mine."[27] The King of Kosala, crossing the border and passing unobstructed through the kingdom, reached the outskirts of the city itself, and sent a message to the King of Benares bidding him either to yield the kingdom or to give battle. But the latter's reply was: "I fight not, let him seize my kingdom."[28] Thereupon the King of Kosala reached the royal palace with his army, and having arrested the King of Benares along with his ministers, had them buried alive up to the neck in the cemetery. But even at this hour, the King of Great Virtue (Mahāsīlava) did not harbor even the slightest angry thought. The story proceeds and it is said that at night two ogres disputing for their respective share of a corpse, approached the King of Benares for arbitration, considering him to be just and righteous. The King fulfilled their request, and they, in gratitude, helped the King to approach the usurper sleeping comfortably in the royal chamber. He awoke the usurper from his sleep and the latter was horrified to find himself alone in a helpless condition before the King of Benares. The King of Benares then related to him the entire episode as to how he could come from the cemetery to the royal chamber, whereupon the usurper's heart moved within him, and he begged for the Mahāsīlava's forgiveness, saying: "O King, I, though blessed with human nature, knew not your virtue, yet the fierce and cruel ogres whose very food is flesh and blood had known about it. Henceforth, I, sire, will never plot against a man of singular virtue, as you are."[29] This indeed was a real moral awakening for the usurper. The next morning, not only did he restore the kingdom of the King of Benares, but he also publicly apologized to the latter, promising to remain a loyal friend and helper for all time to come.

---

[27] *J.*, I. 263.
[28] *Op.cit.*, I. 263.
[29] *Op.cit.*, I. 266-7.

One may or may not accept the historicity of this story, but it does reflect the Buddhist attitude to war, and it shows what the truly effective way of conflict-resolution should be. It certainly provides a practical illustration of the Buddhist maxim: "Conquer anger with love and evil with good."[30] In no other way can a lasting solution to conflicts and disputes be found. War certainly is not a lasting solution, because as the Buddha points out: "Victory begets enmity and the vanquished lives in sorrow."[31]

The fact that the early Buddhist position is antithetical to that of the *Gīta* becomes abundantly clear when we compare the dialogue between King Śakra and his charioteer, Matali, in the early Buddhist text *Samyutta-nikāya,* with the dialogue between Arjuna and his charioteer Kṛṣṇa in the *Gīta* on the specific question of how to treat the evil-doer. The arguments used in the two dialogues are quite similar, and yet what is held superior by Kṛṣṇa in the *Gīta* is shown to be inferior by Śakra in the early Buddhist text.[32] In this text, the demon king Vepacitti displays outrageous conduct and uses abusive words against King Śakra at which his charioteer, Matali tells Śakra that it would simply indicate weakness and fear on his part if he tolerates such abuses of Vepacitti. But Śakra replies that it would be unbecoming of a wise person like him to be stirred by such words and behavior of an ignorant one.[33] Matali tells him that not to fight and control evil is to give encouragement to it, but Śakra emphatically says that to remain awakened and silent at the anger of others is alone the best way to control it.[34] Matali further argues that by so doing he will not only be betraying his fear and weakness but will also earn bad name to which Śakra replies that fame or bad name, praise or slander are immaterial to the really wise one. To resist force with force is only brutal, and is really an indication of weakness. For the wise ones, it is tolerance and forgiveness which matter most[35]. To fall victim to anger is a sin. The real victory lies in victory over anger. One who does not give way to anger does good both to himself as well as to others.[36]

According to the Buddhist concept of *Brahma-vihāra,* one radiates all directions with boundless love or friendliness (*mettā*) towards all beings, compassion (*karuṇā*) for those in distress, rejoicing (*muditā*) with those who are justly happy, and equanimity and detachment (*upekkhā*) towards all beings.[37]

One must not take it to be an imaginary ideal; it is a goal to be definitely realized and quite a few have actually realized it. We must, therefore, adopt this ideal for our practical guidance. Especially during the present time when tremendous developments in science and technology have placed colossal

---

[30] *Dh.,* 223.

[31] *Dh.,* 201; *S.,* I. 83.

[32] Compare *Gīta* chapter 11 with *S.,* I. 221-4.

[33] *S.,* I. 221.

[34] *Ibid.,* I. 221.

[35] *Ibid,* I. 222.

[36] *Ibid,* I. 222.

[37] *M.,* I. 38.

weapons of mass destruction in the hands of men, the humanity has virtually reached the crossroad of self-annihilation and sheer survival. One cannot, therefore, afford to take the question of war and peace lightly. In the recent past, M. K. Gandhi, a great admirer of the Buddha, made it his life-mission to bring home this conviction to his fellow men all over the world that no salvation is possible for them, whether as individuals, communities or nations, unless they tread the path of non-violence and adopt it firmly as the only means of conflict-resolution. He sincerely believed that one nonviolent fighter can exert much greater influence on the world than a million violent men, because what really counts is the moral purity of men rather than their sheer number. He emphatically asserts: "Non-violence is the Law of the human race and it is infinitely greater than and superior to brute force."[38] He further points out that if non-violence or love and compassion are valid moral laws for an individual in his personal conduct, these should be regarded equally valid in his public and political conduct. In the words of M. K. Gandhi: "It is a profound error to suppose that whilst the Law is good enough for the individuals, it is not for masses of mankind."[39] Gandhi challenges the conventional dichotomies between private and public morality, religious and political pursuits, sacred and secular actions, moral rightness and politics expediency and personal salvation and universal liberation. A person of integrity looks upon life as an integral whole, and does not try to artificially compartmentalize it.

From what has been said above, it is evident that the Buddhist ideal of morality has no room for war. Evidences are many where we find Buddha indicating either directly or indirectly his abhorrence of war. He conveys his views firstly by showing the futility, harmfulness and inconclusiveness of war, secondly, by contrasting the use of physical force with the exercise of righteousness and thirdly, by actual demonstration of the life of loving kindness and compassion.

It must, however, be conceded that the true Buddhist ideal of absolute non-resistance, non-violence or peace in the face of any provocation is extremely difficult to practice for an average ruler or a householder. After his enlightenment Buddha himself is found pondering over the question as to whether it is possible to reign with dharma, without killing or causing to kill, without conquering or causing to conquer, without grieving or causing to grieve (S. I. 116). Mara at once, asserting its possibility, prompts him to take up the life of a king (*loc. cit.*). But the Buddha rebukes Mara and adds: "How can one be inclined towards worldly pleasures (*kamesu*) which he has seen to be the source of suffering? Knowing that attachment to the world is an entanglement, a man should learn to surmount it."[40] It is not quite clear whether in disapproving of Mara's advice, the Buddha precludes the possibility of ruling a kingdom

---

[38] P.K.Prabhu and V.R. Rau, eds., *The Mind of Mahātma Gandhi* (Ahmedabad: Navajivan Publishing House, 1969), para. 439. 1.

[39] *Ibid, para.* 439b.

[40] *S.*, I. 117.

altogether without killing or causing to kill etc., for he does not say anything direct on the subject, though he declines to reign on the ground that worldly pleasures are sources of suffering (*dukkham*), and attachment to them is an entanglement or a bondage (*upādhim*). In any case, it seems that the Buddha also considers it very difficult for a king to avoid the duty of punishing criminals. In the *Cakkavatti Sutta,* however, we find reference to Cakkavatti kings conquering and ruling the entire world without punishment and without arms (*D.,* III. 59). This may be the Buddhist concept of an ideal king who rules the land righteously without waging war against others, though it seems to be acknowledged that this ideal is difficult of realization. In any event, it is important to note that even this ideal (*cakkavatti*) king had to abandon his kingship and practice the holy life as a recluse in order to attain the highest goal.[41] Even Śakra, who is portrayed as a great admirer of the Buddha (*S.,* I. 233-235) and is considered extremely kind and compassionate, is found fighting against demons in defense of peace-loving and righteous people (*S.,* I. 216-224).

This indicates that a peace-loving defender is considered moderately good, though he still falls short of moral perfection in so far as he wavers from the true Buddhist ideal. We find no occasion whatsoever when war is approved, appreciated or justified by the Buddha. On the contrary, he takes every opportunity to express his disapproval and deprecation of war in any shape or form.

In light of this Buddhist approach, what we need to do in this violent world is to make a concerted effort to facilitate the emergence of such individuals and groups who are fully convinced of the power of non-violence (to put it negatively) or love and compassion (to speak in positive terms), and who are able and eager to undertake the mission of drawing up and implementing a broad design of renovating the individuals, society and State on the basis of moral and spiritual values enshrined in Buddhism.

---

[41] *D.,* II, 76-77.

CHAPTER 8

TOWARDS A BUDDHIST THEORY OF SOCIAL ETHICS

Sallie B. King

Though its social ethic remains largely unarticulated, on the basis of its most important philosophical and religious claims, Buddhism can be shown to occupy a position in social ethics which balances or harmonizes a number of the antinomies with which we are familiar in Western ethical theory: the individual and society; human rights and social responsibilities; utilitarian and deontological ethical theory. I will attempt to articulate a Buddhist position on each of these issues in turn and then illustrate this Middle Path social ethic with reference to contemporary forms of Engaged Buddhism. Methodologically, I will speak as a scholar of Buddhism in the voice used by contemporary socially engaged Buddhists when they explain themselves to the Buddhist world. That is, I will adopt an evolutionary perspective in which I draw upon key teachings widely embraced in the past and present, i.e., the Four Noble Truths and *pratītyasamudpāda* taught by Śākyamuni Buddha, the Buddha nature concept embraced by Mahāyāna Buddhism and I will also give myself license to perhaps say something slightly new but which I believe to be continuous with these venerable and well-established teachings.

1. The Individual and Society

First let us consider the relationship between the individual and society. With some exceptions, the primary view emphasized in Western social and political thought has been that the individual and society, one individual and other individuals, are by nature locked in conflict: my wants, needs, interests and freedom are inherently in conflict with yours individually and with the groups. This view has developed in such a way that in America today the popular view might be called individualism run amok: the individual has all the "rights" and all the value; indeed, it is difficult on the basis of available American social theory to find a justification for social good if it "costs" the individual anything. Not only do Americans believe the individual self has all the value, Americans also largely believe the individual self is autonomous. With roots in the Biblical notion of the individual soul, and greatly strengthened by the "Protestant principle" which emphasizes that one stands alone before God to justify one's actions in life, taking all the responsibility unto oneself alone, Americans emphasize individual freedom, the individual will, individual choice, and individual responsibility. Thus, if I may be forgiven for painting in very broad strokes, with the important exception of some feminist drought, mainstream American popular thought and much of its social theory may be characterized as affirming the individual (as autonomous and as the seat of value) and downplaying to an extreme the importance of society and social groups.[1]

By way of contrast, and again please forgive me for painting with broad strokes, in popular East Asian Confucian thought, the social group (primarily the family) and society at large are strongly affirmed and the individual very much downplayed. While I believe that the individual and the group are held in a creative tension in the Confucian *Analects*, the popular appropriation of this thought has emphasized the aspect of individual conformity to group norms and the wishes of others to the extent that it has traditionally been quite difficult to express individuality or to stand alone in Confucian society. Moreover, the individual is clearly conceived in Confucian thought as very much a social being such that a concept of autonomy comparable to the Western notion is unthinkable in Confucian terms.

It would be too much to say that Buddhism resolves this dichotomy, or even that it occupies a position in the middle which resolves the apparent conflict between the two extremes. Nevertheless, it does acknowledge in a strong way the role played by both the social and the individual poles in human life.

On the one hand, with its central philosophical principle of conditioned origination (*pratītyasamutpāda*), Buddhism emphasizes the vast extent to which human beings are conditioned by society, by culture, by one's physiology, by the family and other important groups and individuals, and by one's own past actions and habits in this life and others. Philosophically, nothing holds greater weight in Buddhism than this principle. This is so much the case that some commentators and critics have concluded that there is no freedom in Buddhism. Admittedly, passages in some Buddhist texts might lead one to such a conclusion, as when they state that 'so-and-so achieved enlightenment because of the merit accrued over countless lifetimes'; or 'because of the merit accrued over countless lifetimes, so-and-so was able to learn of the Buddha's teachings.'

---

[1] See Robert Bellah, et.al., *Habits of the Heart: Individualism and Commitment in American Life* (New York: Harper and Row, 1985). Bellah does a masterful job of demonstrating that even when we do embrace a social good, we are intellectually uneasy, as we have no conceptual language with which to understand why the social good has value.

Nonetheless, to conclude that there is no freedom in Buddhism or even that freedom plays a small role, is completely absurd and groundless, as is clear to anyone familiar with Buddhism as a religion. For the Buddha to teach human beings at all, for Buddhism to be established as a religion, the freedom to alter the course of one's future life and lives through the application of choice and determined effort is an essential premise. If we were fully conditioned, there would be no point in the Buddha speaking and the idea of human beings actively choosing to intervene in the web of conditioning that binds them could not possibly arise. Without freedom as a MAJOR component, there is no Buddhism at all, no Noble Path, no religious life.

What we have here, then, is a situation in which conditioning as part of *pratītyasamutpāda*, plays a role second to none in Buddhist philosophy, while freedom plays a role second to none in Buddhism as a religion. Conditioning, of course, includes social-cultural conditioning among other forms, and is a major factor constructing our bondage. It definitely limits our immediate possibilities by constructing the particular form which the present moment takes for every one of us and opens a limited number of possibilities for our immediate future. It clearly negates any notion of individual human autonomy. Buddhism is perhaps even clearer and stronger than Confucianism is affirming that the de facto, functional "self" is constructed by factors apparently outside itself That is, the individual is constructed by its family, its society, its culture, its physiology and its own past. As Thich Nhat Hanh might characteristically put it, the self is constructed of non-self parts. Thus, there is no possibility whatsoever of conceiving an individual autonomous human self in Buddhism. In this sense, there is no self; indeed, we delude ourselves in defining ourselves as individuals. Nonetheless, freedom, the ability to free oneself of the web of conditioning, is absolutely critical to Buddhism.

Is this an unresolved contradiction in Buddhism? Not entirely; it is, I believe, an unresolved philosophical issue in Buddhism, but it is too much to say it is a contradiction, In the first place, human effort and freedom are given ample acknowledgment in the discourses of the Buddha, as Kalupahana clearly demonstrates in his forthcoming book, *Ethics in Early Buddhism*.[2] He shows that while there is no single Buddhist term that corresponds to will, there are very many terms which refer to various aspects of effort and creativity, such as determination, strength, striving, exertion, venture, vigor, etc.[3] Of course, it is no detriment to Buddhism that it has no concept of an individual, autonomous will;

---

[2] Dr. Kalupahana was kind enough to show me an electronic version of his manuscript *Ethics in Early Buddhism* in time for me to benefit from it in writing this paper. I believe that our views on the individual and society in Buddhism are fundamentally in accord. However, whereas he analyzes *pratīyasamudpāda* as the middle between autonomy and accidentalism (with which I agree), I here analyze the final Buddhist position as the middle between *pratīyasamudpāda* as conditioning and the freedom to break through conditioning.

[3] *Ibid.*, Ch. 4, "The World and the Will."

indeed, this idea is widely discredited in contemporary Western philosophy.[4] However, it is too much to say that Western philosophy may learn from Buddhism on this point because I believe that Buddhism does not have this point worked out either. Nonetheless, the Buddhist position seems to fall short of a direct contradiction precisely because its position is unarticulated. Buddhism speaks here, as it characteristically but not always does, as existential rather than systematic thought. That is, it speaks here from the perspective of what may be empirically observed in human existence. What do we observe when we look at ourselves? We see conditioning and we see that ability to make a decision, exert ourselves, and drastically alter the conditions of our existence. These are both empirically true. How both of these may be true is not worked out philosophically, but then Buddhism never has dedicated itself to the working out of all philosophical issues. Perhaps this question is of the same nature as those questions which the Buddha declared "tend not to edification."

What does this mean with respect to the individual and society in Buddhism? Whereas Western thought emphasizes individuality, and Confucian thought emphasizes society, Buddhist thought may be characterized as strongly emphasizing both. Both are crucial for our understanding of who and what we are; both are powerful in determining who and what we are. Moreover, they are interactive. Thus, an adequate theory of social ethics must heavily weigh both.

2. Human Rights and Social Responsibilities

We turn now to our second issue, human rights and social responsibilities. Of course, this issue is closely related to that of the relationship between the individual and society, so we may expect that the answer to be worked out here will significantly parallel the conclusion reached above.

To begin with, Buddhists have never traditionally spoken of rights, but have emphasized responsibilities, or obligations, in a sense. The foundation of Buddhist social ethics can be located most firmly in the five lay precepts. Simply put, these state: I undertake to observe the precepts (1) to abstain from the taking of life; (2) not to take that which is not given; (3) to abstain from misconduct in sensual actions; (4) to abstain from false speech; (5) to abstain from liquor that causes intoxication and indolence.[5] These may be understood as restraints that one willingly takes upon oneself for the sake of others and oneself. In this respect, they are an interesting nexus of the freedom and conditioning discussed above.

Let me demonstrate. First, one makes a decision and determines to undertake, for example, the first precept. Second, by not taking life, one not only avoids harming others, one avoids harming oneself by exerting oneself to

---

[4] Its discrediting is largely due to the devastating attack it suffered at the hands of Gilbert Ryle in his *The Concept of Mind* (London: Hutchison, 1949).

[5] Hammalawa Saddhatissa, *Buddhist Ethics: The Path to Nirvāṇa* (London: George Allen & Unwin, 1970; reprint edition, London: Wisdom Publication, 1987), 73.

restrain whatever habitual tendencies one may have to harm others (a habitual tendency established by one's having harmed others in the past and/or by the conditioning power of the violence of one's society), thus de-conditioning that habitual tendency, thereby lessening its power to construct one's future. Thus, the precepts, while recognizing the great power of conditioning, emphasize in this very context one's power to de-condition oneself through decision and unrelenting effort.

Also note that the precepts cut directly through the line between individual and society. It is clearly good for society to be made up of individuals who will not harm others, steal, lie, etc., but in the Buddhist view it is equally and inseparably true that it is good for oneself as well. Thus not only is there no conflict between the individual good and the social good, these goods are one and the same.

Now, classically in Western thought, the language of both "rights" and "responsibilities" is framed in terms of at least potential conflict between the individual and society: "rights" are what society, or others, owe me, and "responsibilities" are what I owe to society, or others. A society which does not respect my "rights" is not Good, and I may be justified in taking steps to ensure that my "rights" will become respected. Likewise, society may be justified in restraining or coercing me if I do not fulfill some of my essential "responsibilities" such as to share the cost of government or to refrain from harming others in my society.

The Buddhist precepts are formulated in the language of responsibility: I undertake not to harm you. The precepts do not say anything about you not harming me! Traditionally, as Kalupahana points out, a universal monarch, if there were one, might have taken this language of moral abstention and transformed it into language of prohibition: you shall not harm another.[6] But let us examine this matter philosophically. Philosophically, the precepts imply that the society will be Good in which its members do not harm each other, steal from each other, lie to each other, etc. This in turn implies that a member of a Good society should have a reasonable expectation not to be harmed, stolen from, etc. Now, one may or may not want to call such a thing a "right," but it is certainly closing in on that ground in a practical sense, if not in the full conceptual sense.

In short, if we choose to use the five lay precepts as our guides towards a Buddhist social ethic, they seem to imply a definition of a Good society as one in which we simultaneously have rights and responsibilities to both not harm others and not be harmed, not steal and not be stolen from, not lie and not be lied to, etc. However, the kind of "rights" we are talking about here are fundamentally unlike "rights" as conceived in Western political theory insofar as they are fundamentally *non-adversarial.* My responsibility not to harm you is in my own interest and your interest is fulfilled by my not harming you. Similarly, my "right," if we want to call it that, not to be harmed by you constitutes an

---

[6] See Kalupahana, Ch. 15, "Law, Justice and Morals."

opportunity for you to promote your own interest by practicing self-restraint. Thus understood, rights and responsibilities are interdependent to the point almost of fusion. In this light, from a Buddhist conceptual point of view, it might be best to drop the separate terms "rights" and "responsibilities" and speak in a unified way of a community of "mutual obligation" in which our individual Goods and the social Good co-inhere such that my obligation to you is also my obligation to myself.[7] While this would be philosophically more accurate from a Buddhist perspective, the Buddhist community will probably want to continue to speak with the larger world using "rights" language, since this is the language to which we have become accustomed in international discourse.

3. Utilitarianism and Deontology

Our third issue is the relationship between utilitarianism and deontology in Buddhist ethical theory. Utilitarianism is a consequentialist theory, which is to say that the moral value of an action is determined by the consequences of that action. If the consequences of an action are good, the action is good; if the consequences are bad, the action is bad. In Mill's classic form of utilitarianism, an action is good if it produces a greater amount of happiness than unhappiness for all persons affected. A deontological theory, in contrast, is a non-consequentialist theory in which an action is considered to be intrinsically good or bad in itself, without reference to the consequences of that action, usually by measuring the action against some absolute standard.

We have seen above that, with some reconceptualization, Buddhist theory affirms both individual and society, both rights and responsibilities. Now we shall see both utilitarian and deontological perspectives to be affirmed in Buddhism, though with considerable conceptual adjustment.

The Four Noble Truths of Buddhism seem to express a utilitarian perspective. The First Noble Truth, *duḥkha,* names the inherently unsatisfactory nature of human existence as the problem. The Third Noble Truth, the cessation of *duḥkha,* offers the hope that the problem can be resolved, and the Fourth Noble Truth maps out the way in which the cure of the problem may be realized. In short, suffering and unhappiness are the problem for which Buddhism is the cure. In other words, suffering and unhappiness are bad, while the elimination of suffering is good. Thus it would seem that any action which eliminated suffering would be good, while any action which produced suffering would be bad. Such a view would fit comfortably within the utilitarian family of ethical theory.

But Buddhism fundamentally has two concepts of the Good. The first, as we have seen, is the elimination of *duḥkha.* The second, which we will now consider, is the realization of *nirvāṇa.* The elimination of *duḥkha* and the

---

[7] Dr. Kalupahana speaks of human society as based upon "mutual self-interest." Since my interest is your interest, and vice versa, "mutual self-interest" could be synonymous with "mutual obligation." See Ch. 5, "Individual and Society."

realization of *nirvana* might appear upon first consideration to be two names for the same thing, and certainly in some respects they are. However, in another respect they differ in a significant way. While the elimination of *duḥkha is* a Good that falls into the consequentialist-utilitarian camp of ethical theory, the realization of *nirvāṇa is* an absolute, or deontological, Good. To see why it is deontological, we will need to consider Buddhism's theory of human being.

Of course, Buddhism's theory of human being evolved over time. But the continuous thread which evolves is the notion that human beings are beings with the potential of enlightenment. This notion was relatively implicit in early Buddhism and became explicit later. Some of the early teachings indicative of this idea are the following: (1) The Buddha was convinced to teach when he surveyed humankind and observed that while some would be uninterested in his message, others would welcome his teachings. (2) The Buddha taught all who would listen, without imposing restrictions by social class, gender, education, or other differentiating characteristics. (3) Persons of all backgrounds were, in fact, confirmed as having attained the fruits of liberation during the Buddha's lifetime. (4) Perhaps most significantly, the Buddha's teachings strongly emphasized the rarity and preciousness of a human birth, urging everyone to take advantage of their human birth, to practice Buddhism and attain release, since release could not be had from any of the other six destinies.

These early suggestions regarding the potential of humankind, of course, became fuel for later debates which directly raised the question of whether all humankind, without exception, was capable of ultimately achieving enlightenment, or not. Suffice it to say, that after considerable debate, the Mahāyāna wing of Buddhism explicitly affirmed the Buddha nature concept, according to which all members of humankind are capable of eventually attaining enlightenment and thus in the present should be regarded as embryonic Buddhas, beings who carry the seed or germ of Buddhahood within. (There is considerably more to the Buddha nature concept than this, but as it is more controversial I propose that we limit our discussion to this part of the concept.) It is worth noting that in China, all forms of Buddhism which did not embrace this affirmation died out relatively quickly.

This theory of human being, in its latent and its fully developed form, has important implications for ethics. I must note that these implications do not seem to have been noted in traditional forms of Asian Buddhism until relatively recently. It may be that it required the encounter with both Western ethical thought and the crises of modernity in order for these implications to come to the fore. Even now, I do not know that they have been explicitly discussed, though they have been acted upon, as we shall see.

Very simply, if it is the case that a human birth is a rare and precious birth inasmuch as it provides an opportunity for realization, and/or if all human beings are embryonic Buddhas carrying the nature of Buddhahood within, then we have the basis for a deontological form of ethics. Buddhahood and/or the realization of Buddhahood is an absolute Good in Buddhism. Two ethical propositions follow from this affirmation: (1) any action conducive to the enlightenment of any human being is a Good action, and any action inimical to the enlightenment of any human being is bad; (2) any action which partakes of the nature of Buddhahood (wisdom and compassion) is a Good action; any action contrary to the nature of Buddhahood is bad. While the first proposition may still be considered to fall within the limits of utilitarianism, the second is clearly deontological since it refers not to the consequences of an action but to the nature of an action itself as measure against an absolute value in determining the moral value of that action.

It can immediately be seen that the admission of a deontological strain in Buddhist ethics must alter our earlier proposal that Buddhist ethics might be of a utilitarian nature. Let us return to the five lay precepts. It can now be seen that to violate the first precept, to harm life, is morally wrong not only because its consequences include the production of suffering for oneself and another, but also because the very nature of the action itself, harming life, is intrinsically incompatible with the nature of Buddhahood. The same is true of the other lay precepts: to steal, to engage in sexual misconduct, to lie, or to intoxicate oneself all both produce suffering for oneself and another and violate the nature of Buddhahood.

Thus the ethical foundations of the five lay precepts can be understood either in utilitarian or deontological terms. But of course from a Buddhist perspective, the ethical analyses that in the West go under two different names and are seen as ma or ethical alternatives constitute a single Buddhist ethical position. It is easy to see why: Buddhahood (the foundation of the deontological ethical absolute) IS freedom from the production, and the suffering, of *duḥkha* (the utilitarian ethical foundation).

Our consideration of the Buddhist concept of human being and the deontological strain in Buddhist ethics also helps us to see how Buddhist ethics differs in important ways from Mill's utilitarianism. Mill defines a good act as one productive of greater happiness than unhappiness for all persons concerned. Thus an arithmetic calculation must be made in which one considers all the happiness produced for some against all the unhappiness produced for others, determines which is greater and considers ethically good that action which produces "the greatest good for the greatest number." There are two aspects of this approach with which Buddhism is incompatible.

First, there is an adversarial element involved in Mill's calculus; one person's happiness is in a competitive posture with another person's unhappiness. We have seen above that the kind of "rights," if one calls them that, embraced by Buddhism differ from Western notions of "rights" in being non-adversarial. In the present case again, the kind of "utilitarianism," if one calls it that, found in Buddhism is non-adversarial. We have seen in our analysis of the five lay precepts that my good is conceived as your good and vice versa.

Furthermore, suffering is simply an absolute bad in Buddhism. Nothing that produces unhappiness for any sentient being could be considered good. Thus nonviolence in Buddhism is an absolute, not a relative or situationally dependent value. To demonstrate the significance of this point, consider the theory of the "just war." Western "just war" theory presupposes an adversarial situation in which a greater good (say, freedom from tyranny) is presumed to arise out of the lesser evil of the morally justified war. But in Buddhism there are no just wars. No matter how great the evil with which a society is confronted, Buddhism does not condone the use of violence -harm perhaps to a few in order to free many from severe suffering -- to rectify that evil. Whereas Mill's moral theory would accept violence in such a case, Buddhism does not. This is not to say that as a matter of historical fact no Buddhists have ever violated this principle; I am simply trying to clarify the ethical principle itself.

I must say that there may be cases in which Mill's calculus may be more helpful than the Buddhist approach. Certainly many would consider the Buddhist perspective in which my good is your good to be simply naive. And it must be asked whether Buddhist ethics can help us to make some of the complex and difficult decisions we face in the modern world. Can Buddhist ethics help us decide the best way to allocate scarce resources, for instance who will receive an organ transplant when the need is greater than the availability of organs? Or can Buddhist ethics help us to choose between competing goods, for example whether to use a pool of tax money for education, hospices, or childcare? I am not prepared to debate these issues here and indeed I am very aware that Buddhism has greater ethical resources for addressing such issues than those to which I have confined myself here. However, I am not sanguine that an ethical posture which fundamentally turns away from the acknowledgment of adversarial or competing goods and bads will be in the best position to address the kinds of issues I have raised.

Second, the fact that Buddhist ethics is composed of a deontological, as well as a utilitarian, strain allows it to resolve certain issues which Mill's ethics is incapable of resolving. The classic example here is slavery. On the basis of Mill's theory, it is impossible to show why slavery is wrong if, for example, it is a minority which is enslaved and their suffering is not too intense, while the majority whom they serve is made very much happier by their service. It is necessary to have a deontological criterion in order to show why such a situation is morally wrong.

From a Buddhist perspective, slavery is wrong for two reasons: (1) presumably the conditions under which the slaves live reduce their opportunity to learn and practice Buddhism, and hence reduce the likelihood that they will be able to realize it fruits; more importantly, (2) to enslave another is an action inherently incompatible with the gentleness and compassion of Buddhahood and an active negation of the embryonic Buddhahood of the slave, and thus inherently the negation of absolute Good as recognized in Buddhism, while to be enslaved is to live in a condition expressive of the negation of one's embryonic Buddhahood and thus again inherently the negation of Good.

In sum, Buddhist ethics has both utilitarian and deontological elements, Its utilitarian element embraces the idea that suffering is bad and freedom from suffering is Good, but expresses this in a form free from adversarial conflict either between individuals or between the individual and society. Its deontological element is based upon the potential of each person to realize Buddhahood, or the recognition of embryonic Buddhahood in each person. However, what might seem from a Western perspective to be two ethical strands in Buddhism is a single strand inasmuch as Buddhahood is the non-production of suffering (compassion) and the non-experiencing of suffering (wisdom).

4. Engaged Buddhism

Turning now to the final component of this paper, let us consider briefly some of the ways in which some contemporary forms of socially and politically engaged Buddhism are expressive of the perspective I have sketched above. Two essential, but unstated, premises of contemporary Buddhist social activism are: (1) every human being is of great, perhaps absolute, value and should be so treated; and (2) every human being has the potential of Buddhahood. The first two premises are related; on their bases, a third premise arises, namely (3) it is good for human beings to express and nurture their emerging Buddhahood.

The first premise, that every human being is of absolute value and should be so treated, seems to me to be rooted in the notion that a human birth is a rare and precious birth, the direct implication of which is that a human life is a rare and precious thing, a thing of great value. It is only common sense to protect, cherish and attend to the well-being of something that is rare and precious. Here the second premise, every human being has the potential of Buddhahood, comes into play. From a Buddhist perspective, to attend to the well-being of human life immediately implies that one must afford each human life the opportunity to study and practice the Buddhist path.

This is the Buddhist foundation of what from a Western perspective is called "human rights work" pursued by Asian Buddhists, often at the risk of their life, liberty, or well-being. Most dramatically, in Vietnam, in Burma and in Tibet, in modern times and even at the present moment -- none of these struggles is over -- Buddhists in vast numbers have risked everything to protect, cherish and attend to the well-being of precious human life. In each case, Buddhists have risked their lives in the attempt to repel or bring down brutal political regimes threatening and destroying human life and well-being. In all three cases, moreover, a politically open society has been seen as essential to human well-being. In Vietnam and in Tibet, this struggle has been inseparable from a struggle to preserve the opportunity to freely study and practice Buddhism. The fact that in all three cases Buddhists have risked and all too often lost their lives in this struggle powerfully demonstrates just how deeply these values are held, how essential they are felt to be.

The ex-untouchable Ambedkarite Buddhists of India converted from Hinduism to Buddhism for expressly social reasons: in order to repudiate the Hindu caste system with its notions of more and less spiritually and socially acceptable people, and its labels of untouchability and outcaste. These Buddhists did not need the fully developed Buddha nature concept to tell them that Buddhism values every single human life as a rare and precious thing -- the

Buddha's repudiation of the caste system with its implicit embrace of human egalitarianism was sufficient to accomplish that. For them, Buddhism is the most important vehicle they know for egalitarianism, for social change based upon egalitarian values, for the enhancement of their own well-being, and for the nurturing of their own potential.

Somewhat similar is *Sarvodaya Shramadana* of Sri Lanka, a vast Buddhist organization which works to "develop" the declining villages of Sri Lanka on the, basis of Buddhist, rather than capitalist or Marxist values. They recognize spiritual liberation as the ultimate good, but believe that its attainment is facilitated among a population freed from grinding poverty with its associated social and psychological ills and is indeed enhanced by the nurturance of the individual's well-being in all its dimensions (within limits set by Buddhist Middle Path moderation, wisdom and compassion).

The third premise, the belief that it is good for human beings to express and nurture their emerging Buddhahood, is explicitly stated by Japanese Buddhists (specifically Risshō Kōsei-kai and Soka Gakkai) and by Thich Nhat Hanh, but is an unstated premise of Buddhist activism more broadly. Here the notion frequently found in tradition that one first needs to free oneself of one's own delusion before one is in any condition to work for the welfare of others is either expressly repudiated or ignored and replaced with the notion that Buddhahood is not something one finds later at the end of a long path, but instead is something one expresses now, in the present moment, to the best of one's ability, and in so doing one makes real the Buddha whom one is striving to be.

Every conceivable kind of spiritual social activism, as long as it is an attempted expression of wisdom and compassion, becomes possible on the basis of this third premise. And indeed, the variety of actions found among Buddhist activists is virtually limitless: work for gender equality and an end to the oppression of women, work to protect animals, work to protect our planet, work with the dying, work with the homeless, work with AIDS patients. Such work of course, is also an expression of such traditional Buddhist ethical values as compassion and *ahiṁsā*. Thus, work to protect the planet is motivated by urgent concern to protect the matrix of all life, and work for gender equality and the protection of women is motivated by compassion for the oppression of women and the desire to open Buddhist practice more effectively to women.

5. Conclusion

In conclusion, I do believe that as a historical fact contemporary Buddhist social activism was largely provoked by Buddhism's encounter with the Western world and with the crises of the twentieth century. (The one exception to this pattern is the Japanese Nichirenite groups, which can and do cite precedent in the medieval founder of their line, Nichiren.) However, at the same time, it is important to recognize that this contemporary activism can be fully understood and justified in explicitly Buddhist terms, as I have tried to show in this paper. Moreover, the kind of ethics that may be seen as underlying this

Buddhist activism constitutes a provocative conceptual alternative to the better established Western theories of social ethics. I hope that the philosophers among us may continue to attempt to articulate this Buddhist social ethic, aided by the activists who demonstrate even more clearly what it all means.

CHAPTER 9

COMMUNITY: VIOLENCE, PEACE, AND THE WAYS OF COMMUNITY

A. L. Herman

1. Protocol

The central question that this book takes up is, "Can the problems of violence and peace in the 21st century be solved through what I shall call "the way of community"?" The answer to that question entails introducing an assumption, an argument and a challenge regarding violence and peace. The assumption is that no one would willingly or knowingly do violence to oneself. The argument is that if one's community is like oneself then no one would willingly or knowingly do violence to one's community. The challenge, if the argument is sound, is then to get humans to see the world as their community, i.e., as themselves. To that end we raise three questions: First, "What is a community?" second, "How does one become a member of a community?" and third, "Can the problems of violence and peace in the 21st century be solved through the way of community?"

In order to answer these questions, Chapter I of this work analyzes the concept of community together with the assumption and the argument previously mentioned. Chapters II through V examines four representative concepts of community, viz., the "biotic community" of Aldo Leopold, the "beloved community" of Martin Luther King, Jr., the "āśramic community" of Mohandas K. Gandhi, and the "karmic community" of Mahāyāna Buddhism, respectively. Following the discussion of each of these communities, we investigate several puzzles and problems to which each of them would seem to lead. Chapter VI concludes this work by pointing to several benefits and puzzles that would appear to arise from trying to solve the problems of violence and peace through the way of community.

2. Something about Community

If all communities share certain properties, properties that make them communities, then what applies necessarily to one community ought to apply, *pari passu*, to other communities. We explore three questions regarding the properties of communities: First, "What is a community?"; second, "How does one become a member of a community?"; and, third and finally, the question that we shall get to in Chapter 11 of this book, "Can the problems of violence and peace in the 21st century be solved through the way of community?" It is this third question, a question about ultimate happiness in this world, that will constitute the central question to be put throughout this study. The argument that we shall be pursuing in order to arrive at an answer to that central question is a variant of a Socratic argument first used by Plato in the fourth century B.C.E. In the dialogue Apology, Socrates, on trial for his life, claims that he's innocent of corrupting the youth of Athens because no one intentionally harms those who could then harm oneself-, this premise gets Socrates to the conclusion that he never intentionally demoralized the youth of the city, so he's not guilty of the charge of knowingly corrupting the young. The argument assumes, consequently, that no one in their right mind would ever knowingly set out to harm himself. Our "community argument" follows this Socratic pattern and it goes like this:

1. No one would intentionally do violence to oneself.
2. One's community is identical with oneself.
3. Therefore, no one would intentionally do violence to one's community:

If the community argument is sound then it is imperative, if our central question is to be answered, that one inquires into just what a community is and how one goes about convincing others that we are all members of a community.

In what follows we explore the properties of community together with suggestions as to how becoming a member of a community is to be carried out. Let's assume at the outset, and very roughly and incompletely, that a community is a group or collection of two or more members who share something-or other and that it's that sharing that essentially defines them as a community (from the Latin *communis*, "common"). And let's also assume that the more obvious things that community members share, whether consciously or unconsciously and in varying degrees or quantities, are a history of, and a loyalty to, the group, as well as a more consciously shared language, feelings, expectations, purposes, respect, stability, integrity, love, or destiny. Thus not only would families, villages, cities, and nations be candidates for community status, but so also would lynch mobs, orchestras, the human body, ecosystems, autos, and cuckoo clocks, with or without the cuckoo. The key to what our concept of community is must lie in the nature of what is shared as well as with the sharing itself.

Aristotle began his Politics with these memorable lines, "Every community is established with a view to some good...every political community aims at good...at the highest good."[1] That "highest good," for Aristotle, was, of course, "happiness." In our investigation we shall be employing Aristotle's notion of community and assume that the kind of community that we are seeking is one that is capable of generating the highest good through some manner of sharing. This allows us to leave out of consideration as candidates for community autos and clocks, as well as nefarious human economic, political, and social groups...

We turn next to four ways of community each aimed at generating the highest amount of "happiness" for itself and/or its members: First, the "biotic community" of the American naturalist and ecomystic, Aldo Leopold (1887-1948); second, the "beloved community" of the American Baptist minister and social activist, Martin Luther King, Jr. (1929-1968); third, the "āśramic community" of the Hindu statesman and prophet of non-violence, Mohandas K. Gandhi (1869-1948); and, finally, the karmic community of Mahāyāna Buddhism. *N.B. In this much-abbreviated work on community, the sections on the biotic, the beloved and the āśramic communities are excluded.*

We turn next to our fourth and final community, the karmic community, which also attempts to answer our two previous questions, "What is a community?" and "How may one acquire membership in it?" together with this central question, "Can the Mahāyāna Buddhist way of the karmic community solve the problems of violence and peace in the 21st century?"

3. Mahāyāna Buddhism and the Way of the Karmic Community: The Law of Karma and the Problems of Karma and Merit

The Mahāyāna Buddhist way of the karmic community may be related to the solving of two problems relating to both karma and the law of karma. These problems of karma result from an individualistic interpretation of both karma and the law governing its recompense. The Mahāyāna solution to these problems will lead to a communal interpretation of the law of karma and to the way of the karmic community. In what follows we shall briefly explore the history of the law of karma in Hinduism, the problems of karma or merit that resulted, and the Mahāyāna solution to these problems using the way of the karmic community. Finally, we shall explore the central question with which this study began now reinterpreted for the way of the karmic community, Can the Mahāyāna Buddhist way of the karmic community solve the problems of violence and peace in the 21st century?

---

[1] Aristotle, *Politics: The Basic Works of Aristotle* (Richard McKeon, Ed.) (New York: Random House, 1941),11-27.

4. The Law of Karma in the *Upaniṣads*

The law of karma is the principle of cosmic justice that holds that all good actions will be rewarded and that all wicked actions will be punished, sometime, somehow, somewhere. This principle is probably related to the Vedic concept of *Ṛta* on the one hand and to the later post-Vedic development of the concept of karma, "action, performance, business," on the other. The law of karma, as a principle of justice and action, probably receives its earliest Indian formulation in the oldest *Upaniṣad,* the *Bṛhadāraṇyaka* (about 700 B.C.E.), where it is said, "Truly, one becomes good by good action and bad by bad action."[2] And the principle is assumed in another classical statement regarding transmigration from the same *Upaniṣad:*

> This is what happens to the man who desires. To whatever his mind
> is attached, the self becomes that in the next life. Achieving that end,
> it returns again to this World.[3]

Finally, the *Śvetāśvatara* (about 400 B.C.E.), states the doctrine of karma in the form in which it is roughly and popularly known to this day:

> He who has the *guṇas* [qualities] and is the agent of actions that will
> bring consequences, he is the recipient of the consequences of
> whatever he does. Taking on all possible forms... he, the *prāṇadhipa*
> ["the ruler of the vital breaths," i.e., the self], is reborn in bondage
> according to his actions. According to his actions, the embodied self
> chooses repeatedly the various forms in various conditions in the next
> life. According to his own qualities and acts, the embodied self
> chooses the kinds of forms, large and small, that it will take on.[4]

The Upaniṣadic law of karma is the traditional metaphysical principle of individual justice in Hinduism. It simply says that if you do the dharma or if you do the adharma then you get the karma, i.e., sooner or later you will receive your due, for as you sow, so shall you reap. This metaphysical principle is directed primarily at the single, isolated, separate, existing individual and it guarantees to that individual moral fairness on a cosmic scale. It receives one of its clearest instantiations in the great Hindu text, the *Bhagavād Gītā* (*BG* for abbreviation).

5. The Law of Karma in the *Bhagavād Gītā*

Soteriological religions such as Hinduism provide Saviors who are able to share their merit or good karma with the faithful. In the *BG* (400-200 B.C.E.) a human incarnation of the Hindu preserver God, Viṣṇu, is born into the world as

---

[2] *Bṛhadāraṇyaka Upaniṣad,* 3.1-3.

[3] *Bṛhadāraṇyaka Upaniṣad,* 4.4-6.

[4] *Śvetaśvatara Upaniṣad,* 5.16.

Lord Kṛṣṇa. He now comes announcing to his friend-cousin-disciple Arjuna, as well as to all the world, the conditions, i.e., the origin, causes, and purpose, of his human incarnation as Savior:

> You and I have passed through many births, Arjuna; I know all of them but you do not.
>
> Though unborn, for the Ātman is eternal, though Lord of all beings, yet using my own nature,
>
> I come into existence using my own māyā.
>
> For whenever there is a decaying of dharma [rightness and order] and a rising up of adharma [evil and chaos], then I send Myself forth.
>
> I come into existence time after time to protect the good, to destroy the wicked, and to reestablish the holy dharma.[5]

Lord Kṛṣṇa here, in a way, is the Hindu personification of the law of karma. Subsequently, Kṛṣṇa reveals to Arjuna one of the ways or yogas by following which he may attain the highest happiness:

> Arjuna, you must see that my devotees never perish...For those who take refuge in Me, whether of lowly birth, or women, vaiśyas or even śūdras, they all go to the highest goal.
>
> Fix your mind on Me; be dedicated to Me; sacrifice to Me; lay yourself devotedly before Me; discipline yourself and with Me as your Supreme goal, to Me you will truly come.[6]

The *BG* concludes with Kṛṣṇa's promise to Arjuna and to all of His future devotees:

> Listen once more to My supreme message, the highest secret of all. You are truly My beloved and so I will tell you what is best for you.
>
> Merge your mind with Me, be devoted to Me, worship Me, revere Me, and you shall come to Me. I promise this to you truly, for you are ever dear to Me.
>
> Abandon all other duties, come to Me alone for refuge. Be not sorrowed for I shall give you liberation from all sins[7].

---

[5] *BG*, 4.5-8.

[6] *BG*, 9.31-34.

[7] *BG*, 18.64-66.

Lord Kṛṣṇa has laid out the conditions under which, it can be argued, any "Savior" must operate and under which any "soteriological game"[8] must be played. Thus Lord Kṛṣṇa has the power to recognize sins, to forgive them when they occur, to recognize true repentance and devotion in His devotees that makes that forgiveness possible, to bring order and righteousness into a disordered and chaotic world, and to do all of this with perfect justice and fairness. In other words, from the beginning of His birth into the world of *adharma* until the saving of His beloved and worshipful devotees from sins and their consequences, to the gathering of those same liberated devotees into "the fair worlds of those of virtuous deeds,"[9] Kṛṣṇa does what He does either in concert with, or under the aegis of, the law of karma. But it is here that the trouble begins for this very concerned and committed Savior in a universe dominated by the law of karma.[10]

6. Two Problems of Karma in the *Bhagavād Gītā*

Lord Kṛṣṇa is able to dispense rewards to his devoted and loving disciples. His grace is operative in the created world where the law of karma also operates; and Kṛṣṇa dispenses the former in accordance with His disciples prayerful requests for liberation from sin and for help in reaching heaven:

> And while performing all actions, having taken refuge in Me, by My grace (*prasāda*) he reaches the eternal, indestructible goal.

> Focusing your thought on Me, you will overcome all difficulties by My grace. But if from egoism you will not heed this advice then you will be utterly destroyed.

> Flee to Me for shelter with your entire being, Arjuna. By My grace you shall attain the greatest peace and the eternal goal.

In the end, of course, Arjuna sees his way clearly and he cries out to his Savior:

---

[8] A "game" here is a physical or mental contest carried out according to rules and undertaken for amusement, recreation, or winning a stake, i.e., a game is any ruled activity for reaching a goal. In this sense, all religions are games.

[9] *BG*, 18.71.

[10] Kṛṣṇa has defined the cosmic breadth of the law when he says to Arjuna at *BG*, 8.16 that all the worlds from Brahma the Creator downwoards are subject to rebirth and therefore are governed by the law of karma. Since the creation consists of all beings including the Gods themselves, we must assume that the law of karma holds sway even over them. Only by reaching liberation and Lord Kṛṣṇa does one pass beyond the reach of the law of karma (or so it seems).

My delusion has been destroyed. I have come to my senses through your grace. With all my doubts gone I shall act according to your word. [11]

The route to enlightenment or liberation for the *BG,* at least as far as the Hindu Savior game is concerned, would seem to be something like this: The disciple, Arjuna, first recognizes a problem he cannot solve by himself, he then begins the search for the solution to the problem and, on the advice of Lord Kṛṣṇa, engages in *bhakti,* devotion, to Kṛṣṇa; the latter on seeing his devotee's earnest and heartfelt yearning grants His disciple His *prasāda;* finally, armed with this grace the worshipful disciple is able to solve the problem with which the entire search began.

But what precisely is it that Arjuna seeks from Kṛṣṇa? His favor or grace, to be sure; but what is this *prasāda?* It really is the power to overcome delusion, as he says, and it is the power to solve his problem, to reach the goal of heaven or enlightenment, or whatever. Why doesn't Arjuna have that power himself? Why does he need, as it were, outside help? The answer to all of these questions lies with the law of karma. Lord Kṛṣṇa, we must suppose, has "earned" his exalted position as Savior through eons of action that produced meritorious karmic consequences, consequences that have been stored and that are now available for dispensing as *prasāda.* In other words, Lord Kṛṣṇa's power comes from his past actions and that power now operates with dispensed or dispensable *prasāda* in accord with the law of universal cosmic justice. The good karma that produced that power has been earned by Kṛṣṇa, it has been stored by Kṛṣṇa, it lies waiting to be used by Kṛṣṇa for those who commit *bhakti* to Kṛṣṇa, and it will be dispensed by Kṛṣṇa to deserving disciples such as Arjuna. All of this is made possible by the law of karma which simply says that everyone ought to get, and ultimately will get, what's coming to them. It says, as we have seen, that sooner or later justice will be done, that the more good that is done, the greater the reward, and the more evil, the greater the punishment.

But now consider two problems of karma that would appear to have arisen with our Savior Kṛṣṇa and His attempts to dispense *prasāda,* i.e., his own karma, within this universe dominated by the law of karma. Call these two problems of karma, first, "the problem of stored karma," and, second, "the problem of the transfer of karma. " Both problems threaten the status of the law of karma as a dispenser (that's what it is because that's what it does!) of justice to individual agents in need of rewards.

7. The Problem of Stored Karma

We have assumed that Kṛṣṇa, over the millennia and through his actions and in accordance with the law of karma, has generated an enormous quantity of good karma. It is important to realize that He hasn't used this karma but has, as

---

[11] *BG,* 18.56,58,62,73.

it were, stored it, banked it, waiting for opportunities to use it, to spend it. It is, after all, his karma, produced by him, now stored and waiting to reward him in accordance with the law of karma. But consider; the practice or possibility of the storage of this kind of good karma is quite inconsistent and threatening to the very law or principle that made the practice possible in the first place: To store the good and not reward the generator of the good is flatly contradictory to the law of karma. The Savior is now in the transfer business, clear and simple; hence, storage is necessary, hence, a store of karma is necessary; and that contradicts the law or principle by virtue of which the karma was made possible in the beginning. In other words, the Savior's karma account is not the Savior's karma account since it will not be used for him but only by him. In other words, his stored merit is no longer his stored merit.

Hand in hand with this problem goes another, and the two problems can be nicely considered together.

8. The Problem of the Transfer of Karma

As we stated, to store the good without letting that store be used to reward the storer of the good is inconsistent with the law of karma. Thus to transfer Lord Kṛṣṇa's good karma to you means that Lord Kṛṣṇa's good karma is no longer His good karma; and, further, to say of Kṛṣṇa's stored karma that it's not going to lead to a reward for Him because it's been transferred to you is, again, to say that Kṛṣṇa's karma is not Kṛṣṇa's karma.

Furthermore, even if you deserve Kṛṣṇa's stored karma, the fact of your deserving it means that you, too, have done good actions that now demand to be rewarded. So what has happened to your deserved karma? To say that it has been topped off with someone else's stored karma entails either of two things: First, that someone else didn't get his reward, i.e., he got less than he deserved, which is unjust; or, second, that you have gotten more than you deserved, which is also unjust.

We might point out here that stored karma is not ruled out *per se* by the law of karma; it is only necessary that what is stored must be used by the same one who stored it, i.e., storer and user must be the same in some sense. For example, you might do many good works in this life but not be rewarded until the next life.[12] So in some sense your good karma has been "stored." However, if you

---

[12] The Hindu Purāṇic tradition has provided for such things as deferred, hence stored, karma: "A man reaps that at that age, whether infancy, youth or old age, at which he had sowed it in his previous birth... A man gets in life what he is fated to get, and even a god cannot make it otherwise." Manmatha Butt, ed., *The Garuḍa Pūraṇa* (Calcutta: Society for the Resuscitation of Indian Literature, 1908), included in Robert O. Ballou, ed., *The Pocket World Bible* (London: Routledge and Kegan Paul, Limited, 1948), 68. Further, karma can be divided between *aravda* karma, on the one hand, which is the result of actions that have begun to produce effects, and *anaravda* karma, on the other, which is the result of actions that have not yet begun to produce effects. The latter, in turn,

reach nirvana, and if your good karma is not used up or exhausted by rewarding you, then this would be inconsistent with the law of karma.

We might point out, again, that transferred karma is not ruled out *per* se by the law of karma; it is only necessary that the person to whom it is transferred is the same person who made it, i.e., transferer and transferee must be the same in some sense. For example, you might do many good works in this life, accumulate karma, but not be rewarded until the next life but you are, nonetheless, the "same" person. To repeat, if your stored karma is transferred to you then there is no problem; however, if you reach liberation and your stored karma is transferred to some other person then there is a problem that we might call "the dilemma of stored karma": If that other person deserves stored karma then, since that person has a reward of his or her own coming that doesn't involve your karma, their being deserving makes the transfer of your karma unnecessary. If that other person does not deserve stored karma, then such a transfer of karma would be unjust. Now, either that other person deserves your karma or not. Therefore, either the transfer is unnecessary or it is unjust. Thus the dilemma of stored karma, the problems of karma, and the storage and transfer of karma seem inconsistent with the ancient law of karma.

If the dilemma of stored karma is not solved then the Hindu Savior game is in trouble since it is said to be efficacious in leading one to heaven only if the available karma is both stored and transferable. And if the problems of karma which are generated from karma's storability and transferability are not solved then the law of karma is in trouble. On both counts, it must appear, the Savior game and the law of karma are in trouble.[13]

---

is divided into *praktana* karma, the results of actions done in previous incarnations, our "stored" karma, presumably, which have not yet begun to produce effects; and *kryamana* karma, the results of actions done in this incarnation which have not yet began to produce effects, another "stored" karma, presumably. See Troy Wilson Organ, *Hinduism, Its Historical Development* (Woodbury, NY: Baron's Educational Series, Inc., 1974), 188.

[13] The storage and transfer of merit is common throughout both Hinduism and Buddhism wherever the individualistic interpretation of the law of karma applies. For Hinduism and the Indian systems generally, see Wendy Doniger O'Flaherty, ed., *Karma and Rebirth in Classical Indian Traditions* (Berkeley, California: University of California Press, 1980), and especially 28-33 (O'Flaherty) and 303-307 (Gerald James Larson); and for Buddhism, see 165-192 *passim* (McDermott). For merit transfer in Buddhism see Charles F. Keyes and E. Valentine Daniel, eds., *Karma: An Anthropological Inquiry* (Berkeley, California: University of California Press, 1983), especially 261-264 and 279-284 (Keyes); see also G. P. Malalasekere, "'Transference of Merit' in Ceylonese Buddhism," in *Philosophy East and West* 17 (1967): 85-90; Minoru Hara, "Transfer of Merit," *Adyar Library Bulletin* 31-32 (1967-68): 382-411; Richard Gombrich, "Merit Transference in Sinhalese Buddhism: A Case Study of the Interaction Between Doctrine and Practice," in *History of Religions* 11 (November, 1971): 203-219; James P. McDermott, "Is There Group Karma in Theravāda Buddhism?", in *Numen* 23 (1976): 67-80, and "Sadhina Jātaka: A Case Against the Transfer of Merit," *Journal of the American Oriental Society* 94 (1976): 385-387; finally, see Edward Conze, "Buddhist Saviors," and

9. Individualism, Saviorism, Communalism, and the Law of Karma

In the preceding sections we have attributed to the *BG* and possibly thereby to Hinduism a strictly individualistic interpretation of the law of karma. In this attribution each individual earns karma or *prasāda* by personal effort and for very personal ends or goals. The interpretation led to two problems of karma which are about to be solved by a new interpretation of the law of karma within Mahāyāna Buddhism.

There are probably three views that one could adopt with respect to the relationship between the person seeking heaven, or liberation, or a solution to a problem and the law of karma. Let's denominate these three possible relationships: Karmic Individualism," a *Upaniṣad*'s view we have briefly dealt with above; "Karmic Saviorism, " the Hindu view we have been exploring above; and "Karmic Communalism," a Buddhist view which we shall take up presently. Let's speak briefly to each one.

10. Karmic Individualism

Karmic individualism is the most radical interpretation of the relation between persons and the law of karma. It rejects the possibility of the transfer of merit between one person and another either because there is no person as such or because there is nothing to pass over or because each individual is entirely "on his own" in matters of enlightenment. This rugged karmic individualism assumes that we each make the goal on our own by each generating his or her own karmic chain with no outside help. The clearest example of radical individualism is probably found in the early *Upaniṣads* and possibly in early Buddhism with the remarks of the Buddha as he lay dying:

> The Doctrine and Discipline, Ānanda, which I have taught and enjoined upon you, is to be your teacher when I am gone. And now, Oh! monks, I take my leave of you; all the constituents of being are transitory; work out your own salvation with diligence.[14]

There is no Savior here to share His or Her generated karma and the passage enjoins the listener/reader to start pulling himself up by his own karmic bootstraps. Gautama the Buddha's view of rugged karmic individualism was to remain a part of early Theravāda Buddhism with its attendant *anātman* and atheistic foundations and arhat-seeking monks. The view has been called "selfish" by the later Mahāyāna critics of "Hīnayāna" and in a sense selfishness

---

"The Development of Prajnaparainita Thought," in *Buddhist Studies 1934-1972* (San Francisco: Wheelwright Press, n.d.), especially 40-42 and 130-132, respectively.

[14] Henry Clarke Warren, trans., *Mahā-Parinibbāna Sutta of the Dīgha-Nikāya in Buddhism in Translations* (New York: Atheneum, 1963/1896), 109.

defines the more rugged karmic individualists very nicely (I see nothing morally reprehensible with a well-argued selfishness!).

The law of karma, according to karmic individualism, applies only to individuals wherein each generates his or her own karma through his or her own present actions in splendid isolation from the karmic influences of others, whether they be living or dead or Saviors or communities of karmic beings.

11. Karmic Saviorism

A milder form of karmic individualism emerges with karmic Saviorism. It appears in the *BG,* as we have seen, above. Here we meet with the notion of shared karma and, with that, the notion of an accumulated karma to be shared. The concepts of stored karma and transferred karma will emerge after 200 B.C.E. in Mahāyāna Buddhism perhaps as a consequence of the Hindu soteriological influence. That influence probably rested, as we have seen, above, on this milder form of karmic individualism wherein each person still pulls up on his or her own bootstraps to achieve desired goals but now there are the helping hands of the Savior, or the Bodhisattva, as we shall see, below, in Mahāyāna Buddhism, that one can count on for some extra pulling and support.

The law of karma, according to karmic Saviorism, still applies to individuals but the action-generated karma is no longer entirely one's own but is constituted by a storehouse of karma or merit generated and accumulated by others. This stored karma is then dispensed according to a soteriological logic to deserving devotees or recipients. The law of karma, under karmic Saviorism, has been considerably broadened and expanded as we move from self-centered karmic individualism to Savior-centered or even God-centered karmic views.

But, as we have seen, this milder or mitigated karmic individualism introduces several problems that it cannot solve, viz., the problems of stored karma and the transfer of karma, which brings us to a new view, a Mahāyāna Buddhist view, about karma and the law that governs its dispersal.

12. Karmic Communalism

Karmic communalism, our third and final view of the relationship between the individual and the law of karma, calls upon all members of a community of beings to share their merit, i.e., their karma, with other members of the same community. Karmic communalism is found as early as the 2nd century B.C.E. in Mahāyāna[15] with the development of the concept of the Bodhisattva. Like the

---

[15] Karmic communalism may also be found in Theravāda Buddhism in the concept of the Saṅgha, the community of monks. Since our interest here is in Mahāyāna and not in the history of Pali communalism, karmic or otherwise, we'll say no more about Theravāda. But see a discussion of Theravāda Saṅgha as a source of merit in David Kalupahana, *A History of Buddhist Philosophy* (Honolulu: University of Hawaii Press, 1992): "If the disciples of the Buddha are endowed with these four characteristics [well-

Avatar-God-Savior of the *BG,* the Bodhisattva comes declaring his love and compassion. But, unlike the Kṛṣṇa of the *Gīta,* the Bodhisattva of Mahāyāna karmic communalism is a member of the community he seeks to save; he has felt their pain, their terror, and he doesn't stand ontologically and majestically above and beyond it or them. The Bodhisattva remembers that he is yet a man or a woman. Kṛṣṇa, though compassionate in his own way, gives no inkling that he remembers any such thing even though he confesses that Arjuna, his cousin, is "truly My beloved:" While both are "Saviors," the Hindu Avatar is not the Buddhist Bodhisattva.

Here is the 7th century C.E. Bodhisattva, Śāntideva, expressing this new way of shared or communal merit:

> Through the merit derived from all my good deeds I wish to appease the suffering of all creatures, to be the medicine, the physician, and the nurse of the sick as long as there is sickness. Through rains of food and drink I wish to extinguish the fire of hunger and thirst. I wish to be an inexhaustible treasure to the poor, a servant who furnishes them with all they lack. My life, and all my re-births, all my possessions, all the merit that I have acquired or will acquire, all that I abandon without hope of any gain for myself in order that the salvation of all beings might be promoted.[16]

In his *Śikṣāsamuccaya,* Śāntideva summarizes the standard that has inspired all previous Bodhisattvas in their one endeavor in life--to put off their own liberation until everyone in the community of beings has been saved:

> A Bodhisattva resolves: I take upon myself the burden of all suffering, I am resolved to do so, I will, endure it. I do not turn or run away, do not tremble, am not terrified, nor afraid, do not turn back or despond...My endeavors do not merely aim at my own deliverance. For with the help of the boat of the thought of all-knowledge, I must rescue all these beings from the stream of Saṁsāra, which is so difficult to cross, I must pull them back from the great precipice, I must free them from all calamities, I must ferry them across the

---

behaved (in Pali *supaṭipanno*), straightforward (*ujupaṭipanno*), methodical (*nayapaṭipanno*), and correct (*samipaṭipanno*)], they are worthy of veneration, hospitality, magnanimity, and respect. They represent an incomparable source of merit (*puññakkhetta*) for the world, since they are the living aspirants to the moral ideal represented by the Buddha... The Sangha or community of disciples would then be a veritable source of merit not in its own right [which is what will happen in Budhisattva-domonated Mahāyāna], but because it *represents* a community that cultivates a noble moral ideal (*dhamma-cari*)," 117-118, emphasis added. See also Sukumar Dutt, *Buddhist Monks and Monasteries of India* (New Delhi: Motilal Banarsidass, 1988), especially chapter 5, "Saṅgha Life and Its Organization in Early Settlements."

[16] Śāntideva, *Bodhicaryāvatāra* 3.6-10, in Edward Conze, *Buddhism: Its Essence and Development* (New York: Harper Torch Books, 1959), 149.

stream of Saṁsāra. I myself must grapple with the whole mass of suffering of all beings. To the limit of my endurance I will experience in all the states of woe, found in any world system, all the abodes of suffering. And I must not cheat all beings out of my store of merit.[17]

The Mahāyāna Buddhist who follows the way of karmic communalism is quick to point out that the law of karma need not be contradicted by the storage and transfer of merit. The latter two practices merely call for an extension of the domain of the law of karma. And that extension, far from being inconsistent with the original law, is rather a logical deduction from it. The original formulation of the 1-lindu law of karma, whether interpreted as Upaniṣadic karmic individualism or Hindu karmic Saviorism, was merely too narrowly stated and too narrowly applied (to single individuals and persons); what Mahāyāna did was to resist that narrow and personal interpretation and to draw out its wider implications (to apply it to whole societies and communities).

Edward Conze gives a fine defense of karmic communalism as he speaks, first, about the original and narrow belief in the law of karma:

> The original belief seems to have been that each one of us has his own series of karma, that the punishment for his misdeeds must be suffered by him, and that the rewards for his good deeds are enjoyed only by him. This excessive individualism was not essential to the karma doctrine, and just as historically the notion of collective responsibility preceded that of individual responsibility, so, in the Vedas it had been assumed that the members of a family or clan all share one common karma.

Conze concludes with this objection to that original belief about the law of karma:

> The individualistic interpretation of the law of karma throws each individual on his own resources, and seems to deny any solidarity between the different persons as regards the more essential things of life, i.e., as regards merit and demerit.[18]

The Mahāyāna interpretation of the law of karma is, according to Conze, less individual-oriented, and more community-oriented: Merit is made to be shared in a community. As such, it would allow, according to Mahāyāna, the storage and the transfer of merit to other *bhaktas*, to other members of the *bhakta* community.

Under karmic communalism it is permissible to store what you cannot use for the future benefit of all sentient beings; and to have transferred to you what

---

[17] *Śikṣāsamuccaya*, 280-281 (*Vajradhvaja Sūtra*) in Edward Conze, et. al., eds., *Buddhist Texts Through the Ages* (New York: Harper Torch Books, 1964), 131.

[18] Edward Conze, *Buddhism: Its Essence and Development*, *op. cit*, 148.

you may not strictly speaking deserve, having produced less merit in your lifetime than you're going to get back after it. But it's all just and fair because the answers to questions about what belongs to whom and who deserves what from whom have all changed radically.

The law of karma, according to karmic communalism, more closely resembles a familiar communalist cry of the 19th century in the West: "From each according to his/her ability; to each according to his/her need." It is upon this foundation that Buddhist communalism, karmic, moral, and social, will in the future be constructed, which brings us finally to our fourth and final concept of community.

13. Mahāyāna Buddhism and the Way of the Karmic Community

Just as karmic communalism lies as a middle path between karmic individualism and karmic Saviorism so also the way of the karmic community is a middle path between the too-much-ness of Aldo Leopold's way of the biotic community and the not-enough-ness of Martin Luther King, Jr.'s way of the beloved community. We discovered that with karmic communalism justice was a matter of community involvement and that what was shared was the karma itself. Karmic communalism has solved two problems dealing with the storage and transfer of merit and as such it has considerably altered the traditional interpretation and scope of the law of karma. This has made possible the transfer of stored merit to anyone who belongs to the community and who, through *bhakti*, requests it. The community of those capable of making such requests could now theoretically include the entire world. This world community of potential merit receivers and merit generators we call "the karmic community."

Once again, the Bodhisattva turns to that store of merit for dispersal to the karmic community since the karma was generated for them, stored for them, and it is now dispersable to them. In the *Aṣṭasahāsrikā Prajñāpāramitā Sūtra* of the 2nd century B.C.E., Subhūti, a merit generator and disciple of the Buddha, lays out the details of the Bodhisattva's task:

> He considers the mass of morality, the mass of concentration, the mass of wisdom, the mass of emancipation, the mass of the vision and cognition of emancipation of those Buddhas and Lords.
>
> In addition he considers the store of merit associated with the six perfections, with the achievement of the qualities of a Buddha, and with the perfections of self-confidence and of the powers; and also those associated with the perfection of the super-knowledge, of comprehension, of the vows; and the store of merit associated with the accomplishment of the cognition of the all-knowing, with the solicitude for beings, the great friendliness and the great compassion, and the immeasurable and incalculable Buddha-qualities.[19]

---

[19] *Aṣṭasahāsrikā* VI in *Buddhist Texts Through the Ages, op. cit.,* 133.

That store of merit has many generators, we are reminded. It comes, Subhūti tells us, from all those who abide by the Dharma, i.e., from Buddhas and Bodhisattvas at all levels of liberation; in addition, the store comes from monks and nuns of the Order, lay persons who engage in meritorious works, Gods, Nāgas, Yakṣas, men and ghosts, etc., and all those who entered *parinirvāṇa* without using up their generated merit. Ordinarily this would produce the problems of karma mentioned in Part 1, above. But now we have members of the karmic community to consider as both the generators, storers and dispersers of all this merit and not the single individuals of traditional Hinduism.

The *Aṣṭasahāsrikā* is quite clear on what and who constitutes the karmic community. In addition to the Gods, supernatural beings, men and ghosts mentioned above, Subhūti also includes animals. The result is that this Mahāyāna karmic community, while theoretically identical to Gandhi's āśramic community (they both share the law of karma, after all), is somewhat smaller than Leopold's biotic community, since it excludes plants and ponds, but larger than King's beloved community, since it includes animals. Is there an advantage to such an addition for the Buddhist karmic community as opposed to these other two communities? There is to the extent that with the law of karma now covering a community that includes *all* sentient creatures it goes beyond King's narrow beloved community of humans only but restricts itself within Leopold's broader biotic community of all living things; as a result, it may now be not only more realistically acceptable to common sense but it may now be more understandably defensible to philosophic sense. However, some problems and puzzles remain.

14. Problems with the Way of the Karmic Community

The central question that we set out to answer in this chapter was, Can the Mahāyāna Buddhist way of the karmic community solve the problems of violence and peace in the 21st century? The answer that we suggested entailed getting everyone to see that they are members of a community and as such they are the community; and since no one would knowingly and voluntarily do violence to himself or herself, and since everyone would help their community knowing it to be themselves, violence would be diminished and peace would prevail. The questions then became, "What is a community?" and "How does one become a member of a community?"

This then led to an investigation of three communities, the biotic community of Aldo Leopold, the beloved community of Martin Luther King, Jr., the āśramic community of Mohandas K. Gandhi, and the ways that each adopted for overcoming the problems of violence and peace. Each of these communities, good as they were, generated other problems that rendered their usefulness questionable in solving the problems of violence and peace.

We then turned to our fourth community and the way of the karmic community. We discussed its history and its relation to the law of karma as a solution to the two problems of the storage and transfer of karma or merit in Hinduism. At this point we suggested that the way of the karmic community was able to solve these two problems as well as several of the other problems that our three previous ways of community generated but could not solve. However, the way of the karmic community generates several problems of its own. Each of these problems relates to puzzles already raised and that seem to be indigenous to all communities.

15. The Problem of Self-transformation

Membership in the biotic community, the beloved community, and the āśramic community seemed dependent, as we saw, on a person being altered or changed in some way or other, as a condition for membership in those communities. Just how these rites of passage are to be implemented was not clear in all three cases. The question might now be asked with regard to the way of the karmic community: How does one become a member of the karmic community?

The question is readily answered since the law of karma has already determined that membership for each member of the community. Thus, you and I are here in the karmic community because of our past lives and the karma generated by each of us in those lives. That past karma and the law governing its dispersal has brought us into this community of sentient beings and it is the ground on which awareness of that community rests. Presumably the awareness that I share karma with other sentient beings is the source of the realization that I belong to the karmic community. And that awareness transforms me from an outsider to an insider who knows that when I harm others I harm myself and when I help others I help myself. But how do I achieve that awareness?

16. The Problem of Karmic Fascism

Membership both in the biotic community, the beloved community, and in the āśramic community seemed to lead, as we saw, to the individual being devoured by the community. But unless the community is strong there can never be peace; and if the community is weak there will always be violence. Recall that the dilemma of community demonstrated that if the community was not strong enough then violence and chaos resulted; and if the community was too strong then, while peace might result, eco- or communal-fascism was the price that one paid for it. Both eco-fascism and communo-fascism waited to devour the individual in the name of peace and security.

But the problem of what we might call "karmic fascism" is easily solved if we keep in mind that we are not talking about an isolated community, a Saṅgha for example, dominated by central rulers who lay down absolutes that guarantee the survival of the group no matter what it takes. What binds the karmic community together is not a common energy, life, or mystical spirit but karma and karma is being generated afresh each moment. The individuals of the karmic community have as their goal the reduction of bad karma and violence, and the production of good karma and peace; as such, individual striving and initiative is most essential. Without such action bad karma enters and the community is destroyed by its own violence.

17. The Problem of "What is Shared Karma?"

Several final questions will be left to another time since I'm not sure that I know the answers to them: What does it mean to say that two or more beings share the same merit or the same karma? Is it like sharing a history, or a future, or a destiny, i.e., sharing memories, hopes, and fears? Is it like sharing a bank account or D.N.A., or the same physical body? Is it like sharing the same mind or intellect where two brains, as it were, become one? "Shared merit" or "shared karma" seems to intend some form of reduction of body, mind, and spirit from the complex to he simple within whatever it is that constitutes the domain of the law of karma.

CHAPTER 10

SEARCHING FOR A MAHĀYĀNA SOCIAL ETHICS

David W. Chappell

1. Introduction

Mahāyāna Buddhist ethics is usually summarized by the "three kinds of pure precepts" (*sanju jingkai*), namely, (1) to prevent all evil, (2) to cultivate all good, and (3) to save all beings.[1] In reviewing the available modern studies of Buddhist ethics in the light of these categories, it becomes clear that the usual focus is to examine Buddhist monastic codes which deal with the category of preventing or avoiding wrong doing,[2] while other studies focus on Buddhist "virtue ethics," the second category.[3] However, the topic of "saving all beings" has generally been neglected, even though this is said to be the distinctive mark of Mahāyāna.[4] Because of this neglect, and because of the increasing request by

---

[1] The usual phrase is *sanju jukai* (the three comprehensive pure precepts). See Gyōnen, *Essentials of the Discipline School* in the newly annotated edition by Sato Tatsugen, *Gendai goyaku Ritsushū kōyō* (Tokyo: Daizō Publishing Society, 1994), 27-93. These three ideals are found in various Buddhist scriptures, as Gyōnen points out, such as is the *Yujia lun* (T.30.51 la-514b), the *Pusa shanjie jing* (T.30.982c) and the *Pusa dizhi jing* (T.30.910b-c), etc. These three categories provide the basic structure for *Asaṅga's Chapter on Ethics With the Commmentary of Tsong-kha-pa. The Basic Path to Awakening, The Complete Bodhisattva* (Lewiston, New York: Edwin Mellon Press, 1986) translated by Mark Tatz. In fact, these categories occur so often and in so many different Mahāyāna texts that Ono Hodo found at least fourteen different Chinese ways of translating the names of the three groups (Ono,186-187).

[2] See Charles Wei-hsun Fu and Sandra A. Wawrytko, eds., *Buddhist Behavioral Codes and the Modern World* (Westport, Connecticut: Greenwood Press, 1994).

[3] See James Whitehill, "Buddhist Ethics in Western Context: The 'Virtues' Approach," *Journal of Buddhist Ethics* 1 (1994): 1-22.

[4] Damien Keown in *The Nature of Buddhist Ethics* (New York: St. Martin's Press, 1992) reviewed these three categories, especially as described in the "Chapter on

non-Buddhists about Buddhist views for improving society, it is the intention of this paper to explore the nature of Mahāyāna ethics in the third category concerned with how to save all beings.

More specifically, the hope is that by exploring this third category, that we might find some portion of Mahāyāna ethics that can be generalized as a social principle to be followed by all of society, without requiring membership in the Buddhist community. This will avoid the sectarian practice that uses religious proselytization as the primary method of saving all beings. Instead of analyzing the ethical principles of those who have left the world (monastics), or exploring how one can serve society by attracting other people to become Buddhists (evangelism), the limited goal of this paper is to discover what social ethics are presented by Mahāyāna that might become a general guide for distinguishing right from wrong behavior in our complex world, and for guiding improved relationships among people. Since Mahāyāna ethics is a vast field,[5] as a first step I shall review some problems inherent in generalizing about Mahāyāna ethics, and then shall focus on the *Upāsaka Precept Sūtra* (T. 30.1488.1034-1075), which is an early Mahāyāna manual of lay bodhisattva ethics that is in active use by contemporary Chinese Buddhists.

The *Upāsaka Precept Sūtra* is sometimes referred to as the *Shansheng jing*[6] in order to connect it to several early Buddhist ethical texts also named *Shansheng jing* that survive in four Chinese translations[7] and which are similar

---

Morality" in the *Bodhisattva-bhumi sūtra*, and concluded t hat "It is principally the addition of the third factor which raises the Mahāyāna moral edifice over the head of its predecessor and allows it to claim superiority in scope" (142).

[5] Among the two hundred Mahāyāna texts containing bodhisattva, precepts, almost all have been ignored in Western studies and only a handful have been analysed or translated into Western languages. See Ono hōdō, *Daijō kaikyō no kenkyū* (Tokyo: Risōsha, 1954).

[6] The currency of this ceremony for Chinese Buddhists is seen in the fact that it was newly edited and printed for a recent ceremony in October 1974 by three of the leading Buddhist masters in Taiwan, Ven. Wu-ming, Ven. Ching-hsin, and Ven. Kuang-yuan. For the name of *Shansheng jing*, see the *Zhuanshou zhushi sangui wujie pusajie* (A Brief Ceremony for Delivering the Three Refuges, Five Lay Precepts, and the Bodhisattva Precepts to Laity) (Taiwan: Haiming Chan Temple, 1994), 30. Attending the ceremony were two visitors who had travelled especially to participate in the ceremony, Mrs. Frieda Shu Luan Huang and Mr. Chang Hsiang 0 Huang. Coming from the Los Angeles Chinese Buddhist community, Mr. and Mrs. Huang had been working for several years to prepare core Buddhist materials in English to assist the development of Buddhist practice in America. One of these texts is the ceremony for receiving the bodhisattva precepts used in this ceremony.

[7] *Liufang li jing*, T.1.16.250-252. It should be noted that this text is not listed as being translated by An Shigao in the earliest catalog of Buddhist scriptures compiled by Tao-an in the fourth century; *Shansheng-jing*, T. 1.17.252-255; *Shansheng jing, Zhang Ahan*, T.1.135.70a-72c; *Shiwen jing, Zhung Ahan*, T.1.135.638-642.

to the *Sigālaka Sutta* found in the Theravāda *Dīgha-nikāya* in Pali.[8] However, the Mahāyāna *Upāsaka Precept Sūtra* (hereafter called *UPS*) is about twenty times longer than these texts, and only has a few traces of these earlier texts in the first and fourteenth chapters. Although this larger Mahāyāna precept text is sometimes called the *Shansheng jing,* it is also called the *Youposai jie jing* (*Upāsaka-śīla sūtra*) and was translated into Chinese by Tan Wuchan in the early fifth century (424-426 A.D.).[9]

Unlike the popular *Fanwang jing* (Brahma Net Sūtra) that is used by clergy as well as by laity, the *UPS* text explicitly focuses on laity, and at the end of most of its twenty-eight chapters it contains the refrain:

> Good son, as the Buddha has said, there are two kinds of bodhisattvas: (1) lay and (2) ordained... It is not difficult for the ordained bodhisattvas to hold the precepts for ordained people, but it is difficult for the lay bodhisattvas to hold the precepts for lay people. And why? Lay people are bound by more unfavorable conditions.[10]

As a consequence, it elevates lay practice above clerical practice, and additionally argues that clergy only keep pure, whereas laity is also able to help others by giving. Since the *UPS* precept text connects itself to the oldest lay ethical tradition of Buddhism by having Sigālaka as its interlocutor, and since it is a Mahāyāna bodhisattva precept text explicitly for laity rather than for clergy, and since it is for ordinary laity rather than for a leader such as Nāgārjuna's *Advice to a King,*[11] and since it is a text still in regular use among Chinese Buddhists in Asia and has recently been introduced to the West, I propose it as a useful starting point in exploring lay Mahāyāna ethics.

2. The Upāsaka Precept Scripture (UPS)

In Chapter One the *UPS* recommends honoring the six directions much like the earlier texts, but contrary to them there is no mention of Sigālaka beginning his practice based on his father's instructions, but instead we read that it is six non-Buddhist teachers who have recommended this practice. The Buddha responds by telling Sigālaka that in his teaching there are also six directions, but

---

[8] *Sigālaka Sutta: Advice to Laity, Dīgha-nikāya,* No. 31, tr. by Maurice Walshe, *Thus Have I Heard* (London: Wisdom Publications, 1987), 461469

[9] T. 24.1488.1034a- 1075b (Jp., *U-ba-soku kai kyo,* tr. by Shih Heng-ching, *The Sūtra on Upāsaka Precepts* (Berkeley: Bukkyō Dendō Kyōkai, 1991).

[10] *Ibid.,* 75. This refrain is repeated at the end of 27 of the 28 chapters, being omitted only in the second chapter. Unless otherwise noted, all future quotations from *The Sūtra on Upāsaka Precepts* will be based on Ven. Heng-ching's translation, with slight revisions sometimes added.

[11] For a lucid translation, see Jeffrey Hopkins, "The Precious Garland of Advice for the King," in *The Buddhism of Tibet* (Ithaca, New York: Snow Lion, 1987, reprint of 1975 edition of George Allen & Unwin), 105-206.

these are to be identified with each of the six perfections (giving, morality, patience, zeal, mindfulness, and wisdom) as a way to increase a person's life-span and wealth. Furthermore, the Buddha introduces a sectarian note by asserting that only bodhisattvas can make offerings to these six perfections. Accordingly, the *UPS* quickly moves away from the ethical advice that pervades the earlier Sigālaka texts and Chapter Fourteen of the *UPS*, and instead shifts attention to the distinctiveness of the bodhisattva path.

> It is through the combination of various good karmas and the arousal of the aspiration for enlightenment that one is called a bodhisattva. To say that all sentient beings possess bodhisattva nature is not correct.[12]

Unlike the later claim in East Asia that all people have the Buddha-nature, this passage shows an early period when Mahāyāna was still in the process of consolidating its own identity. For example, the *UPS* is careful to distinguish bodhisattvas from being another word for laity. Instead, the uniqueness of bodhisattvas as a distinct religious group is emphasized by defining them as only those laity who has aroused the aspiration for enlightenment. The sectarian emphasis in Chapter One is summarized by a hierarchy of eight levels of practitioners: from the bottom to the top, we have beings in the desire realm, next are non-Buddhist teachers, next are Buddhists going from stream-enterers, to once-returners, to non-returners, to arhats, to pratyekabuddhas, and culminating in lay bodhisattvas:

> It is not difficult for an ordained person to arouse aspirations for enlightenment, but it is inconceivable for a lay person to arouse the aspiration for enlightenment. And why? Lay people are bound by more unfavorable conditions. When a lay person arouses aspirations for enlightenment, the four *deva* kings and also kings in the Akaniṣṭha and other heavens pleasantly and with great surprise exclaim, 'Now, we have a teacher of men and gods.'[13]

Arousing the aspiration for enlightenment (*bodhicitta*) is clearly the defining trait of a lay bodhisattva. Not only is it the cause for their superiority as bodhisattvas to all other religious practitioners, but it also expresses the framework and values that guide Mahāyāna lay ethics. Even though the text lists non-Buddhist teachers and other beings as the lowest level, still they are not rejected as evil but are included as practitioners. Accordingly, while following the texts exposition of the Mahāyāna bodhisattva path, we must be on the watch for general guidelines that might be available for all, even the lowest.

Chapter Fourteen contains the ceremony for receiving the six lay precepts, and like Chapter One is structured around offerings to the six directions. Again

---

[12] *Ibid.*, 3.
[13] *Ibid.*, 6.

the story from the earlier recensions that Sigālaka had received instructions from his dying father to honor the six directions is missing. Instead, the *UPS* begins where the earlier texts end, namely, with the instructions that the six directions represent six different groups of people: east = parents; south = teachers; west = wife; north = beneficial friends (*kalyāṇamitra*); lower direction = servants; and upper direction = clergy. In this list a Mahāyāna influence can be seen in only one area: instead of the north referring to worldly friends, the *UPS* text changes it to refer to spiritual companions, the *kalyāṇamitra,* a code word used for those in the Mahāyāna community. The earlier texts emphasize that the benefits of caring for your friends are that they will look after you and your property when you are inattentive, they will be a refuge when you are afraid, they will not desert you when you are in trouble, and they will show concern for your children.[14] By contrast, the Mahāyāna text says that your spiritual companions will teach you to cultivate good teachings and to avoid bad ones, to help you when you are afraid, and will strengthen you against laxity.[15] (This change in the *UPS* implies a teaching not for the general public in Indian society, but for laity within the new Mahāyāna community; not for your friends and neighbors, but for those who have shared values and practices everywhere.

In addition to the inherent benefits of these six relationships, the *UPS* assures us that the consequence of maintaining these relationships will be an increase in wealth and life-span, and support in keeping the *upāsaka* (lay Buddhist) precepts. Whereas the earlier texts end at this point, the Mahāyāna text uses this as an introduction for the ceremony for receiving the *upāsaka* precepts, and immediately launches into the eight preparatory questions about whether or not you have received permission to take the precepts, whether or not you have debts to the saṅgha, whether or not you are sick, etc. After these questions, there is a review of various basic moral virtues that echo the beginning portions of the earlier texts, such as avoiding bad friends and bad habits, avoiding killing, stealing, lying, and sexual misconduct, avoiding selling intoxicants, avoiding entertainments, etc. Following these admonitions, the *UPS* concludes with the ceremony for receiving the six major precepts, and adds on twenty-eight minor precepts. While all of these are morally helpful, none of these are distinctive in content except perhaps for the last minor precept:

> If an *upāsaka* who has taken the precepts comes across a sick person along the road and does not look after and arrange a place for him but deserts him, he commits a fault. He cannot rise from degradation, nor can he purify his actions.[16]

Although it is well known that the Buddha instructed his monks to care for other monks who are sick, this broader and more inclusive instruction to care for

---

[14] Walshe, *op. cit.,* 467-468.

[15] Heng-ching, *Upāsaka Precepts,* 64 (with slight revisions).

[16] *Ibid.,* 75.

any stranger along the road is new and powerful. It is also reminiscent of the story of the Good Samaritan told by Jesus in answer to a lawyer who asked that if we are to love our neighbor, who counts as our neighbor (Luke 10:30-35). Once again the circle of relations for whom we have responsibility has changed from those who have close proximity and familiarity to us to include anyone who has need of help.

After a final encouragement, the *upāsaka* precept chapter ends at this point without explaining these new Mahāyāna injunctions. Accordingly, we must look through the other chapters if we are to understand why and how this change of boundaries has taken place, and how it might extend to all of society.

3. The Aspiration for Enlightenment (*bodhicitta*)

Chapter Two of the *UPS* begins by laying out twelve different pairs of reasons (circumstances, events, shi) that might arouse the thought of enlightenment. Among these we can find something for everyone no matter what their level of maturity or spiritual development.

> 1. The first reasons are materialistic: to increase one's longevity and wealth.
> 2. The next reasons are idealistic: to continue one's bodhisattva nature and to sever the sufferings of others.
> 3. Next is the realization that a person has failed to gain benefit throughout an endless series of rebirths, and that finally the Buddha cannot save a person, but "I have to liberate myself."
> 4. Next is the concern for moral achievements, namely, to practice all good deeds, and not to lose what has been practiced.
> 5. Next is a striving for the best, namely, to surpass the level of humans and gods, and to surpass the two Buddhist vehicles: śrāvakas and pratyekabuddhas.
> 6. Next is the practical commitment to undergo all suffering for the sake of attaining enlightenment, which in turn will provide all benefits.
> 7. Next is the realization that all the Buddhas of past and future are the same as oneself, and therefore that enlightenment is attainable.
> 8. Next is to realize that even though a sixth-stage bodhisattva might regress, he still is superior to the attainments of the two vehicles, and therefore one should seek the highest goal.
> 9. Next is the ideal of wishing to liberate all beings and to surpass the achievements of non-Buddhists.

10. Next is the practice of not abandoning other beings, but instead forsaking all selfish afflictions.

11. Next is the practice of eliminating the present selfish afflictions of others, and preventing future selfish afflictions.

12. Finally there is the practice of cutting off the obstructions to wisdom, and cutting off the obstructions for others caused by their bodies.

Arousing the quest for enlightenment (*bodhicitta*) is the foundational activity for a bodhisattva, and this variety of reasons to support the aspiration demonstrates that the bodhisattva life is not limited to one level of maturity, nor to one mood or moment in life. Furthermore, this list shows that arousing the *bodhicitta is* not a once-and-for-all event, but is a recurring and unending experience.

This list begins with self-interest (for longevity and wealth), and sometimes returns to it (#3 and #6). Often this means being idealistic in wishing for the highest goal (#2, #4, #5, #8, #9). The list ends not with reasons for arousing the *bodhicitta*, but with ways to practice this path in what appears to be complete altruism (# 10, # 11, # 12). Also, buried in the middle of the list (#7) is the encouraging realization of the sameness of oneself and all the other Buddhas, so that success in achieving enlightenment is assured.

Even though the third reason to rouse the *bodhicitta* promotes self-reliance, soon this is balanced in the text by a list of supporting conditions, including the support of spiritual companions (*kalyāṇamitra*) and the instructions of a teacher. Accordingly, none of these reasons for seeking enlightenment are absolute, but all work together to provide logic and guidelines on the path. Accordingly, these twelve pairs of reasons lay out a platform that becomes the ethical framework for the *Upāsaka* precepts.

In addition, practical refinements are added to help implement the goal of attaining enlightenment. Chapter Two ends by telling the practitioner that the largest amount of karma can be overcome based on seeing:

1. The five evils (a polluted and disaster-ridden world, physical and mental handicaps, distorted teachings, strong passions, and a short life) that afflict humans in an evil period in contrast to the spiritual powers of a Buddha;

2. That one's own body suffers when others suffer, therefore one wishes to eliminate their suffering as a dimension of one's own suffering.

Seeing how the spiritual power of a Buddha is superior to the suffering of normal life is the beginning of the Buddhist path, whereas realizing that the suffering of others is one's own suffering is the culmination of the Buddhist path. In addition to taking these two insights as the beginning and end of bodhisattva practice, we should note that taking the suffering of others as one's own is another change of boundaries similar to the injunction to help sick strangers mentioned above.

4. Compassion: The Mahāyāna Ethical Foundation

Having reviewed a variety of circumstances (*shi*) that might precipitate the aspiration for enlightenment in Chapter Two, and after reviewing various kinds of causes (*yin*) in the beginning of Chapter Three, the *UPS* then condenses them all into one primary cause: compassion. Numerous illustrations are given of how compassion arises. In this long exposition, secular life and the religious life are included:

> He arouses compassion because he sees that sentient beings do not love their parents, brothers, wives, children, servants, relatives and clans. Good son, an intelligent person should contemplate that the happiness of *samādhi* in the heaven of neither thinking nor non-thinking is like the suffering of hells which is shared by all beings. He can then arouse compassion.[17]

In addition to emphasizing compassion, the *UPS* makes a distinction between ordinary compassion (*bei*) and "great compassion" (*da-bei*, Skt., *mahākaruṇā*). Ordinary compassion is the kind of compassion that arises before enlightenment, it is limited, it comes and goes, it wavers, it cannot save all beings, and it lacks wisdom. On the other hand, great compassion arises after enlightenment, it is boundless, it does not waver, it can greatly save and help, and it is practiced with wisdom.[18]

This promise of being unlimited, unwavering, vast, and wise as a result of enlightenment echoes the ecstatic value given in early Buddhism to compassion as part of the four immeasurable minds (*siwuliangxin;* or four *brahma-vihāra, sifanzhu*): namely, good-will (*maitrī*), compassion (*karuṇā*), (3) sympathetic joy (*muditā*), and equanimity (*upekṣā*).[19] As the quality of being unborn and undying is celebrated as a feature of nirvana in early Buddhist texts, the four immeasurables express an ethical ideal that had a sense of expansiveness and of completeness, and which was a theme that pervaded the earliest texts.[20] Chapter

---

[17] Heng-ching, *UPS*, 12, T.24.1036b.23-26.

[18] *Ibid.*, T.24.1036b.26-c.5.

[19] For the appearance of the four immeasurables in the early Buddhist scriptures, the Āgamas and Nikāyas, see Thich Minh Chau, *The Chinese Madhyama Āgama and the Pali Majjhima Nikāya (A Comparative Study)* (Saigon: The Saigon Institute of Higher Buddhist Studies, 1964; reprinted by Motilal Banarsidas, Delhi, 1991), 101-103; see Mochizuki Shinkō, ed., *Bukkyō daijiten* (Tokyo: Sekai seiten kankō kyōkai, 1958-1963), 2101a.

[20] The list of four immeasurables appears in at least twelve of the Chinese Middle-length Agamas, namely, Nos. 6, 18, 21, 24, 25, 29, 36, 3 7, 63, 64, 82, and 98, and the descriptions there are mirrored in the Pali *Majjhima-nikāya*.

Three supports this view since it asserts that the six perfections can only be adequately practiced through great compassion. This emphasis is in dramatic contrast to the Perfection of Wisdom tradition that argues that the six perfections can only be properly practiced based on wisdom. Although one might expect that a text on ethics would emphasize compassion over wisdom,[21] it is important also to see that compassion provides a shared ground with conventional experience in contrast to the disjunction from ordinary life that the perfection of wisdom celebrates. That is to say, all people have experienced compassion to one degree or another, and great compassion is merely an extension of this beyond its usual limits.[22]

Chapter Three ends by asserting that "if lay people do not cultivate compassion, they cannot attain the *upāsaka* precepts." On the other hand, it promises that all other good virtues can be attained based on compassion: "If they cultivate compassion, they will perfect morality, patience, vigor, meditation and wisdom." In the moral arithmetic of the universe, in return for compassionate giving, the *UPS* says that the practitioner can thereby "destroy bad karma as large as Mount Sumeru and will soon attain unsurpassed, perfect enlightenment. He will gain rewards as great as Mount Sumeru even from a little good karma." And even though these great rewards may not become available in the immediate present, compassion will also help the practitioner through difficult times:

> Cultivating compassionate thoughts, one can give what is difficult to give, endure what is difficult to endure, and do what is difficult to do. Therefore compassion is the basis of all good dharmas.[23]

At the conventional end of the spectrum, these statements can be connected to the idea that "compassion pays" that is sometimes used at an early level of socialization.

5. Helping Others

Chapter Four of the *UPS* returns to the theme of how a person can awaken to the aspiration for enlightenment, or how one can become repulsed by the cycle of rebirth (*saṃsāra*) and attracted to nirvana. It emphasizes that because of the differences among the minds of beings, so the skillful devices (*upāya*) differ in order to awaken them. In this context, a new aspect of bodhisattva practice

---

[21] See verses 100, 172, 402, etc. in Edward Conze, tr., *The Perfection of Wisdom in Eight Thousand Lines and Its Verse Summary* (Bolinas, California: Four Seasons Foundation, 1973), 17, 23, 52, etc.

[22] This emphasis on continuity with conventional experience can be contrasted with the experience of emptiness found in the Perfection of Wisdom literature which asserts that the experience is not a matter of degree, but is discontinuous with daily life: emptiness dissolves ordinary perception and removes the conventional sources of support.

[23] Heng-ching, *UPS*, 13.

134 David W. Chappell

emerges, namely, the *ability to liberate others*: "A bodhisattva is one who can always awaken the minds of sentient beings." Accordingly, besides nonattachment to oneself and praising the Three Jewels, the seeds for enlightenment involve both having compassion for others, and also "saving sentient beings from immeasurable suffering and afflictions." Finally, the chapter gives lists of bodhisattva practices that include delight in the accomplishments of others.[24] Accordingly, the marks of a bodhisattva involve not just a push toward enlightenment and compassion toward others, but effectiveness in helping others, and being happy when others benefit.

In Chapter Seven on Making Vows, we again find that healing the sick is emphasized, and see for the first time an affirmation on harmonizing those who are separated by disagreements.[25] In the next chapter we read that a true bodhisattva has equanimity for both friends and foes. Also, if he has little wealth, he should give first to the poor, and second to the saṅgha (lit., "field of blessings"), or first to the poor, and second to the rich.[26]

Chapter Nine has many heroic illustrations of bodhisattva activity from previous lives of the Buddha, including using the power of his vows to seek rebirth in difficult circumstances, or to be reborn as a fish, a beast, or a medicine tree, or to sacrifice oneself for others, such as when the Buddha gave his body to save the life of a pigeon. This elevation of compassionate actions to mythic proportions in these *jātaka* tales is matched in Chapter Ten by equating the path to enlightenment with enlightenment itself: "The path of enlightenment is enlightenment, and enlightenment is the path."[27] This in effect raises compassionate and ethical behavior to an absolute level when this behavior represents the bodhisattva vows in the quest for enlightenment. Accordingly, the text is then able to argue that "to benefit others is to benefit oneself"[28] since benefiting others is the bodhisattva path, which is equal to enlightenment.

The theme of "self-benefit, benefit-others" (*zili lita*)[29] in Chapter Ten of *UPS* places considerable emphasis on teaching and speaking, and is expanded in Chapter Eleven by listing a number of related personal prerequisites that should be developed in preparation for teaching others,[30] followed by a list of various positive inner qualities. Finally, Chapter Eleven proposes specific ethical practices, such as not publicizing the errors of others, nor publicizing their secrets, nor what they would be ashamed of. While this follows the traditional Buddhist emphasis on correct speech, the text also echoes the guidelines from

---

[24] *Ibid.*,17-18.

[25] *Ibid.*, 31.

[26] *Ibid.*, 35-36.

[27] *Ibid.*, 41, T.24.1042b.22-23.

[28] *Ibid.*, 43, T.24.1043a.10.

[29] This phrase has become the popular shorthand for this idea (e.g., T.24.1043c.9, 1044b.7).

[30] These include perfecting eight dharmas in order to benefit oneself and others: longevity, an attractive appearance, great physical strength, noble birth, wealth, being male, eloquence, and fearlessness when speaking to large groups of people. See Ibid., 50.

Chapter Seven to harmonize those in contention, and especially to have compassion for one's enemies:

> He always shows kindness to his foes. When friends and foes are suffering, he first saves his foes. He is compassionate to those who scold him. Seeing someone steal his things, he keeps silent and unmoved. He has compassion for those who come to beat him. He sees sentient beings as his parents.... When harm befalls him, he returns it with good.... He is willing to make others happy through his own suffering.[31]

This passage expresses a radical VALUE REVERSAL so that foes are given preferential treatment over friends. In addition to seeking to harmonize those who are divided, bodhisattvas are taught not to alienate those who are at odds with them, and are given guidelines emphasizing the importance of reconciliation. The *UPS* teaching to favor and have compassion for one's enemy provides an important Buddhist background to the nonviolent response of the Dalai Lama to the Chinese who invaded Tibet. Not only is this an act of compassion, but in Chapter Twelve we learn that not making a distinction between friend and foe is also the perfection of wisdom.[32] However, this is not a passive acceptance of foes, nor just to see "all foes as dear friends,"[33] but to actively "benefit one's foes,"[34] with a willingness to transform them.[35]

Having equanimity and compassion for one's enemies, and even seeing them as intimate family members ("dear ones") and favoring them, is not just a matter of resolving interpersonal conflict, such as within the safety of the saṅgha. Rather, it had practical action that had economic and legal dimensions, such as not reporting robbers who steal from you, and having compassion for those who physically fight and attack you. This must raise serious questions when we consider women who suffer sexual aggression, or those like modern Tibetans who have been assaulted militarily and been conquered by force. Even though the Dalai Lama has received the Nobel Peace Prize for his non-violent policies toward China and his freedom from hatred and vengeance, the concept of loving your enemies is not without many ethical problems.[36]

---

[31] *Ibid.*, 52-53, T.24.1045a.

[32] *Ibid.*, 56, T.24.1045c. In Chapter Sixteen and Eighteen the bodhisattva is again told to "benefit both foes and friends without discrimination." See *ibid.*, 81, 90; and T.24.105lb, 1053a.

[33] *Ibid.*, 95, T.24.1054a.

[34] *Ibid.*, 76, T.24.1050b.

[35] *Ibid.*, 57, T.24.1046a.

[36] See the recent publications by Donald W. Shriver, Jr., *An Ethic for Enemies: Forgiveness in Politics* (New York : Oxford University Press, 1995) and by Stephen J. Pope, *The Evolution of Altruism and the Ordering of Love* (Washington, D.C. : Georgetown University Press, 1994).

Regarding the practice of giving, Chapter Twelve makes a distinction between two categories: (1) the field of blessings (the Buddhist saṅgha) and (2) the field of poverty. The bodhisattva gives to the first to increase conditions for happiness, and he gives to the second in order to eliminate the causes for suffering.[37] This balance between giving attention to the Buddhist community and to the world as having equal value is emphasized in a variety of apocryphal Buddhist texts in China that emphasize filial devotion and social welfare.[38] (Since this social compassion extends not only to the poor, but especially the sick, in China the term "field of compassion" (*beitian*) was substituted for the term "field of poverty.")

This balance is seen in Chapter Thirteen which explicitly aims at making other laity into disciples, but which also teaches lay disciple to increase positive thoughts and "to make offerings indiscriminately to all Buddhist and non-Buddhist practitioners as far as he can."[39] It is clear that the ethical framework presented in the *UPS* is not legalistic, nor exclusivistic, but seeks to develop people first in their own life and context, and later, when they are ready, to introduce them to the teachings and practices of Buddhism in terms of which all divisions are to be harmonized and all afflictions pacified.

6. Secular and Non-Buddhist Learning

As seen in the debate over welfare policy in the United States Congress, suffering for the benefit of others involves many practical issues, and so the *UPS* advocates the study of non-Buddhist and secular learning:

> Although secular studies are not beneficial, he learns them for the sake of sentient beings. What he learns should be the best in the world. Although he masters the most superior worldly learning, he does not become arrogant.[40]

Later in Chapter Twelve this theme is repeated as part of the five dharmas to be practiced: faith, compassion, courage, "reading secular texts without becoming weary," and "learning all secular business without becoming tired."[41] Similarly, the text encourages using "worldly languages and means that one knows to transform sentient beings so that they will not be covetous."[42]

The study of non-Buddhist writings is significant in not being primarily aimed at making others into Buddhists, but at developing in others an attitude free from covetousness. Studying non-Buddhist writings not only provides a

---

[37] *Ibid.*, 55, T.24.1045c.

[38] See Kenneth K. S. Ch'en, *The Chinese Transformation of Buddhism* (Princeton: Princeton University Press, 1973), especially Chapters Two and Six.

[39] Heng-ching, *UPS*, 61, T.24.1046c.24-25.

[40] Heng-ching, *UPS*, 53, T.24.1045a.

[41] *Ibid.*, 56, T.24.1045c.

[42] *Ibid.*, 57, T.24.1046a.

basis for interfaith dialogue through studying other religions,[43] but also could embrace developing skill in psychological therapy, or could even include economic theory and political action since its goal would challenge a primary value necessary for capitalism and consumerism, namely, greed. The personal values of cooperation rather than competition, of contentment rather than covetousness, are consistent with the Buddhist goal of inner serenity. However, by extending these values into a social goal by seeking to have others embody these values have consequences that challenge the 45 assumptions of consumerism within American economic and political ideology.[44]

7. The Six Perfections as the Ethical Framework

Chapter Fifteen follows the chapter on receiving the lay bodhisattva precepts, and gives advice on deepening the practice by emphasizing the attitudes of faith, compassion, effort, freedom from jealousy and arrogance, and staying close to the Mahāyāna community of *kalyāṇamitra*. Chapter Sixteen adds to this by emphasizing constant mindfulness and devotion to the Buddha. Chapter Seventeen extends this to an emphasis on making offerings to the Dharma and Saṅgha as well, so that all Three Jewels in the "field of blessings" are properly reverenced. These three chapters all cultivate the internal relations of the Buddhist community, and have little to do with ethical actions in society.

The *UPS* returns to more worldly concerns in Chapter Eighteen which moves back to a balanced emphasis on service to the world and to Buddhism, to dear ones and to foes equally, to Buddhist studies and to secular learning. This non-discriminating practice that seeks neither reward nor favor for one's efforts is only possible, however, by practicing the six perfections. In order to practice giving properly, the bodhisattva has to cultivate the other five perfections: morality, patience, zeal, mindfulness, and non-discriminating wisdom. Accordingly, the ethical framework for Mahāyāna precepts is the practice of all six perfections, which enables the moral injunctions to be practiced in an enlightened way. The cultivation of the six perfections is foundational for the lay Buddhist ethical life, and is the major concern of the last ten chapters of the *UPS*.

Chapter Nineteen is an extended discussion of giving, and is by far the longest chapter in the *UPS*. Much of the discussion celebrates giving as a means for one's own spiritual advancement. Nevertheless, since the text offers guidance both to those who seek wealth, longevity, and a better rebirth, as well as to those developing inner spirituality, it accepts the fact that readers may be at

---

[43] See David Chappell, "Buddhist Responses to Religious Pluralism: What Are the Ethical Issues?" in Charles Wei-hsun Fu and Sandra A. Wawrytko, eds., *Buddhist Ethics and Modern Science* (New York: Greenwood Press, 1991), 355-370 for a review of the range of Buddhist attitudes to other religions.

[44] See John Cobb and Herbert Daly, *For the Common Good: Consumerism* (Boston: Beacon Press, 1989).

different levels of spiritual maturity and is offering helpful guidelines for these different people.

Chapter Nineteen ends with an extended description of various social welfare projects that a lay bodhisattva should undertake, including such practical ventures as learning medicine, building hospitals, road repair, building guest houses, digging wells, planting fruit trees, building bridges, maintaining canals, protecting animals, massaging tired travelers, making shade with umbrellas, providing people with ear picks, consoling the grieving, etc.[45]

The two character phrase for compassion (*cibei*) is usually broken into two parts: *ci* increases a sense of affinity, kinship, or kindness, such as being able to see you enemies as members of your own family. This is achieved through the practice of mindfulness. On the other hand, *bei* involves both awareness and action: it not only increases affinity, but it also relieves suffering. At this point it involves the practice of giving.

> Good son, if a person can see even one hair's breadth of goodness in
> one's foes rather than their unwholesomeness, you should know that
> he is practicing kindness. When his foes are suffering from illness
> and if he goes visiting, takes care of them, and gives them what they
> need, you should know that he is cultivating compassion.[46]

Based on these last chapters, it becomes clear that the study of Mahāyāna ethics cannot be restricted to the study of bodhisattva precepts, but must involve the other practices of the six perfections. Ethics is not only a matter of social restraint to prevent wrong doing, nor even the cultivation of various personal virtues, but also means the development of new understanding, awareness, attitudes, and positive action. Basically, Buddhist precepts focused on restraint, whereas bodhisattva vows, mindfulness, and wisdom developed the perspective, the clarity, and the motivation for evaluating complex social conflicts and for initiating constructive action.

8. Preliminary Conclusions

1. THE VALUE OF THE LAITY. In seeking an introduction to Mahāyāna social ethics that might provide some general principles, the *Upāsaka Precepts Sūtra* was chosen as the focus because of its enduring importance for lay

---

[45] The development of Buddhist social welfare in China is elaborated by Michihata Ryōshū, *Chūgoku bukkyō to shakai fukushi jigyo* (Kyoto: Heirakuji Shoten, 1967).

[46] Heng-ching, *UPS*, 187, T.24.1074c.15-18. In this case, the Taisho edition does not use *bei*: for the final word translated as compassion, but this reading would be consistent with the distinction drawn between the two in the previous line, namely, that "kindness (*ci*) can only increase affinity but cannot relieve suffering. Compassion (*bei*) is not so. It not only increases affinity but also relieves [pain]." (1074c14-15) Accordingly, I follow the reading given by Ven. Heng-ching.

Buddhists from earliest Mahāyāna up to the present. Throughout the *UPS* the life of a lay bodhisattva, is more highly praised than that of ordained bodhisattvas because it has the capacity to give to others both the dharma and physical help. Since the obstacles for practice are also greater, the text repeatedly emphasizes that the effort and achievements of lay bodhisattvas are greater than those of clergy. This provides an important revalorization of lay society that can be a basis for contemporary Buddhist social ethics and is a fitting response to the age-old social critique of Buddhism as undermining the family and being world-denying.

2. FAMILY, FRIENDS, AND TEACHERS. With lay society as the context, the text emphasizes that priority should be given to six relationships as primary. The family emerges as the most important bond, and one's teacher and one's friends are placed in the midst of the kinship bonds of family and marriage, and given equal priority. However, a central question involves identifying who are the teachers and friends to be honored.

As we have seen, the good friends in the non- Mahāyāna Sigālaka texts played a role that parallels the role of the modern state: they will look after you and your property when you are inattentive, they will be a refuge when you are afraid, they will not desert you when you are in trouble, and they will show concern for your children. Accordingly, we can see a parallel between the earlier texts and the modern emphasis on home and nation in the non- Mahāyāna Sigālaka texts. By contrast, the *UPS* consisently worked from within the social framework of the new Mahāyāna support group, the *kalyānamitra,* which is based not on spatial proximity as found in nationalism, but a kinship of shared values: your spiritual companions will teach you to cultivate good teachings and to avoid bad ones, to help you when you are afraid, and will strengthen you against laxity.[47] Friends are redefined from their role as supporters of your family and property to those who can guide you in right understanding and right action.

In the *UPS* the roles of friend and teacher become much closer, since friends are defined not in terms of their ability to protect our property, but to guide us toward enlightenment: "When a lay person arouses aspirations for enlightenment, the four deva kings and also kings in the Akaniṣṭha and other heavens pleasantly and with great surprise exclaim, 'Now, we have a teacher of men and gods.'"[48]Although less sectarian than monastic rules, it is clear that the *UPS* emphasizes that a primary loyalty should be given to those who nurture and influence you for good and for enlightenment. In the *UPS* text, the home relationships of parents-spouse-servants are balanced by the spiritual relationships of teachers-*kalyāṇamitra*-clergy.

3. DEVELOPMENTAL ETHICS. Lawrence Kohlberg has recently argued that all people must grow through several inevitable stages of moral development, beginning with conventional morality (defined by service to

---

[47] Heng-ching, *Upāsaka Precepts,* 64 (with slight revisions).

[48] *Ibid.,* 6.

family and friends), and later moving on to meeting the needs of society. After passing through a period of disillusionment with the hypocrisy and arbitrariness of social structures, conventional morality is replaced by a universal sense of compassion beyond the limitations of the conventional structures of family and society, and moving toward a sense of common kinship free from distinctions between friend and foe, self and others.[49]

Both Kohlberg and the *UPS* show that ethics is much more than moral injunctions and the development of inner virtues. Instead, they discuss a hierarchy of ethical worldviews and values, and seek to move individuals from their limited identities to a more open and universal worldview permeated by compassion and filled with effective actions to relieve the suffering of all.

In both Kohlberg and the *UPS*, the commitment to one's local society and nation dissolves as a primary commitment, and is replaced by a more universal sense of kinship that transcends the distinctions of geography and between friend and foe. However, the difference between Kohlberg and the *UPS* is that for the *UPS* family relations remain at the same primary level as spiritual companions, whereas for Kohlberg they do not. In this sense, the *UPS* balances the family with the universal rather than replaces the family, and so the *UPS* is close to the feminist critique of Kohlberg by Carol Gilligan that emphasizes the ongoing priority of family relationships as exemplified by the unbroken mother-daughter relationship.[50]

The *UPS* developmental view of ethics can also be seen in the advice given to a bodhisattva about how to cultivate lay disciples (Chapter Thirteen), gently leading them from their worldly concerns to a more selfless pattern of service. However, it can also be seen within the advice given to the bodhisattvas themselves about arousing the motivation to seek enlightenment (Chapter Two), since they may begin from selfishness, and also may have moments when their motivation is less than free of discrimination and selfish interest. At a beginning stage, lay bodhisattvas may still be concerned for wealth and longevity, and may still identify primarily with their family and friends. Nevertheless, priority is given to adorning their life with blessings through giving, morality, and zeal in order to avoid trouble and to be successful. But the goal is always to go beyond this conventional level of morality to a more universal compassion that is the distinctive quality of lay bodhisattva practice. Accordingly, the *UPS* embodies levels and stages of ethic action that are reflected in the six perfections, and which are also echoed by such Western theorists as Lawrence Kohlberg who devised six stages of moral development.

4. CARING FOR ENEMIES. Based on this balance between a physical family and a spiritual family, the task of seeking happiness and avoiding

---

[49] See Lawrence Kohlberg, *The Philosophy of Moral Development* (San Francisco: Harper & Row, 1981) and *The Psychology of Moral Development* (San Francisco: Harper & Row, 1984).

[50] Carol Gilligan, *In a Different Voice: Psychological Theory and Women's Development* (Cambridge, Mass.: Harvard University Press, 1982).

suffering becomes redefined. The six major lay bodhisattva precepts function as moral restraints as preventive measures to avoid suffering, as do many of the twenty-eight minor precepts (Chapter Fourteen). The other kinds of actions required in the minor precepts are injunctions to serve parents, teachers and the sick, and to reverence the Three Jewels of Buddhism. Besides these traditional precepts, the major novelty is the last precept instructing a bodhisattva "who comes across a sick person along the road" not to desert him, but to look after him and arrange a place for him. It seems that the precepts preserve an early and conservative view of Buddhist ethics, and it is only this last precept (that may have been added on) that hints at the broad ethical vision of Mahāyāna. Accordingly, to discover more about this social activist position with regard to human suffering beyond one's limited social and saṅgha obligations we must look elsewhere in the text.

Perhaps one reason why Mahāyāna ethics are not adequately reflected in the lay bodhisattva precepts is because precepts are usually forms of restraint, whereas the distinctive values, worldview, and practices that enable bodhisattvas to treat enemies as dear family members and that support social welfare activities are to be found not in precepts but in prose exhortations.[51] This is confirmed by the *UPS* when it defines a bodhisattva in Chapter One not just as someone who does good accumulates good karma, but also as someone who had aroused the aspiration for enlightenment (*bodhicitta*).[52]

In the *UPS* view of the world, bodhisattvas are given the highest value short of the Buddha because of their aspiration for the supreme enlightenment of a Buddha (*bodhicitta*), and the value of all actions is measured in terms of this intention. As a consequence, the motivation to save others, namely, compassion, becomes the highest ethical attitude in the *UPS*.

Within the Mahāyāna worldview of the *UPS*, a warning is given, however, that if one helps others as a method to get a reward, then the practice is not giving, but trade. Accordingly, all the six perfections of a bodhisattva need to be cultivated in order to guide the practice of giving to and saving others. The six perfections are divided into two groups: giving, morality, and zeal adorn life with blessings, whereas patience, mindfulness, and wisdom adorn life with wisdom.[53] The wisdom of a bodhisattva is to see that the others are not separate from ourselves, so that we respond to ease their sufferings and are joyous in their accomplishments. Furthermore, wisdom means that we are free from discriminating between foes and friends, and have no expectations nor need of reward.

---

[51] A focus on bodhisattva, precepts greatly limits the range of Mahāyāna ethics. For example, see the recent volume of seventeen essays edited by Charles Wei-hsun Fu and Sandra A. Wawrytko, *Buddhist Behavioral Codes and the Modern World* (Westport, Connecticut: Greenwood Press, 1994).

[52] *UPS*, 3.

[53] See *UPS* Chapter 12, 54, T.24.1045b.

The motivation for ethical behavior expressed in Chapter Two by the twelve examples of reasons for seeking enlightenment can be broken down into three areas: one is self-interest (wealth and longevity), and another is a striving for excellence and superiority (to be the best, to consolidate moral victories, to be superior to gods, and better than non-Buddhists and members of the two vehicles). These reasons are all expressions of individuation, and represent two-thirds of the list (numbers 1, 3, 4, 5, 6, 7, 8, 9). By contrast, only one-third (numbers 2, 10, 11, 12) affirm helping others. The two most striking examples of these in the *UPS* involve caring for anonymous sick people and enemies.

The ethics of restraint can be argued on the basis of self-interest, and legislated by governments as bringing the greatest good to the greatest number. In addition, virtue ethics can be encouraged and cultivated as expressions of superiority and individual moral satisfaction, as can be seen in the Confucian tradition. However, caring for sick strangers and for enemies, two distinctive recommendations for lay bodhisattvas in the *UPS*, exceed this conventional wisdom.

Although the illustrations offered in the *UPS* might serve as inspirational stories of heroic individual actions, they will hardly be adequate for social norms. Nevertheless, based on the present theories of "tough love" which have demonstrated the necessity of parents providing structure and limits for their children, and healthy families needing boundaries and mutual agreements among their members, loving strangers and enemies "as dear ones" need not involve chaos or total self-sacrifice. Being a lay bodhisattva need not mean total indulgence of the whims of others, and the removal of consequences from their actions. Instead, it only demands that the sick and enemies be seen as kin, as members of our family, as being connected to us, so that their suffering becomes our-suffering.

Etymologically the word kindness is not first of all an emotion, but the recognition that others are the same-kind-as-us. Similarly, according to the *UPS* interpretation of *cibei,* compassion, it is not first feeling with the other (compassion) but first a recognition of affinity, that then leads to helpful actions to relieve suffering. The primary basis for this action is not based on enhancing our own individuation, but instead on compassion. Specifically, we learn that compassion involves two aspects, its transformation of our self-identity to a sense of connectedness with the fate others. Specifically, the character ci in the phrase *cibei* (compassion) means a sense of affinity, kinship, or kindness, such as being able to see you enemies as members of your own family, which is achieved through the practice of mindfulness. This sense of kinship with others, even sick strangers and enemies, is the understanding that Mahāyāna posits as foundational for its ethics. Since this is only achieved through the practice of mindfulness and wisdom, it becomes clear that Mahāyāna incorporates these as essential aspects of its ethical platform.

5. UTILITARIAN RESULTS. Finally, *bei* in the phrase *cibei* (compassion) involves both awareness and action: it not only increases affinity, but it also relieves suffering. At this point it involves the practice of giving and the

achievement of practical results. At this point, Mahāyāna moves beyond virtue ethics to adopt utilitarian criteria.

Bodhisattvas are defined as those who are committed to seeking to become a Buddha, and the *Lotus Sūtra* constantly shows that a Buddha is not just someone who has self-enlightenment, but also has the capacity to teach and save other beings. Thus, a primary criterion for bodhisattva practice is its effectiveness in saving others. The *UPS* adds to this definition by asserting that laity are superior to clergy because they are able not only to teach but also to give materialistic benefits. Saving others involves meeting the physical needs of others as well as the spiritual.

These five conclusions do not begin to address complex ethical problems. Although they provide a certain profile of the lay bodhisattva, their validity and usefulness now need to be measured by trying to apply them as a guide to various ethical decisions. But perhaps this is a task for Buddhists rather than scholars.

CHAPTER 11

THE *SARVODAYA* MOVEMENT'S QUEST FOR PEACE AND SOCIAL AWAKENING

George D. Bond

The *Sarvodaya Shramadana* movement in Sri Lanka represents one of the earliest examples of what has come to be called engaged Buddhism. *Sarvodaya* began as a grassroots development movement that drew its inspiration from Buddhist thought. In this way it contrasted sharply with most other development organizations that were based on combinations of Judeo-Christian and Western materialist ideals. *Sarvodaya* interpreted Buddhist thought and values to establish ideals for social change and development. Breaking with most interpretations of Theravāda Buddhist thought, *Sarvodaya* argued that the dharma entails a dual liberation--the liberation not only of the individual but also of the society. Neither the traditional Buddhist monastic interpreters of the Buddha's teachings nor the reformers had stressed so clearly as *Sarvodaya* the implications of the dharma for social change. *Sarvodaya* has insisted that the welfare of the individual is bound up with the welfare of others, and that for there to be true liberation for the individual there must also be true liberation for the village, the nation and the world. This philosophy--with its obvious implications for peace--has provided the moral compass that *Sarvodaya* has followed for four decades in Sri Lanka. In this paper we examine the history of *Sarvodaya*'s work to realize this ideal of dual liberation through practical programs for the people of Sri Lanka. The path has not been easy for *Sarvodaya* has encountered both obstacles and opponents, and in the process, as *Sarvodaya* has evolved and grown from a small volunteer movement to a large NGO, its vision of what it means to realize these Buddhist ideals in practice has also evolved and grown.

1. *Sarvodaya*'s First Decade: 1958-1968

The *Sarvodaya* Movement began during that period in the late fifties, when Sri Lanka was alive with the enthusiasm of the post-independence Buddhist

Revival. The idea for the movement was born in a series of work-camps held for the students and faculty of Nalanda College, Colombo. The leader of *Sarvodaya*, A.T. Ariyaratne, was a faculty member at Nalanda College, and he organized these work-camps in the village of Kanatolluwa, a poor, low-caste village in the North Central Province of Sri Lanka. The camps were begun as an "educational experiment" to give urban youth the opportunity to experience village life and assist the people there. The seed that was planted with the first work-camps grew and became the *Sarvodaya Shramadana* Movement. The name of the new movement reflected the dominant influences behind it.

(1) The first influence was that of Mahatma Gandhi who coined this term "*Sarvodaya*" to refer to his village development movement in India. The *Sarvodaya* movement in Sri Lanka was strongly influenced by Gandhi and his philosophy of social change and development. The Sri Lankan *Sarvodaya* adopted the Gandhian values of truth, non-violence and self-denial as central principles for its philosophy of development.

(2) The second influence came from the Buddhist philosophy of Sri Lanka and particularly from the interpretation of Buddhism that arose during the Buddhist revival. One of the central themes of the Buddhist revival was the expansion of the role of laypersons in Theravāda Buddhism. The leaders of the Buddhist revival assumed that the goal of the religion, *nibbāna,* was as available to lay persons as it was to monks. This belief led, for example, to the insight meditation movement in which many lay Buddhists began to do *vipassanā* meditation, a practice traditionally taught only to monks and nuns.[1] But whereas the Buddhist revival generally opened the goal of liberation to lay persons, most of the reformers continued to view liberation as an individual goal. *Sarvodaya*, however, took this reform one step further by arguing for the liberation of society as well. This reforming insight is evident in the definition that they gave to the term *Sarvodaya*; instead of defining it as Gandhi had, as "the uplift of all," the Sri Lankans interpreted *Sarvodaya* to mean "the awakening of all." The mission of the *Sarvodaya* movement from the start was to bring about social transformation through "awakening" people and society--by which they meant setting in motion a spiritual development process of empowering people to effect qualitative changes in their lives and in their society. Awakening referred to a holistic process of change; a process that had to be collective and integrated. This understanding of the process of awakening led *Sarvodaya*'s teaching that development had to take place on the individual, family, communal, national and global levels.

(3) The other term in the name of this movement, *Shramadana,* is also important for understanding the nature of this alternative development movement. *Shramadana* means the gift of service or labor. It is based on an ancient South Asian and Buddhist conception of how society should function in harmony. *Shramadana* was the governing insight that grew out of *Sarvodaya*'s

---

[1] For a discussion of the insight meditation movement, see my book *The Buddhist Revival in Sri Lanka* (Columbia, SC: University of South Carolina Press, 1988).

original work camps and became the earliest application of Buddhist ideals to development practice. To begin the process of development in a village, *Sarvodaya* organized *Shramadana* camps or work camps in which an entire village joined forces with volunteers from other villages to build or repair some common facility such as a school or a road. *Sarvodaya* found that one of the biggest problems in poor villages was apathy, but that this apathy could be counteracted by showing the villagers that major problems could be solved by self-effort if everyone worked together. The *Shramadana* camps accomplished major projects of infrastructure development, but more importantly they began the process of "awakening" as people started to understand their situation and to take responsibility for changing it. The *Shramadana* camps provided an intensive microcosm in which the people could live out *Sarvodaya*'s vision and come to a new understanding of how society could work. The importance of the *Shramadana*, camps for *Sarvodaya*'s approach to development is summed up in the slogan, "We build the road, and the road builds us."

During the first decade of its existence, *Sarvodaya* was largely a *Shramadana* or work camp movement, operating at the grassroots level and fueled by volunteerism. This was a time of great enthusiasm. There was very little outside funding--only the voluntary contributions of Sri Lankans and a great pool of volunteer workers willing to assist with village development for the poorest rural people. As a humanistic, grassroots, Buddhist-based development movement, *Sarvodaya* found great acceptance in rural Sri Lanka.

2. *Sarvodaya*'s Second Decade

The second decade witnessed the evolution of *Sarvodaya* from a work camp movement to a Non-Governmental Organization (NGO) with a Buddhist philosophy for grassroots development. During this period *Sarvodaya* articulated its Buddhist philosophy for development work and set up programs that would bring about the kind of dual liberation that it regarded as essential to the *dharma*.

Sarvodaya's interpretation of Buddhist thought emphasized the social and communal aspects. *Sarvodaya* interpreted the goal of "awakening" to mean enabling individuals and society to overcome greed, hatred and ignorance by developing generosity, non-violence and compassion. To explain the Buddhist steps for reaching this goal, *Sarvodaya* focused on two sets of ethical principles: the four "*brahmavihāras*" and the four principles of group behavior, *saṃgraha vastu*.[2] The four "*brahmavihāras*" were traditionally taught in Theravāda as practices of *samādhi* meditation that resulted in the *jhāna*s or lofty trance states. In texts such as the *Visuddhimagga*, these meditations did not necessarily lead to social involvement or have social implications. Rather, the original purpose of

---

[2] Dr. Ariyaratne has discussed these principles in many publications, including *Sarvodaya Shramadana: Growth of a People's Movement* (Colombo: Sarvodaya Press, 1974) and *Collected Works*, Vol. I , 51 *ff* (Colombo: Sarvodaya Press, 1989 -).

meditating on loving kindness, compassion, sympathetic joy and equanimity seems to have been to purify and calm the mind of the meditator. *Sarvodaya*, however, gave these four ethical meditations a distinctly social interpretation. Ariyaratne said, for example, that "One who cultivates loving kindness or *mettā* towards all cannot ignore suffering and evil that abound around him. Here are the hungry, the diseased, the ignorant, the disunited and the exploited who have to be lifted up. One who believes in the welfare of all has to go in search of these people and strive to remove the causes of their suffering."[3] *Sarvodaya* gives the other three "*brahmavihāra*s" a similarly practical and social interpretation focusing on the ethical quality.

Sarvodaya stressed the four principles of group behavior because they also could be interpreted as guidelines for the application of the dharma to society. *Sarvodaya* used these four principles, i.e., *dāna*, generosity; *piya vacana*, pleasant speech; *attha cariyā*, constructive conduct; and *samānattatā*, equality, to provide rationales for *Sarvodaya*'s social programs. Ariyaratne wrote, for example, that "*dāna*, or sharing, stresses the equitable distribution of wealth and exploitation-free society…The concept of '*dāna*' or sharing was not born out of the reaction against an exploiting class…(but) it was purely based on the knowledge that overcoming craving (or *taṇhā*) is the sole means to supreme happiness."[4]

Sarvodaya employed these values to craft an alternative form of development to the dominant Western-materialist model that had been applied in Sri Lanka since the colonial period. Ariyaratne rejected this model because it was based on the profit motive and fueled by human greed. He argued that development should lead to a new society based on cooperation rather than on competition. *Sarvodaya* defined its goal of 'awakening' as enabling individuals and society to overcome greed, hatred and ignorance by developing generosity, non-violence and compassion.

Sarvodaya's model of development focused on the "poorest of the poor" and used a "basic human needs" approach to assist them. The idea of basic human needs, which had been developed by various international development planners, had as its centerpiece a list of the fundamental requirements for an adequate standard of living.[5] *Sarvodaya* devised its own list of the "basic human needs" as seen from the perspective of Buddhist values. *Sarvodaya*'s list stressed that in addition to the standard items such as food, clothing and housing, people also needed "a clean and beautiful environment including a psychological

---

[3] *Sarvodaya Shramadana: Growth of a People's Movement*, 14.

[4] *Collected Works*, Vol. I, 51.

[5] See *Basic Human Needs: A Framework for Action*, John McHale and Magda McHale, A Report to the U.N. Environment Program, Transaction Books, 1978, 12 *ff*. Also *The Planetary Bargain: Proposals for a New International Economic Order to Meet Human Needs*, policy paper of the Aspen Institute for Humanistic Studies, 1975.

infra-structure," and "cultural and spiritual development."[6] Because *Sarvodaya*'s concept of development was closely tied to its understanding of awakening, it held that true development involves more than economic, political and social factors; it also involves moral, cultural and spiritual factors. These Buddhist elements were as essential to development, in *Sarvodaya*'s view, as the secular elements. All of these elements together contribute to a process of integrated development leading to the awakening of the individual and the society.

During the second decade, *Sarvodaya* embarked on an ambitious campaign to spread the movement; they called this the "100 Villages Development Campaign". The campaign was so successful that by the end of the decade *Sarvodaya* was active in some 2000 villages across the island. In 1969, as a result of the successes of the movement, Ariyaratne received the Ramon Magsaysay International Award for Community Leadership. This recognition from abroad brought increased prestige to the movement and its leaders. In 1972 *Sarvodaya* was legally incorporated as a Non-Governmental Organization and in that year received its first outside funding. Two European foundations NOVIB and FAIM granted some 250,000 Rupees to *Sarvodaya* for its development work. In that year also, Dr. Ariyaratne resigned his faculty post at Nalanda College to devote full-time to leading the growing *Sarvodaya* movement.

3. *Sarvodaya*'s Third Decade

During the third decade of its existence, from the mid-70s to the mid-80s, *Sarvodaya* continued its rapid growth as a movement. It had become a national movement and now found itself thrust into national issues.

By the end of the 1980s *Sarvodaya* was engaged in development work in some 8000 villages throughout Sri Lanka. To oversee and coordinate this village work *Sarvodaya* found it necessary to build a huge infrastructure of administrative centers, development education centers, vocational training centers, rural leadership training centers and experimental farms. *Sarvodaya* extended its movement to all parts of the island, even the predominantly Tamil areas of the North. It became by far the largest NGO in Sri Lanka and the only organization--including the government--that was able to work and travel in all parts of the country as the civil war intensified.

One reason for this rapid expansion of the scope of *Sarvodaya*'s work was the rapid increase in donor funding that occur-red during this period. In 1980 *Sarvodaya* received only 30 million rupees in philanthropic funding but by 1988 it was receiving some 185 million rupees annually. In 1974 there had been only

---

[6] *Sarvodaya*'s list of the ten "basic human needs" included: 1) a clean and beautiful environment including a psychological infrastructure, 2) a safe and adequate water supply, 3) basic requirements of clothing, 4) a regular balanced diet, 5) a simple abode, 6) basic health care services, 7) transport and communication services, 8) fuel, 9) continuing education for all, and 10) cultural and spiritual development. This list is discussed in *Collected Works,* Vol. II, 80.

four donor foundations, but within a few years there were over twenty. This level of funding not only made *Sarvodaya* the largest NGO in the country, but also gave it increased responsibility for solving the pressing problems of the country.

This responsibility intensified in August 1983 when the country erupted with terrible ethnic riots. In retaliation for terrorist activities in the northern part of the country, Sinhalese mobs--at least some of which were organized by right-wing politicians--attacked Tamil civilians and property throughout the southern part of the island. Houses and shops were burned to the ground, people were killed and thousands of others were forced to flee to refugee camps. When this occurred, Ariyaratne and *Sarvodaya* took the lead in caring for the refugees and in seeking to bring peace to the country. In October 1983, *Sarvodaya* organized a national conference of religious and civil leaders to explore ways to solve the conflict. Over two thousand leaders filled the Bandaranaike Memorial International Conference Hall and drew up a "People's Declaration for National Peace and Harmony." This Declaration was drawn up by *Sarvodaya* and expressed many of the basic principles of the movement. For example, the document echoed Buddhist teachings about peace such as the verse from the *Dhammapada* stating that, "Hatred does not cease by hatred; only by non-hatred does hatred cease." In language that reflected *Sarvodaya*'s view of peace and development, the Declaration said that the aim of the conference was "to create a suitable spiritual, mental, social and intellectual environment for arriving at possible solutions in a friendly dialogue, based on the principles of truth and non-violence."[7]

At the conclusion of the conference, *Sarvodaya* declared that it would conduct a peace march from Kataragama in the southern part of Sri Lanka to Jaffna in the north, a distance of 1000 miles. This march would begin on December 6, 1983 and last 100 days. In a country racked with violent conflict, such a march constituted a brave effort at peace. *Sarvodaya* explained the rational for the march by saying that "History records that the Buddha undertook a series of walks in his 45 years of existence for the well being of humanity...He walked long distances to settle disputes among warring communities on more than one occasion. Once the Buddha visited Sri Lanka to bring peace between two communities who were preparing for war."[8] The other obvious precedent for this march was the marches of Gandhi in India. When the day for the march came, Dr. Ariyaratne and thousands of Sri Lankans eager for peace began the long march at Kiri Vihara near Kataragama. Before they had gone very far, however, President J.R. Jayawardene called on them to postpone the march and they complied with his urgent request. Other peace marches were conducted in the next few years by Dr. Ariyaratne and his supporters. Two marches were held in 1985 and 1986 to Sri Pada in an effort to bring peace in the hill country. Other marches were made to the Temple of the Tooth in Kandy.

In addition, *Sarvodaya* became one of the major relief agencies during this period. Western foundations who dealt with Sri Lanka appealed to *Sarvodaya* to use its network of development centers to coordinate the relief supplies and funds for the refugees of this violence. This led to a great increase in the scope of *Sarvodaya*'s work during this period.

Largely as a result of this noble work during the third decade of *Sarvodaya*'s existence, Ariyaratne received additional international awards. In 1982 he received the King Baudouin Award for International Development from the government of Belgium. In 1986 he became the recipient of the Alan S. Feinstein World Hunger Award from the United States. The awards reflected the heightened national and international status that both Ariyaratne and the *Sarvodaya* Movement had attained.

4. *Sarvodaya*'s Fourth Decade

Sarvodaya has entered its fourth decade and has continued to work for its goals of peace and awakening. The present decade has presented *Sarvodaya* with several challenges which had not arisen before. These challenges might be seen as byproducts of *Sarvodaya*'s success and its becoming the predominant development movement in the country. So far, *Sarvodaya* has met the challenges successfully, but the challenges have raised important questions that *Sarvodaya* must solve in the future. The two major challenges that *Sarvodaya* has encountered can be considered under the heading of challenges from the Sri Lankan government and challenges resulting from their relations with donor foundations.

(1) *Sarvodaya* and the Government of Sri Lanka: *Sarvodaya*'s relations with the government of Sri Lanka had always been cordial until 1989 when President Premadasa came to power. Premadasa and Ariyaratne had been allies in working for development during the previous part of the decade when Premadasa was serving as Prime Minister under President J.R. Jayawardene. When Premadasa became President, however, he launched an all-out attack on Dr. Ariyaratne and the *Sarvodaya* Movement. This attack was carried out on many fronts at once.

- The Government-controlled media carried fallacious stories and editorials charging *Sarvodaya* with corruption, immorality and fraud. [These charges which had no basis in fact were repeated in countless ways in the papers, on television and radio.]
- The Criminal Investigation department took many *Sarvodaya* workers into custody for "questioning" and held them for various periods of time--the worst case being two women who were held without any basis for 2 years.
- In general, various government departments were ordered not to have any dealings with *Sarvodaya*, this included everything from not issuing passports to staff members who needed to go abroad to

> not supplying water from government pumping stations in drought zones.
>
> - The capstone of President Premadasa's attacks on *Sarvodaya* was the appointment of a Presidential Commission of Inquiry into Non-Governmental Organizations. Although in theory this commission was to investigate all NGOs, in actuality it was intended to destroy *Sarvodaya*. The commission had as its agenda proving that all of the charges of corruption and wrong doing that the press had made about *Sarvodaya* were true. The commission spent over two years investigating *Sarvodaya* in exhaustive detail. During this period, almost all of *Sarvodaya*'s work had to cease because Ariyarame and his colleagues were forced to spend countless hours providing reams of information demanded by the commission. The tension that this process of defending themselves against the commission was compounded by the actual death threats that Ariyaratne and *Sarvodaya* officials received during this period.

The government's motives for this campaign of attacks were doubtless complex. However, it seems clear that a major factor behind them was the success and power of *Sarvodaya* and Dr. Ariyaratne. The new President was threatened by Ariyaratne's popularity among the rural masses and resented the way that these voters held Ariyaratne in high regard as a spokesman for Buddhist values and ideals in the country--possibly a more important spokesman than the president. The government also felt threatened by the size and resources of the *Sarvodaya* Movement. In a revealing editorial written during the height of the governments campaign against *Sarvodaya* the government press asked whether *Sarvodaya*, as an NGO that had received foreign funds intended to assist the country, should be allowed "to use against a people's elected government the nearly 100 million worth of property, buildings and vehicles that they have country-wide?"[9]

(2) *Sarvodaya*'s relations with its donor foundations: Since *Sarvodaya* became an NGO in the mid-seventies, most of its funding has come from international foundations such as NOVIB (Netherlands), CIDA (Canada), FNS (W. Germany), NORAD (Norway), Helvetas (Switzerland), ITDG (UK) and also some American donors such as USAID, the Ford Foundation and the Asia Foundation. Although at times these donors sought to steer *Sarvodaya* away from its distinctive development goals, for the most part the donors allowed *Sarvodaya* freedom to do what it thought best. After all, *Sarvodaya* had been spectacularly successful at pursuing its own path and the foundations liked supporting a winner. When the government attacked *Sarvodaya* and brought it before the presidential commission, however, *Sarvodaya*'s relations with its donors began to change. To be sure, the foundations stood by *Sarvodaya* during

---

[9] "It is damaging for Non-Governmental Organizations to get involved in politics," *Sri Lanka Daily News,* April 6, 1992.

the attacks by the government, but when the attacks ended the foundations began to bring out their own challenges to *Sarvodaya*'s programs.

The donors sought to impose on *Sarvodaya* what were seen as "World bank-type financial and administrative systems," and to force it to comply with their foundations' expectations about the meaning of development.[10] Although *Sarvodaya* had from the outset defined development in qualitative terms, the donors now brought pressure on *Sarvodaya* to adopt a quantitative approach and to accept quantitative measures of developmental success. The donors demanded also that *Sarvodaya* further centralize its administration and organization. When the leaders of *Sarvodaya* pointed out that these demands ran counter to *Sarvodaya*'s philosophy and ideals, the Project Director from NOVIB replied, "We are not interested in philosophy. For NOVIB development is a business. There is nothing idealistic about it."[11]

As a part of this attempt to reform *Sarvodaya* in their own image, the donors sought to disentangle what they regarded as *Sarvodaya*'s development organization from the *Sarvodaya* movement. They said, "There is a sense of religion and perhaps even of politics about the 'movement aspects' of *Sarvodaya* which donors are reluctant to support." In short, the donors wanted to transform *Sarvodaya* from a movement into an efficient development agency.

To put *Sarvodaya* back on a "proper" course the donors demanded that more frequent evaluations of *Sarvodaya*'s work be made. They appointed management consultants, assessment missions and monitors who visited *Sarvodaya* to audit the progress of development. These monitors and assessors descended on *Sarvodaya* several times per year and required to be shown everything from the records at the headquarters to the most distant field work sites. During their visits all other work at *Sarvodaya* centers effectively ceased while the *Sarvodaya* officials tried to meet the demands of the monitors. This process of evaluation became so oppressive that in the two years prior to 1993, some eight monitoring missions descended on *Sarvodaya*. Ariyaratne has said of this period, "In a less than two year period as many as 123 recommendations were imposed on *Sarvodaya* which were humanly impossible to implement. The senior staff of *Sarvodaya* had hardly any time to look at and contribute to what was happening in the villages."[12]

The imposition of these monitors on *Sarvodaya* represents a classic instance of the clash between Northern donor foundations and Southern NGOs. The monitors who came to *Sarvodaya* were Western educated experts in economics and management. Some were paid as much as a thousand dollars per day -- in addition to their per diem in the best hotels. These people sat across the table from *Sarvodaya* workers, very few of whom had university degrees and who were paid approximately $1000 per year. The monitors asked questions and

---

[10] *Future Directions of Sarvodaya*, 10.

[11] *Ibid.,* 12.

[12] *Ibid.,* 18.

dictated the terms and as one official told me, "The *Sarvodaya* workers hardly knew what to say."

Often these monitors behaved with arrogance toward the *Sarvodaya* workers, demonstrating clearly that they had no interest in the philosophy and ideals of *Sarvodaya* but only wanted to see results. One monitor who was visiting a village went so far as to demand that the village worker who had mentioned the spiritual dimension of development show her the spirituality contained in the work.[13]

Relations between *Sarvodaya* and the donors reached a crisis in 1993 when NOVIB announced that it would reduce its funding to *Sarvodaya* by 42%. This reduction was made despite a long-term commitment that the consortium had made to *Sarvodaya*. NOVIB cited various reasons for the cut including that the Dutch government was not satisfied with *Sarvodaya*'s audit reports. The reductions were devastating to Ariyaratne and *Sarvodaya*. Coming as they did hardly three months after Premadasa had died and the Sri Lankan government had ended the campaign of persecution of *Sarvodaya*, the reductions constituted another crippling blow to the *Sarvodaya* movement. It is difficult to avoid concluding that the government's attacks had influenced NOVIB's opinion of *Sarvodaya* and that NOVIB had been waiting for the first opportune moment to withdraw from its long-standing ties with *Sarvodaya*. As a result of the reduction in funding, the leaders of *Sarvodaya* had to take drastic action. *Sarvodaya* retrenched over one thousand staff members. This number included two-thirds of the district level staff and large numbers of the village workers. This reduction in funding by the donor consortium brought *Sarvodaya* to a standstill. *Sarvodaya* district centers throughout the country that had recently been busy with activities now stood empty. Facing this financial crisis, Ariyaratne and his colleagues were forced to re-evaluate their future course.

5. Conclusion

To conclude, we can note that *Sarvodaya* needs to address several challenges in order to face the future and survive. These challenges can be summarized as follows:

1. The challenge of funding created by the break with its philanthropic donors;
2. The related challenge of rediscovering/reaffirming its own identity as a movement; and
3. The challenge of charting a course that will address the new context and the future.

First, with regard to its philanthropic donors, *Sarvodaya* needs to work out a plan that will enable it to survive with integrity. The consortium approach did

---

[13] *Ibid.*, 16.

not work out because: (a) the donors did not understand *Sarvodaya*'s philosophy of development, and (b) because of this, (they) sought to control the movement. In *Sarvodaya*'s recent strategic planning, the solution that it has proposed amounts to an exit strategy from donor support altogether. They propose to continue with donor support for another three year period, but during this time to develop ways to become financially independent from WESTERN donors -- such as an endowment fund and more income producing projects. Whether these plans to become self-supporting are viable remains to be seen -- certainly it would seem that the scale of *Sarvodaya*'s work would need to be further reduced.

Second, as *Sarvodaya* declares its independence from Western foundations and tries to chart its own course, it will be essential for it to reaffirm its own identity and its goals for development. Raising the question of identity forces *Sarvodaya* to confront the question of whether its identity has changed as it has evolved and grown. Have the values and the ideals on which *Sarvodaya* was founded changed with its evolution? Ariyaratne has appeared to assume that *Sarvodaya*'s identity and ideals have not changed as the organization has evolved. In his speeches and writings in recent years, he implies that the old ideals are still operative, that the movement has not changed. When *Sarvodaya* encountered the recent funding crisis with the consortium, Ariyaratne's first reaction was to say that they would simply do without donor support and "restart the movement." He reported that he told the donors, "If we have no funding, we will restart the movement...We cannot abandon our vision just to please the donors."

But is this possible? Experts on organizational behavior have observed that an organization's values are integrally related to its form, so that "It is completely inappropriate to consider the form of an organization separately from its values."[14] And there is no question that the form of *Sarvodaya* changed considerably as it grew with the support of the donors from a volunteer movement into a large NGO having a huge bureaucracy and infrastructure.

As *Sarvodaya* cuts its ties to its donors and seeks to chart its own course, it is essential that it rediscover and reaffirm those values and ideals that gave it its distinctive mission -- ideals such as selfless service and simplicity of life based on Buddhist values.

Third and finally, *Sarvodaya* needs to draw on these values and ideals to craft a plan for addressing the social, political and economic contexts of the present and the future. From its Gandhian/Buddhist identity, *Sarvodaya* has to bring forward those values and ideals that will enable it to address the current situation most appropriately. It needs to find out whether Asian values and approaches can provide more viable alternatives for development.

Fortunately for *Sarvodaya*, the present time seems auspicious for a rediscovery of those values. At one time, *Sarvodaya*'s values represented an

---

[14] Zadek and S. Szabo, "Valuing Organization: The Case of *Sarvodaya*," in *New Economics Foundation* (1993): 26.

alternative that was foreign to the views of most development planners. Today, however, some development thinking seems to be endorsing *Sarvodaya's* original objectives. For example, the *Human Development Report* for 1994 from the UNDP calls for a "new development paradigm" which "puts people at the center of development, regards economic growth as a means and not an end...and respects the natural systems on which all life depends." This report goes on to describe this new paradigm in terms that sound as if they had been borrowed from *Sarvodaya's* literature, saying that development should enable "all individuals to enlarge their human capabilities to the full and to put those capabilities to their best use in all fields--economic, social, cultural and political."[15]

Sarvodaya stands today along with the rest of the developing world at an important crossroads; and *Sarvodaya* seems to have valuable guidance for moving ahead from this crossroads. Since it has pioneered this "new development paradigm," perhaps *Sarvodaya* can show people how this form of integrated development can solve the problems of a post-modern world. And just as it has faced the many prior challenges during its history, *Sarvodaya* seems ready to face the present difficulties. It has reaffirmed its goal of a dual liberation of persons and society. Whereas in the first decades, *Sarvodaya* was content to focus on village development, Ariyaratne now talks more about the need to create a new social order. He draws upon his Buddhist values to critique the present social order which has been built on capitalist and materialist values by saying, "You can organize greed and call it development; you can organize hatred and call it peace and you can organize ignorance and call it science.[16]" *Sarvodaya* seeks today to reemphasize the need for a new middle path, a path between the extremes of materialistic development of the world and spiritualist retreat from the world. *Sarvodaya* needs to apply its methods and values to contemporary problems so that in establishing this middle path it realizes again the truth of its development slogan "We build the road and the road builds us."

---

[15] United Nations Development Program, *Human Development Report* (1994): 4.

[16] Statement made in a speech to the Central Bank of Ceylon, July 20, 1994.

CHAPTER 12

SKILFUL MEANS, MORAL CRISES AND CONFLICT RESOLUTION

Stewart McFarlane

What I want to argue in this paper is that skilful means (*upāya kauśalya / fangbian / hōben*) are fundamental to an understanding of Buddhism as a soteriology. Secondly I want to show that the particular Mahāyāna articulation of skilful means in texts and historical cases offer a challenge and a corrective to conventional understanding of Buddhist ethics and notions of Buddhist leadership.

In the mainstream Mahāyāna understanding of the term, skilful means may be defined as the enlightened teacher's ability to understand the spiritual condition and mental state of a person and to teach them on a level appropriate to their level of understanding, and in doing so lead them out of a state of suffering and ignorance and into a higher level of understanding. The emphasis in the term and in most textual accounts and examples is on the skill and ability of the teacher to manipulate a situation in which the deluded being is in a position to achieve higher understanding or at least to avoid actions which will lead that being to greater suffering.

I think it is a mistake to suppose that the method of skilful means is confined to Mahāyāna traditions. There are examples of the Buddha's own employment of skilful means in Pali texts which conform closely to the later fully articulated Mahāyāna understanding of the term. One of the best examples is the story of Nanda, the fullest version of which appears in the *Jātaka*. The monk Nanda, who is Śākyamuni 's half brother, is having difficulty maintaining his zeal for the holy life because he misses his wife so much. This is not surprising since the Buddha called him forth into the holy life just after Nanda's wedding. To strengthen the Nanda's resolve, the Buddha takes him up into the heavenly realm of Śakra in the Brahmaloka and shows him the millions of heavenly maidens there. Nanda is suitably dazzled by their beauty and thinks his wife resembles a "wretched ape" in comparison. He asks the Buddha how he can return and win these maidens and is assured that by following the holy life he can enter the Brahma-realm. Nanda vows to do this and pursues his training with vigor. Later on he is shamed by some of the elder monks for this mercenary attitude, and abandons his desire for the maidens. Later still he becomes an *arahant.*[1] The point about the story is that the Buddha skillfully manipulates Nanda by setting one level of desire against another. And further, like the famous story of the burning house and the toy carts in the *Lotus Sūtra*, the Buddha promises what he has no intention of delivering, in order to disengage someone from a situation which will entail long term suffering. His deception is justified because it spiritually benefits the recipient. The logic of this episode from the Theravāda texts is exactly the same as that of the skilful means stories in the *Lotus Sūtra*.

Similarly, a story from the commentary on the *Aṅguttara-nikāya* concerns the poor girl Kisagotami whose baby dies, and who is distracted with grief that she cannot accept the child's death as a reality, someone suggests that she ask the great teacher Śākyamuni for a cure for the child. The Buddha says she must get three mustard seeds, but they must come from a house in which no-one has died. She goes around the entire village, borrowing the seeds but eventually realizes that there is no family that has not known death. She takes the child's body to be cremated, and returns to the Buddha for further Dharma teaching.[2]

Like the incident with Nanda and the famous parable of the burning house from the *Lotus Sūtra,* the Buddha appears to promise what he has no intention of delivering: a life disporting with heavenly maidens, the resurrection of a dead child or a toy cart or lesser way to Liberation. What he gives instead is a means to overcome suffering and death permanently. The implication in all these texts is that the deception is justified because it succeeds in detaching the person concerned from their deluded standpoint which will cause them to suffer, and brings them to a higher level of understanding which puts an end to suffering and delusion. In all these cases the Buddha understands the orientation or obsession of the person he is dealing with and addresses their problem at that level. He does not deliver a standard Dharma discourse or make impossibly high spiritual and mental demands on the subject. He is employing the method of using method to take out a thorn, and taking the interests or obsessions of these persons seriously and directing them to a higher level of understanding. Similarly when he intervenes in the dispute between the Śākyans and Koliyans over water rights, he does not offer the rival armies an abstract discourse on nonviolence and harmlessness, but confronts them with the consequences of armed conflict. He simply asks them whether the possible gain of water is worth

---

[1] E. B. Cowell, ed. and trans., The *Jātaka*, London: PTS, 1973, Sec. 182, 63-65; see also F. L. Woodward, trans., *The Minor Anthologies of the Pali Canon, Part 2: Udāna and Itivutta* (London: Oxford University Press, 1948), 25-28.

[2] E. A. Burtt, *The Teachings of the Compassionate Buddha* (New York: Mentor Publ., 1955), 43-36.

the loss of their best warriors and leaders.[3] Rhetorically and psychologically the method is exactly that of the skilful means scenarios in later Mahāyāna texts.

Another similarity to be found in these and other skilful means scenarios is the gravity of the situation in which the sufferer is to be found. In the *Lotus Sūtra* a house which is about to be consumed by fire and the victims are not even aware of the danger. Or in the case of Nanda, a monk is seriously considering leaving his practice and the *sangha*. In later Mahāyāna examples of skilful means, intentionally exaggerated accounts are given to heighten the sense of crisis. Dramatic and rhetorical, sometimes almost theatrical effects are created in the texts to heighten the sense of crisis and desperation, and so to increase the impact of the efficacy of skilful means and the power of the particular teacher who resolves the crisis. In many scenarios the sense of crises is created by situations of real or potential conflict. Their resolution is far from what would be expected of standard Buddhist ethical responses. The text, "Skilful Means in the Mahāyāna" (*Dacheng fangbian hui*)[4] contains many such examples of desperate situations which require drastic measures and extreme skilful means to resolve them. The tone and style is established in the following passage:

> Good man, as an illustration considers a fighter, who hides the sword, he carries and escorts a group of travelers. None of the travelers know this man's secret stratagem. They despise and pity him, showing no respect, and say to one another, "He has no weapons and no partner, and is not even strong or powerful. He cannot even save himself from danger; how can he help others? It is impossible for him to defeat any bandit. He will certainly run into trouble." When a gang of bandits suddenly appears from an uninhabited marsh, the fighter stands ground firmly and draws his hidden sword. In one move he kills them, and conceals his sword. In the same way, good man, a *bodhisattva* who practices skilful means conceals his sword of wisdom and joins other beings, amusing himself with the five sense pleasures as a skilful means to convert those beings. When people see the *Bodhisattva* amuse himself with pleasure, not knowing it to be skilful means they pity him and think him dissipated, saying, "Such a person cannot save even himself from saṃsāra, let alone all sentient beings. It is impossible for him to defeat demons." However, the *Bodhisattva* is skilled at using skilful means and the sword of wisdom. When he has attained his object [of saving beings] he will with the sword of wisdom cut through all hindrances and will attain a pure Buddha-land....[5]

---

[3] Hazra, K.L., *Royal Patronage of Buddhism in Ancient India* (Delhi: D.K. Publications, 1984), 34.

[4] J. Takakusu and K. Watanabe, eds., *Taishō shinshū daizōkyō* [newly revised *Tripiṭaka* of the Taishō era] (Tokyo: Taishō Issaikyō, 1922-1933), text 38 in the *Mahāratnakūṭa* collection, T.11.310.594-607.

[5] *Op. cit.*, T.11.310.597 b.

160   Stewart McFarlane

I realize that the above account with its highly dramatic imagery sounds more like something from a Chinese or Japanese warrior story, or even a Kurosawa movie, and I shall say something about the possible reason for the vivid nature of the example later. The passage is assuredly from an important treatise on skilful means to be found in the Chinese *Mahāratnakūṭa* collection. The importance and popularity of the text in China is demonstrated by the fact that it was translated from Sanskrit into Chinese three times between 300 and 1000 CE.

In other Mahāyāna texts similar transgressions of conventional Buddhist moral norms are justified in terms of the demands of compassion and skilful means. An early text on skilful means, translated into Chinese in the later Han dynasty (between 25-220 C.E.), describes how a Brahmin convert to Buddhism is part of a caravan of traders when he meets a friend who is scouting for a gang of 500 bandits who attack such caravans. The bandit warns his friend of the ambush so he can save himself, and the Buddhist kills him.[6] He reasons that if he warns the traders they will kill the bandit and carry the karmic responsibility for his death. But if he does not warn them, the scout will guide the bandits to attack the traders and there will be great loss of life. The Buddhist therefore takes the course which is the lesser of three evils and accepts responsibility for his action. Later Mahāyāna texts use the same kind of ethical or karmic dilemmas in similar situations to illustrate the notion of skilful means and its ethical adaptability, The "Skilful Means in the Mahāyāna" text quoted above goes on to provide more fascinating examples. It describes how the Buddha, in a previous existence was leading some traders on a voyage when he learned that one of their number plans to kill and rob them. To prevent this he kills the man with a spear.[7]

What do these examples tell us about Buddhist ethics generally and about Buddhist notions of leadership specifically? Even admitting the exaggerated dramatic effect created by these examples and the sense of crisis and urgency which the scenarios intentionally invoke, they do present something of a challenge to a conventional view of Buddhist ethics and of Buddhist notions of leadership. Do they provide realistic possible models for Buddhist leadership? I would suggest with some caution, that they do, and that such notions of leadership which are proactive, dynamic and sometimes skillfully abrogate conventional ethical norms, are appropriate in certain crisis situations.

Despite the possibilities for exploitation which such examples present, no less an authority than Asaṅga, under the inspiration of Maitreya, argues in the *Bodhisattvabhūmi* that the *bodhisattva* is justified in transgressing Buddhist and conventional ethical norms in the interests of skilful means. The text has

---

[6] *Op.cit.*, T.3.156.161b-162a; see also Paul Dernieville, "Le bouddhisme et la guerre, " in *Choix D'Etudes Bouddhiques* (Leiden: E.J. Brill, 1973), 293.
   [7] *Op.cit.*, T.11.310.604c; see also Garma C. C. Chang, *A Treasury of Mahāyāna Sūtras: Selections from the Mahāratnakūṭa Sūtra* (University Park and London: The Pennsylvania State University Press, 1983), 456-457.

survived in Sanskrit as well as in Chinese and Tibetan translations. The translation here is from the Sanskrit:

> There are certain offences of nature which the *bodhisattva* may practice through his skilful means, whereby he commits no fault and indeed produces much merit. For instance, the *bodhisattva* sees a thief or bandit ready to kill many hundred beings, even great beings such as *śrāvakas, pratyekabuddhas,* or *bodhisattvas.* Seeing this he refines his thought and reflects, "If I kill this being I will be reborn in hell, but I am willing to suffer it. This being may later act in such a way as to avoid hell". Resolving in this way the *bodhisattva,* with kind thoughts toward the being, one with him in his heart, with compassionate regard for his future and abhorring his act, he kills him. He is free from fault and produces much merit.
>
> So too is the *bodhisattva* when there are kings or great ministers who are excessively cruel and have no compassion for beings, intent on causing pain to others. Since he has the power he makes them fall from command of the kingdom, where they cause so much demerit. His heart is compassionate, and he intends their welfare and happiness. If there are thieves and bandits who take the property of others, or the property of the saṅgha or a *stūpa,* making it their own to enjoy, the *bodhisattva* takes it from them reflecting, "Let not this property be a disadvantage and misfortune to them for a long time." So he takes it and returns it to the saṅgha or to the *stūpa.* By this means, the *bodhisattva,* though taking what is not given, does not have a bad rebirth, indeed much merit is produced.[8]

Though these arguments and examples are presented in much less dramatic style than the previous accounts, the hypothetical cases presented by Asaṅga are still examples of crisis situations. I think the murder and robbery of *śrāvakas, pratyekabuddhas* and *bodhisattvas* qualifies as a crisis, as does the misrule of cruel and oppressive kings, or the illegitimate appropriation of the saṅgha's property. In his examples, the emphasis is not so much on the teaching of those involved and leading them out of suffering, but upon what actions are permitted for a sufficiently advanced level *bodhisattva,* under the general exercise of skilful means. The message is not that everything is permitted to everyone. It is not antinomian, but in certain crisis situations, desperate and dharmically legitimate actions are appropriate. Note also that in these situations the notion of responsibility and karmic responsibility or ownership of deeds still applies in that the *bodhisattva* is required to think, "I may be reborn in hell for this act". As Asaṅga points out, the *bodhisattva*'s expectations are not realized, and in fact he

---

[8] Asaṅga, *Bodhisattvabhūmi* (Wogira, U., ed.), Tokyo, 1930, 165-167; see also Tatz, M., *Asaṅga's Chapter on Ethics, With the Commentary of Tsong-Kha-Pa,* "The Basic Path to Awakening", "The Complete Bodhisattva" (Lewiston, NY: The Edwin Mellon Press, 1986), 70-71.

produces much merit in so acting. But Asaṅga's point is that whatever objectively arises from the action, the *bodhisattva* subjectively must maintain an attitude of compassion and abhorrence for his action and accept responsibility for it. Only in that way is much merit produced. The implication seems to be that if the *bodhisattva* were to perform such actions from self-interested motives, or even from disinterested motives, but with an attitude that his actions were justified and would produce much merit, then they would not count as skilful means and would result in woeful consequences. We are not here talking about a Buddhist version of a "just war" ethic in which the *bodhisattva* feels himself to be justified in desperate and violent actions. On the other hand, Asaṅga is providing a serious hypothetical case here. In fourth and fifth century India, the only system of government, as far as I am aware, was a hereditary monarchy. When Asaṅga talks about causing kings and ministers to fall from power, one of the few ways to achieve that is armed revolution and probably regicide. Those options are of course not specified, the text as it stands is radical and challenging enough. The karmic or dharmic justification continues to pervade this hypothetical in that the Bodhisttvas overthrows the offending kings and ministers as much out of compassion for them, to prevent them from offending further, as for their suffering subjects.

Interestingly when the monk dPal-gyi-rdo-rje acted on just this sort of textual precedent and assassinated King gLang-dar-ma in 842 in order to prevent further persecution of the *saṅgha,* he appears to have adhered very closely to Asaṅga's hypothetical model. Despite the fact that his act was widely welcomed by the Buddhist population because the *saṅgha* which was being persecuted by King gLang-dar-ma, dPal-gyi-rdo-rje accepted the responsibility for his action and refused to participate in further ordination ceremonies, acknowledging that he had committed *pārājikā* offence.[9]

Western Buddhological scholarship has frequently recorded its unease at these teachings as expounded in the Mahāyāna. Not surprisingly Catholic scholars such as La Vallee Poussin[10] and Lamotte[11] were critical of what they saw as antinomian tendencies in the Mahāyāna. Such passages do not of course conform to conventional western understandings of ethics. They are not intended to illustrate even conventional Buddhist ethics. They are rather taking fundamental ethical and soteriological categories in Buddhism and applying them to situations of extreme crisis and real conflicts between different ethical demands. These passages are intentionally and rhetorically forcing us to confront situations approximating those in which real ethical decisions or life choices have to be made.

---

[9] Tatz, *op.cit.,* 297.

[10] Louis de La Vallee Poussin, Louis de, "Notes Bouddhiues 7. Le Vinaya et la Purite D'Intention. Academie Royales de Belgiques," *Bulletin de la Classe des Lettres,* 1929, Bruxelles, Vol. 15, Series 5, 202-214.

[11] Etienne Lamotte, *L'Enseignement de Vimalakīrti* (Universite de Louvain, 1962), 145, note 4.

Buddhist ethics are unlike traditions of ethical reflection in the west in a number of important ways. First of all western ethics, particularly under the influence of Kant and his successors, adhere to the notion of ethics as universal and universalizable. That the same fundamental ethical requirements and obligations apply to all humans. Buddhist ethics cannot be universal in this way because the universe of beings in the Buddhist worldview exists in a hierarchy, structured according to the karmic and spiritual development of beings. Different ethical standards, requirements and levels of responsibility apply to different levels of being. Also the hierarchical nature of beings means that different degrees of gravity and karmic consequences attach to offences against such beings. For Kant and the dominant western traditions of ethics, the theoretical position declares that killing is murder and is always of equal gravity. For Buddhists, killing a monk, or even worse an *arahant is* more serious offense than killing an ordinary person; Buddhist ethics are also developmental as well as hierarchical. Levels of responsibility increase with one's increasing moral and spiritual purity. Higher standards of behavior are expected of members of the *saṅgha* than of lay people. The hierarchical and developmental nature of Buddhist ethics makes ethical generalization and prescribing, in anything but the most formal sense (such as the *prātimokṣa*) extremely difficult. Buddhist ethics are also situational and are fundamentally concerned with intention or the psychological and volitional factors behind actions rather than with the actions themselves. For Kant, when confronted by the murderer who asks the whereabouts of his next victim, it is still wrong to lie, even to save the victim's life[12]. For Asaṅga it is perfectly obvious that you lie to save the person's life.

When we look in detail at the examples cited by Asaṅga and in the other texts we see that despite their challenging and dramatic nature fundamental Buddhist ethical considerations are still observed. There is a particular concern with the correct intention behind the *bodhisttavas* response to the situation. Is he intervening actively on the right grounds and motives? The mechanisms of karma, however modified, due to the particular circumstances of the participants, are still felt to apply in these passages. In that sense Buddhist ethics are more universal than Kantian ethics, because karma operates across a wider range of beings than do Kant's categorical imperatives.

In terms of moral theorizing, the Buddhist emphasis is on an ethic of intention. The moral and spiritual capacities of beings are crucially determined by their orientations, intentions and actions over past lives, i.e., karma formation. Due to these factors, beings exist in a spiritual and moral hierarchy, which is nevertheless fluid and developmental in character. Various consequences follow from such an ethical outlook. First generalizing to a set of absolute imperatives is very difficult in such a view. Which level of beings and in which state is one prescribing for? The notion of universal moral absolutes derivable from fixed principles is difficult to sustain. As general rules or actions guides, killing, lying

---

[12] Immanuel Kant, *Critique of Practical Reason* (Abbott, T.K., trans.) (London: Longmans, 1909), Appendix, 361-364.

and stealing are unwholesome and unskillful actions which will have grave consequences for the offender. But as we have seen, in particular circumstances then such actions may be necessary, providing the person who so acts is prepared to accept the consequences of their actions. The motivation for such actions must of course be selfless, disinterested and compassionate. This means that at the very least, the *bodhisattvas* so acting must have a sufficiently high level of self-awareness for their motives to be pure. They must also possess sufficient insight and skill so as to correctly understand the seriousness of the crisis and the skill to know how to act appropriately to remedy it. This brings us back to the notion of a moral and spiritual hierarchy. Beings of sufficient skill, insight, compassion and purity of motive are not common. One cannot on the basis of a Buddhist skilful means position, formulate a universalizable set of moral guidelines which could be observed or prescribed for all beings. The situation, the context and the capacities of the beings involved, determines what actions are appropriate. None of this fits in easily with traditional western forms of ethical theorizing. These tend to rest on Kantian notions of prescribability and universalizability. In other words can a particular moral viewpoint or response be generalized such that you can unconditionally will everyone to act in that way in similar circumstances. Others tend to be consequentialist or utilitarian in a quite restricted and materialist sense of asking whether a certain viewpoint, action or policy, if generally applied secures the maximum benefit in terms of happiness or material benefits for the majority of the population. Traditional Christian ethical formulations also recourse to divine authority and the notion of the universal love of God as that which underpins particular ethical positions. From a Buddhist perspective all these ethical perspectives fail because they are not universal enough. They do not allow for the diversity of beings and species, and tend to assume that only humans are worthy recipients of moral consideration. Furthermore they fail to allow sufficiently for the psychological factors which shape human actions and responses. Fear, dependence, aggression, desire, obsession, motive, intent, will are all the kinds of factors observed in the course of mindfulness and meditation practice as well as being identified and analyzed in the *Abhidharma* and *Vijñānavāda* texts. In comparison with Buddhist ethics traditional western ethical positions tend to have a restricted view of human potential and development, and tend to ignore the possibilities for genuine selfless and compassionate action. Western utilitarians restrict human worth to forms of material or emotional provision and happiness, without addressing the need for spiritual fulfillment. If the notion of the common good or the greatest happiness for the greatest number could be given a particular Buddhist dimension, to include spiritual happiness and the opportunity to lead a dharmically fulfilled life, and if consequentialist and pragmatic considerations could be extended to include karmic processes, then the types of argument developed by western Utilitarians could be applied to the calculations undertaken by exponents of skillful means. The Buddhists' calculations have to allow for karmic consequences over possible future lives, for all those involved. And Buddhists have to be more self reflective and self aware than act utilitarians so as to ensure that their own motivations to action are pure and compassionate. Any self-deception underlying the motive to act will mean that the offense because karmically unwholesome and damaging for those involved. Rather than confronting the complexities of Buddhist moral reflection and action, some western scholars have preferred to dismiss Buddhism as ethically incoherent[13] and antinomian.[14]

The examples discussed above do offer radical and challenging models of leadership and of course are easily open to abuse and casuistic exploitation. One area of particular concern and interest is the whole question of Buddhist ethics and sexual behavior. Attention has been drawn to recent cases of Buddhist leaders engaging in sexual relations with followers, and in some cases legal action has been taken. It would of course be misleading to suggest that this is a problem entirely confined to the transmission of Buddhism in the West. John Stevens gives examples of some of the problems and resolutions with regard to Buddhadharma and sexuality which have emerged in Buddhist history.[15] With the increasing access to information, the attention of the press and widely reported legal cases, the problems are being highlighted and discussed openly in the public domain, probably for the first time in the history of Buddhism. The passage in the *Bodhisattvabhūmi* immediately following that cited, discusses a case where a *bodhisattva* may suspend Buddhist ethical norms and have sex:

> The lay *bodhisattva* may engage in the dharma of sexual embrace with a single woman, if her thought is overwhelmed with the agony of sexual desire. The *bodhisattva* reflects, "Let her not give rise to resentment and much demerit. Let her be caused by me to abandon unwholesome states, and let what is desired be a cause for good." With a thought that is only compassionate he engages in the dharma of sex. There is no fault and he produces much merit.[16]

One of the first things to note about this passage is how cautious Asaṅga is in his account of the conditions under which a *bodhisattva* may have sex. First, he specifies that this can only apply to a lay *bodhisattva*. Presumably it is unthinkable for a monk to have sex. Note that no such qualifications applied to the previous list of permissible transgressions. Second, the woman must not be married. Third she must be in a sufficiently desperate state of desire to as to threaten her mental stability. Fourth, the *bodhisattva* only concurs with her desires out of a motivation of compassion and in order to prevent resentment, and to resolve an unwholesome state. Finally in the scenario envisaged by

---

[13] A. C. Danto, *Mysticism and Morality* (London: Penguin Books, 1972), ch. 4.

[14] Lamotte, *op. cit.;* see also R. C. Zaehner, *Our Savage God* (London: Collins, 1974), 63-66.

[15] Stevens, J., *Lust For Enlightenment: Buddhism and Sex* (Boston & London: Shambhala, 1990); see also B. Faure, *The Rhetoric of Immediacy* (New Jersey: Princeton University Press, 1991), Ch. 11.

[16] Asaṅga, *op. cit.,*167; see also Tatz, *op. cit.,* 71.

                          Stewart McFarlane

Asaṅga the sexual encounter seems to be envisaged as a one encounter. This is not the case in the typically dramatic case described in the "Skilful Means in the Mahāyāna" text of the *Mahāratnakūṭa*. Here a woman encounters a handsome *brahmacārin* as he emerges from the forest after purifying and training himself for over four billion years. She declares she will die from desire if she cannot have him. Taking compassion on her and to prevent her death, he lives with her for twelve years after which he resumes his celibate training and advanced *jhāna* practice, and is subsequently reborn in the Brahma realm. The final twist is brought with the disclosure that this *brahmacārin* was in fact Śākyamuni Buddha in a previous life and the woman was Yaśodharā his wife.[17]

The recent high-profile cases of sexual relations do not appear to conform to either set of precedents. In both cases cited, the *bodhisattva* engages in sex to prevent resentment and suffering, whereas the sense of betrayal and resentment generated by recent cases seems to indicate the opposite of this effect. Furthermore the motivations of the *bodhisattvas* are described as selfless and compassionate. The crisis of sexual desire is ascribed to the woman in both these cases. And the *bodhisattva* has sex in order to fulfill her needs and to resolve her crisis. Neither *bodhisattva* is described engaging in these practices habitually or in a serial fashion. And although in the case of the Buddha in a previous life twelve years sounds like a serious ongoing relationship, compared to his life of purification in the forest of over four billion years, it almost counts as a one night stand. In the *kalpa* in question we are clearly dealing with a different relative time scale. There is insufficient space here to discuss homosexual transgressions, and the texts cited offer no precedent. Bernard Faure's view is that historically, monastic Buddhism was more tolerant of homosexuality than heterosexuality.[18]

By way of a general conclusion to this paper I would say that the cases of skilful means cited in Mahāyāna texts are intentionally dramatic and challenging, and encourage us to see that the most difficult ethical decisions must be made in times of crisis and extreme circumstances. Although specific moral norms are abrogated in these crisis situations, fundamental assumptions about the operation of karma and the acceptance of responsibility for actions, as well as the need for insight, understanding and compassion for those involved, remain in place. The *bodhisattvas* in these scenarios are seen by virtue of their wisdom and compassion as possessing the moral authority power and psychological resilience to act appropriately and compassionately. Many provide perfect models of crisis management and creative leadership. The textual examples deliberately involve *bodhisattvas* in "worldly" situations of conflict, violence, political struggles and sexual encounters. In other words they are located in situations where a standard monastic response is inappropriate and the *prātimokṣa* are of little application. They could be regarded as extreme cases of the sort of problems which confront people all the time. Something of the same

---

[17] Chang, *op.cit.*, 433.
[18] Faure, *op. cit.*, 238.

psychological subtlety and creative leadership, in addition to wisdom and compassion is actually required of all *bodhisattvas,* which technically includes all Mahāyāna Buddhists, since all Mahāyāna Buddhists take the *bodhisattva* vow to save all beings. In the political sphere Asaṅga's precedent would seem to suggest that when confronted with a systematically unjust and oppressive regime, a *bodhisattva* is justified in taking direct and possibly violent action in overthrowing that regime. If of course the *bodhisattva* had it in his power to overthrow that regime nonviolently, perhaps through the disclosure of damaging confidential information, then that would of course be preferable.

The sort of scenario I have in mind would be a Watergate type situation or a Clive Ponting case. The latter was a British civil servant who revealed to the press that the Prime Minister and Secretary of State for Defense had lied to Parliament and the British people about the circumstances of the sinking of the General Belgrano which marked the beginning of the armed conflict with Argentina in April 1982. Ponting's disclosure did not of course bring down the Conservative government (the British people having by then become accustomed to being lied to), but at least the jury who tried Ponting had the sense to acquit him despite a virtual directive from the judge to convict.

Such a sanction as that provided by Asaṅga does leave the Buddhist world in a difficult position with regard to the Chinese occupation of Tibet, accompanied as it is by persecution of the *saṅgha* and ordinary Tibetans. I personally think that economic and political sanctions should be brought against the Chinese in order to get them out of Tibet. It is clear that the Dalai Lama himself is opposed to armed resistance or an invasion by an allied force. But it is interesting to compare the situation of Tibet with that of Kuwait when invaded by Iraq. Western economic interests were threatened, and U.S., coordinated U.N. response was immediate. The Chinese invaded Tibet in 1959 and still the U.N. has taken no effective action. Of course Tibet has no oil.

On the level of individual acts of violence and abuse of living beings; Asaṅga and the other texts cited clearly legitimize direct action against assailants to prevent such violence. I am happy to report that some British Buddhists are active in the recent direct action, in the form of human blockades of ports, to prevent the exporting of livestock for slaughter in continental Europe, forcing the government to reconsider this practice. I look forward to similar blockades of slaughter houses and animal testing laboratories in the U.K. In final conclusion I would say that Asaṅga and the other texts considered, do offer some guidelines and models for what forms an engaged and karmically responsible Buddhism might take.

CHAPTER 13

BUDDHIST CONFLICT MANAGEMENT

Ron Burr

1. Introduction

This title perhaps oversimplifies more than most. This paper is about Buddhist conflict management. However, qualifications are necessary.

The immediate context of this paper is my consultation in the first of what promises to be a series of workshops on conflict management sponsored first and foremost by the *Sarvodaya* organization founded by Dr. A. T. Ariyaratne.[1] However, this paper is meant to address Buddhist applications to conflict management in general, and not specific to the context of Sri Lanka. The title "Buddhist Conflict Management" oversimplifies the extent to which there is a common lore in human relations training, begun in the west but now international, which includes conflict management. The *Sarvodaya*-sponsored 'training' is, in the first instance, Buddhist in that this common lore is being given a Buddhist application to a more or less Buddhist context. Furthermore, some theories are offered from Buddhism to support the 'training'.

Secondly, the term Buddhist needs to be clarified in a couple of ways. The concept of Buddhism used in this paper is primarily that of the Pali Nikāyas, that is, the earliest Buddhist texts. It must remain thus, so as not to revert to something more specific just to Sri Lanka. However, certain values common to the Sri Lankan reading of Early Buddhism are present in the text.

The motif of this paper is primarily an account of how training has been designed and implemented in the *Sarvodaya* case. This being the first workshop for training Buddhist monks to do conflict management or at least the first in an admirably planned series by *Sarvodaya*, it seems worthy of reporting in some detail.

---

[1] I applaud the *Sarvodaya* leadership and the Asia Foundation for putting resources into the training of Buddhist monks for conflict management. I also congratulate the trainers and all those involved in designing this workshop for the care and effort they have given to this fine beginning.

Because of attention to this motif, a more traditional approach to the subject suggested by the title of this paper cannot be expected. Traditionally, one's outline would include early on: what is meant by Buddhism in this paper, in more detail than has been presented so far. Next the outline would take up what is meant by conflict herein, at what point conflict or response to conflict becomes negative and so worthy of management, what is meant by management, and so on.

Since this paper is partially about what is often called an experiential workshop, in contrast to a seminar, the topics just mentioned are addressed in the course of participant discussion. That is, they are not presented solely in lecture form as might be expected at a seminar. Often participants are asked to provide their own self or group-generated accounts of topics prior to the time a trainer interjects any additions or differences from the front. So, responses to the topics mentioned above emerge as an account of such a workshop unfolds. Incidentally, this is where much of the interest lies for readers of this paper-- especially those who are familiar with human relations training in general, or conflict management specifically. Who those social activist monks are and what they think about conflict provides, I think, valuable data to the peace-making, peace-keeping field.

After a brief account of experiential learning and a rationale for providing conflict management workshops, I relate my observations of the first *Sarvodaya* Conflict Management workshop.

2. Experiential Learning

Experiential learning is the method of choice for learning about conflict management. There are of course theoretical issues, of the sort previously mentioned, needing to be addressed. However, the greatest learning deficiencies for those entering the field of conflict management are those having to do with skill and attitudes requisite to facilitating others through the resolution of negative responses to conflict. Almost secondarily, theoretical learning is added along the way. Thus, experiential learning is a topic for "philosophical praxis",[2] in the sense of this term used by Friere: "the action and reflection of men upon their world in order to transform it."[3] The role of an educator in this field, according to Friere, is one of "problem-posing."[4]

The reader is asked to remember that well designed, experiential workshops are cumulative in participant learning. Simple learnings are expected in the beginning, to be built upon as the workshop continues. Beginning with the learning and practice of certain training fundamentals greatly increases the

---

[2] G. E. Kessler, *Voices of Wisdom* (Belmont, California: Wadsworth Publishing Company, 1995), 161. (Kessler's emphasis).

[3] Paulo Friere, *Pedagogy of the Oppressed*, trans. Myra Bergman Ramos (NY: Herder and Herder, 1970), excerpted in *ibid.*, 165.

[4] *Ibid.*

likelihood of success among the apprentice conflict managers being trained. Others of these fundamentals follow in this section: being aware of goals, having ample time for formal review after each session, following an experiential learning model beginning to end, and having ample time for attitude and skill-building activities.

2.1. Goals

The obvious rationale for accentuating goals is that both learner and facilitator are most likely to be able to aid in the learning if they know what the intended learning is. As Lewis Carroll said: if you don't know where you are going, it doesn't matter what road you take. Seasoned facilitators of experiential learning clearly know and transmit which goals of the workshop they are furthering with each of their modules. I recommend making a poster and starting each training session with a statement of the goals for that session along with how those goals relate to participant needs.

2.1.1. Design

If some form of audience assessment is not possible, trainers should carefully think through what they believe the needs of participants are in relation to the topic of the workshop. They should then formulate clear, concise, and if possible, behavioral goals that express how participants' training needs are to be met. Subsequently, they should find training modules to achieve those goals. Those training modules should then be organized in consideration of order of what is being learned-simple to complex, underlying to overlaying; variety of training methods; the most active modules occurring at times when participants may be groggy; and, stages in some theory of group process, e.g., FIRO theory in which groups cycle through stages of inclusion, control and affection.[5]

2.1.2. For Conflict Management Training

Reasonable goals for the workshop topic under discussion might include the following.

Participants have the opportunity to:

---

[5] W. C. Schutz, *FIRO: A Three Dimensional Theory of Interpretation Behavior* (NY: Rinehart, 1958). This theory has the advantages of 'face validity', being easy to explain, and also being easy for apprentice trainers to remember. More recent and comprehensive versions appear frequently. See, e.g., S.A. Wheelan's *Group Processes: A Developmental Perspective* (Boston: Allyn and Bacon, 1994), who believes that there is a "process of group development across all types of groups." (14). The stages in this process are said to be dependency and inclusion; counter-dependency and fight; trust and structure; work; and, termination.

1. Get acquainted with other social service workers,
2. Increase skills in brainstorming ideas and solutions,
3. Develop a working definition of conflict and related concepts,
4. Identify conflicts along a spectrum of importance,
5. Consider a range of causes of conflict; and select the most important ones,
6. Write and analyze personal case studies of conflict situations,
7. Consider negative and possibly positive aspects of conflict,
8. Discuss Buddhist perspectives of conflict,
9. Apply a method of analyzing conflict,
10. Apply a method of 'mapping' conflict,
11. Practice active listening,
12. Consider other forms of listening, such as empathetic listening,
13. Learn to identify submissive, aggressive, and assertive behaviors,
14. Recognize good negotiation and mediation practices,
15. Discuss Buddhist concepts of peace, using them to draft a definition of peace,
16. Discuss various ways of resolving conflicts, stressing non-violent methods.

2.2. Norms

Those new to training often appreciate at the beginning of a workshop having agreements about some expected behaviors.[6] These help everyone keep the workshop on track by holding themselves and others to attitudes and behaviors that all have agreed are most likely to produce those results indicated by the workshop goals. Here is a set of such norms which is often used in workshops conducted by the author:

RESPONSIBILITY FOR OWN LEARNING
ATTEND ALL SESSIONS
HIGH PARTICIPATION

---

[6] Agreement about values, norms, and ideologies reduces member anxiety and increases the ability to predict and understand the events that occur." (Wheelan, *op. cit.*, 27). "Norms represent collective value judgment about how members should behave and what should be done in the group. Norms are necessary if the group is to coordinate its efforts and accomplish its goals. Without behavioral predictability, chaos reigns." (38). It does anyway.

APPROPRIATE RISK TAKING
SUPPORTIVE OF OTHERS
CONFIDENTIALITY
FUN/WORK

Given sufficient workshop time, participants may become involved in providing their own similar list of norms, for which they would have an increased level of commitment. In lieu of this opportunity, brief explanations for the facilitator's choices are given.

2.3. Experiential Learning Model

An experiential learning model is often displayed at the beginning of a workshop, after the goals are shown, as the way most likely to produce the attitude and skill building requisite to accomplishing those goals. It is usually displayed as a cyclical figure of four stages with arrows drawn among them. The four stages follow a learning theory popularized by Kolb. The four stages are, as I present them: 1) Experience, 2) Review for observations about what was felt, experienced or observed, 3) Generalizations about what was learned in terms of what was most significant, and 4) Projections toward future situations--or, experience as in number one--about how what has been learned may be applied in order to be more effective in such situations. Theoretical support for offering experiential learning to adults for enhancing their skill and attitudes includes reference to motivation, acquisition of habits and other facets beyond the scope of this paper. Readers are referred to the vast literature on experiential learning now contained in libraries around the world.

At the end of each training module experienced facilitators often have participants write answers to review questions, which elicit information regarding those four stages in relation to the goals of the modules. These records are then maintained and saved by each participant until the closing sessions. At that time the participants can review the whole workshop to see, among all they have learned, the important items about which they are willing to contract with themselves for acting on after the workshop. This review also makes it easier for them to contribute intelligently to the workshop evaluation.

2.4. Evaluation of Experiential Learning

Workshop evaluations are often constructed in consideration of the goals. They can provide quantitative data for quick summary, and for donors, as well as qualitative data which may give more information to trainers about ways to improve. The evaluation form may begin with these instructions: please mark on the scale following each goal the extent to which you were able to meet this goal in this workshop. Participants then complete the evaluation with regard to each goal. A line with 10 divisions and a clear designation of which end is "completely" and which end is "not at all" makes it easy to compile numerical data for quick evaluation by trainers and donors. These data may be kept and continuously compiled or even displayed, so that answers are forthcoming about how human and monetary resources are being utilized in training.

3. Why Conflict Management?

There are turning out to be many ways to work for peace, the elusive, yet most important indication of social stability. In last years conference here Ken Kraft challenged those attending to see an inseparable relationship between peaceful inward endeavors and working outwardly for peace. He further offered a typology for this work. There are, he says, the three realms of "authentic Buddhist peace work": [7] 1) individual practice (like deepening insight, cultivating equanimity, and practicing non-harming; 2) personal relations and ordinary actions of daily life;[8] and, 3) the primarily public realm of deliberate social action.[9]

Indicative of the ethical complexities which may signal the adaptation to our times of Buddhist social ethics, is Ken's noting that most decisions come in the form of dilemmas. We have not a single ethical choice against which to apply the Buddha's path, but most of the time at least two, of which one must be chosen, and about which there is a possible Buddhist viewpoint on either side. Again, if "Seeds get lodged, but you can't really measure the result," and, "There's a kind of cognitive dissonance that gets planted," even our good friends, our *kalyāṇamitta* won't be of any help.[10] Our ethical and metaphysical causal connections will simply be confused. The general challenges with which Ken's paper ended are these: 1) for globally oriented activists to identify the meaningful connections with other activities and features of life;[11] and, 2) to actualize our East-West visions of spiritual democracy and democratic spirituality. [12] Certainly, the *Sarvodaya* conflict management training is a complex combination of the goals and challenges present in the account of Buddhist inner peace combined with Buddhist social action.

The *Sarvodaya* strategic plan for 1995-1998 speaks to the democratic sentiment, expressed by Dr. Kraft, in the following way. The upshot is that *Sarvodaya* has been openly democratic since inception:

> *Sarvodaya* evolved from the bottom up as a democratic organization with elected office-bearers at the level of the Lanka Jathika Sarvodaya Shramadana Sangamaya (1 1980). Independent national

---

[7] Ken Kraft, *Practicing Peace: New Perspectives from Western Buddhism* (Honolulu: University of Hawaii Press, in press), 2. Citations are from the conference draft of Dr. Kraft's paper, and will be revised after I see the published version.

[8] *Ibid.*, 3.

[9] *Ibid.*

[10] *Ibid.*, 28.

[11] *Ibid.*

[12] *Ibid.*, 30.

organizations like Suwasetha and Women's Movement and all the executive bodies at the village level societies are elected from membership. Therefore, *Sarvodaya*, at all levels and in every respect is a democratic organization where citizens participation is the most distinct characteristic.[13]

In their "situation analysis"[14] at the beginning of the latest *Sarvodaya* strategic plan, reference is made to poverty, war and unachievable lifestyle expectations as problems that have remained in effect in the last two decades of Sri Lankan existence. The interrelated problems of poverty and unachievable lifestyle expectations easily escalate from conflict, to dispute, to some sort of violence. Both of these are in the background of the religious and ethnic violence presently alive in Sri Lanka. Part of the *Sarvodaya* strategic plan is to address all of these. That plan envisions a role for *Sarvodaya* in "National Re-integration", a form of "social engineering", and furthermore a role in continuing to grapple with the children and refugees of war.[15]

Their strategic plan also articulates the Mission of *Sarvodaya* in the coming years. This articulation is under the umbrella of the way *Sarvodaya* Shramadana has been defined since its inception: as, "the awakening of all in society ... through the sharing of labor and other voluntarily gifted resources for the personal and social awakening of all ..."[16] In its most concise terms the mission is to: "create a new global social order based on the values of Truth, Non-violence and Self-denial, and governed by the ideals of participatory democracy."[17]

Conflict resolution occurs as one of three priorities in the context of the Mission Statement, in the *Sarvodaya* strategic plan. The first of these priorities is to help communities develop the capacity "to insulate community level productive activity", and give this activity "security" against "the exigencies of external shock."[18] In conjunction with the part of the *Sarvodaya* mission to be an impetus and model for peace, their second priority is "to play a more assertive conflict resolution and peace-making role. " Although there are many ways in which this may be accomplished, the training being described herein is meant to play a central role in furthering this priority. The third priority is to produce and

---

[13] *Towards Self Reliance and Sustainability: Sarvodaya Strategic Plan for 1995-1998* (Moratuwa, Sri Lanka: Self-published, September 1994), 14.

[14] In my paper for this conference last year, "Preventing War and Promoting Peace: with Reference to Buddhist Non-essentialist Traditions" (University of Hawaii Press, in press), I provided a detailed description of the process of situation analysis (called in my paper 'gap analysis') as it applies to community development work. *Sarvodaya* is a clinic for those who want to study this process.

[15] Sarvodaya Strategic Plan, *ibid.*, 9.

[16] *Ibid.*

[17] *Ibid.*

[18] *Ibid.*

perpetuate a method of economic development that is an alternative to the most competitive, material oriented, forms of free market economics.

Leaving the *Sarvodaya* program aside for a moment, and writing from my own experience of 'situation analysis' in years of community development-peace work, the ability to manage conflicts and disputes before they erupt in violence is widely thought to be a central feature of preventing war, and so making and keeping peace. Much more will be added about conflict management as we proceed.

4. *Sarvodaya* Conflict Management Learning

What follows is the author's account of the inaugural *Sarvodaya* conflict management training. I would not be able fully to delineate which parts of this account are interpreted consciously and which unconsciously. In some cases my comments and evaluations are explicit.

I recorded what was said a provided through a translator. Excerpts of this are given below. I also conducted some of the modules, which were in turn translated into Singhala. I provide excerpted memories of these. In addition, I made recommendations for what I believe would improve future workshops in this series.

Topics of the modules I have excerpted are: get acquainted activities, expectation elicitation, brainstorming, defining conflict, drafting personal cases of conflict, evaluating conflict in terms of seriousness, evaluating conflict at to good or bad, causes of conflict, Buddhist views of conflict, 'analysis' of conflict, conflict 'mapping,' effective listening, a middle path between aggressive and submissive behaviors, peace discussions with Dr. Ariyaratne, cooperation versus competition, conflict management cycles, and mediation.

4.1. Initial Session

On the afternoon prior to the ceremonial opening day of the *Sarvodaya* workshop, the participating monks gathered to register and then have an initial get acquainted session. For getting the monks relaxed about being in the workshop and together, the facilitators decided on three exercises. Sitting in a circle, still with their desks in front of them, they were instructed to tell their name, temple, district, and work they are doing. The monks reported being school teachers, directors of schools and social programs, students for advanced degrees in Buddhism, *Sarvodaya* workers, anti-drug workers, one originator of his own NGO, family counselors, an environmental worker in a village, a supervisor of four preschools, a member of an organization working for the poor, a coordinator of a Buddhist institute for 25 years (whose predecessor had been killed); the national coordinator of monks for *Sarvodaya* also studying for a masters in Buddhism. Among those attending but not Buddhist monks were a law student, a university student volunteer, a member of the committee of elders for a village, and a retired government worker now a full time volunteer for the

Sarvodaya Legal Aid Office. Second get-acquainted activity: The desks in front of each participant were announced-by one of the facilitators as being a barrier between people, and they were removed. Participants were instructed to find one or two other participants about whom they knew the least and find out something of value to them or about them, then if they were to have time to move on to another and do the same.

Expectation elicitation: Participants were asked individually to write on a small note card the following: why they came; and, what they expect. The rationale provided for doing this was that the program could be tailored to suit their desires, and that the cards would be displayed on a board throughout the workshop. The largest number of responses (6) indicated an interest in knowing more about what conflict is, some wanting a comparison between western and Buddhist ideas of same. Two wanted to know more about the Sarvodaya Legal Aid office (outside the scope of the workshop). Two wanted to know more about *Sarvodaya*; and two about helping with family conflict in rural areas. Other interests mentioned were: racial conflicts; law and human behavior; how to resolve mental problems; developing skills already being used at village level; how to teach conflict resolution to Dhamma schools; how to utilize law; how to resolve social problems and conflicts; and, how to prepare for the 20th century. I suspect that the interest in *Sarvodaya* Legal Aid Services was because of their boldly displayed banner at the beginning, owing to the workshop being organized under their domain. This was to become more clear the following morning at the opening ceremony.

Third get-acquainted activity. Participants were asked to think of an incident that made their life go on a different path, or perhaps changed their life. Then as time and inclination allowed each would have the time to stand and relate this incident. The purpose was to further relax the atmosphere and build trust. I had hypothesized that the majority would be stories about the decision to join the order. This was not the case. To give only a few: one said he saw his younger brother drunk and reading "dirty books" with a friend. At that point he decided to begin a drug prevention program. Another related a similar situation in which he went from merchant to merchant until no store sold "dirty books" in his village. Another said that upon seeing a butcher hack a piece of meat he realized the pain the animal had undergone and became a vegetarian. Sri Lankan monks are not normally vegetarian.

The next day's starting time and activity was announced and day 1 was over.

4.2. Day 2

Early morning meditation and yoga. Monks and facilitators arose at 5:30 for 6:00 - 7:00 meditation and yoga. Standing breathing, stretching and face-head massaging was done for about one-half hour. While this was done the facilitator made comments about overall mental health. After some floor stretching the facilitator got participants in seated posture for a talk about meditation and then a brief meditation itself. In the talk he said that there are three characteristics of good mental health, all of which are fostered by meditation: memory, sensitivity (including empathy), and perseverance. Meditation was scheduled to be an integral part of each day as each individual's approach to personal conflict management. I remarked in my introduction, above, some general rational for this point of view. Meditation often preceded or followed the monks' routine of chanting.

4.3. Opening ceremony

To begin the introductions, a member of the Sarvodaya Legal Aid Services office said that this would be the first of at least 20 planned workshops on conflict resolution. She said that eventually 600 monks would be trained to be mediators in their villages, in cooperation with Sarvodaya Legal Aid offices now being set up. She said that the sponsorship of the Sarvodaya Legal Aid Services has come from the Asia Foundation (funded by USID) since 1985, and that the idea for the conflict resolution seminars came from the president of the Sarvodaya, Dr. A.T. Ariyaratne, who would speak next.

Dr. Ariyaratne said that in 1972 there was a village leadership program for Buddhist monks initiated under the leadership of a very able senior monk. After both that monk and his chief disciple died, just about the end of the initial ten-year grant period in 1982, the leadership program dissipated. Ed Anderson of the Asia foundation picked up the project for an additional six months, recognizing peaceful ordinary people instead of market economics as stressed by most other donor agencies. The monks present are not just teachers, he said, they also live and work in the lay society which has complex problems. Hence the need for this training. The monks teach dhamma to those of us who must live in the suffering of ordinary society. This training will hopefully combine the dhamma with ways to cope with everyday life. Three focuses aid this effort: 1) human rights education; 2) training in those skills requisite to managing anything; and, 3) conflict resolution.

Dr. Ariyaratne commented on the *Sarvodaya* plan for the near future. The immediate focus would be on 1,000 pioneering villages. In time, volunteers from those 1,000 will go to 4,000 others; and volunteers from those eventually will add another 5,000 to the total. He said the basis of the work must be a spiritual vision. This is why a thousand monks will be trained. They should not be second to lay people in certain areas like human rights and conflict resolution. Everyone in Sri Lanka has an opinion about how to solve the major ethnic conflict, without searching very deeply into the problem. *Sarvodaya*, he said, wants also to influence other major areas of importance like nutrition. Along with creating a middle path society neither affluent nor poor, in nutrition the goal is "neither hungry nor over fed". Also, he said, harmful things have been done legally, e.g., poisoning the environment. Another two important areas of focus are: strengthening village economies and technology. In forty years, fossil fuels may become rare; so *Sarvodaya* will work to develop alternatives, such a solar energy.

In his summary, he indicated that there are young monks, wondering which way to go, and *Sarvodaya* can help to guide them. *Sarvodaya*, he said, must also form interfaith groups at the village level.

When the donor representative, Ed Anderson of the Asia Foundation, spoke, he initially followed on Dr. Ariyaratne's comments about the international donor community and the sort of project beginning this day. He and his colleagues at the Asia Foundation thought the conflict resolution for monks project was a "great idea". But the other members of the donor community consistently gave blank stares and asked what Buddhist monks could possibly have to do with conflict resolution. Fortunately, Mr. Anderson said, he and his colleague disagreed with them. He said there is a need to reach an understanding of certain modern techniques: 1) management of conflict situations in the community, 2) understanding of current thought on human rights; and 3) basic familiarity with law. Additionally, he said, adhering to principles of humanity found in all religions: love, kindness, compassion, and the desire to lift people from their suffering. With these principles in mind, he concluded, let them guide us in all our discussions.

Opening activity--Brainstorming. Knowing that so many exercises in this conflict resolution workshop refer to brainstorming, this day's training began with an exercise to reinforce brainstorming. Like so many of the modules they were to see, participants were assured that they could participate in it now and then conduct it themselves tonight. It brought a smile from those eager for some practical learnings. Two of us spoke as we wrote two posters one in each language. Mine said at the top: BRAINSTORMING, Goal: Quality ideas and solutions; Rules; 1) Quantity now; Quality later; 2) No censorship--write down every idea without comment; 3) Have a short time limit; 4) Encourage creative, even strange ideas; 5) Get inspired by others' ideas. All of these have the purpose of producing a quantity of creative ideas for later evaluation and insertion into problem-solving processes.

In the brainstorming warm-up activity, groups of 5-6 participants were assigned a simple object and told to brainstorm as many practical uses for it as they could in just 2 minutes. The 'winners', they were jokingly told, would get to readout their list. The winning group read out a list of 15 uses for a brick. We rewarded them with the opinion that if 15 uses of a brick could come from their group in 2 minutes that they could solve almost any problem that would ever occur within their group by starting with brainstorming solutions.

Activity 2: what is conflict, brainstorm? In the same groups participants were asked to brainstorm as many responses as possible, in two minutes, to the question, "What comes to mind as conflict?" The winning team read out 52 responses, after which all of the teams were asked to underline the most important items on their list, for all of them, by consensus. The combined list was recorded in front as they were reported. It included: competition, opposition; hatred; blighted expectations; untrustworthiness; fear; shock, desire; spiritual degeneration, spoiled character; loss of compassion; loss of stability, loss of friendship; social decay, loss of happiness; loss of foreign aid; arising of a beastly culture; social discord; division; injustice; intolerance of others views; religious conflict; communal conflict; territorial conflict; cultural conflict; separation from loved ones; being together with unloved ones; environmental destruction; opportunism reigning; jealousy, and, mental pollution.

For the second part of this activity participants were requested as individuals to produce a single definition of conflict. These are sample individual definitions that were posted: In our competitive world, wishing to satisfy one's desires, jealousy and hatred arising, at moments of weakness, engaging in conflict with society and others; two opinions or two parties engaging in an unfortunate incident; a clash of needs and non-solution; failure to understand the truth, due to inability to satisfy one's physical and mental and social aspirations; arises from breakdown of trust; lack of understanding of others, and not respecting the different ideas and peculiarities of others; lack of truth and moral law; wrong thoughts, and carrying them out; killing and the public exhibition of terror; and, mental tension that arises due to lack of parental love.

Day 2-first activity after lunch: writing personal cases. Participants were requested to think about some conflicts they have confronted and to write them on a piece of paper. Individually they were to write one full page about a conflict they have faced. It would not be necessary to explain that conflict only to describe it. If they were to think they haven't faced such conflict, they were encouraged to recall even small disagreements, e.g., over just distribution of something between others, that must have occurred in their purview. Five minutes were allowed for this.

Facilitators requested the formation of new teams the same size as before (roughly five people). Participants were requested to read-their case to the others in their small group. The cases were to be saved for other uses, throughout the workshop.

Afternoon activity two: Conflict line. Now that the participants had heard the different accounts of conflicts in their group, the facilitator combined groups of five into groups of ten people. The individuals in each of these groups were requested to order themselves by consensus in a line that reflected how they ranked the gravity of the conflicts described in their individual cases. The purpose was to introduce the notion of a spectrum of conflict. Trainers sampled the cases selected for various positions on the line and facilitated discussions of the choices and their reasons. The following example is from the first group's report: of the most gravity was a case in which a death threat was delivered in a village, after which an actual killing occurred. The monk reporting was arrested concurrently and later released. Least weighty for this group was a member's experience with trying to explain a poem in an eighth grade classroom, in which a boy piped up that the poem was a lie. Somewhere in the middle of importance for them was the dilemma of trying to teach with love and compassion. If you do, students won't do their homework. But if you don't, they won't come to class.

One of the trainers commented that what was low for this group was about a single incident, whereas what was in the middle was about a habit. He asked the group what was to be learned from this. Comments were about the difference and gravity of problems. The easiest often are psychological, and the worst--as indicated by this groups most important item--include threats to life.

In another group the least important involved a difference of opinion that was difficult to resolve. When the trainer asked right off about why this order was chosen, again the answer came that problems range from psychological pain to, at least threat of, physical injury. As this group was queried about the reasons for their rankings, beginning from the lower middle of the line, they ranged upward from family conflict between parents and children, to a larger grouping of people involved, to a public conflict, to an institutional problem in which a temple sermon was called into question by a monk who threatened to take the problem to the board. Next highest on the scale of gravity for this group was another institutional problem in which fighting broke out and some people were hospitalized. The story indicating the most serious conflict for this group was an account of an incident during the insurrection in which the police came and dragged a village member away. In addition to the previously mentioned criteria of importance, this group reportedly found another criterion: the sheer numbers of people involved.

For a third group the easiest conflict in their stories was of two female teachers arguing in a school. The next story in line involved asocial injustice in which an inappropriate person was selected for a job. Somewhere in the middle was a case in which funds had been raised for some temple event which did not require the use of all the funds. An argument ensued among the board about what to do with the money left over--bank account, building fund? Second from the top was a religious conflict having to do with what the monks of this group termed "unethical conversions". Some Christians came to their village and gave gifts to all those who would convert. They reportedly rented a house, brought folks in from outside, and started prayer services. Lots of people reportedly came because they were giving things away. A group of young Buddhists went to them and threatened them, telling them to go away. They did it again, received a last warning, and then did it again. When the young Buddhists went out and drove them away, the police came and arrested the young Buddhists.

The 'Christians' simply went to another village where the same thing reportedly happened. In addition they tried to buy off the monks with scholarships, then tried to debate with one of the monks, claiming that the *New Testament* was the same as Buddhism. Finally the monk had them chased off. The other groups disagreed with this group about what they thought was the conflict of the most gravity. This group had ranked number one a case of a conflict in a work camp which eventually had to be resolved by a mediation board. A trainer had remarked that the gravity of this situation was marked by the length of time taken to resolve it. However, the members of other groups suggested that the proselytizing case was worse for two reasons: because it threatened the culture of the nation, and because so many people were potentially involved. A trainer chimed in that difference of opinion, as in this case of religious disagreement can have some of the most serious results. In contrast, personal disagreements between individuals rarely take on an organized form.

It was announced that we were about to take up the topic of how to act against conflicts. However, a trainer said that a bit more organized and detailed lecture material, about the spectrum of would be presented before we moved on. Part of what follows are my additions to what the trainer said. J.W. Keltner[19] assumes in a recent book that disputes and conflicts "are part of a larger struggle process which is a basic function of living and involves all of us. . ."[20] He has proposed a six-stage model to help understand the ways that "mild differences may escalate to disagreement, to dispute, to campaign, to litigation, and finally to fight or war."[21] One of the manifest purposes of having such a model is to help people have an early warning, to be able to diagnose their situation, and to choose remedies appropriate to the 'stage' in development of the conflict. Factors that influence the stages in this model are: "the processes we use with each other, our behaviors, our relationships, our goals, our orientation to each other, our communication, our decision making, possible outcomes, and our intractability potential.[22]" Elsewhere, the author adds another influence on this process: intervention possibilities.[23] The trainer closed the session by reiterating that our solution, if solution is called for at all, changes with the stage in the development of conflict.

Afternoon activity three-Debate: conflict good or bad? A trainer instructed participants to divide themselves into several groups based on whether they thought conflict to be largely negative, or largely natural and so good (or at least acceptable). The groups were to prepare their cases and then select a member to represent them in debate by occupying one of two chairs in the center of the room, in order. As a reminder of the two sides in the debate, one chair is designated negative, the other positive. Any occupant of a chair must vacate in less than 50 seconds to give spokespersons from other groups a chance to speak.

---

[19] J. W. Keltner, *The Management of Struggle: Elements of Dispute Resolution through Negotiation, Mediation and Arbitration* (Cresskill, New Jersey: Hampton Press, Inc. 1994). "Instead of the term conflict I want to use, as much as possible, the term "struggle." Conflict seems much to restrictive and negative in its general implications, and it has many contradictory implications and referents in our society. Because of these wide variances in perception and usage, I intend to use the term "struggle" to apply to all those situations in which people alone or in groups are in disagreement with each other or operatin in opposition to each other." (p. 1, Keltner's emphasis). "… rather than eliminate struggle we should manage it so that it does not become destructive. " (2). **"Peace ... does not mean the absence of struggle! It means the management of affairs, including the whole range of struggle, in such a way that there is not destruction of the human condition and potential."** (*ibid.,* Keltner's emphasis).

[20] *Ibid.,* 4.

[21] *Ibid.*

[22] *Ibid.*

[23] *Ibid.*

A monk opens with the view that conflict is good. Looking at the history of the world, great cultures, races and individuals were born out of the challenge of conflict. Without it there would be no great creation.

Monk 2: But look at our country. Fighting with Tamils in the north. Many lives lost. Economic development down the drain. Decline in such a situation is much greater than the gain.

Monk 3: Our paths are always through such conflict to progress. The south has had much terror, but the result has been a new and better government.

Monk 4: Countries need peace. The value of life is very high. From conflict comes the loss of life and property.

Monk 5: If not for the interest conflict brings, people would not come together. Because of two people we are born.

Monk 6: An intelligent group of people in here, before lunch, brainstormed thirty-two bad things about conflict.

Monk 7: Anyway, vision comes forth out of conflict: Sparta, the Buddha's philosophy.

Monk 8: Conflict itself is unimportant. The great teachers were trying to overcome it. The only people who profit from conflict are arms dealers.

Monk 9: Minds conflict--that is good.

Monk 10: After conflict no one is left living.

Monk 11: Because of war we love our country, our army, our nation.

By the time the last monk spoke there had obviously developed some levity in the room. A trainer intervened to ask for a verdict on the matter.

A monk offered what he said was a 'moderate' viewpoint. We are going to have conflict. So what is the point to saying that it is either good or bad. Good seems to arise out of some conflict. But we must see to it that negative effects are minimized.

A trainer reinforced this view, saying that it is not the conflict that is bad, but the way we use it, like electricity.

A monk asked for an example of a conflict used well. Reference was made to a poster which had earlier been hung on the wall. In the story depicted on the poster, two clans are on the brink of war about the diversion of the river Rohini, upstream. The Buddha intervenes and asks which is more important, blood or water. The two clans respond by settling the conflict. Another example offered is the case of a mass murderer being converted by Buddha. He is depicted in the story simply as a good man who had been misled.

A bit of "expert", lecturette material would have been helpful at this point. An example follows. One author notes the many advantageous, if not indispensable, roles of conflict in our lives. Conflict is a way to "delineate areas of common values", provides and opportunity to "clarify psychological boundaries, " and then the resulting "shared values and norms" add to a group's stability.[24] Conflict can help balance the extreme positions or view held by

---

[24] Wheelan, *op. cit.*, 15

people, thereby becoming an "energy source" which helps "drive the system" of a group.[25]

As an explanation for the inevitability of conflict as a stage in the development of groups, the following has been offered. Group members naturally aspire to develop independence within the group, and so begin to offer their own "goals and ideas about group structure. Coalitions begin to form among members with similar ideas and values. Splits occur as a result, and conflict inevitably ensues."[26] There are many paradoxes in this account of conflict. One is that this individuation process, leading to conflict, may initially be meant to reduce anxiety by helping the group get clear about goals and structure of the group. It is a way of assuring that divergent points of view are accommodated in a group with common interests.[27]

Another paradox is that conflict has been held to be helpful in developing trust. But the appeal is to our memory of our own experience: "It is easier to develop trust in another person or in a group if we believe that we can disagree and ... not be abandoned or hurt for our differences ... marriages become more solid and real after the first fight."[28] This could be held to hold across the board for relationships among people and groups, that having worked out conflict is an impetus to solidarity. "It provides energy, a commonly shared experience, and a sense of safety and authenticity, and it allows for deeper intimacy and collaboration."[29]

Even, or perhaps especially, a view which assigns so important and inevitable role to conflict in the stages of group development, will also recognize its harmful effects in relationships or groups wherein development is stunted. The appeal here is to experience as well:

> Longstanding wars, feuds, divorces, and the breakup of business partnerships are examples of the potential negative outcomes of conflict. Thus, while this stage cannot be avoided, since it is the only route to mature collaboration, most of us would rather bypass the conflict stage of group development. As with individual development, however, groups that avoid this stage remain dependent, insecure, and incapable of true collaboration, unitary action, or productive work.[30]

On this view, our experience teaches us the intuitive lesson that the importance and inevitability of war provides both the energy for cycling into closer relationships, and failing this, spiraling into levels of destruction of individual and social constituents.

---

[25] *Ibid.*, 16.
[26] *Ibid.*
[27] *Ibid.*
[28] *Ibid.*
[29] *Ibid.*
[30] *Ibid.*

Video of a social activist monk. During a protracted break, a video was shown of a monk who did a lot of social service work in southern Sri Lanka. Much of his work required some form of conflict management. In the spirit of experiential learning, participants were instructed to interact with it in their minds and be ready to provide an analysis of it later. In my view, some of the power of this video and these instructions was lost by not being closely tied to the following activity.

After PM break--Activity/discussion, causes of conflict: Buddhist perspective. Groups were instructed to produce short reports about a Buddhist perspective on causes of conflict. Follows some sample responses. *Conflict first arises in the mind. In a sermon Buddha said first to look at our own mind and see if what we are doing is right. Secondly, people get into conflict over things they want. Third, conflict can spread to the whole world. The root of all conflict is greed. *An instance of greed causing conflict is the problems that arise over money. There is also a Buddhist teaching about conflict arising because of diversity among people and groups. *Ways that conflict arises: 1) social--when state doesn't look after society; 2) individual--the root of which is greed. To be rid of conflicts we must see reality, the world as it is. If there is a violation of moral law in one area, the whole society can be affected with conflict breaking out everywhere. The way out is to be fully aware and to follow moral precepts--more meditation, more loving kindness, look inside yourself, and always try to help society. *Conflict starts between individuals: hatred, greed, delusion. Human beings try to change the world because they want to be close to what they desire and far from what they do not desire. In Buddhist mythology, the state was formed because poverty was the root of crimes. Humans are bound up in illusion. All problems are in their minds and are psychological.

Comments by Dr. Kalupahana. One of the resource people present at this inaugural training for Buddhist monks, was Dr. David Kalupahana, of the University of Hawaii. He was asked to speak about the Buddhist point of view on causes of conflict. What follows is a brief digest of his comments.[31] They are provided in the first person, to give a sense of the way he delivered them, and the end at the bottom of this paragraph. Some of my own observations on the previous session. I got the feeling that, as discussed in the early session, some thought conflict to be natural in the sense of being found in nature. Is it right that Buddhist teaching describes what conflict is in this sense? Does the world divide naturally into 'conflicting' pairs, groups, or camps? In Taoism there are many such divisions: genders; poles in electricity, positive and negative; yin and yang. Conflict is viewed as natural for them. The competing view in Buddhism is that conflict only arises in a cultural world created by humans. What is in nature is not really conflict. Buddha taught that we should avoid the two extremes that

---

[31] I interviewed Dr. Kalupahana on audiotape, shortly after he had delivered his comments in Singhala. This interview is being transcribed into written form, and I hope to revise what follows in a more accurate version.

occur even in language and take a middle path. The world of culture made by humans is a small one, so we must avoid the extremes. Salvation found in nirvana is beyond culture. Some monks have accepted conflict as natural. But it does not, said Dr. Kalupahana, exist in nature, only in the human world. A trainer agreed, saying that if you walk down the road and a limb falls on your head, hurting you, that is not conflict. Someone hits you with a limb, it is conflict.

4.4. Day 3

After meditation and breakfast: Activity, analysis of conflict. A trainer introduced this module by stating that the main purpose of this analysis was to be to find causes. He went on to discuss what will be meant here, operationally, by 'analysis'. It will simply be a list of causes for various conflicts which were noted in the cases written and discussed by individuals yesterday. He read a sample case and asked for the cause. During the August, '89 riots there were complaints of noise coming from a temple. The police investigated, found some firearms and arrested three boys. The chief incumbent was surprised with a charge of possessing weapons in the temple. The chief priest was thought to have undergone unnecessary difficulties because of this incident. Directions were given to groups to think of as many causes of conflict, in such a case, as they could. They were given five minutes, after which the group with the most causes reported their number to be fifty-three, among them: suspicion; violence; injustice; fear; selfishness; anger; envy, haughtiness; need; pride; degrading others; looking down upon others; self preservation; preservation of power and wealth; uncriticalness; cruelty; aggressiveness; domination, misunderstanding; ungratefulness; mental aberration; insatiable desire; praising oneself / looking down on others; poverty, love of power; quick anger; competition, economic inequality, generation gap; ignoring responsibilities; breach of traditions; nationalism; religiosity-, destruction of values; social oppression, dogmatism; partisanship; intoxicants.

A trainer observed that with so many causes, many of which overlap, it might be possible to narrow the field to a few 'fundamental', or 'root' causes. Participants were requested to go through their longer list for ten minutes with an eye to narrowing the list to the very primary causal factors. Reports followed.

The first report highlighted unilateral thinking--holding that some view is one-hundred percent true. The problem is that someone else will be holding that a conflicting view is one hundred percent true. This group also believed that a majority of the conflicts that occur have as a cause some sort of duplicity. Another cause is poverty, in a broad sense: material, mental, energy. The last mentioned cause by this group was social discrimination.

The second report was made on the chalkboard in relation to a diagram which had all further causes-individual, social and environmental--arising from ignorance. This ignorance flowed into individual causes through mental, bodily and speech-causes,

The third report also consisted in a diagram in which the world, at the top, was dispositionally conditioned by an underlayer of economic, social, political, environmental, religious and cultural factors, as well as factors related to diversity. At the bottom of the diagram, as the root of all of these factors, was (again) ignorance.

A fourth report listed ignorance, egoism, craving, inequality in society/and in needs, and individual nature.

A participant expressed having learned by his own experience that "you cannot pin it down to one cause."[32] A trainer remarked that multiple causes need to be integrated reasonably, and that this is supported by some writings.[33] He represented this integration in a pie chart, with curved arrows above and below representing a movement among unnecessary issues and more genuine ones. An example of an unnecessary squabble is the case of two lovers who fight because one of them has not written to the other one often enough while away. On the pie chart were 5 'pieces':

1. 'Relationship': He explained that interpersonal factors which sometime lead to conflict are like snoring and smoking, and that they derive partly from a lack of patience with each other.
2. 'Data', having to do with receiving the wrong information: An example used was thinking that someone else can use your airline tickets.
3. 'Needs', also referred to as interest-conflict, an example of which would be having one chair with two people who wanted to sit on it.
4. 'Structural', indicating rules and procedures which are perceived to preclude our doing what we want to do, or to restrict our creativity.
5. 'Essential ideas': This alludes to all of our 'sacred cows', or more literally to ideological or value conflicts.

As a test of recognition, the trainer closed out this lecture material with a brief case of two families who only can see the worst in each other. In anger one day, one family member spits on a member of the other family and a fight

---

[32] According to the bias of my paper at last year's conference (*ibid.*), this is an important insight. I also believe that a training setting is an important impetus for this learning. Without such experience just detailed, the approach of these monks might have been considerably more intellectual. The likely outcome of a more intellectual approach would have been a unilateral declaration of the single cause of conflict being ignorance. The problem with such a unilateral declaration, as I presented it in my paper, is a practical one. In order to make and keep peace we must cooperate with those of other traditions which claim other root causes for conflict. I believe a facilitative stance on causes of conflict is to assume that they are multiple.

[33] Notably Christopher Moore's *Mediation Process*.

ensues. The police have to come to break it up. Without providing a cause in this story, the trainer asked the participants to guess at cause(s). Answers came back which mainly focused on caste. A good lesson in basic problem solving--not to give up to soon on hypothesizing. The trainer offered that it may have been a bit of all of hem.

Activity, further analysis--conflict mapping. A trainer suggested that since many conflicts in our society arise out of needs and interests, it might be helpful to learn a method of 'mapping' these out in a situation. He presented such a method.

First, it was suggested that we give the conflict a name, providing it is an appropriate characterization. Giving a conflict the wrong designation can impede coming to agreement. In the example of a youngster who wants to borrow the family car, what if the father doesn't want to lend it? What will this be called? What is a neutral description? What would be a neutral description in the problem of a teacher who comes consistently late to work? Suggestion: "the issue about teacher-arrival"?

A second rational stage in mapping a conflict is to get clear about who are the parties to the conflict. If in the car case, above, the mother needs the car as well, we immediately have a different problem.

Next it seems reasonable to map out the needs and interests of the parties involved.

However, the mapping will not be complete without a last stage in the mapping which elicits ways in which fears of the parties involved may impede their movement toward settlement. So, what are their fears?

This 'map' might be displayed on a poster as follows. In the title of the poster will be the neutral name of the conflict which is inoffensive to all parties. Below this in serial order will be listed the name of each party, then next to their name, their needs or interests, and nest to that their fears. In the "who uses the car" case, the son's needs may be such things as impressing friends, impressing girls, and avoiding the stuffy bus. His fears might include that the father will refuse, and that his journey won't get made at all.

Groups were instructed to choose one of the cases participants wrote on day one and map out the conflict. After covering their results, a trainer discussed with the group the usefulness of this mapping. For one thing it helps us see the other persons point of view, and so have some sympathy for their needs and interests. This makes possible all parties having a sense of what would be a 'middle way' in the matter. It may even make it possible for the parties to ask each other for clarification on their needs and fears, thereby making the whole process more human. A trainer recounted an example from the authors Fisher and Ury, about two kids arguing over the only orange in the house prior to going to school. . The monks were asked about how to settle the matter. After many suggestions, a monk asked, "Well why does each of them want it?" This is the key to this example. The son wants the juice; and the daughter has a teacher wanting to demonstrate how to make marmalade. He needs the inside; she needs the peel.

First activity after lunch, listening. In order to be able to do well at mapping--getting agreement about the name, and finding out the parties' needs and fears, a good facilitator must be superlative at listening.

Brainstorming may be the first skill one is likely to learn in a problem solving oriented training about conflict management. However, the ability to listen effectively is surely the most basic skill in helping others to help themselves. One likely place to begin a consideration of listening is with a discussion of why effective listening is an issue at all. Why or how is there ineffective listening? This is a subject which requires little input from trainers, because participants generally have vast experience with being listened to ineffectively. What that looks like or means just needs to be elicited from them, which can be done with the whole group from the floor. Title a poster paper "Barriers to Effective Listening" and write down what they say, things like: physical difficulties (like poor hearing, or a tick), distractions, poor eye contact; physical barriers (like desks); and key psychological barriers (like disinterest, prejudging, stereotyping, and forming responses).

There are three levels of effective listening: content, feeling and values. The most basic of these, what is called active listening, is assuring a speaker they have been heard by repeating back the content of what they have said, <u>to their own satisfaction</u>, before stating one's own opinion. This is <u>the </u>fundamental place to start training conflict managers how to listen. It is also the fundamental way to show others that we care about what they have to say, and so care about them. Unfortunately, even this basic skill is not taught in school to anyone but communication majors. And even for them, much more time is spent teaching them to be good speakers.

A trainer reported that the Buddha had remarked about how distance affects communication. One should not be too far away, too close, too high above, too low, and not directly in front of those we are communicating with. So, Buddhists continue to be extra aware of body language in communication. For example lay people in Thailand Cambodia and Laos are careful to *wai* (put their hands together in front of their faces) when they greet monks. Monks in training practiced communicating close, far, above, below, overly direct, and back to back. This occasioned more levity than communication.

Focusing again on listening, a trainer remarked that Elizabeth Harris came to Sri Lanka to visit the rebels in Jaffa. When she went there to meet their leader she said she came not to talk but to listen. The trainer said a similar story is told of Mandela, commenting about peacemakers--that they come first to listen. Buddhists have added reasons to listen carefully, in that they have been taught to value highly staying very aware in the moment.

A good introduction to get participants interested in practicing active listening is to begin with having them generate a list of interesting topic about which to have a conversation- After that they can practice, in groups of three, being each of an active listener, one being actively listened to, and an observer.

Subsequently trainers have groups discuss what they learned in the process and then turn their discussion to uses for active listening. Groups often report the usefulness of active listening to show care, to summarize agreement, to get clarification, and to avoid misunderstanding.

A trainer closed this module for *Sarvodaya* by saying: 1) make sure to summarize and paraphrase; 2) whenever you paraphrase and summarize, you remember better; and 3) when you listen carefully, the speaker speaks better.

Activity after PM break--being assertive, rather that aggressive or passive. A trainer introduced this subject as an important aspect of human behavior. What do you do, he asked, if someone talks and talks, and won't stop to listen? What do you do about people who make requests that are hard to fulfill such as asking you to provide them a certificate that they attended a program when they didn't? Then there are people who will talk a long time about problems we know we cannot help with. How would we characterize a person with little moral fiber, bent at will by others, who might say or do nothing in response to the challenges just mentioned? One possibility is "submissive" (others are "timid", or "passive"). If 'submissive' were written at one end of a line, representing the far reach on a spectrum of <u>not</u> taking action to protect one's own interests, what would we call the extreme other side of the line? How would we characterize a person who acts to further only his or her own interests, always at the expense of the interests of others? The trainer suggested that "aggressive" seems to fit as a depiction of those people.

Assuming that we want to be like neither of those types of people, when there are conflicting interests at stake, what would be a middle path between these two extremes? The trainer said that this is often referred to among conflict managers as "assertive behavior". Assertive people are able to delay seeking a solution that is solely in their own favor. They can wait until they have heard the interests of others in order to see if all interests can be satisfied--at least to some extent. They are also able to stand firm, until their own interests are considered, in the face of others who wish prematurely to preempt decision-making. This sort of person is more likely to be involved in conflict resolutions that stand the test of time.

A trainer proposed a case for consideration. A junior monk in a temple is approached by a big donor to that temple and asked to borrow the temple's statue for a short time. The policy is not to let it outside. One possible reply: "It is a historical relic. If the district government official comes by and it is not here, I will have to tell him that you took it." This would be near the middle, that is be somewhat assertive. Other assertive possibilities are just to say no and not give reasons. He has a right to do that. Or, he could say no with understanding-, I understand that you want it badly, but I cannot lend it." He could also take the time to explain his interests, and listen to the other person's; although the answer may turn out to be the same. Or, there may be the possibility of appeal to policy makers.

Although it was not done during this module, trainers often have participants role play handling a situation in all three ways: submissively, aggressively, and assertively. With four people in a group, each member gets the experience of behaving in each of the three ways, as well as feeling what it is like to have others behave that way to them. Lessons learned in that manner are often thought to be more useful at the level of reactions and practical skills, than theoretical information alone stored in memory.

4.5. Day 4

After meditation, chanting and breakfast--discussion on peace with Dr. Ariyaratne. A trainer
introduced this discussion by reviewing the workshop goal of being able to resolve conflicts without their resulting in harmful struggles. The final aim of conflict resolution, he said, is peace, a word that is so misunderstood. We pay great attention, in the press and elsewhere, to wars. Yet we have given only a fraction of that amount of attention to peace issues. He said that Dr. Ariyaratne would be giving some thoughts on the matter of peace, and then anyone who wanted would be able to discuss with him their own thoughts on what he said.

The following are Dr. Ariyaratne's words to monk-participants as recorded by means of a translator. They are in the first person, as he delivered them.

We need to be able to resist entanglement in society which leads to peace being disturbed. When peace was disturbed in the North of our country [the 1983 Tamil uprising], I went directly to the area to see the president. When I was not able to do so, I returned and called his office requesting a curfew. The president refused and said of me that I was against the Singhalese and against the nation.

I went back to the area, talked to the district and got them to set up refugee camps, without instructions from others to do so. At that time I saw that the Tamils were also divided among themselves over such things as caste. Thinking about peace after this, my thoughts have been these.

Our aim as individuals is liberation. Our immediate environment is our family. Next is the village, that is, rural or urban communities; and, next is our nation. From the point of view of my own liberation, why do I want peace and to make peace among others? Because I have compassion for them. To have peace among others, they must also do many things. But I can give them compassion.

At any two moments our personality stays uniform and continues in a process of dependent origination, conditioned by causes prior to birth, in the environment after birth, as well as from other mental and bodily factors.

I was just chatting with Burr about market economics. Maximization of production is the aim in that. Though mostly misunderstood, there is a way to promote efficiency, or quality in Buddhist terms. Involved in highly efficient means, we must never lose track of the aim of doing everything for the awakening of ourselves, our families, villages and for the benefit of having compassion in our minds for everyone. We have been cutting trees for firewood and energy. In forty years time we may not have this source of energy any more, and have to look for others. Still in Sri Lanka, there is a disturbance of the environment and we must inform the government that we need to take a middle path. Villages are becoming economically divided. In the U.S. seventy times the energy is being used as in developing countries, which contributes to poverty elsewhere. Why do these things happen?

Science has now been developed to the point that scientists are interfering with nature at the cellular level. Also they are attempting to produce humans under laboratory conditions. Doing this violates certain natural conditions. How far are our man made laws in accord with the laws of nature? International government organizations should not, any more than anyone else should, make laws that are out of accord with the laws of nature. There are Buddhist versions of natural, phenomenal laws. They refer to laws in the seed, in the seasons, with the working of karmic forces, and with mental factors...

In today's family environment, in this country, eighteen percent are having problems--principally owing to wives going to work as never before. Twenty percent more are in physically challenging circumstances, such as a war zone. Practical approaches, strategies, need to be developed to reduce the negative affects of these trends.

I have been able to get Tamils to visit Buddhist temples, and Buddhists to go to Hindu temples--as one of many strategies we have been using. Now I am looking at the whole country, in which power is mainly invested in the government. According to the Buddhist 'law of righteousness', government is to be the peoples' representative. Phenomenal laws are influencing the people. The people can show the way to the government. We must find the right mix in the laws of nature, government, and people in order to influence the future toward a just peace. I plan to build an institute, to have others focus on the social work and I will concentrate on these peace matters, along with those who want to come here and join me.

Question: Of the four happinesses in Buddhism one of them is prosperity, or being rich. How is this related to an open economy?

Answer: The '83 uprising was a brainchild, of the national government, that got out of control. This is why the president did not immediately meet my request for a curfew. Such things are accepted, in an open economy, if they seem to result in short term gains. Non-violence and self-denial are <u>qualities</u>. They cannot be centralized. They are in the minds of people. Only what can be quantified can be centralized.

These days there are many contaminants in our foods, like preservatives, which centralized bodies overlook because they relate to profits. Privileged individuals are granted big loans, which village cooperatives apply for but are denied. If centralized government, the private sector, and the people get together, however, it is possible to have an open economy. But we do not really have one now.

Question: What about the future of the conflict in the northeast?

Answer: There is no instant solution. We must educate people, go to them and unite the common people of both communities.

Question: What about the *Sarvodaya* workers who have been lulled?

Answer: This was not reported accurately. Under the Indian government we were allowed to distribute food up there. Even Supreme Court judges up there were refugees at the time. Other groups up there did not, for various reasons, like it that *Sarvodaya* was there distributing food. If they were influential they would spread rumors about us. Media often are not interested in reporting our side, like for example this training being done here, because we steer clear of being part of any particular political party.

Question: How are these government policies, for example the ones about the environment, affecting the masses.

Answer: Things are changing from the old days of the ~power pyramid' with the king at the pinnacle of power and influence. In the future, the villagers can be linked through science, computers and spirituality, as well-without going through the government.

After AM, cooperation vs. competition module. A trainer opened this module by saying that in every conflict there is the potential for struggle. However, there are concepts and practices we can learn which will lessen the possibility that this potential for struggle will have negative effects on relationships, families, communities and society. The concept is win-win, or cooperation. Competition seems important in many sports. But, apart from them other forms of play should teach children to be cooperative. Even businesses said to be in competition with each other for the same markets will often cooperate for the sake of the future of their industry, or to regulate themselves instead of having government regulate them. Certainly the various divisions inside of such organizations can greatly reduce the overall efficiency of their organizations by competitive, win-lose behavior against each other.

Even when our effectiveness requires our being able to cooperate, still certain individuals, departments or societies believe that they will get more if they can win at the expense of others. This is a dangerous, short -term view; and, it is as dangerous for those who think they can get away with it as it is for those who supposedly lose. In the long run, our belief is that win-lose behavior is a - downward spiral of mutual retaliation to keep others from succeeding at our expense. In the end, there may seem to be win-lose behavior; but actually, after the retaliation is over, there is only lose-lose. That is, there is no win-lose, really only win-win and lose-lose.

There is a companion concept to win-lose. It is the belief by those who attempt to win over others that for every triumph there is a loser, as though all human behavior could be factored into a "zero-sum". However, in many of our endeavors it is possible for us to achieve our visions and goals in cooperation with others, so that they are not hampered from, and perhaps even are aided in, achieving their goals too. Good conflict managers are always on the lookout for these sorts of solutions to situations of conflict and potential struggle.

Of the examples related in the workshop, here is one. Imagine two donkeys tied together in a field with grass all around. For a day they happily eat all of the grass around them until they are standing in a circle of barren ground. What to they do now? Suppose each of them begins to pull in the direction of the grass in front of their face, and that it is in opposite directions. At first it looks like it may be possible to ignore the other one, or perhaps even win at the expense of the other, who would be left in the barren circle. However, since they are pulling in opposite directions, neither one of them gets the grass; when all they really need to do is move in the same direction, whatever it is.

As an observer of this module, I believe it would have been more effective with the addition of some practical experience. Simulations exist which allow participants to experience what happens when they attempt to win at the expense of others. Afterward they are able to review what they have done and decide for themselves, which most of them do, whether they would have gained much more in the simulation by having cooperated with others. My opinion is that such theoretical material about cooperation versus competition as just summarized, is much more effective ff it is offered to people who have experienced an overly competitive environment. After lunch, module--the conflict 'circle'. A trainer presented a cyclical model of managing conflict. Imagine it as a circle, with stages connected by arrows, which eventually cycle back to the first item in the stage--conflict. Once conflict occurs, the first stage in its management for it to be understood, or analyzed. Next will come the suggestion of many hypotheses as to how it can be managed. Next will be the choice of one of those hypotheses, hopefully with the agreement of the parties to the conflict. This hypothesis will be acted upon, and subsequently there will be an evaluation made. If the conflict is successfully managed at this point, the cycle will be broken. If it is not, the cycle will be repeated.

Similar to my comment about the cooperation module, my opinion is that in a workshop setting, ff theoretical material is important enough to present, it is important enough for the participants concurrently to have skills and attitudes developed in relation to that material.

Mediation module. What does a mediator do? A trainer provided the following suggestions: 1) skillfully enter into the situation; 2) take up the task of trust building: between the mediator and the parties as well as among the parties. The mediator must associate with them, 3) bring both, or all, sides to agreement about accepting mediation, 4) study the conflict. How many factors are involved, for example. How are each experienced differently by the parties; and 5) negotiate the resolution of struggle.

Negotiation begins with how they are going to sit. There will be cultural factors involved here as elsewhere. Sitting across from each other may, for some, be overly direct. They may need to sit side by side, with the mediator across from them.

The role of mediator is different from the role of a judge. It is to help people understand their issues, then to help other parties understand them. A mediator may spend considerable time with each party in private. If possible a mediator may be equally a friend of each.

A mediator may fulfill the following roles as well: 1) active participator; 2) breaker of deadlocks; 3) skill and attitude developer or trainer; 4) idea or solution investigator or explorer; 5) conveyer of solutions; 6) one who brokers agreement; 7) recorder of agreements. A mediator helps show parties the realities or practicalities of situations. A mediator the sort of leader who if the parties succeed, they did it themselves. But if failure occurs the leader is ready to be the scapegoat. Things a good mediator does not do are: 1) sit in judgment; 2) settle agreements with his or her own power 3) show partiality to one party over another; or 4) breach confidentiality.

Participants practiced being a mediator while others role played various cases of conflicts: such as the river Rohini case. Attention was paid to how the parties sat, and especially to repeating back what each side said and summarizing any areas of agreement that emerged.

Discussion ensued about the way that famous leaders can play other roles in times of struggle. There is the case of the Buddha coming upon a dispute in one of the great monasteries of the time. The dispute was about hygiene habits of some of the monks. The Buddha simply left and went to the forest. The monks had to work it out among themselves in order to have the Buddha return. This was compared to instances in which Gandhi fasted until struggle abated.

The Buddha is depicted as being a conflict manager in other situations as well. There is a legend about him helping in Sri Lanka in a dispute over a jeweled chair. In the *Majjhima-nikāya* the Buddha is portrayed as recommending to those involved in disputes that they should: 1) pick the correct time to enter as a mediator; 2) speak softly and kindly; 3) see to it that the truth is told; 4) use only words that are fruitful or useful; 5) speak with compassion.

The participants were asked to consider the simple case of their neighbor being angry and to propose some approaches. One suggestion was to talk to him about his good activities. Another was to show kindness to him and his family, not overlooking kindness to his children. If communication has broken down, it was suggested that one might be able to talk to the neighbor's family or friends.

A trainer then adapted this discussion to one of greater scope, at least in terms of numbers of people involved. He said that if India is angry with Sri Lanka, the latter may offer aid in times of crisis. This may go on more than once, say three times, before any reciprocation is observed. Letters may be written, and may go unanswered for a few times, before a response would come. It might be possible to exchange some things with them useful to each party, but not useful to furthering their struggle. It is important to notice that there are always alternative solutions to maintaining or deepening the struggle.

The main feature of good solutions, it was suggested, is various forms of justice. There is substantial justice, process justice, justice equitable to all parties, compensatory justice (for past damages), and subtractive justice or justice which includes sanctions. With regard to the latter, it is often difficult to determine that one side alone has done wrong. If this surety cannot be achieved, and sanctions are to be imposed, they should be imposed on all who deserve them.

Evenings of this workshop were spent in informal presentations by various speakers and facilitators, with questions from the monks. My last evening with them I discussed just war theory, *jihad*, and the hope that Buddhism in Sri Lanka will not develop a concept similar to these, because such concepts have so often become an excuse for the abuse of mass violence.

I clearly observed in this training how very capable and ready these monks were to add these skills and this role to the other ways they contribute to their society. One great advantage to training them to be trainers in conflict resolution themselves may not have been considered as yet by those in support of this training. Many of them will eventually go through a train the trainers workshop and learn to conduct workshops similar to the one described above. In addition to the elevated credibility they will bring to the training of monks, there is the added factor of how much greater will become their own mediation skills because of having to internalize them at the level of trainers. I believe their commitment to peaceful mediation as a response to struggle will be an internalized beacon of light to those considering more militant approaches.

CHAPTER 14

BUDDHIST THOUGHT IN *SARVODAYA* PRACTICE

A. T. Ariyaratne

Among various facets of contemporary Buddhism two aspects have always attracted me. One is the living Buddhism among the rural masses as understood and practiced by them in their daily life. Second, the applicability of Buddhist teachings as a whole to meet the numerous challenges modern Sri Lankans face as individuals, families, communities and a nation. These challenges are not confined to a Sri Lankan context only. They also have a direct relationship to what is taking place in the international scene as a whole. Therefore, what I am attempting to do in this paper is to describe as concisely as possible how through the *Sarvodaya Shramadana* Movement of Sri Lanka, Buddhist thought and its applications have developed during a period of four decades beginning from the mid-nineteen fifties.

The word *Sarvodaya* was coined by Mahatma Gandhi from two Sanskrit words *sarvam* and *udayam*. He believed that post-independent India should develop on a vision of working for the "welfare of all." He believed in a "welfare society" as opposed to a "welfare state" of the western model. After independence he could not live long enough to guide the nation towards this ideal of *Sarvodaya* through concrete action programs. However, his close followers led by Acharya Vinoba Bhave and Shri Jayaprakash Narayan developed programs such as the Bhoodan (Land Gift), Gramdan (Village Gift), and Shanth Sena (Peace Army) movements and during their life times these were very successful.

Sri Lanka adopted the word *sarvodaya* from India and was inspired by what was already achieved by the Gandhian Movement in that country. However the *Sarvodaya* movement in Sri Lanka was nurtured and developed independent of the Indian experience in most aspects. This was primarily due to the Buddhist cultural background of Sri Lanka.

The word *sarvodaya* itself was given a different connotation and meaning. The Buddha is the Supremely Enlightened or Awakened One. All Buddhists strive to attain *nibbāna,* the ultimate state of enlightenment or awakening. In his first discourse the Buddha speaks of "the arising of vision (*cakkhum udapādi*), the arising of knowledge (*ñānam udapāti*), the arising of wisdom (*paññā udapādi*), the arising of nescience (*vijjā udapādi*), and the arising of light (*āloko udapādi*)." This indeed is a call to awaken your eye (of truth), awaken your knowledge, awaken your wisdom, awaken your science (of understanding), and awaken the light (within you). As such, the word *Sarvodaya* was interpreted in the Sri Lankan *Sarvodaya* Movement as the "awakening of all."

1. Levels of Awakening

The concept of human awakening for practical formulation of programs is organized into six levels all of which are, however, inter-related.

> Awakening of human personalities (*pauruṣodaya*)
> Awakening of families (*kuṭumbodaya*)
> Awakening of village communities (*grāmodaya*)
> Awakening of urban communities (*nagarodaya*)
> Awakening of nations (*deśodaya*)
> Awakening of the world community (*viśvodaya*)

Each of these levels of awakening is categorized into many sectors again for practical purposes even though all these are interrelated and interdependent. The six broad sectors into which *sarvodaya* has developed its activities are spiritual, moral, cultural, social, economic and political. In all these six sectors there should be an awakening process taking place from within individuals and extending to the world community in a harmonious way for real progress and peace.

The Buddha, in his first sermon, exhorts monks to go forth into the world and work for the welfare of the people. A cardinal principle in Buddhism, i.e., seeking people, going forth in search of them, was adopted by *Sarvodaya* as its working ethos. Identifying needs wherever they are, and working with the people in order to meet such needs was the main objective of going to the people. *Sarvodaya's* philosophy and program of work was thus fashioned deriving inspiration from the Buddha's teachings.

The *Sarvodaya* assumption is that the practical aspects of Buddhist philosophy the people followed in the past could also be profitably utilized to sustain them in the present time. *Sarvodaya* tested this assumption while working in the villages of Sri Lanka. As an example I can cite the pattern of agricultural life in the rural areas, which has a number of practices inspired by Buddhist teachings.

There are numerous teachings attributed to the Buddha and his principal disciples. Some of these teachings have become unidentifiable elements of a popular living psychology of people. For example when something unusual or tragic occurs in their community or any other part of their country or the world an illiterate woman hearing this sad news may involuntarily utter with her hand on her cheek the words *"aniccaṁ dukkhaṁ anattāṁ."* She may know only vaguely that these words have a profound philosophical meaning pertaining to all living things. Impermanence, pain and non-substantiality are inescapable realities of every conditioned existence. In a positive sense the Buddha's unique teaching of the principle of "dependent arising" (*paṭiccasamūppada*) would be the subconscious philosophical or psychological base from which the woman responded to the shocking news she heard.

The story of Kisagotami comes to my mind here. Kisagotami's only son had just died. She, overcome by intense pain of mind, went around asking people to provide her with a medicine to bring back the dead son to life. Finally she was asked to go to the Buddha. The Buddha asked her to fetch a handful of mustard seeds from a house where no death had taken place. Kisagotami went from one house to another, and finally realized that death came to all.

It is this process of realization in the individual, arising out of contact with others that *Sarvodaya* has based itself in developing its practical programs. The awakening of the individual arises through realization. He comes into contact with others through a social interaction process, and in him there dawns the understanding. It is this understanding that illuminates his entire chain of actions thereafter. In the story of Kisagotami, she herself identified the truth, i.e., the inevitability of death in the context of living. *Sarvodaya* attempts to transfer such basic Buddhist teachings to the day-to-day experience of our people.

As a corollary of this realization *Sarvodaya* believes in self-help. Buddhism exhorts its followers to strive hard without becoming dependent on help from outside. The importance of self-help is emphasized while at the same time underscoring the group effort that ultimately brings the social process to a meaningful conclusion. *Sarvodaya* strived to achieve this balance between individual self-reliance and group self-help.

2. Application of Philosophy

The problem faced by *Sarvodaya* is how best to identify these Buddhist thoughts in the psychological environments of people, develop these with the help of enlightened scholarship amongst us, relate them judiciously and selectively to the myriad of problems human beings and communities face at present, weave them into a comprehensive philosophical framework, and through processes of formal and non-formal education help people to absorb these refined philosophical thoughts again into their living culture. The sum total of this exercise is what *Sarvodaya* calls developing a "vision." It is this vision that *Sarvodaya* has converted into a Mission with the participation of over 10000 village communities out of a total of 24000 village communities in Sri Lanka.

Sarvodaya Shramadana means "awakening of all" in society worldwide. This is sought to be achieved through the sharing of labor and other voluntarily gifted resources for the personal and social awakening of all beginning with individuals and families at the community level. The critical mass of awakening in many communities will effect change at the national level and subsequently at the global level. In very concise terms, the mission of *Sarvodaya Shramadana* is to create a new global social order based on the values of truth, non-violence and self-sacrifice and governed by the ideals of a participatory democracy. The decentralization of power and resources, upholding of basic duties and rights, satisfaction of basic human needs, protection and nurturance of a healthy environment, non-violent conflict resolution and tolerance of cultural, religious and linguistic differences will be given pride of place in such an order. The economic principle would be one of a sustainable (no-poverty, no-affluence) society based on the sharing of resources and their prudent and mindful use.

It should be observed from what I have stated so far that the mission of the *Saryodaya Shramadana* Movement was not to engage in an academic exercise to prove or disprove a particular view point from scholarly debates and treatises. On the other hand it was a genuine endeavor, however small, on the part of some concerned and committed human beings, like the present writer himself, to bring about a transformation for the better in the lives of millions of human beings the world over who have not yet been benefited by the development strategies practiced by the present decision makers.

In this endeavor, in the Sri Lankan context, we have attempted to learn as much as possible from the Buddhist teachings and practices and apply them to achieve our objectives. *Sarvodaya* may have failed to reach the high academic standards in our written expositions about our work as expected by well-known expatriate Sri Lankan scholars such as Gananath Obeysekera ("Social and Ethical Transformation in Modern Theravāda Buddhism - A Polemical Essay"). Yet in the *Sarvodaya* philosophy and practice as evolved up to now in 37 years numerous individuals and village communities have come to accept that there is some hope for themselves in this self-development approach.

The attempts made by these scholars need a response because their assumptions are based on wrong premises. To describe *Sarvodaya* as a Movement started by "goodhearted but naive western intellectuals who see the movement in terms of their own utopian fantasies of a benevolent social order" is to mislead others as to what *Sarvodaya*'s philosophy and program is. Obeysekera, in order to prove his points resorts to highly personal and irrelevant arguments. One is that "Ariyaratne with his educated Protestant background writes in English" which is, according to him, a characteristic of what he calls a "Protestant Buddhism."

I do not want to dwell at length on such criticism coming from academics without any basic understanding of Buddhist Practice and *Sarvodaya* programs of work. I really wanted to draw your attention to criticism often leveled at *Sarvodaya* and the nature of arguments marshaled in order to prove them. I wrote both in English and Sinhala (more in Sinhala) depending on the audience I wish to address.

3. *Sarvodaya* Approach

Sarvodaya in selecting Buddhist principles and practices had two important considerations: (1) their immediate and long-term benefit and relevance to modern day problems, and (2) the extent to which such principles and practices were incorporated into our own socio-economic life. Such principles and practices identified from past socio-economic life were not "just" incorporated in our program of action. These were amended or even were reformulated to suit modern contexts. In Buddhism we have the principle of *ehi passiko,* which loosely interpreted could mean "come, test it," 'of, "experience it yourself and then accept it." That was *Sarvodaya*'s test method of both principle and experiences taken from Buddhist philosophy.

Unfortunately, Obeysekera who states that we have only *Shramadana* (sharing of labor) as a successful strategy, taken from Buddhist practice, has not seen and experienced our programs in action. Those come under six broad heads, namely, spiritual, moral, cultural, social, economic and political life, which attempt to cover every aspect of human life. The difference between a family gathering or any other strategy such as *kayya* (a corporate social action - in give and take spirit - found in agricultural life) may have and should have their parallels in other countries. But in Sri Lanka, in the past, nurtured by Buddhism, such practices gained a distinctive Buddhist flavor. What *Sarvodaya* has done is to carefully select such practices and reformulate these to suit modern social situations. This has to be understood by experiencing the *Sarvodaya* process personally. Empirical realization is the touchstone of such principles and practices. It is very difficult to understand them second or third hand, for example, by way of paid research assistants to collect data for you, while you analyze them seated in a university room, perhaps in the United States. As one of our own sociologists Prof. Nandasena Ratnapala has remarked "second or third hand research or research by means of *podiyans* (ill-paid research assistants) is not the way to understand *Sarvodaya* experience. (Janashruti Vidyava, 1995)

Let me examine some of the efforts made by *Sarvodaya* in relation to both theory and practice to achieve the above-mentioned goals.

It has become a fad these days to talk about a multi-ethnic, multi-religious, multi-linguistic society and the importance of providing for all these divisions in society so that no discrimination against any group is permitted under the law. While accepting the reality of the existence of this multiplicity of groups and the importance of accepting all as equals before the law *Sarvodaya* emphasizes and advocates the positive principle of striving to achieve the "well-being or the awakening of all." The compartmentalization and separation of life needs to be overcome. Unless an individual develops in one's own mind respect towards all life such an individual cannot successfully awaken his or her own personality. The cultivation of this mental attribute of *mettā*, or loving kindness, as advocated by the Buddha, is indispensable for the spiritual progress of any individual. More importantly the establishment of this principle in the minds and hearts of a critical mass of people in all countries of the world, I believe, is the surest way to set about building a tolerant and peaceful world order.

This process of activity is not based on a vision of a glorious past conceived in our fantasy. We have observed how the philosophy of Buddhism can be translated into action in the real experiences of the people. Buddhist teachings backed by small group action strengthened the rural life of our people. What *Sarvodaya* did was to understand the significance of such teachings and small group action, relate them to one another in the context of modern experience.

The four *brahma-vihāras* (sublime abodes), namely, *mettā* (loving kindness), *karuṇā* (pity - what *Sarvodaya* applies as compassionate action), *muditā* (sympathetic joy), and *upekkhā* (equanimity), are the foundations on which *Sarvodaya* advocates the promotion of personality awakening. The more a human society has individuals mindful of their own personality awakening as a spiritual objective the better placed will such a society be to achieve justice, peace and progress. In the *Karaṇīyametta-sutta, Mettānisaṁsa-sutta, Mahāsudassana-sutta, Khaggavisāṇa-sutta,* and many other *suttas,* Buddha strongly advocates these four qualities to be constant companions of a good Buddhist. *Sarvodaya* appeals to all human beings: "Respect life. Engage yourself in service to others to remove the causes that bring about physical and mental pain and fear in them. Cultivate detached joy resulting from such selfless activity and learn to face loss and gain, fame and blame, comfort and suffering with equanimity."

4. A Concern for All

This approach of *Sarvodaya* has successfully worked in the villages where *Sarvodaya* is active. *Sarvodaya* development programs are active in more Buddhist, Hindu, Muslim and Christian villages than those done by their respective religious organizations. Non-Buddhist people have subscribed to the *Sarvodaya* philosophy of working for the well-being or awakening of all from their religious perspectives. They participate as one human family in *Shramadana* (gift of labor) and *Shanthi Sena* (peace brigade) camps, Relief Rehabilitation Reconstruction Reconciliation and Reawakening projects and programs conducted in civil war affected areas, leadership and occupational training programs, and in all other *Sarvodaya* activities.

This approach based on Buddhist teachings emphasizes the oneness of human beings without any emphasis on factors that divide the community into fractions. Race, caste, gender, belief etc. had no relevance in such an approach. Compassion for all even extending to cover animals and the environment made *Sarvodaya* activity reach all communities and all religions because respect for life and compassion were the foundation on which such activity was based.

The people were motivated to identify their basic needs and discover the extent to which such needs are satisfied. Such an exercise involving small group action did not basically differ from a Buddhist to a Hindu, a Christian or a

Muslim village. Leadership was identified and in such an exercise the role of the clergy in each religion was given due recognition. Religious rituals were usefully utilized in order to motivate and involve people in development programs. *Sarvodaya*'s approach is now well documented. A study done by ICED at the University of Connecticut (ed. by Phillip Coombs - 1990) shows how in Buddhist and Christian villages the respective religious rituals are utilized for involving people's participation. The manner in which religious amity is supported by the temple, church, the dewale and the mosque is also attested to in other studies. The practical levels to which *Sarvodaya* has accomplished its objectives could be viewed only by involving oneself in this total context.

It is natural for one to refer to the question as to the present troubled situation in Sri Lanka and question *Sarvodaya*'s role in this context. The question may be posed that if *Sarvodaya*'s activities had been going on successfully how could three insurrections, one still having its heavy toll of human suffering in North Sri Lanka take place. In 1971 and 1988 - 89 when the two youth insurrections took place in the south of Sri Lanka, none of *Sarvodaya* trained youth took part in such violence. As the complex forces of these youth insurrections were directly related to the centralization of political power, *Sarvodaya* could do very little to arrest them. The source of destruction emanated from the highest and centralized political and governmental structures over which *Sarvodaya* had no control. But in keeping *Sarvodaya* youth away from violence and coming to their help once the insurrection ceased, *Sarvodaya* did its expected role. Many a youth involved in the 1971 insurrection received help from *Sarvodaya* and re-joined the mainstream political and social life.

The same phenomenon can be seen at work today. In the case of the turmoil that is going on in the North and East, *Sarvodaya* is doing what it can in order to rehabilitate the almost destroyed country. In times of racial clashes particularly in 1983, in the South, and thereafter in the North, *Sarvodaya* committed itself to help and succor human beings and did its best to alleviate their sufferings. In a very dark age of our recent history, almost under siege, *Sarvodaya* strived to protect human rights. We could do all such activities because of the great inspiration the philosophy and program received from Buddhism.

Meetings of *Sarvodaya* workers are known as Family Gatherings. This is to inculcate the idea that in spite of our differences we are one species (*Vāseṭṭa-sutta*) and as such we should consider ourselves as one human family. In all family gatherings and other *Sarvodaya* programs time is set apart for a common meditation and religious observances. Common meditation is based on *ānāpānāsati bhāvanā* (mindful breathing) and *mettā bhāvanā* (meditation on loving kindness). In religious observances, according to the numbers of people present, the smaller religious groups are given the first opportunity to observe their faiths so that psychologically they can overcome any sense of minority or inferior feelings they may have. This in a way we believe is a continuation of the Aśokan tradition of respecting adherents of all religious faiths as admonished by the Buddha himself.

5. *Shramadana* Camps

Dāna (giving, gifting, sharing) is a very important principle in Buddhist teachings. It is so in other world religions as well. *Sarvodaya* calls all people to share whatever they are capable of with others as their contribution to build a better society. Gifting manual labor (*sramadāna*), land (*bhūmidāna*), knowledge *jñānadāna*), skills (*silpadāna*), spiritual knowledge (*dhammadāna*) and so on are the ways in which anybody rich or poor, educated or uneducated can contribute to the *Sarvodaya* effort.

A *Shramadana* camp provides the physical, psychological, social and the working environment in which these gifts as well as other forms of group conduct can be practiced. Hundreds of such camps are held throughout the year on different locations. The physical output of such camps may be access roads to villages, renovation or construction of village tanks and irrigation systems, community drinking water projects, environmental and reforestation schemes, community health work, housing and so on. On the other hand the practice of sharing, pleasant language, constructive work and equality in association bring about a social benefit that cannot be expressed in monetary terms. At this stage what we call psychological infrastructure building is attempted.

For a lay Buddhists, the practice of not only *dāna* but also *sila* (morality) and *bhāvanā* (meditation) is important. The *Shramadana* camp environment provides an excellent opportunity to initiate particularly the young and youth to these practices. Our societies are fast moving towards embracing the unchecked materialism of modern economics. In a free market open economy the religious and spiritual heritage of our societies has been brushed away leaving room for competitive and possessive instincts of individuals to flourish. Youth, women and children are the first victims of this societal malaise. Alcoholism, drug addiction, crimes, child prostitution, spread of sexually transmitted diseases and AIDS are taking dangerous proportions. All macro structures in the political and economic fields knowingly or unknowingly are contributing to aggravate this situation. The formal and non-formal educational activities conducted by *Sarvodaya* in camps and other places are doing their utmost to combat these evils and create public opinion against them.

6. Participation and Inclusion

In the context of the modern day it is through education coupled with meaningful social action that we could deal with such social problems. Buddhism had taught us that the correct understanding of the problem (a form of *sammā-diṭṭi*), is the first step towards the solution. Based on this understanding a program in which small groups carry out basic social action has to be formed. *Sarvodaya* recognizes the importance of such small groups beginning from the family-kinship network, neighborhood groups, the village, the street community in urban areas, and attempts to mobilize these to achieve its desired objectives.

Participation of the people is the foundation of the social action programs of *Sarvodaya*. Such participation is conceived in (1) understanding a problem, (2) formulating a plan of action to deal with the problem, (3) putting that plan into effect, (4) evaluating the implementation and correcting the plan it, if necessary, and (5) sharing its results.

Personality and family awakening can successfully take place only if the village community is on a path to village awakening. After our countries went under alien rulers for centuries our village communities were exploited and marginalized. While numerous macro rural development schemes were implemented with foreign aid and grants, the benefits of most of these accrued to the already rich and powerful, thus increasing the gap between the marginalized and the privileged. The top-down plans simply did not work. *Sarvodaya* on the other hand does not believe that our present economic and political structures modeled on the western experience will ever change the situation for the better. The present system needs a radical transformation that permits our own indigenous genius, cultural traditions and ethos of the people to emerge in the form of a new system. *Sarvodaya* learnt a great deal from the Gandhian concept of *grām svarāj* (village self-government). The philosophical basis for the Sri Lankan experiment was greatly enriched by the early Buddhist literature as well.

The teachings contained in some of the Buddha's discourses such as the *Mahā-maṅgala-sutta, Parābhava-sutta, Mahā-parinibbāna-sutta, Cakkavatti-sīhanāda-sutta, Aggañña-sutta* and *Vyaggapajja-sutta* are those that inspired the *Sarvodaya* thinking on village re-awakening. The basic principles on which a sustainable and progressive society may be founded, serving both the *attha* (economic) and *dhamma* (moral) well being of the people, can clearly be developed from these teachings.

The Buddhist teachings, emphatically stated here, are not taken by *Sarvodaya* merely because of their philosophical importance. Whatever teaching had a practical social relevance, it was immediately adopted by *Sarvodaya*. Take for example the idea that a human being differs from another not because of birth but because of action. The Buddha put this idea into practice by his admission of those considered as of low birth into his community of monks. *Sarvodaya* revived this Buddhist practice by starting its initial program among a community of socially discarded people.

Thus working with the underprivileged became an important approach of *Sarvodaya*. Such underprivileged people could come from the socially depressed, economically deprived, politically exploited communities living in any part of the country. It became *Sarvodaya*'s responsibility to assist these people to assert their value as human beings and help them to share with others the material and non-material resources in society on an equal basis.

Another aspect of *Sarvodaya*'s philosophy and practice is manifest in the Movement's attitude towards women. The Buddhist teachings state that the Buddha was born to the benefit not only of men, but also of women. The path to freedom is open to men as well as women. To King Pasenadi of Kosala, who was worried about the girl child born to his queen, the Buddha said that "A woman child may prove to be a better offspring than a male" (*Saṁyutta-nikāya* 1.86).

An American scholar who had experience at the grass-root level observes this aspect in the following manner. "It is not surprising, therefore, that the revitalization of the Buddhist social ethic brings with it an increased openness to the role of women" (Joanna Macy, *Dharma and Development*, 1983).

The *Sarvodaya* Movement from its inception understood the value of women in development and in every village organized mothers groups to mobilize women. In this program they were imparted with knowledge and skills, made to participate in their own programs and finally empowered them with a status as equal members of society. The process of empowerment and conscientization had taken place since *Sarvodaya*'s birth in our country. The empowerment of women is thus a vital aspect of *Sarvodaya*'s philosophy and practice which owes its inspiration to Buddhist teachings.

7. Different Paradigm

Mahatma Gandhi in his Panchayat Raj says: "You cannot build non-violence on a factory civilization, but it can be built on self-contained villages. Rural economy, as I have conceived it, eschews exploitation altogether, and exploitation is the essence of violence. You have, therefore, to be rural-minded before you can be non-violent. If my dream is fulfilled, and if every one of the seven lakhs of villages becomes a well-living republic in which there are no illiterates, in which no one is idle for want of work, in which everyone is usefully occupied and has nourishing food, well-ventilated dwellings and sufficient Khadi for covering the body, and which villages know and observe the laws of hygiene and sanitation, such a state must have varied and increasing needs, which it must supply unless it would stagnate...."

The UN Human Development Report 1994 accepts the need for a new development paradigm: "To address the growing challenge of human security, a new development paradigm is needed that puts people at the centre of development, regards economic growth as a means and not an end, protects all life opportunities of future generations as well as the present generations and respects the natural systems on which all life depends."

Both from the Gandhian point of view and from the experience of the last five UNDP Development Decades it is quite clear that full human development and happiness cannot be achieved by centralization. The need of the times is decentralization. Centralization as a system is inconsistent with a non-violent structure of society. Non-violence, peace, kindness, contentment and happiness are qualitative states. These can best be nurtured and sustained at decentralized levels such as the individual, the family and the small community. *Sarvodaya* believes that a new social order devoid of present global dangers can only be built if the existing macro socio-economic and political structures can be transformed to serve these levels rather than by being in a position to control them.

We are reminded at this stage of the statements made by the Buddha in the presence of Vassakara, the prime minister of Magadha, why the Vajjins were a strong republic. The seven principles of the Vajjin's social conduct that contributed to their strength and prosperity over two thousand five hundred years ago are equally relevant to our time if we can take the bold step of decentralization of our political and economic structures. In fact *Sarvodaya* has incorporated these seven principles of non-decline into the rules of the *Sarvodaya* village level societies.

Although the principles refer to a group of Republican kings, explaining their political pattern (*Dīgha-nikāya* 11, 72-76), the principle does have an immediate relevance to modern democracy. According to the Buddha these principles, when practiced would promote the progress of those who participate in it. *Sarvodaya* has recognized the importance of those principles in the people's practical life in two main ways.

1. By promoting their participation in small group activity in which such principles are practiced. The people make themselves conscious and aware of their economic and social problems and plan their own programs to solve such problems themselves.
2. The people are made conscious at the grassroots level about their rights and privileges. The democratic process of give and take, toleration, sharing power and others are put to work in small and medium group activity. The people learn what constructive social protest is and practice such strategies.

8. Communication Technology

We who live in modern times have a much greater advantage over the ancient village republics of India such as the Vajjins or Lichchavis. There are certain modern developments in science and technology which they could not have even dreamed of. There is a wealth of scientific knowledge and technological know-how that modern man has mastered which can be used by decentralized societies. Of very special significance to the subject of decentralization that I am now discussing is communication technology. The so-called communication highway is now becoming a reality. The most important question we have to ask ourselves at this stage is who is going to get the real benefit out of these modern discoveries and inventions? If the current national and international structures are going to remain as they are then we will have no doubt who the beneficiaries will be. On the other hand we have to raise another question as to how best the present disadvantaged and marginalized people of the world could get benefited from these advancements in science and technology. My answer is the vision of highly decentralized communities in the world getting networked together bypassing the centers of power. This vision has to be translated into concrete organized action in every field of development and they have to be built on moral principles we have outlined above. If we fail to do this, organized greed, ill will and ignorance (of spiritual realities) will bring our world still nearer to total destruction.

If this challenge has to be faced successfully, village communities have to be empowered socially, economically and technologically. Social empowerment includes community capacity building, early childhood development, community health and environment, conflict resolution and peace making, disaster management, applied research and communication, gender and development, and development education. Economic empowerment includes development of skills in savings and credit management, rural enterprise development, management training, and rural enterprise support services such as introduction of new products, and consultancy and marketing services. Under technological empowerment, appropriate rural technology, agricultural and agro-industrial skills, grain storage technology, vocational and technical training, solar power technology and applied research and communication technology are included.

When the above three categories of empowerment are taken as a whole, a village community is expected to graduate in five phases of development. These are the psychological infrastructure building phase, social infrastructure building phase, legal incorporation phase, economic development phase, and self-sufficiency phase. Right through these phases *Sarvodaya* villages interact with one another and generally a cluster of ten villages work together as a unit. When one thousand such clusters reach a certain level of development, it is believed that the totality of the processes thus released will influence the decision makers to re-orient their top down development programs to conform to the people's participatory development process released from the bottom up.

Basically, over 80% of the people in the world who belong to the poor and lower middle classes are not so much interested in growth rates and GNPs. They are primarily interested in ensuring for themselves optimum levels of security pertaining to their physical security, environmental security, food security, health security, economic security, and political security.

9. Priority Areas

What does Buddhist philosophy offer in the above-mentioned areas of improving the quality of life of people? In our experience, there is an abundant wealth of information and guiding principles pertaining to all those subjects under consideration. Take for example early childhood development. Buddhist texts vividly describe the factors affecting the conception of a child, growth of the child in the mother's womb, the birth of the child, its progressive development through infancy, childhood, adolescence, and adulthood. This ancient knowledge supplemented with modern scientific findings can easily provide us future directions for healthy early childhood development.

The Buddhist teaching has led and inspired *Sarvodaya* to formulate the outlines of its own development philosophy. The basic assumption here is that every individual's basic needs should be first satisfied. The material as well as the non-material resources should be utilized first and foremost to satisfy the basic needs of all. The secondary and tertiary needs can be identified at the next stage.

This is followed by two other principles: (1) As far as possible the relationship between human beings and the environment should be mutually supportive and enriching. (2) Exploitation of human beings should not be made under any condition. Respect for life and the upholding of human rights emanate from this principle.

Development should be decided by the people and should include social, economic, political, spiritual, psychological and cultural areas of human life. It should not be a one-sided process looking only at economic improvement. The people should be in a position to participate and share the fruits of development as far as possible controlling the rise of excess needs while leaving a fair share of whatever material necessary to satisfy other's basic needs.

We are living in a world where a considerable proportion of the world's population is ageing. Considerable efforts are being made to prolong life. However, everything that has a beginning also has to come to an end. That is inevitable. Therefore, we should not only learn the art and science of living longer, but also that of facing death that is inevitable. In the Buddhist tradition the practice of *anicca bhāvanā* (meditation on impermanence) is an essential component of spiritual training. In the educational system every human being is given an understanding of what the human personality is. *Paṭiccasamuppāda*, or the doctrine of dependent arising, consisting of twelve interdependent causal factors, gives this understanding. This twelve-fold formula represents an explanation of a person in bondage. It also explains in the negative form, or when understood in the reverse order, the process of freedom from this bondage.

Another example is food that is a basic human need. According to the Buddha, while material food is the first and foremost nutriment, there are three other nutriments we should be mindful of. The second nutriment is the sensory perceptions, stemming from the fact that people are sensory-bound. The third nutriment is mental dispositions or volitions. Kalupahana calls this intentionality or the individual's decision-making or goal-setting capacity. Finally, consciousness, which is generally associated with memory, is the last nutriment. All these four nutriments are founded on craving (*taṇhā*). Craving contributes to suffering. Hence, to overcome suffering, one has to eliminate craving.

This simple but profound teaching which is very much a part of our culture goes diametrically against what takes place in our world as development. What has gone on as development is nothing else but an intense effort to create increased craving in human minds and releasing forces of mass production involving vast quantities of nonrenewable and limited natural resources to satisfy that craving. The result is uncontrollable pollution of the environment, destruction of ecological systems, disruption of cultures and economies which were sustained for centuries, breakdown of human families and communities, social unrest and conflict both at national and international levels, and in shom breakdown of all life support systems.

10. Middle Path and Cosmic Laws

According to Buddhist teachings, what is important is avoidance of both self-mortification and self-indulgence. In the present day world context, *Sarvodaya* advocates the concept of a no-poverty, no-affluence society. This is the middle path advocated by the Buddha. Such a society need not destroy nature, value systems, or cultures. As Mahatma Gandhi expressed, the world has no resources to satisfy the greed of one man, but the world has enough to satisfy the needs of all men. Therefore, the *Sarvodaya* development strategy advocates right livelihood (*sammā ājīva*) where the satisfaction of basic and secondary human needs take priority in all development efforts. A participatory democracy and a sustainable economy can be built only if human beings make up their minds to find harmony between sensory satisfaction and spiritual happiness.

It is appropriate at this stage to mention the five cosmic laws the Buddha enunciated as guiding principles to be followed in human affairs in dealing with human beings, other living creatures, and nature. These are the cosmic laws pertaining to genetic composition (*bīja niyāma*), the cosmic law pertaining to seasons (*utu niyāma*), the cosmic law pertaining to social phenomenon (*dhamma niyāma*), the cosmic law pertaining to causation (*kamma niyāma*), and the cosmic law pertaining to the mind (*citta niyāma*). As we are living in an age when everybody speaks of globalization, global village concepts and global trade and so on, it is appropriate for Buddhist scholars to devote time to expand on these cosmic laws and discover ways and means of applying these profitably to global human conduct and behavior in all areas of human activity.

The issue of conservation of bio-diversity is high on the world development agenda at this time. Can the law of *bīja niyāma* throw some light into the debate? Serious climatic changes are adversely affecting our overpopulated and over-polluted world. Can the principle of *utu niyāma* lead us to some possible solution? There are a lot of disruptions, rivalries and even bloodshed, not only between countries and within nations, but within families as well. Can the principles of *kamma niyāma* and *dhamma niyāma* enlighten us to find a new way to bring about harmony and peace? The psychological imbalances and disturbances may be the cause that led certain human beings to act in an insane manner in recent incidents like the gas attacks in Japanese subways and bomb attacks in Oklahoma in United States which resulted in loss of a large number of human lives and injuries to many times more. Can the law of *citta niyāma* provide us a lead to bring about more peace within human minds? These are areas that need a great deal of research and study, not purely for academic purposes but with a view to finding solutions to crying problems humanity as a whole faces.

The greatest message that *Sarvodaya* gives to the world in the 21st century is the message of peace and tolerance. Such a message can only be realized when it begins in the human heart. It should thus begin in the individual and then flow to the family, community, society and the world. Toleration of others, equality and sharing of resources and power without the exploitation of human being by others are the final objective. Violence should be eschewed at all levels. It is in such a context where we learn to tolerate our differences and refrain from exploiting others that a new world order may be created. *Sarvodaya* is searching for strategies to build such a world order. It possesses a tested strategy to achieve this objective. Can we all coming from all parts of the world realize the importance of this objective and muster sufficient courage and strength to put this strategy to action? In this unique exercise all of us may not reach Nirvana; but I am sure for most of us the world then could be a more satisfactorily fulfilling and beautiful place in which to live.

Part 3

Environment

CHAPTER 15

FROM NATURE TO BUDDHA NATURE: TOWARDS A BUDDHIST ENVIRONMENTAL ETHICS

Nona R. Bolin

It is generally understood that the ecological crisis is a symptom of our technological and scientific age. Both analyses and solutions usually provide schema that attempt to locate causal conditions and/or effective remedies. East and West are struggling with a similar ecological problem in the area of applied ethics, and the problem is being addressed with comparable strategies and methods of conceptual rigor. Contemporary Western philosophy has sought to extend its traditional ethical principles to include obligations towards the environment through the employment of broadly interpreted deontological or consequentialist principles. This generally involves proffering arguments that animals and the environment fall within the scope of rights, interests, value and respect. Even though the environmental problem is pressing and impacts on everyone in our global society, its urgency has shown the limitations of Western ethics perhaps more than any past ethical incongruity. Consequently, it seems particularly important that contemporary thought formulate some adequate guidelines. But these will not prove satisfactory as long as ethics is restricted to its traditional manifestations. The French philosopher Michel Foucault has maintained that modern philosophy cannot formulate a comprehensive ethical code because its understanding of ethics is constituted by thought's self relation instead of the relatedness of thought to nature or the world. Thinking that systematically turns to the worldless thinker, instead of existence in a world, will remain impotent to even understand the issues. The crisis of the environment may be so recalcitrant that our traditional ethical theories, religious and secular, provide little direction.

The two most important Western attempts to depart from traditional ethical systems in order to envision a responsible environmentalism are ones which challenge the very notion of ethical agency. Through a brief examination of these theories, this paper will engage a more radical questioning of the very possibility of an ethics that falls outside of traditional metaphysics, both in the

West and in the East. Invoking basic Buddhist doctrines, I will follow a way of interpreting Buddhist teaching in order to provisionally approach an environmental ethics through the basic Buddhist doctrine of the *anattā* and the "Four Noble Truths." This engagement with Buddhist thought is not a matter of providing a better or more adequate approach to the question of environmental ethics. Rather I am engaging in an inquiry which may give some direction to what may be a provisional approach towards a Buddhist environmental ethics.

I use the word "provisional" with emphasis on the qualified conjunction of Buddhism and *ethics*.

1. Eco-feminism

> If we do not love life on our own account and through others,
> it is futile to seek to justify it in any way.
>
> Simone de Beauvoir

Eco-feminism is an offspring of the analysis of Western patriarchy and its dominion over otherness. While *woman* is the paradigmatic example of the *other*, this notion is broad enough to include the marginalized or oppressed on which the sovereignty of Man has been established.

The ageless association of Woman with Nature facilities a "natural" identification of the two within the Western onto-theo-logical tradition such that many feminist theorists have come to explore this association in order to expose the co-subordination of both. The denigration of woman and the theory by which it is condoned, is echoed in the way "Nature" has been understood and the way the rape of the earth has been, and still is, sanctioned.

Religious eco-feminists understand the Judeo-Christian tradition as claiming that 'Man' is the spiritual image of the Creator. At the same time, women are thought to be materially created and their embodiment is associated with birth, death and the cycles of historical time. Women are derived from a second order of reality and one associated with absence of goodness. While some feminist theologians challenge the orthodox interpretations by seeking different hermeneutical approaches to religious texts, others seek a transvaluational representation of women through a revival of healthier associations of woman and nature. A number of feminists who have no nostalgia for religious revelation apply deconstructive analyses to the tradition, analyses that undermine oppressive foundational principles. The rational subject, seen as inevitably gendered, is the mainstay of domination, and thus becomes the target of deconstructive strategies. Since it has maintained its rule through a supporting theory of ethical agency, all systems that purport to be universal and absolute are shown to be irrevocably gendered.

> We have been perceived for too many centuries as pure Nature;
> exploited and raped like the earth and the solar system; small wonder
> if we now long to become Culture, pure spirit, mind. Yet, it is

> precisely this culture and its political institutions which have split us
> off from itself in so doing it has also split itself off from life,
> becoming the death culture of quantification, abstraction, and the will
> to power which has reached its most refined destructiveness in this
> century. It is this culture and politics of abstraction which women are
> talking of changing, of bringing into accountability in human terms.[1]

While I believe that some versions of eco-feminism resonates with some readings of Buddhist ontology, I will not pursue those connections in this paper.

2. Deep-Ecology

In order to distinguish itself from its less weighty rival, "shallow ecology," the theory of "deep ecology" attributes to all natural diversity its own intrinsic value. Shallow ecology is limited in its anthropomorphic approach to attribute only extrinsic value to what is *other*.

Arne Naess, the Norwegian philosopher who coined the phrase "deep ecology" and is its major proponent, attempts to embrace a wider ethical framework that extends beyond the limitations of traditional deontological and utilitarian theories. Naess rejects the extension of human interests in favor of an extension of the subject who has interests. One need no longer appeal to some consideration of *otherness* to sustain an environmental ethics. Instead, the ethical subject itself undergoes transformation. According to deep ecology, the sense of an expanded self challenges the traditional notion of the ego and egoism. Once the boundaries of the self are deepened, the appeal to selfless or altruistic action is unnecessary. Environmental ethics is an enlightened self-relation with no interference of *otherness*.

Following a basically Hobbesian theory of human nature, Naess maintains that self-interest is the normal human condition. Consequently, self-sacrifice is not a realistic prescription. The extensive moralizing of the ecological movement has been built on altruistic incentives of a traditionally defined ethical agent. It has fostered the false impression that sacrifice is necessary to sustain a viable environment. "Duty" and "respect" towards what is not one's own are untenable and will not suffice to provide the basis of a successful environmentalism. Hence, Naess concludes that self-interest must be mined as the impetus of a reformulated ethical egoism with one important difference. "Self must undergo a fundamental transvaluation and personal identity must enlarge to minimalize the alienating" man-in-the-world" model to a "relational total-field image."[2]

---

[1] Adrienne Rich, *Of Woman Born* (New York: W.W. Norton, 1976), 285.

[2] Arne Naess, "Identification as a Source of Deep Ecological Attitudes," in *Radical Environmental Philosophy and Tactics*, ed. Peter C. List (Belmont, California: Wadsworth Publishing Co., 1993), 30. Also see "The Shallow and the Deep, Long-range Ecology Movement" in the same publication, 19-24.

In developing his theory, Naess borrows from the so-called "Gaia Hypothesis." In an abbreviated form, the Gaia Hypothesis emphasizes the enveloping atmosphere as an integral part of the overall eco-system. The air which makes respiration possible is the invisible, unobtrusive and unobvious medium by which we live, act and speak. Air permeates the earth's surface and is the net of our connection with all of its other occupants. Air is the breath of the organism by which the planet is sustained. That breath is in turn produced by plants and microorganisms that contribute to the breath of organic existence. Reflection on the surrounding biosphere shifts the locus of essential vitality from the human to the vast organic entity of which one is a part. The expanse of breath is seen to constitute a new understanding of *space*. No longer the pre-Newtonian container of isolated bodies existing in their own isolation, space becomes the medium of interconnectedness that deepens our awareness of the extended boundaries of self. In Hindu terms this model of space is reminiscent of the jeweled net of Indra in which each knot is a jewel that reflects all others.

Naess' use of the Gaia Hypothesis, and his differentiation of the narrow and the comprehensive self, explicitly invoke the doctrine of the *Ātman*. Specifically Naess employs Gandhi's use of *mahā-atman*. While Naess claims to avoid both Eastern and Western mysticism and the religious practices that attach to Hinduism, he nonetheless stresses the dissolution of an individuated self who becomes enlightened to the unity of *Ātman* and *Brahman*. As in the Hindu tradition, the intrinsic worth of the totality of existence is "something shown in intuition" and it is this truth that is foundational. It admits of no proof. Naess recognizes that this type of enlightenment will require a fundamental change in social and political beliefs and practices in Western culture. His theory falls short of suggestions as to the means of implementing this change.

3. The Ethical Subject

As a philosophical discipline, ethics requires the centrality of a *self, agent* or *subject* which constitutes the formative locus of the relation between subject and object, agent and patient. This bipolar relation may be considered a relation of one self to another self, or the relation of a self to an *other*. But at a more foundational level, it is a self-relation of one's self to one's self. So while ethics is generally understood to be a means of self-regulation, it is also a means of self-constitution. The prescriptive project of ethical legislation includes what is often called "self-determination" through presuppositions of both autonomy and mastery. The ethical self is then both agent and patient since the subject is its own object of prescriptive enforcement. The ethical subject has no authority outside of its own configuration and establishes itself as Law. Whether it acknowledges itself as ultimate Subject or acknowledges some other Subject as the ultimate authority, morality rests upon the all too human foundation of *subjectivity*. The movement towards authenticity is the movement that directs the formative self towards conformity with universal principles. All who share the place of authority, all *subjects* form a transcendental subjectivity. Individual moral agents constitute "kingdom" or totality of moral legislation.

Self-actualization is a constitutive possibility for autonomous human existence such that the moral or even potentially moral being is not reducible to mere descriptive history and social orderings. The ethical subject transcends the world of description, the world of mere *things,* and attains sovereignty of its rightful reign by means of its own most possibility of subjectivity. While cultural, social and historical determinations are necessary in contributing to the ontic formation of selfhood, a higher and more proper sense of self is invoked in the transition from the *is* to the *ought,* from the mundane to the moral. The formation of this subject takes place through accountability. The moral self is not merely accountable. He must have the capacity to give an account of himself, what he has made of himself.

> In short, for an action to be moral, it must not be reducible to an act or a series of acts conforming to a rule, a law, or a value. Of course all moral action involves a relationship with the reality in which it is carried out, and a relationship with self. The latter is not simply 'self-awareness' but self-formation as an 'ethical subject', a process in which the individual delimits that part of himself that will form the object of his moral practice, defines his position relative to the precept he will follow, and decides on a certain mode of being that will serve as his moral goal. And this requires him to act upon himself, to monitor, test, improve and transform himself. There is no specific moral action that does not refer to a unified moral conduct; no moral conduct that does not call for the forming of oneself as an ethical subject; and no forming of the ethical subject without 'modes of subjectification' and 'ascetics' or 'practices of the self' that support them. Moral action is indissociable from these forms of self-activity, and they do not differ any less from one morality to another than do the systems of values, rules and interdictions.[3]

Perhaps we do not yet know how to approach an ethics without the centrality of the ethical subject. Such an approach constitutes a provisional inquiry into an ethics that does not follow the tradition of the metaphysics of the predominant philosophies of either Western or Eastern metaphysics.

4. Buddhist Ethics

When one considers "ethics" within a Buddhist perspective, any number of approaches arises. Its rich doctrines embrace many possibilities. The various schools and movements of Buddhist philosophy provide different and often times competing theories about the interpretation of the status of its ethical

---

[3] Michel Foucault, *The Use of Pleasure,* Volume II of *The History of Sexuality* (New York: Pantheon Books, 1985), 28.

tenants, such as those of the "Eightfold Noble Path." This inquiry will take a different direction, the path of questioning the very possibility of a Buddhist *ethics.*

While it is apparent that the Buddha accepted a differentiation between right and wrong, it is important to consider how these differences are to be understood and how they arise. At the level of right action as prescribed by the Eightfold Noble Path, morality may be identified with questions concerning certain social practices and ways of livelihood and interaction. As a general set of prescriptions and restrictions by which behavior is evaluated, praised or blamed, these teachings are guides to a meaningful life. But they are not means to some other-worldly reward. In this respect we are to understand and interpret these maxims as we would look at any social or secular ethical principles. In this regard, the Buddhist approach to life shows little distinctive difference from many others. But the question of ethics pursued here must be pushed back to more elementary Buddhist *truth* in order to question the very possibility of ethical agency and the ontological status of all ethical value.

The inquiry into Buddhist ethics must resist the imposition of the Western metaphysical structures of 'meta-ethical' determinations. Generally understood, foundationalist theories concerning the nature of the Good serve as the basis of absolutist and relativist theories that in turn supply the norms of human action with a universally applicable code of behavior. Within such parameters, Buddhist ethics would appear to be relativistic or even nihilistic. But these judgments do not accept Buddhist doctrines on their own terms, and remain content to approach its teachings through categories that are unquestioned and maintained to be universal in scope. It may, however, be important to contrast Buddhist *ethics* with the tradition that it rejects, namely Hinduism. A detailed comparison is beyond the scope of this paper, although, I will pursue this through the theory of the *subjectivity* of the *Ātman.*

Like the Western metaphysical tradition, Hindu metaphysics maintains that a certain type of awareness is the gateway from morality to enlightenment. The transcendental arena of the enlightened is accessed through an awareness of unity and totality, and the incorporation of one's authentic existence into this place. The identification of *Ātman* as *Brahman* allows the two perspectives of inside and outside to merge through the acquisition of the knowledge of the self. But when one considers the possibility of a Buddhist *ethics* the problematics of an authentic self which becomes aware of itself as such, becomes the focal point of contradistinction. If this notion of the *self* essential to ethics as I have maintained that it is, and this is also true of Hindu ethics, then Buddhism, via the central doctrine of the *anatta,* cannot call for a "new" or "alternative" approach to ethics. Indeed, the very appeal to a Buddhist *ethics* may lead to a suspicion that what is being reinscribed is some oblique appeal to a notion of ethical agency or the *Ātman.* In a parallel fashion, it is clear that many approaches to explain the doctrines of reincarnation and *karma* have conjured up reference to a *self* in order to give some consistency to seemingly incommensurate doctrines.

Following the Buddhist rejection of the Ātman, our central issue becomes whether or not an *ethics*, traditional or otherwise, can accommodate the absence of a central agency, an absence that cannot even be called a *non-subject* or a *non-presence?* This is the question which inevitably surfaces when one pursues a Buddhist *ethics* through the doctrine of the *anattā.*

The very question of the possibility of "ethics" interjects itself at the commencement this of inquiry. But it is the movement of this questioning that draws one *towards* the enigmatic nature of this issue as it appears to resist solution. Nonetheless, following this inquiry, this *towards* and its *resistance* is the very issue that demands our patience on the path. The importance of this path of inquiry, the tension and discomfort of the question, leads us *towards* a way disconnected from any anticipation of an arrival at a place of metaphysical repose.

Traditionally, questioning carries with it a general notion of ignorance and discomfort. Answers, theories, resolutions entail a place where questioning ceases and may no longer arise. Living in the perpetual state of questioning provides little appeal. Yet, the culmination of inquiry is suspect in the Buddhist tradition since all positions are provided with some grounding metaphysics.[4] But if a Buddhist *ethics* is at all possible it must be such that it has no supporting metaphysical categories. Rather it must be an *ethics* attuned to its own overcoming, to the transitoriness or the norms and values of its own teachings. This overcoming would alert the inquirer to the dangers of attachments to universals, absolute, relative or otherwise, that situate the ethical agency which espouses them. The unfinished one who seeks self in the ethical self intensifies the questioning when the answer, any answer, is itself questioned. The Buddhist's question must forestall the metaphysical solution.

The *Ātman,* and the awareness thereof, carries with it the possibility of *enlightenment* and invokes a state of stasis beyond the questioning and striving within the world of *saṁsāra.* Hindu enlightenment is granted to the being who has as its own most possibility a selfhood beyond inquiry, no longer bound to the ignorant state of the questioner. This notion of *enlightenment* presupposes a fundamental sameness of self, realizing its own totality in a place of authenticity. It is this self that is the traditional ground of the ethical self. While the differences may be subtle, Eastern and Western metaphysics are not such distant relatives.

However, since Buddhism does not take its departure from a theory of the *Ātman,* or any related theory of the self, one may be tempted to conclude that the question of morality cannot arise. However, the question of morality inevitably takes a detoured path, an eight-fold one.

---

[4] Nona K Bolin, "Sorcery East and West: Nāgārjuna and Derrida" presented at the American Philosophical Association meeting, Spring, 1994, Kansas City, Kansas.

5. Buddhism and Suffering

Buddhism begins with the basic truth that suffering exists. Suffering discloses an ontological possibility of sentient existence that is not determined by a self-like possibility, a possibility of being that is not self-referential or relational to some transcendent future to which the individual may truly and authentically relate its existence. The world does not present itself as an instrument of redemption, but as a place of purposiveless. The being whose basic constitutive component is its openness to suffering finds itself in the inescapable milieux of social and worldly determinations. This being does not transcend or exist apart from this ontic; everyday existence. It has no alternative form of being. It has no foundational presence.

Unlike Hinduism, Buddhism posits no transcendental subjectivity to encompass time and space by means of some trans-historical possibility. The rigorous refusal of appeal to a transcendental ego is an acceptance of situatedness in the temporal and the finite. This acquiescence bares the radical contingency that all existence is. Groundless contingency reveals the primordial lack or *nothing* that inhabits being. Covering this lack or supplementing it with a fabricated ego, the human being seeks a purpose and explanation for the suffering that befalls it, denying that suffering is an essential part of its non-essential being. But this fabrication is not a matter of individual volition or even what may be called "self-deception". Life as we find it covers over its abyssimal *essence* and proffers an illusionary assurance of security. Life flees from its own perdition and conceals its own transience. The veiling of lack is simultaneously the fabrication of a subject that desires an existence apart from worldly suffering through appeal to an "inside" immune to the viscidities of the body, and which is in turn identical to, or essentially connected to, an "outside," a place of releasement. (In Hinduism, the inside and the outside form the Ātman/Brahman identity). Life shapes the ego through manifestations that present a security of position and possibility. The *self* to which life retreats is not "false" or "illusionary". Attachment to life makes possible certain "realities." The historical manifestations of possible ways of life precede each existence and provide a continuity of contest and possibility.

The Buddhist "ethical self" accepts its place within these possibilities. This *ethical being* is never the transcendent self of foundationist metaphysics. The "ethical self" is only and always found in human and historical situations, and never occurs outside or beyond the karmic conditions of existing in a world with others. Thus Buddhism does not posit some time or space wherein ethical affect is absent or irrelevant. But Buddhism is not a matter of abolishing or demeaning ethical norms. Such a move would be regulated by some appeal to a metaphysical solution.

The truth of suffering is revelatory in that the being who recognizes this basic truth has an existential possibility irreducible to the karmic matrix of historical existence. However, awareness and acceptance of suffering cannot transcend the finitude of existence. Buddhist *enlightenment* does not transport the individual out of itself towards some *better, higher* or more authentic place of repose. The difference that allows the possibility of enlightenment is no alternative <u>mode</u> of existence. The possibility of enlightenment is the possibility of disruption, not in the active sense of doing something to stay the karmic world, nor in some ascetic sense of resolve. The difference of Buddhist enlightenment reveals the condition of human existence as split, in the sense that the existence of the ontic, ethical self never truly coincides with any existence of absolute and universal values. The tension of this difference that forbids the possibility of unity, is suffering of a primordial sort. It discloses the fabricated self and the inherent lack of being that is essential to its own constitution. When human existence is at odds with its own mode of existence, the most primordial form of suffering is engendered in recurrent human possibilities. The karmic continuance of the ego is accompanied by the denial of constitutive ambiguity. Suffering both veils itself and reveals itself in the ego. Thus the inquiry into suffering reveals that suffering cannot be subordinated by conceptual analysis. It exceeds and exudes all doctrine, teaching, and explanation, and veils itself accordingly. Suffering preoccupies itself with itself in order to forget itself Yet this preoccupation recoils and searches out the suffering that it veils. Inquiry seeks itself through recoiling from the very self that is its only refuge. *Enlightenment* always already *is saṁsāra.* The refusal of metaphysical comfort takes one down the path to the awareness of one's own existence. This path has no more closure than the existence it seeks. The path is one of the middle way.

6. Towards the Region of Environmental Ethos

The existence of suffering in the absence of resolution or justification, the truth of suffering in the face of failure to rectify suffering, is inseparable from the teachings of the Buddha. The transformative power of suffering does not bring about its elimination. But the transformative possibility that it does bring about is compassion.

Is it possible to face suffering without the metaphysical *hope* of overcoming suffering? The attempt to alleviate suffering may lead to obscured, even invisible consequences that engender and renew suffering in the karmic world of repetition. Can we be concerned with suffering and engage suffering without imposing on it some system of meaning? The issue of living with compassion, absent of explanation and expectation, relates back to the issue of the *anattā.*

To take up one's identity in the conflict of primordial suffering is to recognize the abyssimal place of one's own being. Questioning is constitutive of this impermanent and contingent existence. Questioning depends upon a futurial place of the *towards* that forgoes stability in a present. Detachment from the definitive, correct and adequate allows residence in a place where we already are, but a place that is distant and unfamiliar to our everydayness. The place of Buddhist questioning is not the Socratic place of the dialectic. Nor is it any place of mediation. Often read as a dialectician, Nāgārjuna solicits the power of questioning, not through a dialectics of questioning and answering, but through a disruptive questioning that disturbs common epistemological comforts, common divisions and established distinctions. In taking no position, Nāgārjuna seeks the place of the between, the strange *middle* of disruption. Through his enigmatic questioning of all foundational positions, Nāgārjuna conjures the way to an obscure path in which this questioning resonates with the tension of existence. The *towards* of this inquiry opens up possibilities that disrupt the interplay of forces that allow attachment. In this region there is an uncanny belongingness.

This region is not without its correlate in the West. The Greek word *e'thea* is used in Homer to refer to a place where animals and wild creatures abide. It has a distinct opposition to culture. In the *Iliad* (6.506-11) Homer recounts the story of a captured horse who breaks free from the stable and breaks towards the plains. Breaking stride he runs with the exhilaration of a regained freedom. The horse is on his way to his own element. He has never been successfully broken. The place of this region is called the *ethea* of animals and refers to the place outside the domain of Greek culture, to the place of the barbarian who resists domestication. Both barbarians and animals, accustomed to their own places and ways of life, were difficult to change or *civilize.*

The *related word, ethos,* is also found in Plato to refer to that part of the *psyche* that resides behind, within the recesses of a hidden retreat that is ownmost and never disclosed. It is the place of primary belonging, one's home (*oikos*). The Indo-European root of *ethos* (*Swedh*) means "one's own." It is the place of identity, but this reference to identity has an unsettling connotation of a place of both identity <u>and</u> difference, an area of residing tension. It carries the notion of a "middle" but a middle between two irreconcilable boundaries. *Ethos* names neither one nor the other but the residing difference between. It names the breach deep within the soul that is one's ownmost. The attempt to cancel out this tension is to be exiled from one's ownmost region.

If this region is the place of all being, a place that is lived <u>with</u> others, interconnectedness may bring us to the site of the possibility of an environmental *ethics.* This is not the connectedness of selves in an originary Self. It is the connectedness of those who suffer. If "ethics" is now understood in its more originary sense, one owns up to one's own being. This sense of ethics as *ethos* is preparatory for the recognition that all beings belong to the *ethea.* While this environs is the place where the self is formed, the site of suffering; it is also the place where the self is overcome, the site of releasement. It is the place of the compassionate Buddha.

> We must first turn, turn back to where we are in reality already
> staying. The abiding turn, back to where we already are, is infinitely
> harder than hasty excursions to places where we are not yet and never

will be, except perhaps as the monstrous creatures of technology, assimilated to machines.[5]

---

[5] Martin Heidegger, "The Nature of Language," in *On the Way to Language* (New York: Harper and Row, 1971), 85.

CHAPTER 16

ENVIRONMENTAL CRISIS AND SURVIVAL

Lily de Silva

When one stands on the beach at twilight and surveys the ocean stretching as far as the horizon, with the star-studded firmament arching above, one is awe-struck by the tremendous vastness of the cosmos as compared to the human being who is but an infinitesimal speck in this mighty, infinitely gigantic universe. With that awe-inspiring wonder, when attention is paid to the human being, one is wonder-struck by the potentials of this minute creature who has the capacity to perceive, conceptualize and understand this vastly complicated organization and structure of the universe. Modern scientific man has unraveled many of the mysteries of nature, but in the process has brought about unprecedented pollution rendering nature inhospitable to his very existence. In this paper we propose to explore the wisdom contained in the teachings of the Buddha who has, in known history, reached the supreme apex in understanding the place of man in the natural environment and the way to transcend nature.

The Pali words which come closest to nature are *yathābhāta* and *loka*. Man is expected to understand the reality of himself (*yathābhāta*) as a part and parcel of nature and his environment, the world (*loka*). *Lujjatīti loko*,[1] the world, is so called because it constantly undergoes change, because it disintegrates. So does man undergo change as part and parcel of nature. But man in his ignorance and arrogance considers himself as superior to nature and exploits natural resources for his comforts and advantage according to his technological skill. So long as he did this within reasonable limits to satisfy more his needs rather than greed, nature was hospitable. So long as his philosophy was 'to be,' 'to live,' rather than 'to have,' 'to possess,' nature was kind. But at present nature seems to lodge a protest and revolt when man's wanton greed 'to possess' exceeded manageable limits.

---

[1] *S.*, IV, 52.

Sabbe sattā āharaṭṭhitikā,[2] all beings subsist on food, gross food to satisfy his hunger (*kabaliṅkāra āhāra*), and food for his senses (*phassa āhāra*), besides the psychologically nourishing components of the volitional drive (*manosañcetanā*) and consciousness (*viññāṇa*).[3] The first two types of food come from the natural environment consisting of fauna and flora. Man in his voracious greed to satisfy his hunger for pleasure, wealth and power has exploited natural resources with such unprecedented gusto that nature's capacity to rejuvenate and replenish life supporting resources has been outstripped with disastrous effects on man himself The air we breathe is so polluted in major centers of civilization that some cities are called "asthma capitals of the nation," water is rendered so impure that it has to be boiled and strained before it is made drinkable in many parts of the world. The use of chemical manure, insecticides, pesticides and weedicides has impaired the natural bacterial balance of the topsoil so drastically and robbed it of its fertility that the quality of the crops has been reduced in flavor, nutritional value and shelf life. Non-renewable natural resources are fast dwindling, and deforestation the world over is causing climatic changes and weather patterns adverse to human well-being. Acid rain is reported from some parts of the world, and ozone depletion casts a gloom of skin cancer and other deadly diseases due to exposure to radiation. Scientists predict global warming with the possibility of inundating the worl4fs major centers of activity situation in., coastal regions within the first half of the next century. Man himself is responsible for this state of affairs, and it is also his own responsibility to search for solutions for the well-being of his own species. Hence inquiries into the wisdom of ancient seers, besides of course technological enterprises for cutting down pollution for sustainable development.

> The world is led by the mind, it is dragged hither and thither by the mind.

> The mind is one phenomenon under the power of which everything goes.[4]

When the history of human civilization is perused in the light of the above statement made by the Buddha, it becomes abundantly clear that human ideas have shaped the destiny of mankind and of the external world in this long march from savagery to civilization. In the Stone Age, when man was a hunter and food-gatherer, his activities hardly disturbed nature. In the age of animal husbandry, he led a nomadic life in search of pastures. During the age of settled agriculture life, man modified the face of nature with vast irrigation schemes, terraced paddy fields and plantations. Thus far man cooperated with nature and

---

[2] *D., III,* 211.

[3] *D.,* IV.

[4] *Cittena niyyati loko cittena parikissati, cetassa ekadhammassa sabbeva vasam anvagū. S.,* I, 39.

nature was benign to him. With the dawn of science and the industrial revolution, man became much more knowledgeable regarding the secrets of nature, and man's attitude towards nature became much more aggressive and exploitative. The present era of human history is characterized by the discovery of nuclear energy and space travel. Fired by the enthusiasm to conquer limitations imposed by nature, materialistic man of science still goes forward undaunted by the hazards he is faced with, searching for technological remedies to alleviate the eco-crisis he has brought upon the planet. But the philosopher and the religious-minded theologian searches his own conscience to find out where he went wrong. What are the attitudes and lifestyles which have brought mankind to this brink of disaster?

The *Aggaññasutta* of the *Dīghanikāyas*,[5] which relates the episode of the evolution of the world and society, emphasizes the fact that moral degeneration of man causes the degradation of his personality as well as his environment. The primordial beings were self-luminous, subsisting on joy, endowed with the ability to move in the skies, and were sexually undifferentiated. The earth was covered over with a honey-flavored, butter-like creamy substance. One being conceived the idea to taste this earth substance and was overcome with greed for its flavor when he did taste. Others followed suit and they started partaking of this substance in greater quantities with more and more greed. As time advanced their bodies became coarser and coarser, and they gradually lost self-luminosity, the ability to subsist on joy and move about in the sky. This moral degradation of man had its effect on the external environment, too. The honey-flavored, butter-like earth substance diminished and vanished, and was replaced by a variety of mushroom and subsequently by an edible creeper. During these successive periods the beauty of the beings varied according to the intensity of their greed. Some were comely in appearance while others were plain. Those who were handsome became proud and conceited and they looked down upon the others, and this attitude gave rise to further adverse effects on their personalities and in the food resources in the external environment. Sexual differences manifested themselves on these beings and spontaneous birth was substituted by sexual reproduction. Self-growing rice appeared on earth and through laziness to gather each meal man grew accustomed to hoarding food. As a result of this hoarding habit, the growth rate of food could not keep pace with the rate of demand. Thereupon land had to be divided among families. After private ownership of land became the order of the day, those who were of a more greedy disposition started robbing from the plots of others. When detected they denied. Thus through greed, vices such as stealing and lying became manifest in society. To curb wrong-doers and punish them, a king was elected by the people (referred to as the "Great Elect", *Mahāsammata*), and thus the original simple society became much more complex and complicated. To make the growing demands made by a morally deteriorating society, social institutions were organized to safeguard justice and fair play as far as possible. The fertility

---

[5] *D.*, 27.

of the soil diminished and self-growing rice became extinct. Man had to till the land and cultivate rice for food. That too was enveloped in chaff which needed cleaning before consumption.

The point we wish to emphasize by citing this evolutionary legend is that Buddhism believes that, though change is a factor inherent in nature, man's moral deterioration accelerates the process of change and brings about conditions which are adverse to human well-being and happiness.

The same truth of the importance of the human mind is reiterated in the first stanza of the *Dhammapada:*

> The mind precedes all phenomena, mind is supreme and everything is mind-made. If one speaks or acts with an impure mind suffering follows him like the wheel following the hoof of the draught animal.[6]

The simile eloquently expresses how burdensome it is to endure the effects of an evil mind. The mind creates conditions within the human personality and in his environment for the experience of weal or woe depending on its moral caliber.

The *Cakkavattisīhanādasutta* of the *Dīghanikāya*[7] further elucidates the truth that when rulers neglect their moral obligations to provide employment opportunities to secure the well-being of their subjects and thus maintain law and order in the country, crime and evil become rampant in society. As a result human health deteriorates and life expectancy gradually gets lowered. If the process continues without being checked, incestuous and unnatural sexual behavior, wanton greed and wrong views assail society. So much so that immorality is committed without a sense of shame and it is commonly accepted as the order of the day. Those of immoral behavior even become social celebrities.

Even the word morality becomes obsolete. This moral degradation casts its adverse effects on the external environment as well. The earth fails to produce flavorsome, nutritious food. Delicacies such as butter, ghee, honey and treacle disappear and crude foods of very poor quality take their place. Hatred, fear and suspicion grip society and even family members become estranged with the spread of such negative emotions. Weapons are proliferated and strife, terrorism and war menace society. Lawlessness (*dassukhīla*)[8] continues unabated until man himself realizes his folly and turns over a new leaf.

According to a discourse in the *Aṅguttaranikāya*[9] when profligate lust wanton geed and perverse values grip the heart of man and immorality becomes widespread in society, weather patterns get disrupted. When seasonal rain fails,

---

[6] *Manopubbaṅgamā dhammā manoseṭṭhā manomayā manasā ce paduṭṭhena bhāsati vā karoti vā tato naṅ dukkhaṅ anveti cakkaṁ va vahato padaṁ. Dh.* I .

[7] *D.,* 26.

[8] *D.,* I , 135-136.

[9] *A.,* I , 160.

crops get adversely affected with various kinds of pests and plant diseases. Through lack of nourishing food, the human mortality rate rises.

Thus several *suttas* of the Pali canon demonstrate the fact that early Buddhism believes in the existence of a close relationship between human morality and the natural environment. This idea of the interdependence of man and nature has been systematized in the theory of the five cosmic laws, *pañca niyāmadhammā*. [10] The five are physical laws (*utuniyāma*, lit. season law), biological laws (*bījaniyāma*, lit. seed law), psychological laws (*cittaniyāma*, lit. mind law), moral laws (*kammaniyāma*, lit. action law) and causal laws (*dhammaniyāma*, lit. reality law). [*Dhammaniyāma* is translated as "causal laws" because *Saṁyutta-nikāya* [11] states as synonyms *dhammaṭṭhitatā dhammaniyāmatā idappaccayatā*.] Causal laws operate within the first four spheres as well as among them.

This means that the physical environment of any given area conditions the growth and development of its biological component, i.e., fauna and flora. These in turn influence the thought pattern of the people interacting with them. Modes of thinking and ideas determine moral standards. The opposite process of interaction is also possible. The morals of man influence not only the psychological make-up of the people but the biological and physical environment of the area as well. Thus the five laws demonstrate that man and nature are bound together in a reciprocal causal relationship with changes in one necessarily bringing about changes in the other.

Modern large-scale industries have advanced with such incredible productive capacity that they supply much more than the available demand. To keep these industries going without a reduction in profit, business magnates resort to producing goods of inferior quality with a much shorter life-span than they could produce. Take for instance the automobile industry. A car purchased during the early decades of this century was road-worthy for a number of decades, but recent new cars are trouble-free for a few years. These large-scale industries producing low-quality goods are environmentally disastrous. On the one hand they consume much of the non-renewable resources of the world which took millions of years to form and which could satisfy the needs of many more generations to come, and on the other hand they contribute to air pollution through fossil fuel burning much more rapidly than quality products.

The human being also suffers a great deal in this industrialized age. Machines have robbed man of his creative ability. The ancient man used his fingers to sew, to weave, to carve, to sculpture, etc. These developed the necessary brain power which collectively brought about the industrial revolution in the long run. But now industry itself seems to have gone beyond its utility value. Hence the cry for appropriate technology, reminding one of the middle path (*majjhimā paṭipadā*) approach so much valued in Buddhism. Just as even good nourishing food taken excessively causes high blood pressure, obesity, etc.,

---

[10] *Atthasālini*, 272.

[11] *S., II, 25.*

even so science and technology have gone beyond man's enduring capacity. There are psychological, social and environmental limits to growth.

Let us take the psychological aspect first. As most men are reduced to button-pushers in vast industrial complexes where practically everything is automated, man feels frustrated and alienated by the monotony of his work. His creative ability is frustrated and he finds no job satisfaction. Curiosity and creativity are innate precious qualities or drives in man, and when he feels that he is getting a wage for work which he barely understands and which hardly gives him the satisfaction of seeing something which he himself created, he feels alienated from the whole set-up. Here we are reminded of the ivory combs displayed in our museums. How much satisfaction and pride of accomplishment that creative artist would have enjoyed having produced that beautiful work of art. Compare him with the worker in a plastic ware (comb) factory. What job satisfaction does he get? He is just a laborer, no master of himself. Today we need not hunt down elephants for ivory, but there are plenty of bovine horns which could be utilized for manual production of combs if only man turns to small scale handcraft which gives much-needed dignity and a sense of self-fulfillment to the frustrated alienated man.

Social limits to growth are obviously plain in the family situation today. Mostly men move into urban areas from villages in search of livelihood. This is one of the important causes for family disruption. Children in such families tend to grow without proper parental love, care and guidance. Such children clique themselves and roam the streets together, often becoming a social nuisance. While some of them become juvenile delinquents, parents themselves drift apart and the family which is the fundamental unit in society just gets dissipated with enormous unhealthy consequences. Rural migrants into urban areas suffer boredom and loneliness without the warmth of their family relationships. They tend to take to alcohol and resort to prostitutes. Though driven by economic necessities to begin with, being unable to cope with the demands of physical and psychological needs, they succumb and seek the easy way out through unwholesome means, thus getting bogged down in misery more and more. These are the unhappy consequences of urbanization and large-scale industrialization. To circumvent these repercussions there is the growth of suburban residential areas where factory workers could commute daily from their homes. Decentralization of factories is another means, but it decentralizes pollution too with factory effluents. Thus, social limits to growth is seen in many aspects of life once again pointing to the value of the middle path approach propounded in Buddhism. Neither in manual labor nor in industrialization could we find social stability and peace, hence the need for the _via media_ of appropriate technology.

Another aspect of the social limits to growth is seen in the utilization of leisure. These days when domestic labor-saving devices are readily available, the middle class housewife has to keep herself occupied either by going out to work or by cultivating a suitable hobby. To cope with the soaring cost of living and inflation often both husband and wife are driven to seek employment through sheer economic necessity. But this is not an altogether healthy phenomenon as children tend to get neglected, and the woman's role as homemaker tends to suffer with insidious consequences. Woman's role as homemaker is of prime importance for the health of both spouses and of children, and thereby of the entire society. Therefore it is the bounden duty of society to attach monetary value to handicraft and cottage industry to encourage women to take to hobbies such as knitting, sewing, embroidery, lace-making, pottery, painting, sculpture, etc. Such hand-made goods should be valued much higher than factory products, thus affording a source of income while providing women to utilize their leisure meaningfully with a sense of fulfillment.

Some social habits cultivated by modern man are not only injurious to himself, but to those around him and also to the environment at large. Take the habit of smoking for instance. Smoke inhaled causes deposits of tar-like nicotinous substances in the respiratory system giving rise to cancer and other related diseases. Now it is discovered that what is called passive smoke is also injurious to health. A non-smoker who lives in the company of a smoker is also exposed to health hazards. When calculated the millions or billions of cigarettes consumed daily in the whole world, one can guess the volume of nicotine fumes that are released into the atmosphere. Moreover tobacco growers know how tobacco plantations render the soil infertile, and this is another extremely vulnerable aspect in the environmental issue caused by unhealthy social habits of man.

Over-population is another tremendous burden the world has to carry today. Perhaps from the scientific point of view it can be said that the evolutionary process has been accelerated. From the Buddhist point of view, the human world is not the only sphere where life exists, there are *peta* worlds as well as *deva* worlds. It may be that beings from such spheres also have found birth in the human world. Whatever the source from where more beings come to inhabit the world, the man of science has come out with various methods of birth control to cope with the growing population problem. Buddhism as a way of life cannot afford to turn a blind eye to these problems too. Medical science itself has shown the dangers of methods such as birth control pills; it has also discovered the rhythm method for women with a regular menstrual cycle. Thereby they can avoid the fertile period and resort to the 'safe period.' This reminds us of the Buddhist exhortation for laymen to observe the eight precepts during the four main phases of the moon. It is not known whether these lunar phases have any effect on woman's fertility, and it is our contention that this is an area which needs proper scientific investigation. Until such time, it may be useful for those who believe in Buddhist values, and in modern science, to practice celibacy during the four main phases of the moon and also abide by the rhythm method. This means control over sense pleasures even within family life in order to limit births according to one's economic and social circumstances.

This brings us to the four types of pleasures delineated by Buddhism for the layman. They are *atthi sukha, bhoga sukha, anana sukha,* and *anavajja sukha.*[12] The first spells the pleasure of economic security. Every human being must have the wherewithal to get his basic needs satisfied. Without proper food, clothing, shelter and medicine, life could be burdensome and miserable, to say the least. *Atthi sukha* may vary according to the skills one has acquired early in life and according to one's intellectual capacity and resourcefulness. One has to learn to cut one's coat according to his cloth. But a person with wanton greed will not be able to enjoy the pleasure of economic prosperity or security, because the more he gets, the more he wants. It is like filling a bucket with a hole. Therefore Buddhism teaches the value of contentment (*santutthi paramam dhanam*).[13] When perseverance (*utthānaviriya*) is tempered with contentment one can go up the ladder of worldly prosperity without disappointment and frustration. This is the secret of righteous success, and when one has more to spare one should learn to share with others. This is *bhogasukha.* Wealth that is shared gives great satisfaction and cuts down jealousy on the part of others. One gathers friends and well-wishers when wealth is enjoyed sharing with others. *Anana sukha,* or the pleasure of debtlessness, does not merely mean the absence of monetary obligations. It means the pleasure one derives having discharged one's responsibilities in all social roles. As parents we can be debt-free only if we have fulfilled our responsibilities towards our children. They have to be emotionally nourished with the love we shower on them. They have to be taught what is right and wrong mainly through example. They have to be educated wherewith they can be weaned economically. According to Buddhism, parents should take an interest in choosing a suitable spouse for the child and thus wean from emotional dependence too to a large extent. It is the mother who cannot wean the child emotionally who becomes a problem mother-in-law to the child's spouse. As a child, one has obligations towards one's parents and maybe grandparents, too. The *Sigālovāda sutta*[14] shows the duties an individual has to perform in all social roles; by dutifully attending to them, one can have a debt-free, untroubled conscience. *Anavajjasukha* is the highest of all pleasures derived by the enjoyment of the first three pleasures. It is the pleasure of having done no wrong. One's mode of livelihood too should be free of blame as Buddhism declares all trade in meat, poison, weapons, liquor and slavery as blameworthy. These are also environmentally harmful.

Sigālovāda sutta[15] exhorts the layman to collect wealth as the bee collects pollen from the flower. This is a very eloquent simile from the environmental point of view. When collecting pollen the bee neither robs the flower of its beauty nor destroys its fragrance. Having thus collected pollen it manufactures honey which is far more precious as food and medicine. Similarly man is

---

¹² *A.,* II, 69
¹³ *Dh.,* 204.
¹⁴ *D.,* III, 188-191.
¹⁵ *D.,* III, 188.

expected to utilize the resources nature provides without polluting and harming nature, to make life richer and happier. This can only be done if man tries to satisfy his needs and not his greeds. Overexploitation impoverishes natural resources, impairing nature's replenishing capacity. Wastage in the modern world is another detrimental factor, reminding us of the prudent use of nature's bounty in a little episode of the *Vinayapiṭaka*.[16] Ānanda explained to king Udena how, when monks get new robes, the old ones are utilized as coverlets or bed sheets, the old sheets are used as mattress covers, the old mattress covers are used as rugs, old rugs as dusters, and old tattered dusters are kneaded with clay to repair cracked floors and walls. Thus nothing is wasted and such economical use of resources should serve as a shining example for modern man in this age of disposables.

From the Buddhist point of view, the environmental crisis is nothing but the external manifestation of the internal moral crisis of modern man. This is the pathos of luxury and power. Man in his greed for wealth and pleasure exploited natural resources with unprecedented avarice. If we were to take the example of deforestation in one country only we can see how large-scale felling of trees in Thailand resulted in entire villages being submerged under tons of mud when torrential rain fell on denuded mountaintops. Such disasters are not rare occurrences in other parts of the world as well, not to speak of the fertile topsoil erosion and the escalation of crop failures. Thus it is man himself who suffers when he is overpowered by greed, aggression and delusion. Therefore an attitudinal change is imperative if the present eco-crisis is to be surmounted.

Man's inhumanity to animals can be seen in the way livestock farming is carried out today. In deep litter poultry farming, the birds cannot even move about, they are fed for eggs or meat and one can just imagine the torture they go through long before they are slaughtered. Thus man has become inhuman and insensitive to the pain of others. Such humans would do anything for money, and it is no wonder that crime, terrorism and war are rampant in the world today. Hired murder is a public secret resorted to by Mammon worshipping unscrupulous affluent men holding high positions in the world.

Nature can cope with the biological human waste matter through its process of decomposition. But nature cannot cope with the psychological venom man pours out into the atmosphere. The normal exhaled breath of man contains carbon dioxide and it is utilized as plant food by the vegetable kingdom. But it is our contention that the breath also contains psychogenic noxious gaseous properties caused by negative emotions. For we know that emotional changes cause changes in our breathing pattern. We sigh in grief, we gasp in pain, we yawn in laziness, we snort in anger, and we are short of breath in excitement. These changes are due to glandular secretion of hormones and their toxic substances must be exhaled with the breath. When large masses of people breathe out such venom the whole atmosphere gets polluted and nature is unable to purify this type of impurity. Terra firma is covered over with a biosphere

---

[16] *Vin.*, **III**, 291.

consisting of fauna and flora, and an atmosphere into which is fused what we prefer to call the psycho-sphere. It is this psycho-sphere or the collective consciousness of mankind that governs the world, hence the Buddhist assertion *cittena niyyati loko,* the world is led by the human mind. The vegetable kingdom suffers a great deal when this collective consciousness is unwholesome. In the *Gāmaṇicaṇḍajātaka*[17] it is stated that the flavor of fruits and vegetables diminish when the farmers neglect their moral obligations. According to modern scientific experiments plants grown with equal horticultural care but in an atmosphere of love and in hostile settings show contrasting differences in growth. Love encourages healthy growth whereas hostility stunts and gradually withers them off. Thus Buddhism would argue that the environmental crisis is an indication of the moral crisis in man. A change of heart is a sine qua non to surmount the environmental crisis, hence the search for solutions by all major religions of the world today.

Man and nature are intertwined. The planet protected by the ozone layer above forms one whole ecosystem causally and interdependently bound together by physical, biological, psychological and moral laws. When man acts collectively with impure minds to outweigh morally wholesome behavior, physical laws react adversely to man's health of body and mind. This is the message given by *suttas* such as the *Aggañña, Cakkavattisīhanāda* and *Aṅguttara* I, 160. The same morally responsive psychological involvement of man with the world outside is succinctly expressed by the statement: Knots within and knots without mankind is enmeshed in knots.[18]

The only way out of this mess is to establish ourselves on morally wholesome behavior and cultivate a non-aggressive attitude towards nature with a philosophy of 'being' / 'living' rather than 'having' / 'possessing'.

> Sow a thought and reap an act
> Sow an act and reap a habit
> Sow a habit and reap a character
> Sow a character and reap a destiny.

---

[17] *J.,* 257.

[18] *Anto jaṭā bahi jaṭā jaṭāya jaṭitā pajā. S.,* I , 13.

CHAPTER 17

TWO PERSPECTIVES ON BUDDIRST ECOLOGY

Donald K. Swearer

The world's environmental crisis has prompted religiously committed, socially concerned people throughout the world to search their traditions for resources to address its root causes and its symptoms. Buddhists are no exception. The compatibility between the Buddhist worldview of interdependence and an "environmentally friendly" way of living in the world, the values of compassion and nonviolence, and the example of the lifestyle of the Buddha and the early Saṅgha are cited as important contributions to the dialogue on how to live in an increasingly threatened world. This essay seeks to contribute to this discussion through an examination of classical and contemporary sources. The classical sources include paradigms of the cosmos and of human society in the Pali Suttas. The contemporary sources focus on the activities of concerned Thai Buddhists, in particular the writings of Buddhadasa Bhikkhu My interest in this topic is prompted in part by visits to Thailand in 1990 and 1994.

During the past half century, economic and social configurations have changed dramatically throughout the world as a consequence of vast increases in population, urbanization, industrialization, and technical achievement. These changes have, to a certain extent, created a common economic culture determined by the necessities of the modern nation state and the business interests of the transnational or multinational corporation. This economic culture is primarily "materialistic" in nature in the sense that human wellbeing tends to be defined in terms of the production and consumption of goods. It is commonplace, for example, to measure the "wealth" of a nation in terms of its GNP (Gross National Product).

The consequences of the development of our economically defined modern culture are manifold. It has, for example, led to a general increase in life expectancy among many populations of the world as a consequence of improved health services more adequate housing and so forth. In respect to material aspects of life more people share in the benefits of the increased production and use of various kinds of goods. Yet, even from an economic perspective the increase in the production and use of goods has been a mixed blessing. In general, even though by GNP measurements the world has seen a significant increase in the amount of material wealth, critics are quick to point out the gross disparity between the rich and the poor not only in "developing" countries such as Thailand, but "developed" countries like United States. For instance, in Thailand since 1988 conflicts over water use between the wealthier industrial-urban sector and the poorer agricultural-farming sector have prompted numerous protests by farmers over low water supplies.[1] These came to a head in the drought year of 1993. Internationally, it can also be pointed out that despite improvements in agricultural technology hunger has emerged as a persistent and pervasive worldwide problem. The capital intensive "green revolution" with its dependence on chemical fertilizers and pesticides has produced more systemic, long-range problems than it has solved.

Developments in various kinds of technologies have lead to dramatic breakthroughs in everything from space exploration to microscopic laser surgery. At the same time, however, it has contributed to a sense of the hopelessness and violence of modern society whether it be the plague of drug addiction in urban ghettos, the endemic spread of the AIDS virus, pervasive armed conflict, or the seemingly insurmountable problem of waste disposal, especially the threat of the widespread nuclear contamination of living space or the chemical contamination of water and food supplies.

Our modern economic culture has also had a generally deleterious effect on classical moral values and religious worldviews and on traditional ways of understanding human existence and what constitutes the good or happy life. In the face of a perceived threat to traditional ways of being by modern economic culture, some seek a return to the verities of a simpler era believed to be embodied in an earlier historical age or represented by an idealized, mythic time of primal beginnings. Religious fundamentalisms whether Christian, Jewish, Muslim, Hindu, or Buddhist can be interpreted as a retreat from the confusions and threats of the modern world to the simple truths and values of an earlier age. But there are other, more creative and constructive religious responses to modernity than today's various fundamentalisms. Thoughtful religious adherents the world over are seeking to understand and interpret their traditions in ways that preserve the lasting insights and values of their faith, but at the same time engage the realities of existence in today's world rather than retreating from them. In the first half of this essay I propose to explore some of the classical teachings of the Theravāda Buddhist tradition relevant to the environmental concerns shared by people around the world today. Then I shall examine some of the specific teachings relative to Buddhist ecology found in the writings of Buddhadasa Bhikkhu, the most noted interpreter of Buddha-dhamma in Thailand.

---

[1] See *Bangkok Post*, Monday, November 13, 1989, "EGAT Warns of Low Water Level in Dam," 1&3.

1. Buddhism, Development & the Environment

In the past several years the news media in Thailand has devoted a considerable amount of attention to the conflicts between the goals of national and commercial development, the well-being of the majority of the Thai people (especially the rural, farming populations), and the health of the environment. In particular, the Seventh National Development Plan has been criticized for following in the footsteps of its predecessors by emphasizing material growth at the expense of a more balanced development and an equitable distribution of wealth. As Dr. Ananda Kanchanapan of the Faculty of the Social Sciences at Chiang Mai University put it, "Development in Thailand has emphasized the GNP and doing so has undernimed the moral and spiritual integration between the social and natural environment.[2] An article in the *Matichon* newspaper which I cite as representive of this point of view charged that development in Thailand benefitted the elites at the expense of the environment and proposed a reformist Buddhist perspective that would challenge selfishness and greed and the excessive life-style that resulted from "too much wealth, too much power, too much to eat and drink, too many cars and mistresses."[3]

Thailand's religious and cultural traditions offer many resources for the creation of a balanced and equitable model for development, one appropriate to the ecological challenges of our times. Fundamentally, the classical Theravāda Buddhist view envisages the human and natural environment as one, organically interrelated whole. This view is supported by such seminal Pali Suttas as the *Aggañña-suttanta* ("The Sutta of the First Beginnings"), the *Sigālovāda-suttanta* ("The Sutta of the Layperson's Ethical Code"), and the *Dhammacakkappavattana-sūtta* ("Setting the Wheel of the Law in Motion"). We shall examine the resources in these texts for the construction of a Buddhist ecology of both the human and natural environment.

As its title suggest, the *Aggañña-sutanta*[4] a story or myth of the origins of the world. In the beginning, according to the text, the world was in a state of "radiance" or undifferentiated perfection. As the cosmos evolved or devolved from this state of perfection, differences and distinctions arose: human beings emerged made of mind; earth with savor, endowed with color, odor, and taste formed on the cosmic waters. Humans then tasted the earth and through the arising of greed their self-luminance faded away; they became more and more

---

[2] Paraphrased from a lecture delivered at the McGilvary Theological Faculty of Payap University on October 27, 1989 ("Quam Khawcai Kiewkap Sangkhom Thai: Khabuankan Chai Amnat lae Kanyaek Chiwit Ook Pen Suan").

[3] It is interesting to observe that the first issue of *Generation* (October, 253 2), an expensive, elite journal contained a lead article, "The Buddha's Tears: The Decline of Buddhism in Thailand (Namtatthakhot: Anicca Buddhasasana nai Muang Thai)," 39-55. In the article some of the more important voices for reform of the Thai Saṅgha and Thai society are mentioned including Buddhadasa Bhikkhu and Sulak Sivaraksa.

[4] *Dīgha Nikāya* 3, 80-98.

solid, manifesting differences in gender and comeliness. The savory earth was replaced by fragrant, clear-grained rice in abundance. Gender and comeliness differentiation led to lust, and the division of rice land into private plots led to greed and stealing. In short, the perfection of a totally integrated human and natural world becomes, marked by division, dissension and strife, thereby necessitating the election of just ruler and the institution of a structured social order.

The Buddhist creation story, as we can see, asserts that the ideal or perfect world is one unmarked by distinctions and divisions of any kind, but that in the imperfect or fallen world in which we live a harmonious and just society is ensured by a righteous ruler or government and an appropriate scheme of social organization.[5] Unlike the Indian Brahmanical case, in the Buddhist story the class structure is neither ascribed at the creation nor granted by birth, but has only a functional or instrumental value. The same claim holds true for the ruler as well. His position comes into being by necessity, i.e., the "sinfulness" or ignorance and greed of human beings. He sustains his rule through personal righteousness, and by ruling justly.

The ruler selected to resolve the conflicts which had developed is referred to in the text as the Great Elect (*mahāsammata*) and the Lord of the Fields, but above all as one who ruled by the Dhamma, hence, a *dhammarājā*. The stock description in the Pali texts is a righteous monarch (*dhammiko dhammarājā*). Buddhaghosa explains the term *dhammiko* as one who rules with justice and impartiality, and applies the term *dhammarājā* because the king does not acquire his power through fraud or violence, but through rightful succession and adherence to the precepts of the righteous kings.[6]

As is true of many traditional religious worldviews, the personal virtue and just rule of the king and his governors is reflected in the patterns of nature. That is, when the rulers are just and virtuous nature is bountiful, the moral and natural orders being inextricably bound together. Such a vision is articulated in the 13th century Thai cosmological treatise written by King Lithai of Sukhothai:

> The grain, the water, fish and food, gems and precious ornaments, the seven gems and nine gems, silver and gold as well as silk and satin will be plentiful. The *devatā* will make the rain fall in the right season and the right amount, not too much nor too little. The grain in the fields and the fish in the water will not suffer from lack of rain. The days, nights, months and years will be clearly defined. The *devatā* who are the guardians of homes and of the city will take good care since they respect and honor rulers who are righteous. When there are

---

[5] The class structure proposed in the Sutta is the classical four-fold division of priest, warrior, merchant, and servant. A special case is also made for the monk or bhikkhu, those who pursue trans-mundane goals rather than mundane goals no matter how worthy.

[6] B.G. Gokhale, "Dhammiko Dhammaraja. A Study in Buddhist Constitutional Concepts," *Indica* (1953): 162.

rulers who are not righteous the rain and water will go wrong. The plowing and planting will be ruined from the lack of rain. The fruits and plants which grow from the earth will lose their nutritive essence and delicious taste. The tree trunks that grow will lose their healthy look. The sun, wind, rain, the moon and stars will not regulate the seasons in the normal way. This is because the rulers do not follow the Dhamma.[7]

Far from being an antique relic from a bygone age, classical cosmological treatises the likes of the *Aggañña-suttanta* and the *Tribhūmikathā* bring important ecological insights to bear on contemporary problems of development. Some of these insights are the following: (1) that the human and natural world are inextricably one; (2) that possessiveness motivated by lust, ignorance, and hatred divides and destroys the natural harmony of things; (3) that distinctions within the sphere of human ecology are required by necessity and function rather necessitated than by birth and privilege; (4) that the moral/human and spiritual/natural realms are mutually self-reflective.

It may seem odd that to refer to the *Sigālovāda-suttanta* as a text from which we might derive insight into a Buddhist ecological perspective.[8] After all, the text proposes a code of behavior between specific social and familial groups: mother, father and children; teacher and student; wife and husband; among friends; between master and servant; and between holy men (*samaṇas*) and their disciples. What has a code of lay ethics, as this text is often characterized, to do with Buddhist ecology? There are, in my view, two very important perspectives in this text relevant to the subject of this essay. The first is its very structure. The second is the moral attitude or virtue which underlies its specific ethical advice.

First, it is important to note that in the *Sigālovāda-suttanta* the Buddha suggest a moral transformation of the traditional Indian Brahmanical view of the universe. As the story opens the Buddha happens to observe a young boy, *Sigāla* in the process of making offerings to the deities of the four quarters, the zenith, and the nadir on behalf of his deceased father and in accordance with Brahmanical custom. The Buddha uses the occasion to explain that in the religion of an Ariyan (i.e., in the practice of the *Buddhasāsana*) the six quarters are worshipped in another way. He then proceeds to interpret the six quarters as groups or types of people: parents (east), teachers (south), wife and children (west), friends and relatives (north), servants and workers (nadir), brahmans and mendicants (zenith). From an ecological perspective it is important to keep in mind that the Buddha retains the cosmological structure of the classical Indian worldview but grounds it in a moral rather than a sacrificial understanding of the universe. In the text two templates are superimposed on one another: the cosmic/natural and the human/moral. The two are inextricably intertwined. The

---

[7] Phya Lithai, *The Three Worlds According to King Ruang* (*Trai-bhumikatha*), ed. and trans. by Frank E. & Mani B. Reynolds (Berkeley: Asian Humanities Press, 1982), 75.

[8] See *Dialogues of the Buddha* (*Dīgha Nikāya*), Pt. 3, 171 *ff.*

world in all of its "quarters" is essentially an interdependent whole, and its very functioning as a natural order depends on the way in which we as moral beings treat one another in our various positions, functions, and statuses.

How are we to treat those around us, our parents, children, friends, superiors, inferiors, etc.? The text stipulates specific kinds of behavior, we are to share with friends, praise our wives, be attentive to teachers, and so forth. Underlying all of these specific actions, however, is a moral quality of sympathy (*anukampā*). *Anukampā* is literally the attitude or virtue of being moved (*kampā*) in response to other beings and things (*anu*). As T.W. Rhys Davids explains the term, "*Anukampanti* (a verbal form of the nominal) is the typeword for the protecting tenderness of the stronger for the weaker, and means vibrating along-after. It thus in emotional force is even stronger than our compassion of sympathy. And because the pulsing emotion is other-regarding, a feeling-together whatever the loved one feels, it is justifiable to render it often by love."[9] In short, the virtue or attitude of *anukampā* derivative from the *Sigālovāda-suttanta* might be characterized as the ideal ecologically oriented moral concern- -a tenderness toward the weak, a "vibrating along-after" be the object a beloved friend, an animal, or, for that matter, a tree. In the second section of this paper I shall draw a close relationship between this understanding of empathy and those Buddhist monks and laity working actively to protect (*anurakkhana*) Thailand's forests.

The third text from which I propose to derive an ecological lesson is one of the best known in the Theravāda canon, the so-called "First Sermon" or the *Dhammacakkappavattana-sūtta*. In this text the Buddha's teaching is characterized as a Middle Way between the extremes of indulgence and ascetic abstinence. The Sutta sets forth the classic description of the Middle Way: the Four Noble Truths and the Noble Eightfold Path. This formulation of the essence of the *Buddhadhamma* characterizes existence as suffering (*dukkha*), locates the cause of this suffering in ignorance and craving, and spells out the solution to suffering through moral (*sīla*), mental (*samādhi*), and spiritual (*paññā*) training (*sikkhā*). In the case of the First Sermon, I would also like to suggest two points of great relevance to a Buddhist ecology. The first is the basic affirmation that a Buddhist way of life is a Middle Way, a balanced way which avoids all kinds of excesses. A Middle Way attitude toward life rests on the assumption that the various elements of life exist in integrated balance. A similar attitude is reflected in the balance struck between the eight limbs of the Noble Eightfold Path. It is not sufficient for one to pursue the higher meditative goals of the Buddhist path. These mental and spiritual attainments are inextricably part of one's social and moral development.

The second point is the emphasis in the text on the negative effect of heedlessness or lack of awareness, and the correspondingly positive effect of

---

[9] See Introduction to the *Sigālovāda Suttanta in Dialogues of the Buddha*, Pt. 3, Sacred Books of the Buddhists, Vol. 4, trans. T.W. Rhys Davids (London: Luzac & Co., 1957), 171-187.

heedfulness and awareness. Walking the Buddhist path is coming to know oneself and one's surroundings including the natural environment, and to act attentively. The same claim can be made for the basic moral precepts of the Buddhist life: not to kill, steal, fornicate, lie, or consume intoxicants. Violence is a form of heedlessness, as is being in an inebriated state, or stealing. Lack of awareness or heedlessness is certainly at the heart of developmental excesses destructive to the balance of life, including the environment.

2. Bhikku Buddhadasa

The aforementioned principles and moral virtues relevant to the design of a Buddhist ecological perspective receive extensive expansion and elaboration at the hands of Buddhadasa Bhikkhu, Thailand's most prominent interpreter of the *Buddhadhamma*.[10] Buddhadasa was born in 1906 as Nguam Panich. He began his monastic career at the time Thailand was moving toward a constitutional monarchy. In 1932, the year which marked that change, Buddhadasa established his now famous monastery in Chaiya, southern Thailand, known as Wat Suan Mokkhabalarama, The Garden of Empowering Liberation. There he began a remarkable teaching career which established him as significant and creative interpreter of Theravāda Buddhism. Although Buddhadasa died on July 8, 1993, his teaching legacy continues to influence the development of Buddhism in Thailand and other parts of the world.

Buddhadasa's interest in Buddhism and the environment is part of a much broader movement in Thailand. Several NGOs including the Santi Pracha Dhamma Institute, the Seikyadhamma Association, and the International Network of Engaged Buddhists have organized monks and laity to work on behalf of the protection of the environment. Many noted Buddhist reformers and social activists, e.g. Sulak Sivaraksa, Chatsumarn Kabilsingh, Prawes Wasi, Phra Dhammapitaka, have been actively involved in these organizations or have sought to define the inherent interrelationship between Buddhism and nature and to articulate a Buddhist justification for environmental action.[11]

---

[10] For an introduction to the thought of Buddhadasa, see Bhikkhu Buddhadasa, *Me and Mine, Selected Essays of Bhikkhu Buddhadasa,* ed. Donald K. Swearer (Albany: SUNY Press, 1989).

[11] Numerous publications in the area of Buddhist ecology and Buddhist environmentalism have been published in recent years. Examples directly connected with Thailand include Susan M. Darlington, "Monks and Environmental Conservation: A Case Study in Nan Province," *Seeds of Peace,* 9.1: 7-10; Leslie E. Sponsel and Poranee Natadecha-Sponsel, "The Role of Buddhism in Creating a More Sustainable Society in Thailand," (London: SOAS, 1994). Noteworthy publications in Thai include Phra Thepvedi [Phra Dhammapitaka], *Phra Kap Pa [Monks and the Forest]* (Bangkok: Khrongkan Vanaphitdak, 2535/1992). Dhammapitaka, Dr. Chatsumarn Kabilsingh, and others appeal, in particular, to the exemplary importance of the life of the Buddha and the early Sangha as a resource for defining the relationship between human beings and the natural environment.

An issue which preoccupied Buddhadasa toward the end of his life was the destruction of the natural environment (Thai: *thamachat;* Pali: *dhammajāti*). One of his informal talks at Wat Suan Mokkhalarama. was titled, "Buddhists and the Care of Nature" ("Buddhasasanika Kap Kan Anurak Thamachat"). Much of the content of this section is based on two of Buddhadasa's talks given in March of 1990 and printed in the booklet by that title, (Buddhadasa Bhikkhu. *Buddhasasanik Kap Kan Anurak Thamachat.* Bangkok: Kamol Kimthong Foundation, B.E. 2533/C.E. 1990). 1 shall begin our consideration of Buddhadasa's notion of "caring for nature" in a manner consistent with his abiding interest in language by examining the last two terms in the title of his talk, *anurak* (Pali: *ana-rakkha*) and *thamachat* (Pali: *dhammajāti*).

Within the context of the worldwide concern for environmental destruction, the Thai term, *anurak*, is often translated into English as "conservation." In fact, the dozens of Thai monks involved in efforts to stop the exploitation of forests in their districts and provinces have been labeled, *phra anurak pa*, translated as "forest conservation monks." *Anurak,* as embodied in the life and work of Buddhadasa and several forest conservation monks, however, conveys a richer, more nuanced meaning closer to its Pali roots; namely, to be imbued with the quality of protecting, sheltering, or caring for. By the term, *anurak,* Buddhadasa intends this deeper, dhammic sense of *anu-rakkha,* an active "caring for" that issues forth from the very nature of our being. In this sense, *anu-rakkha* is linked with a pervasive feeling of human empathy (Pali: *anu-kampā*)[12] for all of our surroundings. If you will, caring is the active expression of empathy.

One cares for the forest because one empathizes with the forest just as one cares for people, including oneself, because one has become empathetic. But how does one become empathetic? *Anurak,* in this sense is fundamentally linked with non-attachment or liberation from preoccupation with self which is at the very core of Buddhadasa's thought. He articulates this theme by various Thai and Pali terms including *mai hen kae tua* (not being selfish),[13] *cit wang* (non-attachment or having a liberated heart-mind), *anattā* (not-self), *suññatā* (emptiness). In a talk to the Dhamma Study Group at Siriraj Hospital in Bangkok in 1961 he stated unequivocally the centrality of non-attachment to Buddhist spirituality: "This is the heart of the Buddhist Teachings, of all Dhamma: nothing whatsoever should be clung to: (*sabbe dhammā nālaṁ abhinivesāya*)."[14]

---

[12] Western students of Buddhism often translate *anukampa* as "sympathy." In my own view "empathy" is a more apt translation. I have in mind the image or metaphor of a tuning fork that resonates empathetically with its environment. I construe empathy in a strong, dispositional sense.

[13] It is noteworthy that one of nine pamphlets published by the Dhamma Sapha, a group recently formed to disseminate Buddhadasa's teaching, is *Kan Tham Lai Khwum Hen Kae Tua* [Rooting Out Selfishness] (Bangkok: Dhamma Sapha, n.d.)

[14] Buddhadasa Bhikkhu, *Heartwood from the Bo Tree,* trans. Santikaro Bhikkhu (Bangkok: Usom Foundation, 1985), 13. This book has been recently reissued

We truly care for our total environment and for our fellow human beings only when we have overcome self-preoccupation and those qualities which empower it, e.g. desire, ignorance, hatred. Many of Buddhadasa's essays reflect his profound commitment to this truth, for example: *Khwam Mai Hen Kae Tua Champen Samrap Rabop Kanmuang Khong Lok* (1989) [Overcoming Selfishness is Essential to a Political System], *Kan Rapchai Phum Tham Hai Lok Santi* (1960) [Serving Others Makes the World Peaceful], *Kan Tham Ngan Dum Cit aang Phu'a Sangkhom* (1975) [Working with Liberated Heart and Mind For the Good of Society]. Note the persistent linkage between non-attachment, selflessness, and the capacity to be truly other-regarding. Caring (*anurak*) in Buddhadasa's dhammic sense, therefore, is the active expression of our empathetic identification with all life forms, sentient and non-sentient, human beings and nature.

Caring in this deeper sense of the meaning of *anurak* goes beyond the well publicized strategies of the conservation monks to protect and conserve the forest such as "ordaining" trees, as important as these strategies are in Thailand today. This is where the second term, *dhammajāti* comes into the picture. The Thai term, *thamachat,* is usually translated as "nature. " In its more nuanced Pali sense, however, *dhammajāti* denotes everything that is linked to *dhamma* or that is *dhamma*-originated (*jāti*). That is to say, *thamachat* includes all things in their true, natural states, a condition that Buddhadasa refers to as the "normal" or "nomative" (*jāti*). To conserve (*anurak*) nature (*thamchat*), therefore, translates as having at the core of one's very being the quality of caring for all things in the world in their natural or true conditions; that is to say, to care for them as they really are rather than as I might benefit from them or as I might like them to be.

From an ethical perspective this means that our care for nature derives from an ingrained selfless, empathetic response. It is not motivated by our need to satisfy our own pleasures as, say, in the maintenance of a beautiful garden, or even the laudable goal of conserving nature for our own physical and spiritual well-being or for the benefit of future generations. To care for nature in these pragmatic, functional terms has immense value, to be sure. Buddhadasa would not dispute this fact. A carefully tended garden is both meaningful to the gardener and inspirational to the viewer; furthermore, human survival may depend on whether or not we are able to conserve our dwindling natural resources and solve the problems of our increasingly polluted natural environment. Laudable as these two senses of conserving nature are, however, they lack the profound transformation or spiritual sense of what Buddhadasa means by *anurak thamachat.*

---

by Wisdom Publications. Those who criticize Buddhadasa for being a modernist, eclectic thinker should keep in mind that he has never relinquished the centrality of the concept of non-attachment. While this notion is certainly pan-Buddhist and figures prominently in the ethical emphasis of modern Buddhist apologists, the concept of non-attachment is also fundamental to classical Theravāda *sīla-dhamma.*

The concept of active caring for other human beings has a prima facie value.[15] The word itself evokes numerous examples from our own experience, e.g., the parent who cares for a child, the mutual caring among friends, the responsible caring of citizens for the well-being of the state. But what does Buddhadasa mean by caring for nature, *thamachat*? By *thamachat* Buddhadasa certainly does not mean to essentialize or romanticize the concept of nature. Quite the contrary. For Buddhadasa, things in their natural, true state are characterized by their dynamic, interdependent nature (*idap accayatā, paṭiccasamuppāda*). Everything is linked in a process of dependent co-arising, or as Buddhadasa says so often, "We are mutual friends inextricably bound together in the same process of birth, old age suffering, and death."[16] In other words, the world is a conjoint, inter-dynamic, cooperative enterprise (Thai, *sahakorn*. Pali, *sahakaraṇa*) in which we transcend all manner of artificial distinctions such as employer / employee, capitalist / laborer and get about the business of saving the world.[17]

While some linkages are obvious to us, e.g., our relationships with family and friends, other are more attenuated or hidden. For example, only in recent years has it been commonly recognized that the destruction of the Brazilian rain forest or the ocean dumping of toxic waste affects the entire world's ecosystem, or, in more immediate and personal terms, that whether I personally conserve water, electricity, fuel oil and so on affects not only my utility bills but the entire cosmos. To care for (*anurak*) nature (*thamachat*), therefore, stems from a realization that I do not and cannot exist independent of my total environment. I am not "an island unto myself," or, in Buddhadasa's terminology, I do not and cannot exist unto myself (Thai. *tua ku khong ku*) because to do so contravenes the very laws of nature (*dhammajāti* = *idappaccayatā*).

Buddhadasa extends the sense of a cooperative society (*sahakorn*) *to* the cosmos.

> The entire cosmos is a cooperative. The sun, the moon, and the stars live together as a cooperative. The same is true for humans and animals, trees and the earth. Our bodily parts function as a cooperative. When we realize that the world is a mutual, interdependent, cooperative enterprise, that human beings are all mutual friends in the process of birth, old age, suffering, and death, then we can build a noble, even a heavenly environment. If our lives are not based on this truth then we'll all perish.[18]

---

[15] For example, see Nel Noddings, *Caring. A Feminine Approach to Ethics and Moral Education* (Berkeley: University of California Press, 1984).

[16] Buddhadasa used this phrase in many of his talks. See, for example, *Buddhasasanik Kap Kan Anurak Thamachat* [Buddhists and the Conservation of Nature], 34.

[17] *Buddhasasanik Kap Kan Anurak Thamachat*, 34 -35.

[18] *Ibid.*, 35.

My own personal well-being is inextricably dependent on the well-being of everything and everyone else, and vice versa. In Buddhadasa's view this is an incontrovertible, absolute truth (*saccadhamma*). To go against this truth is to suffer the consequences. Today, we are suffering the consequences. As Buddhadasa expressed it in terms approaching an apocalyptic vision: "The greedy and selfish are destroying nature.... Our whole environment has been poisoned, prisons everywhere, hospitals filled with the physically ill, and we cant build enough facilities to take care of all the mentally ill. This is the consequence of utter selfishness (Thai. *khwdm hen kae tua*).... And in the face of all of this our greed and selfishness continues to increase. Is there no end to this madness?"[19]

In Buddhadasa's view, caring for *thamachat* means not only that we care for other human beings and for nature, but also that we care for ourselves. In a manner typical of Buddhadasa's interpretation of Buddhadhamma, he makes a distinction between inner truth and outer truth. Outwardly *thamachat* means physical nature. But the inner truth of nature is *dhammadhātu* (the essential or fundamental nature of *dhamma*), namely, the dependent co-arising nature of things (*paṭiccasamupāda, idappaccayatā*). "When we realize this truth, the truth of *dhammadhātu*; when this law of the very nature of things is firmly in our hearts and minds, then we will overcome selfishness and greed. By caring for this inner truth [*anurak thamachat phainai* = *dhammadhātu*], we will then be truly able to care for nature (*anurakkha dhammajāti*).[20]

Buddhada's teachings about caring for nature represent a thoughtful Buddhist ecological perspective (*nivesavidaya*); the simplicity of his lifestyle amidst the natural surroundings of Suan Mokkhabalarama, moreover, provides a compelling testimony to the viability of putting these teachings into practice. Caring for nature (*anurak thamachat*) is not a theory. It is a way of life.

---

[19] *Ibid.*, 15-16. I have given a free rendering of the Thai in order to convey my understanding of Buddhadasa's meaning.

[20] *Ibid.*, 12-13.

CHAPTER 18

ETHICS OF WEALTH: BUDDHIST ECONOMICS FOR PEACE

Suwanna Satha-Anand

> It is hardly an exaggeration to say that, with increasing affluence, economics has moved into the very centre of public concern, and economic performance, economic growth, economic expansion, and so forth have become the abiding interest, if not the obsession, of all modern societies. In the current vocabulary of condemnation there are few words as final and conclusive as the word "uneconomic." If an activity has been branded as uneconomic, its right to existence is not merely questioned but energetically denied.
>
> E.F. Schumacher, *Small Is Beautiful*

> The problem with "Western economics," is that it is purely material, totally forgetting about spirituality, about moral values; then, where is peace? There is, of course, the difficulty of agreeing on moral values. If we use that as an excuse to simply eliminate moral values, then, where is peace?
>
> Buddhadasa Bhikkhu, *On Buddhist Economics*

1. Introduction

Rahula Sri Walpola stated over thirty years ago, "The common belief that to follow the Buddha's teaching one has to retire from life is a misconception. It is really an -unconscious defense against practicing it."[1] Although thirty years have passed and a lot of literature on the "application" of Buddhist teachings has come out, it is fascinating to see how little attention has been paid to serious application of Buddhist principles in the modern practice of daily life. Perhaps the most ironic of all is the fact that the leadership in Buddhist countries have, at best, paid only lip service to the ideals of the Buddhist traditions. Buddhist developing countries "happily" march on towards economic success, mostly and faithfully following in the footsteps of Western models of economic practice. In

---

[1] Walpola Rahula, *What the Buddha Taught* (New York: Grove Press, inc., 1974), 77.

the case of Thailand, after 30 years of economic development, we have become one of the top ten countries in the world where there is the highest level of income gap between the rich and the poor.[2] In the past five years Thailand has become *the* leading importer of German-made Mercedes Benz in Southeast Asia. Pet dogs of the Thai elite are eating imported beef from France, while malnutrition among the poor is a problem which stubbornly stays on. Key Thai intellectuals have predicted that there will be wide-spread unrest and uprisings by the rural poor, and a bloody scenario is not a remote possibility.[3]

Then came Buddhadasa Bhikkhu, a reformist monk from Southern Thailand, who asked, "The problem with 'Western economics' is that it is purely material, totally forgetting about spirituality, about moral values; then, where is peace?"[4]

There are, of course, multiple and complex factors which are conducive to peace, both in the "inner" and "outer" senses of the term. However, when we take Buddhadasa Bhikkhu seriously, we are confronted with the challenge to focus the attention on one fundamental issue, namely, the absence of spirituality and moral values in the economic realm. I take his position to mean that the quest for "moral values" and "spirituality" in economics is the key to peace. Let us investigate.

2. Values of Neutrality and Neutrality of Values

Perhaps the most arrogant claim human beings ever made in history is the claim that they can discover (or rather create) a system of knowledge which is value free. Since the seventeenth century, science and technology have reigned supreme on this stage which claims to be beyond value judgment. This very knowledge, together with economics, has created so much visible wealth and comfort for a large number of human beings that its sacred validity is beyond question. However, upon closer scrutiny, tins "sacred validity" seems to have concealed some very fundamental unexamined assumptions which have led to innumerable conflicts and violence between man and man, as well as between man and nature. A leading Thai monk scholar puts it in the following way:

> Economics has been said to be the most scientific of the social
> sciences. Indeed, economists are proud of how scientific their subject

---

[2] These statistics were presented to a group of teachers at an academic gathering at the Faculty of Education, Sri Nakarin-wirot University, Prasarnmitr campus, by Khun Pipop Thongchai, Manager of the Foundation for Children, a well-respected non-government organization in Thailand, in November 1994.

[3] This possibility is presented by Professor Prawase Wasi, a highly respected medical doctor who has been an active voice of conscience for Thai society in the past decades. In 1993-1994 he gave several interviews to the newspapers predicting possible bloody scenes in Thai society in the near future if nothing is seriously done for the benefit of the rural poor.

[4] See Buddhadasa Bhikkhu, *On Economics* (an in-depth interview by Dr. Leonardo Chapela) (Surat Thanee Province: Suan-mokh, 1991), 12 (a typed manuscript).

is: that they take only those things which can be measured and quantified into their considerations. It has even been asserted that economics is purely a science of numbers, a matter of mathematical equations. In its effort to be a science, economics tries to eradicate all questions of abstract values as unquantifiable, and seeks to be value-free. But in opposition to this trend, some critics of economics, even a number of economists themselves, say that actually, of all the social sciences, economics is the most value-dependent. It may be asked how it is possible for economics to be a value-free science when its starting point is the perceived needs of human beings, which are a function of the value-systems of the human mind. Furthermore, the end-point or goal of economics is to answer those perceived needs to peoples' satisfaction and satisfaction too is an abstract value. *So economics begins and ends with abstract values.*[5]

One might say that "Western economics" values the fact that it is "value-free," thus making economics one of the sciences. On the other hand, "Buddhist economics" makes explicit the fact that economics is value-laden and should be. This is because economic sufficiency is the prerequisite of a peaceful society.[6] And peaceful society is desirable. The question remains, of course, what kind of values should serve as the basis and purpose of social co-existence. This problem will be taken up in detail as we proceed.

At this point, we should explicated more clearly how the neutralization of all values through the money economy has served as an illusory basis for the seeming objectivity of economics as a science. E. F. Schumacher explains:

> In the marketplace, for practical reasons, innumerable *qualitative distinctions* which are of vital importance for man and society are suppressed; they are not allowed to surface. Thus the reign of quantity celebrates its greatest triumphs in 'The Market.' Everything is *equated* with everything else to equate things means to give them a price and thus to make them exchangeable.[7]

Money is, of course, that "ultimate tool' which is the greatest equalizer of all things. According to Georg Simmel, the under-celebrated author of *The Philosophy of Money*, money is the ultimate tool because, relative to all other tools that man has made, money and money alone can be used to achieve *any* end whatsoever.[8] A ploy cannot be eaten, a silk dress cannot till the land, but

---

[5] Pra Debvedhi (Payut Payutto), *Buddhist Economics* (Bangkok: The National Identity Board, Office of the Prime Minister, 1994), 15.

[6] See a discussion of the Buddhist analysis of the decline of a society as a result of insufficient economic condition of the people in Chaiwat Satha-Anand and Suwanna. Wongwaisayawan, "Buddhist Economics Revisited," in *Asian Culture Quarterly* 7.4 (Winter 1979): 31-41.

[7] E.F. Schumacher, *Small is Beautiful* (London: Perennial Library, 1975), 15.

[8] Georg Simmel, *The Philosophy of Money,* ed. David Frisby (New York: Routledge, 1991), 210-217. Simmel explains the infinite use of money in the following:

money gained from selling horse dung can be used to buy Dior perfume. Money gained from arms sales can be used to feel orphans. In this sense, money is the greatest tool man has ever made. Precisely because money is the ultimate medium through which everything else can be exchanged, and in a sense transformed, money assumes the role of God.

Although one might say that the essence of money is its being a "pure medium," money functions through numbers. As the "neutrality" and "objectivity" of numbers are never questioned, the objectivity and neutrality of money is also guaranteed. Once a created object or produce reaches the "market," it becomes a product with "economic" value. This very economic value makes that particular object "valuable" as an item which can be exchanged into something else. In this process, the "value" of a thing is "objectified" into numerical quantity, namely $20 or $500, depending first on its use value, then on its exchange value. Thus, value is transformed into a price, and the neutralization of values has turned a full circle, with the almost magical help from money.

For "practical reasons," money makes indefinite exchanges possible and quantifiable; for moral reasons, money creates a lot of confusion. As the market suppresses innumerable qualitative distinctions which "are of vital importance for man and society," money helps perfect that suppression. If one thinks *only* in economic terms, that is, how much money one is going to make, there is no reason *why* one should choose to keep one's farmland over selling it to a condominium developer. If one thinks only of how much money one is going to make, there is no reason to choose a teaching profession over drug dealing. However, if moral reasoning is to be taken into consideration, choosing a *right* livelihood is crucial. In this sense Buddhist economics has to re-negotiate and regain a space for "qualitative distinctions" which is key to a peaceful relationship between men.

So it seems that although economics does begin and end with abstract values, namely, demands or desires and consumption or satisfaction, the process between these two end points has been taken up by quantitative calculation, to the extent that economics has been believed to be a science. In this sense the values of neutrality (in the name of science and objectivity), has taken precedence over moral issues in economics and has effectively concealed the process of neutralization of all values. No doubt that a society which moves on with basically economic force should face so much confusion of the soul which manifests itself in so much strife and violence.[9]

"thus, the value of a given amount of money is equal to the value of any object for which it might be exchanged plus the value of free choice between innumerable other objects, and this is an asset that has no analogy in the area of commodities or labor" (213).

[9] See an enlightening explanation of this observation in Robert L. Heilbroner, *The Worldly Philosophers* (New York: Simon and Schuster, 1972), 16-25. The most crucial point is, "For the market system is not just a means of exchanging goods; it is a mechanism for sustaining and maintaining an entire society" (25).

3. Right Livelihood: A Return of Moral Values in Economics

As Buddhadasa puts it, the difficulty of agreeing on moral values has been used as an *excuse* to simply eliminate moral values in the economic realm. Within the scope of this paper, it is not feasible to delve into the intricacies of philosophical debates as to which or any ethical consideration should reign supreme. However, what will be attempted is an exploration of *one* possible system of ethical consideration for economics. It is believed that although Buddhist economics might not be taken as *the* answer for modern-day economics, the discussion should highlight what is crucially missing in everyday economic practice. This is done with the hope that a search for *right* view could initiate a meaningful quest for all.

It is fascinating to see that so much of the literature on Thai Buddhism has dealt with the way of the monks, and much less on the way of the laymen, particularly on the noble ways (*ariya magga*). *Right livelihood* (*sammā ājīva*) is prescribed as the fifth of the eight ways, starting from *right understanding* (*sammā-diṭṭhi*) to *right concentration* (*sammā samādhi*). According to Buddhadasa. Bhikkhu, *sammā* means "righteous," which indicates being "correct" and "sufficient".[10] In the economic sphere, having *sufficient* is a prerequisite for physical well-being as well as a pre-condition for peace and order in a given society. In the *Cakkavattisīhanāda-sutta* of the *Dīgha-nikāya*, the decline of a human society is described in the following way.

The first society was under a monarchical rule. The king was a good ruler and, therefore, the country prospered for thousands of years. Whenever there was a crisis, the powerful monarch would do as his predecessors had done before him.

Then, a particular king failed to act like his predecessors in one of the most important tasks of a ruler, that is, "whosoever in they kingdom is poor, to him let wealth be given." Instead, "on the destitute he bestowed no wealth. And because this was not done, poverty became widespread."

Thus, the country became full of poor people. Then, one of the poorest stole something. He was brought before the land. The monarch questioned the man and learned of his poverty. Due to his compassion, the king gave that man enough to live on.

Soon this event became widely known. Then, there was another man who was not poor, but he had the idea to increase his wealth. He stole something, got caught, and was brought before the king. He then *lied* to the king to obtain something beyond his need. And he was successful.

This example soon became known by all in the country. There were many who followed this misconduct. It happened again and again until the lung could no longer offer his wealth. He therefore decided to put an end to this stealing and lying. He executed the next one who was arrested and brought before him.

---

[10] Buddhadasa Bhikkhu, *op.cit.*, 9-10.

From then on, those who stole began to arm themselves. Whenever they robbed anyone, they murdered their victims for fear of being arrested and executed.

At this point the Buddha said, "Thus, brethren, from goods not being bestowed on the destitute, poverty grew great ... stealing ... violence ... murder ... lying ... evil speaking ... adultery ... abusive and idle talk ... covetousness and ill-will ... false opinions ... incest, wanton greed and perverted lust ... till finally lack of filial and religious piety and lack of regard for the head of the clan grew great."[11]

From this story it is obvious that the first cause of all evils is the king's failure to observe the significance of the economic condition of the people. In other words, poverty is the cause of immorality and crimes, such as theft, falsehood, violence, hatred, cruelty, etc. In this sense, the king had not acted *righteously* because he failed to provide *sufficiently* for his people. In order to eradicate crime, punishment is not the best policy, but the economic condition of the people should be improved. Therefore, one might say that the first principle of a Buddhist economics is *sufficiency*. This sufficiency indicates neither inadequacy nor excess. In view of this principle, one might say that the glorification of the excessive is a hallmark of economic success in the modern world. However, this very excessiveness is also a pre-condition for strife and violence in much the same way as sufficiency is a pre-condition for peace.

This story also testifies to the fact that Buddhism does not overlook the significance of economic matters. But the Buddhist concern focuses on the moral dimension of economic practice. Now let us investigate the second meaning of the term *sammā*, namely, being correct.

Being correct in right livelihood includes identifying what is wrong or ill-livelihood. The Buddha identified six types of wrong livelihood (*mijā ājīva*). They are: cheating, tempting, trickery, deceiving, and profiteering [12]. In addition to these, there are five types of trading which are considered incorrect. They are: arms dealing, animal trading, flesh trading, intoxicating chinks trading and poison trading[13]. Although it might be unfair to say that the money economy encourages people to cheat or deceive as a livelihood, the overwhelming emphasis on the making of money as the sole purpose of all economic activities does help soften rather than strengthen these exhortations. However, when it comes to incorrect trades, it seems that all of these trades are big money earners. In the case of Thailand, from 1982 to 1991, the military budget amounted to 17.35% of the total expenditures of the central government, while the Ministry of Public Health received 4.45% over the same period[14]. Revenues from sales of

---

[11] See Walpola Rahula, *op. cit.*, 81-82. See also Chaiwat Satha-Anand, *op. cit.*, 41-42.

[12] *The Tripitaka* (The Thai edited version), Vol. 14, 192.

[13] *The Tripitaka* (The Thai edited version), Vol. 22, 237.

[14] Chaiwat Satha-Anand, *Thai Military Expenditure 1982-1991: Vision and Policy Thoughts* (Bangkok: Chulalongkorn University, forthcoming), Table 10, 43 (from a typed manuscript).

locally brewed alcohol amounts to billions of baht annually. This is not to mention the millions of baht made from the "flesh trade," if this term includes the human flesh of young prostitutes. It is clear that all these trades make much sense economically, but not morally.

Perhaps due to the astronomical economic success in Thailand in the past decade, as well as to the moral and spiritual atrocities thereof, there has been quite a large quantity of literature on Buddhist economics presented by both Thai monk scholars as well as by Western economic experts. It is interesting to note that among the key works on this issue, the Buddhist attitude towards wealth is expressed in the following manner:

> People having wealth or possessions, even having a great deal of wealth, is not incompatible with Buddhism. It is not whether one has much or a little of wealth, but how the wealth and property is used; is it used for the benefit of others, for society; or is it used for one's own personal benefit?[15]

Or, according to Professor Swearer, who wrote the following in his introduction to his volume on *Ethics, Wealth, and Salvation: A Study in Buddhist Social Ethics*:

> They (the contributors to the volume) believe not only that Buddhism gives at least a provisional affirmation to material prosperity, but that there are many instances in which wealth is highly praised and there are many norms for handling wealth which intimately link lay and monastic society. Instead of a single-minded condemnation of wealth, according to the contributors, Theravāda Buddhism offers a "middle way," or sees the acquisition and renunciation of wealth in a dialectical relationship.[16]

In a real socio-cultural context, this "dialectical relationship" must be very delicate, and a well-balanced and appropriate relationship quite difficult to achieve. Even during the time of the Buddha himself, there were many cases of offerings from the laymen and laywomen which were deemed inappropriate by the Buddha."[17] In some sense, the 227 rules of conduct for monks in the *Vinaya* are not only a prescription for monks' practice in relation to the lay world, they are also a system of rules which prescribe an appropriate utilization of things

---

[15] Buddhadasa Bhikkhu, *op. cit.*, 7.

[16] Russell F. Sizemore and Donald K. Swearer, eds., *Ethics, Wealth, and Salvation: A Study in Buddhist Social Ethics* (Columbia: University of South Carolina Press, 1992), 1.

[17] Chantravrathit Pongpan, *Setthi in the Tripitaka*, an unpublished M.A. thesis submitted to the Department of Oriental Languages, Faculty of Arts, Chulalongkorn University, B.E. 2522. In this thesis there are citations of several recorded cases of lay offerings to the monks which were deemed inappropriate by the Buddha, and thus prohibited.

"material" for a *sufficient* well-being of monks. This middle way between the acquisition and renunciation of wealth should continue to be a problematic for monks and laymen; otherwise, many inappropriate acquisitions might be offered to monks with good or ill intentions.[18]

If one looks at the way of the monks "realistically," one should readily understand the necessity or practicality of the Buddhist position that "at least provisional affirmation of material prosperity" is important. This is because monks are meant to *depend on* laymen for material support. Historically the first devoted Buddhist laymen and laywomen belonged to the trader class. Canonically, the Buddha's most important sermon on how to *use* one's wealth was given to Anāthapiṇḍika the "millionaire." His instructions are as follows:

> Noble disciples in this *dhamma-vinaya* should spend their wealth which they have acquired with diligence and accumulated with their own labor and sweat, with legitimate means in such a way as to bring about their own well-being. They should take good care of their parents, keeping them happy. They should take good care of their children, their wives, their slaves, workers and servants, keeping them happy.... Then they should spend their well-earned wealth on their friends.... Then they should spend their well-earned wealth on protection from dangers from fire, water, kings, robbers or un-beloved descendants.... Then they should spend their well-earned wealth to make five lands of sacrifices, namely, sacrifices for their relatives, visitors, ancestors, taxes and the gods.[19]

It might be interesting to note that this sermon offers a *complete* picture how to spend one's wealth. The fact that it can be this complete is probably due to Anāthapiṇḍika's enormous wealth. In this sense, not all laymen are supposed to complete their spending picture in this way. However, the messages are quite clear. First, one's wealth has to be "well-earned," namely through one's own labor and through legitimate means. Second, one's wealth should be spent on layers of relationships from one's self, one's parents, children, servants, friends, protection from dangers, and *then* the five kinds of sacrifices. In another sermon, the Buddha instructed the young man Sigala that he should spend one-fourth of his income on his daily expenses, invest half in his business, and put aside one-

---

[18] In the past two years, Thai daily newspapers have been spiced with the scandal involving several allegations of sexual misconduct of Pra Yantra, a high-profile monk preacher. Once the case was submitted to the Supreme Patriarch, one of the key evidences against Pra Yantra was his use of a credit card at several night clubs in Australia and New Zealand in 1994. Only then a question was raised as to the appropriateness of "offering" a credit card for a monks' personal use.

In many monks' living quarters in Thailand, lay people witness first-rate, high-priced audiovisual equipment. In some famous temples in Bangkok, younger monks refer to going to certain monk's living quarters as "going to the discotheque."

[19] *The Tripiṭaka* (The Royal Thai version), Vol. 22, 44-45.

fourth for any emergency[20]. Taken together, these two sermons hardly portray a Buddha who is against wealth as such. It is the *ethics* of acquiring wealth and the *ethics* of spending wealth which are the major concern. One can say that these instructions indicate what "being correct" means in the term *sammā ājīva* or *right livelihood.*

Another point which should be added here is that *right livelihood* includes an overcoming of "selfishness." This point can serve as a direct critique of the existing practice of economics whose unquestioned assumptions about unlimited human desires in a sense *celebrates* unbridled selfishness. As Buddhadasa Bhikkhu puts it:

> As long as the economic system is based on selfishness, encourages selfishness, supports and protects selfishness, justifies and legitimizes selfishness, it would fail. Buddhist economics, therefore, must overcome selfishness in both the worldly and spiritual spheres.[21]

It is important to note that economics needs a moral dimension if it is to be understood as a human activity which can lead to the "overcoming of selfishness." The aims and purposes of economics is, on the one hand, not simply to get rich or grow in number and size, or to accumulate the most means to satisfy one's desires, whether banal or subtle, but it involves the "taking care" of other people within different circles of relationship as exemplified in the above sermon for Anāthapindika. On the other hand, earning wealth is not condemned, but legitimate ways of earning needs to be the pre-condition. Otherwise, not only does it not make "economic sense" to be unethical in many circumstances, it also can easily create a devastating moral situation for all[22].

At one level, the Buddha instructed people how to spend their wealth wisely; at another level, he offered a new *definition* of what "wealth" means. In the *Dāna-sutta* (the *sutta* on money), the Buddha discussed *ariya sab* (noble wealth) in the following passage:

> Behold, O monks! There are seven kinds of wealth. What are they? They are 1) *saddhā* (faith), 2) *sīla* (morality), 3) *hiri* (shame), 4) *otappa* (fear of sin), 5) *suta* (being well-learned), 6) *cāga* (charity), and 7) *paññā* (wisdom).[23]

---

[20] Walpola Rahula, *op. cit.*, 83.

[21] Buddhadasa Bbikkhu, *op. cit.*, 5.

[22] A highly respected Thai economist and former Governor of the Bank of Thailand, Dr. Puey Ungpakorn wrote a mini-treatise on the *dhamma* of economic activities in *Sasana-dhamma and Development* (Bangkok: Komol Keemthong Foundation, B.E., 2530). In short, he argues that immorality bears heavy economic casualties for the whole society.

[23] *The Tripitaka* (The Royal Thai version), Vol. 23, 5.

It is only natural for the Buddha to argue for new definitions of what wealth means. This attempt is necessary for it points to the inadequacy of the "worldly" understanding of wealth as owning tangible means of livelihood and satisfaction of desires. To be true to the spirit of Buddhism, a vision of more noble wealth should be created to counter-balance the worldly version, as well as to uplift the human spirit to search for higher value in life.

4. Implications of Buddhist Economics

If economics is not seen as a "scientific" calculation of production, distribution, and consumption of material goods, but is seen as a human activity for the "overcoming" of selfishness, what would be the implications of Buddhist economics on these three processes of economic practice? First of all, as E. F. Schumacher puts it, production will not be seen as a profit-making process of making "products" for sale as goods in the market. Rather, the emphasis will be on the production process *as human work*. In his words:

> The Buddhist point of view takes the function of work to be at least threefold: to give a man a chance to utilize and develop his faculties; to enable him to overcome his ego-centeredness by joining with other people in a common task; and to bring forth the goods and services needed for a becoming existence.[24]

In modern production processes, it is obvious that "efficiency" is understood as involving the ability to produce the largest number of products within the shortest time, bearing the least monetary cost, while making the most profit. In this calculation there are violent tensions between the employers and the employees, between man and his work, between man and nature. In this scheme of calculation nature exists only as "natural resources," or something that will create wealth for man. In Buddhist economics, on the other hand, production processes cannot be separated from human work, a process whereby a human being interacts with the material world and with other human beings, in order to develop his faculties, to overcome his ego-centeredness, and to bring forth needed goods and services. "Efficiency" is then not correlated to profit-making products, but to the developing of the human potential.

In a "free market" society, distribution of goods is determined through price mechanisms. Resources in society are distributed only to those who are capable of buying them. This process is seen as "just" in everyday economics. In Buddhist economics, the emphasis is not as much on the price mechanism of goods, but on the distributive giving of wealth to different people in various circles of relationships. The values of giving (*dāna*) and compassion have to come into play. According to Professor Swearer:

---

[24] E. F. Schumacher, *op.cit.*, 54-55.

> The giving of gifts to those in need, to one's family, and to the religious establishment is an extraordinarily prominent practice in Theravāda Buddhism.... According to the Theravāda texts, by far the most important form of giving, called *dāna*, is that directed to the Buddha and the *Sangha*. In fact, we may go so far as to suggest that religious giving is of such importance in Buddhist thinking about wealth that *dāna* and not some concept of structural justice is the central concept in Buddhist social and political philosophy.[25]

If Professor Swearer's analysis is taken seriously, it would mean that in Buddhism, the question of justice as *interpersonal* consideration cannot exist in isolation from the question of giving and compassion. This is perhaps due to the belief that the issue of justice as *personal* consideration is already taken care of in the doctrine of *kamma*. However, the question whether Buddhism lacks the concept of "structural justice" still remains open for future exploration.

The last step in the economic quest of man is, of course, consumption, which is taken to mean the satisfaction of desires. Perhaps here lies the central difference between Western economics and Buddhist economics. In the former way of thinking, desires are the given. It is not within the realm of economics to "control or question" desires. It is the essence of economics to *satisfy* desires. In contrast, Buddhism seeks to *bridle* desires as a way to happiness. There are two ways to achieve satisfaction: one is to seek ways and means to satisfy one's desires, and the other is to seek ways to reduce one's desires, thus making it easier to achieve satisfaction. The former is conventional economics and the latter is Buddhist economics.

If we relate these two different approaches to achieving satisfaction to the problem of global environmental destruction, we can easily see why Buddhist economics is a much-needed quest for all humanity. It does not need repetition here to point an accusing finger to the successful atrocities of modern technologies, which are under the strong directorship of modern Western economics. It is no accident, therefore, that the movement for deep ecology seeks spiritual and metaphysical support from many Eastern religions, with Buddhism as one of the major candidates.[26]

5. Concluding Note

It might not be feasible to think that peace, in the physical, structural or spiritual sense of the term, is possible outside the realm of economic consideration, or ultimately speaking, outside the consideration for human happiness. But one needs to develop *right understanding*, or *sammā-diṭṭhi*, about economic practice and about happiness. If human beings insist on being stupid

---

[25] Sizemore and Swearer, *op. cit.* 13.

[26] See for example an article by Richard Sylvan and David Bennett, "Taoism and Deep Ecology," in *The Ecologist* 18.4/5 (1988).

about being happy, namely believing in the famous advertising campaign by Kloster beer that this amber liquid is "Happiness you can drink!", then peace is not being given a chance. This is not to condemn this particular brand of beer, not to advocate a Spartan way of life; the crucial point is simply that it is not wise to reduce the potential of being fully human to the potential of a living meat for consumption.

Buddhism is often presented and explained as a religion which aims at the cessation of suffering. If one would only put it positively, one can say that Buddhism offers a systematic prescription for happiness.

According to Buddhism there are four kinds of happiness for laymen:

1) The first happiness is to enjoy economic security or
   sufficient wealth acquired by just and righteous means (*atthi-sukha*).
2) The second happiness is spending that wealth liberally on
   himself, his family, his friends, and relatives and on
   meritorious deeds (*bhoga-sukha*).
3) The third happiness is to be free from debts
   (*anana-sukha*).
4) The fourth happiness is to live a faultless, and a pure life
   without committing evil in 27 thought, word or deed (*anavajja-sukha*).[27]

It is obvious that to *be ethical* about acquiring and spending wealth is itself a kind of happiness. To be free from debts and to lead a pure life is also happiness in itself. This is not to mention the unsurpassed happiness of *nibbāna*, which is the ultimate goal of Buddhism. In conclusion, one might say that:

1) Buddhism gives affirmation to the importance of wealth
   for "sufficient" well-being,
2) Buddhism offers an ethics for the earning and spending of
   wealth.
3) Buddhism offers alternative ways to achieve happiness by
   reducing desires rather than simply by satisfying desires.
4) Buddhism challenges the human spirit to achieve more
   "noble" wealth of faith and wisdom.

---

[27] Walpola Rahula, *op. cit.*, 83.

CHAPTER 19

THE LOTUS AND THE WHEEL: ALTERNATIVE POLITICS, ALTERNATIVE DEVELOPMENT

Meenakshi Gopinath

How can you buy or sell the sky -- the warmth of the land? The idea is strange to us. We do not own the freshness of the air or the sparkle of the water. How can you buy them from us? We will decide in our time. Every part of this earth is sacred to my people. Every shining pine needle, every sandy shore, every mist in the dark woods, every humming insect is holy in the memory and experience of my people.... We know that the white man does not understand our ways. One portion of the land is the same to him as the next, for he is a stranger who comes in the night and takes from the land whatever he needs. The earth is not his brother, but his enemy, and when he has conquered it, he moves on.... The sap which courses through the trees carries the memories of the red man.... Our dead never forget this beautiful earth for it is the mother of the red man. We are part of the Earth and it is part of us. The perfumed flowers are our sisters, the deer, the horse, the great eagle, these are our brothers.... the water's murmur is the voice of my father's father. The rivers are our brothers, they quench our thirst...the air is precious to the red man for all things share the same breath.... We know that the white man does not understand our ways.... The earth is not his brother but his enemy and when he has conquered it, he moves on.... Perhaps it is because I am savage, I do not understand. What is man without the beasts? If all the beasts were gone, man would die from a great loneliness of spirit - for whatever happens to the beasts soon happens to man....

Teach your children what we have taught our children, that the earth is our mother. Whatever befalls the Earth befalls the sons of the Earth.... All things are connected like the blood that unites one family. Man did not weave the thread of life: he is merely a strand in it. Whatever he does to the web, he does to himself....

Where is the thicket? Gone

Where is the Eagle? Gone

The end of living and the beginning of survival.

When the American Indian Chief Sealth made this famous statement in 1854 in his native Duwamish, before the Treaty Commission, he echoed a worldview whose death knell had already been sounded in the west by the Enlightenment ideal that made man the measure of all things.

The Romantic reaction notwithstanding the Cartesian - Newtonian paradigm which envisioned man becoming the master and possessor of Nature had become the foundation of the modern world's notion of Progress.

The mechanistic implications of this *weltanshauung* have found strong reverberations in our twentieth century notions of development. Most modern development theories by over emphasizing economic indicators tend to overlook substantial existential concerns. The development trajectory followed by countries of the North, and increasingly of the South, has resulted in an eco-crisis of unprecedented proportions. The threats to the global environment take many forms and the examples read like a litany of assaults - deforestation, desertification, pollution caused by erosions and effluents from industrial plants, extinction of marine and plant species, problems of acid rain, depletion of the ozone layer and the risk of climate change, disappearance of several indigenous ways of life, damaging demographic imbalances, overcrowding and consequent urban crime and squalor; and growing immiseration of large sections of the population. Ironically, all this has happened through a period of what is called impressive economic growth, with substantial increases in industrial production particularly after 1940, and improvement in the standard of living.

From the second half of the twentieth century the world had to suddenly confront the fact that there were definite limits to growth, finite resources, and that Mother Earth's patience was running out. Brakes had to be put on the Promethean spirit. The scenic route to progress was no longer an evolutionary inevitability. Hard choices had to be made and made fast.

Today the anthropocentric view of the universe stands challenged as never before. Ecologist Edward Goldsmith warns that in the light of trends related to global warning, pollution, famine and disease, to expect that human beings will survive the next sixty years is a sheer act of faith. However the warning signals seem lost on a public numbed by the onslaught of ecological bad news![1]

From the perspective of the less developed part of the world, where I come from, the hegemonic model of development, supported by the world capitalist system caters to the wasteful patterns of consumption of the North at the cost of the underdeveloped South. An even more distressing aspect of this is how erstwhile frugal and fairly equanimous societies, being converted into markets, are being sucked into a maelstrom of acquisitiveness, greed and rapacity by

---

[1] See Allan Hunt Badiner, "Is the Buddha Winking at Extinction," presented at the Conference on Ecological Responsibility, New Delhi, 1993.

mindlessly imitating the consumption patterns of the North. Comprador political and economic elites in the third world commit unwitting populations to irreversible choices of incongruous life styles in the name of growth and material well-being. Here, the connection between minority power, privilege and wealth and the impoverishment and disempowerment of the majority, the marginalization of indigenous populations and environmental degradation can be quite easily made. In most post- colonial societies, consequently questions of environment and development are linked to issues of social inequality and the cornering of increasingly scarce resources by the elites, whose face is turned away from their roots and community towards the metropolitan centers of economic power. The progressive commodification of erstwhile tribal or community relations result in an on going increase in conflict levels within these societies.[2]

As North - South disparities grow and as inequalities become exacerbated within the communities of the south, environmentalists in parts of the developing world agonize over the fact that for the rich both within and outside their societies there is indeed, relatively speaking, a 'free lunch' which is more often than not at great cost to the environment.[3] Even a cursory look will provide some stunning examples. Calculations show that if the petroleum used in one U.S. city, namely New York, was available to the world's poor in the form of kerosene, firewood consumption in the third World could be replaced. But of course whether the women who spend hours collecting firewood and breathing all that smoke will ever have access to kerosene will depend upon the world market, health of national economics, international trading system, and debt burdens which restrict the import capacity of nations.

The Netherlands, for example, is the most densely populated country in the world and also one of the richer ones. Its economy thrives because it uses an enormous amount of resources from the Third World at very low prices. A recent study pointed out that a Dutch person uses six hectares of land, most of it in the third World for every hectare used in the country itself .[4]

The South is caught in a double bind. An unequal entrant into the world capitalist system it has the terms of trade hopelessly skewed against it. It has bartered its psycho-spiritual reserves for material gratifications generated by the purveyors of cultural imperialism - the media and the hidden persuaders of the New Information Order. The red signals seem to read: No economic independence: No spiritual fulfillment.

---

[2] This is not to suggest that there are no heterogeneous tendencies or dispossessed populations in the North. Postmodernist discourse has drawn attention to non-totalizing trends. However, post-colonial societies display disparities in a much more dramatic form.

[3] See Anil Aggarwal, "Who says the rich do not get a Free Lunch?,"' CSE lecture series, New Delhi, August 1993.

[4] *Ibid,* Preface.

Now that 'being rich' has been elevated to the level of a value world-wide, the lure of affluence introduces a new kind of helplessness - the inability to break out of the syndrome of wants generated by an acquisitive mass society and its hegemonic culture which attempts to standardize the texture of lives in more subtle and insidious ways.

Is there then a way out of this impasse? For our societies of the developing world the imperative lies in altering the metaphor of development. We must engage in the explosive and subversive exercise of fashioning a counter culture in the most fundamental sense; a counter-culture which renews the now frazzled link between the microcosm and the macrocosm, between the particular and the universal and between the individual and her environment. On one level this would involve 'breaking the terrain' of the totalizing discourse on the economy. On another level it would involve an act of collective remembering - of recovering from the vast reservoir of our spiritual traditions and heritage an apposite perceptual landscape that will help effect this metanoia.

I believe that the idea of universal responsibility unfolding in contemporary Mahayanist discourse (and articulated most effectively by H.H. The Fourteenth Dalai Lama) provides an invaluable conceptual framework for the much needed liberatory alternative.

On the issues of development and environment, engaged Buddhism can find common ground with Gandhi's concepts of *svarāj* (freedom) and the role of the *satyāgrāhi* (seeker after truth) to provide eco-social insights that are empowering and activist. My attempt here is to highlight that common ground.

I use the symbols of the lotus (*puṇḍarika*) and the wheel (*cakra*) to illustrate this possible confluence. The lotus as the symbol of Buddhism indicates, the ability to transcend the limitations of one's environment while being co-existent with it, also the unfolding of the manifold potential of the human spirit through awareness. The *cakra,* the spinning wheel propagated by Gandhi, was a symbol of freedom from colonial domination and the harmonizing of the internal and external environment of social beings in the process of non- violent production. Spinning yam was for him both a spiritual and political act - stressing the dignity of labor and the protest against the inhuman application of technology for domination and power over people.

Universal responsibility underscores, giving the richest possible expression to the altruistic impulse of the *bodhisattva,* with compassion and loving kindness. An activist engagement with the here and now is implicit in its precepts. From the stand point of Buddhadharma responsibility is universal for two reasons - first because of the inter-dependence of all human beings and phenomena, and second, because compassion generates the altruistic attitude, and therefore, the special responsibility to see that whatever we do helps others, and that our acts do not cause suffering but create conditions that lead to the alleviation or end of suffering. From the time we take birth we enter irreversibly the realm of responsibility. All individual actions have effect. They affect themselves, they affect others (society) and they affect the environment on which we depend for sustenance and survival. This environment consists of nature (the ecosystem) as well as the social conditions and institutions that relate to our every day life.

In as much as universal responsibility demands bringing about an alleviation of suffering, it demands that we identify and renounce whatever causes or perpetuates suffering. This leads it inevitably to grapple with ever-complex social issues of injustice, inequality, want, poverty, and their causes. This leads it inevitably into questions of both spiritual and material needs, and the use, production and distribution of resources. Universal responsibility takes Buddha-dharma quite squarely into the realm of the political. Here, one must emphasize that from such a perspective, politics is to be seen as the art of the possible and not as the politicking of political parties within the electoral system.

The *pañcasīla* principles, the five moral precepts of Buddhism, would exhort that such political engagement be non-violent, and ensure equitable distribution of wealth. In the "Discourse on the Lion's Roar of the Universal Monarch" (*Cakkavatti-sīhanāda-sutta*), the Buddha says that once a king allows poverty to arise the people always steal to survive. Economic justice is therefore bound up with right livelihood. The precept against sexual misconduct could well extend to working against the exploitation of women and other violent manifestations of patriarchy. The precept of abstinence from false speech could underscore the need to expose the deceptive shibboleths of mass culture protected by the media and false advertising, The fifth precept's exhortation against clouding the mind through intoxicants could translate into a systematic struggle against the structure of false needs generated by an overtly consumerist, hence violent culture, destructive in the long run of individual and social health.[5]

Does engaged Buddhism or what Julia Martin has called 'compassionate activism' minimize the importance of the middle path? To embrace universal responsibility is also simultaneously to reject the extremes of self-indulgence or self-flagellation as it is to reject extreme beliefs which cling to the material world or deny it completely. By interpreting the meaning of life lived according to the middle way, Buddhism presents itself as a serious alternative basis for environmental thought and action. Peter Timmerman's assertion[6] that to be a Buddhist today is a geopolitical act for the obvious reason that every one of our acts now adds or subtracts from the load of human affairs which burden the earth, seem to square with the concept of universal responsibility. It is also:

> A geopolitical act because given the continuing devotion to consumerism, one of the most radical acts we can perform in our society is to consume less, to sit quietly meditating in a room, or to try and think clearly about who we are trying to be. And finally being a Buddhist is a geopolitical act because it provides us with a working

---

[5] See Sulak Sivaraksa, *Seeds of Peace* (Berkeley: Parallax, 1992), 72-79.

[6] See Peter Timmerman, "It is Dark Outside," in Martine Batchelor and Kerry Brown, eds., *Buddhism and Ecology* (New York: Cassell, 1992), 75.

space within which to stand back from our aggressive culture and consider alternatives.[7]

From the standpoint of universal responsibility, the separation between rights and duties is transcended. One assumes rights in the context of the responsibility to act, employing always skillful means as antidotes to ignorance, delusion, greed and hatred. Excessive greed finds expression in life orientations bound to extreme sensuality and hedonism (*kāma taṇhā*) and in limitless expansion and possessiveness (*bhava taṇhā*). Hatred is expressed by a destructive and violent attitude towards oneself, others and the natural world (*vibhava taṇhā*). Destructive patterns of consumption generate unending cycles of desires and satisfactions. The psychological roots of ecological disaster and recovery are factors very much related in the Buddhist context to the search for an environmental ethic.[8]

The Buddha urged his disciples to remember the doctrine of karma. The law of karma states that all our thoughts, words and deeds shape our experiences in the future. What each one of us is experiencing now is the outcome of the imprints of what we have thought, said and done in the past. So, far from being a doctrine of fatalism, karmic understanding encourages us to take responsibility for our present situation as well as for how our lives will unfold in the future. The praxis of universal responsibility, like *satyāgrāha,* combines contemplation and action, and emphasizes the congruence of thought, speech and action as the sine-qua-non of eloquent and effective activism.

From the Buddhist point of view the generally recognized parameters of development, by stressing gigantism, foster greed and competition in society. E. F. Schumacher's persuasive arguments for sustainable development and for the study of economics as if people mattered has accorded to his seminal work, *Small is Beautiful,* the status of a kind of manifesto on 'Buddhist economics'. Although essentially non-Buddhist in the methodology he adopts, Schumacher has admirably pointed out that a non-violent and gentle attitude towards nature is the ecological stance of Buddhism.

From the Buddhist perspective, it is not only people that matter, but all life, the animate and the inanimate worlds and the complex web of inter-relationships -- both seen and unseen -- between them. Buddhist literature is replete with expressions of veneration for nature laying down the special responsibility of the human species to protect and preserve the delicate balance.

In the *Sutta-nipāta,* one of the earliest texts, the Buddha says:

> Know ye the grasses and the trees.... Then know ye the worms and the moths and the different sort of ants. Know ye also the four-footed animals, small and great, the serpents, the fish which range in the

---

[7] *Ibid.*

[8] Padmasiri de Silva, "Buddhist Environmental Ethics," in Allan Hunt Badiner, ed., *Dharma Gaia* (Berkeley: Parallax, 1990), 17-18.

water, the birds that are borne along on wings and move through air -
- Know ye the marks that constitute species are theirs, and their
species are manifold.[9]

The community of monks was forbidden by the *vinaya* to cut trees, eat the
meat of animals of the forest, or contaminate water resources. Among the early
expressions in Buddhist literature showing the interdependence of human kind
and nature, there was also a deep awareness of the need to protect species to
preserve the earth:

> Come back, O Tigers! To the woods again
> and let it not be leveled with the plain.
> For without you, the axe will lay it low.
> You without it for the ever homeless go.[10]

The *Mettā-sutta* echoes a well known and much loved teaching which
exemplifies the duty enjoined on all Buddhists:

> Thus as a mother with her own life guards the life of her own child,
> let all embracing thoughts for all that lives be shine.[11]

The Buddha under the bodhi-tree calling the earth as witness to his resolve
not to swerve from his goal of *nirvāṇa,* is one of the most moving examples of
the essential non-duality of the physical and spiritual worlds stressed in
Buddhist thought. Hence, a paradigmatic shift in our perceptions on
development and indeed economics would have to start:

> From the premise of non-duality - recognizing that at root the
> distinction between agent, act and object is merely conceptual. It is
> nothing but a grammatical convenience that has been tragically
> mistaken to represent three intrinsically separate entities or
> substances. In fact there are no things apart from the agents that act
> upon them and no agents apart from the things upon which they act.
> Whether we are admiring a tree or cutting it down, we stand in
> dynamic unbroken and unrepeatable relationship with that tree. Each
> situation of life is an interdependent seamless whole, entirely devoid
> of the divisions imposed on it by our alienated and anxious
> consciousness.[12]

In fact the philosophy of *pratītya-samutpāda* (dependent arising) would
inevitably lead -- as Stephen Batchelor has so vividly pointed out -- to the

---

[9] *Sutta-nipāta,* translated by V. Fausboll (London: H. Milford, 1968).

[10] *Khuddakapāṭha* (London: Pali Text Society, 1960).

[11] *Ibid.*

[12] See Stephen Batchelor, "Buddhist Economics Reconsidered," in *Dharma Gaia, op. cit.,* 179-180.

rejection of an anthropocentric view of the universe. The doctrine of *śūnyatā* (emptiness) asserting the absence of inherent existence of substances and phenomena of the finite and infinite world, emphasizes the relational and the correspondent nature of all existence. Consequently, the Buddhist experience of reality, if anything,

> (It) has tendered to be 'acentric.' For ultimately nothing in the universe deserves pride of place. No matter how noble something may be, as soon as it is placed at the center of things it becomes susceptible to deification, reification and all the subsequent distortions and abuses that have characterized things at the center of human history.... Paradoxically, however, *placing nothing at the center is tantamount to placing everything at the center.*[13]

The first step towards an alternative perspective on development would be to stress interconnections and interrelationships as the basis for a new ethics before looking at the impact of policies on the quality of life and environment. So far there is a tendency to look at development in aggregate terms - GDP being given pride of place over more humane indicators. Presently, attention is mainly given to the total production of goods and services regardless of the effects on nature and environment. Hence rapid depletion of forests, soils or fisheries shows up in the GDP statistics as something positive. The un-sustainability of such a system needs to be highlighted.[14] Until environmental and economic processes are brought into harmony within the overall perspective of inter-dependence a myopically *sectoral* approach will govern development initiatives. The *sectoral* approach lacks the understanding that it is the over-all through-put of energy and materials that matter, that energy and materials never disappear. Consequently if we only address the parts, and not the whole, we run the great risk of just moving an environmental problem from one place to the other.

Environmental problems of the south, the debt burden, the unstable prices of raw materials, the prevailing agreements on trade and tariffs, the net transfer of capital from the South to the North falling commodity prices, the North continuing to make imports of manufactured goods from the South difficult through levies and quotas as long as issues like these are not properly addressed, there is no real meaning in trying to tackle problems of forest destruction, soil erosion or waste management. All these issues are inter-related, but their relations are obfuscated, reified or fetishized by the hegemonic views of development. These interrelations are mystified in the perceptual landscape of the individual who has to make "life style choices at the expense of ways of

---

[13] *Ibid,* 180.

[14] The principle of "polluter pays" decided upon by the OECD in 1972 is still to be implemented in full measure. Also "green taxes", which means lower taxes on income and higher taxes on energy and consumption of natural resources, have yet to get on the formal political agenda of governments the world over.

seeing and being. These life style choices come to people in the developing world like packaged identities. Like a fancy dress wardrobe of apparent but spurious variety, they standardize wants, are diversionary and escapist in nature, serve the insatiable appetites of a consumerist culture for new sensations and harbor the familiar mechanisms of alienation.[15]

The Buddhist environmental ethic moves beyond merely laying bare the hidden 'mystified, capitalist relations of production in the new world economic order. For that pertains to the social world alone. At root it is concerned in a deeper sense with the search for a more comprehensive meaning in the relationship between human kind and nature. It is not only critical in relation to the ecosystem, but demolishes the notions of selfhood which is fore-grounded in the technological ethic of our century.

> When the conviction that there is a social, enduring self co-existing with millions of solid enduring others in a world of solid enduring things, falls away, a universe of magically inter-related processes and events is revealed. That dreadful, alienating sense of separation dissolves, opening us to the freedom that is our birthright.[16]

In this sense, the ecological crisis we witness today is from a Buddhist standpoint a rather predictable outcome of our deluded state wherein we feel separate from one another, separate from the environment that sustains us, and separate from the things we use and enjoy. A Buddhist perspective of environment stresses the elimination of this delusion for highlighting the idea of interpenetration and interdependence.

Several *sūtras* from the Pali canon show that early Buddhism emphasizes the close relationship between human morality and the natural environment. The later commentaries talk of the *pañca niyāmadhamma,* or theory of the five natural laws. These emphasize how physical and environmental factors condition the thought patterns and moral standards of humanity and how they are, in turn, conditioned by them.

Nāgārjuna's doctrine of emptiness was also developed to emphasize how things do not merely depend for their existence upon their own immediate set of causes but upon *everything* in the universe. The *Avataṁsaka-sūtra*'s metaphor of Indra's Net, a vast grid of interconnected mirroring spheres, each one reflecting the other, uses poetic imagery to convey the tenet of the mutual interpenetration and interfusion of all phenomena.

---

[15] See "Gandhi and Counter-Culture", in *Gandhi Marg* 1.7: 396. See also Alvin Gouldner, *The Dialectic of Ideology and Technology* (New York: Seabury, 1976).

[16] See Stephen Batchelor, "The Sands of the Ganges", in *Buddhism and Ecology,* 35.

> There are myriads of forms and hundred of grasses throughout the
> entire earth, and yet each grass and each form itself is the entire
> earth.[17]

The contemporary Vietnamese monk and poet Thich Nhat Hanh emphasizes the interconnection of all living things thus:

> When we look at a chair, we see the wood but we fail to observe the
> tree, the forest, the carpenter, or our own mind. When we meditate on
> it we can see the entire universe in all its interwoven and
> interdependent relations in the chair. The presence of the wood
> reveals the presence of the sun. The presence of the apple blossoms
> reveals the presence of the apple. Meditators can see the one in the
> many and many in the one.[18]

The Buddhist precepts stand validated by contemporary research in the field of subatomic physics. The mathematical interpretation of this subatomic world no longer refers to actual reality, but only to "potentialities", and physical laws simply express the "connectivity" of statistical pointer readings.[19]

Einstein's words echo this sentiment resoundingly:

> A human being is a part of the world called by us 'universe', a part
> limited in time and space. He experiences himself, his thoughts and
> feelings, as something separated from the rest, a kind of optical
> delusion of his consciousness. This delusion is a kind of prison for us,
> restricting us to our personal desires and to affection for a few
> persons nearest to us. Our task must be to free ourselves from this
> prison by widening our circle of compassion to embrace all living
> creatures and the whole of nature in its beauty.

Armed with mindfulness and the capacity of awareness to shed the illusions of our epoch, Buddhism is confronted with the challenge of entering the realm of the social and indeed the political. The dictates of loving kindness and compassion demand that *the perfumed* garden of contemplation not be insulated from the 'cries of the world'. The *bodhisattva* robes need to be embellished by the dust of the barren lands. This would undoubtedly involve finding in Schumacher's words, "the right path of development, the Middle Way between

---

[17] See Dōgen, *Moon in a Dewdrop*, edited by Kazuaki Tanakashi (New York: North Point Press, 1988), 18.

[18] Thich Nhat Hanh, *The Sun My Heart* (Berkeley: Parallax, 1988), 90.

[19] With Heisenberg's Principle of Uncertainty (or indetermination), we now reach the outer units of scientific possibilities by doing away with determination and causality in view of the impossibility of determining simultaneously the position and velocity of a particle. The deeper we penetrate the microcosmic world, the more difficult direct observations become -- along with the fact that the observation itself interferes with the behavior of the phenomenon.

materialist heedlessness and traditional immobility, in short of finding Right Livelihood".

Engaged Buddhism must launch its non-violent *satyāgrāha* against the consumerist culture taking roots in the South. From here too may arise the leadership for this movement ' for here the most devastating effects of the eco-crisis and its impact on the lives of people are felt. Also the South may draw from the reservoir of its traditions, now perilously close to extinction, the flickering light of insights and beliefs that accord respectability to simplicity and non-violent living. The Gandhian trajectory could prove a useful map for today's engaged Buddhist.

The Activism of *Svarāj*

At the heart of the Gandhian notion of *svarāj* is the rejection of the basic premises of modern industrial society which, according to Gandhi, foster greed, violence, inequality and the self-indulgence of the few at the cost of the many. *Svarāj* (or freedom) not only involves an active engagement in the reordering of a colonized society, but also simultaneous individual transformation by embracing truth and non-violence. Rejecting all attempts to reduce the uniqueness of being human to biological, psychological or sociological considerations, Gandhi sees human destiny to be in the ethico-religious quest for self-transformation. This quest for self-knowledge, far from being pursued in the isolation of a Himalayan cave, occurs here and now and provides the basis for man's relationship with the outer world. This is characterized by an organism's vision emphasizing inseparable unity, harmony and non-injury.

In his articles in *Young India,* Gandhi says:

> *Svarāj* for me means freedom for the meanest of our countrymen.... I am not interested in freeing India merely from the English Yoke. I am bent on freeing India from any Yoke whatsoever.... The word *Svarāj* is a sacred word, a Vedic word, meaning self-rule and self-restraint, and not freedom from all restraint which 'independence' often means.[20]

What Gandhi meant by *pūrṇa-svarāj* (complete freedom) is:

> ...an awakening among the masses, a knowledge among them of their fine interest and ability to serve that interest against the whole world.... harmony freedom from aggression from within or without, and a progressive improvement in the material condition of the masses.[21]

---

[20] See R. K. Prablu and R. R. Rao, eds., *The Mind of Gandhi* (Ahmedabad: Navajivan Pub. House, 1967), 317.

[21] *Ibid,* 318.

Svarāj blends both the introspective and activist components in the path to self-reliance and freedom.

The integration of introspective practice with social and political awareness and action is emphasized in Buddhism as well. As Ariyaratne has shown with the success of his *sarvodaya* movement in Sri Lanka, (by recasting a Gandhian notion and translating it as the "awakening of all"), development is not merely the transfer of technology, or sophisticated power plants, but the significant *metanoia* at all levels - personal, spiritual, political and economic.

Individual transformation as the pre-requisite for social transformation is also the cornerstone of the *prajñā* (wisdom) and *śīla* (morality) of the Buddhist commandments.

Gandhi employed the Hindu notion of *dharma to* reiterate that the 'freedom' of the individual in order to be abiding can and must coexist with the virtuous ordering of society. *Dharma* as that which holds together and sustains, subsumes the universal laws that uphold the cosmos, the moral order in society and the precepts of social behavior.

> The great truth: 'As with the individual so with the universe, is applicable here and elsewhere, says Gandhi. If we are ever torn by conflict from within.... *Svarāj* can have no meaning for us. Government of self, then is primary education in the school of *Svarāj*.[22]

The *prajñā* and the *śīla* of *svarāj* were enshrined in the vows taken by the *satyāgrāhi*s (those engaged in the activist pursuit of truth) at Gandhi's Ashram. At core they embody an eco-politics that is synchronous with what could be a Buddhist perspective of development. Their political orientation is however more explicit than the *bodhisattva vows* of working for the happiness of all sentient beings.

Some Buddhist scholars emphasize that the primary Buddhist position on social action is one of total activism, an unswerving commitment to complete personal transformation and complete world transformation, and that this activism becomes fully explicit in Mahāyāna with its magnificent literature on the Bodhisattva career [23]. If, as claimed, it is squarely in the center of all Buddhist traditions to bring basic principles to bear on actual, contemporary problems to develop ethical, even political guidelines for action, then the *Satyāgrāhi*'s vows can provide valuable additional insights.

---

[22] This ten-fold path of virtuous evolution exhorts individuals "not to kill, not to be covetous, not to rape, not to lie, abuse, slander or gossip, nor to bear envy, malice, or false convictions," and are matched by injunctions to prolong life, be generous, maintain proper sexuality, tell the truth, reconcile conflicts, speak gently, speak meaningfully, be loving, rejoice in others' fortune, and hold authentic views.

[23] See Robert Thurman, " Nāgārjuna's Guidelines for Buddhist Social Action," in Fred Eppsteiner, ed., *The Path of Compassion* (Berkeley: Parallax, 1985, 1988), 120.

For Gandhi, the route to *svarāj* lay in turning the totality of one's responses to the relentless pursuit of truth. Truth here is perceived as all those attributes through which the essence of existence manifests itself. From the perspective of Buddha-dharma this would involve a deep understanding of the nature of impermanence and the consequent dissolution of the 'I' or ego.

In social terms the pursuit of truth implies the assertion that meaning and significance can be found through the mediation of non-deterministic temporal realities (echoes of dependent co-arising?). Only through the web of inter-relationships which are purposive but never manipulative can truth render itself transparent to the seeker. This involves a caution towards fixed positions and ready-made identities and the cultivation of the maximum possible degree of openness.[24] At root it builds on the conviction that millions of individual explorations in this direction will at some point of critical mass precipitate a social transformation. Buddhist teaching maintains this openness by enabling us to recognize the changing nature of all human projects at reordering the world, by urging us to keep what Suzuki Roshi calls "our beginner's mind". And all along universal responsibility urges us to continue to strive for the alleviation of suffering. Integral to Gandhi's application of *karmayoga* (individual action for the welfare of others in a spirit of renunciation to the fruits of action) was its emphasis on *advaita* or non-differentiation between the self and other aspects of creation, on inter-connectedness and inter-penetration.

The vow of *ahiṁsā*, or non-violence, is too well-known to merit further elaboration here. Gandhi variously translated this also as 'love', 'compassion', and charity and saw it as a necessary element in his quest for self-realization. "My uniform experience has convinced me", he says in his autobiography, "that a Perfect vision of Truth can only follow a complete realization of *ahiṁsā*." Gandhi's emphasis, while conceding that perceptions of the truth may vary, lay in a *way of seeking truth,* of reconciling differences with means that sub-serve the need for preserving cohesion in society. From the standpoint of Buddha-dharma this would involve entering the four abodes of *mettā, karuṇā, muditā* and *upekṣā*, since one of Buddhism's transcendent virtues is upholding a non-violent view towards all forms of life.[25]

For Gandhi *ahiṁsā* involved *ātmaupamya,* or identifying oneself with others. The Mahāyāna meditative techniques of exchanging oneself with others, especially in the *lam-rim* practices of Tibetan Buddhism, similarly enters into the spirit of compassionate activism. *Svarāj* was for Gandhi the self-reliance of individuals who practiced the way of realization by complete openness even to the British, the ultimate "other" for colonial India. The politics of the

---

[24] See P. V. Pillai, "Gandhi and Counter Culture", in *Gandhi Marg* 1.7 (1979): 397.

[25] *Mettā* is the loving respect for all beings that liberates me from self indulgence; compassion, or *karma,* involves a commitment to improve the common lot; *muditā* is the pleasure derived from service to others; and *upekhā* is equanimity or detachment that keeps the ego in check.

bodhisattva too would be informed by dissolving the notion of the "other". Such a deconstructionist approach would move away from the oppositional mode of conventional politics. This would involve identifying the problem to be overcome and not the group/class/party that needs to be vanquished. Thus Gandhi's non-violent approach to conflict resolution lay in converting the ostensible 'opponent' towards a desirable perspective through love. Gandhi said in the *Bombay Chronicle:*

> My love of the British is equal to that of my own people. I claim no
> merit for it, for I have equal love for all mankind without exception.
> It demands no reciprocity. I own no enemy on earth. That is my
> creed.[26]

The vow of *asteya* (non-stealing) assumes tremendous significance in today's world. It defines the parameters of appropriation or acquisition from nature or produced wealth. No one has unlimited rights especially when her contribution is limited. *Asteya* exhorts self-restraint in the individual to ensure social equality. When I take more than what I need, it is at someone else's cost. It is theft. To accumulate for some unforeseen future need is to appropriate more than my share of the immediately available. That too is theft. It unleashes a cycle of irrational wants, leads to dehumanization alienation and violence and to the depletion of environmental resources. Accumulated property or power can only be held in trusteeship (*sammāyasa*). If the trustee uses it for herself it is misappropriation.

Asaṅgraha is the corollary of *Asteya* and stresses non-covetousness. Covetousness results in increasing dependence on others, or in the tendency to dominate, control or subjugate through possessions, and often for the sake of external possessions. The individual's relationship to objects needs to be that of a sagacious user and not an un-satiated appropriator.

The extension of the logic of this non-acquisitiveness and non-indulgence to the realm of the senses and corporeal existence is the essence of the vow of *brahmacarya* (continence).

Śarīra-śrama (the notion of bread-labor) was used by Gandhi symbolically to instill a consciousness of the dignity and equality of labor, and as an antidote to the social ills of living off the labor of others and to managerial elitism. The *Bhagavād-gīta* had given the term *yagya* to physical labor, reiterating that he who eats without performing this, eats the fruits of sin. Gandhi extended it to include the notion of labor as the Great Leveler or Great Equalizer to overcome social arrogance by demonstrating to a class and caste-ridden society that no form of work or labor can be demeaning.

Bhayavarjana (fearlessness). At the root of all fear is the body. The mind fears for the body, for the conditions the body may find itself in and the effect they may have on the mind. Fear is the loss of something related to the body or

---

[26] *The Mind of Maāatma Gandhi, op. cit.,* 323.

the ego. It is also born of ignorance of the transient nature of all things. The vow of fearlessness was a necessary prerequisite to opening the doors of perception.

In the vows of *sarva dharma samānatva* and *sparśabhāvanā* are enshrined the principles of tolerance to all religious persuasions, and the struggle against all manifestations of discrimination on the basis of caste, color or creed. The importance of these vows in today's strife-torn world of apartheid, religious and racial conflict, cannot be overstated.

The vow of *svadeśī* (self-reliance) draws on the essence of all the other vows, and brings together with an extraordinary relevance the threads of individual striving, peace and justice. It eludes any easy definition but broadly signifies a dynamic notion of self-reliance, in realms spiritual, material and social. It reiterates the sanctity of man's link with his immediate environment both in terms of nature and other men. It is also another way of showing that each man can and *must* contribute his little in his own way and not take refuge under a 'free-rider' rationale. In the attempt to identify himself with creative endeavor, man must as a first duty dedicate himself to the service of his immediate neighbors. Pure and selfless service to those who come within the orbit of one's everyday life can never by its very nature result in disservice to those who are far away. To abdicate one's responsibility to the proximate for the lure of far pavilions is to strike at the root of social cohesion. *Svadeśī* symbolizes the bringing of human patterns of consumption in tune with the resources of the immediate environment in such a way that the equations of right and responsibility remain direct and non-abdicatory.

The concerns of *svadeśī* must inevitably lead to a critique of gigantism. The notion of development which is implicit is one which favors the embracing of responsibility and the rejection of abdication. It upholds democracy and decentralization to empower people in their efforts to transform themselves to co-exist with the human and natural environment in a non-violent and harmonious manner. Primarily it subverts the received notions of power which are based on hierarchical and patriarchal constructions of reality. In rejecting domination and ego-centrism, it sees the moral force emanating from service to humanity as the preferred energy for social ordering. Here it is in time with the perspective of engaged Buddhism. The collective energies of the saṅgha replace the coercive power of the nation-state and diffuse exclusive boundaries, by ever widening the parameters of responsibility, from the proximate gradually to the more distant. As Gandhi said, "The most effective exercise of power is that which irks least. Power rightly exercised must sit as light as a flower."

The political journey of the *bodhisattva,* as that of the *satyāgrāhi,* begins with a unique empathy for the pain of the phenomenal world, indeed of our planet. At another level it deconstructs all concepts of essence and selfhood, in the understanding of *śūnyatā*; and then returns to an engagement with the world itself -- with form, with *tathatā.* *Saṁsāra* becomes *nirvāṇa,* in the altruistic effort to liberate sentient beings from suffering.

At one level people engaged in a meditative awareness begin to see pain as a motivating factor to work on themselves and on issues.[27] Armed with a philosophy which is life-affirming, it becomes easier to see that personal pain and global pain are very much inter- related. Gandhi saw self-suffering as an essential component of *ātma-upamya.* Apart from allowing us to feel the pain of others it burnishes reason. A chastened reason equips us to act non-violently for the alleviation of suffering.

The altruism of the *bodhisattva* is embellished by loving kindness. To open the heart to absolute emptiness is also in Nāgārjuna's precepts to open the heart to unbounded love. As Vimalakīrti describes it:

> ...the love that is never exhausted because it acknowledges void-ness and selflessness the love that is tolerance because it protects both self and others; the love that is enterprise because it takes responsibility for all living things the love that is liberative technique because it shows the way everywhere ... the love that is high resolve because it is free of passions; the love that is without deceit because it is not artificial, the love that is happiness because it introduces living beings to the happiness of a Buddha. Such, Mañjuśrī, is the great love of a *bodhisattva.*[28]

Gandhi too emphasized love as the most potent aspect of nonviolent living. The seeker after truth, must widen the circle of love till "it embraces the whole village, the village in turn must take into its fold the district, the district the province, and so on till the scope of our love becomes co-terminus with the world."[29] Gandhi cites the Buddha's exhortation to conquer anger by 'non-anger' and emphasizes that by this he was drawing upon a positive quality, namely, the supreme virtue of love.

Paulo Frier postulated that wasting one's hands of conflict between the powerful and the powerless means to side with the powerful, not to be neutral. This is the real challenge for the engaged Buddhist. Her nonviolent *satyāgrāha* for right livelihood demands that she extend herself against a status-quoist position. *This involves overturning the existing notions of power and embracing change.*

Using the win/win approach as opposed to the you win/I lose notions, where power is used as domination and victory over a potential equal or opponent, the engaged Buddhist is mindful of the Buddha's words of caution.

> Victory creates hatred. Defeat creates suffering. The wise ones desire neither victory nor defeat. Anger creates anger. He who kills

---

[27] See Christopher Titimuss, "Inter-activity: Sitting for peace and standing for Parliament", in *The Path of Compassion, op.cit.,* 185.

[28] Robert Thurman, *The Holy Teaching of Vimalakīrti* (University Park: Pennsylvania State University Press, 1976), 57.

[29] From *Young India* (June 27, 1929): 214.

will be killed. He who wins will be defeated. The wise ones desire neither victory nor defeat.[30]

The Gandhian position is akin to this:

> By its very nature, non-violence cannot 'seize' power, nor can that be its goal. But non-violence can do more; it can effectively control and guide power without capturing the machinery of government. That is its beauty.[31]

The practice of dissolving the ego - through meditation and service - is the powerful Buddhist alternative to the prevalent notions and structures of power. This gentle subversion is the potent vow of its politics.

The outstandingly original contribution of Buddhism has been its emphasis on seeing that the *real is what inheres in change.* Embedded in this dynamic of phenomenality, it rejects hypostasizing any particular social arrangement or construct. Consequently continual self-renewal and the shedding of shibboleths fall within the intellectual and social responsibility of the Buddhist. In directing us to focus on our interconnection with other beings it asks us to act in mutuality to experience true development. In the words of Sulak Sivaraksa is to see it as the continuity between the inner and the outer world. Taken a step further it would mean overturning a model of development whose continued power and success depends upon the indifference of the many to the predicament of a large section of the population of the world. The world can never be at peace unless people redefine the notions of security in their every day lives and societies cease to regard economic growth as the *summum bonum* of development.

Nobel Laureate Eli Wiesel's aphorism merits collective remembering. "The opposite of love is not hate but indifference. The opposite of education is not ignorance but indifference. The opposite of beauty is not ugliness but indifference. The opposite of life is not death but indifference to both life and death."

Could 'overcoming indifference' then not be the political manifesto of the engaged Buddhist of today - and the ethic of her program of empowerment?

> *The knell of mere survival.*
> *The Beginning of Living.*

---

[30] From *Aṅguttara-nikāya,* cited in *The Path of Compassion, op. cit.,* 18.

[31] *Towards New Horizons,* by Pyrarelal, preprinted from *Mahātma Gandhi, The Last Phase* (Ahmedabad: Navajivan Pub. House 1959), 91.

CHAPTER 20

BUDDHIST ATTITUDES TO AND TREATMENT OF NON-HUMAN NATURE

Peter Harvey

1. Humanity's Place in Nature

Buddhism sees humans as one type of sentient being, along with gods, *asuras*, animals, ghosts and hell-beings, who share the conditioned, limited realm of *saṁsāra*, the round of rebirths. Humans are not seen as special creations by a God, or as having been given 'dominion over' animals, etc. nevertheless, a human rebirth is seen as a very rare and fortunate one, and in the above listing of rebirth types, humans comprise one group, while all animals (i.e., land animals, birds, fishes, worms, insects: *M.*, 3:167-9) comprise another. To that extent, humans are 'set apart.' This is because they have a greater freedom and capacity for understanding than animals (and a greater motivation for spiritual progress than gods). Thus most moral and spiritual progress, or its opposite, is made at the human level. The relatively special place of humans in the Buddhist cosmos means that they can be seen as at a 'higher level' of existence than animals. To be reborn as an animal is a result of bad karma, and to be a human result from good karma. This, however, is not seen to justify a domineering exploitation of animals. Humans are superior primarily in terms of their capacities for moral action and spiritual development. The natural expression of these is not an exploitative attitude, but one of kindness to lesser beings, an ideal of *noblesse oblige* (Hall, 1902: ch. 19). This is backed up by the reflection that each human will have been some type of animal in many past rebirths, and that each animal will have been a human in many past rebirths. As a human, one may be in a more fortunate position than animals, but this is only a temporary state of affairs. Therefore, one cannot isolate oneself from the plight of animals; one has oneself experienced it (*S.*, 2: 186). Moreover, in the ancient round of rebirths, one will have previously crossed paths with every being one comes across, from a human down to an insect. In some past life they will have been a close relative or friend, and have been very good to one (*S.*, 2:189-90). Bearing this in mind, one should return the kindness in the present.

The Western concept of 'nature' is one which places humans and human artifices over and against the 'natural' world of animals, plants and the physical environment. In the present century, industrialization, etc., has led to many environmental problems, and thus to reflection on how humans should act and live so as to be in a less destructive, and self-undermining, relationship with 'nature.' Yet even this view tends to divide such 'nature' from what is 'human'. The classical Buddhist perspective, though, has seen a more appropriate division as that between sentient beings, of which humans are only a special case, and the non-sentient environment, the 'receptacle-world' (*bhājana-loka*), in *Sarvāstivādin* terminology. In this division, plants would generally come on the non-sentient side of the line, but there is some ambiguity here, and differences of view. . The key quality, then, is sentience, the ability to experience and to suffer, and the related ability, in this or a future life, to transcend suffering by attaining enlightenment. Whether sentient or insentient, though, everything in the conditioned world is subject to Conditioned Arising, the natural process of law-governed arising-according-to-conditions. In this sense, *everything* (except the unconditioned, *Nirvāna*) is natural, or 'part of nature.'

This even applies to the gods, which in most religions are counted as part of the 'super-natural.' Gods are seen as existing at various levels, with some sharing the earth with humans. Buddhist texts refer to certain gods living in large trees (*Vin.*, 4: 34-35) and even in healing herbs (*S.*, 4: 302; *M.*, 1: 306): thus one should not anger such a being by damaging or destroying his or her home (Hall, 1902: ch. 20). Other gods dwell on the land. Thus a Thai custom, upheld even in the busy modern city of Bangkok, is to build a small 'spirit house' next to a building erected on a previously open plot of land. This is to house any gods displaced from the land: to be considerate to them and thus not rouse their anger. In Ladakh, a ceremony at the first planting of the year likewise seeks to pacify the spirits of the earth and water, as well as worms and fish, all of which might be disturbed by agricultural activity (Batchelor and Brown, 1992: 43).

It is held that karmic effects sometimes catch up with people via their environment. Thus, at *A.*, 2: 74-6, the bad actions of a king and his people are said to lead to poor rainfall and thus poor crops. Right actions have the opposite effect. The environment is thus held to respond to the state of human morality; it is not a neutral stage on which humans merely strut, nor a sterile container unaffected by human actions. This clearly has ecological ramifications: humans cannot ignore the effect of their actions on their environment. This message is also strongly implied by the *Aggañña Sutta* (*D.*, 3: 84-93), on the initial stages of the development of sentient life on earth. This occurs when previously divine beings fall from their prior state and, through consuming a savory crust floating on the oceans, develop physical bodies, and later sexual differentiation. At first their environment is bountiful, but it becomes less so the more they greedily take from it. They feed off sweet-tasting fungus, and then creepers, but these in tam disappear as the beings differentiate in appearance and the more beautiful ones become conceited and arrogant. Then they feed off quick-growing rice, gathering it each day as they need it. But due to laziness, they start to gather a week's supply at a time, so that it then ceases to grow quickly, necessitating cultivation. Consequently, the land is divided up into fields, such that property is invented, followed by theft. Here, then, is a vision of sentient beings and their environment co-evolving (or co-devolving). The beings are affected by what they take from their environment, and the environment becomes less refined and fruitful as the beings morally decline.

All this takes place according to the principle of Conditioned Arising, which in Mahāyāna Buddhism was interpreted to mean that everything is 'empty' of inherent nature. That is, nothing can exist on its own, with an essence, for each thing depends on other things to condition its arising, existence and meaning. In Eastern Buddhism, the inter-relationship of all things (and thus of humans and their environment) is particularly strongly emphasized. In the *Avataṁsaka-sūtra* is an image, the 'Jewel Net of Indra,' explained by Fazang, a master of the Huayan School, as follows. In this infinite net, a jewel is placed at each knot, such that each jewel reflects every other one, including their reflections of every jewel, and so on to infinity (Cook, 1989: 214). This is seen as a simile for reality as a web of interdependence, in which each thing is 'interpenetrated' by every other. Each item is made possible by, and reflects 'every other, for they all condition it in one way or another. Nothing can exist by itself, but it also makes its own contribution to the whole. Thus the *Sūtra* says, 'Every living being and every minute thing is significant, since even the tiniest thing contains the whole mystery'. Cook sees this perspective as one of 'cosmic ecology' (1989: 214).

In the lands of Eastern Buddhism, the traditional ideal has been one of harmony with nature. This has been particularly emphasized by the Chan / Zen School, in such actions as blending meditation huts into the landscape, not wasting any food in monasteries, landscape painting, landscape gardening, and nature poetry (Suzuki, 1959: chs. 11 & 7). Great attention is paid to seemingly insignificant aspects of nature, for insight into them can give an intuitive appreciation of the indescribably and mysterious 'suchness' which runs through the whole fabric of existence. This can be seen in examples of the famous *haiku* poetry form:

<table>
<tr><td>On a dry branch
A raven is perched:
This autumnal eve!</td><td>The old pond,
A straw sandal sunk to the bottom,
Sleet falling.</td></tr>
</table>

Attunement to nature is also found among the poems of the early Arahats in the *Theragāthā*, a Theravāda text. Mahā-Kassapa says, 'With clear water and wide crags, haunted by monkeys and deer, covered with oozing moss, those rocks delight me' (v. 1069-70). Sāriputta affirms, 'Forests are delightful, where (ordinary) people find no delight. Those rid of desire will delight there; they are not seekers after sensual pleasures' (v. 992). That is, the enlightened appreciate nature in a non-attached, non-sensual way. Fearlessness could also be developed, as when meditating in the vicinity of fanged animals (v. 524). For such wilderness-meditators, the environment could itself be a teacher, especially of constant change and impermanence, and as an example, such as the mountain being seen as an image of unshakeability (v. 1000). Thus Mahānāma says that he is 'found wanting by the mountain with its many shrubs and trees' (v. 115).

2. Meat-eating

It is thus clear that the Buddhist ideal for humanity's relationship with animals, plants and the landscape, is one of harmonious co-operation. Buddhism has always encouraged good treatment of other sentient beings, and the first of the five ethical precepts is to abstain from 'onslaught on living beings (literally: breathers).' That is, to avoid intentional killing or harming of any sentient being. This is based on sympathy, *anukampā*: not wishing to inflict on others what one would not like to experience oneself. Relevant to the first precept are such activities as animal sacrifice, pest control, animal husbandry, meat eating and animal experimentation. Here, only the latter two will be discussed. Of course, the main reason why animals are killed is to eat them. Buddhist texts and Buddhist leaders have sought to discourage this. The emperor Aśoka made fifty-six official 'no slaughter' days per year, protecting both animals and fish.[1] He gave up hunting trips, the favorite sport of Indian rulers, banned the killing of a wide variety of non-food animals, birds and fishes, and drastically reduced, then eliminated, the slaughter of animals to feed the large royal household.[2] In Sri Lanka, a number of Buddhist kings prohibited the slaughter of animals, either wholly, or in certain circumstances. In Japan, the emperor Temmu, in 675 C.E., restricted the use of certain types of hunting devices and eating the meat of cows, horses, dogs and monkeys (Chapple, 1992: 57).

Nevertheless, vegetarianism is less widespread among Buddhists than non-Buddhists often assume. In fact, the Buddha's emphasis was on the avoidance of killing. So it is worse to swat a fly -- an immediate act of killing -- than to eat the carcass of an already dead animal. Only in certain Mahāyāna texts is vegetarianism advocated. The position in early Buddhism, and in Theravada lands, is as follows.

In the Buddha's day, vegetarianism was practiced by Jains, who once accused the Buddha of knowingly eating an animal that had been specifically killed for him. The donor denies this, and the Buddha explains that a monk may eat meat provided it is 'pure in three respects'. If the monk has not seen, heard or suspected that the animal had been killed specifically for him (*Vin.*, 4.237-8). Elsewhere, the Buddha explains that a monk receives food as a gift from a donor, and his loving-kindness for donors and other creatures is not compromised by

---

[1] Pillar Edict V: Nikam & McKeon, 1959: 56
[2] Pillar Edict V and Rock Edict I : Nikam, & McKeon, 1959: 55-6.

such eating, if it is 'blameless' by being 'pure in three respects' (*M.*, 1.386-71). He goes onto emphasize, though, that a donor generates much bad karma even ff he or she kills a being so as to give alms to himself or a monk. This is on five grounds: I) giving the order to fetch the animal, ii) the pain and distress caused to the animal as it is dragged with a rope around its neck, iii) giving the order to kill the animal, iv) the pain and distress of the animal while it is being killed, v) the offering of the meat to a monk if it is of an unsuitable type not allowable for a monk (e.g., dog flesh: *Vin.*, 1.218-19). Here, it can be noted, the evil of the act resides both in the actual actions of the killer and the suffering of the killed.

It is notable that the Buddha actually resisted an attempt to make vegetarianism compulsory for monks (*Vin.*, 2.171-2). In order to foment a schism, his jealous cousin Devadatta proposed that all monks should be vegetarian and should follow a number of previously optional ascetic practices, such as living at the root of a tree. The Buddha refused, reaffirming that the practices were optional and meat was acceptable if it was 'pure in three respects'. Devadatta then attempted to lead his own order, under these rules, seeking to gain support from those who 'esteem austerity'. Elsewhere, such a purely external way of assessing someone's spiritual worth is seen as unreliable (*A.*, 2.71). Prior to his enlightenment, in his ascetic phase, Gotama had himself tried the teachings of those who taught 'purity through food', i.e., living off small amounts of only one type of food, be it jujube, beans, sesame or rice. Such externally oriented practices only made him thin and weak, though (*M.*, 1.80-1). The link between vegetarianism and extreme asceticism is also found at *M.*, 1.342-3, where it is included among the practices of self-tormenting ascetics, along with such things as eating once a week, never sitting down, and pulling out of the hair. Such ascetic acts are not seen to 'purify' a person (*Sn.*, 249), and meat is not what is to be seen as 'tainted faire', but 'hurting living creatures, killing, cutting and binding, stealing, telling lies...' are (*Sn.*, 242).

It is notable, above, that the Buddha did not even regard vegetarianism as among the optional ascetic practices for monks. If they were given flesh-food, and it was 'pure' as described above, to refuse it would deprive the donor of the goodness-power (*puñña*) engendered by giving alms-food. Moreover, it would encourage the monks to pick and choose what food they would eat. Food should be looked on only as a source of sustenance, without preferences. To believe that being a vegetarian is itself spiritually purifying would seem to be an example of the spiritual fetter of 'attachment to virtues and vows'. It is certainly the case that feelings of moral superiority are a common danger among vegetarians: though it can be avoided! Likewise, vegetarians can in time become disgusted with meat, but this can be seen as a case of negative attachment. In any case, as the above suggests, there are many worse actions than eating meat.

The above discussion is concerned with what is acceptable for a monk or nun, who must, with few exceptions, eat what is given to them. The considerations for a lay Buddhist are similar, but not identical. A layperson has more control over his or her food supply, ingredients must be directly obtained or bought. Laypeople, within the limits of their means, make many preference-directed choices over what they eat. So for a layperson to avoid flesh-food (except, perhaps, when he or she is someone's guest) is not to refuse what someone has graciously offered, and not, as such, more 'picking and choosing' than is normal for a layperson. A lay vegetarian must, though, be wary of feelings of judgmental moral superiority, and negative attachment to meat. The latter is best dealt with by not refusing meat if one is someone's guest. While it is in some ways more feasible, then, for a layperson to be a vegetarian than a monk, one feature of Buddhism weighs against this leading to vegetarianism being more common among the laity. Normally, higher standards of behavior are expected of a monk than a layperson. If even monks are not expected to be vegetarian, a layperson might well think, 'why should I?'

It is clearly the case, though, that any lay Buddhist should not kill an animal for food, or tell someone else to do so. Either action clearly breaks the first precept. The question arises, though, as to whether buying meat from a butcher is participating in wrong action by encouraging it. One passage (*A.*, II.253) says that a person will be reborn in hell if he kills and encourages others to do so. 'Encouraging' alone is not specified as having this effect, but in any case, such encouraging would normally be seen to be of a direct form, for example 'why don't you go hunting?'. Clearly, to ask a butcher to kill an animal for one is to break the first precept. In the West, most food animals are killed in large abattoirs, and 'butchers' only sell the meat. Most Buddhist countries lack such large-scale slaughter-houses (they would be seen as hells on earth) and so obtaining meat is more likely to have the attendant danger of being directly involved in an animal's death. This probably helps to reduce the extent of meat-eating.

To make one's living as a butcher, hunter or fisherman clearly comes under the category of wrong livelihood' (*A.*, II.208), to be avoided by all sincere Buddhists. Not uncommonly, raising livestock for slaughter is also seen as 'wrong livelihood'. Certainly one finds that, in Buddhist societies, butchers (slaughterers and meat salesmen) are usually non-Buddhists, often Muslims. By making a living by or from killing, they are seen as depraved people, and are often treated as outcasts. Buddhist fishermen are more common, though they have a low status in society due to their livelihood. As fish are seen as a lower form of life than land animals, it is seen as less bad to kill them. The excuse is sometimes made that they are not <u>killed,</u> but just die when taken out of the water. This is evidently a case of trying to distance oneself from what is recognized as an unwholesome action. In Southeast Asia, people often catch their own fish, which clearly breaks the first precept; but if a living is not made from this, it is not seen as wrong livelihood'.

In Theravāda countries, vegetarianism is universally admired but little practiced.[3] There is a minority witness of vegetarians, however -- such as the one-time governor of Bangkok --, and most people have an uneasy conscience

---

[3] See Gombrich, 1971: 260-62; W. King, 1964: 281-84; and *World Fellowship of Buddhists Review*, 1983.

when they <u>think</u> about meat-eating. Most lay-people eat meat, though some abstain on observance days, or during periods of meditation. A few monks let it be known that they would prefer vegetarian food, and, in Burma, some nuns are vegetarian in periods of more ascetic practice (Kawanami, 1990: 27). In general, it is seen as preferable to eat the meat of an animal which is less intelligent, and/or smaller (large animals take more effort to kill, thus more sustained bad intention is involved: see Conze, 1959: 70), than the opposite. Thus it is worst of all to eat beef (in Burma prior to British colonization, it was a crime to kill a cow, as it was in the period 1960-62). It is seen as less bad to eat pork, then goats or chickens, and less bad again to eat eggs. Nevertheless, eggs are always regarded as having been fertilized, so to crack an egg is seen as killing a living being. This means that, in Sri Lanka at least, no eggs are used in Buddhist monasteries, and pre-cracked 'Buddhist eggs' are sold to the middle-class pious Buddhists. It is seen as least bad to eat fish, an unintelligent form of life that needs little effort to kill. Fish is by far the most common form of flesh eaten, as is reflected in a Thai saying on the abundance of their country, 'There is fish in the water, there is rice in the fields'.

In the Mahāyāna tradition, texts are found which argue for vegetarianism. Such advocacy was clearly facilitated by the climate of opinion that the Buddhist emphasis had helped to created. Jain criticism of meat-eating by Buddhists may have played its part, but the Mahāyāna emphasis on compassion seems to have been a key factor. Thus the *Mahā-parinirvāṇa Sūtra* says that eating meat 'extinguishes the seed of great compassion' (Kapleau, 1981: 34). Ruegg (1980) notes that vegetarianism was first emphasized in texts, such as this, which focused on the idea of the *tathāgata-garbha*, or Buddha-potential, in all (or most) beings. The above Sūtra has the Buddha explicitly saying, 'I order the various disciples from today that they cannot any more partake of meat'. More ambiguously, the *Bodhisattva-prātimokṣa* is cited as saying that flesh food should not be given to a monk, but if it is, he should eat it (Bendall & Richardson, 1971: 143). A late addition to the *Laṅkāvatāra Sūtra* (Suzuki, 1932: 211-23) has a series of arguments against meat-eating, and has the Buddha <u>denying</u> the scriptural idea of it being 'blameless' to eat meat that is 'Pure in three respects'. Such a direct contradiction of an earlier scriptural idea is unusual in Mahāyāna texts; non-acceptable ideas are generally subverted, reinterpreted, or seen purely as a 'skillful means'. The arguments of the *Sūtra* can be summarized as follows: 1) all beings, in some past rebirth, have been a close relative or friend. One should thus look on all beings as if they were one's only child, with loving-kindness, and not eat them; ii) the smell of a meat eater frightens beings and gives a meat-eater a bad reputation; iii) eating meat by Buddhists means that the Dharma will be spoken ill of, and the Bodhisattvas will lose their hearers; iv) meat stinks; v) meat-eating prevents progress in meditation, and leads to arrogance, as so onions, garlic and alcohol (here the influence of Hindu yoga ideas seem apparent); vi) the meat-eater sleeps uneasily, with bad dreams (d. loving-kindness is said to lead to good sleep); he is anxious, with bad digestion and bad health. A Bodhisattva will get goodness power and health through eating grains, beans, honey, oil, ghee, molasses and sugar, etc.; vii) meat-eating leads to a bad rebirth as a carnivorous animal, or a low caste human, vegetarianism leads to a good rebirth; viii) ff no meat is eaten, no-one will destroy life, as there will be no market for the bodies. Here, various types of argument are used: an appeal to love, and to the duty of returning past kindnesses (i); prudence (ii); the need to protect the Dharma (iii); disgust (iv); spiritual pragmatism (v); mental and physical health (vi); karmic effect (vi and vii); and good indirect consequences of abstinence (viii). The *Sūtra* concludes that there is goodness-power in avoiding flesh-food, that the arguments defending meat eating are spurious, and that the Buddha never ate meat (though he probably did so, given what earlier texts say).

Early in the fifth century A.D., after a period of Mahāyāna influence, the Chinese pilgrim Faxian reported that the markets of the Buddhist heart-land had no butchers' shops, though outcasts did sell meat elsewhere (Legge, J., 1956: 43). Outside India, it is in Eastern Buddhism that Buddhist arguments for vegetarianism have had a notable effect. The emperor Wu, in 5 11, included a ban on meat-eating among other animal-protection legislation. His actions helped lead to the long-term reduction of meat-eating by Chinese Buddhists, and the virtual end of meat-eating in Chinese monasteries and temples (Welch, 1967: 112-113). Such a requirement for vegetarianism by monks and nuns is enshrined in the supplementary monastic code of Eastern Buddhism known as the *Brahmajāla Sūtra* (Dharma Realm, 1981). Among pious lay-people, vegetarianism has been common, being seen as an implication of either the first precept or the Bodhisattva vows (Welch, 1967: 365). For Chinese Buddhists, to see Theravāda monks eating meat often comes as a shock, as it is seen as very un-monkly behavior! Chinese attitudes have also broadly prevailed in Korea and Japan. It is claimed that Japan was 'essentially a vegetarian country' until the middle of the nineteenth century (Kapleau, 1981: 34). Certainly, beef was not eaten. Since the opening of Japan to the West, in 1868, though, western meat-eating habits have gradually come to have a considerable influence. The monasteries, especially Zen ones, remain formally vegetarian, though it has been observed that trainee monks do eat meat when away from the monastery (Kapleau, 1981: 27).

In Northern Buddhism, while the tradition is Mahayana, the harsh, cold climate, yielding little plant protein, has meant that most people, except for some bLamas, eat meat (Bell, 1928: 217-34). Those Lamas who eat meat, though, may do a ceremony to help the dead animal gain a good rebirth. A common livelihood is as a nomadic herdsman up on the high pastures of Tibet or on the steppes of Mongolia, so livestock play an important part in the economy of these regions. Nevertheless, people often abstain from meat on observance days, when, in pre-communist Tibet, slaughtering was banned, and butchers are despised. The most direct method of killing an animal, with a knife, is generally avoided, suffocation being the preferred method. While Theravādins prefer to eat small creatures, the Tibetans reason that it is better to kill a few large animals (cattle, sheep and goats) than many small ones (Ekvall, 1964: 75). The fact that this fits in with the abundance of fish in Theravāda lands, and cattle, etc., in Tibet, is surely no accident! The widespread avoidance of fish and fowl is also related to the practice of disposing of human remains by compassionately making them available to birds and fish. Tibetans are noted for their kindness to animals, and even have scruples about eating honey, for this is seen as entailing both theft from and murder of bees.

In the West, vegetarianism among Buddhists is more common than in many parts of Buddhist Asia. This is due to Western expectations of what 'non-harming' Buddhists should do, a general increase in vegetarianism in the West, along with ease of obtaining good vegetarian food, and the influence of the Eastern Buddhist model, particularly via America. In Britain, when food is offered to Western monks trained in the Thai tradition, Thais often give meat dishes, but Westerners give vegetarian ones. This is gradually having the effect of the Thais offering more vegetarian ones.

3. Animal Experimentation

In the modern world, animals are 'used' in large numbers in product testing, and in medical research and training. From a Buddhist perspective, this might be seen as analogous to the animal sacrifices of ancient Brahmanism. Whether sacrificed in the name of religion, or of 'science' and 'knowledge', the intention was/is, in part at least, to bring benefit to human beings. Nevertheless, there is clearly a conflict here with the first precept. The use of animals in medical research at least has strong utilitarian arguments in its favor. Buddhist ethics, though, are not generally based on the principle that the ends justify the means (except in certain versions of Mahāyāna 'skillful means' theory). From the traditional Buddhist perspective, it is more certain that killing an animal is wrong than that generating better drugs, etc., from experiments on it is good (cf. King, 1964: 281). Should a Buddhist take drugs which have been tested on animals? If the Theravādin attitude to meat-eating is applied in this area, it would be acceptable. Mahāyāna vegetarianism might imply that it was unacceptable. What of actual involvement in drug testing on animals? Theravāda principles would rule it out as against the first precept. The Mahāyāna principle of skillful means might suggest it was acceptable, where really necessary. The Western Zen monk Saido Kennaway regretfully accepts that many developments in modern drugs and surgery have depended on animal dissections and experimentations. He goes on to say that,

> From a Buddhist point of view, anyone prepared to do this has to know and accept the karma of his actions. This would entail trying to do as little harm as possible, using alternative methods if available, killing only if absolutely necessary, treating the being with tender respect and making sure the knowledge is put to good use (Shasta Abbey, 1980: 23).

Of course, much testing is not necessary, but arises from an atmosphere of commercial secrecy and rivalry. It might also be pointed out that many modern ills arise as the result of chosen lifestyles, e.g., from smoking, drinking and diet. One might ask if animals should pay the price of alleviating the products of human folly (Story, 1976: 369-71). But, from a Buddhist perspective, that does not rule-out compassionate help for those who thus suffer. One thing that most Buddhists would agree on, whether or not they accept or oppose medical experiments on animals, is that angry and violent means of opposition, by groups such as the Animal Liberation Front (active in the U.K.), are unwholesome and indicative of attachment to views. Action more in line with traditional Buddhist behavior would be to liberate animals by <u>buying</u> them from establishments that would otherwise experiment on them. Jainism is faced with a similar dilemma to Buddhism. In India, where Jains are very active and influential in the pharmaceutical industry, animals are used for drug testing if really necessary, but are then 'rehabilitated' by recuperation facilities maintained by the laboratories; if possible, they are then released back into the wild (Chapple, 1992: 59).

As regards debate on this issue in Buddhist countries which engage in such research, information is unfortunately lacking. Among Western Buddhists, there is the Buddhist Animal Rights Group, in Britain, and the Buddhists Concerned for Animals group in America (*World Edlowship of Buddhists*, 1984: 73-9). The latter focuses on animal experimentation, as well as factory farming and trapping.

4. Species Preservation

The values of traditional Buddhist societies generally ensued that the environment and the species it contained were not over-exploited. The influence of consumerism or state capitalism, however, is currently having corrosive effects. In response, active environmentalist movements have started in such countries as Thailand, where positive action to save the dwindling forests have been taken by monks such as Ajahn Pongsak Tejadhammo (Batchelor & Brown, 1992: 92), and even by the Government, which has officially banned logging. Nevertheless, as Bhikkhu Bodhi argues (Sandell, 1987: vii), further work needs to be done to articulate the practical implications of the Buddhist perspective, in new ways, to the leaders of Buddhist lands currently under the sway of the Western model of development.

Western environmentalism focuses much attention on preventing the extinction of species. It is questionable, though, whether Buddhist principles give strong support to this particular concern. In an eons-old world of change and impermanence, it is to be expected that species will become extinct -though extinctions are particularly rapid at present! The Buddhist concern has always been for the suffering of individual sentient beings, whereas a 'species' is a non-sentient abstraction. Nevertheless, Buddhism sees it as bad to kill any sentient being, particularly when it belongs to a species whose members are of developed intelligence/sensitivity. So, while Buddhist principles might not strongly support saving 'the whale', they support saving whales!

It is indeed sad that countries with a Buddhist heritage pose particular threats to certain endangered species. The tiger and rhinoceros are threatened by the demands of traditional Chinese medicine, and the varieties of whales are threatened by the Japanese. It is pleasing to note that Taiwanese Buddhists sometimes buy 'pet' tigers to rescue them from the pot. What of Japanese whale-hunting? This can be seen as the product of several factors. The fact that Japan is an island has meant that the sea has been looked to as a great food-provider. The preference for sea-foods was probably also strengthened by Buddhist concerns over meat-eating, for fish are seen as a low form of life. Kapleau reports one whaler as saying 'If whales were like pigs or cows, making lots of noise before they die, I could never shoot them. Whales die without making a noise. They're like fish.' (1981: 47) (of course, distressed whales do make a noise, but it cannot be heard above the water). With more powerful boats, and an increasing secularism, there has been much whale killing. In the post-war period, this was initially encouraged by the American occupying force, so as to help feed the starving population. Today, though, whale meat is not much eaten, and the carcasses are largely used for pet food and industrial products. To an average Japanese, killing a whale is no worse than killing a cow, though of course a pious Buddhist would not want to do either. The intelligence of members of the whale family should also elevate their importance in a Buddhist scale of values. Given the Buddhist concern for 'all sentient beings', Japanese whaling, and the Japanese emphasis on memorial rites, it is perhaps not surprising that Buddhist monks sometimes carry out memorial rites for the whales killed by Japanese whalers. Kapleau reports one such in 1979, put on by a Zen temple, and with government officials and executives of a large whaling company in the audience (1981: 46-50). Unfortunately, the service did not seem to contain any discouragement of whaling, but was more like a way to salve people's consciences. In this respect, the rite seems similar to the popular *mizuko kuyo* rites for aborted fetuses.

BIBLIOGRAPHY

Batchelor, M. & K. Brown, eds. *Buddhism and Ecology*. London & New York: Cassell, 1992.

Bell, C. *The People of Tibet*. Oxford: Clarendon Press, 1928.

Bendall, C. and W. H.D. Rouse, trans. *Śikṣā Samuccaya*. 1922. Delhi: Motilal Banarsidass, 1971.

Chapple, C. "Nonviolence to Animals in Buddhism and Jainism." In *Kraft* (1992): 49-62.

Conze, E. *Buddhist Scriptures*. Harmondsworth: Penguin, 1959.

Cook, F. "The Jewel Net of Indra," in J. B. Callicott & R. T. Ames, eds. *Nature in Asian Traditions of Thought.* Albany: State University of New York Press, 1989.

Dharma Realm Buddhist University. *The Buddha Speaks the* Brahma Net Sūtra. Talmage, Ca.: Buddhist Text Translation Society, 1981.

Ekvall, R.B. *Religious Observances in Tibet.* Chicago & London: University of Chicago Press, 1964.

Gombrich, R.R. *Precept and Practice.* Oxford: Clarendon Press, 1971.

Hall, F. *The Soul of a People* (on Nineteenth Century Burma). London: Macmillan, 1902.

Kapleau, Roshi P. *To Cherish All Life; A Buddhist View of Animal Slaughter and Meat Eating.* Rochester, N.Y.: The Zen Center, 1981.

Kawanami, H. "The Religious Standing of Burmese Nuns," *Journal of the International Association of Buddhist Studies* 13 (1990): 17-39.

King, W.L. *In the Hope of Nibbāna.* LaSalle, Ill.: Open Court, 1964.

Legge, J. *A Record of Buddhist Kingdoms.* New York: Dover, 1965.

Nikam, N.A. & R. McKeon, eds. and trans. *The Edicts of Aśoka.* Chicago and London: University of Chicago Press, 1959.

Ruegg, D. S. "*Ahiṁsā* and Vegetarianism in the History of Buddhism." In S. Balasooriya et al, eds., *Buddhist Studies in Honor of Walpola Rahula* (London: George Fraser, 1980), 234-41.

Sandell, K., ed.*Buddhist Perspective on the Eco-crisis.* Kandy, Sri Lanka: Buddhist Publication Society, 1987.

Shasta Abbey. *Buddhism and Respect for Animals.* Mt. Shasta, Ca.: Shasta Abbey Press, 1980.

Story, R. "The Place of Animals in Buddhism." In his *Dimensions of Buddhist Thought: Collected Essays Vol.3* (Kandy, Sri Lanka: Buddhist Publication Society, 1976), 363-73.

Suzuki, D.T. *The Laṅkāvatara Sūtra.* London: Routledge and Kegan Paul, 1932.

Suzuki, D.T. *Zen and Japanese Culture.* New York: Bollingen Foundation, 1959.

Welch, H. *The Practice of Chinese Buddhism, 1900-1950.* Cambridge, Mass.: Harvard University Press, 1967.

World Fellowship of Buddhists Review 20.3 (1983): "Another Buddhist's View on Buddhists Eating Meat," appendix, 1-8.

World Fellowship of Buddhists Review 21.4 (1984): "Buddhists Concerned for Animals," 73 -9.

CHAPTER 21

VARITIES OF RELIGIOUS ECOLOGY: A TYPOLOGY OF BUDDHIST ENVIRONMENTALISM

Ian Charles Harris

The emergence of eco-religiosity, a specifically religious concern for the environment, is a major development within most religious traditions in the late twentieth century. The reasons for this are undoubtedly complex and, as yet, little scholarly work has been undertaken to delineate the component features of the movement. As such, it is far too early to be in a position to evaluate the long-term prospects or future direction of the movement which, in all certainty, has its origin in the elites of 1960s liberal Christianity. The first clear indication of eco-religious discourse comes from such circles though, in time, we may witness a broadening out of the debate into other forms of Christianity, and ultimately beyond the confines of that faith into the other major religions. The real turning point is reached in the 1980s with a "burgeoning of theological literature." [1] Particularly relevant for our purposes, the first significant manifestation of environmental concerns within organized Buddhism may be placed towards the end of this decade, although it is clear that several retrospectively influential writings[2] may be identified before that period. The push by some Christians for dialogue with other faiths, an enterprise often driven by the political agendas of its liberal wind, undoubtedly did much to contribute to the development of indigenous eco-religiosities amongst the dialogue partners. A particularly noteworthy example of this in process in action is the series of declarations published at the end of the 25th anniversary meting

---

[1] See Peter Beyer, *Religion and Globalization* (London: Sage Publications, 1994), 206.

[2] I am thinking particularly of Gary Snyder in this context. On Snyder's impact on the development of ecoBuddhisin, cf. my "An American Appropriation of Buddhism" in Tadeusz Skorupski and Ulrich Pagel, eds., *Buddhist Forum,* Vol. 4, Tring Institute of Buddhist Studies [in press].

of the World Wildlife Fund in Assisi in 1986.[3] Perusal of the declarations by representatives of most of the major faiths shows a remarkable uniformity of attitude given the significant differences that clearly exist in other areas of doctrine and practice.

When one seeks to explain the high level of congruence between historically distinct traditions the special significance of the environment as a global issue emerges as a decisive factor. As Beyer points out, "environmental issues concretize the problematic effects of the global societal system more clearly than others."[4] It is hardly surprising that a certain uniformity of outlook occurs when the point at issue has a character of this kind, not the least because the phenomenon of globalization, it has been claimed, leads to a transformation of the traditional conceptions of location in time and space. Giddens,[5] for instance, argues that modernity results in the uprooting of localizable referents in such a way that customary dimensions of social and cultural life are transformed into global or "empty" space. Perhaps it is the implicit appreciation of our geographical "emptiness", under the conditions of modernity, that encourages the concord that has come to characterize the arena of inter-religious eco-dialogue. In other words, contemporary factors may force traditional religions, such as Christianity and Buddhism, to move into a closer intellectual and emotional harmony the more they move away from the geographical locations that give them their cultural/historical form.

In a sense, analysis along these lines represents a modest reformulation and updating of the old perennial philosophy thesis, i.e., that if we strip away the peculiarities of culture and history all religions are revealed as pointing to the same few eternal truths. However, another reading of the situation is possible. We may turn away from the particularities of tradition entirely and focus instead on the specifically "religious character" of environmentalism itself. It is a commonplace that religions serve to articulate the problematic character of human existence while at the same time offering a decisive route to its resolution. Contemporary environmental ethics, despite the various shades of meaning separating its differing formulations, shares in this endeavor by relating our present difficulties to discontinuities in the structure of the natural world. The aim is to re-establish the original purity of nature. This can be achieved for we possess, either as a species or, from the perspective of deep ecology, as part of a greater bio-spheric community, the power to rectify the man-made dangers presently oppressing the planet. Looked at in this light environmentalism shares significant insight. Conversion experience and missionary zeal are, of course,

---

[3] The earliest example that I have found of dialogue in this area is a W.C.C. conference of 1979, cf. R. L. Shinn, ed., *Faith and Science in an Unjust World,* Vol. 1 (Philadelphia: Fortress Press, 1980), particularly the article by M. Palihawadana entitled "Buddhism and the Scientific Enterprise," 138.

[4] *Op. cit.,* 208.

[5] Anthony Giddens, *The Consequences of Modernity* (Stanford: Stanford University Press, 1990), 17 *ff.*

well-attested in the phenomenon of eco-commitment and strong soteriologies are often reflected in the this-worldly activism that emerges as the result of such commitment. In other words, eco-religiosity need not be subsumed under some presently existing tradition but may be regarded as a virtual religion in its own right. It is, perhaps, more accurately a religion-in-the-making.

As I have already noted, attempts to discriminate between different manifestations of the religio-environmentalist spirit are still in their infancy. Kearns,[6] working within the field of North American Christian studies, has sketched out a tripartite typology which, with some adaptation, is presented by Beyer in his discussion of environmentalism and globalization. The first type is said to reflect an intuition that the whole of creation represents a vast, spiritually satisfying system of inter-related entities in which the continuity of sentience is not disjointed by arbitrary distinctions such as that between human and non-human life forms. This emphasis on radical holism is characteristic of the writings of the Passionist priest Thomas Berry,[7] and the creation spirituality movement of Matthew Fox,[8] amongst others, we shall characterize with the term eco-spirituality. The second, or eco-justice, strand occurs in its most fully articulated form within the context of the World Council of Churches.[9] In this formulation environmental concerns are envisioned a part of an integrated package of measures in which social, political and spiritual needs are held in harmony. The incorporation of ecological concerns within an agenda that has its roots in the earlier liberation theology movement is said to represent a further elaboration of the concept of justice in the life of the church. Our third and final type derives from the Old Testament notion of stewardship. Self-appointed 'stewards' of creation are typically found in the more theologically conservative ranks of Christian believers.[10] As such they argue that the answer to the present environmental crisis is to be found in a return to the ways of the past -- ways that are most effectively articulated by the biblical tradition itself. Christians are urged to avoid the pitfalls of modernism for salvation in its environmentalist

---

[6] Laurel Kearns, "Redeeming the Earth: Eco-Theological Ethics for Saving the Earth," paper presented at the Association for the Sociology of Religion Annual Meeting, Washington, D.C., 1990. Also "Saving the Creation: Stewardship Theology and Creation Spirituality," paper presented at the American Academy of Religion Annual Meeting, Kansas City, MO., 1991. Both are quoted by Beyer, *op. cit*, 217 *f.*

[7] E.g., Thomas Berry, *The Dream of the Earth* (San Francisco: Sierra Club Books, 1988).

[8] E.g., Matthew Fox, *The Coming of the Cosmic Christ: The Healing of Mother Earth and the Birth of a Global Renaissance* (San Francisco: Harper and Row, 1988).

[9] Cf. for example, World Council of Churches, *Signs of the Spirit, Official Report of the Seventh Assembly, Canberra, Australia, 7-20 February 1991* (Geneva and Grand Rapids, MI: World Council of Churches Publications/ Eerdmans, 1991), 55*f.*

[10] E.g., Granberg-Michaelson, Wesley, *Ecology and Life: Accepting our Environmental Responsibility* (Waco, TX: Word Books, 1992).

sense can only come from a return to tradition. The term eco-traditionalism therefore seems appropriate for this type.

Let us now turn to contemporary writings in the field of Buddhism and the environment to discover how helpful this threefold typology may be in analyzing the shape and nature of the Buddhist debate. It should be pointed out that the amount of material in print is not vast and any conclusions must be regarded as highly provisional. Nevertheless, there does seem to be a natural division into four distinct categories:

1. Straightforward endorsement of Buddhist environmental ethics by traditional guardians of doxic truth, of whom H. H. Dalai Lama[11] is perhaps the most important representative. The material in this first group tends to avoid discussion of those areas of Buddhist doctrine that may be used as support for the ethical claims made.
2. Equally upbeat treatments by mainly Japanese and North American scholars and Buddhist activists, such as Noritoshi Aramaki,[12] Joanna Macy,[13] and Brian Brown,[14] premised on the same assumptions as in category 1. The point that distinguishes the two is that in this group authors seek to identify the most appropriate Buddhist doctrinal bases from which an environmental ethic may proceed, e.g., the Huayan doctrine of interpenetration, tathāgatagarbha, etc.
3. Critical treatments, which, while fully acknowledging the difficulties involved in reconciling traditional Asian modes of thought with those employed by scientific ecology, are optimistic about the possibility of establishing an authentic Buddhist response to environmental problems. The work of Lambert Schmithausen[15] is particularly relevant in this respect.

---

[11] Tenzin Gyatso, His Holiness the 14th Dalai Lama, "A Tibetan Buddhist Perspective on Spirit in Nature," in Steven C. Rochefeller and John C. Elder, eds., *Spirit and Nature: Why the Environment is a Religious Issue* (Boston: Beacon Press, 1992), 109-123.

[12] Aramaki Noritoshi, *"Shizen-hakai kara Shizen-sasei e - Rekishi no Tenkai ni tsuite"* (From Destruction of Nature to Revival of Nature: On a Historical Conversion), *Deai* 11.1 (1992): 3-22.

[13] Joanna Macy, "The Greening of the Self," in Alan Hunt-Badiner, ed., *Dharma Gaia. A Harvest of Essays in Buddhism and Ecology* (Berkeley: Parallax, 1990): 53 -63. Also *Mutual Causality in Buddhism and General Systems Theory: The Dharma of Natural Systems* (Albany, NY: State University of New York Press, 1991).

[14] Brian Brown, "Toward a Buddhist Ecological Cosmology," *Bucknell Review* 37.2 (1993): 124-137.

[15] Lambert Schmithausen, *Buddhism and Nature: The Lecture Delivered on the Occasion of the EXPO 1990 (An Enlarged Version with Notes)* (Tokyo: The International Institute for Buddhist Studies, 1991) [Studia Philologica Buddhica, Occasional Paper

4. Forthright denial of the possibility of Buddhist environmental ethics on the grounds that the doctrinal standpoint of "canonical" Buddhism implies a negation of the natural realm for all practical purposes. Noriaki Hakamaya[16] is the most significant and vigorous exponent of this final position.

One result of comparison between Christian and Buddhist categories is the apparent lack of an obvious eco-justice strand within contemporary Buddhism.[17] The questions of social justice have been an issue for Buddhists in the modern period, most notably in the writings of Thai reformists such as Bhikkhu Buddhadasa and Sulak Sivaraksa.[18] Nevertheless, it is rare to find environmental concerns playing any significant role in their thought. I am unable to consult works in Thai though I am reliably informed that ecological considerations are beginning to manifest themselves within the practice of Buddhist monks, particularly in the north-east of the country.[19] Whether more theoretical approaches from the Thai Buddhist perspective exist I cannot say, indeed, I hope that those attending the conference will be able to shed light on this matter. All I can say is, at this stage, it is impossible to be certain about the prospects for a Buddhist perspective on eco-justice.

When we move to the second type, i.e., to the area of eco-spirituality, we shall find far more fruitful ground for comparison, not the least because Christian and Buddhist approaches to the topic, more often than not, can be traced to the geographical environment of the west coast of North America, or at any rate to those parts of the intellectual thought universe that exhibit strong lines of affiliation to the counter-culture. Here the boundaries between world historical religious traditions begin to lose any definite form. Nominal representatives of both traditions regularly work together, speak from the same

---

Series VII]. Also, *The Problem of the Sentience of Plants* (Tokyo: The International Institute for Buddhist Studies, 1991) [Studia Philologica Buddhica, Occasional Paper Series VI].

[16] Hakamaya Noriaki, "Shizen-hihan toshite no Bukkyō" (Buddhism as a Criticism of Physis / Natura), in *Komazawa-daigaku Bukkyōgakubu Ronshū* 21 (1990): 380-403. Also "Nihon-jin to animizmu", in *Komazawa-daigaku Bukkyōgakubu Ronshū* 23 (1992): 351-378.

[17] To be fair, Joanna Macy (1991, 198 *ff*) touches on the topic in the later chapters of her book thought not to any significant degree.

[18] Sivaraksa's "True Development" in Hunt-Badiner, ed., *op. cit.*, 169-177 [adapted from a paper delivered to the World Conference on Religion and Peace, Melbourne, Australia, 1989], merely notes the existence of a growing emphasis on ecology within Buddhism but fails to develop any significant connections with social justice.

[19] Cf. J. L. Taylor, *Forest Monks and the Nation State: An Anthropological and Historical Study in North Eastern Thailand* (Singapore: ISEAS, 1993).

platform, and sit on the editorial boards of the same journals.[20] Thomas Berry, for example, is both a Catholic priest, old China hand, and the author of a number of works on Buddhism.[21] It would be incorrect to view this essentially American cooperation as an example of the Christianization of Buddhism any more than it is credible to talk of the Buddhist subversion of Christianity. On the contrary, with eco-spirituality we are, perhaps, witnessing one of the first blooms of environmentalism as a global virtual religion, drawing on the doctrinal and motivational resources available in the two traditions, yet fully independent of any of their institutional structures.

Not surprisingly, the philosophical, and specifically ontological, orientation of eco-spirituality shows considerable uniformity across old religious boundaries. We have already had cause to note the tendency in Christian circles to visualize existence in a thorough-going holistic fashion. The same holds good for Buddhist writers in this second category, as I hope that I have already demonstrated in an earlier publication.[22] To give a flavor of the extreme holism demonstrated by *the material,* Brown, in an essay on the *ālayavijñāna / tathāgatagarbha* doctrine as a sufficient basis for a Buddhist environmental ethic, argues that:

> An adequate environmental ethic must be grounded upon a cosmology capable of rendering the universe as a coherent whole in which human consciousness is an intrinsic self-expression of that larger reality...Such a cosmology and attendant ethic is indicated by the *Ratnagotravibhāga*'s general analysis of tathāgata...the inherent tendency of tathāgata to know itself as the perfectly pure essence, the Suchness of all things, embryonically moves toward perfect self-realization as the one universal reality, or dharmakāya.[23]

Similar arguments have been offered by those who aim to use the Huayan doctrine of the mutual interpenetration of all things for a similar purpose. The intention here is to show that since all things are interrelated we should act in a spirit of reverence towards everything. However, the category of "all things" includes insecticides, totalitarian regimes and nuclear weapons, and the

---

[20] For example, Matthew Fox, an ex-Dominican, officially silenced by the Vatican in 1991, and now an Episcopalian Canon of Grace Cathedral, San Francisco, has co-organized seminars oriented around eco-spiritual themes with Joanna Macy, professor of Philosophy and Religion at the California Institute of Integral Studies, and writer with a long-standing interest and involvement in the Sri Lankan, Buddhist inspired, rural development, *Sarvodaya* movement [cf. n. 40 *infra*].

[21] Cf. Thomas M. Berry, *Religions of India: Hinduism, Yoga and Buddhism* (Chambersburg, PA: Anima Publications, 1992); and his *Buddhism* (Chambersburg, PA: Animal Publications, 1989).

[22] Ian Harris, "Causation and Telos: The Problem of Buddhist Environmental Ethics," *Journal of Buddhist Ethics* 1 (1994): 46-59.

[23] *Op. cit.,* 131-132.

argument possesses some obvious problems. In fact, it suffers from being rather vacuous from a moral perspective.

Ethics has traditionally sought to arrive at judgments about those states of affairs that are valuable and those that are not. Unless generally accepted criteria are employed such that one may arrive at moral judgments, there will be a tendency for everything to appear equally valuable. This is clearly an unsatisfactory state of affairs. J. S. Mill makes much the same point in his attempt to undermine the classical doctrine of natural law. If the *ius naturale* implies a conception of nature as "the sum of all phenomena, together with the causes which produce them" [which it does in our case], then "there is no mode of acting that is not conformable to nature in this sense of the term."[24] As such, there is little difference between saying "all things are equally valuable" and holding to the proposition that "everything is devoid of value." If we now return to eco-spirituality and to its central intuition, we will remember that holism was invoked in order to prove the inherent value to all beings. In the light of what has been said, much still needs to be done to establish this in a fully satisfactory manner. By way of an aside, it is worth noting that both Buddhist and Christian eco-spiritualities owe a considerable debt to the deep ecology movement, which also, incidentally, flourishes on the western seaboard of North America. Critical appraisal of the axioms of deep ecology also reveal a major difficulty associated with the concept of radical holism.[25]

Before leaving the subject of eco-spirituality we should note another potential problem, this time arising from within the Buddhist context itself. Brown and others come dangerously close to overturning the radically pluralist ontology on which early Buddhism seems to have been based. By dissolving the apparent distinctiveness of entities within a realm of over-arching and total interrelatedness signified by Mahayanist terms like *tathatā*, these scholars move close to a rejection of the basic Buddhist insight into *anattā*. This is, in fact, the reason that Hakamaya[26] [category 4, above] cannot admit the possibility of a purely Buddhist environmental ethic. In his view, any attempt to posit a hypostatized and unified reality as the source from which all particularities emerge is ultimately non-Buddhist for it is in fundamental conflict with the doctrine of non-self (*anattā*). He terms this error *dhātuvāda*. It has to be said that Hakamaya places very high levels of restriction on those manifestations of the tradition that can be regarded as authentic.[27] However, the insistence odes ensure

---

[24] John Stuart Mill, *Three Essays on Religion: Nature, the Utility of Religion and Theism*, Third Edition (London: Longmans, Green and Co., 1885), 15.

[25] Cf. Sylvan, Richard, "A Critique of Deep Ecology," Part I, *Radical Philosophy* 40 (1984): 2-12; Part II, *Radical Philosophy* 41 (1985): 10-22. In particular, cf. Part II, 10 *f.*

[26] For a survey of Hakamaya's writings relating to this matter, cf. Swanson, Paul, ""Zen is not Buddhism." Recent Japanese Critiques of Buddha-Nature", *Numen* XL.2 (1993): 115-149.

[27] This point is made by Schmithausen, *Nature* (1991), 56, in fact, the rejection of *dhātuvāda* ruled out most forms of East Asian Buddhism.

that causation along the flow of tune, the Abhidhammic; understanding of dependent origination (*pratītyasamutpāda*), another cardinal Buddhist doctrine, is conserved as a workable concept. In fact, the deconstruction of causation understood in this way, one of the tendencies inherent in extreme holism, holds very considerable and negative consequences from the ethical perspective.[28]

Our final eco-religious type is of the eco-traditionalist variety. I would not wish to suggest for a moment that Lambert Schmithausen shares the same attitude as the conservative Christians[29] mentioned earlier. Having said this, it is the case that his attempt to uncover an authentically Buddhist environmental ethic proceeds from a re-evaluation of textual resources. This was clearly a feature of the eco-spiritualist type, although in this case textual studies are generally conducted after intuitions about the Buddhist conception of the natural world have crystallized. Texts may then be assembled to give confirmation to the original insight. Schmithausen proceeds in a far more cautious way. He is always anxious to avoid the charge that he is imposing extraneous motives onto the results of his historical investigations.[30] As such, his method involves an uncovering of textual hints concerning an ancient past, so that the earliest strands of the Buddhist tradition may be re-established. Thus, in a discussion of the possibility of attributing sentience to plants, he concludes that the earliest strata -of Buddhism, "where the border-line status of plants [i.e., between sentience and insentience] served to reduce inhibitions against injuring them ... should now be introduced to re-establish them."[31] In another article, this time focusing on the rather negative portrayal of the status of animals in canonical sources, Schmithausen suggests "that in an age where establishing ecological ethics has become imperative [such teachings] ... ought to be de-dogmatized by being relegated to their specific didactic contexts."[32] In other words, he does not wish to avoid, in any straightforward way, the difficulties presented by the textual tradition. His endeavor requires the proper contextualization of primary materials. This seems to me to be the hallmark of a properly conservative method that avoids the temptations associated with the modernizing tendencies present in eco-spirituality. There is no invention of tradition here.

In this connection it will be as well to mention the tendency in some quarters to idealize the ecological credentials of pre-modern Buddhist cultures. Both western scholars and Buddhist spokesmen from the Asian heartlands of the tradition[33] have engaged in this activity from time to time. I have already noted[34]

---

[28] Cf. Harris (1994), *op.cit.*

[29] It should be noted here that Beyer (*op. cit.*, 218) admits that eco-traditionalism in the Christian context reflects an "attempt to liberalize [Christian] groups that are generally more theologically conservative."

[30] Cf. *Sentience* (1991), p. 1, n. 1.

[31] *Ibid.,* 106.

[32] Lambert Schmithausen, "How can Ecological Ethics be Established in Early Buddhism?" [unpublished article], 22.

[33] Some of the statements in the Buddhist declaration at Assisi express this highly Romantic attitude, cf. Ven. Lungrig Naingyal Rinpoche, "The Buddhist

that in general, such arguments remain to be supported by hard historical evidence and, in any case, the claim that pre-modern societies were ecologically aware in the modern sense is a clear example of anachronism.[35] Nevertheless, it must be recognized that this is regarded as a perfectly valid exposition of the ecological merits of Buddhism in the eyes of its proponents even if, as Huber observes in his clear-headed treatment of the Tibetan evidence, "we should, as scholars, be careful not to distort the historical and ethnographic record of those societies in order to strengthen our case."[36] Given the evidence, it seems reasonable to conclude that we may include both textual re-examination and the more romantic quest for cultural examples of ecological rectitude as both part of the category of eco-traditionalism.

Having worked through our threefold typology it seems that three of the four original Buddhist categories have been accommodated, admittedly in a rather messy fashion. Only the first group of writings on the environment has failed to be admitted into the scheme. Works of this kind often adopt an inspirational tone that proceeds from an assumption, generally unsupported by any textual, historical or cultural evidence, that the compatibility of Buddhism and environmental ethics is a self-evident fact. As such, no further justification is needed. In fact, such an attitude may be observed as a sub-theme in much of the material already covered, with the exception of Schmithausen and Hakamaya. In so far as any argument is employed to support this view, it goes something like this: a positive orientation towards environmental matters is a good thing; Buddhism itself is a good thing; therefore, Buddhism supports and is compatible with ecological activism. I shall term this fourth type of response eco-apologetics. The motivation -underlying Buddhist apologetics is not easy to characterize. In my view three ingredients may be at work in the thinking of its proponents, though not necessarily all at the same time.

In the first place, we should be aware of the influential, and still largely unchallenged, assumption of Lynn White Jr.,[37] that the present eco-crisis is

---

Declaration on Nature" in *The Assisi Declarations: Messages on Man and Nature from Buddhism, Christianity, Hinduism, Islam and Judaism* (London: World Wide Fund for Nature, 196), 3-7. Also cf. Yuthok K Gelek, "The Tibetan Perception of the Environment," paper presented to the Sixth Conference of the International Association of Tibetan Studies, Fagernes, Norway, 1992 [quoted in Poul Pedersen, "Nature, Religion and Cultural Identity: The Religious Environmentalist Paradigm," in Arne Kalland and Ole Bruum, eds., *Asian Perceptions of Nature: A Critical Perspective* (London: Curzon Press, 1995), 4-5. The Dalai Lama's own exhortations on the subject take a similar line.

[34] Ian Harris, "How is Environmentalist Buddhism?," *Religion* 21 (1991): 101-114.

[35] Cf. Pedersen, *op. cit.,* 7 *f.*

[36] Toni Huber, "Traditional Environmental Protectionism in Tibet Reconsidered," *Tibet Journal* 16 / 3 (1991): 63-77.

[37] Lynn White, "The Historical Roots of our Ecological Crisis," *Science* 155 (1967): 1203-7. The major criticism of White's thesis has come from Christian theologians who have been anxious to demonstrate the existence of textual resources

                                    Ian Charles Harris

primarily the result of factors that have their roots in the Judeo-Christian worldview, most notably in the idea of man's dominion over nature. White concludes that the correct course for future generations is to turn away from our European religious heritage to embrace those traditions that offer a more positive -view on our inter-relations with the natural world, i.e., to the religions of the East.[38] This is intriguing, not least because White offers very little evidence to support the claim that Eastern modes of religiosity are more eco-friendly. Analysis reveals that the thesis rests on the same romantically uncritical attitudes that we have already discussed with regard to the eco-traditionalist type. True, Asia has in modern times sustained a far lower level of economic activity than the West, but should we conclude that this is the natural consequence of ancient religious ideologies? There are clearly other factors in the equation, and it may be worth noting that the reports of early European travelers, even the most romantic admirers of Asia, often dwell on the very obvious levels of pollution and dirt in the Asian cities to which they otherwise were devoted. Hardly ideal credentials from the ecological perspective!

A second ingredient that undoubtedly plays a role in the crystallization of eco-apologetics: is the growing and increasingly complex nature of intercourse between Christianity and its client faiths, particularly those beyond the boundaries of Europe and North America. I refer to the phenomenon of inter-faith dialogue -- a process, interestingly enough, that parallels eco-religiosity itself in terms of its historical starting point and subsequent development. This is not really surprising, for both reflect, in slightly different ways, globalizing influences. As we have already noted, eco-religiosity has its roots amongst the liberal Christian elites of the 1960s, i.e., precisely the same group that was in the vanguard of the dialogic endeavor. Having admitted this, there can be little surprise in the fact that the eco-crisis should figure as a major agenda item in meetings between Christians and representatives of other faiths, particularly in the situation in which theologians, in part as a reaction to the challenge of White and his supporters, were working out their own specific responses to the problem. Faced with the task of responding to an agenda of this kind, representatives of all traditions will inevitably speak with one voice. To break ranks on an issue that appears so crucial to the survival of the planet is inconceivable. No religious tradition, indeed no system of thought or culture, is likely to be in favor of an impending environmental catastrophe. To indicate

---

within the Christian tradition that support an environmental ethic. Robin Attfield's work springs to mind in this context. Very little criticism has emanated from the quarters that have benefited the most from the thesis, i.e., from Hindus, Buddhists, etc.

[38] It is perhaps unsurprising that White's implicit "hierarchy" of religious traditions coincides with the outlook of many religiously active people in the West, and particularly in North America today where Buddhism is becoming more and more the religion of choice. This, in turn, helps to explain the ecological currents at work in counter-culturally influenced Western Buddhism, cf. *supra* the discussion of eco-spirituality.

otherwise would be an act of gross folly. Nevertheless, it must be appreciated that predictions of eco-catastrophe have their origins elsewhere. They are essentially scientific,[39] although scientists have often, and this is noteworthy, sought allies from outside their own discipline, even from the ranks of their traditional opponents, the followers of religion. On the conceptual and symbolic levels at least, the problem of the environment is scientific, not religious, though an interface between the two competing interpretations of the world may, and is, being constructed perhaps, in part, because of the deep historical roots of our romantic attachment to the world. In one sense, then, the reason that unanimity exists amongst religious dialogue partners is that the matter under discussion is essentially secular, even if it is, from time to time, dressed up in a religious garb. As such, the divisions that may be revealed in the discussion of more central matters are masked. This is not the only mechanism at work on such occasions. Simple courtesy, the lack of time to consider the implications of some of the declarations made at such events, and even occasionally, a straightforward desire to curry favor in influential circles may also contribute to agreement, particularly when the point at issue does not pose any obvious threat to the doctrinal integrity of the respective traditions. It is not beyond the bound of possibility that factors of this kind have influenced the views expounded by Buddhist representatives in inter-faith dialogue.

Use of phrases like "curry favor" may suggest a certain cynicism in the mind of this writer. I hope to show that this need not be the case. In order to do so, let us turn to our third and final ingredient -- *realpolitik*. Buddhism, in its ancient heartlands, has been under threat from a variety of forces including modernism, totalitarianism, tourism, etc. Responsible leaders of such communities may be required to look beyond their traditional sources of support in order to protect the way of life of the people they represent. Tibetan Buddhism is an obvious example. It is difficult to image that Tibetan communities in exile in India could flourish successfully without support from the government of India, other foreign donor countries, and a variety of charitable non-government organizations. In particular, the inevitable under-employment in refugee communities, e.g., amongst Tibetans in India, is a well-documented fact. Now, significant financial and moral support is available to create employment in areas considered worthwhile by international donors and, not unsurprisingly given the global dimension of environmentalism, ecologically beneficial projects of rural development occupy a high priority in the minds of aid administrators and their political masters. In the last few years the Tibetan government in exile has initiated a program of environmental awareness with a

---

[39] In this context, we should beware of the naive assumption, an assumption strongly promoted by many scientists themselves, that science somehow describes nature "as it is." Science as a symbolic system of interpretation, in this sense, shares many of the characteristics of traditional religious explanations of the world. In this connection cf. Elizabeth A.R. Bird, "The Social Construction of Nature: Theoretical Approaches to the History of Environmental Problems," *Environmental Review* 11.4 (1987): 255-64.

specific emphasis placed on education. To this end teaching resources for school children are being prepared and a number of practical projects have been sponsored. The program has the blessing of H. H. Dalai Lama who now regularly takes the opportunity to publicize his environmental credentials on the international stage.[40] At the time of writing I only have anecdotal evidence that the program is supported by international aid funds,[41] though the case of the *Sarvodaya* movement of A. T. Ariyaratna in Sri Lanka[42] indicates that this would not be the first time a Buddhist-inspired environmental initiative has been sponsored in such a way. How are we to view this from the Buddhist perspective?

Under the special circumstances of exile, leaders such as the Dalai Lama will be required to raise funds, often from within that same international aid sector, to ensure viable levels of economic and cultural activity for their people. Employment and cultural and environmental enrichment are likely to follow from the injection of significant sums of money, and it can be argued any change wrought by such investment will not be in fundamental conflict with the best interests of Buddhism. However, there is a fine distinction to be maintained between activities that fall into this category on the one hand and those that flow from the central insights of Buddhism itself on the other. In the present case we can speak of a general mutuality of interests between donor and recipient. Each benefits, in their own way, from the arrangement. The receipt of aid for development work should therefore be distinguished from the genuine expression of authentically Buddhist traditions, and this is the reason that I employ the term *realpolitik* in the context of Tibetan eco-apologetics. It is not because I believe that anything sinister or underhanded is involved, but merely that there may be a very subtle motivation to confuse the two categories, i.e., to make the claim that an environmental ethic is central to the Buddhist scheme of thing when it is, in fact, a peripheral, though clearly important, issue.

---

[40] I expect to be criticized for this statement. In defense, may I add that the comment is devoid of any personal animosity -- the Dalai Lama is clearly a man of the highest integrity. Nevertheless, as an international figure he must face in two directions at once, i.e., to his Buddhist countrymen on the one hand and towards influential international elites on the other. An enthusiastic endorsement of the contemporary agenda of the second group, with its emphasis on the global nature of the world's problems, may be the most effective means of eliciting their support for the Tibetan people's fight to regain their homeland.

[41] I hope to have the necessary documentation by the time of the conference. Reference is also made to a joint Thai Tibetan project into the perception of nature under the patronage of H. H. Dalai Lama in Sivaraksa, *op. cit.,* 175.

[42] For details of the movement, cf. Joanna Macy, *Dharma and Development: Religion as a Resource in the Sarvodaya Self-Help Movement* (West Hartford, CN: Dumarian Press), 1983. For a more critical treatment, cf. Richard F. Gombrich and Gananath Obeyesekere, *Buddhism Transformed: Religious Change in Sri Lanka* (Delhi: Motilal Banarsidass, 1990), 245 *f.* It also appears that internationally sponsored activities of this kind are under way in Thailand, cf. J. L. Taylor, n. 18 *supra.*

It is now in order for us to draw together the various strands of the foregoing discussion. Buddhist ecological ethics, even at this early stage in its development, is not a monolithic entity. Three reasonably clear-cut forms exist, i.e., an eco-spiritualist type, an eco-traditionalist type, and an eco-apologist type, though it must be added that there may be considerable overlap between the three in practice. A fourth category, concerned with matters of eco justice, may be in the process of formation, although how far this will crystallize remains to be seen. In the view of the present author all present some difficulties, particularly with regard to their level of philosophical coherence; however, I hope that this brief sketch will stimulate further debate. With this in mind, I shall finish by raising three inter-related queries:

1. Does it make sense to speak of tradition specific eco-religiosities any longer?
2. What impact, if any, has the agenda of Western liberal elites had on the development of an ecologically aware Buddhism?
3. Is there an environmental ethic that stems from authentically Buddhist sources?

CHAPTER 22

KOREAN BUDDHIST LAND-WISDOM IN THEORY AND PRACTICE: THE CASE OF PINE BROAD TEMPLE AGAINST MODERN DEVELOPMENT

Jae-ryong Shim

1. Mountain Temple and the Korean Seon Buddhism

1. 1 The Korean Buddhist Monastic Landscape

To discuss the relevant attitude of the Korean Buddhist monks, as well as the laypersons toward nature or the natural environment represented by the mountainous terrain of the Korean peninsula, we may as well take stock of the general landscape of the Korean Buddhist mountain-temple compound. Then we will embark upon our journey to Korean Buddhist temples having historically alleged the traditional love of nature, coupled with Chinese Taoist occult geo-science, namely, the technique of reading the directions of wind and water for the proper allocation of residence of both the living and the dead.

Most of the small scale Korean Buddhist temple compounds are demarcated by the one pillar gate (*ilju-mun*) at the front entrance, which carries the name plaque. Climbing one steep mountain after another, and finding the one pillar gate surrounded by the subtle fragrance of incense, a traveling Buddhist practitioner or any tourist may finally feel relieved, taking a deep breath, to rest at the end of his difficult hike. A short distance from the first gate stands the gate of the Four Heavenly Kings (*sacheonwang-mun*) marking another entrance to the temple precinct proper. At the four ferocious looking *deva*s, even infidels would tremble and deeply bow down before them, truly repenting their past deeds.

But they will soon be relieved to find within the inner court a lecture hall (*beop-dang*) where they are always welcome to listen to the Buddha dharma's universal compassion and wisdom for the suffering beings. Nearby at a monastic quarter they can quench their thirst with fresh water, or a hot vegetarian dish may be served if their visit to the temple coincides with mealtime. If also, they are fortunate enough to stay overnight at the quarter, they will be awakened at three o'clock in the morning by the sonorous bell ringing and deep resounding drum beating at the bell tower (*jong-gak*) usually across from the main hall of the Great Hero (*daeung-jeon*) where the main hero Buddha Sākyamuni , other Buddhas and bodhisattva are enshrined. Most regular rituals are held in this main hall of worship.

To the left of the main hall of worship, the Hall of Judgment with the Ten Kings of Hell and the deceased soul saving Bodhisattva Kṣitigarbha (*myeongbu-jeon*) stands for the bereaved family members to console their deceased parents and loved ones. To the right side of the court is another Hall with 500 *arhats* (*nahan-jeon*) which accommodates Buddha's chief disciples for the monks' as well as lay people's adoration and emulation. At the center of the inner court is erected a pagoda, in which either the Buddha's or eminent monks' relics are preserved. On special occasions like the Buddha's birthday or the Buddha's *parinirvāṇa* (death), a splendid ceremony is performed with thousands of Buddhist monks and laypersons attending, chanting, singing, and dancing around the pagoda.

Behind the main hall a small shrine for the Mountain Deity or the Seven Dipper Stars of Taoist Pantheon (*sansin-gak* or *chilseong-gak*) is usually hidden from the visitors' view. People never forget to pay tribute to the mountain deity, upon whose dominion the Buddhist temple stands. They also pray for longevity and secular success of their family members at the Taoist Pantheon. After all Korean Buddhist temple complex still retains physical evidence for its remarkable process of syncretic naturalization and adaptation to indigenous belief systems.[1]

The Pine Broad Temple of our direct concern, however, as one of the main monastic compounds in Korea, does not have the above-mentioned shrines for mountain and/or Taoist deities. Instead the Pine Broad Temple is replete with its own traditional array of buildings, where past masters and patriarchs of Korean Buddhist Seon Order had practiced meditation and preached Buddha dharma. Hence, the befitting title for this temple as the Saṅgha-jewel.

It is especially proud of the Sixteen Masters, whose portraits are hung in the National Preceptors' Hall (*kuksajon*). The Hall of Dharma Lecture (*seolbeop-jeon*) standing side by side with the Society of Cultivating Seon Meditation Hall (*suseon-sa*) high above and separated with a somewhat elevated terrace from the hall of main hero, seems to symbolize the conspicuously higher authority of the Korean Son patriarchal tradition, which originated seven hundred years ago during the Goryeo dynasty and is still practiced. Ordinary people are prohibited from the Society, where resident Seon monks are always practicing meditation

---

[1] Sometimes another third shrine for the solitary saint (*Dokseong-gak*) is seen along with the above two shrines. Often these three shrines are merged into one single building, in which the three deities are enshrined together.

and inquiring about the *hwadu* (Zen stories). No wonder that the Pine Broad Temple enjoys an unceasing prosperity and fame due to their efforts. In addition to the professional institutes for meditation and lecture for ordained monks, the Pine Broad Temple is currently running a popular short-term practice session every summer for ordinary lay persons, teaching the pure gospel of the Buddha to hundreds and thousands astray souls in the cities, giving them a temporary retreat from hectic city life, and above all, instilling in them the importance of serenity and tranquility acquired from the silent lectures of rocks, trees, streams, fresh air, birds, and animals which live in the mountainous natural environment. Mountain-temples are, in short, the essential sources for spiritual replenishment for the 'hungry and tired' city-dwellers.

Rick Fields, a narrative historian of Buddhism in America, aptly remarks:

> Yet in all the Buddhist countries of the world, it is *only in the still remote mountains of Korea* (or more precisely, South Korea) that life of the original Chan community continues to this day.[2]

It is no wonder that virtually in every corner of the mountainous Korean peninsula is built either a large Buddhist monastic complex or a small hermitage that maintains the original Seon spirit. We may, however, wonder why only South Korea still maintains the original Chan life of strict discipline and spiritual poverty, not influenced by the urbanization and industrialization of global modernization process.

From the comparative perspective, one may say that among the four Asian countries heavily influenced by the Zen Buddhist tradition, Japanese Zen had already lost its original vitality due to its relatively early industrialization and moreover, probably still earlier secularization process of Japanese Buddhism, Japanese Buddhist monks marry and have their succeeding sons run the temple by a hereditary system. Meanwhile Chinese and Vietnamese Zen, as well as other Buddhist traditions, have recently been destroyed by anti-religious communist ideology and practice.

But another explanation is still required as to why in Korea alone, Seon Buddhism has maintained a special affiliation with deep mountains and scenic spots of natural beauty. Keeping this question in mind, we are ready for the historical journey reflecting upon and assessing the uniquely Korean phenomena of "mountain temples."

1.2. Mountain and the Korean Seon Buddhism: A Historical Reflection

From the time of introduction to Korea during the end of Unified Silla dynasty and the beginning of Goryeo kingdom, Korean Seon Buddhism had

---

[2] Rick Fields, *How the Swans Came to the Lake: A Narrative History of Buddhism in America* (Boulder, CO: Shambala, 1981), 351. Quoted with this author's emphasis added.

found its monastic grounds at the so-called Nine Mountains, remote from the capital center of political power, for Seon attracted favors from the rebellious, local lords around the provincial mountains at the downfall of the Unified Silla.

But this initial affiliation of Korean Seon with mountains had yet to be supplemented by another important ideological underpinning by the geomancer-Buddhist Seon monk Doseon (827-898). Without his geomantic theories and practice, we can hardly explain the idiosyncratic affiliation of Korean Buddhism with mountains. Doseon is solely responsible for the major design of the Buddhist monastic landscapes in the entire Korean peninsula.

Doseon (827-898), born at Yeongam County in Jeolla Province, trained in the Mahāyāna Hwaeom Doctrine and later turned to Seon attracted many monks and lay disciples[3]. His chief contribution, however, lies in his propagation of geomancy in relation to the foundation of the Goryeo kingdom. Doseon's geomantic technique analyzed, according to the Chinese Kiangsi Method, the surface features of a region and was used more in identifying locates for building palaces and government offices than in choosing sites for graves.

Doseon, in addition, created two novel geomantic theories worthy of our examination, for they assume a character quite distinct from that of China and because his theories became widespread and exerted an immense power during the Goryeo dynasty down to the present day Korea. The theory, *jigi soewang seol*, states that vital energy of the earth flourishes as well as declines, meaning that in the lie of the land there is prosperity or decline, auspiciousness and inauspiciousness. Extending this theory it could easily be interpreted to mean that by choosing the auspicious locale for building houses, capital cities, tombs, etc., individuals or the country could prosper or decline in prosperity. Another complementary theory, *bibo satap seol*, states that topographical defects could be remedied; locations with weak earth veins or inauspicious mountain forms can be artificially cured of their defects by constructing a temple or erecting stūpas. This attempt to combine geomancy and Buddhism was very natural at that time because Buddhism was the state religion of Goryeo [4].

Wang Geon (r. 918-943), the founder of the Goryeo dynasty, believed in Doseon's geomantic theory. Influenced further by Doseon's divination of the auspicious topographical features of Gaegyeong (present Gaeseong, near

---

[3] For a complete biography of Doseon, see Choe Yujeong's Stele Inscription (1150) at Jade Dragon Monastery [*Dong Munseon* 117:18b-22b; *Chosen kinseki sōran* 1:560-561].

[4] Geomancy, already accepting the yin-yang and five elements theories, aligned with the Buddhist notion of "wholesome root produces wholesome fruit." Hence, Doseon's novel theory stated that the erection of monasteries and stūpas could alter the geomantic situation. At times, allied with prognostication texts, geomancy also acquired a revolutionary character, heralding the coming of a new utopian world. With the coming of rational Neo-Confucianism in the Joseon dynasty, the geomantic practice of selecting an auspicious tomb site for ancestors never lost its influence. The ugly mountainous terrain pockmarked by gravesites in the present Korean peninsula is a legacy of geomancy.

Pammunjeom at De-Militarized Zone) as the region blocking wind, and of Seogyeong (present Pyeongyang, the capital of North Korea) as the region acquiring water, Wang Geon moved the capital of the new kingdom from Gyeongju at the south-eastern comer to Gaegyeong at the center of the Korean peninsula. But in fact Wang Geon's political philosophy was eclectic, subscribing not only to geomancy but also to such diverse sources as the mountain spirits, Buddhism, and Confucian thought, etc. He had yet referred to geomancy in three out of the Ten Injunctions which he issued for the sake of posterity. We take the three articles for our critical examination in relation to the Korean Buddhist practice of building mountain-temples.

> Second Article: Construction of all temples must conform to Form and Configuration of Doseon's geomantic theory. Doseon said that temples built at places not designated by him would drain the land of its virtue, and in due process, cripple the dynasty. I am worried that future kings, princes, princesses and courtiers might build Wondang (temples for fulfillment of wishes). In the late Silla dynasty, many new temples were constructed, leading to a decline of the land's virtue and the dynasty's collapse. Posterity must take it as a warning.

> Fifth Article: By virtue of the invisible help of mountains and rivers of the Three Han, I accomplished the great task of founding the state of Goryeo. The western capital (Pyeongyang) is the base of the land vein of our country because of its harmonious water virtue. Peace and eternal prosperity of the dynasty require that kings visit the western capital in the middle months of every season (in the 2nd, 5th, 8th and 11th month) and stay there for more than 100 days.

> Eighth Article: Beyond Geum River in the south of Charyeong mountain range, mountain forms and land configurations are inauspicious. Adverse geomantic locale has also affected people's character. If people living in that region are employed in government positions or enter the court as a result of matrimonial alliances, they will prove to be a source of chaos and conflict. As they resent the unification of the land, they will assassinate the king and hold aloft the banner of rebellion.

One can easily interpret that Wang Geon utilized Doseon's geomantic theories in the 2nd article with the objective of strengthening the economic foundation of the state by restricting the number of temples. Wang Geon must also have had intended to obtain popular support by the synthesis of the then popular religion of Buddhism and geomancy, without, at the same time losing a chance to scrutinize the mushroom-growth of temples at the new capital Gaegyeong, the western capital Seogyeong, as well as at other geopolitical strategic places.

In the fifth article, geomantic theory was used as a major political objective; it consolidated a strategic base at Seogyeong to launch military operations against the northern territory. Geomancy in the Goryeo dynasty was so central in the royal politics that all historical references to geomancy pertain to the problem of the site of King's temporary residences.

The eighth article, proscribing employment of people from Latter Baekje, seems to express Wang Geon's grudge against them because of their long rivalry. However, his political application of geomantic theory has had tremendous repercussions on the present Korean people; it boosts a discord rather than concord, and parochial conflict rather than national harmony among the Korean populace.

2. The Case of the Pine Broad Temple against Modern Development

During the 1980's[5] the Korean Song Gwang Sa (Pine Broad Temple) Buddhist community waged a war against two fronts; one against the fever of modernization and another, against the ever increasing number of modern nomadic hordes, i.e., city-dwelling tourists and garbage-makers. The war is still going on under various names. This is an interim report and an assessment.

While the Pine Broad Temple community was engaged in the tenth project of reconstructing the main hall of worship, relocating and renovating some of the old, dilapidated buildings in their monastic compound, it was taken by surprise to hear that the government's economic planning board decided to drill an underground tunnel behind the Jogye Mountain at the foot of which the temple complex was situated. The underground tunnel was to channel the massive water reservoir of the Juam. Dam to Gwangju City (the capital of the southern Jeolla Province), to provide the ever-thirsty citizens with abundant, fresh tap water. In order for the massive water reservoir to be built for agricultural and industrial purposes, a large number of resident farmers had to be relocated, enormous number of land tracts had to go underwater, and long meandering highways opened to an elevated terrain. Traditionally the farmers primarily consisted of lay Buddhist supporters and they suffered the plight of leaving their homeland.

In the meantime, the Pine Broad Temple Buddhist community also had to suffer, for its income would dwindle due to the overall industrialization, concomitant with the urban migration of the farmers, resulting in a decrease of rural population. Through the newly built highway hordes of tourists, instead of farmers, would migrate to the provincial park's Jogye Mountain Resort, which lies adjacent to the Pine Broad Temple monastic compound, harassing and disturbing the serene Buddhist sanctuary. The underground hydroduct being inimical to the untouchable, sacred terrestrial formation of the Jogye Mountain

---

[5] The modernization process in Korea began during the 1960's, initiated by the military junta. But a massive industrialization project was implemented mostly in the south-eastern part of the Korean peninsula, while the south-western part of Korea, where the Song Gwang Sa is located, was to be included in the modern development project starting from the 1980's.

according to the geomantic configuration, the highway would also irrevocably and visibly damage the Buddhist monastic sanctuary's landscape.

Monks at the temple were naturally alarmed at the forthcoming change of the monastic landscape. They held a general assembly of all senior and junior monks belonging to the treasured Saṅgha-jewel[6] monastery (*seungbo sachal*) the Song Gwang Sa. Collectively they mobilized every possible means of preventing the massive modernization project of the government, as well as protecting the integrity of the Buddhist sanctuary's geomantic configuration.

I do not have the time and intention of recording in detail the protracted development of the Song Gwang Sa's confrontation with the government's modernization project.[7] It suffices us to report that eventually the Buddhist community had partially succeeded in relocating the hydroduct far away from the previously determined site, but at the cost of allowing a highway to be built leading up to the tourist village which was close enough within the distance where you can hear your friend calling from the monastic compound. Ironically, the Pine Broad Temple community welcomed the opening of the highway, while vehemently rejecting the underground hydroduct.

They were partially successful, to the extent that the integrity of the geomantic configuration of the Pine Broad Temple was kept safe and unharmed by their petitioning to the government's economic planning board to relocate the underground hydroduct far from the monastic sanctuary. We may as yet assess the Korean Buddhist allegiance to the Taoist geomantic land wisdom as a whole. And the effect of the newly built highway is yet to be seen in the ensuing years, for an ever increasing number of tourists throng to the Buddhist temple complex, thereby threatening the natural habitat, disturbing the environmental equilibrium, and ultimately disrupting the uniquely serene and tranquil atmosphere of the practicing Buddhist monks in Korea and from abroad, even though the tourists may add some additional income for the community.[8] We have no way of

---

[6] In Korean Buddhist tradition, the three Buddhist religious symbols, i.e., Buddha, Dharma and Sangha, are represented by three temples. The Tongdo-sa Temple at Yangsan represents the Buddha-jewel, for there the teeth-relics of the Buddha Sākyamuni are enshrined. The Haein-sa Temple at Hapcheon houses the Dharma-jewel, for the National Treasure, Eighty-Thousand Pieces of Wood Block Printing Tripitaka (*palman daejanggyeong*) are kept. And finally, the Songgwang-sa Temple, the Sangha-jewel, which is famous for the harmonious congregation of practicing monks, which originated from the Society of Meditation and Wisdom (*Jeonghye-sa*). This Society dates from the 12th century Goryeo dynasty, founded by the National Preceptor Bojo Jinul (1158-1210), who was the actual founder of the present Korean celibate Buddhist Monks' Jogye Order.

[7] The concrete and minute records of the Song Gwang Sa's confrontation and eventual success will make, I believe, an interesting case for a careful investigation for concerned environmentalists, developers and social scientists.

[8] Tourists are required to pay a nominal fee for entering the temple complex in addition to their payment for entering and utilizing the provincial park. But the entrance fee is divided by both the temple and the government Bureau for Management of Cultural

ascertaining and providing evidence for the genuine attitude of the resident monks of the Song Gwang Sa temple toward the ancient land wisdom contained in the geomancy. It is, however, certain that most of the Korean Buddhist 'mountain-temples'[9] were built according to the general geomantic plan of the 9th century Korean Seon (Zen) Buddhist monk Doseon,[10] exceptions being a few urban temples built in the two capitals of the Unified Silla and Goryeo kingdom, namely, Gyeongju and Gaeseong.

3. A Tentative Assessment: The Case of the Song Gwang Sa Buddhist Temple in terms of Global Healing

Nobody in present day Korea seriously and consciously subscribes to the geomantic theories invented by Doseon and utilized by Wang Geon a thousand years ago, although some pious sons still invite a geomancer to determine their ancestor's grave site. But the physical existence of the Buddhist mountain-temples behooves us to re-examine the ancient geomantic land wisdom in the age of environmental consciousness and global healing.

Now we ask: what possible lessons can we learn from the Pine Broad Temple case against the massive modernization project motivated by economic profit, which completely disregards the Buddho-geomantic tradition of Korean mountain-temples?

Diverting the underground hydroduct far away from the monastic sanctuary by appealing to the geomantic theory, the Pine Broad monastic community also constantly reaches out to the cities, operating all sorts of propagation centers (*pogyo-dang*) at major urban centers. Some monks have organized groups of reading Buddhist scriptures (*gyeongjeon ikgi moim*) exhorting Buddhists, as well as non-Buddhists to read the gospel of the Buddha in the vernacular. Some other monks run a meditation center in the midst of the metropolitan area for ordinary people. Still other monks work in the suburban areas promoting organic farming without the use of chemical fertilizers and insecticides.

In short, Korean Seon Buddhist monks are not solitary recluses in the deep mountain sides, meditating only on the 'illogical, nonsense stories,' but they are very much active in every facet of the contemporary modern world, fully

---

Properties. Still, the Buddhist temple community benefits in terms of financial income after the traditional fanner-supporter group had left for urban areas.

[9] Most of the famous Korean Buddhist temples are located deep in the mountains far away from the social and cultural centers of urban cities. Hence, the usual nomenclature is mountain-temple, *sansa*. The Korean Buddhist temples nested deep at the foot of these mountain ranges starkly contrast the Western religious landscape: one can see a towering cathedral pompously piercing the sky all in the artificially planned urban centers.

[10] Doseon's contribution to Korean Buddhism is conspicuous in terms of his effort to propagate the geomantic land wisdom in connection with his helping Wang Geon, the founder of the Goryeo kingdom. Hence, Doseon is supposed to be the progenitor of the Korean geomantic theory and practice.

conscious of their responsibilities in participating and engag the global problem of environmental destruction as well as nature in harmony with human needs. Buddhism, especially S Korea, is never expected to escape from the urgent problem The modern form of suffering, they claim, can be cured original insight into the interdependence of all things: man, r Keeping the five fundamental Buddhist precepts alone ca effectively cure the insatiable human greed -- that of environm natural resources and super-international marketing of consume another element of Korean S Buddhism urges us to turn our att existence of mountain-temples in Korea: it fights against modernization projects, protects the geomantically auspicio monastic compound securely nestled in the serene mountain sid developers' bulldozer ever encroaching and distorting our natur

The unique geographical location of the Korean Bud represented by the Song Gwang Sa at Suncheon, Jeolla Nam render us an idiosyncratic land wisdom by which we can pr environmental problem we face in the modern world. It is our analyze all the possible implications of the Buddho-geoma practice of land use toward our common goal of global healin need to sort out further the economic, political, spiritual and issues of geomantic land use, this author would like to finis quoting a traditional Korean poem.

> At the end of ten years' work
> I have a hut with a straw roof.
> The clear wind lives in one half,
> and the bright moon in the other.
> Therefore no space to invite the hills---
> they will have to stay outside.
>   by Song Sun (1493-1583)[11]

Listening to this poem, even the visiting tourists may find in temples of Korea, a silent lesson of caring for the natural en "letting the hills to stay outside") without human meddling.

---

[11] English translation is Richard Rutt's from *The Bamboo Grove. Introduction to Sijo* (Berkeley: University of California Press, 1971), 152. having no association with geomancy, we can glimpse the essence of the A attitude toward Nature, and caring for the natural environment untouched b greed. The author of this *sijo* was not a Buddhist recluse, but a mature polit the government of the Joseon dynasty.

CHAPTER 23

SOME WOMEN OF THE *GAṆḌAVYŪHA-SŪTRA*

Rebecca Clare

1. Introduction

In this paper I propose to consider several of the female characters in the *Gaṇḍavyūha-sūtra* (henceforth GVS) in the light of the wider philosophical concerns of the text. The sutra develops the idea that the *dharmadhātu* (the realm of ultimate reality) and the *lokadhātu* (the worldly or conventional realm) are the same, and presents a markedly non-dualistic metaphysic within which there is no ontological basis for discrimination against women on the grounds either that they are somehow 'other' than men or that they have close links with the natural, *samsaric* world, and are therefore not especially suited to the spiritual life. It has been pointed out elsewhere[1] that dualistic traditions (i.e., traditions that assert a strong distinction between the secular and the sacred, the material and the spiritual) are more likely than non-dualistic (or 'integrative') ones to present negative portrayals of women, and indeed there is a wealth of Buddhist literature which seems to support this suggestion. Where a wide divide is proposed between *saṁsāra* and *nirvāṇa*, or between the lay life and the monastic life, it is often the case that women are associated with the *samsaric* and the lay life rather than with the spiritual and the monastic life.[2] However, the GVS is an example of a text which collapses the metaphysical distinction between the sacred and the secular, the lay life and the monastic life, and which,

---

[1] Carol Christ, for example, has commented that: "As women begin to question their historic subordination, they also challenge the adequacy of the dualistic, hierarchical and oppositional ways of viewing the world ... women's quest is for a wholeness in which the oppositions between body and soul, nature and spirit or freedom, rationality and emotion are overcome." See C. P. Christ, *Diving Deep and Surfacing* (Boston: Beacon Press, 1986).

[2] See D. Paul, *Women in Buddhism: Images of the Feminine in the Mahāyāna Tradition* (London: University of California Press, second edition, 1985), especially part 1.

as we shall see, presents relatively positive portraits of women and their spiritual abilities.

2. The *Gaṇḍavyūha-sūtra*

The GVS, known in the Chinese and Japanese *Tripiṭaka*s as the final portion of the *Avataṁsaka-sūtra*, but standing as an independent scripture in the Sanskrit, has been described by Conze as a link between the *Yogācāra* and *Tantra* traditions:

> While providing a cosmic interpretation to the ontological ideas of the Yogācārins, it shared with *Tantra* a fascination with the play of cosmic forces.[3]

It is the story of a spiritual quest in which the hero, a young man called Sudhana, visits a number of spiritual guides (one hundred and ten in the original version, of which the extant version describes fifty-three). Each of the guides tells him what they know of the spiritual life before directing him to a further guide who can tell him more. Implicit in all this is the premise that there may be many paths to enlightenment and many ways to achieve spiritual progress; each of the guides approaches the spiritual life in a different way whilst recognizing that other ways may be equally valuable. Thus the spiritual life presented in this sutra is not rule-bound or dogmatic, but is infused with the teaching of *upāya kauśalya* (skillful means) wherein each progresses according to his or her capacities and inclinations. Cleary has commented that the sutra teaches that:

> Those who are within a fixed system have not the slightest inkling of the scope of consciousness that lies beyond the bounds of their perceptions as conditioned by their training and development. It suggests that all views that are conditioned by cultural and personal history are by definition limiting.[4]

There is no attempt at all in the sutra to suggest that some might be precluded from attaining enlightenment because of their lifestyle or age or gender; it is assumed that these things have no bearing upon one's spiritual capabilities. The spiritual guides are of all ages, both sexes, and many occupations. For example, there are several monks, a nun, a grammarian, kings and priests, boys and girls, sailors and householders, perfumers, a goldsmith, a courtesan, the Buddha's mother, a god and many goddesses. All are shown to be aware of the need for *upāya kauśalya* in their teaching, and many describe the various circumstances in which they have taken birth in order to help other beings.

---

[3] Quoted in J. Snelling, *The Buddhist Handbook* (London: Rider, 1992), 153.

[4] T. Cleary, tr., *Entry into the Realm of Reality* (*The Gaṇḍavyūhasūtra*) (Shaftesbury: Shambhala, 1989), 1.

The 'integrative' concerns of the sutra are reflected in the teachings of many of the guides, young and old, male and female, monastic and layperson. In some Mahāyāna sūtras,[5] non-dualist teachings about *śūnyatā,* nondiscrimination, the identity of *saṁsāra* and *nirvāṇa,* and so on, are explicitly used to deconstruct discrimination against women; however, this is not the case in the GVS. The GVS has gone beyond the stage where argument on this point is necessary, and there is no doubt that women are capable of attaining great spiritual heights. Here, then, we have a sutra in which women and men are presented as bodhisattvas and dharma- teachers on an equal footing and in which it would be odd indeed to find anybody disputing such equality.

Again, several Buddhist sutras[6] teach that a woman can only progress so far along the bodhisattva-path, and that when she reaches a certain stage of spiritual development (the exact level varies from text to text) she must change into a man, either in this life or in a future life, in order to make further progress. However, according to the GVS, enlightenment is for all and this completely precludes the need to change sex at any time. Some Mahāyāna sutras[7] attempt to counter sex-based discrimination by standing the theme of change of sex on its head and depicting sex change precisely as a means to indicate the fluidity and emptiness of sexual characteristics. Since nobody in the GVS, however, asserts that sexual characteristics are real or fixed, there is no need to change sex in order to show otherwise. Here, then, we leave behind changes of sex from female to male, just as we abandon any notion of discrimination towards women. This is a sūtra which shows us the potentialities of women as dharma-teachers when they have been freed from the constrictions of having to argue for their right to be dharma- teachers.

Out of the fifty-three spiritual friends in the extant GVS, twenty-one are female characters. Of these, eleven are goddesses, and the other ten are:

1. Asā, a laywoman;
2. Maitrayanī, a girl;
3. Prabhūtā, a lay devotee;
4. Acalā, a girl;
5. Siṃhavijṛmbhitā, a nun;
6. Vasumitrā, a courtesan;
7. Gopā, a girl;
8. Māyā, the Buddha's mother;
9. Bhadrottamā, a laywoman; and
10. Śrīmatī, a girl.

---

[5] For example, see the tale of the Goddess in Chapter Six of the *Vimtalakīrtinirdeśasūtra* in E. Lamotte, tr., *The Teaching of* the *Vimtalakīrti, Sacred Books of the Buddhists* XXXII (London: PTS, 1976), 153-172.

[6] See Paul, *op. cit.,* Chapter Five.

[7] Again, see the *Vimtalakīrtinirdeśasūtra,* Lamotte, *op.cit.,* 169-172.

In the remainder of this paper, we will consider the accounts given by Acalā, Gopā, Māyā and the Goddess Sarvajagadrakṣāpraṇidhānavīryaprabhā.[8]

3. Acalā

The Acalā of the GVS is an *upāsikā* (a Buddhist lay devotee) living in the kingdom of Sthira, and Sudhana is directed to her by King Mahāprabha. This is how she is introduced:

> A crowd of people said, 'Acalā the *upāsikā* lives in the house of her honored parents, surrounded by relatives, and teaches the dharma to great crowds of people'.[9]

Acalā, a young girl who still lives at home, is a lay devotee rather than a nun, yet gives dharma-instruction to great crowds of people. In some Mahāyāna sūtras, this would be the cue for an eminent monk such as Śāriputra to appear and challenge her right to teach;[10] instead, the GVS describes the light which illuminates Acalā's house, the blissful trance which Sudhana enters as he approaches, and her great beauty:

> Nobody ... could equal her beautiful body and scent .... Her radiant complexion was unequaled ... except by the radiance of the tathāgatas and anointed bodhisattvas.[11]

This stands in great contrast to the descriptions of female bodies frequently given elsewhere in Buddhist literature, which often dwell upon the supposed vile, impure nature of women's bodies.[12] In the GVS, there is no talk of impurity or illusion, or of the foul nature underlying the superficial beauty. Quite simple, Acalā, a young female dharma teacher, is exceptionally lovely. Unlike in many Buddhist texts,[13] female beauty is not placed in opposition to spiritual progress;

---

[8] For a discussion of *Āśā Prabhūtā, Siṁhavijṛmbhitā* and *Vasumitrā*, see Paul, op. *cit.*, 94-105 and 137-162.

[9] My translations of the GVS are based on the Sanskrit edition by P. L. Vaidya, ed., *The Gaṇḍavyūhasūtra, Buddhist Sanskrit Texts 5* (Darbhanga: The Mithila Institute of Post-Graduate Studies and Research in Sanskrit Learning, 1960). Page references and line numbers refer to this edition, here, 131.3 1 - 132.2.

[10] See, for example, the case of the *Nāgā* princess in the *Saddharmapuṇḍarīkasūtra* in H. Kern, tr., *The Saddharmapuṇḍarīka, or The Lotus of the True Law, Sacred Books of the East* XXI (Oxford University Press, 1884), 252-254.

[11] Sanskrit in Vaidya, *op.cit.*, 132, 10*f*.

[12] For example, the *Strīyartasūtra*; see N. Schuster, "Yoga-Master Dharmamitra and Clerical Misogyny in Fifth Century Buddhism," in *The Tibet Journal* IX. 4 (1984): 33-46.

[13] See, for example, the *Aṅguttara Nikāya* 3.67-68, in F. L. Woodward & E. M. Hare, trs., *Gradual Sayings* (London: Pali Text Society, 1951-55).

in fact, it is compared with the radiance of enlightened beings. The text goes on to make this connection between Acalā's beauty and the dharma explicit. Rather than being a trap or a distraction to those who would practice the dharma, Acalā's great beauty has a positive effect:

> Nobody could be found in all the world who was capable of looking on the *upāsikā* Acalā with lustful thoughts. There was no being in the whole world whose defilements did not come to an end the moment they saw her. Just as the one hundred thousand gods in the sphere of desire do not practice defilements, so beings, on seeing the *upāsikā* Acalā, do not practice them. There were no beings in the whole world who were satiated on seeing the *upāsikā* Acalā, except for those who were satiated with wisdom.[14]

Rather than acting as a catalyst for defiling thoughts, the female body is here presented as an antidote to them. The juxtaposition of the descriptions of her great beauty and of her beneficial effect upon beings who see her implicitly indicates that there is nothing about female sexual attractiveness *per se* which promotes attachment.

Sudhana then pays homage to Acalā, and asks her to tell him about the path of the bodhisattva. Acalā herself is, of course, a bodhisattva, and relates how she came to start out on the bodhisattva path. It should be noted that although many of the female characters (and, indeed, male characters) in the GVS have a mythic and magical quality which makes one hesitate to place them in the category of "real" or historical women, many of them give accounts of the beginnings of their spiritual progress which have much more of the quality of historical narrative about them. The goddesses and bodhisattvas who tell such tales usually describe how, as a young girl (often a princess), they met the Buddha or another great dharma-teacher, and were inspired to practice the *bodhisattvayāna*. The characters whom we meet in the present sūtra are women who have been practicing the bodhisattva-path for eons, and as such they all have miraculous powers and extraordinary insights. Whilst not wanting to suggest that we can place these women accurately within history, or even necessarily that they ever existed at all, the fact that they are advanced bodhisattvas with great powers certainly does not preclude putting them forward as inspirational role models for "real" women.

According to Acalā, she was once the daughter of King Vidyuddatta. She tells of a spiritual conversion that took place after her parents and the palace entertainers had fallen asleep and which thus parallels and echoes the Buddha's own great decision to embark on the spiritual life after the entertainers in his father's palace had fallen asleep. Acalā relates how she looked up at the night sky and saw there the Buddha and many bodhisattvas, pervading the whole universe. She wondered how such a body could be attained, and the Buddha

---

[14] Sanskrit in Vaidya, *op.cit.*, 213, 26*f*.

predicted that she would overcome passions and attachments and attain the wisdom of Buddhahood. Since that time, says Acalā:

> I have not had a single passionate thought, still less had sexual intercourse, for as many *kalpas* as there are atoms in India. I have not had a single angry thought towards my own relations, let alone towards innocent strangers. I have not had a single thought towards my self, still less considered anything as mine. I have not had any thoughts of illusion, or of difference, or of harmony.[15]

It is made clear here that Acalā, despite being a woman, is not lustful or sexually insatiable or any of the other qualities attributed to women by earlier, monastic texts. Moreover, she has conquered anger and ego, and has reached a point of wisdom where she perceives neither harmony nor difference, i.e., where she has come to reject the notion of opposites and fixed states. She goes on to say that since that time:

> There is not even one being I have met in whom I have not caused the thought of supreme, perfect enlightenment to arise. There is not one *śrāvaka* nor *pratyekabuddha* whom I have spoken to who has not thought of deliverance. Good son, since then I have not had even one thought of doubt or duality or discrimination or variety or rejection or acceptance of adoration or resistance towards even one word [of the dharma].[16]

Not only has she reached great spiritual heights herself, but she has helped other beings to attain the thought of enlightenment. Explicitly now, she describes the integrative framework wherein her own remarkable progress is situated. Rejecting dualities and discrimination (*vikalpa*), she has reached a point of equilibrium and equanimity which admits of no doubts in her spiritual practice. She tells Sudhana how she has always been with the Buddhas since that time, and how she has worked constantly on behalf of other sentient beings. She performs a miracle which causes Sudhana to see countless worlds made of lapis lazuli, containing billions of Buddhas practicing skillful means and pervading the entire universe. Finally, Acalā directs him to the next in the series of spiritual teachers, a mendicant called Sarvagāmin.

In Acalā, then, we see a young girl whose sex is unproblematic in terms of her quest for Buddhahood. Although the text dwells on her physical attractions, these are not seen as hindrances. In fact, her great beauty is a skillful means intended to attract other sentient beings to the spiritual life.

4. Gopā

---

¹⁵ *Ibid.,* 13 4, 28*f.*
¹⁶ *Ibid.,* 135, 16*f.*

Gopa is a young girl of the Śākya clan who lives in the city of Kapilavastu. When Sudhana meets her, she is surrounded by eighty-four thousand young women, all of whom are on their way to enlightenment:

> All those eighty-four thousand women were irreversible in their progress towards supreme, perfect enlightenment ... they were free from all attachments and their minds had rejected all the pleasures of *saṁsāra*. They had become pure in the non-attachment of the dharma-realm and their minds were approaching omniscience. They were free from all hindrances and deceptions ... and they acted as emanations from the dharma-realm.[17]

Not only Gopā, then, but all of her female companions, are advanced bodhisattvas, unshakeable in their path to enlightenment. Many earlier Buddhist texts[18] depict women as symbols of the attachments of *saṁsāra*, whereas in the GVS it is strongly emphasized that *these women* are free from attachments and that they have no truck with worldly pleasures. The idea that they might be involved with *saṁsāra is* negated; in fact, these women are characterized by non-attachment and freedom from hindrances, representing the purity of the *dharmadhātu.*

Sudhana then asks Gopā to tell him about the path of the bodhisattva. She tells him her story: long ago, there was a great king called Lord of Wealth, who had a wife, Lotus Born, and a son called Lord of Glory. In an incident echoing the pleasure drive undertaken by the young Siddhartha Gautama, Prince Lord of Glory went out for a drive to a nearby park. In the same city there lived a courtesan called Beautiful and her lovely daughter Splendor of Delight in virtuous Conduct, who was beautiful, wise, kind and modest. When the daughter saw the prince, she fell in love with him and asked her mother to give her to him. Her mother, however, was worried and told Splendor of Delight that prostitutes should not become attached to one man only, but are supposed to give pleasure to many men.

The young girl then had a vision of a buddha which inspired her to speak to Prince Lord of Glory. Her opening words to him describe her role as a prostitute, much desired by worldly men:

> I am distinguished in the world for my desirable body;
> I am celebrated in all regions for my good qualities.
> My power of wisdom has no equal;
> I know all arts, pleasures and illusions. Many thousands of men
> Look at me with lust.[19]

---

[17] *Ibid.,* 302, 30*f.*

[18] For example, the *Theragāthā*; see K.C. Lang, "Lord Death's Snare: Gender Related Imagery in the *Theragāthā* and the *Therīgāthā,*" in *Journal of Feminist Studies in Religion* 11.2 (1986): 63-79.

[19] Sanskrit in Vaidya, *op.cit.,* 313.27 - 314.2.

However, the following lines dismiss preconceptions about the link between female sexuality and attachment to the world:[20]

> But, prince, I have no passion For the people of this world.
> I have no hostile thoughts,
> Nor do I revere any beings,
> I have no animosity or hatred.
> My thoughts are concerned with the benefit of all beings.[21]

Despite the lust of thousands of men, Splendor of Delight has no desire for them. Here, the traditional, oppositional relationship between sex and spirituality is deconstructed and replaced with a more balanced, integrated view. The theme of integration is continued in the final stanza: Splendor of Delight neither adores any beings nor despises them. Her thoughts are not attached in either of these ways, but are simply, as befits a bodhisattva, concerned with the welfare of all beings.

Splendor of Delight goes on to praise the young Prince's face and body in sensuous, colorful terms, dwelling on his strength, radiant complexion, lustrous hair and fine features. Her speech is the speech of a love, as she offers herself to the Prince and asks him to accept her. Prince Lord of Glory praises her beauty, asks to whom she belongs, and expresses his hopes that she is good, wise, loving and, above all, that she loves the dharma well enough to practice it for countless eons. Her mother, the courtesan Beautiful, then reappears to tell the prince about her daughter. Splendor of Delight, it transpires, was born from a jeweled lotus on the same day as the prince himself. The courtesan eulogizes her daughter's great beauty and talents, which include mathematics, literature, archery, medicine, languages, and music and dancing. No man except for the Prince, says Beautiful, is worthy of her. The Prince then tells Splendor of Delight that he is on the path to supreme, perfect enlightenment. He is worried that she will prove a hindrance to his practice of non-attachment, and that she will be made unhappy by his devotion to the dharma. The young woman, however, is determined, and she promises to be his companion on the spiritual path, steadfast in her endurance of the most terrible trials. She says:

> You have set out for supreme enlightenment,
> Creating endless compassion for beings.
> Having received all beings kindly,
> Take me too, with compassion.
> It is not for enjoyment, or wealth,
> Or desire, or pleasure,
> That I want you, best of beings, for my husband,

---

[20] See Paul, *op. cit.*, 79 & 156, for comments on the link between prostitution and the spiritual life in the GVS.

[21] Sanskrit in Vaidya, *op.cit.*, 314, 3f.

But to share the spiritual path with you.[22]

Again, we see that even Splendor of Delight's desire for the prince is not based upon worldly desires, but upon the wish to follow the bodhisattva-path. The prince, she implies, need not reject women simply because he wants to follow the dharma. Hearing her words of wisdom, the Prince is delighted and gives her many valuable presents. Beautiful speaks further verses praising her daughter:

> Giving the utmost pleasure to touch,
> Her limbs are extremely soft,
> When the sick touch her,
> They recover instantaneously.
> The beautiful scent of her limbs
> Surpasses the best perfumes;
> All those who smell it
> Become established in pure conduct.
> Her body shines like gold,
> Radiant like the center of a lotus.
> All angry beings
> Become kind when they have seen her.[23]

The three verses are divided into two halves: first, Beautiful praises her daughter as if describing her to a potential client - she is wonderful to touch, beautifully scented and as radiant as a flower. However, in each case, the effect of Splendor of Delight's great beauty is a spiritual one; touching her brings recovery from sickness, inhaling her scent brings purity of conduct, and seeing her brings kindness. Sensuality and spirituality merge together as Beautiful recommends her prostitute daughter to the bodhisattva Prince.

The Prince and the prostitute leave together to see the Buddha, who is teaching in a nearby park. The Buddha gives a special teaching for them and they attain advanced levels of spiritual practice, and Splendor of Delight becomes an irreversible bodhisattva. She and the prince go to see his father to tell him about the appearance of the Buddha, and the King is so delighted that he gives his throne to the Prince and sets off to listen to the Buddha. The King and many of his former subjects become homeless wanderers, following the Buddha and attaining great spiritual powers, whilst his son becomes a great and powerful king with an abundance of wealth, extensive armies and many sons. The bodhisattva Lord of Glory, erstwhile champion of the solitary, unencumbered life, has now become a layperson, a king with a beautiful prostitute as companion. In this new role, he furthers the spread of the dharma by building temples and performing miracles, and many of his subjects become followers of the Buddha.

---

[22] *Ibid.*, 323, 26*f*.
[23] *Ibid.*, 325, 18*f*.

The story that Gopā tells, then, if full of reversals and tensions. The beautiful prostitute becomes an irreversible bodhisattva; the young male spiritual seeker becomes a great bodhisattva-king, and the king becomes a homeless mendicant. In this way, preconceptions about appropriate ways of spiritual living are called into question; all the lifstyles in this episode are presented as equally valid, and, to a large extent, as interchangeable. A beautiful young courtesan can become a great bodhisattva just as well as a powerful king or a homeless wanderer. There is no monopoly on the spiritual life; it is one's attitude of mind that is important, rather than one's occupation or status. We see the Splendor of Delight, although employed as a prostitute and thus representing the ultimate in female sexual attraction, has a mind which is pure and unattached and is therefore well able to stand alongside the male characters in Gopā's tale as an advanced bodhisattva. In this extract, then, it is evident how the rejection of opposites (particularly sensuality and spirituality) and denial of fixed structures entail that women, even prostitutes, are included on an equal footing with men on the path to enlightenment.

Gopā then explains that she is, of course, Splendor of Delight, whilst Queen Lotus Born, mother of the young prince, is now Māyā, the mother of the Buddha. Gopā describes how she and her prince paid homage to many buddhas and attained many spiritual powers during the course of thousands of eons. She then directs Sudhana to Māyā, the mother of the Buddha and the next in the series of spiritual guides.

5. Māyā

Māyā, of course, is a familiar figure in Buddhist literature. There are several accounts of her confinement, for example, which largely negate any positive female experience of pregnancy and parturition, and which tell how Māyā died shortly after the birth of the Buddha in order to avoid becoming impure.[24] In the GVS, however, the portrait painted by Māyā of that same experience of giving birth is quite different. When Sudhana meets Māyā, she is seated on a beautiful throne. She is a great bodhisattva who practices skillful means in order to help all beings through her inexhaustible compassion. She has the power of appearing in any form she chooses to enable her to help others, she is omniscient, a tathāgata, omnipresent and supremely wise. Sudhana requests a teaching about the path of the bodhisattva, and she tells him that she is the mother of all buddhas. Māyā describes the birth of Siddhartha:

> Good son, I was then living in house of King Śuddhodana. When the
> time came for the bodhisattva to descend from tusita heaven, from

---

24 See R.L Clare, *Women and Buddhism, with particular reference to the soteriological possibilities presented in the Saddharmapuṇḍarikasūtra, the Vimalakīrtinirdeśasūtra and the Gaṇḍavyūhasūtra* (unpublished Ph.D. thesis, Cambridge University, 1995), 27-28.

> each of a countless number of pores, as numerous as the smallest
> atoms in a buddha-land, like the birth-qualities of all the bodhisattvas
> and tathāgatas, he produced brilliant spheres and rays of light which
> illuminated the whole world and shone through all the pores in my
> body, having entered through my head.[25]

Elsewhere in Buddhist literature, birth is depicted as a dangerous and potentially polluting experience; some accounts stress that the Buddha, although born from Māyā, was not made impure because he avoided contact with her bodily fluids.[26] In the GVS, however, Māyā's body, far from being impure, is radiant with pure light. Māyā then describes miracles and visions associated with her pregnancy; she saw many bodhisattvas and buddhas and all the buddha-lands. Her pregnant belly was, simultaneously, as vast as space and also the usual human size. Then: In every instant of thought, all the assemblies of bodhisattvas at the feet of all the tathāgatas in all the world in the ten directions, entered my belly to see the transformation of the bodhisattva in the dwelling-place of my womb.[27]

In this passage, Māyā's womb is portrayed as a holy place, suitable accommodation for tathāgatas and bodhisattvas. It is the place from which the Buddha Śākyamuni chooses to make his entrance into this world, and indeed Māyā describes how he gives dharma-teachings whilst still in her womb. She then relates how she is the mother of all buddhas in all universes and at all times, using her great power of skillful means in order to facilitate the entrance of buddhas and bodhisattvas into all the various worlds.

Pregnancy and giving birth, uniquely female experiences which are described in less than flattering terms elsewhere in Buddhist literature, are portrayed as spiritual experiences, full of magic and miracle, in the GVS. There is no mention of impurity or pollution, and Queen Māyā does not die; rather, she exists (because of her own spiritual powers) at all times and in all places, giving birth to countless enlightened beings. In Acalā, we saw that a young girl can have a great spiritual vocation; in Gopā, we saw that a prostitute can be a great bodhisattva; here, in Māyā's tale, we see that motherhood can be a spiritual path, too. There is no suggestion here that motherhood entails closer links with *saṁsāra*, that it involves or symbolizes attachment to the worldly and is an obstacle to following the dharma. Māyā shows that pregnancy and motherhood can themselves be understood as ways of following the dharma.

Māyā says that she has told Sudhana all that she can, and directs him to Surendrabhā, one of a whole series of goddesses who appear in the *Gaṇḍavyūha-sūtra* as spiritual guides.

6. Sarvajagadrakṣāpraṇidhānavīryaprabhā

---

[25] Sanskrit in Vaidya, *op.cit.*, 345, 12*f.*
[26] Clare, *op.cit.*, 27-28.
[27] Sanskrit in Vaidya, *op. cit.,* 346, 12*f.*

In the course of his spiritual pilgrimage, Sudhana is directed to a number of bodhisattva-goddesses who each teach him what they know about the bodhisattva path. Some of their tales are extremely lengthy, and there is much room for further research into these accounts. Here, we have space to examine briefly one of the goddesses' narratives in conclusion to the investigation of the presentation of female characters in the GVS.

Sarvajagadrakṣāpraṇidhānavīryaprabhā (henceforth SPV) is the penultimate goddess visited by Sudhana. She possesses immense skillful means which manifest particularly in making her body appear to sentient beings as an inspiration to lead the spiritual life. The appearance of her body brings deliverance to many beings and exhibits all the marks of true knowledge and enlightenment. The purity of her body is emphasized:

> She had come from the indivisible realm of *dharmakāya* (the body of
> the dharma). Having become an unsupported tathāgata, her body was
> naturally undefiled, inherently sinless and pure, [like] the body of the
> dharma.[28]

We end with a female tathāgata, a fully enlightened being. It is implicit in many of the accounts of female characters in the GVS that they are also tathāgatas, and here it is explicitly stated. SPV uses her female body, pure and undefiled, to attract beings to the realm of Thusness which she has already visited. Her female body is a pure reflection of the dharma-body, and it is by looking upon her female form that beings are enabled to perceive the body of the dharma.

Furthermore, it is not just that SPV sees fit to use a female body as an emanation of the *dharmakāya,* nor that she does not contemplate changing her female sex. She goes on to tell Sudhana the story of how she became an enlightened being, and we learn that she was in fact a man when she set out on the path to enlightenment. She was, she says, a young Prince called Conqueror, who took pity on the prisoners his father had cast into jail and petitioned his father for their release. The king was not easily convinced, even though Prince Conqueror told him that he would undergo any kind of suffering and torture in order to secure their freedom. The Prince released them all from jail, at which the king became enraged and swore to kill his son unless the prisoners were returned to the dungeons. At this point, the queen intervened, begging that her son should have two weeks in which to help people before the king killed him. The Prince spent the two weeks performing compassionate and generous acts, which led to a great buddha visiting the kingdom to teach the dharma. Thousands of people attained great spiritual powers, after which the Prince, with the permission of his parents, gave up his wealth and became a follower of the Buddha. After that, the Prince was born many times in order to help other beings,

---

[28] *Ibid.,* 265, 15*f.*

and accumulated more and more wisdom, until finally he took on the female form of the night goddess.

Here, then, we have an instance of sex change from male to female, where the female exemplifies a higher state of spiritual progress than the male, and where it is the female body in particular which is portrayed as a fit receptacle for the *dharmakāya*. There is no comment in the GVS on this sex change; changing from man to woman is not seen as an event which needs explanation. There is no sense of a need for justification of the incident, and no reasons are given to explain the choice of a woman's body. It is simply taken for granted that female sex does not debar one from the status of tathāgata.

7. Conclusion

Although many Buddhist texts do present negative views of women and do suggest, for various reasons, that women cannot become advanced bodhisattvas or buddhas,[29] such views are by no means unchallenged within Buddhist Sanskrit literature. We have seen that the GVS is a rich source of positive portraits of women, wherein female characters are dharma-teachers, bodhisattvas and tathāgatas, and, significantly, are all of these without abandoning any of the characteristics of their sex. Pregnancy, motherhood, daughterhood, the beauty of the female body; all of these are celebrated in the GVS and it is nowhere suggested that these things are in opposition to the spiritual life. On the contrary, the *dharmadhātu* can be found in the womb just as in the monastery. Sudhana discovers that the spiritual life excludes prejudice and discrimination. Of course, this is not an insight which he gains from twentieth century liberal ideas about the equality of all human beings, or from feminist notions of the rights of women (valid as these concepts may be); rather, the integrative philosophical dynamics of the GVS itself form the framework for positive and equitable attitudes to women and their spiritual abilities.

---

[29] Śāriputra, for example, takes this position in the *Saddharmapundarikasūtra*. He says: "A woman has never attained *Buddhahood* ... women cannot attain the five states ... of *Brahman* ... of *Śakra*.... of a great king.... of a ruler of the world, and ... of a *Bodhisattva* who is incapable of sliding back." Translated from the Sanskrit edition by P.L. Vaidya, *Saddharmapundarikasūtra*, *Buddhist Sanskrit Texts* No. 6 (Darbhanga: The Mithila Institute of Post-Graduate Studies and Research in Sanskrit Learning, 1960), 161, 9*f.*

Part 4

Health

CHAPTER 24

IS BUDDHISM PSYCHOTHERAPHY?

Daniel E. Ponce

> When people are spiritually lost, their psyches are mangled and tied
> in knots, so to speak, so then they mangle and tie their bodies into
> knots in order to straighten out their psyches.
>
> William Elliott (1994)

ABSTRACT

In the West, psychotherapy is a specific psychosocial *practice* done by professionals with patients/clients in order to alleviate psychological *suffering* by whatever name it maybe called (e.g., "disorder," "dysfunction," "psychopathology," "disease," "conflict," "crisis," "problem"). Buddhism is an Eastern *spiritual practice* done by members of the Buddhist community (*sangha*) to realize *enlightenment,* an experience attained by its founder, Gautama Buddha. As more and more Western psychotherapists develop an interest in Buddhist principles, some are beginning to apply these principles as if Buddhism is just another "brand" of psychotherapy, albeit subtly and unwittingly. Conversely, a lot of Buddhist teachers (especially first or second generation Western teachers trained by Eastern Masters) and their students are increasingly using their practice as a form of psychotherapy. The paper will argue that not only is it a mistake to confuse/misuse Buddhism as another form of psychotherapy, but that this fundamental misperception is at the root of a lot of scandals and tragedies that have rocked Buddhist (and other spiritual disciplines with Eastern origins, as well) communities in recent years. A conceptual model is presented that could be used in identifying and clarifying the source(s) of confusion. Finally, using the model as a guide, recommendations are made to prevent future tragedies from occurring.

Shorn of obfuscating partisan polemics, all Western modes of psychotherapy have, as their fundamental reason for being, a premise and a promise to relieve psychological pain and *suffering.* In the U.S. alone there are about 418 brand names of psychotherapy (T. Karasu, *et al.*, 1984) all of which claim they have the wherewithal to alleviate suffering. Psychotherapy is a multi-million dollar *business* subsumed under Health and Human Services and is ostensibly provided by trained and licensed professionals in the field (e.g., psychiatrists, psychologists, social workers, nurses, professional counselors) and many more that are not certified or monitored by any governmental agency. As a formal discipline, psychotherapy is a recent development in the West, its inception generally attributed to Freud and the psychoanalytic movement (circa late 1800's and early 1900's) which purported to alleviate suffering through psychosocial means (i.e., the so-called "talking cure").

Buddhism, on the other hand, is a spiritual practice that has Eastern roots, whose *raison d'etre* is the realization of *enlightenment* or *awakening,* an experience attained (more accurately, "realized" since strictly speaking, in sophisticated Buddhist teachings, there is nothing to "attain," nobody to "attain it," and no experience to "experience") by its founder, the Indian Gautama Buddha (born 563 B.C., died 483 B.C.). It is practiced by the individual members of the Buddhist community, following Buddha's last-minute exhortation to his disciples during his death throes to "Work with diligence. Be lamps unto yourselves. Betake yourselves to no external refuge. Look not for refuge to anyone beside yourself. Hold fast to the truth as to a lamp." (Ross, 1981). Parenthetically, not looking "for refuge to anyone beside yourself" applies even to the Buddha himself and his teachings. Buddhism, as originally conceived and practiced by its founder therefore, is most definitely *not* an entrepreneurial system ran by an elite corps of professionals trained to provide relief from psychological pain and suffering. Although cessation of suffering *could be* a beneficial *side effect,* it is not the main activity or aim of the practice. As a matter of fact, in some sects like Tantric Mahāyāna Buddhism, suffering is viewed not as an unwelcome or undesirable vicissitude of life that must be eliminated, but rather as an important, even necessary catalyst or ingredient toward one's quest for enlightenment (Bharati, 1975). Some Buddhist adepts are even slyly hinting that the Buddha's statements about the nature of, and the relief of sufferings, which, on the surface could be argued as the main source of the current confusion between Buddhism and psychotherapeutic practice, are really at a deeper level, an elegant skillful means (*upāya*), a clever "come-on" by the Buddha to hook the uninitiated, since presumably, left to their own resources they will not have the sufficient and necessary motivation to undertake spiritual practice. By making it appear as if alleviation of suffering constitute one of its noble truths, the Buddha appealed to the masses desperate to find something that would relieve them of their anguish and misery. It is the equivalent of Madison Avenue advertisement "hucksters" convincing us that we have a "problem" in order to sell us something to "solve" the problem, when no problem really exists.

I am purposely highlighting the differences between Buddhism and psychotherapy at the outset in order to lay the groundwork of the thesis that will be developed in this paper which is, that the *confusion* and *inappropriate use* of Buddhism in a psychotherapeutic context (albeit unconsciously and unwittingly) by both the members (variously called "students," "disciples," "lay practitioners") and their leaders ("Masters [*Roshis*]," "teachers [*senseis*]") are mainly responsible for the unfortunate scandals that have led to tragic consequences in several Buddhist communities. At the risk of sounding a bit too premature therefore, the answer to the question posed by the title of this presentation is not only an emphatic "No!," but a caveat is being stated right from the start that not recognizing that Buddhism and psychotherapy belong to different levels of realities is to court certain disaster.

1. Sources of Conflicts and Confusion

Using the American experience as an exemplar, there are many sources of conflicts and confusion that have plagued the transplantation of Buddhism from the East to the West. Some of these problems are quite obvious and gross (e.g., language and translation problems; individual personality problems), some quite subtle (e.g., the "business" side of the operations are rarely discussed openly until it becomes a problem). In and by themselves, these problems would probably gradually fade away, chalked up eventually as "part and parcel of growing-up pains." But together, they created an aggregate *critical mass* that precipitated a rash of scandals that shook up the fledgling Buddhist community in America. These scandals took the form of accusations of abuse of power, or the trappings of power (e.g., financial and material excesses by the leaders; sexual exploitation by leaders of their members; physical and emotional abuses, etc. for an excellent and balanced summary, see Butler, 1990). These tragedies wiped out some Buddhist communities, and some, though seemingly surviving the shock, continue to experience on an individual and collective basis, the aftermath of the shocks, a condition that has been called in a psychiatric context, "post-traumatic stress disorder."

There are two sources of conflicts and confusion that are of particular relevance to the purpose of this paper. The first has to do with *cross-cultural issues* of transplanting Buddhism as an authentic spiritual practice from one indigenous culture (e.g., Japanese, Korean, Chinese, Thai, Malaysian, Tibetan, etc.) to another (e.g., American). The second, which is the focus of this paper, is the *confusion* by both leaders and members of two *radically different* though *seemingly* related practices, Buddhism and psychotherapy. The cross-cultural problem is beyond the scope of this paper and is mentioned here only to indicate that it is a very important but rarely discussed factor. I briefly touched on this issue in an article I wrote regarding the introduction of Zen Buddhism in an overwhelmingly Spanish/Catholic culture like the Philippines (Ponce, 1978).

Let me now address the second issue which is the failure to make a distinction that Buddhism and psychotherapy are two entirely different levels of practices altogether. Before I proceed any further, I would like to introduce at this time a conceptual model that I will be using as a point of reference in my analysis. The model was developed by Ken Wilber (1984) and is his adaptation of the so-called "Great Chain of Being" that has been mentioned by others through antiquity. The following is my own slightly modified version of Wilber's model.

In the schema, each concentric circle represents a particular level of "being" or "reality" (e.g., matter, life, mind, etc.) and a particular discipline that has, as its object of study, that particular domain (e.g., physics has, as its "object of study," matter; biology, life; psychology, mind, etc.). The letters on the left side of the figure (i.e., "A"; "A+B"; "A+B+C") represents a key concept in the schema of the idea that each level *incorporates* but *transcends* the preceding level. To phrase it somewhat differently, each higher level contains *all* the elements of the previous lower levels (i.e., structures, functions, capacities, etc.), but in addition, contains something *unique* and not found in previous levels. For instance, the level of "mind (psychology, A+B+C)" contains both "life (biology, A+B)," and "matter (physics, A)" but matter does *not* contain life, and life does *not* contain mind. The numbers on the right side of the schema represent the "levels (e.g., Level 1, 2, 3, etc.) of beings or realities."

To make the schema less abstract, the following is an application of the schema in a theoretical approach called General System Theory (von Bertalannfy, 1968) which, in psychiatry has been dubbed the "bio-psycho-social approach," now the overwhelmingly preferred way of presenting and discussing diagnosis and treatments of choice, particularly in the examination process called "board certification (by the American Board of Psychiatry and Neurology, Inc.)." This is an examination procedure that has not only prestigious significance, but serious economic import as well to the practicing psychiatrist since fee schedules are increasingly being tied to board certification.

As in Figure 1, a higher level, say the "person" level will contain the "nervous system," the "organ/organ systems," the "tissue," "cell," "organelles," "molecule" (and we could even include the "particle," and "sub-particle") levels, but any level below it is *discontinuous* with it. That is to say, it is logically impossible for lower level domains to "become" the next higher level. A cell *cannot* become a tissue: the *whole is* greater than the sum of its *parts,* indeed. A medical technician possesses competencies of a medical aide, but in addition, has something "more and different;" a nurse possesses competencies of both aide and technician, but in addition, has something "more and different" a doctor has all the competencies of all of them, and in addition, has something "more and different."

In logic, this principle has been invoked by Sir Bertrand Russell (Whitehead, 1910) in resolving logical paradoxes in his Theory of Logical Types, which in essence states that there is a logical discontinuity between a class and its members. A class cannot be a member of itself, nor can one of the members be the class. The word "matches" cannot be a member of the class it is referring to the actual matches that are used to light fires. Along the same lines, the General Semanticists (Korzybski, 1933) have, as their theoretical centerpiece, their famous dictum "the map is not the territory."

To summarize, the "Great Chain of Being" model assumes that problems, conflicts, paradoxes, etc., will arise if: 1) there is lack of, or insufficient recognition and distinction of the different levels of being and realities; 2) there is mistaking of levels for each other; and 3) there is inappropriate application of lower-level reality standards to measure or judge higher-level realities.

2. Buddhism is not Therapy

Psychotherapy (generically and specifically) belongs to Level 3 (psychology/mind) in the Great Chain of Being. Level 3 is the realm of the "mind" or the "psyche" and its attributes'/4sensation, perception, cognition, awareness, consciousness, symbolization, memory, beliefs, attitudes, habits, predispositions, etc. The one unique factor present in this level which is not present in Level I (physics/matter), and Level 2 (biology/life) is consciousness or the ability of being aware of being aware. It is only at this level that dualities and polarities make their appearance, and become "real" in a manner of speaking: pleasure/pain; bad/good; right/wrong; true/false; correct/incorrect; teacher/student; father/daughter, etc. Language and the symbolic process is the main medium and instrument par excellence of creating this world of separation, and differentiation. In turn, this makes possible awareness of "time" and "space" (man is the only being that can be "late" for appointments), and abstract standards and ideals (e.g., "wisdom," "compassion," "freedom," "well-being"). These standards and ideals form the basis of systems of morality, ethics, esthetics and other man-made agreements. Dualities and polarities enable the existence of problems, conflicts, paradoxes, in short the stuff that anguish, misery, and suffering are made of. Correspondingly, solutions to problems, resolution of conflicts, and the dissolution of paradoxes, all of which are the subject matter of the practice of psychotherapy, reside in Level 3. All of these Level 3 attributes and characteristics are simply non-existent" or "unreal" at Level 1 (physics/matter) and Level 2 (biology/life). There are no "true mountains/false mountains" or "friendly amoeba/hostile amoeba." Level 1 and 2 are also discontinuous: one can calculate quite accurately the trajectory and probable landing site of kicking a dead cat. Not so with a live one.

Strictly speaking, Buddhism as an authentic *spiritual* practice belongs at Level 6 of the Great Chain of Being, which is 3 levels "higher" than Level 3, the level of psychotherapeutic practice. At Level 6 (mysticism/spirit), Levels 1-5 are incorporated but transcended. Rules, roles, relationships, and realities that are valid and operating at Levels 1-5 are transcended, and are therefore, to a certain extent, *no longer appropriate.* The import of the latter becomes important when we discuss the implications of confusing Buddhism as another form of psychotherapy. Level 6 is represented by the 10th Ox-herding picture in classical Buddhist literature which depicts the "stages" of spiritual practice, the picture where the "being" returns to the "marketplace" (i.e., exposed to the vagaries of the previous levels but no longer bound by their constraints) (Johnson, 1982). In Level 6, there are no longer "problems to be solved" or "moral/ethical dilemmas," because dualities and polarities have ceased to be significant (not in the sense of having been "eliminated," "mastered," or "solved," but rather in the sense that nightmares "vanish" as one wakes up, or the snake that one was deathly scared of "goes away" as one realizes that it is really a coiled rope). Ontological and epistemological concerns so characteristic of Level 3 (psychology/mind) and Level 4 (sociology/group mind) though present, (immanent), are no longer relevant and demanding of focus or attention (transcended). Dōgen Zenji, a Soto Zen Buddhist Master was to the point when he described his enlightenment experience as "dropping of body and mind." (Suzuki, 1980).

These "attributes" (now in quotes because at Level 6, attributions are no longer valid, since attributions separate inseparables, i.e., the thing/being from their attributes) of Level 6 which "characterizes" authentic spiritual practice probably explain why in authentic Eastern spiritual practice (regardless of persuasion--Buddhist, Daoist, Sufist, Vedantist) there is a glaring and remarkable lack of a system of describing two of the hallmarks of Western world view: *psychopathology,* which implies dualistic notions of normalcy/abnormalcy, health/illness, order/disorder and *developmental psychology,* which implies "stages of development," an example of linear time/space description. These unspoken, usually unrecognized, differences have been particularly irksome to a lot of Western students/disciples of Eastern spiritual teachers/Masters because Westerners are so used to "norms," "standards," "criteria," "yardsticks," hence are more prone to react with moral indignation or ethical righteousness if they perceive any transgression or deviation from Level 3-4 rules. This sets the stage for Level 3-4 and Level 6 collision.

3. When Level 3 and Level 6 Collide

In turning to Buddhism ostensibly as a spiritual practice, many American students will be doing so out of some perceived psychological or social (i.e., Level 3-4) hurt or deficiency. They will either be casualties of, or refugees from conventional Western answers to their perceived pain or inadequacies, which, undoubtedly they have tried, but found wanting. Examples of these "answers" are drugs; material pursuits (money, fame, sex, power); psychotherapy; and traditional forms of religion like Judaism and Christianity. Regardless of their reasons for turning to Buddhism, they will be bringing to the situation the three conditions mentioned earlier that are conducive to creating conflicts and problems: 1) ignorance of the different levels of being and realities; 2) confusing different levels for each other; and 3) unwittingly using lower-level standards (e.g., Level 3-4, psychological and/or social) to measure and judge higher level realities (e.g., Level 6, spiritual). Even the most intellectually sophisticated student will probably still revert back to psychological or social levels when confronted with highly emotionally-charged issues as "sex," "money," "power," "justice," demanding painfully at times, moral, ethical, and esthetic accountability from leaders who are perceived to have transgressed the "accepted" boundaries. Perhaps understandably and rightfully so. Caterpillars who have not "achieved" butterfly status will not only not comprehend butterfly behaviors, but deem their behaviors literally and figuratively *impossible.*

For their part, even the most enlightened Eastern Buddhist teacher will probably be susceptible to category errors, and also be subject to insensitivity to level nuances. Never mind that the errors may be due to unawareness or mistaken assumptions regarding the ability of the students to function at Level 6 when they can only function at Level 3. Understandable as this myopia might be, they lead to teacher-student conflicts nonetheless. So-called "crazy wisdom (Feuerstein, 1991)" behaviors by Eastern teachers (or by their Western proteges or surrogates), where the teacher uses anything and everything to induce enlightenment in the student, up to and including morally reprehensible behaviors by Level 3 or 4 standards, may be appropriate for a culture Or community that intuitively understand and in fact, *expects,* such a behavior. Not so, in a culture that still is, like it or not, hidebound to Level 3 or 4. The result can be truly catastrophic when the teacher hides under the guise of "crazy wisdom" to justify what, in truth, are really deplorable Level 3 or 4 behaviors. Ironically, a Western Zen Roshi, himself *the* most famous (or infamous, depending on one's point of view) case of the clashing of levels, Richard Baker Roshi summed it up quite well: " A lot of people are trying to see Buddhism as a form of psychology, or trying to make Buddhism into psychology. What I am always pointing out is that psychology is very different, that *there is no psyche* in *Buddhism* (emphasis added)" (*Tricyle,* 1994). When asked how he would handle psychological problems that are presented to him by the student, Baker's response was succinct and to the point: " I send them to a psychotherapist. "

4. Where to Go from Here

The prediction of Padmasaṃbhāva (quoted in Fields, 1981), the great Tibetan seer, made many centuries ago is now upon us ("when the iron bird flies, and horses run on wheels/the Tibetan people will be scattered like ants across the world,/the dharma will come to the land to the land of the Red Man"). It seems safe to say that Buddhism is no longer in its infancy in America and in the West, hence the relevant question appears to be Alice's question to the Cheshire puss: "Will you tell me please which way I ought to go from here?" (Carroll, 1960). Having identified potential sources of past and concurrent conflicts and focusing on one, confusing Buddhism as another mode of psychotherapy, I would like to conclude this paper by making the following recommendations: First, I think leaders, teachers or Masters of Buddhist communities ought to take the initiative in educating prospective students/disciples of the significant *differences* between psychotherapy and Buddhism, emphasizing that they are truly *worlds of realities* apart from each other. This has a precedent in medical practice and it is called "informed consent," an orientation procedure where the patient is informed and educated as much as possible about the proposed medical procedure/intervention so that there is literally "informed consent." I think this will significantly eliminate or at least diminish teacher-student conflicts that stem primarily from ignorance, misunderstandings, or misperceptions. Second, Buddhist teachers should be adept not only at teaching and guiding students to *function at* Level 6 (mystical/spiritual) but to identify behaviors at various lower levels, and if the teacher is not trained or comfortable in dealing with Level 3 or 4, to do what Baker Roshi does, refer them to those that are trained to do so. Third, Buddhist teachers should have on-going "consultations" from "experts" of other (albeit) lower levels to minimize getting "enmeshed (a technical term in psychotherapy meaning to get unconsciously embroiled in the patient's psychological/social problems)." The psychotherapeutic phenomena of transference/ counter-transference (projection of feelings or attitudes from past figures onto the therapist, in this case, the teacher) are particularly important to recognize in order to avoid their pitfalls. Yogi Amrit Desai, founder and former spiritual leader of Kripalu Yoga Fellowship, one of the biggest and better-known Eastern-based spiritual community in the U.S. (established in 1972, with more than 300 resident disciples, and servicing 15,000 guests a year) had this to say about the dangers of not recognizing the transference / counter-transference phenomena in teacher-disciple relationships: "Unfortunately, in some ways the teaching of the Eastern guru-disciple relationship of love, selfless service, and surrender reinforced co-dependence and suppression. Many residents transferred their feelings about parental authority to me, the spiritual authority. I did not then have any understanding of the process that psychotherapy calls 'transference.' So, much was not said at the time...I thought I was being loving to others, and they thought they were being loving to me" (A. Cushman, 1994).

Unfortunately for guru Desai, this realization came too late for him. He voluntarily resigned his position as spiritual director of Kripalu shortly after making his statements on "transference." He finally acknowledged (charges were initially made in 1985) that he has had inappropriate sexual contact with three women disciples through the years (*Yoga Journal*, 1995). Requesting consultation from lower level experts does not necessarily imply a diminution of a teacher's higher-level accomplishment or stature. Even Einstein had to secure the services of a tax accountant to prepare his income taxes.

Finally, the student/"buyer" is, in the final analysis, *still* ultimately responsible for insuring that he or she is not gypped or sold a bill of goods. In too many cases, so-called mature and responsible adults will still play "victim" and totally disavow any accountability for negative things that happen, blaming the teacher entirely. This may be acceptable Level 3 or 4 behaviors, but if one is truly determined to do spiritual practice at Level 6, then it is best to heed what the Buddha said: "Let us all be lamps unto ourselves."

REFERENCES

Bharati, A. *The Tantric Tradition.* New York: Samuel Weiser Inc, 1975
Butler, K. "Encountering the Shadow in Buddhist America." *Common*

Boundary 3 (May/Jung 1990): 14-22.

Carroll, L. *The Annotated Alice*. New York: Clarkson N Potter Inc, 1960

Cushman, A. "Shrinking the Guru." *Yoga Journal* (November/December 1994): 119.

Elliott, W. "Going East." *The Quest* 7 (Winter, 1994): 20.

Engel,G. "The Clinical Application of the Bio-psychosocial Model." *Am J Psychiatry* 137 (1980): 535-44.

Feuerstein, G. *Holy Madness*. New York: Paragon House, 1991.

Fields, R. *How the Swans Came to the Lake*. Colorado: Shambhala Books, 1981.

Johnson, W. *Riding the Ox Home*. London: Rider & Co, 1982.

Korzybski, A. *Science and Sanity*. Pennsylvania: Lancaster Press, 1933.

Ponce, D. "The Sound of Two Hands Clapping: Zen Buddhism and Christianity in the Philippines." *Journal of Buddhist-Christian Studies* 5 (1978): 235-241.

Ross, N. *Buddhism: A Way of Life and Thought*. New York: Vintage Press, 1981.

Suzuki, S. *Zen Mind, Beginners Mind*. New York: Weatherhill, 1980.

"The Long Leanung Curve: An Interview with Richard Baker Roshi." *Tricycle* 4 (Winter 1994): 30-36. Whitehead, A and B. Russell. *Principia Mathematica*. Cambridge: Cambridge Univ. Press, 1910.

Wilber, K. *Quantum Questions*. Colorado: NSW Science Library, 1984.

"Yogi Desai Resigns from Kripalu." *Yoga Journal* (February 1995): 120.

CHAPTER 25

THE ROLE OF BUDDHISM IN MENTAL HEALTH IN THE MODERN WORLD

Padmal de Silva

1. Introduction

Buddhism has a rich and sophisticated psychology, which has been studied in some detail in recent years.[1] Some parts of the canonical texts, as well as of later commentarial writings, are examples of explicit psychological theorizing, while most of the others include psychological ideas and much material of psychological relevance. For example, the *Abhidhamma-piṭaka* contains a highly systematized psychological account of human behavior and mind; the English translation of one of the *Abhidhamma* books, the *Dhammasaṅgani,* was in fact given the title *A Buddhist Manual of Psychological Ethics* by its translator, Caroline Rhys Davids, when it was first published in London in 1900. The practice of Buddhism, as a religion and a way of life, involves much in terms of psychological change. The ultimate religious goal of the *arahant* state reflects and requires major psychological changes. In addition, as can be seen from an examination of the basic Buddhist teachings, the path towards the achievement of this goal, the Noble Eightfold Path, also involves steps many of which can only be described as psychological.

While the rapid popularization of Zen Buddhism in the West no doubt provided a special impetus for the relatively recent interest in the study of Buddhist psychology,[2] quite independent of this several scholars had begun to appreciate, and to examine closely, the psychological aspects of Buddhism. The works of these scholars concentrated on specific aspects of Buddhist psychology

---

[1] See for example, P. de Silva, "Self-Control Strategies in Early Buddhism," in J. Crook and D. Fontane, eds., *Space In Mind: East-West Psychology and Contemporary Buddhism* (Shaftesbury: Element Press, 1990); see also, D. Kalupahana, *Principles of Buddhist Psychology* (Albany: State University of New York Press, 1987).

[2] See for example, D. H. Shapiro, *Precision Nirvāṇa* (Englewood Cliffs, NJ: Prentice-Hall, 1978).

and attempted to compare them with modern psychological notions and/or to analyze Buddhist concepts in terms of theoretical frameworks derived from contemporary Western psychology. For example, Govinda[3] analyzed the basic principles and factors of consciousness as found in the *Abhidhamma-piṭaka,* and Johansson[4] offered an analysis of some fundamental psychological concepts of Buddhism (*mano, citta,* and *viññāṇa,* all of which refer to different aspects of "mind") using a psycho-semantic paradigm. He subsequently undertook a similar exercise for the concept of *Nibbāna*[5] and attempted to elucidate it using the semantic differential paradigm of Osgood. Kalupahana[6] has provided probably the most detailed discussion of the psychological concepts of Buddhism. In his work, he draws illuminating parallels with the psychology of William James. One of the parallels particularly highlighted by Kalupahana is the notion of the stream of thought or consciousness. Kalupahana's analysis also emphasizes the close links between the philosophy of Buddhism and its psychological notions.

2. Buddhism and Mental Health

While studies such as the above are of much value in the examination of the basic psychology of Buddhism, the special relevance of Buddhism for mental health and psychological therapy has been commented on by many authors.[7] In the following paragraphs, several topics falling within this area will be discussed. This discussion will focus, on Early, or Theravāda, Buddhism. Many of the general points that will be made, however, are equally applicable to other schools and forms of Buddhism. It is perhaps worth noting that there is already a rapidly growing literature on other schools of Buddhism, especially Zen, from the standpoint of psychological therapy.[8]

---

[3] A. Govinda, *The Psychological Attitude of Early Buddhist Philosophy* (London: Rider, 1969).

[4] R. E. A. Johansson, "Citta, mano, viññāṇa: A Psycho-semantic Investigation," in *University of Ceylon Review* 23: 165-215.

[5] R. E. A. Johansson, *The Psychology of Nirvāṇa* (London: Allen & Unwin, 1969).

[6] Kalupahana, *Principles of Buddhist Psychology, op. cit.*

[7] See for example, P. de Silva, "Buddhism and behavior modification," in *Behavior Research and Therapy* 22: 661-678; P. de Silva, "Early Buddhist and modern behavioral strategies for the control of unwanted intrusive cognitions," *Psychological Record* 35: 437-443; P. de Silva, "Self-control strategies in Early Buddhism," *op. cit*; D. Goleman, "Meditation and consciousness: an Asian approach of mental heath," *American Journal of Psychotherapy* 30: 41-54; also W. L. Mikulas, "Buddhism and behavior modification," in *Psychological Record* 31: 331-342; W.L. Mikulas, "Eastern and Western psychology: Issues and domains for integration," *Journal of Integrative and Eclectic Psychotherapy* 10: 229-240.

[8] Shapiro, *Precision Nirvāṇa, op. cit.*

Buddhist psychology is relevant to mental health in today's world in two ways. First, it has techniques which can be used for the remediation, or therapy, of psychological and behavioral problems. Second, it has techniques, as well as an overall stance, that can help in the prophylaxis, i.e., prevention of psychological disorders. We shall examine and comment on these in some detail in the following.

3. Meditation

One major aspect of Buddhist psychological practice which has obvious relevance to mental health and which has already gained entry into modern psychological therapy is meditation. In the Buddhist texts, meditation is given pride of place as an essential aspect of the individual's religious endeavor. The ultimate aim of this endeavor is to reach a state of perfection, and personal development is an essential part of this quest. Whereas restrained and disciplined conduct is part of this training and preparation, meditation is considered a crucial ingredient. It is worth noting that the Pali word for meditation is *bhāvanā*, which literally means 'development' or 'cultivation'. In Buddhism, meditative efforts are seen primarily as a means of personal development.

Two forms of meditation are described in the canonical texts: *samatha* (tranquility), and *vipassanā* (insight). For the sake of completeness, a brief account is given below of what these two forms of meditation consist of.[9]

The word *samatha* means 'tranquility' or 'serenity'. *Samatha* meditation is aimed at reaching states of consciousness characterized by progressively greater levels of tranquility and stillness. It has two aspects: the achievement of the highest possible degree of concentration and the progressive calming of all mental processes. This is done through increasingly concentrated focusing of attention, where the mind withdraws progressively from all stimuli, external and internal. In the end, states of pure and undistracted consciousness can be achieved. The *samatha* meditation procedure starts with efforts at concentrating the mind on specific objects and progresses systematically through a series of states of mental absorption, called *jhāna*. *Vipassanā*, or insight, meditation also starts with concentration exercises using appropriate objects to focus on. In this procedure, however, once a certain level of concentration is achieved so that undistracted mindfulness can be maintained, one goes on to examine with steady, careful attention, all sensory and mental processes. One becomes a detached observer of one's own activity. The aim is to achieve total and immediate awareness of all phenomena. This leads, it is claimed, eventually to the full and clear perception of the impermanence of all things and beings. It is held that *samatha* meditation by itself cannot lead to enlightenment or perfection, *vipassanā* meditation is needed to attain this goal. Whereas the former leads to temporarily altered states of consciousness, the latter leads to enduring and

---

[9] A. Sole-Leris, *Tranquility and Insight* (London: Rider, 1986).

thorough going changes in the person's mental functioning and paves the way for achievement of the *arahant* state.

The claims made in Buddhism for meditation have clear relevance to mental health in general, and to psychological therapy in particular. The meditative experiences of both types, when properly carried out and developed, could be expected to lead to greater ability to concentrate, greater freedom from distraction, greater tolerance of change and turmoil around oneself, greater ability to be unaffected by such change and turmoil, and sharper awareness of and greater alertness to one's own responses, both physical and mental. Meditation would also lead, more generally, to greater calmness or tranquility. Although the ultimate goal of perfection, the *arahant* state, requires a long series of regular training periods of systematic meditation, along with major restraint in conduct, the more mundane benefits of meditation should be available to anyone who seriously practices it.

From a therapeutic perspective, this means that Buddhist meditation techniques can be useful as an instrument for achieving certain clear benefits in the sphere of mental health. Primarily, meditation would have a role as a stress-reduction strategy, comparable to the modern techniques of relaxation.[10] There is a substantial and growing literature in present-day clinical psychology and psychiatry that shows that meditation does in fact produce beneficial effects in this way.[11] Studies of the physiological changes that accompany meditation have shown several changes to occur which, together, indicate a state of calmness or relaxation.[12] These include: reduction in oxygen consumption, lowered heart rate, decreased breathing rate and blood pressure, reduction in serum lactic acid levels, and increased skin resistance and changes in blood flow. These peripheral changes are generally compatible with decreased arousal in the sympathetic nervous system. There are also central changes, as shown by brain wave patterns. The amalgam of these physiological changes related to meditation has been called the "relaxation response."[13] This kind of evidence clearly establishes the role of meditation as an effective relaxation strategy.

Meditation techniques have been used systematically for numerous clinical problems, and recent work has moved towards the scientific evaluation of the efficacy of these techniques. Indeed, if meditation is to establish itself as a viable and worthwhile stress-control strategy in modern mental health care, the only way this can be achieved is through subjecting it to such systematic and

---

[10] H. Benson, *The Relaxation Response* (New York: Morrow, 1975); Goleman, "Meditation and consciousness," op. cit.

[11] P. Carrington, "Modern forms of meditation," in R. L. Woolfolk, M. Lehrer, eds., *Principles and Practice of Stress Management* (New York: Guilford, 1984); and D. H. Shapiro, "Overview. Clinical and Physiological comparison of meditation with other self-control strategies," *American Journal of Psychiatry* 139: 267-74.

[12] R. L. Woolfolk, "Psycho-physiological correlates of meditation," *Archives of General Psychiatry* 32: 1326-1333.

[13] Benson, *The Relaxation Response*, op. cit.

rigorous evaluation. The available data show that systematically carried out meditation has definite value for certain problems with certain client populations. The problems for which meditation has been used in clinical settings include general stress and tension, test anxiety, drug abuse, alcohol abuse, and sleep problems. [14] Some impressive research has also shown the usefulness of mindfulness meditation (a form of *vipassanā* meditation) training in the management of chronic pain. [15] It is interesting that the early Buddhist texts contain explicit references to the value of this form of meditation for the control of pain. [16] Similarly, the Buddha also recommended meditation as a means of achieving trouble-free sleep. [17]

It is perhaps worth dwelling briefly, at this point, on the use of mindfulness meditation for pain control. Kabat-Zinn reports that ninety chronic patients who were trained in mindfulness meditation in a ten-week stress-reduction program showed significant improvement in pain and related symptoms. A control group of patients who did not receive meditation training did not show such improvement. The authors explain their rationale for selecting this strategy for the treatment of pain as follows: "In the case of pain perception, the cultivation of detached observation of the pain experience may be achieved by paying careful attention and distinguishing as *separate* events the actual primary sensations as they occur from moment to moment and any accompanying thoughts about pain. [18] " It is this detached observation of sensations that mindfulness meditation, as described in the Buddhist texts, helps one to develop. This makes such meditation a strategy particularly well suited to pain control. It is significant that the references to pain control by mindfulness meditation in the original Buddhist texts appear to make this very point. [19] A notable example is found in the account about the monk Anuruddha, who fell quite ill. When some visiting monks asked him about his pain, his reply was that the pain-generating bodily sensations could not perturb him, as his mind was firmly grounded in mindfulness. The implication here is that meditation can reduce, or "block out", the mental aspect of the pain, that is, although the physical sensations of pain may remain, vulnerability to subjectively felt pain is reduced. This account is

---

[14] Carrington, "Modern forms of meditation," *op. cit.;* J. Kabat-Zinn, A. O. Massion, J. Kristeller, L. G. Peterson, K. Fletcher, L. Pbert, L., C.O. Linderking, and S. F. Santorelli, S.F., "Effectiveness of a meditation-based stress reduction program in the treatment of anxiety disorders," *American Journal of Psychiatry* 149: 936-943.

[15] J. Kabat-Zinn, "An outpatient program in behavioral medicine for chronic pain patients based on the practice of mindfulness meditation: Theoretical considerations and preliminary results," *General Hospital Psychiatry* 4: 33-47; J. Kabat-Zinn, L. Lipworth, and R. Burney, "The clinical use of mindfulness meditation for the self-regulation of chronic pain," *Journal of Behavioral Medicine* 8: 163-190.

[16] *Saṁyutta-nikāya* (4 volumes, L. Peer, ed.) (London: PTS, 1884-98).

[17] *Vinaya-piṭaka* (4 volumes, H. Oldenberg, ed.) (London: PTS, 1879-83).

[18] Kabat-Zinn, "The clinical use of mindfulness meditation," *op.cit.,* 165.

[19] de Silva, "Self-control strategies in Early Buddhism," *op. cit.*

from the *Saṁyutta-nikāya,* which appears to maintain this position quite explicitly in a different passage.[20]

It must be stressed, however, that meditation techniques are not to be taken as a panacea for all psychological disorders. They were intended in early Buddhism for self-development, and the texts refer, as seen above, to their additional beneficial effects in certain contexts and conditions. The point here is that the nature of the meditational endeavor, and its results as part of a Buddhist's self-development, suggest a useful role for it in the remediation for certain psychological disorders, especially stress-related ones, and also for the psychological aspects of certain physical conditions. The available clinical literature provides favorable evidence. Further studies, especially systematic and rigorously controlled clinical trials, will no doubt shed more light on what specific uses meditation can have in therapeutic settings.

4. Other Strategies for Behavior Change

There is a second aspect of Buddhist psychology that is of particular relevance from a therapeutic perspective. The literature of Early Buddhism contains a wealth of behavior change strategies, which can only be described as behavioral, used and recommended by the Buddha and his disciples. This is an aspect of Buddhism that had been neglected by modern scholars until recently.

It is only in the past few years that these behavioral strategies have been highlighted and discussed.[21] These strategies are remarkably similar to several of the established techniques of modern behavior therapy. Thus, Buddhism can be said to have a close affinity to present-day behavioral psychology. The ways in which the overall approach of behavior modification and that of Buddhism may be said to be broadly similar have been discussed by Mikulas[22] in an important paper. Some areas of similarity highlighted by Mikulas include: the rejection of the notion of an unchanging self or soul, focus on observable phenomena, emphasis on verifiability, stress on techniques for awareness of certain bodily responses, emphasis on the here and now, and wide and public dissemination of teachings and techniques. Given this broad similarity, and the general empiricist/ experientialist attitude of Buddhism as exemplified by the *Kālāma Sutta*[23], in which the Buddha advises a group of inquirers not to accept anything on hearsay, authority, or pure argument, but to accept only what is empirically and experientially verifiable, it is not surprising that specific behavioral strategies were used and recommended in Early Buddhism. It is also entirely in keeping

---

[20] *Saṁyutta-nikāya,* Vol. 4, *op. cit.*

[21] de Silva, "Buddhism and behavior modification," *op. cit.;* de Silva, "Early Buddhist and modern behavioral strategies," *op.cit.*; de Silva, Self-control strategies in Early Buddhism," *op.cit.*

[22] Mikulis, "Buddhism and behavior modification," *op.cit.*

[23] *Aṅguttara-nikāya* (4 volumes, R. Morris and E. Hardy, eds.) (London: PTS, 1885-1900), Vol. 1.

with the social ethic of Buddhism, which recognizes the importance of behaviors conducive to one's own and others' well-being as a goal in its own right. When and where specific behavior changes are required, both in oneself and in others, these are to be effected using specific strategies.

The *behavioral* nature of these strategies needs to be stressed. When a certain response needs to be altered, an attempt is made to change it at a behavioral level - that is, directly, by operating on the behavior itself, and not indirectly, *via* other means. This is precisely the approach of modern behavior therapy. [24] Behavior therapy distinguishes itself from other therapeutic approaches by concentrating on the problem behavior directly. There is no attempt to change the target response indirectly, either through the exploration of assumed unconscious factors or through pharmacological substances acting *via* the nervous system. The problem behavior itself is operated upon. The same applies to the behavioral strategies found in Early Buddhist literature. This is not to suggest that this is the only means of behavior change accepted or recommended in Buddhism; as noted in an earlier paragraph, major behavior changes are expected to occur through personal development, including restrained conduct and systematic meditation training. On the other hand, quite independent of this overall personal development, the Buddha and his disciples did not hesitate to resort to, and advocate, direct behavioral ways of changing responses where needed.

The range of behavioral strategies found in the literature of Early Buddhism is impressive.[25] These include the following: fear reduction by graded exposure and reciprocal inhibition, using rewards to promote desirable behavior; modeling to induce behavior change; stimulus control to eliminate undesirable behavior; use of aversion to eliminate undesirable behavior, training in social skills; self-monitoring; control of intrusive thoughts by distraction, switching/stopping, incompatible thoughts, and prolonged exposure; intense, covert focusing on the unpleasant aspects of a stimulus or the unpleasant consequences of a response, in order to reduce attachment to the former and eliminate the latter; hierarchical approach to the development of positive feelings towards others; use of cues in behavioral control; use of response cost to aid elimination of undesirable behavior; use of a family member in carrying out a behavioral change program; and, cognitive-behavioral methods (e.g., for grief). Details of these, including references to the original texts, have been cited elsewhere and will not be repeated here.[26] It will be useful, however, to provide

---

[24] J. R. Wolpe, *The Practice of Behavior Therapy*, 4th Ed., (New York: Pergamon, 1991).

[25] de Silva, "Buddhism and behavior modification," *op. cit*; de Silva, "Self-control strategies in Early Buddhism," *op. cit.*

[26] de Silva, "Buddhism and behavior modification," *op. cit.;* de Silva, "Early Buddhist and modern behavioral strategies," *op. cit.*; de Silva, "Self-control strategies in Early Buddhism," *op. cit.*

one example of this behavioral approach in Buddhism and to highlight its similarity to modern parallels.

For the control of unwanted, intrusive cognitions, which particularly hinder meditative efforts and can therefore be a major problem for a Buddhist, several strategies are recommended. These include: switching to an opposite or incompatible thought, ignoring the thought and distracting oneself, and concentrating intensely on the thought.[27] As can be seen, all of these bear close similarity to strategies used in modern behavior therapy for the problem of intrusive cognitions, especially obsessions. The first (switching to an opposite, incompatible thought) is basically no different from the thought-switching or thought-substitution technique described by de Silva and Rachman,[28] Rachman and Hodgson,[29] and others. In this technique, the client is trained to switch to thinking a thought different from the unwanted intrusion. The Buddhist technique has the added refinement that the thought to be switched to should be both incompatible with the original one and wholly acceptable in its own right. For example, if the unwanted cognition is associated with lust, one should think of something promoting lustlessness; if it is associated with malice or hatred, one should think of something promoting loving kindness. The second Buddhist strategy mentioned above (ignoring and distraction) is essentially similar to the distraction techniques advocated by modern therapists.[30] The client is instructed to engage his or her attention on a different stimulus or activity. The Buddhist texts also offer suggestions as to what distractions might be usefully employed; these include both physical and cognitive ones. For instance, one might recall a passage one has learned, concentrate on actual concrete objects, or undertake an unrelated physical activity. The third technique (concentration on the intruding thought) is similar to the modern strategy of satiation/habituation training.[31] Present-day therapists may instruct the client to expose him/herself to the thought repeatedly and/or for prolonged periods of time. The Buddhist texts advise one to face the unwanted thought directly and continuously, concentrating on that thought and nothing else. Similar comparisons can be made between most of the other behavioral strategies found in the Buddhist texts and those established in present-day behavior therapy for similar purposes.

The importance of the presence of these behavioral strategies in the Buddhist texts is manifold. First, it highlights the fact that Buddhism has something to offer in the area of day-to-day management of behavioral problems, often as a goal in its own right, for the individual's own and his/her fellow

---

[27] For a fuller account, see de Silva, "Early Buddhist and modern behavioral strategies," *op. cit.*

[28] P. de Silva, and S. Rachman, *Obsessive-Compulsive Disorder - The Facts* (Oxford: Oxford University Press, 1992).

[29] S. Rachman, and R. Hodgson, *Obsessions and Compulsions* (Englewood Cliffs, NJ: Prentice-Hall, 1980).

[30] Wolpe, *The Practice of Behavior Therapy, op. cit.*

[31] de Silva and Rachman, *Obsessive-Compulsive Disorder, op. cit.*

beings' benefit and happiness. They are applicable irrespective of whether or not one has committed oneself to a life devoted to the goal of personal development. Second, these strategies are well defined, easy to use, and, above all, empirically testable. Indeed, the Buddhist approach is one of testing various strategies until an effective one is found. The Buddha's advice to the Kālāmas on the importance of not accepting any view on the basis of heresy or authority, but only on empirical grounds, reflects this approach. The Buddha's own quest for enlightenment followed this path; having tried out various methods and teachings available at the time, he rejected each of them as they failed to lead to his goal and eventually developed his own path.[32] Third, the techniques are for use on oneself as well as for influencing the behavior of others; examples are found of both types of uses.

In terms of present-day mental health practice, the relevance of this aspect of Buddhism is abundantly clear. A range of well-defined strategies is available for dealing with common behavioral problems. The fact that many of these are similar to modern behavior therapeutic techniques in remarkable ways implies that their validity and utility are already established, as many of the latter have been subjected to rigorous clinical and experimental investigation.[33] Those Buddhist strategies that so far have no counterpart in modern behavior modification should be tested empirically. If evidence is then found for considering them clinically useful, they can be fruitfully incorporated into the repertoire of techniques available to the present-day practitioner.

5. Relevance for Mental Health Prophylaxis

As noted in previous paragraph, another potential application of Buddhist psychology in mental health lies in the area of prophylaxis. There is much scope for this which needs to be seriously studied. Several Buddhist strategies appear to have a clear potential role in the prevention of certain kinds of psychological disorders. For example, systematic training in meditation, leading to greater ability to achieve calmness and tranquility, can help enhance one's tolerance of the numerous inevitable stresses in modern life. One may, in other words, achieve a degree of immunity against the psychological effects of stress and frustration. This brings to mind the notion of stress inoculation training of Donald Meichenbaum.[34] One should be able to inoculate oneself against the breakdowns that conflicts and stresses in life can cause. Meditative exercises found in Buddhism should enable one to make significant progress in this direction, mainly through achieving a high threshold for stress tolerance. In

---

[32] D. Kalupahana, and L. Kalupahana, *The Way of Siddhartha* (Boulder: Shambhala, 1982).

[33] S. Rachman, and G. T. Wilson, *The Effects of Psychological Therapy*, 2nd Ed. (Oxford: Pergamon, 1980).

[34] D. Meichenbaum, *Stress Inoculation Training* (New York: Pergamon, 1985).

addition, the facility and skill in self-monitoring that one can acquire with the aid of mindfulness meditation could provide a valuable means of self-control. The role of self-monitoring in the self-regulation of behavior is well-documented in modern clinical psychology. The overall self-development that Buddhism encourages and recommends also has something, one might say a great deal, to offer for prophylactic purposes. For example, if one trains oneself not to develop intense attachments to material things and to those around one, which is a major feature of the overall stance of Buddhism, one is less likely to be vulnerable to psychological distress and disorders arising from their loss, including abnormal and debilitating grief reactions. A further example is the emphasis placed in Buddhism on the four *brahma-vihāras,* or sublime moods. These - *mettā* (loving kindness), *karuṇā* (sympathy), *muditā* (congratulatory benevolence) and *upekkhā* (equanimity) - enable one to interact with one's fellow-beings in a peaceful and conflict-free manner, and thus are a clear means of preventing maladaptive behaviors and cognitions such as jealousy, excessive anger, frustration and envy. Total renunciation of all worldly comforts is not required in order to achieve this land of mental attitude, as the Buddha clearly acknowledged.

Thus, some of the meditation exercises and other personal development strategies found in Buddhism, as well as the overall attitude of Buddhism to life which such strategies help one to develop, can potentially enable a person in today's world to develop an outlook on life and patterns of response that will help him/her to cope with the problems of living with greater calmness and assurance and with reduced vulnerability to common psychological disorders. This kind of primary prevention is clearly a major contribution to mental health. And it has particular relevance in today's hectic, competitive and conflict-ridden world.

6. Conclusions

To recapitulate then, there are several ways in which Buddhist psychology has implications for mental health in today's world. First, Buddhist meditation techniques have already begun to be used, and shown to be effective, in the remediation of certain clinical problems. This practice is growing and is being investigated clinically and experimentally. Second, Buddhism possesses an array of other behavior change strategies, which also have a similar role in the remediation of psychological problems. Third, there is much potential for the use of Buddhist strategies for psychological prophylaxis. This applies particularly to meditation techniques. The overall stance of Buddhism on life and one's interactions with one's fellow-beings is also of relevance here. In sum then, Buddhist psychology has a clear contribution to make to mental health practice in today's world. Some use of it is already being made, and there is room for a greater and more explicit role.

CHAPTER 26

PSYCHOLOGICAL TRANSFORMATION OF MIND: THE FOUNDATION FOR OVERCOMING DIS-EASE

Leslie S. Kawamura

According to the *Nanhai ji gui neifa zhuan*,[1] when Yijing (635-713) visited India, Buddhism was divided into two movements, the Hīnayāna and the Mahāyāna. The Mahāyāna was established by Nāgārjuna and by extending his system known as the Mādhyamika, the Yogācāra was developed into a unique form of Mahāyāna by Asaṅga (395-470) and his brother, Vasubandhu (400-480), on the basis of works known as the "Five Treatises of Maitreya." The Chinese Faxiang School claims six sutras and eleven commentaries as basic texts upon which the Yogācāra is systematized.

The term *yogācāra*, used to describe a particular school of Mahāyāna Buddhism, was probably derived from the title of Asaṅga's encyclopedic work, the *Yogācābhūmi-śāstra*. However, this school is also known as the *Cittamātra*, the *Vijñaptimātra*, or the *Vijñānavāda* in India and the *Dharmalakṣaṇa* [Faxiang] in China. These terms describe specific paradigms found within the system and consequently fall short of the mark of describing the school as a whole. When these terms are translated into English as the "Mind-only School" (*cittamātra*), the "Yogācāra idealism[2] (*vijñaptimātra* or *vijñānavāda*), or the "*Dharmalakṣaṇa* School" (which is no translation at all!), there may be a tendency to go even farther astray, because as a school of Mahāyāna Buddhism, the term *yogācāra* must represent, first and foremost, a path to Enlightenment.

One may question the basis for my discomfort with the English translations of the terms. First, it is not a problem that *cittamātra* is one of the major topics within the Yogācāra. Although the translation "mind-only" is a lexically correct

---

[1] T.54.2125.205.

[2] I am in agreement with Thomas Kocumuttom in rejecting the idea that Yogācāra is an Idealism. See his book A *Buddhist Doctrine of Experience* (Delhi: Motilal Banasidass, 1982), 140-141.

352   Leslie S. Kawamura

translation of the term "*cittamātra*," if the English rendering "mind-only" is to mean that "only a mind exists" or "only mental phenomena exist," then it is a misleading interpretation, because on the basis of such an interpretation, one could conclude that the point of the Yogācāra is to establish an ontology of the mind. However, in this paper an attempt is made not only to heed Agehananda Bharati's insight that "...contemporary analysis and common sense would...unite with Buddhism, against the static Aristotelian-Christian ontology,"[3] but also to show that the Yogācāra is a practical method by which one can overcome human dis-ease (*duḥka*) and thus gain the Enlightened state, the only state that allows one to gain peace for oneself and thus opens new passages to benefit others.

Secondly, the Yogācāra school, without doubt, is centered around terms like *citta, manas, vijñāna*, and *vijñapti*, but in the Yogācāra, these terms do not refer to the material stuff making up what we call mind or consciousness, but rather they are function terms,[4] i.e., they refer to mental activities that become the object of mental integration (*samādhi / dhyāna*) by which an appreciation of (*prajñā*) and compassion towards (*karuṇā*) all sentient beings, oneself as well as others, arise. In other words, these terms draw our attention to the fact that it is experience that counts in life and it is the mind that counts (*cittamātra*) in experience. In the words of H.V. Guenther:

> There is no point in saying that not only my awareness but also that of which I am aware is mental. Similarly, it is meaningless to assert that the colors which I see are physical. The mental and the physical are special constructs within the field of experience.... Once we appreciate that it is the experience that matters, we will never bring up any questions of things existing unexperienced.[5]

Keeping in mind the fact that the Yogācāra is a method by which one gains mental control and keeping in mind that in experience it is only mind that counts, throughout this paper, I shall use the terms Buddhist Mentalistic Trend to refer to the Yogācāra system and Buddhist Mentalists to refer to those who follow this trend. By so doing, I shall avoid the dangers involved in pre-judging the meaning of the terms like *citta, manas, vijñāna*, and *vijñaptimātra* which according to Vasubandu's *Triṁśikā* are synonyms.[6] Furthermore, the words "Buddhist Mentalistic Trend" are obscure enough that they do not exclude the aspect of "practice" which the term *yogācāra* implies, and they are still exact

---

[3] Agehananda Bharati, *The Tantric Tradition* (1965, London: Rider & Co, 1970), 57, n. 34.

[4] Sylvain Levi, *Vijñaptimātratāsiddhi, Deux Traites de Vasubandhu, Viṁśatikā [La Vingtaine] et Triṁśikā [La Trentaine]* (Paris: Libriaire Ancienne Honore Champion, 1925), 16: *pratītyasamutpannatvaṁ punar vijñānasya pariṇāma-śabdena jñāptiṁ.*

[5] Herbert V. Guenther, *Buddhist Philosophy in Theory and Practice* (Baltimore: Penguin Books, 1971), 16.

[6] See Sylvain Levi, op. *cit.*, 3: *cittaṁ mano vijñānam vijñāptiśceti paryāyāḥ.*

enough to indicate that the main trust of the trend is for the Buddhist Mentalists to penetrate the workings of the mind. This means that the Buddhist Mentalists are interested in the problem related to mares experience and mental processes involved therein.

The whole field of man's experiences is summarized in the first verse of the *Trimśika* as follows:

> The conventional use of the self and phenomena appear in various ways in the transformation of consciousness. That transformation is threefold.[7]

In other words, everything within the field of our experience, i.e., all that we believe to comprise our subjective and objective worlds, is a mental construct which comprises our world of experiences in the threefold transformation of consciousness (*vijñāna-pariṇāma*). The subjective and objective worlds are none other than consciousness as a perceptual process (*vijñāna*) being manifested as *citta* (mind), but they are postulated (*upacāra*) as if they were otherwise. That is, *citta* does not refer to some static entity, but it refers to a perceptual process (*vijñāna*), and this *vijñāna*, which is a dynamic process, takes on an existential status (*dravyatas*) in a relational structure that comprises reality (*pratītyasamutpanna*). Therefore, "consciousness" is to be understood as a term that refers to the mental processes (*vijñāna*) constituting a person who is caused to be aware (*vijñapti*) *of* one's "presence" in a world the value or meaning (*artha*) of which is determined by one's attitude (*manas*). This distinction between making the mentalistic trend speak about consciousness in term of ontology and having the mentalists express consciousness as a process can be farther clarified in the following words of John Phillips Jr. when he states:

> The theory is cognitive rather than associationistic; it is concerned primarily with structure rather than content - with *how* the mind works rather than *what* it does....[8]

How the mind works or, what amounts to be the same, the structure of mind can best be described by the words "relatively invariant".[9] We talk about a structure as *invariant* in so far as there are certain specific patterns which functionally encode an organism (or event) to be what it is, although the patterns differ between different organisms (or events). For example, a single-celled organism has certain situational patterning which are unique to it and which

---

[7] S. Levi, *op. cit.*, 13: *ātma-dharmapacāro hi vividho yaḥ pravartate / vijñāna-pariṇāme 'sau pariṇāmaḥ sa tridhā //*

[8] John L. Phillips Jr., *The Origin of Intellect, Piaget's Theory* (San Francisco: W. H. Freeman and Co., 1969), 6.

[9] The term "relatively invariant" is borrowed from David Bohm, *The Special Theory of Relativity* (New York: Benjamin, 1965), see especially 185-186.

differ greatly from the situational patterning of a more complex organism, such as a person. We speak about structure as *relative* in so far as, although at any specified time/space a certain pattern may be understood to be a particular existence (*rūpa*), that particular existence is without essence (*anātman*), is transient (*anitya*), and as a consequence, is bound to be disappointing (*duḥkha*). Thus, when the Buddhist Mentalists talk about a perceptual process (*vijñānavāda*) as the central concern for dealing with experience (*cittamātra*), they do so with the understanding that whatever constitutes an experience (*vijñaptimātra*) is pre-conditioned by or is relative to one's own cognitive capacity, be it degenerating (*abhūtaparikalpa*) or elevating (*prajñā*). This means that the Buddhist Mentalist's *weltanschauung is* not so much 'person *qua* person' but rather 'person *qua* awareness.' In other words, the Buddhist Mentalists do not discriminate between the physical and the mental as separate and unique categories, but what is called the "physical" and what is called the "mental" are nothing more than different perspectives of viewing the situation of "being in the world" and "being of the world."

From early times, the historical Siddhārtha as an Enlightened Being (*buddha*) has been concerned with the welfare of the many. That is, Siddhārtha saw the uncertainty of life and life's process as the foundation of human suffering, because those who do not understand that life and life's process are uncertain and forever in flux believe them to be dependable and durable. Ordinary people do not see how one's perceptual process gives meaning to the world rather than derive meaning from it. Consequently, in discussing the structure of mind as a process of transformation, the Yogācāra developed a system of praxis by which one gains insight into the "how the mind works."

In the verse of the *Triṁśika* quoted above, the transformation of consciousness was stated to be threefold:

1) The specificity of a person's "being in the world" is technically known as the first transformation, *ālayavijñāna*;
2) One's interaction with oneself is the second transformation, *kliṣṭamanas*;
3) One's interaction with the world, both internally and externally, is the third transformation, *viṣaya-vijñapti*.

These three transformations that constitute the totality of one's existence, both physically and mentally, indicate that it is not only meaningless to talk about an awareness which is divorced from one's bodily existence, but it is also meaningless to talk about the validity of human experience which is outside of one's own perceptual sphere. Further, these three transformations comprise eight facets of perception unlike the usual six, viz., the visual, the auditory, the olfactory, the taste, the tactile, and the categorical perceptions. Consequently, the reason for the re-examination of the traditional Abhidharmic view of perception by the Buddhist Mentalistic Trend lies in the fad that when the six sensory perceptions are described in their triadic relationship of sensory object (*viṣaya*), sensory organ (*indriya*), and sensory cognition (*vijñāna*), there is no basis from which the view that a "self exists" (*ātma-dṛṣṭi*) can arise. This means that as a consequence, there could not be a mistaken notion about a permanent self from which one must be liberated and from which all human disease arises.

According to Sthiramati, the reason for discussing the three fold transformation of consciousness is to relinquish the two obstructions, emotional (*kleśāvaraṇa*) and intellectual (*jñeyāvaraṇa*),[10] and these two obstructions must be removed because they obstruct one from benefiting oneself and from benefiting others."[11] The emotional obstructions are particularly troublesome because bate and anger, for example, do not offer peace and happiness to one as is evident in the words of Śāntideva found in his *Bodhicaryāvatāra*:

> When one is mentally feverish with hate,
> The mind cannot experience peace.
> In not being able to gain either happiness or joy
> One will lose sleep and become very unsteady. [Verse 6.3]

And

> By anger friends are made weary, and even if one attracts
> Them, by gifts, they cannot be made to stay.
> In short, anger does not offer one
> The slightest chance to be happy. [Verse 6.5][12]

The way in which the roots of these emotional obscurations can be removed is also clearly explained by Śāntideva:

> An ordinary enemy, even if he is banished from a country
> Will remain in some other country and, when he has recovered,
> Will return from there increased in strength.

---

[10] S. Levi, ed., *Trimśikā, op. cit.*, 15: *pudgala-dharma-nairātmya-pratipādanaṁ punaḥ kleśa-jñeyāvaraṇa-prahāṇārtham /*

[11] See Sthiramati's *Madhyāntavibhāgaṭīkā, Exposition systematique du Yagācāravijñāptivāda*, ed. by S. Yamaguchi, Tome 1. Texte (Nagoya: Hajunkaku, 1934), 64: *de la khyab pa ni byang chub sems dpa'i rigs can rnams kyi nyon mongs pa dang shes bya'i sgrib pa ste zhes bya ba ni khyab par byed pas khyab pa ste / don mtah' dag la sgrib pa'i phyir ro // don mtha' dag ni bdag gi don dang gzhan gyi don to // yang na nyon mongs pa dang shes bya'i sgrib pa rnam pa gnyis btags pas byang chub sems dpa' rnams kyi sgrib pa la khyab par byed pas khyab pa zhes bya'o //*

[12] See *Bodhicaryāvatāra of Śāntideva with the Commentary Pañjikā of Prajñākaramati*, Buddhist Sanskrit Texts, No. 12, ed. P. L. Vidya (Darbhanga: Mithila· Institute of Post-Graduate Studies and Research in Sanskrit Learning, 1960), 82: *manaḥ śamaṁ na gṛhṇāti na prītisukham aśnute/ na nikrāṁ na dhṛtiṁ yāti dveṣaśkye hṛdi sthite // 3 // suhṛdo 'py udvyante 'smād na ca senyate / saṁkṣepān nāsti tat kiṁcit krodhano yena susthitaḥ // 5 //*

But the way of the emotion is different. [Verse 4.45]

Each emotion is destroyed by the eye of discriminating awareness.
Once removed from one's mind, where could it go?
Where would it rest to gain strength to harm one?
Of I do not strive assiduously due to my weak constitution, it will be
the end of me. [Verse 4.46][13]

The meaning of these verses is quite clear. In a sense, *kleśa*s (negative emotions) are like enemies constantly lurking about in search of an opportunity to attack. But unlike ordinary enemies, who may find a new residence, rest up, and return again, once the *kleśa*s have been uprooted by discriminatory awareness, they will have no where to go and hence will not be able to return. However, even when one overcomes anger or hatred, for example, they return to Obstruct whatever peace and joy we may have. Why is this so? It is so because even though hatred and anger may seem to have been removed, they are not actually uprooted until discriminating awareness (*prajñā*) comes into play. Thus, in order to overcome the frustrations and disease that one faces in encountering the various emotions, one must cultivate the eye of discriminating awareness and in order to do so, one must understand how the three transformations of consciousness (*vijñāna-parināmaṇa*) is foundational to the occurrence of all negative and positive qualities that make up our existences.

The three transformation of consciousness[14] refer to the eight perceptual operations that consist of the *ālayavijñāna* as a "Perceptivity tending to distinct perceptual judgment, but as yet undetermined and being merely the dynamic aspect of a stratum that will allow all possible differentiations,"[15] the *kliṣṭamana*s by which the dynamics comprising the substratum is taken to be an 'I' or a 'mine,' and the usual six perceptual operations (viz., visual, auditory, olfactory, taste, tactile, and categorical judgements) that are outwardly directed. Although it is important to know the complexity of the *ālayavijñāna* and also what is the dynamics of the *kliṣṭamana*s, taking its stand on the *ālayavijñāna*, in

---

[13] *Ibid.*, 46: *nirvāstitasyāpi tu nāma śātror deśāntare sthāna-parigrhaḥ syāt / yataḥ punaḥ saṁbhrtaśaktireti na kleśa-śātror gatiridṛśī tu // 45 //*

and 47: *kāsau yāyānman manaḥ stho nirastaḥ sthitvā yasmin madūdhārtham yateta / nodyogo me kevalaṁ mandabuddheḥ kleśāḥ prajñādṛṣṭisādhyā varākāḥ // 47 //*

[14] The three transformations are related to the eight perceptual operations as follows: 1st transformation - *ālayavijñāna* (substratum awareness); 2nd transformation – *kliṣṭa-manas* (emotionally tainted mind); 3rd transformation *viṣayavijñāpti* (six cognitions of six epistendc objects through six faculties).

[15] See Herbert V. Guenther, *Kindly Bent to Ease Us*, Vol. 1 (Emeryville, Cal.: Dharma Publishing, 1975), 262.

the process of identifying the substratum as a particular existence,[16] for the purpose of the subsequent discussion, the following views will be adopted:

1)   Any perception is localized in some existential basis,
2)   the location is emotionally charged (unwholesome Or wholesome), and
3)   the locus of perception is the surrounding world.

This means that any perception, i.e., experience, is located in the corporeal basis-of-personal-existence, and this means that the *ālayavijñāna* has the function of biological appropriation[17]. In this context, the Buddhist Mentalists are to be credited for having emphasized the relevance of existence to praxis in their discussion of the structure of mind. That is, the point from which all Buddhist praxis must begin and end is one's own existence. In short, "(t)he only cognitive system we know first-hand is our own."[18]

In more recent times, there seems to be a gradual shift taking place in the Western hemisphere in its view of the individual and the world that contains one. Whereas previously the individual was pitted against the world, there seems to be a gradual shift towards understanding the individual and the world in terms of mutual causality or interdependency. That the individual and one's relation to the world is mutually caused has been the foundational principle of Buddhism from its very inception. This means, as Joanne Macy aptly points out, that:

> An entity does not contain coded within it from the start all the information required for it to evolve into what it has or will become. Its present and future do not preexist in it as past, nor are its patterns or potentials precast. They derive from interaction.[19]

She also cautions that this change in perspective does not come without certain repercussions, because any change is a challenge to one's cherished views:

> To think of our selves as changing patterns as fluid as water, as ephemeral as flame, runs counter to conventional assumptions. Language and society, indeed our very perception of a world "out

---

[16] For detailed discussions on these topics, see *Triṁśikā, op. cit.*, 18-22, and Asanga's *Mahāyānasaṁgraha*, in G. M. Nagao, ed., *Shodaijoron, Wayaku to Chukai* (Tokyo: Kodansha Inc., 1982) (Vol. 1), 1987 (Vol. 2). See also Vol. 1, chapter 1, 59-270.

[17] The idea that the *ālayavijñāna* is a "corporeal-basis-of-personal-existence" is an important interpretation made by L. Schmithausen. See his extensive study of the term *ālayavijñāna* in his book. *ālayavijñāna* (Tokyo: The International Institute for Buddhist Studies, 1987).

[18] Joanne Macy, *Mutual Causality in Buddhism and General Systems Theory* (New York: State University of New York Press, 1991), 148.

[19] Joanne Macy, *op. cit.*, 95-96.

there" distinct from a self "in here," encourage the notion that as
selves we are separate and distinct individuals, anchored in separate
and distinct bodies. If we conclude, as would be natural, that we exist
independently in our own right with an identity that endures intact
through time, then change can appear as a threat from which we need
to protect ourselves.[20]

However, in protecting ourselves from the threat of change, we position
ourselves to counteract all and any possibilities for spiritual growth. Further, our
need for an "identity that endures intact through time" becomes the cause for
blinding us from seeing that such beliefs causes disease. Such a struggle to avoid
change is known as *āvaraṇa*, an obstruction, in the Buddhist Mentalistic trend.

Of the many texts belonging to the Buddhist Mentalistic trend,
Vasubandhu's *Madhyāntavibhāgabhāṣya*, [21] especially the second chapter,
presents a comprehensive discussion on. the obstructions, that is the two
obstructions emotional (*kleśāvaraṇa*) and intellectual (*jñeyāvaraṇa*) mentioned
above[22]. The two obstructions, emotional and intellectual, are understood to
trupede one against the attainment of liberation and they are called
"afflictions"(*saṃyojana*) in view of the fact that they plague all possible worlds.
As "afflictions" they are classified into the following nine[23]

1)   Cupidity-attachment (*rāga*);
2)   anger (*pratigha*);
3)   arrogance (*māna*);
4)   lack of intrinsic awareness (*avidyā*);
5)   the three which together are called "wrong views" (*dṛṣṭi*), i.e.,
     belief that the [five] psycho-physical
     constituents constitute a substantive self (*satka- dṛṣṭi*), perverted
     pride (*mithyā- dṛṣṭi*), and belief in the extreme
     views (*anta-gra- dṛṣṭi*);
6)   the two which together are called "opinionatedness regarding
     ideologies (*parāmarśa*), i.e., opinionatedness regarding
     ideologies (*parāmarśa*) and opinionated-ness concerning

---

[20] Joanne Macy, *ibid.*, 107.

[21] See G. M. Nagao, *Madhyāntavibhāgabhāṣya* (Tokyo: Suzuki Research
Foundation, 1964), 28-36 for the second chapter. Vasubandhu's *bhāṣya* has been
translated into Chinese by Paramārtha: *Taisho*, Vol. 31, No. 1599, and by Xuanzang:
Taisho, Vol. 31, No. 1601; and into Tibetan, *Sde-dge Tibetan Tripiṭaka bstan-hgyur*
(Tokyo: Tokyo University, 1979), Sems-tsam 2, No. 4027, 1-10, Peking No. 5528, Vol.
108, 119-133.

[22] See note 10 above.

[23] The discussions to follow concerning the thirty-seven facets of enlightenment
and the ten perfections are summaries of Mi-pham's commentary on the
Madhyāntavibhāga. See Sonam Topgay Kazi, *Collected Writings of Jam-mgon ju Mi-
pham-rgya-mtsho* (Delhi: Offset Press, 1976), Vol. 3; *Byams chos-sde nga-sogs*, leaf No.
680, line 5 to leaf No. 693, line 2.

ideologies regarding ethical behaviour and compulsive performance (*śīla-vrata- parāmarśa*);
7)   indecision (*viciktsā*);
8)   jealousy (*īrṣyā*); and
9)   avarice (*mātsarya*).

Of these, the first two are closely linked with *kleśāvarāṇa* and become obstructions.

1)   Cupidity-attachment (*rāga*) *is* an obstruction, because an attached mind does not see the faults of *samsāra*.
2)   In the same manner, anger (*pratigha*) obstructs the mind from dwelling peacefully in a tranquil flow.

The remaining seven obstruct one from seeing reality as-it-is. In particular,

3)   Arrogance (*māna*) obstructs one from knowing and from becoming free of the referential object, i.e., the five psycho-physical constituents that are grasped as substantive (*pañca-upadāna-skandha*), because one is firmly rooted in the perverted view (*mithyā-dṛṣṭi*) of thinking "I am a substantive self' (*sakta-dṛṣṭi*).
4)   Loss of intrinsic awareness (*avidyā*) obstructs one from knowing the modus operandi of the five psychophysical constituents upon winch the attachment to a belief in. a self as substantive is based and thus one is unable to realize its nature as-it-is.
5)   Wrong views (*dṛṣṭi*) obstructs the direct experience (*sākṣin*) of the reality of the extinction of suffering (*samudayā-satya*). One does not become liberated, because owing to the strength of that perverted view of thinking that the five psycho-physical constituents comprise a substantive self, one fears that the self will become extinct when suffering is extinguished. Also, one rejects the attainment of that reality of extinction, because owing to over-evaluation, one negates the reality of that extinction of suffering as not existing and as not something to attain, because one believes that impermanence means extinction of the self.
6)   Opinionatedness regarding ideologies (*parāmarśa*) prevents the reality of the path (*mārga-satya*) from in one's existence, because one cannot comprehend the purity of the Buddha path when one is ensnared other perverted ideologies regarding ethical behavior and compulsive performance (*śīla-vrata-parāmarśa*).
7)   Doubt (*viciktsā*) prevents one from knowing the virtues of the three treasures of Buddha, Dharma, and Sangha because by harboring two minds, one does gain certainty.
8)   Jealousy (*īrṣyā*) prevents one from knowing the referent of gain and fame; one who is jealous cannot tolerate the gain made by others because one who is attached to one's own gain and

fame is unable to fathom correctly the referent of life's gain and
fame.

9)   Avarice (*mātsarya*) prevents one from knowing that material
things in life are annoying because by clinging to whatever little
material thing one has as the greatest one cannot know what is
enough.

So long as one has not overthrown those afflictions, one will be chained to
existence and will not gain liberation. So what is the method by which one can
gain liberation from the disease that those afflictions produce? One must
understand their antidotes, i.e., one must understand how they obstruct the
thirty-seven facets of enlightenment (*bodhipakṣa*), the ten perfections (*daśa-
pāramitā*), and the ten stages of a bodhisattva (*daśa-bhūmi*) and in so
understanding one will be able to counteract the negative forces of the afflictions.

In regard to the thirty-seven facets of enlightenment, the four sustained
attentiveness (*catvāri smṛty-upasthānāni*) are obstructed by attachment to purity,
pleasure, a belief in an eternal self and ownership as the basis for postulating
and giving structure to body, feeling, mind, and substance because one lacks the
expertise of knowing (*akauśala*) that these are impure.

The four correct exertions (*catvāri prahāṇāni*) are obstructed by laziness
and so on.

The four footholds for higher cognition (*catvāri ṛddhipādāḥ*) are obstructed
by shying away from the attainment of meditation because one takes up the
unfavorable state of languor and rejects the favorable state of earnestness.

The five powers (*pañcendriyāṇi*) are obstructed by a lack of trust and so on
regarding ones own existence.

The five strengths (*pañca-balāni*) are obstructed by becoming oppressed by
the individual obstacles because the capacity of trust and so on are weak even
though they have been generated.

The seven adjuncts to enlightenment (*sapta-bodhyaṅgāni*) are obstructed by
shying away from the penetrating insight by which one understands the
mistaken belief that the five psycho-physical constituents constitute a
substantive self (*satkāya- dṛṣṭi*).

The eightfold path (*aṣṭāṅga-mārga*) of the majestic ones are obstructed by
the attachment of taking up an inappropriate life-style that arises simultaneous
with the three gates [of thought, speech, and action].

The ten perfections (*daśa-pāramitā*) are obstructed in the following manner.
The perfection of an act of giving (*dāna*) is obstructed by avarice that prevents
one from gaining the fruit of an act of giving, i.e., the wealth of great bliss.

In the same way, the perfection of discipline *śīla*) is obstructed by violating
proper manners that causes the attainment of a favorable state as its result.

The perfection of patience (*kṣānti*) is obstructed by anger that prevents one
from being friendly to sentient beings.

The perfection of endeavor (*vīrya*) is obstructed by laziness that prevents
one from increasing virtues (*guṇa*) and decreasing faults (*doṣa*).

The perfection of contemplation (*dhyāna*) is obstructed by desultoriness that obstructs one from guiding those who do not trust the teachings and who must be guided into this teaching by the transcending powers (*ṛddhi*) that have [contemplation] at their basis.

The perfection of appreciative discrimination (*prajñā*) is obstructed by confusion that prevents one from leading those who are to be trained through teachings of the dharma to a life of freedom.

The perfection of appropriate action (*upāya-kauśalya*) is obstructed by a lack of skill (*upāya*) that prevents one from making the wholesome roots of in-exhaustive gift-giving, etc.

The perfection of vow (*praṇidhāna*) is obstructed by not taking up a vow that prevents one from continuing anything wholesome.

The perfection of strength (*bala*) is obstructed by weakness regarding the adversaries of the perfection that prevent one from making wholesome acts and their results definite and certain.

The perfection of knowledge (*jñāna*) is obstructed by taking the doctrine at face value without having understood the deep intention of the teaching. Consequently, one is prevented from enjoying the Mahāyāna teachings that results from knowledge and sentient beings are prevented from reaching maturity by means of one sharing un-mistakenly the teaching with others.

The *dharma-dhātu* that is all encompassing is distinct in- view of the purification that results from insight that occurs on each of the ten bodhisattva stages but is not distinct m view of the fact of tile sameness of self and others. As one progresses through the stages one by one, the obstruction that must be removed in each of the stages is removed. How is this so?

On the first bodhisattva stage, the *dharma-dhātu* is experienced as all encompassing. The *dharma-dhātu* is itself empty. Through this experience the self is realized to be the same as the other and the other is realized to be the same as the self and in. view of the fact of emptiness, there is no haughtiness regarding self and others. Consequently, the perfection of giving is practiced and thus the bodhisattva comprehends the two benefits of benefiting oneself and benefiting others.

On the second bodhisattva stage, the *dharma-dhātu* is experienced as the highest, because the brilliance of the *dharma-dhātu* is experienced in its naturalness. Consequently, one thinks, "Although attainment is common to all, we must continue our practice to attain the purification of all aspects." Here purification of all aspects means to remove the delusions that are emotively toned and not emotively toned. Consequently, in. this second stage, the perfection of ethical behavior is practiced and thus the bodhisattva makes oneself into a pure vessel.

On the third stage, the doctrine is experienced as a majestic flow of the *dharma-dhātu*. Realizing that the act of listening to the teachings is none other than the majestic flow of the *dharma-dhātu*, the bodhisattva habituates oneself in the perfection of endurance even if one has to hurl oneself into the scorching flames of tri-chilocosm in order to gain the teachings.

On the fourth stage, one experiences the *dharma-dhātu* without being attracted to it because the bodhisattva realizes that the *dharma-dhātu* has no eternal substance to it. Even the craving for the teachings is abandoned; consequently, this fourth stage, the perfection of effort is practiced, because the bodhisattva dwells in. the practice of the *bodhyaṅgas* once the activities of body, speech, and mind have been transcended.

On the fifth stage, one experiences the *dharma-dhātu* as being same to the beings. That is, the existential status of the buddhas of the three times, the bodhisattvas, and oneself are seen as not different. The *Daśabhūmika-sūtra* explains the ten kinds of sameness of purity of mind (*cittasya viśuddhi-samatā*) as follows:

1) Sameness of purity of mind with teachings of the buddhas of the past;
2) sameness of purity of mind with teachings of the buddhas of the future;
3) sameness of purity of mind with the teachings of the buddhas of the present;
4) sameness of purity of mind regarding discipline;
5) sameness of purity of mind regarding sentient beings;
6) sameness of purity of mind regarding the removal of doubt and opinionated views;
7) sameness of purity of mind regarding what constitutes and what does not constitute a path;
8) sameness of purity of mind regarding what is removed on the path;
9) sameness of purity of mind regarding the factors of enlightenment; and
10) sameness of purity of mind regarding helping sentient beings become mature.

In view of these ten types of sameness, the bodhisattva realizes that one is existentially not different in one's authentic beings from the buddhas, because the authentic being (*dharma-kāya*) is none other than what is characterized as the transformation of the *ālayavijñāna*. Consequently, on this stage, the bodhisattva habituates oneself in the perfection of contemplation.

On the sixth stage, the *dharma-dhātu* is experienced as neither impure nor pure, because there is nothing pure or impure in. an interdependently originating situation. Consequently, on this stage, a bodhisattva habituates oneself m the perfection of appreciative discrimination.

On the seventh stage, the *dharma-dhātu* is experienced as non-differentiated, because on this stage the bodhisattva realizes that the differentiating characteristics, explained in the *sutra*s, are not different. Because the bodhisattva experiences the *dharma-dhātu* as non-differentiated by knowing that the differentiating characteristics are all the same, one habituates oneself in the perfection of appropriate actions.

On the eighth stage, the *dharma-dhātu* is experienced as neither increasing nor decreasing because the *dharmadhātu*, being the very purity itself, cannot be distinguished as possessing impurity or purity Consequently, it is just as it is. There is an acceptance of no increasing nor decreasing with regard to that which has no defining characteristics, because the bodhisattva gains the knowledge that phenomena is fundamentally non-originating (*anutpattika-dharma-khanti-lābhat*). A bodhisattva, from the eighth stage onward, possesses four kinds of mastery (*caturdha-vaśitā*):

1) Mastery regarding non-discriminating awareness
    (*nirvikalpa- vaśitā*);
2) mastery regarding the pure [Buddha] realm
    (*kṣetra-panbuddha- vaśitā*);
3) mastery regarding primordial wisdom (*jñā-vaśitā*), and
4) mastery regarding action (*karma- vaśitā*).

On the eight bodhisattva stage, a bodhisattva possesses the first two of the four and consequently one habituates oneself in the perfection of the vow in. order to keep the wholesome active uninterruptedly.

On the ninth stage, the *dharma-dhātu* is experienced as the mastery regarding primordial wisdom, because the bodhisattva gains the four well-defined knowledges of the dharma, of the subjects for discussion, of how to speak distinctly, and of how to present the present case. Thus, on this stage, the bodhisattva habituates oneself in. the perfection of power, because one possesses the specific power of strength.

On the tenth stage, the *dharma-dhātu* is experienced as the mastery regarding action because the bodhisattva can act for the sake of the sentient beings in just the way one wishes owing to one's capacity to respond (*nirmāṇa-kāya*). Consequently, the bodhisattva habituates oneself in. the perfection of knowledge, because one possesses the specificity of enjoying the dharma and of bringing sentient beings to maturation.

When one understands the two obstructions, emotional and intellectual, as impediments against the attainment of liberation and as "afflictions" (*saṃyojana*) that plague all possible worlds, one is equipped with the necessary expertise to examine how, in. the experience of human interaction, it is the mind that counts. The term "mind" does not refer to some material stuff making up what we call mind or consciousness, but rather it is a function term and consequently, as pointed out earlier, it refers to the mental activities that become the object of mental integration (*samādhi / dhyāna*) *by* which an appreciation of (*prajñā*) and compassion towards (*karuṇā*) all sentient beings, oneself as well as others, arise. It is only when the individual is in complete control of one's own mental health that the condition for peace in the individual and the society can be gained. Thus although the praxis established by Vasubandu may be centuries old, its application is as current now as it was then.

CHAPTER 27

BUDDHIST MEDITATION AND MENTAL HEALTH

Kwan Kah Yee

1. What is Psychological Illness?

Psychiatric signs and symptoms can be regarded as being deviations from normal behavior and experience. Abnormality of thinking, feeling and behaving does not necessarily signify mental illness. The extent to which behavior or experience is pathological depends upon its context in the personality of the individual or in the circumstances in which it is manifest. For example, anxiety immediately before an examination is normal, but the same degree of anxiety without an appropriate cause can be symptomatic of illness.

Normality is used here to mean the behavior and experience of the majority of people. For example, excessive conformity to social standards and a lack of conformity to social standards are both extremes of the characteristic of conformity, and as such are both abnormal. These extremes of conformity can be simply features of an individual or they can be symptoms of illness, and a full assessment of personality and of the illness is required before the distinction can be made. In addition, the degree of conformity can only be judged in the context of the behavior, involving cultural and social factors.

Normality also depends upon the consistency of the individual's behavior and experience. Anxiety in a person who habitually over-reacts to stress may be normal, whereas the same degree of anxiety in an otherwise placid person can be abnormal.

2. What Psychological Illnesses Would Benefit from a Healthy Lifestyle Most

Some mental conditions are mild whose symptoms are understandable and can be empathized with. They are called neuroses. The psychoses are serious illnesses in which the symptoms are not understandable, cannot be empathized with, and in which the patient often loses contact with reality. The distinction is crude, has exceptions, but is serviceable.

The psychoses are further divided into organic and functional. Organic psychoses are those in which a demonstrable or inferred lesion is present, e.g., tumors, vascular changes, infective, traumatic or congenital factors. The treatment of such conditions should be directed towards the underlying medical condition, and therefore should be the job of physicians specialized in various organic fields of medicine. Examples of organic psychoses are acute delirium and chronic dementia.

Function psychoses, on the other hand, are those in which function is disturbed but no lesion can be demonstrated. Diagnosis of an illness as function should rest on finding positive psychological symptoms and not merely upon exclusion of physical findings. Common function psychoses include affective disorders such as manic-depressive psychosis and schizophrenia with paranoia, etc. They usually need life-long psychiatric treatment by a professional psychiatrist.

The group of illnesses most likely to benefit from a healthy lifestyle are neuroses such as anxiety neurosis, post-traumatic neurosis syndrome, psychosomatic disorders such as phobias, etc., character disorders, hysteria, obsessional neurosis and to a lesser extent psychopathic states. For peoples suffering from functional psychoses, a healthy lifestyle would help them to code with stress better, although it may not affect the prognosis and progress of their disease. However, it is a saying in medicine that we "cure occasionally, relieve sometimes but comfort always."

3. The Effect of Stress on Mental Health in Modern Society

However, prevention is better than cure. Stress is a fact of life. In Singapore, in one year alone, the Counseling and Care Center, one of the leading centers in Singapore in helping people to deal with stress, may be approached to address more than 20 groups of people from all walks of life on the subject of stress. Teachers, office workers, executives, students, housewives, nurses or police officers all agree that their life is generally stressful. They cannot tell what exactly is the problem -- all they know is that they seem to feel an accelerated pace, competition and pressure. Living in an environment of social and technological acceleration can make us feel the psychological effects of impermanence. We feel as if the future is rushing upon us and there is nothing we can do to stop it or even slow it down. The present gets replaced by the unfamiliar future at such a rapid rate that we are forced into a state of continuous adaptation. The constant need to adapt produces an underlying feeling -- largely unconscious -- of apprehension and longing for stability. On the labor front there is pressure to mechanize and computerize. An older member of the university faculty voices her fear of computers and other sophisticated gadgets, not because of what she might do to them, but what they might do to her!

Stress is any kind of pressure that affects a person in his daily life. This effect may be healthy or unhealthy depending upon the reaction to stress factors. That pressure can be defined as wear and tear of daily living or an applied force or system of forces that tends to strain or deform the body.

The majority of people actively seeking help for stress falls within the 20-39 age range. This is the period when we experience a need to come to terms with various changes in our life, such as leaving school, college or university, getting a job, settling into a career, and for some of us adjusting to marriage and family life or to single-hood.

Work being a competitive situation, many find work and job stability stressful. Financial stress is next. Many wage-earners find it difficult to cope with the rising cost of housing and general inflation. With affluence, things such as upgrading one's standard of living and holidays abroad become a need rather than a luxury Affluence brings with it higher expectations of life. This can be a problem if one is unrealistic. Parents begin to expect their children to achieve academic excellence that may be beyond their capacity. Children expect more from and of their parents, thinking they can afford to be like their friends' parents and neighbors. Young people marry with higher expectations of marriage based on what they believe spouses should be to each other, rather than on a realistic understanding of each other.

Family relations form another kind of stress prevalent in cities. This includes difficulties in bringing up children, caring for the aged sick, family communication and the marital relationship. The married would leave their family of siblings to set up their own homes, leaving the single siblings to care for aging parents.

4. Ways to Manage Stress

Stress is not always harmful. So we would rather manage stress than reduce stress. We are inclined to have the faulty notion that we can manage life without adequate preparation and understanding. When that happens, life becomes one big stress.

There are some general truths about stress:

- What is stressful depends on the individual.
- Circumstances have a major bearing on what is stressful.
- That which is predictable is less stressful.
- The ability to control situations can minimize stress.

It is the way an individual reacts that generates stress for himself. Some spend most of their lives aggressively involved in a chronic, incessant struggle to achieve more and more in less and less time, and they are required to do so against the opposing efforts of other things or other persons. They are more prone to stress than those whose reactions to situations tend to be more moderate and regulated. The latter will try to assess their reactions and the situation before taking action.

Having irrational beliefs and mental attitudes also contributes to stress. To quote a few: everybody must like me; people must love me because I need love; everything I do must turn out right; criticism makes me useless; I must be able to control events, situations and people; people must never let me down; people have no right to change; it is a sip of weakness to have problems in life; when things go wrong, there must be something wrong with me; I must accomplish something significant to be somebody; etc.

Life events such as loss through death, divorce or retirement, illness, unhappy events, or other role and status changes cause social stress. Life's events -- whether positive or negative, additions or subtractions -- can serve as stressors. A man given a promotion has to adjust to a new role and added responsibilities. A woman married finds herself in a new role that carries with it certain expectations. Couples who have children may rejoice over additions to the family. However, they will have to double as partners in a marriage and as parents to their children. Each addition to life requires some adjustment and this can create stress. They have effects on people and if the reaction is not appropriate, stress occurs.

5. Persons with Stress May End up in the Following Ways

Fear of the future: Fear is a tension that comes when a person is in the presence of or expects to be in the presence of danger or pain. It usually causes anxiety. The person feels a sense of uncertainty and fear that may not be linked directly to an external threat. He has feeling of worry, apprehension and unease. The anxiety may become severe enough to cause him to withdraw from people, places and situations.

Frustration of the past: Frustration results from blocked goals and is brought on by the high expectations others have of us. If it is not properly handled, it may result in depression. The person may experience hopelessness, despair, apathy, sadness and crying spells, lethargy and sleep disturbances, feelings of worthlessness, over-sensitivity and guilt, loss of interest in activities and people, negative thoughts about self, experiences and the future, and in the extreme form suicidal thoughts and attempts. Depression may last for a few months and profession help is urgently needed.

Emotional instability and mental illness: The person may be happy one week and moody the next week. Other people's remarks may provoke excessive anger or sudden outbursts of temper. Or the person could be hysterical over situations and events. All of these suggest difficulty in controlling emotional reactions. If the emotional instability is severe or the person is subjected to prolonged stress, he may lose touch with reality and experience a mental breakdown. He hears voices, becomes inappropriate in his reactions and behavior, and may be violent and experience mental torment.

Physical symptoms and diseases: High blood pressure, heart attack, gastric ulcers, headache, migraine, neckache, backache, sexual dysfunction and even premature aging have been attributed to stress.

6. Relaxation and Stress

When you are under stress, you sometimes feel you are not in control over people, situations and yourself. This feeling helps to increase the stress and the body reacts by tensing up.

To regain some control, it seems easier to begin by controlling your breathing and body. Once you feel a sense of control, you will feel relaxed and this very relaxation makes you feel even more in control. It brings relief for when the body relaxes, you feel less stressed and more capable of managing the various stresses that affect you daily. A relaxed body leads to a relaxed mind. And as you lose tension you begin to react appropriately to pressures that come your way.

7. Concept of Positive Mental Health

Being free from mental illness does not necessarily mean one is enjoying good mental health. Mental health is general well-being of a person, his mind and his emotions. It is the ability for an individual to maintain harmonious relationships with others and to participate and contribute in a constructive way to the evolution of his social and physical environment (the World Health Organization's definition). Mental health is a condition which permits the optimal development, physical, intellectual and emotional, of the individual, so far as this is compatible with that of other individuals (World Federation for Mental Health's definition).

Good health means having so-and body and mind, able to enjoy life and happiness, able to cope with the demands and stress of modern living, able to adopt desired lifestyle and able to live to a ripe old age meaningfully.

A mentally healthy person feels comfortable about himself, feels right about other people and is able to meet the demands of life.

Self-understanding: The mentally healthy person has a realistic appraisal of himself, his strengths and weaknesses, his good and bad points and accepts them for what they are worth. He can cope with frustrations, worries and emotions of fear, anger, love, jealousy and guilt.

Able to give love: The mentally healthy person is able to like and trust people and expects them to reciprocate with the same feelings. He is tolerant of others' shortcomings just as he is of his own. He does not expect others to be perfect, either. He can form satisfying, meaningful relationships.

Able to cope: The mentally healthy person is able to make necessary adjustments if he cannot change the situation. He gives of his best in whatever he undertakes, and if the result is dissatisfactory he tries to do better the next time. Life's daily challenges, changes and traumas are taken in his stride.

8. Principle of Achieving Positive Mental Health

Healthy personality development depends greatly on attachment between the child and mother or mother substitute. Children between the ages of six months and two years that are deprived of continuous mothering become impaired in their capacity to form deep and lasting relationships with others. With love, acceptance, a sense of belonging, purpose and security, the child gains confidence to face life and venture out into the world.

Parents should examine their reasons for wanting a child and work out how they will share the care and responsibility. Unless parents are mature and stable individuals and have a stable marriage, the child will suffer. Pressure applied to children in school can be harmful, so parents must be realistic.

In conclusion, looking after your physical health, knowing yourself, learning to cope with life, trying to control your emotions, and cultivating a warm social life are the mundane ways to mental health.

9. Develop Spiritual Values

A religion or at least an adequate personal philosophy can make a difference and enhance one's life. It can be a source of comfort and strength in times of crisis and stress.

Do not be afraid of or shy away from seeking help from others, such as a trusted friend, colleague or counselor, or a religious leader who may be able to provide valuable support during a crisis.

10. Buddhist Meditation

Now let us look into the psychological and practical significance of Buddhist meditation on mental health. There are many ways of meditating. Many religions practice various forms of meditation. In the Theravāda school there are the classic forty subjects of meditation. In Mahāyāna schools more meditation methods are mentioned, from the classic twenty-five ways of mentioned in the *Śūraṅgama-sūtra* to the legendary one hundred and eighty thousand methods. Even with the same subject of meditation there are so many ways to practice it. This paper will confine the discussion on one method of Buddhist meditation alone, so that the method and its impact can be analyzed in depth.

The method of meditation referred to in this paper is know as "*ānāpāna sati*." Again there are many ways to practice *ānāpāna sati*, so the way described here is according to Webu Sayadaw of Myanmar. I learned this method of meditation from his student, the late Venerable Ananda Mangala Nayaka Maha Thera Saddharmakeerthi Sri Pandita Dhammaloka Vansaddvaja since 1970 when I was a student studying medicine at the University of Singapore.

11. Mundane Solutions for Mental Health

So far we have discussed only the mundane ways of dealing with stress and mental health. These methods may all sound very logical and useful, but in practice one often finds that it is the less stressful persons that benefits most from these methods. Those more prone to stress usually say, "I know it is good for me and I understand the logic of it, but I just do not know how to practice it and use it to manage my stress." Doctors spend much time to explain and persuade patients to modify their lifestyles, but often find that their patients are not doing what they advise. What these doctors fail to realize is that being able to understand something is quite different from being able to practice it. Most of us know how to appreciate good music, but how many of us know how to produce it?

A person who thinks before he speaks, before he acts, is in a mundane sense a wise person. But consider this: a person who does not think before he speaks or before he acts is a slave of his body, because his body's needs dictate his expression and action. A person who thinks before he speaks and acts is merely a slave of his mind, because his mind's need dictates his expression and action. So they are both slaves. Both are not free to act and react. In discussing the ways to manage stress above, it is the way an individual reacts that generates stress for himself. And stress is the key to mental health. But ff one is not free, how can we hope to modify our action and reaction?

Many realize that their bodies are beyond their control, few realize that their minds too are beyond their control. All thoughts are products of the mind. These include conception, idea, impression, notion, perception, image, view, cogitation, consideration, contemplation, deliberation, reflection, and more important, thoughts, including logic and reasoning. So one cannot use logic and reasoning to conquer thought because thought cannot conquer thought. So one needs to learn to think before one things, so to speak!

12. What Are the Mind's Needs?

To be free from slavery and imprisonment is not to let the mind's need dictate our action. Then we need to know who our enemies are, i.e., what the mind's needs are and how these needs enslave us.

Lobha: Whenever we are involved in gain and lass we are not balanced because we are emotionally involved. The mind will then easily control and enslave us. When we lose something it is easy to understand that we should be miserable. But when we gain something, we start to become anxious to keep it and protect it from loss. Sometimes a rich man is more miserable than a poor man because he has more to lose.

Dosa: Whenever we are involved in liking and disliking we are not balanced because we are emotionally involved. When we like something, we often dislike something else simultaneously. It is unavoidable. A person that likes brightness usually dislikes darkness. If a person likes all things equally, then he likes nothing. When we are with things that we like, we are happy. But this happiness does not last long. For impermanence is always present, and as things change one has to face things that he dislikes. Emotions ranging from discomfort, allergy, dissatisfaction, displeasure, distaste, disgust, antagonism, repulsion and bitterness, to hatred, ill-will and anger may arise. With all these emotions we surely become easily enslaved by the mind. It is common knowledge that when anger strikes, even a so-called wise man will lose control.

Moha: There are three more groups of activities that the mind uses to control us, collectively known as *moha*, or delusion. These are:

> Sloth, topper, Laziness and weariness: the inertness of the mind which refuses to move;
> restlessness, worry and fear: the wondering mind;
> doubt, indecision, ignorance and perplexity: these prevent us from sustaining any progress.

Together with *dosa* (usually translated as "hatred," although it means much more) and *lobha* (usually translated as "greed," but it should mean "craving or lust for power") they are known as the Five Hindrances. They are the means by which the mind enslaves us.

Let us look at an object as an example. First, when you are seeing an object, either you will crave it, you will lust for it, or you will be greedy about the object you see. If not so, you will become angry about what you see, or you will be averted to what you see, or you become allergic to what you see. If not, then you will become slothful, lazy and fall asleep, getting bored with it. Or you get worry about it. What is this? Will it fall on my head? Is it a good omen or bad? Restless will come, failing which you will remain undecided.

13. Meditation as a Means to Master Our Life

So what is meditation for? Meditation is something to do with thought. Meditation is an exercise to enable us one day to become the master of our mind, to be free from the mind's control.

Meditation is to be able to know that though arises and, as it arises, to detect it in that arising; so meditation is to take stock, to tackle the thought process. Unless we ask the mind to hold an object, we do not know where the mind is. The mind is just like a river, but when the mind holds an object, then you get waves. So when the mind holds an object, only then can we train the mind.

It is important to meditate on an object that is relatively free from greed, hatred and delusion, or else emotions will arise and the mind will take over the control of you.

In *ānāpāna sati*, the meditation we are talking about, the object is "the awareness (*sati*) of the breathing-in (*āna*) and breathing-out (*pāna*)."

Please note that the object is not the breath but the awareness. So when you practice this form of meditation, do not say, "I am breathing in, I am breathing out." Simply "sit" at the point where you can be aware of the breath and be aware that "now the breath is present, now the breath is not present." Why not present? Because breathing is not a continuous process. There are three phases: the in-breath, the out-breath and the in-between, a "gap" or a pause where the lung, the chest and the diaphragm are not moving. Awareness of the presence of the breath is awareness. Awareness of the absence of the breath is also awareness. Just like seeing light is seeing, seeing darkness is also seeing. Meditating this way also helps us to see awareness as it is and get rid of the "I."

There is nothing to gain since the awareness of breath is with us all the time, in any situation at any posture and is with us whatsoever we are doing. Since it is available to us all the time, there is no gain or loss. The only time when we lose the breath is when we pass away, but then who cares about meditation or stress after passing away? With breathing, there is no liking or disliking, since very few persons like or hate their breathing. There is also no delusion, since breathing is a natural phenomenon.

Vitakka (initial application): When we hold our attention to the awareness of the touch of breath, since we are holding the mind on an object the inertness of the mind disappears. This is the antidote to sloth and torpor.

Vicāra (sustained application): Now go on repeating, noting the awareness of breath. Doubt will disappear. This is the antidote to doubt.

Pī ti (joy): Since there is no more sloth and torpor or doubt, a kind of comfort that is not dependent upon gain / loss or like / dislike naturally arises. Ill-will-goes away.

Sukha (bliss): As ill-will goes away, one feels safe, protected and satisfied. Bliss appears. Restlessness and worry disappear.

Ekaggata (unification of mind): After removing these four hindrances, your mind is now only observing the object of meditation. Greed or attachment and craving disappear temporarily. It is a temporary phase of rising above the clouds, of transcending temporarily above your worldly things and entering an area of calm.

Now these five things are called *aṅga* or limbs. These are the five qualities of *jhāna*, of absorption, of meditation hearing fruit. Thus meditation is the ability to cultivate the habit of growing in the "mindfulness of breathing-in and breathing-out."

14. Awareness of the Wandering Mind and Bringing it Back: *sammā-vāyāma* (Right Effect)

When you sit down to meditate, say "I am going to become aware of the touch of breath." Ok, sit down. Now your mind wanders. You hear a sound, thinking of something, smell something, or feel itchy. Now that is called wandering mind. If you feel that, it is very natural. You become aware of it. This is very good. Why? You are meditating. That is why you become aware. My object is this, my mind wonders. I-lave I become aware, i.e., am I meditating?

So now, what must I do? Bring back the mind. My mind wanders there; oh, I know my mind wanders. Bring it back, bring it back to the touch of breath. Mindfully I brought back the touch of breath. That is called *samma vāyāma*, the right effect.

15. Meditation has Nothing to Do with Miracles or Religion

Now, this is not a miracle, this has nothing to do with religion. Whether you are Buddhist, Christian, Muslim, Hindu or Atheist, you can do it.

How do you feel when you go above the clouds in a plane? How would you see the world on the top of a mountain? The cars you see are like little ants. And the rivers are like some small lines. You get a new perspective of the world.

When you reach this calm of meditation, you get a new dimension and you see this world in its true nature of greed, hatred and delusion. You see above the clouds and then you discover that you are able to do this at any given time; if you have a lot of problems, you can go above the clouds. This is tranquility. We normally say, "He is disturbing me," or "This is disturbing me." But in meditation we say that nobody disturbs you, you disturb yourself or you allow yourself to be disturbed. It is a functioning within you and it is a functioning for which you have no greed, hatred or delusion. Therefore, your state of mind is going above the clouds, transcending gradually to this point.

So meditation must be a thing which you can use anywhere, at any time, or all the time. So, no matter where you are, whatever position you are in, are you able to become aware of the touch of your breath? Whether you are standing, sitting, walking, lying down, are you breathing? Yes. Therefore, the object is with you. Actually, if the power of meditation is only applicable to setting in the lotus posture, it will be limited.

16. How to Find Time for Meditation in a Busy World

Sleep: Keep your awareness at the touch of breath until you fall asleep.

Waking up: Do all the daily routines such as brushing, washing, dressing, etc., by reflexes. Keep the awareness at the touch of breath until all the routines are done, instead of having a wandering mind.

Work: Use your mind for work and in between two minutes or three minutes, and keep your awareness at the touch of breath.

Housework: Do it by reflexes and put the awareness at the touch of breath.

During traveling: In the bus, etc., put the awareness at the touch of breath.

Eating: Put awareness at the touch instead of letting the mind wander.

Applications: Remain calm, relax and be aware during any task by meditation. You can achieve much more with a non-distracted mind.

17. *Samādhi* and *Vipassanā*: Two Aspects of Meditation

Until now we have been discussing *samādhi*, the way to achieve non-distracted one-pointed-ness.

Now let us look into *vipassanā*, the ability to scan, to process, to investigate, to analyze, to dissect your achievements and see in them the ultimate truth of science. It is impermanent. It ceases to be. It is not that powerful. Therefore, to be detached from achievement is wisdom. To achieve is ego. To claim it is possession, but to be detached and observing the phenomenon is to be a wise person. Such a one is not caught up in the flood of time, in the flood of achievement.

To see this world as one, without the division of race, of creed, of religion, to see the world in its absoluteness as one, not as two, three, or so many religions, to see all people as one, is the quality of equanimity.

In *vipassanā* one can start from practicing the thirty seven factors of enlightenment, starting from the Four Foundations of Mindfulness.

18. *Satipaṭṭhāna*: The Four Foundations of Mindfulness

1) *Cittānupassanā*: awareness (consciousness) of the touch -- mind: the awareness of breathing is a state of mind.

2) *Kāyānupassanā*: awareness of the sensation of touch -- body: breathing in and breathing out are bodily actions.

3) *Vedanānupassanā*: touch is a sensation -- sensation: the awareness of touch is a form of sensation.

4) *Dhammānupassanā*: touch is a phenomenon -- phenomenon: breathing is a phenomenon.

19. Obstacles in Meditation

Now when you meditate, you can get what are called fearful thoughts, fearful moments. Then you must tell yourself at that time that it is mind-made, it is not permanent. There is nothing to fear. It is part of the positive and negative karmas. You must gain confidence to say that it is you, not somebody else. Otherwise, not doing the meditation, following the "spirit," you can fall into trouble. Leaving the meditation and starting to talk to him is dangerous.

Many people write books describing their experiences in meditation. A spiritual man may be expressing through mundane words the spiritual experience. Then they put others into misunderstandings. What a spiritual man would say in his spiritual depth in words, which are normal, may be misinterpreted by others when they read them since they do not have his spiritual depth. So I do not intend to describe in detail how to practice *vipassanā* meditation. Instead, I would like to tell you that you can achieve positive mental health by learning meditation alone.

20. Ways to Make Full Use of Meditation towards Mental Health

Sīla: Precepts are systemic cultivations of thought, expression and action. By willingly refraining from killing, stealing, sexual misconduct, lying and taking intoxicants, one gradually develops the habit of living with less craving, attachment and ignorance. There is no guilt or punishment involved. It is merely a form of discipline and pursuit willingly taken up by individual to develop a habit of non-greed, non-hatred and non-delusion in order practice calm (*samādhi*) and seeing a thing as it is (*vipassanā*).

The development of the insight (*paññā*) of knowing that things are unsatisfactory and impermanent, and that there is no entity that can be truly "me", is entirely up to the individual at his own pace. There is no point in forcing oneself to use logic and reasoning to understand the abstract concept of "no self." Realization has to be cultivated and developed, just like a little boy has to mature gradually. Force-feeding only causes indigestion. A regular balanced diet over time will transform a boy into a mature adult.

With insight, agitation will be overcome by detachment, a distracted mind will be overcome by calm, and emotion will be overcome by tranquility. There will no longer be the stress of the future rushing upon us, but instead will be the realistic approach of coming to tennis with changes by adaptation and modification. As craving is understood and brought under control, the aggressiveness of chronic, incessant struggle to achieve ceases and is transformed into a more moderate and regulated reaction. One will learn to assess his reactions and the situation before taking action. As one learns to see things as they are, situations become more predictable and less stressful as a result of the ability to control situations. As stress becomes more manageable, there will be less neurosis due to fear, frustration and emotional instability from irrational expectations and sudden or adverse life events.

21. Study on the Relation of Meditation and Stress

Five meditation retreats were conducted at Seck Kia Eenh, a Buddhist temple where the Malacca Buddhist Association is located, situated at 57, Jalan Gajah Berang 75200 Malacca, West Malaysia.

A total of 196 participants were involved in the study, 88 males and 108 females between the ages of 7 and 62 years. Members and devotees of the temple were informed of the meditation retreat one month in advance, and anybody interested was able to register under a Dhamma Group Committee. They were told to stay in and practice eight precepts, i.e., the participant population was self-selected among temple devotees. However, not all participants were Buddhist. At least 6 were Christian, and some were Taoist. These did not practice the eight precepts. A few (11) were students. The majority were either housewives or working adults. A few ~9) were retired. Not all the participants were from Malacca. Some came from Kuala Lumpur, Penang,

Johore, East Malaysia, Singapore and Jātaka. The meditation retreats were conducted over weekends in English.

The majority of the participants had no previous experience with meditation. Of 88 males and 108 females, only 5 males and 9 females had some experience of meditation retreats, but none of them had reached the first *jhāna*, and none of them had reached the state of *pīti*.

22. Method Used in the Study to Measure Stress

Have you ever felt pressured and tense without knowing exactly what was happening to you? You may visit doctors for medication, find relief for a while, and then continue to feel the same as before.

This suggests that you should examine whether stress is the cause of these symptoms. Very often we are unable to recognize stress. And that may well be the basic problem -- that we do not know what the problem is. Attempts have been made to design checklist and evaluation formats for detecting stress. Another means of discovering stress is by assessing your anxiety level.

In this study anxiety level was rated from an adaptation from Morse.[1] Participants were asked to answer yes or not to 33 questions. A "yes" to a question scored one point. Some questions related to subjective feelings, and some related to symptoms as a result of stress, i.e. half were subject and half were of objective verifiable facts. The stress levels were classified into extreme (25-33), high (17-24), moderate (9-16) and low (0-8). All participants were rated with the standard questionnaire adapted from Morse. All participants were rated before they practiced meditation and rated by the same questionnaire again three months later.

23. Type of Meditation Practiced

The meditation retreat started with asking why the participants came for the meditation, followed by an explanation of the principles of meditation. Participants were taught to locate the point where they can feel their breathing-in and breathing-out, known as the touch, where it was felt most prominently. They were told to focus on that touch. But instead of focusing on I am breathing in, I am breathing out," members were told not to differentiate the in-breath and the out-breath, but just to note the awareness of the presence or absence of the breathing. They were told that the ability to note the presence of breath is awareness, and the ability to note the absence of breath is also awareness. No particular postures were taught, and members were free to meditate in any posture. They were guided to develop various stages of meditation, from initial application, sustained application, joy, bliss, and unification of mind until the beginning of the 2nd *jhāna*. All members were encouraged to reach the 2nd *jhāna*

---

[1] Donald R. Morse, *Stress for Success* (New York: Van Nostrand Reinhold, 1979).

together. They are not required to achieve beyond the 2nd *jhāna*. This is how they learn of *samādhi*.

After almost all participants reached the 2ndihana, they were guided to practice *vipassāna* in stages and to finally go through all thirty-seven factors of the enlightenment. Then they were reminded of the relationship among *sīla*, *samādhi* and *paññā*, especially highlighting *sīla* or precepts. *Sīla* is the safeguard to prevent us from falling into mental hindrances.

Then they were told when they should meditate and were reminded of the importance of practicing meditation regularly. This was followed by a general discussion, a question and answer section, and individual guidance.

In order to assess the results with less bias, those participants who teamed other forms of meditation before were encouraged to drop their method and follow this method as closely as possible. Fortunately, most participants found this method more precise and more effective than their old method of meditation, so it required minimum persuasion to get them to change methods.

24. Results of the Study

Stress scores before various retreats and three months after the retreats showed that the majority of the participants improved. The average percent of improvement seemed to be proportionate to the initial stress rating or score. The average percent of improvement was 34.02%.

The average percent of improvement seems unrelated to the number of the participants, sex, age, which city or region they came from, or religion. For example, there was a Christian that improved from the score of 20 to 4. There was a child that can practice *vipassanā*.

25. The Lack of a Control Group

Unfortunately, there was no control to compare to in the study. The possibility that the whole result was due to a placebo effect cannot be ruled out. However, the participants found that the meditation was so useful that many of them continue to hold weekly meditation sessions in the temple organized by the participants themselves. At any one time, 50-80% of the participants tamed up for the weekly meditation sessions. These sessions had attracted another 80 to 100 others who had not participated in the study, with some coming as far away as Brunei, mainly because they saw a change in the lives of these participants. They became happier and emotionally more stable. Many of them became more successful in their careers and in their studies. For example, a former bankrupt participant has since become a half-millionaire. A student with a problem of being refused admittance by schools has since graduated with good results and is now a practicing lawyer.

This group of participants is still being followed up. The group that has been followed up for more than two years has not shown any sign of losing their interest in meditation, and their stress scores are still gradually but steadily decreasing.

26. Conclusion

Meditation is a scientific way of observing and investigating the mind so that we become the master of the mind instead of being the salve of our emotions through self-understanding and realization. This helps us to develop the ability to control situations and minimize stress, and to avoid being aggressively involved in an incessant struggle to achieve, so that our reactions can be more moderate and regulated and we can assess our reactions and the situation before taking action. Fear, frustration, emotional instability, and physical as well as mental illness can be prevented by cutting down irrational, unrealistic expectations, and by developing a coping mechanism ready to anticipate any sudden changes in life events. When you reach this state of calm meditation, you get a new dimension and you see this world in its true nature.

Part 5

East Asian Buddhism

CHAPTER 28

THE ROLE OF REPENTANCE - OR LACK OF IT - IN ZEN MONASTICISM

Steven Heine

This paper critically examines the role of repentance or confession in Chan / Zen monastic theory and practice and discusses its significance for understanding the Buddhist approach to peace. The paper is an extension and (penitent) criticism of the paper I presented on a similar topic at the Sixth Seminar held in November 1993, titled "On Repentance (*Zange*): A Zen Synthetic Approach to Peace." In that paper I considered an assortment of criticisms leveled at the social and political implications of Buddhism, especially Zen, which have come from both within and outside of the tradition, including Zen scholars Ichikawa Hakugen and Hakamaya Noriaki and Pure Land philosophy Tanabe Hajime, Japanese writers Mishima Yukio and Ōe Kenzaburō, as well as Western philosophers and historians. These critics have focused on the passivity and complacency or status quo-ism of the social aspect of Zen, its complicity in nationalism and tacit endorsement of Japanese imperialism before and during the war, and its apparent misuse or twisting of the traditional notions of emptiness and naturalism to support *nihonjinron* theory and the myth of Japanese uniqueness. But at the same time I tried to show, rather optimistically following Tanabe, that the notion of repentance as the sense of regret for and correction of wrongdoing could serve as a synthetic and dynamic conceptual and practical model for overcoming some of these problems and integrating Zen and Pure Land, self-power and other-power, and Buddhist great and little traditions, as well as Buddhist and Western religious approaches toward social responsibility.

Considering Sen. Fulbright's definition of peace as being "not a negative, static concept.... [but] a positive method of adjusting the endless conflicts inherent in the nature of restless and energetic men," and in light of the way this view seemed to dovetail with Buddhist views on impermanence and compassion, I argued:

> In addition to Tanabe, both Zen advocates and critics put a strong
> emphasis on the role of individual repentance (*zange*), change of
> heart, spiritual "turning," or transformation in the religious quest that
> could be considered, if appropriately interpreted, to provide a key to
> an active, positive method of adjusting endless conflicts. The Zen
> meditative, self-power path may not be particularly known for
> stressing the idea of repentance, which seems to be primarily
> associated with the Pure Land devotional, other-power path ...
> However, repentance does emerge as an important theme in Zen
> thinkers ... The notion of repentance stems from early Buddhist
> *vinaya* practice and is also highlighted in Tendai meditation as well
> as popular medieval Japanese *setsuwa* literature. Understood in its
> authentic self-reflective sense rather than as a facile, automatic
> confession, repentance can become the basis of a synthesis of the Zen
> and Pure Land, as well as the Mahāyāna and Theravāda, and
> Buddhist and Christian, world-views in relation to peace.

The present paper takes a closer look at the historical context of repentance
in Zen monasticism based on traditional and modern textual and social sources
to better determine the viability and applicability of the notion for understanding
the peace issue. It focuses on two distinct but interconnected tendencies. First,
except for a couple of prominent exceptions such as the *Platform Sūtra* and the
Sōtō sect's "Shushōgi" and perhaps due in part to the *Platform*'s emphasis on
"formless (*musō*) repentance" and the non-production of evil, there tends to be a
lack of evidence in traditional monastic codes or recorded sayings texts for
Zen's involvement in *zange*. Furthermore, and perhaps more importantly, there
is little direct refutation of the practice that was so prevalent in many other kinds
of medieval Buddhism, although, again, the *Platform*, as well as some passages
by Dōgen, could be seen as providing a justification for this. The second
tendency is that there has been a prevalence of references to the notion of *zange*
in recent discussions by Zen writers of contemporary social issues such as the
problem of social discrimination against former outcaste (*hinin*) and
untouchable (*burakumin*) communities. The first tendency may indicate an
indifference or neglect of repentance based on the priority of spiritual
transcendence over the need for ritual confession, but the second tendency
supports the view that *zange* can reflect an approach to conflict-resolution that
may be considered applicable to peace. These tendencies appear to refer to two
different, even conflicting, yet overlapping meanings of repentance: the first
tendency refers to a ceremonial performance, which is used in Zen though not
emphasized in its classical texts, in which repentance is ritually made *toward
Buddhism*, as in the case of correcting oneself or suffering punishment after the
violation of Buddhist precepts; the second tendency refers to a more general,
socially-oriented sense of repenting *for Buddhism*, especially due to its lack of
having corrected or taken full responsibility for its contribution to social
discrimination. Whereas the first kind of repentance operates within the closed
circle of the monastic institution, the second kind open-endedly extends

traditional monastic ritual into the realm of social responsibility and commitment.

Therefore, this paper starts from the observation that although Zen monasticism does employ traditional Buddhist repentance rituals on a daily, monthly, and yearly basis, when compared to some other sects of East Asian Buddhism (as well as non-Buddhist religions), it appears that Zen literature and ritual have placed a relative lack of emphasis on this practice. There may be valid reasons for such a de-emphasis, and the notion of "formless repentance" could be interpreted as offering a rationale for maintaining consistency with other aspects of Zen's self-power ideology and skeptical view of the efficacy of formal, external ritual. Yet the Song Zen texts that generally do not speak of the need for repentance also do not provide a follow-up to the *Platform Sūtra*'s critique or a further explanation for the de-emphasis on the ritual even when they endorse other forms of ceremonialism. An important implication of this apparent indifference is that the failure to view repentance as a sustained mechanism for self-reproach, self-criticism, and self-correction, not that it always functions in such a positive way, may have hindered the development of a cogent Zen moral code (as opposed to monastic rules of etiquette). This statement is not meant to imply the converse, that is, that an emphasis on repentance necessarily leads to ethical responsibility; the Jōdo Shinshū has shown more interest and commitment than Zen in rectifying the discrimination problem beginning in the 1920s, but this may reflect the fact that the overwhelming number of untouchables were assigned to this sect, especially the Nishi Honganji branch, in the Tokugawa era *danka* system. The implications for other forms of Buddhism must be examined on a case-by-case basis. The point is that the de-emphasis in Zen has perhaps helped promote some antinomian tendencies, or at least tendencies that are non-ethical in the sense that they reflect a turning away from a direct confrontation with ethical responsibility and decision-making. Perhaps Zen has cultivated this attitude deliberately, at least on a rhetorical level, in the name of a "trans-ethical" perspective that transcends conventional standards of good and evil in a quasi-Nietzschean sense, but this rationale has a hollow ring in light of Zen's now acknowledged participation in discrimination, nationalism, imperialism, and corporatism.[1]

On the other hand, in recent years *zange* has been evoked by some Zen thinkers as a means of coming to terms with the issue of Buddhism's contribution to social discrimination against former outcastes and untouchables who have been defined as impure by religion and persecuted and denied basic rights by society. The notion of repentance, which seeks to eradicate the roots of defilement and sinfulness, is closely linked to the way that the notion of karma as an explanation of the origin and consequences of evil and defilement is applied to the social structure, as well as to methods for accruing merit. In the past, Buddhism had a tendency of defining outcastes as being burdened with evil

---

[1] Daizen Victoria, "Japanese Corporate Zen," in *The Other Japan: Postwar Realities*, ed. E. Patricial Tsurumi (Armonk, NY: M.E. Sharpe, 1988), 131-138.

karma because of their occupations which involve working with animal flesh, such as butchers, leather-workers, etc. Therefore, perhaps as an unintended and unexpected result of this identification, outcastes were perceived by society as worthy of victimization. Now, the tendency is to reverse the errors of the past by assigning to Buddhism itself the problematic karma, if any, as well as the need for repentance for having helped propagate attitudes which have, even if unintentionally, violated the rights of outcastes. Because the issue of discrimination is often interconnected with the issues of nationalism and militarism in modern Japanese society, which similarly reflect a suppression of minority or stigmatized groups, the development of a self-reflective and self-critical attitude towards the former problem may well offer some clues as to how to apply Zen repentance-based ethics to the question of peace.

In this paper I am using the term *zange* in a generic sense[2] to refer to a cluster of related ideas and terms stemming from early Buddhist monastic texts, a number of which are sometimes translated into Sino-Japanese in other ways, but all of which are closely affiliated with the way that *zange* is frequently used by referring to "remorse, regret, lamenting, repenting for deeds done or omission ... [making] clear the idea that repentance had rewards and the lack of it, punishments."[3] These terms include two main rituals followed by Buddhist monastics. The first is the ritual of *uposatha* (or *fusatsu*), *or* fortnightly (at the middle and end of the lunar month) confession in front of the assembly of monks during the recitation of the *prātimokṣa* list of 250 precepts, a "monastic process of examination, confession and rectification for restoring those who had broken the rules [which] function[s] within a finite context of present human activity involving the mutual agreement of a group of practitioners."[4] During the *uposatha* the monks and nuns confess the wrongdoings in their external behavior and receive standard, prescribed punishments, although confession is also encouraged between the occasions of the ritual. The second ritual is the *pravāraṇa* or mutual, public confessing at the end of the rainy season, a time for monastics who have spent months together to clear the air before making contact with the lay community. Both of these ceremonies are generally followed in Zen practice though the timing of the *pravāraṇa* cycle may vary from the schedule listed in the early canon. *Zange* also refers to the act of penance or contrition (Skt. *kṣama, kṣamayati*), implying a sense of patience and confession, and to the

---

[2] According to Chappell, five kinds of repentance are (1) communal repentance to the *saṅgha* to ensure monastic conformity; (2) personal repentance of karmic history; (3) mythological repentance to a super-mundane Buddha; (4) meditation repentance of incorrect perceptions and attachments; and (5) philosophical repentance of wrong concepts and discrimination. See Chappell, 253.

[3] See Lewis Lancaster, "The Terminology of the *Platform Sutra* in the Chinese Buddhist Canon," in the *Report of International Conference on Ch'an Buddhism* (Taiwan: Fo Kuang Shan, 1990), 55.

[4] David Chappell, "Formless Repentance in Comparative Perspective," in *Report of International Conference on Ch'an Buddhism* (Taiwan: Fo Kuang Shan, 1990), 254.

determination to make reforms (Skt. *deśanā*). It is also important to recognize that East Asian Buddhist views on repentance were no doubt influenced by and assimilated with indigenous approaches to eliminating evil and wrongdoing, such as Confucian ideas about shame and ritual, and the purification rites, exorcisms, faith healings, and memorial ceremonies practiced in Taoism, Shinto, and folk religions (Wu), as well as *zange* practices in some New Religions, such as Ittōen, which has, for example, a communal toilet-cleaning rite.[5]

In light of the various meanings mentioned above, as well as an intriguing typology of Buddhist repentance rituals developed by David Chappell, I suggest that *zange* can be understood by making several basic distinctions. One distinction is between *zange* in the generic sense encompassing a remorse and punishment for wrongdoing and *zange* in an explicitly ceremonial, liturgical sense, as in the *uposatha* and *pravāraṇa* rituals, which in turn also include distinctions between voluntary and required, individual and communal aspects of repentance. Another distinction is between *zange metsuzai*, to borrow the term featured in "Shushōgi" which implies the purification of evil karma through the power of forgiveness of compassionate buddhas, bodhisattvas, and patriarchs, and *zangedō*, to borrow the term which forms the center of Tanabe Hajime's later, postwar philosophy, which implies a personal, existential struggle with one's sense of wrongdoing. Ironically, the Zen text created in the Meiji period by the Sōtō sect by culling and editing Dōgen's sayings seems to suggest a mechanical and devotional model of repentance, and Tanabe's Pure Land approach appears more individualistic and intuitive, keeping in mind that his message was directed to the nation, as well as to his fellow philosophers whose prewar writings contributed to militarist ideology, which was suffering defeat and humiliation in the war. The distinction between *zange metsuzai* and *zangedō* can also be used to encompass the distinction mentioned above between repentance toward Buddhism due to perceptual transgressions and repentance for Buddhism because of its wrongdoings in society at large.

1. Uses, Abuses, and Non-uses

As indicated above, Zen monasteries generally observe the basic Buddhist repentance rites on a monthly and annual cycle, and also include remorseful reflection as part of daily sūtra-reading or meditative walking exercises (*kinhin*). Yet, save for some famous exceptions, Song Chinese and Kamakura Zen texts, including transmission of the lamp histories of lineal succession, recorded sayings of individual masters' sermons and lectures, and Han collection prose and verse commentaries, do not speak extensively of the need for, or benefits or lack of same, of repentance in depicting Zen hagiography, practice, or

---

[5] Winston Davis, *Japanese Religion and Society: Paradigms of Structure and Change* (Albany: SUNY Press, 1992), 189-225.

philosophy. Even the main monastic code, the *Zen'en shingi*[6] contains only brief references, and the plans of the typical monastic compound contain no repentance hall [7]. Among the exceptions to this absence or de-emphasis on *zange* are Northern school texts such as the *Dasheng wusheng fangpian men* and *Lengqie shizu ji*; two *Shōbōgenzō* [8] fascicles, the "Keisei-sanshoku" and "Sanjigo"; Ming dynasty monastic revival texts by Zhuhong; anecdotal, *monogatari*-like writings referring to social leaders, such as samurai in Tokugawa Japan, who saw the error of their ways and repented before converting to Buddhism. Nevertheless, Zen stands in contrast with several other medieval Buddhist traditions that did strongly emphasize repentance: Tendai (Tiantai) in China, which, integrated repentance involving ritual ablutions in sacred chambers into the practice of the Four Samadhi-based on Zhiyi's distinction in the *Fahua sanmei Zhanyi*[9] between formless repentance in the realm of principle (*ri*) and form repentance in the realm of phenomena (*ji*);[10] repentance practices based on a variety of mythological *sūtras* dedicated to the supernatural powers of bodhisattvas who have the capacity to grant mercy, as followed in devotional and esoteric Buddhism;[11] and folk Buddhist *setsuwa* tales of religious awakening.[12]

What is the reason for the de-emphasis in Zen? It is possible to see two of the texts which put an emphasis on repentance at the same time providing a rationale to turn away from the need for confession, particularly in the phenomenal sense of *zange*. This is especially the case in the *Platform Sūtra*'s focus on formless repentance. At first, the *Platform Sūtra*'s view, which stresses that evil karma must be seen as originally empty and thus part of the purity of self-nature (*jishō*), seems to coincide with the Tendai distinction between *ji-zange*, or repentance for misdeeds committed in the realm of phenomenal reality, and *ri-zange*, or recognition of the absolute nature of reality, which is that all

---

[6] See Kagamishima Genryū, Satō Tatsugen & Kosaka Kiyū, *Yakuchū Zen'en shingi* (A Japanese Translation of the Zen Monastic Rules) (Tokyo: Sōtōshū shūmuchō, 1972), 169 & 307.

[7] Martin Collcutt, *Five Mounntains: The Rinzai Monastic Institution in Medieval Japan* (Cambridge: Harvard University Press, 1981) and T. Griffith Foulk, "Myth, Ritual, and Monastic Practice in Sung Ch'an Buddhism," in *Religion and Society in T'ang and Sung China*, eds. Patricia Buckley Ebrey and Peter N. Gregory (Honolulu: University of Hawaii Press, 1993), 147-208.

[8] Dōgen, *Shōbōgenzō*, 2 vols., eds. Terada Tōru and Mizuno Yaoko (Tokyo: Iwanami, 1970 and 1972).

[9] T.46.949a-955c.

[10] See Daniel Stevenson, "The Four Kinds of Samadhi in Early T'ien-t'ai Buddhism," in *Traditions of Meditation in Chinese Buddhism*, ed. Peter N. Gregory (Honolulu: University of Hawaii Press, 1986).

[11] M. W. De Visser, *Ancient Buddhism in Japan*, Vol. 1 (Leiden: Brill, 1935), 249-409.

[12] Margaret Helen Childs, *Rethinking Sorrow: Revelatory Tales of Late Medieval Japan* (Ann Arbor: University of Michigan Press, 1991).

things are empty of own being, including sin. The main difference, however, is that whereas Tendai acknowledges the role *of ji-zange* while advocating its transcendence, the *Platform Sutra* denies *ji-zange* as part of delusion that prohibits a realization *of* transcendence.

The main sections dealing with the theme *of* formless repentance in the *Platform Sutra* are nos. 22 and 33. Section no. 22 "explains the formless repentance that eradicates the sins *of* the triple world." According to this passage:

> If your past, present, or future thoughts as well as moment-to-moment thoughts are not stained by delusion, and *if* in a single instant you cast aside previous evil actions by virtue of self-nature, this itself is confession (*zan*, seeking forgiveness).... What is repentance [made up of two kanji, *zan* and *ge*,[13] regret]? Confession (*zan*) is the non-production [of evil] throughout your life. Regret (*ge*) is to realize your previous evil karma and never let this slip from your mind. There is no reason to make a verbal confession before buddhas. In my teachings, forever to engage in non-production is the meaning of repentance.[14]

This passage emphasizes the need to discard any trace of form repentance as so much distraction and delusion; that is, verbal confession is counter-productive because the key is to realize the non-production of evil based on the original purity of self-nature. The view that self-nature is inherently free from defilement is further highlighted in Lewis Lancaster's translation of several important lines in the above passage:

> Remorse [*ge*] is being free of purposeful action (Skt. *apraṇihita*) for the whole of your life. Repentance is *knowing that with regard to the past there is no evil action* and never let this slip from your mind.[15]

Section no. 33, "a verse of formlessness that will eradicate the sins of deluded people," continues this theme:

> Though [the ignorant person] hopes that making offerings
> and attending memorial services will bring boundless happiness,
> This only perpetuates the three karmas (of past, present, and future)
> in his mind.
> If you seek to eradicate sins by practices based on the pursuit of
> happiness,

---

[13] A prime example is using two kanji, *gen* and *da*, which, when written as a single kanji becomes *chiku*, beasts.

[14] Philip B. Yampolsky, *The Platform Sutra of the Sixth Patriarch* (New York: Columbia University Press), 144-45. Chinese, 10, translations are altered.

[15] Lancaster, 58, a revision of both Yampolsky and Wing-tsit Chan. Emphasis is added.

> Then even if happiness is attained in the future the sins will not be
> eliminated. If the mind is liberated from the very causes of sin,
> This is the true meaning of repentance within each self-nature. If you
> awaken to the great vehicle and truly repent,
> Then you will surely attain a state of sinless-ness.
> Contemplation of the self by those who are studying the Way
> Is the same as the awakening of those already enlightened.[16]

Here, the *Platform Sūtra* argues that true repentance is to awaken to a state of sinless-ness, resembling the notion of innate enlightenment (*hongaku shisō*), prior to the production of evil karma. According to Chappell's insightful analysis, the *Platform Sūtra* creates a reversal from earlier notions of external, ceremonial repentance by stressing the priority of the internal, mental world, from which vantage point offerings and memorials are trapped in the pursuit of worldly benefits that only perpetuates karma in the name of terminating it. In addition, Chappell sums up the differences between the *uposatha / pravāraṇa* ceremonies and the *Platform Sūtra*: the former are based on rectifying wrongs in the sense of incorrect external behavior with regard to the Buddhist precepts in the immediate present through penance, exclusion, probation, restitution, or confession, whereas the *Platform Sūtra* is based on casting aside wrong thoughts and attitudes throughout the past, present, and future by realizing the purity of self nature and that the true precepts stem from the threefold buddha-body within each person [17]. Furthermore, the *Platform Sūtra* points to the identification and equalization of those still practicing and the already enlightened, or of practice-attainment (*shushō ittō*) in Dōgen's terminology.

Dōgen similarly stresses that the realization of authentic spiritual attainment requires going beyond the ritualization of repentance when he cites his mentor Rujing's utterance: "To study Zen is to cast off body-mind. It is not burning incense, worship, recitation of Amida's name, repentant practice (*shū-zan*), or reading sutras, but the single-minded practice of *zazen*-only" (Dōgen, 1, 217, "Gyōji" fascicle; also cited in the "Bendowa" fascicle, *Eihei Kōroku*[18], and *Hōkyōki*). However, the message of "Shushōgi," a short text compiled from Dōgen's writings by Meiji era Sōtō leaders, is somewhat different. The aim of this text is to provide an accessible theological framework in modern times for monastics and laypersons alike. Although the content of "Shushōgi" does not necessarily correspond to the intentionality of the source materials, it is very important for understanding contemporary Sōtō thought. Section no. 2 titled "*zange metsuzai*" seems to stand in contrast, or even opposition, with the *Platform Sūtra* in that it supports repentance in the conventional ritualistic sense, yet its message can also be seen as converging with the Tang text in providing a rationale that vitiates the need for a systematic approach to *ji-zange* confession:

---

[16] Yampolsky, 153. Chinese translations are altered.

[17] Chappell, 255.

[18] Dōgen, *Eihei kōroku*, ed. Yokoi Yūhō (Tokyo: Sankibō busshorin, 1978).

> Although karmic retribution for evil actions must come in the past, present, or future, to make repentance transforms things and accrues merit, and it results in the destruction of wrongdoing (or sin, *metsuzai*) and the realization of purity ... If you repent in the manner described, you will invariably receive the invisible assistance of the buddhas and patriarchs. Keeping this in your mind and following the rules for your bodily behavior, you must repent before the buddhas whose power will lead to the elimination of the causes of wrongdoing at their roots.[19]

This passage emphasizes the virtue of repentance in transforming evil deeds based on the power of forgiveness and the compassion of buddhas, It appears close to a mythological, supernatural perspective yet still requires self-discipline and meditative training. Yet, like the *Platform Sutra*, "Shushōgi" suggests that wrongdoing can be fully eliminated and a state of sinless-ness attained. In other words, both the *Platform Sutra*'s notion of non-production of karma and "Shushōgi's notion of the destruction of karma (*metsuzai*) imply that ultimate human nature (or Buddha-nature or *hongaku*) remains untainted and unaffected by the effects of evil actions. The underlying ethical problem is that by emphasizing the priority of transcendence these approaches may overlook some of the unintended consequences that arise without constraints from a de-emphasis on recognizing and feeling remorse and repentance for actual wrongdoings in the phenomenal realm of karmic causality.

2. The Roots of Social Discrimination and Its Implication for Peace

The *vinaya* rituals of *uposatha* and *pravāraṇa* function within a closed circle in the sense that they refer to repentance for transgressions committed against the Buddhist saṅgha and its *prātimokṣa* rules. Correction of behavior is based on confession and punishments that encourage a return to strict adherence to the rules. Both the *Platform Sutra* and "Shushōgi" seek to move beyond the ritual circle by emphasizing the transformative capacity of self-nature or Buddha-nature. The strength of these approaches lies in their clarification of the soteriological significance of formless repentance, but the weakness lies in their neglect of the ethical implications of de-emphasizing form repentance based on the *zange metsuzai* approach. Recent reflections by concerned Buddhists on the issue of discrimination however, suggest the emergence of another view of repentance that transcends the ritual circle by virtue of the ritual, that is, it transmutes the notion of *ji-zange* repentance into an open-ended commitment to social rectification and responsibility based on *zangedō* (literally, the "way" of repentance).

For example, a recent report on discrimination commissioned by Eiheiji temple, titled "Sendara mondai senmon i'inkai hōkoku," speaks of the need for

---

[19] Azuma Ryūshin, *Sōtōshū: Waga ie no shūkyō* (Sōtō Sect: The Religion of Our Families) (Tokyo: Daihōrinkaku, 1993), 147-9.

Zen's repentance, an intensely profound repentance (*fukaku-kibishii zange*), for the mistreatment of the *burakumin* community.[20] This report and other analyses of the impact of discrimination generally begin with a specific focus on abuses in the practice of *kaimyō*, the bestowing of posthumous ordination names at the time of a funeral. The next step is an investigation of the roots of discrimination in basic Buddhist doctrines and attitudes that gave rise to particular abuses.

Most sects of Japanese Buddhism, for which the association with funeral ceremonies as the main social function is so pronounced that the religion is often referred to by the general populace as "funeral Buddhism" (*sōshiki bukkyō*), are now involved in examining the hypocrisy of the *kaimyō* practices. The *kaimyō* system is an important part of funerals in which laypersons are treated as if they were monks through the use of external symbols (shaved heads, robes, ablutions, etc.). Although *kaimyō* do not identify social status directly, they have a built-in hierarchical approach in that different kinds of names are given to advanced and junior monks, monastics and laypersons, males and females, as well as to a variety of ranks and roles in society, from nobility to poverty.[21] The naming of *burakumin* people extends and perverts the entire process by deliberately identifying their untouchable status in disguised fashion in a way that purports to guarantee their salvation.

Buddhist commentators have been forced to consider what has given rise to such a hypocritical exploitation of Buddhist ceremony. There have been several important accounts of the historical and ideological roots of discrimination. For example, in *Sei to sen* (Sacred and Profane) Noma Hiroshi, a respected modern novelist and follower of Shinran who befriended and supported several *burakumin* writers, stresses two main points: the impact of the Indian caste system on Buddhist conceptions of karmic defilement and social stratification; and the Shinto view of ritual contamination (*kegare*, the kanji for which is also pronounced as *e* in the derogatory term, *eta*) and abhorrence of death. It is also important to understand the role of Buddhism in relation to untouchability in India, Tibet, and Korea. Zen scholars such as Ichikawa Hakugen (Rinzai) and Hakamaya Noriaki and Matsumoto Shirō (Sōtō) have focused on the notions of original enlightenment and non-duality in traditional Mahāyāna and Zen texts which can ironically foster social discrimination in the name of pointing to the attainment of liberation through epistemological non-discrimination. Matsumoto, for example, shows how the rhetoric of equality and universality in Buddha-nature doctrines is undercut by the category of *icchantikas*, exceptions to the rule who are said to be incapable of spiritual attainment. Another key topic is to analyze the transition form the ambiguous role of outcastes in medieval times,

---

[20] "Sendara mondai senmon i'inkai hōkoku" (Report of the Research Group on the Problem of Caṇḍala), no. 10, ed. Eiheiji Sendara Mondai Senmon I'inkai, *Sanshō* 606 (1994): 31.

[21] Shimada Hiromi, *Kaimyō: Naze shigo ni namae o kaeru no ka* (Posthumous Initiation Names: Why are Names Changed Poshumously?) (Kyoto: Hōzōkan, 1991), 67-71.

when they were often given comfort by Buddhism, especially in Eizon's Ritsu sect to the institutionalized and rigidified discrimination in the Tokugawa era, when Buddhism tended to become a source of rather than release from oppression, in part because of the role the religion was assigned in the *danka* system which functioned as an administrative arm of the shogunate.

One focal point has been the topic of *sendara* (Skt. *caṇḍala*), a term for untouchables in the Indian caste system that was appropriated in Buddhist texts as a designation for those whose evil karma prohibits them from being receptive to the Buddha's teachings. This category is discussed in the *Lotus Sūtra*, chapter 14 ("Peaceful Practices"), and in the *Shōbōgenzō* "Sanjigo" fascicle as well as in *Eihei kōroku* (7.47, 6.24, 3.66) and elsewhere. It may have been initially intended as a Way of evaluating the evil karma of murderers and mercenaries. But eventually in Japan the term became a tool to identify and discriminate against those who perform legitimate social functions in killing or handling dead animals even if these activities are not necessarily sanctioned by the saṅgha. This issue is further complicated by the historical situation that many untouchables were further "tainted" by being forced by the Tokugawa shogunate into the position of torturers, executioners, or disposers of the corpses.

An interesting example of how a traditional expression, value-free in its original context, has been subverted and used on behalf of discrimination is a *kōan* cited in the *Eihei kōroku* (9.67) in which a butcher, asked for the best slice of meat, responds that all slices are equally valuable. The conventional interpretation highlights the notion of non-duality and the innate equality of each portion of the whole. Yet in Japan the *kōan* anecdote has been extracted out of its original philosophical context and used, even though the term may not have fully carried the same stigma in the original Chinese setting, in an underhanded and insidious fashion to condescendingly label *burakumin* as "butchers."[22]

Thus, the Buddhist approach to personal liberation has been somewhat subverted and reduced to a "you get what you deserve" or a "blame the victim" justification for social oppression, providing a pseudo-historical mythology that rationalizes the devaluation of "vile occupations." (According to the writings of B. R. Ambedkar, untouchables in India were long reluctant to convert to Buddhism for this reason). "Although from the Kamakura period on one could find Buddhist writings on the idea of spiritual equality among people, Tokugawa Buddhism in no way opposed the official status structure of feudal society, including the segregation of its outcaste segments."[23] Repentance for these deep-seated trends requires a wholehearted and open-ended investigation of the roots of discrimination, and a willingness to challenge and change, rather than apologize for, the problematic Buddhist doctrines and institutions. Yet the continued existence of so-called *eta-dera* (*eta*-temples) and *eta-za* (*eta*-seats) in many areas, well over a hundred years after *burakumin* were legally "liberated"

---

[22] "Sendara mondai," 14.

[23] De Vos and Hiroshi Wagatsuma, *Japan's Invisible Race: Caste in Culture and Personality* (Berkeley: University of California Press, 1966), 88.

in 1871, testifies to the great difficulties involved in weeding out centuries of ingrained behavior.

The issue of discrimination is related to nationalism/imperialism in that both mentalities to an extent reflect Zen's tendency to comply tacitly and at times overtly, or at least to fail to resist and protest, the manipulation and exploitation of minority and stigmatized groups both within Japan and on the continent that is imposed by a hierarchical, authoritarian order. In a similar vein, in the 1920s the Jōdo Shinshū made an appeal for egalitarianism based on a notion conflating Buddha-nature theory with imperial ideology that all followers of the Emperor are indistinguishable. Through much of the twentieth century, with some exceptions,[24] Zen has preferred to cloak itself in the ideology of the "great (imperial) family" (*dai-kazoku*),[25] and it needs to confess by examining and correcting its willingness to allow the abuse of its ideals. Overturning these problems at their roots involves a recognition and acknowledgment as well as sustained examination not only by and for Buddhism but, according to Tanabe's postwar call, on the part of the whole nation:

> At present our nation faces the task, imposed on it externally, of performing *zange* for its past nationalism. That we, as a vanquished nation, should now be forced by others to do what we should surely have done before and of our own accord, occasions the very height of shame and remorse. Yet even at this late hour we can at least perform our *zange* out of deep inner conviction and to ensure our inner freedom. A liberalism imposed from the outside is both nonsensical and contradictory. The opportunistic advantage we take of this relative "other-power" to announce our own liberalism and culturalism is hardly less shameless and unconscionable a posture. The turning point for a new beginning lies in *zange*. Without it, we have no way to rebuild our nation.[26]

---

[24] See Victoria's book.

[25] Ichikawa Hakugen, *Bukkyōsha no sensō-sekinin* (Buddhists' War Responsibilities) (Tokyo: Shunjūsha, 1970).

[26] Tanabe Hajime, *Philosophy as Metanoetics*, trans. Takeuchi Yashinori with Valdo Viglielmo and James W. Heisig (Berkeley: University of California Press, 1986), 296.

CHAPTER 29

HOW CAN GRASSES AND TREES ATTAIN BUDDHAHOOD? AN ASPECT OF THE JAPANIZATION OF BUDDHISM

Fumihiko Sueki

1. Introduction

It is often said that Japanese people love nature. Old Japanese poems are full of praises of the beauty of nature, and Japanese artists have been fond of painting mountains, rivers, flowers and birds. On the other hand, environmental problems are serious in Japan as in other countries. The attitude of Japanese people towards nature is complicated and full of contradictions.

In this paper, I would like to investigate an aspect of this problem from the standpoint of Buddhism. Buddhism is the main religion that concerns nature in Japan because Shinto has come under the influence of Buddhism in its theories and Confucianism is focused upon the problems of human society.

In this paper, I will investigate mainly the problem of the attainment of Buddhahood by grasses and trees (*sōmoku jōbutsu*). In Japan, this idea has developed and spread widely.[1] Japanese classical literature often reflects this idea, *Noh* plays in particular. "Every grass, tree and land, all will attain Buddhahood" is one of the most famous set phrases appearing in *Noh* plays.[2] Although it is sometimes said that this phrase is a citation from the Buddhist sutra *Chūin-kyō* (Ch. *Zhongyin jing*), we cannot find it in this sutra. Modern

---

[1] On the development of this idea in Japan, see Asai Endō, *Jōko Nihon Tendai honmon shisō-shi* (Kyoto: Heiraku-ji shoten, 1975); Hanano Mitsuaki, "Sanjū-shika no kotogaki no senja to shisō ni tsuite," in *Tōyō gakujutsu kenkyū* 14-6, 15-1, 15-2, 16-2 (1975-7); William LaFluer, "Saigyo and the Buddhist Value of Nature," in *History of Religions* 13-2, 14-2 (1973-4); Miyamoto Shōson, "Sōmoku kokudo shikkai jōbutsu" no bussho-ron-teki igi to sono sakusha," in *Indo-gaku Bukkyō-gaku kenkyū* 9-2 (1961); and Sakamoto Yukio, "Sōmoku jōbutsu no Nihon-teki tenkai," in *Nakano kyōju koki kinen ronbun-shū* (1960).

[2] See Miyamoto Shōson's above-mentioned article.

scholars think that it was formulated in Japan. The oldest text which contains this phrase is the *Shinjō sōmoku jōbutsu shiki* written by Annen (841-?), a Tendai monk of the Heian period. This text is important in the history of Japanese Buddhism, not only because it contains this phrase, but also because it is the oldest text to focus upon the problem of the attainment of Buddhahood by grasses and trees. Before Annen, this problem was discussed in the *Toketsu*, a collection of questions on Tendai doctrine posed by Japanese Tendai monks with answers by Chinese Tiantai masters. Both the *Toketsu* and Annen's work presuppose the theory of the attainment of Buddhahood by non-sentient beings that has been advanced by Zhanran (711-782), the sixth patriarch of the Chinese Tiantai school.

In this paper, I venture to use the term "Japanization" of Buddhism. When I treated the thought of Annen before, I called him "the philosopher who Japanized Buddhism."[3] What does the "Japanization of Buddhism"' mean? Recently Peter Gregory used the term "Sinification of Buddhism" concerning Zongmi's thought.[4] On the other hand, the Japanization of Buddhism has not been discussed much until today, in spite of its importance. Although scholars often lump together Chinese, Korean and Japanese cultures under the single term "East Asian culture", these three cultures are quite different from each other. The situation is the same in the case of Buddhism. It is true that East Asian Mahāyāna Buddhism has characteristics in common with Tibetan Buddhism and Theravāda Buddhism in Southeast Asia; however, when we compare Chinese, Korean and Japanese Buddhism in detail, we find that their ways of thinking are quite different in spite of their superficially similar appearance.

The problem of the attainment of Buddhahood by grasses and trees is one of the most suitable cases for comparing Japanese Buddhism with Chinese Buddhism.[5] This is because we can in the *Toketsu* compare the questions posed by Japanese monks and the answers given by Chinese masters together with Annen's criticism of the answers. When we compare Chinese and Japanese attitudes toward this problem, we will be able to get some insight into the Japanization of Buddhism.

In this paper, I will first examine the theory of Zhanran (Section Two) and then examine the *Toketsu* (Section Three) and the work of Annen (Section Four). After Annen, a new development in the theory appeared in Japanese Tendai in connection with the doctrine of innate enlightenment. We will consider it in Section Five.[6]

---

[3] See my article "Annen: The Philosopher Who Japanized Buddhism," in *Acta Asiatica* 66 (1994).

[4] See Peter Gregory's book *Tsungmi and the Sinification of Buddhism* (Princeton, NJ: Princeton University Press, 1991).

[5] Korean Buddhism exceeds the discussion here.

[6] Ths paper is based on Chapter Five of my book *Heian shoki Bukkyō shisō-shi no kenkyū* (Tokyo: Shunjūsha, 1995).

2. Zhanran

The idea of the attainment of Buddhahood by grasses and trees cannot be found in India, although some texts indicate that plants were thought to have lives and minds.[7] It was in China that the idea became an issue of dispute.[8] In China they did not use the term "attainment of Buddhahood by grasses and trees" but "attainment of Buddhahood by non-sentient beings." It was first advocated by Huiyuan, Zhiyi and Jizang in the Sui dynasty and was developed during the Tang dynasty. Zhanran is the most representative person who developed this idea in the Tiantai tradition during the Tang dynasty; his ideas also had a great influence upon Japanese Buddhism. His thought on this subject can be found in the *Mohe Zhiguan fuxing zhuanhong jue* (abbr. *Fuxing*) and the *Jingang bilun* (abbr. *Jinbilun*).[9] Here we will consider Zhanran 's idea first in the *Fuxing* and next in the *Jinbilun*.

The *Fuxing* is a commentary on *Mohe Zhiguan* of Zhiyi (538-597), and the idea of the attainment of Buddhahood by non-sentient beings can be found in a passage which comments on the famous phrase "every form and scent never fails to accord with the Middle Way. This phrase already entails the meaning of the attainment of Buddhahood by non-sentient beings, because it means that forms and scents, that is, objects of the senses, whether sentient or non-sentient, accord with the Middle Way, that is, the absolute truth. We can put the phrase in another way by saying that every phenomenal thing, sentient or non-sentient, attains the absolute, that is, Buddhahood. Zhanran says as follows:

> Now from the standpoint of identity (*soku*), we say that each form and scent never fails to accord with the Middle Way. Although ordinary people think that this form and scent refer to non-sentient beings, they on the one hand admit the accordance of forms and scents with the Middle Way, but on the other hand are astonished to hear of the Buddha-nature in non-sentient beings. [10]

The accordance of forms and scents with the Middle Way means nothing but the existence of Buddha-nature in non-sentient beings. In the following passage, Zhanran explains the meaning of the existence of Buddha-nature in non-sentient beings from the following ten viewpoints:

---

[7] On the issue of plants in Indian Buddhism, see L. Schimthausen's books *Buddhism and Nature* (Tokyo: Reiyūkai, 1991) and *The Problem of the Sentience of Plants in Earliest Buddhism* (Tokyo: Reiyūkai, 1991).

[8] See Kamata Shigeo's book *Chūgoku Kegon shisō-shi kenkyū* (Tokyo: Tōkyō daigaku shuppankai, 1965) and Sakamoto Yukio's the afore-mentioned article published in 1959.

[9] See Ikeda Rosan's article "Kongōbe-ron no shomondai," in *Komazawa daigaku Bukkyōgakubu kenkyū kiyō* 32 (1974).

[10] T.46.151c.

(1) From the viewpoint of the [Buddha] bodies (*shin*). The Buddha nature has three Buddha bodies and the Dharma body, one of the three bodies, inheres even in non-sentient beings; therefore, Buddha-nature inheres even in them.

(2) From the viewpoint of the [Buddha] substance (*tai*). Since the three bodies have the same substance, the reward body and the accommodative body also inhere in non-sentient beings because the Dharma body inheres in them.

(3) From the viewpoint of phenomena and noumenon (*ji-ri*). From the viewpoint of phenomena, a distinction exists between sentient beings and non-sentient beings; from the viewpoint of noumenon, on the other hand, there is no distinction between them.

(4) From the viewpoint of the land [and the body] (*do*). From the viewpoint of delusion, a distinction exists between the mind / body and its environment (*e-shō*); from the viewpoint of noumenal wisdom, on the other hand, there is no distinction between them.

(5) From the viewpoint of the teaching and enlightenment (*kyō-shō*). From the viewpoint of the teaching, there is a distinction between sentient beings and non-sentient beings; from the viewpoint of enlightenment, on the other hand, there is no distinction between them.

(6) From the supra-worldly and worldly viewpoints (*shin-zoku*). From the supra-worldly viewpoint, the substance of sentient beings and of non-sentient beings is one; from the worldly viewpoint, on the other hand, they are of two substances.

(7) From the viewpoint of inclusion (*shozoku*). Since everything in this world is encompassed within the mind of sentient beings, there is no distinction between sentient and non-sentient beings.

(8) From the viewpoint of cause and effect (*in-ga*). From the viewpoint of cause (practice), we see a difference between sentient beings and non-sentient beings; from the viewpoint of the effect (Buddhahood), on the other hand, Buddha-nature is one and the same in them.

(9) From the viewpoint of expediency (*zuigi*). From the viewpoint of expediency, the Buddha preaches a distinction between sentient and non-sentient beings.

(10) According to the teachings. In the three earlier teachings, the Buddha denies Buddha-nature in non-sentient beings; in the final, perfect teaching, on the other hand, the Buddha admits Buddha-nature in them.[11]

---

[11] T.46. 151c-152a is summarized.

The first and second of these statements are assertions from the viewpoint of the Buddha bodies, while the others, except the seventh, distinguish between two standpoints, that is, the standpoints of equality and differentiation. From the second standpoint, a distinction exists between sentient beings and non-sentient beings; from the first standpoint, we find no such distinction. Since the standpoint of equality is thought to represent a higher view than the standpoint of differentiation, the equality of sentient and non-sentient beings is superior to their distinction.

In this way, Zhanran admits the existence of Buddha-nature in non-sentient beings. However, here a new question arises: if insentient beings have Buddha-nature, how do they bring it to maturity and attain Buddhahood? Do they actually become Buddhas? Since Zhanran does not answer this question in the *Fuxing*, it is necessary to examine the *Jinbi lun*.

In the beginning of the *Jinbilun*, Zhanran presents his subject and asserts, "Even the mind / body and environment of beings in the Avīci hell lie wholly within the mind of the holiest sage [Buddha], and the body and land of Vairocana Buddha do not surpass one moment of thought of an ordinary person."[12]

This assertion amounts to a restatement of the principle of the mutual inclusion of the ten realms and the three thousand realms in a single thought-moment in Zhiyi's philosophy. According to the principle of the three thousand realms in a single thought-moment, one moment of thought of an ordinary person contains three thousand realms, including sentient and non-sentient beings. In this way, Zhanran's idea of the attainment of Buddhahood by non-sentient beings is a kind of idealism that subsumes non-sentient beings within the mind of sentient beings. From this standpoint, he denies the idea that each blade of grass, tree, stone, and speck of dust has its own cause (practice) and effect (Buddhahood). It is impossible for grasses and trees to attain Buddhahood apart from the mind of sentient beings.

Thus, Zhanran's idea of the attainment of Buddhahood by non-sentient beings does not mean that grasses and trees aspire to enlightenment, practice and attain Buddhahood by themselves. Not only Zhanran but also other Chinese masters had similar ideas about this problem. Even in the Chan tradition, which sometimes asserts non-sentient beings are Buddhas, the main problem is not the enlightenment of grasses and trees *per se* but of human practitioners. It is a matter of course that the main problem of Buddhism is the attainment of enlightenment by you and me, not by grasses and trees. The attainment of Buddhahood by grasses and trees is seen as contingent upon the enlightenment of sentient beings. In Japanese Buddhism, however, the situation changes. Japanese Buddhist philosophers assert that grasses and trees attain Buddhahood by themselves. In the following sections, we will consider the problem in the case of the early Japanese Tendai school.

---

[12] T.46.781a.

3. The *Toketsu*

In Japan, Saichō (767-822) and Kūkai (774-835) were the first ones to acknowledge Buddha-nature in non-sentient beings. After Saichō's death, his disciples considered this issue from a new perspective. They argued that if non-sentient beings have Buddha-nature, they must individually be able to aspire to enlightenment, practice and realize Buddhahood. Some Japanese Tendai monks mentioned this issue in letters containing questions about Buddhist doctrine that were sent to Chinese Tiantai masters (i.e., the *Toketsu*). The answers from the Chinese masters do not seem to have satisfied the Japanese monks, and their divergence of views shows a difference in the ways of thinking of Chinese and Japanese Buddhism. It was Annen who criticized the Chinese answers and developed the distinctive ideas of Japanese monks.

First, we will examine the questions and answers in the *Toketsu*. In the *Toketsu*, the problem of the attainment of Buddhahood by grasses and trees can be found in the following locations:

    [1] Q Enchō A: Guanxiu   the 17th question and answer
    [2] Q Enchō A: Weizhuan   the 17th question and answer
    [3] Q Tokuen A: Zongying   the 9th question and answer

Here we will examine [1] and [2]. In [1] and [2], Enchō's questions are the same. After citing the first and second of the ten viewpoints given in the *Fuxing* which we examined above, he poses three questions:

(1) Why do non-sentient beings not have perception, while sentient beings have it?

(2) If sentient beings aspire to enlightenment, practice and realize Buddhahood, non-sentient beings must do the same. Why not so?

(3) If one kills sentient beings, one's deed is a grave sin. If one cuts down non-sentient beings, one's deed must also be a grave sin. Why not so? [13]

Here Enchō regards sentient beings and non-sentient beings on an equal level. He cannot admit any difference between them. Although such an idea seems quite strange from the standpoint of Buddhism, it must have been a very important problem for Enchō, and probably for Japanese Buddhists at that time, since Annen also took up the same issue and expanded on Enchō's viewpoints.

Now, how did Guanxiu and Weizhuan answer Enchō's question? At first, Guanxiu seems to admit the equality of sentient and non-sentient beings, because he says: "One cannot choose between sentient beings and non-sentient

---

[13] ND.78.174a is summarized.

beings, because they have the same Dharma-body."[14] However, he does not share the same standpoint as Enchō. He rather seems to misunderstand Enchō's question when he restates the matter as follows:

> Seeing that sentient beings aspire to enlightenment, practice and realize Buddhahood, it is impossible that non-sentient beings do not do so, because non-sentient beings follow the enlightenment of sentient beings. When a sentient being attains enlightenment, all other beings also attain enlightenment without excepting non-sentient beings.[15]

Guanxiu's addition that non-sentient beings follow the enlightenment of sentient beings is quite different from what Enchō wanted to say. While what Enchō wanted to know was whether the perfect equality of sentient beings and non-sentient beings was possible, Guanxiu presupposes the superiority of sentient beings over non-sentient beings. Their ideas are quite divergent. In this way, Guanxiu's answer is not responsive to Enchō's question. He takes the human body as an example:

> Human bodies are made of four great elements [that is, earth, water fire and wind]. Human bodies are [included within the category of] sentient beings, while the four elements are non-sentient beings. Thus human bodies are both sentient and non-sentient. When a human individual aspires to enlightenment, practices and attains Buddhahood, the four elements also aspire to enlightenment, practice and attain Buddhahood. This means that both sentient beings and non-sentient beings aspire to and attain Buddhahood.[16]

What he says is not difficult to understand, but it probably did not persuade Enchō, who wanted to know if non-sentient beings could attain Buddhahood independently of sentient beings. What does Guanxiu say about those non-sentient beings which are not parts of the bodies of sentient beings? He says: "If a human being causes the non-sentient elements inside him [that is, his body] to attain Buddhahood, all non-sentient beings in the world of transience outside him will also attain Buddhahood because they are included within his environment."[17] This is Guanxiu's conclusion. He does not admit the attainment of Buddhahood by non-sentient beings by themselves independent of sentient beings. What he asserts is that non-sentient beings can attain Buddhahood only because they form the environment of sentient beings and are non-dual with them. This is far from what Enchō asked.

---

[14] ND.78.174a.
[15] ND.78.174a.
[16] ND.78.174a.
[17] ND.78.174a.

Weizhuan's answer to Enchō's question is simpler than Guanxiu's. He answers this question from the standpoint of the threefold contemplation in one mind. He says: "When one penetrates the threefold contemplation in one mind, one will not see [any distinction between] sentient and non-sentient beings or [between] Buddhas and sentient beings."[18] What he means is that any distinction between sentient and non-sentient beings is meaningless from the ultimate standpoint of threefold contemplation in one mind. His answer may be right from the standpoint of the orthodox Tiantai tradition; however, it does not seem responsive to Enchō's question.

Thus, the examination of the *Toketsu* makes clear the difference in the view of nature between Enchō and Chinese Tiantai masters. While Enchō regarded non-sentient beings in nature on an equal level with sentient beings such as humans, Chinese Tiantai masters adhered to the principles of Tiantai philosophy and focused on human practice for the attainment of enlightenment. Is it possible to generalize and say that this suggests a difference in attitudes towards nature between Chinese and Japanese people? It is needless to say that we have to be cautious in making such a generalization, however, I am inclined to suspect that the example of the *Toketsu* offers some insight into this larger issue.

4. Annen

Annen lived in the last half of the ninth century but the details of his life are not well know, although he left behind voluminous works. He has been known as the person who brought the systematization of Tendai esotericism to completion; however, I have argued that he was one of the greatest philosophers of Japanese Buddhism and one who greatly advanced the Japanization of Buddhism.[19] Until this year Annen's work *Shinjō sōmoku jōbutsu shiki* (Private Notes on Discussions of Theories on the Realization of Buddhahood by Grasses and Trees) (abbr. *Shiki*) had not been published in moveable type but was available only in a wood-block edition from the Tokugawa period.[20] I have just had it published together with a modern Japanese translation and notes.[21] I think that it was written early in Annen's career.

The *Shiki* has a complex structure. Annen cites various disputes on the problem of the attainment of Buddhahood by grasses and trees, and after every citation he criticizes and discusses the positions maintained by each disputant. The contents of the texts are as follows:

---

[18] ND.78.202a.

[19] See my aforementioned article published in 1994.

[20] There are only a few studies of the *Shiki*. See Misaki Gisen's article "Annen *Shinjō sōmoku jōbutsu shiki no yōten*," in *Tendai gakuhō* 19 (1977); Shinkawa Tetsuo's book *Annen no hijō jōbutsu gi kenkyu* (Tokyo: Gakushūin daigaku, 1992); Chapter Five of my above-mentioned book. My article "Annen *Shinjō sōmoku jōbutsu shiki* ni tsuite," is included in Chapter Five of my own book.

[21] Refer to my afore-mentioned book published in 1995.

[1] Discussion in Buddhist schools
    [1.1] The Tendai school
    [1.2] The Kegon school
    [1.3] The Sanron school
[2] The *Toketsu*
    [2.1] A question by Enchō and an answer by Guanxiu
    [2.2] A question by Enchō and an answer by Weizhuan
       [2.3] A question by Tokuen and an answer by Guanxiu
    and a question by Kōjō and an answer by Zongying
[3] Recent Japanese disputes
    [3.1] A dispute in the Jōgan era (859-876)
    [3.2] Questions and answers by certain monks
    [3.3] Hypothetical questions and answers
[4] Presentation of the perfect teaching

The last part, in which Annen tried to present his own, ultimate view, is incomplete, as are some of his other writings from his early years. It does suggest, however, that he was inclined toward Esoteric Buddhism in his search for a solution to the problem.

Now we will examine some parts of the *Shiki*. In [1.1], Annen cites ten questions and answers that suggest the disputes current in the Tendai school in his day. Then he criticizes two points in the questions and answers he has cited. Both of the two points concern the seventh answer. The seventh question and answer are as follows:

> Question: When grasses and trees attain Buddhahood, do they have the three elements of enlightenment?[22] And at that time do they have the thirty-two physical marks of Buddhas?
> Answer: No.

Annen criticizes this answer and asserts that grasses and trees possess three elements of enlightenment and the thirty-two physical marks when they attain Buddhahood. He cites two passages from the *Fuxing* and the *Jinbilun* in order to substantiate his assertion, although they do not seem to agree with his intent. In any event, his idea is very clear. He is not content with the idea of grasses and trees attaining Buddhahood simply as the environment of sentient beings. He asserts that grasses and trees become individual Buddhas in their own right, possessing the three elements of enlightenment and the thirty-two marks of Buddhas.

In this way, Annen further developed the thinking underlying the questions posed by Japanese Tendai monks in the *Toketsu*. In the second part of the *Shiki*,

---

[22] The three elements of enlightenment are (1) self-enlightenment (*jikaku*), (2) making others attain enlightenment (*kakuta*), and perfect enlightenment (*kakuman*).

he criticizes the answers given by Chinese Tiantai masters for not acknowledging the individual attainment of Buddhahood by grasses and trees. For example, he criticizes Weizhuan's answer to Enchō as follows:

> The intention of the question from Japan is to ask, not asking whether both sentient beings and non-sentient beings are standing outside the contemplation [of sentient beings], but whether grasses and trees individually aspire to enlightenment, practice and attain Buddhahood by themselves. The response of the reverend master [Weizhuan] does not answer this question. Although it resolves the question of the origin of the perfect contemplation of sentient beings, it cannot resolve the question of whether or not non-sentient grasses and trees also aspire to enlightenment, practice and contemplation as do sentient beings.

When Enchō and others sent letters to Chinese masters, they only had simple questions about the attainment of Buddhahood by grasses and trees. Annen, however, had strong confidence in the idea that grasses and trees individually aspire to enlightenment, practice and attain Buddhahood by themselves. He criticized the views of Chinese masters and established a new standpoint different from Chinese Buddhism, one which was transmitted by the subsequent Japanese Buddhist tradition.

When we follow Annen's discussion, it becomes difficult to distinguish non-sentient beings from sentient beings in terms of their capacity for Buddhist practice. Thinking as he did, it is natural that he maintains that grasses and trees also have mind. Indeed, he says in the seventh criticism in [3.2] that there are no being without mind. Everything has mind, and there is no distinction between sentient and non-sentient beings. Sometimes sentient beings change into non-sentient beings and vice versa. Although, because of worldly delusion, we speak of non-sentient beings, in truth there are no such things. Everything is sentient. This is Annen's conclusion.

5. Development in Japanese Tendai Tradition

Annen's conclusion in the *Shiki* seems very strange from the orthodox standpoint of Buddhism. As stated above, it is a matter of course that the main problem of Buddhism is the attainment of enlightenment by you and me, not by grasses and trees. Even if we admit Annen's idea that grasses and trees aspire to enlightenment, practice and attain Buddhahood, how do they do so? Do they truly aspire to enlightenment, practice and attain Buddhahood as human beings do?

Although Annen tried to answer this question in the last part of the *Shiki*, he failed to complete the text. Probably it was too difficult a question even for Annen himself to answer. His answer to this question can be found in his later work *Bodaishin-gi shō*.[23] In that text, Annen examined the problem of the realization of Buddhahood by grasses and trees as part of his examination of the Sanskrit character "A". According to Esoteric Buddhism, "A" is the origin of all things including grasses and trees. Annen again used a fourfold system of interpretation to examine this problem:

    1.   Superficial interpretation: Not only "A" but also all characters and words in the world have the meaning of the bodhi-mind.

    2.   Profound interpretation: Since all phenomenal things are the characters and words of Vairocana Buddha, all phenomenal things including grasses and trees aspire to enlightenment.

    3.   More profound interpretation: From the standpoint of the four *maṇḍala*s, the aspiration to enlightenment and practice of all things are admitted.

    4.   Most profound interpretation: Since not only sentient beings but also non-sentient beings are nothing but Suchness following conditions, all aspire to enlightenment and realize Buddhahood. [24]

In this way, the problem of the realization of Buddhahood of grasses and trees is ultimately solved from the standpoint of Suchness. However, the discussion of the *Bodaishin-gi shō* about this problem is so complicated that it was probably not very convincing.

After Annen, the problem of the attainment of Buddhahood by grasses and trees became one of the main subjects in Japanese Tendai philosophy. The idea that grasses and trees individually attain Buddhahood by themselves became a common idea in Japanese Tendai. From the later Heian period on, there developed a new tendency in Tendai philosophy called the teaching of innate (or original) enlightenment, whose characteristic is the perfect affirmation of this phenomenal world, and which is considered to be one of the extremes in the Japanization of Buddhism. In the literature of the teaching of innate enlightenment we can also find a new development of the idea of the realization of Buddhahood by grasses and trees.

Here I would like to refer to a short treatise called *Sōmoku hosshin jōbutsu ki* (Discourse on the Aspiration to Enlightenment and the Realization of Buddhahood by Grasses and Trees) as an example of this tendency. It is ascribed to Ryōgen (912-985) and Kakuun (953-1007) but is actually a later work by an unknown author. This work consists of four questions and answers. The main idea of the work is presented in the first answer:

---

[23] I have translated this part of the *Bodaishin-gi shō* into modern Japanese. See my book *Annen Genshin* (Tokyo: Chūō kōron sha, 1991).

[24] T.75.486a-c is summarized.

> Grasses and trees have the four aspects of coming into existence,
> abiding, changing, and perishing. These are nothing but the aspiration
> to enlightenment, practice, enlightenment, and the *nirvāṇa* of grasses
> and trees. Are they [grasses and trees] not a kind of sentient being?[25]

This is a decisive answer to the question to which Annen could not give a satisfactory answer: how grasses and trees aspire to enlightenment, practice, and attain Buddhahood. The aspiration to enlightenment, practice, enlightenment, and the *nirvāṇa* of grasses and trees are not strange and mysterious deeds, but the natural change of plants according to the four seasons, that is, sprouting, blooming, growing luxuriantly thick, and withering. It is not necessary to transform natural phenomena in order to enter the world of Buddhas. This phenomenal world is nothing but the world of Buddhas. Such a way of thinking is typical of the teaching of original enlightenment. In this way, the theory of the attainment of Buddhahood by grasses and trees became a part of Japanized Buddhism and became popular in Japan.

6. Conclusion and Further Problems

The above investigation has made clear the difference in attitudes toward nature between Chinese and Japanese Buddhism. In Chinese Buddhism, the main problem was not the attainment of enlightenment by grasses and trees, but by human beings. The attainment of Buddhahood by grasses and trees was a problem subsidiary to that of the attainment of Buddhahood by sentient beings. In Japanese Buddhism, however, it is asserted that grasses and trees attain Buddhahood by themselves. Beyond that, it is said that the natural changes of grasses and trees are nothing but their aspiration to enlightenment, practice and attainment of Buddhahood. I think we can call such an attitude a kind of Japanization of Buddhism.

Then, what effect has such a theory had upon Japanese culture? Love of nature by Japanese people would have some relation with it. On the other hand, it may sometimes have made them irresponsible for their own deeds, because human activities are not held to be more important than the natural changes of grasses and trees.

---

[25] NB.41.14 lb.

CHAPTER 30

BEYOND MANHAE (1869-1944) AND SEONGCHEOL (1912-1993): SEARCHING FOR A NEW BUDDHIST IDEAL

Woo-sung Huh

Buddhism occurred in northern India in about 525 B.C.E. and it formally entered Korea in 4th century. Since then, Buddhism has expressed itself through various types in its effort to deliver the sentient beings from the ocean of suffering. The last one hundred years of the history of Korean Buddhism has also witnessed various types of Buddhism. If a particular type of Buddhism advocated and practiced by an influential Korean Buddhist is so self-evidently true that no doubt and challenge is permissible, then no search for a new Buddhist ideal is necessary. This essay is written with the convictions that there is no such absolute type and that we need to search for a new ideal of a worthy Buddhist through the careful examination of Manhae's and Seongcheol's types of Buddhism.

One cannot say that there are only Manhae (1879-1944) and Seongcheol (1912-1993),[1] or that their types are representative of all other types of Korean Buddhism occurred in the last one hundred years. I have chosen Manhae and Seongcheol for the reason that their understandings of Buddhism are very consistent and show a sharp opposition to each other in the light of many important issues raised and debated in the history of Buddhism since its first occurrence in Indian soil. In addition, these two types contain precious values long-cherished in the history of Buddhism: so precious that one cannot accept only one type by simply dismissing the other. These two types of Buddhism should be examined, compared, and contrasted, in order to dialectically sublate them in search of a new Buddhist ideal.

The key words in Manhae's Buddhism are sudden enlightenment/gradual enlightenment, the action of a bodhisattva, a nation, the Korean people, the

---

[1] For transcription of Korean terms, the editor follows the basic rules established by the Ministry of Education in 2002.

Independence of the country, anger, parting, sadness and tears, whereas the key words in Seongcheol's Buddhism are Discovering Buddha-nature, sudden enlightenment/sudden practice, Hwadu study in Seon (Zen) practice, Old Buddhas and Old Patriarchs, the renunciation of the secular society, "a man of Dao, action-less and disengaged" (*muwihan doin*). Manhae put a great emphasis on the salvation of sentient beings in their historical, social and political context and advocated what one might call a Confucian Buddhism or a political Buddhism, thus a type of engaged Buddhism. On the other hand, Seongcheol attempted to establish a pure and absolute Buddhism which greatly emphasized individual effort to discover the (self-) nature with no remnant of false thoughts in his consciousness or mind.

Keeping all these key words and main features in our minds, this paper will focus upon several issues construed vital to the comparison of both types of Buddhism: the priority issue between Seon practice (*Zen*) and Doctrinal teaching (*gyo*); the issue of the orthodox succession of Buddhas and Patriarchs; the worthier way of renunciation between the Sacred Knowledge of Tathāgata and the action of a bodhisattva; and the tension between the moment of self-contentment, or the Eternal now and a lacked or parting moment suffered through the engagement in the socio-historical matters. This paper will also deal with how Manhae and Seongcheol perceived their time, which exercised a great influence on their views of Buddhism and a worthy Buddhist.

Manhae placed a great emphasis upon the action of a bodhisattva, whose primary role was to become engaged in political and national matters. One of its examples was to fight against the Japanese Imperialism, and it finally culminated in what he called "Minjung Buddhism" (Buddhism of the People). In contrast to Manhae's Minjung Buddhism, Seon Master Seongcheol attempted to return to the ideal of an *arhat*. He found his sole concern in "realizing one's own nature" by means of Seon practices, thus naturally showing less social concern.

To reveal differences, contrasts, and even inner criticisms in their views of Buddhism, and finally to go beyond both of them in search of a new ideal, this paper will discuss their views of Seon, its relationship to Gyo, and the comparison of "salvation through action" and "salvation through knowledge," and their attitudes towards history and politics. In this discussion, the author will try to give two widely opposed answers to the thematic questions suggested by sponsors of this seminar and he will also point out that the struggle between the ideal of an *arhat* and the ideal of a bodhisattva, occurred in the era of the emergence of Mahāyāna Buddhism, is not dead and gone, but is happening in the contemporary Korean Buddhism.

1. Manhae's Political Buddhism

Manhae was a Buddhist monk, poet, and patriot. The motif of his entering the priesthood was not simply the problem of life and death. He gave more importance to the independence of the nation than to the enlightenment or the succession of the Buddha-Patriarchs lineage. In his biography, there is only one record of spending a season in the Seon practice (*angeo*), which reveals that he did not have many Seon practices as compared to other traditional Seon masters. Instead, he usually stayed in Gyeongseong (Seoul) and actively engaged in various social and political activities, many of which were related to colonial policies adopted by the Japanese Colonialist.

He was born on September 29, 1879, in Hongseong, south Chungcheong, the second son of Han Ungjun. He studied classical Chinese at a village school. He was married at fourteen and at eighteen he went to a hermitage on Mount Seorak, where he studied Buddhism and became a monk in 1905. In 1908, he went to Japan to observe the modernization process of the Buddhist church. In his essay "On the Revival of Korean Buddhism" (*Joseon bulgyo yushin-non:* 1910), rejecting the traditional ills of Korean Buddhism, he preached that Buddhist reform was definitely needed, that without it Buddhism and the country could not survive.

It was through active struggles, not through passive meditations, Manhae discovered the historical realities of colonial Korea. That struggle took the form of a countermovement against the Japanese infiltration of the Korean Buddhist church and in 1914 published a digest of Buddhist doctrine in the vernacular. At the time of the 1919 Independence Movement, he helped draft the "Declaration of Independence" and signed the document as one of the thirty-three patriots. In prison he wrote another essay expounding the importance of Korean independence in the preservation of peace in East Asia. Released in March in 1922, he continued his patriotic activities through public speeches and writings till his death of palsy on June 29, 1944, in the eastern suburbs of Seoul.

In May 1926 he published his single volume of poetry, *The Silence of The Beloved* (*Nim ui chimmuk*), comprising eight-eight poems plus "The Foreword" and "To the Reader." Nim is a complex word in Korean: in love poetry it is the beloved, in allegorical poetry, the king, and in religious verse, the absolute. In addition to poetry, Manhae wrote novels. In the area of Buddhism, he taught on *The Teaching of Vimalakīrti* (*Yuma gyeong*), and published it with his partial commentary on it. He also established various Buddhist organization and edited and published Buddhist journals, and he contributed articles to major newspapers. All of Manhae's works are included in his *Collected Works* (6 volumes, 1973).

In 1967 a monument to him was erected in Seoul's Pagoda Park and a leading literary quarterly, *Changjak gwa bipyeong* (Creation and Criticism), established the Manhae literary prize (1973) in his memory.

1.1. Manhae's Sense of the Time

Manhae exerted his effort on responding to challenges posed by his time, rather than peacefully residing in what one may call 'Eternal now.' "Timely Mean" (*sijung*) is basically a Confucian term, but Manhae understands it as a Buddhist one. The spirit of 'Timely Mean' is, to begin with, revealed as his sharp awareness of the present. In his "On the Revival of Korean Buddhism," defining today's world as the world of the present, not as that of the past nor of the future, he laments that there is no voice of revival in Korean Buddhism.[2] How is Manhae aware of his time? It is the era of the beloved's absence, and his reality is a reality in which the beloved is silent or non-existent:

> You have gone. Ah, my love, you have gone.
>
> Shattering the green brilliance of the mountain, hard as it might be, cutting off all ties, gone along the narrow path that opens out to the maple grove.
>
> ---
>
> Love too is man's lot; even though we have prepared with fear of parting at meeting, parting comes upon us unawares and the startled heart bursts with a fresh sorrow.
>
> ---
>
> Ah, even though you are gone I have never said good-bye.
> The sad melody of my song of love curls around your silence.[3]

It is the time when justice, freedom, equality and human rights are lost the time when the evil and enemies are flourishing. But it is also the moment that we should fight for good works and wait for their results, because this moment belongs to the realm of causality.

Manhae expressed what he saw as non-existent in the following poem:

> After you are gone, I cannot forget you because that is more for me than for you.
>
> I do not have any crops, since I do not have any land. Nothing to eat, I went to my neighbor' to borrow millets or potatoes, the master said, 'there is no personality to a beggar. To help you is a sin.' Having heard this, I saw you in my tears on my way home back.
>
> I have no home and I do not have the census register for other reasons. A general attempted to defile my chastity, saying "without the census register, one cannot have human rights. What sort of chastity do you have, without human rights?"
>
> After fighting against him, exactly at the moment when the anger against him became my sadness, I saw you.
>
> Ah, I realized that all kinds of morals, ethics, and laws are the smoke to sacrifice sword and gold. When I was in hesitation whether I

---

[2] Manhae, *Collected Works,* 2: 35.

[3] Manhae, *Collected Works,* 1: 42, translated by S.E. Solberg in *The Silence of Love: Twentieth-Century Korean Poetry* (edited and with an introduction by Peter Lee) (Honolulu: The University of Hawaii Press, 1980), 8.

should earn eternal love, or ink the first page of the history with my
hand, or drink wine, at that moment I saw you.

("I saw you": author's translation.)[4]

This poem is full of what is non-existent thus of what should be restored,
for example, land, crops, food, personality, life, census register, human rights
and chastity. The non-existence is "lacking" of something, not of nothing. This
nonexistence is not the source of happiness or rejoicing in Dao, which becomes
possible after realizing the *anattā* (selfless) doctrine or getting enlightened.
Rather it becomes the origin of anger and sadness. His awareness of what is
lacking, includes morals, ethics, laws, and the relationship between sword and
gold.

All kinds of human institutions, morals, ethics, and laws, exist only for
those who do have sword and gold. Moreover, these sword and gold are only in
vain in themselves. The sense of this lacking is expressed as "the absence of my
Beloved." The power to make something non-existent is called the Māra (*ma*).
Human history, for Manhae, is the world of various evils, because beings of this
world love the round of life and death. But a bodhisattva does not leave behind
this world. In the *The Teaching of Vimalakīrti*, Manjuśrī asks, why are you
without a retinue? Vimalakīrti answered, "all Māras and all adversaries are my
retinue. And why? Māras praise the round of rebirth (*saṁsāra*) and the round of
rebirth constitutes the retinue of a bodhisattva. Adversaries praise all kinds of
false views and a bodhisattva does not avoid any kind of false view. That is why
all Māras and adversaries are my retinue" (3: 304-5).[5] On this phrase, Manhae
makes his comments.

> Why are all Māras and adversaries a retinue? The reason is as
> follows: Although all Māras enjoy the round of rebirth, a bodhisattva
> goes in and out the round of rebirth. Although adversaries love all
> kinds of views, a bodhisattva does not move into a special view,
> leaving behind various false views which also come from the same
> original foundation (3: 305).

The world of the round of rebirth is the place full of beings who have
various false views. Therefore, all Māras and adversaries are my retinue.

---

[4] Manhae, *Collected Works, 1:* 57-58.
[5] Etienne Lamotte, *The Teaching of Vimalakīrti* (Sara Boin, trans.) (London:
PTS, 1976), 119.

1.2. The Non-separation of Buddhism and Politics

Manhae cannot admit the traditional Confucian criticism raised in China and Korea that Buddhism is the teaching of disregarding the filial piety and the loyalty to the king. But this false criticism is made only when one saw the apparent form of "leaving home."

One does not know even a bit of the real aspect or content of Buddhism.[6] Manhae does not interpret psychologically the notions of Buddha-field (*bulgukto*) and the purification of the Buddha-field (*jeongbulgukto*), the suitable action for a bodhisattva. Thus he sees "Buddha-field" as a society or a nation, "the purification of the Buddha-field" as the action of making better or purifying a society or a nation,[7] thus implies the non-separation of politics from actions of a Buddhist.

Manhae's principle of the non-separation of Buddhism from politics is deeply related to his insight that even a Seon master cannot escape the fate of a society or a nation. This insight is well expressed in a poem,

> "The Year-end" (*semo*). Under the mountain, there is a small cottage,
> where the household is practicing Seon. The first circle surrounding
> them is white snow, cold wind, or warm sunshine. The next two
> circles are human existence, war, isms, revolution, and etc.

The thing which moves forward most powerfully is the exercise of the right of the powerful ones and the creditors. The sun sets. This year has passed, leaving behind everything as traces. All kinds of phenomena are variously surrounding the household, the Seon-practitioner. In those phenomena are included the phenomena of nature, war, -isms, and revolutions. The strongest movement is the one of the powerful and the creditors. The political movement is so thoroughly penetrated into all comers of a nation that even a monk in a mountain cannot be immune to it. Manhae's awareness of political power sharply distinguishes him from a traditional Seon master.

1.3. Manhae's View of Seon and Gyo: the Theory of the Equality of Sudden Enlightenment / Gradual Enlightenment

That Manhae emphasizes the Bodhisattva activities to save beings and the non-separation of Buddhism and politics, has him give a sea change to the traditional understanding of Seon practice, doctrinal teaching (Seon-Gyo) and their relationship. The essence of Seon practice is to make one's mind always awakened and to shed light on the reality of one's mind, which for Manhae should not be misunderstood as getting a mysterious level after losing objects. "Once one's mind becomes purified, the principle (of all things) is penetrated

---

[6] "Buddhism and Filial Piety," 1938; see 2: 337.
[7] See *Collected Works,* 2: 239.

into all at once. This is the origin of Seon practice." (2: 53). He said: "Seon is substance (*che*), philosophy is function (*yong*). Seon is to clarify something by itself Philosophy is a research. Seon is sudden enlightenment (*dono*) and philosophy is gradual enlightenment (*jeomo*)." Some 20 years later, Manhae expresses a similar view of Seon and Gyo:

> Setting aside Seon practice and doctrinal teaching, one cannot talk of Buddhism, because Seon practice and doctrinal teaching are Buddhism, and Buddhism is both Seon practice and doctrinal teaching. Seon practice refers to the pure metaphysical principle, and doctrinal teaching refers to Buddhist speeches and writings. One attains knowledge by means of doctrinal teaching, and attains stillness (*jeong*) by means of Seon practice. Only achieving the stillness, one is able to cross the ocean of suffering of life-death to reach to the other shore of nirvana. Without doctrinal teaching one cannot get guiding principles in saving beings. Therefore, as Seon practice and doctrinal teaching are like two wings of a bird, the success and the decline of Buddhism rely on the flourishing and the degeneration of Seon practice and doctrinal teaching.[8]

As can be seen in the above quote, Manhae believes that Buddhism should contain both aspects: sudden enlightenment and gradual enlightenment. The essence of sudden enlightenment is to purify one's mind in order to get reality of all things; through the gradual enlightenment, one can get Buddhist speeches, writings, the guiding principles, and learn philosophy with the purpose of saving beings. This understanding of Buddhism may be called the theory of sudden enlightenment/gradual enlightenment.[9] In view of his analogy of two wings of a bird, his theory of Seon practice/doctrinal teaching may also be named the theory of equality of Seon practice/doctrinal teaching, or the Seon practice and doctrinal teaching in tandem (*Seongyo ssangsu*).

At least on the theoretical level, Manhae attempts to give careful balance to both aspects of Seon Buddhism so that each supports the development of the other. He does not seem to accept the priority of Seon practice over the doctrinal teaching. Instead he warns of the danger of the excessive emphasis upon the sudden enlightenment. Without the aspect of gradual enlightenment, one easily falls into indifference to sufferings of other beings and into the compulsion to seek quietude and isolation which often a traditional Korean Seon practitioner take as the purpose of Seon. Manhae develops his view of the Bodhisattva activities and the true deliverance. He quotes a passage from *Vimalakīrti sūtra*: "For a Bodhisattva to taste the flavor of the trances (*dhyāna: Seonmi*) is bondage (*bak*). On the contrary, to be reborn in a skill-in-means is deliverance (*hae*)." Then, he makes the following comments: "To taste the flavor of the tranquil

---

[8] *Ibid.*, 2: 168, in "A Proposal for Reform of Korean Buddhism."

[9] Manhae once refer-red to "Hwadu" study as the only means of Seon practice. But he also say 1700 Hwadus "nothing more than means (*upāya*)." *Ibid.*, 2: 313.

trances and to avoid the deliverance of beings is bondage. In order to deliver beings to come in and out of the round of re-birth through a good skill-in-means is the deliverance of a bodhisattva."[10]

Manhae also made a reference to the "Ten Ox-herding Pictures," (*ship'u-do*) whose author is said to be a Zen master of the Song Dynasty known as Kaku-an Shi-en (Gwak am sa won) belonging to the Rinzai school. He is also the author of the poems and introductory words attached to the pictures. The ten steps in Zen practice are as follows: Searching for the Ox, Seeing the traces, Seeing the Ox, Catching the Ox, Herding the Ox, Coming home on the Ox's Back, the Ox Forgotten-Leaving the Man alone, the Ox and the Man both Gone out of Sight, Returning to the Origin-Back to the Source, and Entering the City with Bliss-bestowing Hands *Ipjeon susu*). The final step is translated by Manhae as follows:

> Bare-chested and bare-footed he comes out into the market-place;
> Daubed with mud and ashes, how broadly he smiles! There is no
> need for the miraculous power of the gods. The dead trees are in full
> bloom.[11]

Manhae understands by this poem that a bodhisattva "enters the city-market defiled with full of dust and ashes, bestowing compassionate hands in order to deliver beings in the ocean of suffering."[12] He composes his own poem in responding to the rhyme of the above-quoted stanza:

> Coming in and out anywhere I please, crying and laughing cannot
> make any trace on my cheeks. In the ocean of suffering I want to
> make the lotus flower bloom in the fire.[13]

The comments and poems made by Manhae on the "Ten Ox-herding Pictures," clearly state that a Bodhisattva ought to come in and out of the ocean of the suffering and the muddy field in order to make a lotus flower bloom in the fire. He gives a shout: "You ought to know that carrying water and firewood is no more than mysterious function (*myoyong*) and the sound of rivers and the cloud of the mountain are the reality."[14] But one should remember that for Manhae the realm of carrying water and firewood should be enlarged and extended to include the historical-political realm. A traditional master with a very narrow realm of the mysterious function would spend days and nights in Seon practices in mountains, and thus he cannot possibly comprise the historical-political realm through the step of "Entering the City with Bliss-

---

[10] *Ibid.*, 3: 310, and *The Teaching of Vimalakīrti*, 126.

[11] *Ibid.*, *1:* 236, quoted from D. T. Suzuki, *A Manual of Zen Buddhism* (New York: Grove Press, 1960), 134.

[12] *Collected Works*, 1: 233.

[13] *Ibid.*, 1: 236.

[14] "On the Revival of Korean Buddhism," *Collected Works*, 2: 56.

bestowing Hands." He would not realize the great liberation (*daehaetal*) of love which is expressed in the following poem:

I heard the Master preach.

"Don't be chained to love and suffer. Instead, cut off the ties of love and you will rejoice in your heart." So he said in a loud voice.

That master is a fool.

He does not know: True it hurts to be tied with love, but it will hurt more to cut the ties of love, it will hurt more even than death.

In the tight binding of love's bonds lies their unbinding.

Thus great liberation is to submit to the bonds themselves. My love, I was afraid the rope of your love might be weak so I doubled the strands of my love for you.

(The Seon Master's Sermon)[15]

1.4. The Relationship between the Absolute and the Relative

Manhae's Buddhism admits both the absolute world and the relative world and gives an appropriate value to the latter. The relative world is not absolute but refers to the realm of the principle of causality where all sorts of good and bad actions get their fruits. In *Vimalakīrti-sūtra*, Buddha preaches: "Neither being (*sat*) nor non-being (*asat*), all dharmas are born dependent on causes (*hetun pratī tya samutpānnah*; there is in them no self (*ātman*), no sensing subject, no activator (*kāraka*); but good (*kuśala*) or bad (*akuśala*), no action wither."[16]

On this passage in the form of Chinese rendition, Manhae comments, "Since dharmas are empty in themselves, they are not real substance (*shilyu*). But due to the fact that since cause-effect is very clearly functioning in dharmas, they are not sheer nothingness (*jinmu*). Therefore, although there is no definite form of being and non-being and although there exists no substance of an activator nor of a receiver, the results of good and bad actions do not wither" (3: 260). Manhae would believe that "the field of effort (*prayoga*) is the Buddhakṣetra of the Bodhisattva."[17] According to Manhae, the traditional religion holds a wrong view that only when one leaves home to go to the mountain, one can taste the flavor of Dao (*domi*) and that only when one transcends the human life one really becomes a man of Dao (*doin*). But this is not true. A religion should be

---

[15] P.H. Lee, 24.

[16] *The Teaching of Vimalakīrti*, 9- 10.

[17] *Ibid.*, 17.

engaged in the deliverance of beings. Therefore, it enters the world to lead them to the true life.

In short, as Manhae asserts, a religion is "to realize the infinite life in this finite world of dust and ashes." The absolute should face the relative and one has to realize that the absolute and the relative is not separate (2: 132). With respect to the absolute and the relative, there have been the following questions: Does the absolute exist? If it does, what are its main features? How is it related to the relative? These questions form a part of the most important questions in philosophy and religion. In view of this, Manhae's statements that the absolute and the relative face each other, and that there exists no separation between them, are philosophically very significant. How then does the absolute face the relative? How is the infinite life realized in the dusty world (*jinse*)? The religious and luminous life (*jonggyo-jeok gwangmyeong-jeok*) is expressed in the institutions, laws, and morals of the world. Manhae argues:

> Its (religious) life is not a secular (*saesokjeok*) life but a luminous life. It does not take the glories of this world as the only objective. It nor recognizes wealth and rank as the absolute value but the light itself as the absolute. Religion seems to be quiescence and annihilation (*jeokmyeol*) in that it takes the contentment (*manjok*) of the luminous life as the sole purpose. But it is really a great fullness and great function. Institutions, laws and morals of the world are temporarily revealed expressions of this [luminous] life and luminosity. Although they are not absolute, they are, of course, precious and important. Has the so called Buddhism of stillness ever explained and taught that one should realize Dao by breaking up the law of the nation, or by destroying family and escaping [secular] life? No. It only emphasized that [the true] life lies above the [secular] life (2: 132-133).

According to this paragraph, Buddhism has the luminous life in the light of which wealth, rank, and fame become relative. The luminous life is not the status of the empty quiescence, but is a great fullness and function, out of which it flows into the dusty world. Since the locus of the fullness and function is institutions, laws, and morals of the world, these social entities are not meaningless but significant. If there is any problem with those entities, it is only because they are not permanent and absolute expressions of the luminous life but temporary and relative expressions of it. Buddhism cannot be a religion of quiescence and annihilation in that it is related to such relative phenomena as institutions, laws and morals; it is absolute because it transcends them. Manhae calls his Buddhism "Buddhism of the People" (*minjung bulgyo*). He strongly maintains that Buddhism should meet people and be assimilated with them.

2. Seongcheol's Pure and Absolute Buddhism

2.1. The Recovery of Pure Buddhism

The life of Seongcheol was simple. He married at nineteen and left home at twenty-five. Once he said, "The one who, after discovering (self-) nature (*Gyeonseong*), destroying all false thoughts, and realizing the No mind-field, has attained the great resting place, can have a peaceful body and mind even in the turmoil of myriad things as in the steep mountain and deep valleys where even a shadow of a man ceases to exist."[18] For the last fifty years and more, Korean people have experienced historically great event such as Independence (1945), the Korean War (1950), the Student Revolution (1960), the Military coup (1961), the Purification Movement of Buddhism (1950s and 1960s), the Gwangju Movement for Democracy (1980), and the establishment of Civilian Government (1991). But during all these historical events, Seongcheol usually stayed in hermitages and monasteries in the mountains. It appears that even in the non-peaceful time of our history he was able to rejoice in the ultimate joy of No mind-field and he believed that one should be able to do so.

Through all his life, what Seongcheol mostly wanted to do is to rediscover and establish the standard of "Discovering the Self-nature," which, as he claimed, Korean Buddhism has lost for some time. It is the work to rediscover the Immediacy, that is, to discover the purity of Seon in the thoughts of Old Buddhas and Old Patriarchs. His life-long intention is very well demonstrated in a passage of *Seonmun jeongno* (The Right Way of Zen), where he explains that the right dharma has been devastated due to heretical theories in the long history of its succession; he wants to show the right way of Seon for the eternal dharma; and the best way to attain Enlightenment is the Hwadu practice (*Gwanhwaseon*).

What he has presented in *Seonmun jeongno,* as the standard or content of Discovering the Self-nature, consists of four qualities, which an enlightened person is expected to have:

> "To Keep Integrity [in no-mind] Whether Awakened or Sleeping,"
> "Thorough Penetration Both in and Out," "No-mind and no thought"
> and "Permanent Quiescence and Permanent Illumination." For
> Seongcheol, the pure state of mind which is attainable only after all
> false thoughts perished is so important that he even argues that if one
> does not admit these qualities, one does not know what Seon really
> means.[19]

In an interview entitled "To Sacrifice Everything for Truth," Seongcheol was asked the motive of the publication of *Seonmun jeongno,* he replies to the

---

[18] *Seonmun jeongno,* 92-93.
[19] *Eternal Freedom* (Yongwonhan jayu), 149.

effect that once the standard of Discovering the Self-nature has disappeared, everyone began to say that he could achieve Discovering the Self-nature and Becoming Buddha (*Gyeonseong seongbul*). As a result Buddhism has been fallen into a great confusion, and its life has been almost extinguished. A great deal of damage has been done as the days have passed. Finally, it reaches to the point that there exists no longer Discovering the Self-nature and Becoming Buddha. With this keen awareness of Buddhism in crisis, in order to establish the standard of the Discovering the Self-nature and to present its real feature for the future of Buddhism, Seongcheol intends to go back to Old Buddhas and Old Patriarchs and to see how these people in old days studied and preached, and collected what they taught.[20] He is a fundamentalist in going back to the fundamentals of Buddhism and a revivalist in returning to the Old Buddhas and Old Patriarchs.

According to Seongcheol, although attaining Right [Buddha-] Eyes is very difficult task, everyone is able to realize the Buddha-nature if he exerts all his powers on it. If he gives up the realization of the Buddha-nature, then he despises and abandons himself. On the basis of the theory of sudden enlightenment/sudden practice, Seongcheol criticizes the sudden enlightenment/gradual practice proposed by Bojo Jinul (1158-1210), who has been respected as the systematizer and re-founder of Seongcheol's own sect. Jinul's theory did not reach the standard of Discovering the Buddha-nature. Those who follow his theory are called the 21 follower of the teaching of "intellectual understanding" or "conceptual understanding" (*jihae*).[21]

The state of Discovering the Self-nature is achievable only when all false thoughts, including those most infinitesimal ones in *ālayavijñāna*, or the eighth consciousness, have been permanently eliminated. To explain this pure state, Seongcheol employs the simile of "clouds and the sun."

Although the sun of the wisdom of True Suchness is always illuminating the dharma world with its limitless rays, sentient beings are not able to see her because the dark clouds of the three fine and six coarse and the blue sky is uncovered, the great perfect enlightenment is attained and the original (self-) nature that is True Suchness is seen completely when all false thoughts up to the three most infinitesimal ones are extinguished without remainder.[22]

Attaining of the state of No-mind / No-thought by extinguishing all false thoughts, seeing pure Buddha-nature by eliminating ignorance, this is none other than "Discovering the Self-nature," Becoming Buddha. It is also the Ultimate Marvelous Enlightenment, the Highest Authentic Enlightenment, Nirvana without Remainder, "Buddha Ground," Tathāgata and Liberation which have been referred in such perennial paradigms of Buddhist teachings as *Zongjing lu* (*Jonggyeong rok*), *Dacheng qixin lun* (*Daeseong gishin-non*), *Nirvāṇa sūtra* (*Yeolban-gyeong*) and *Yogācārabhūmi-śāstra* (*Yuga saji-ron*). Such a sudden

---

[20] See *Let Us See Correctly Our Own Self* (*Jagileul baro bopsida*), 191-193.
[21] *Seonmun jeongno*, 1-3.
[22] *Ibid.*, 7.

enlightenment to the Buddha-nature brings the instantaneous perfection of all meritorious qualities-sudden cultivation. Thus, there is no need to perform any kind of moral duties in order to make this sudden enlightenment more perfect and more complete.

Taking into consideration of all what Seongcheol has said concerning "Discovering the nature," it appears that the ultimate state or the great Nirvana refers to the pure state of mind or consciousness, and the state where one can experience the subsequent eternal happiness, or the great stillness. He exerts wholeheartedly his time and energy in actualizing this pure state of mind through his body and mind, and in teaching other fellow monks. And he puts forward his realization and the way on how to achieve it in the form of the theory of sudden enlightenment/sudden practice (*dono-donsu*).

The realization of the self-nature is also called "the No-hindered Knowledge" (*muae-ji*) or "the Natural Knowledge" (*jayeon-ji*), or "the Sacred Knowledge of Tathāgata" (*yeorae seongji*).[23] Seongcheol view of the Śākyamuni Buddha is also based upon his understanding that Discovering the Self-nature was in the beginning achieved, taught and transmitted to the next generations by the Buddha, thus without him nobody could know the way to realize this state of mind.

2.2. The Absolute and Infinite World and its Fundamental Criticism on the World of Sentient Beings

The state of "To Keep Integrity [in No-mind] Whether Awakened or Sleeping" is called the absolute, infinite, and eternal world. Seongcheol thinks that the purpose of believing in a religion is to attain this state and to abide in it, after leaving behind the relative world. Seongcheol argues:

> I think that the aim of a religion is to come out of the relative and finite world and to enter the absolute and infinite world to gain the eternal happiness. Since the relative and finite world is the world of becoming-perishing, the absolute and infinite world is the world of nirvana, the fundamental purpose of a religion is to cross from this shore to the other shore and to rejoice in happiness. The eternal happiness cannot be realized in the relative and finite world. The fundamental desire of human beings ties in the eternal happiness. But one cannot attain this happiness without entering the absolute and infinite world. Therefore, one cannot avoid aiming at entering the absolute and infinite world in order to gain the eternal happiness. This is the fundamental aim of all religions regardless of what they are.[24]

---

[23] *Ibid.*, 48 and 68.

[24] *One Hundred Days Sermon* (*Baek'il beommun*), 1:34.

In the same page, a passage found in the *Qixin lun* (*The Awaking of Faith*), "to free from all sufferings and to gain the ultimate bliss," is similarly interpreted by Seongcheol. What is strikingly important here in Seongcheol's view of the absolute and the relative, is the unbridgeable gap between these two worlds. Being separated, there is no significant relationship between them. As to the relationship between the absolute and the relative, Manhae argues that a religion is to realize the infinite life in the world of dust and ashes; the luminous life of a religion should have the feature of a great fullness and function; the locus of its fullness and function is the institutions, laws, and morals of the world; and the relative world is only the temporary and relative expression of it. Seongcheol would argue, contrary to Manhae, that only after one leaves the nation and the family, one is able to realize Dao. Therefore, Seongcheol's emphasis upon absolutism and "leaving home" would prevent him from accepting Manhae's view of the Buddhist practice that requires the final step of the Entering the City with Bliss-bestowing Hands to fulfill the entire process of Buddhist practice. Seongcheol further rejects the view that a bodhisattva should come in and out of the re-birth world, since sentient beings love to stay there. Instead, for Seongcheol, the Great Quiescence free and unhindered is the preservation and self-cultivation.[25]

Seongcheol's emphasis upon the pure Buddhism and the state of no traces of all false thoughts, seems to develop a strong sense of mistrust of all kinds of actions in the secular society. He cannot admit as the proper place for the Seon practices the secular world, which is primarily based upon desire, lust and false thoughts. This world cannot be the proper locus of peace, freedom, and happiness in their true senses. Seongcheol argues: Listen to this eternal sound of the bell, after leaving behind all kinds of transient desires:

> Here on the earth, all sages, clever men, heroes, and great men; they are haughty; this is funny. The unification of the six nations achieved by the first Emperor of the Chin, the conquest of the world by Alexander and Napoleon; all these things are one of the most shaky business, since they are foams over foams.

> Oh, a raging folks captivated by self-desires. Let us listen to the eternal sound of the bell, after leaving behind useless desires in a vain dream. The cry of wild geese, flying in pairs in the clear sky and in the rays of the full moon, celebrate us, and the echo of peace and freedom overflow the universe.[26]

The eternal sound cannot be heard as long as one has even a bit of desire, since desire is always transient. Sages, clever persons, heroes and great men on the earth are captivated by desire. In their minds there still exist false thoughts and afflictions.

---

[25] *Seonmun jeongno*, 97.
[26] *Jagileul baro bopshida*, 17.

According to Seongcheol, the teaching of the perfectly pure state of mind or consciousness is unique to Buddhism that it cannot possibly be found in other teachings such as Confucianism and Daoism. Old [Buddhist] people claimed that the three teachings, Confucianism, Buddhism and Daoism were not different from each other but there was a unity among them. But Seongcheol refuses to accept this claim. The reason is twofold: Confucianism and Daoism are teachings functioning in the world of sentient beings; all theories presented in and actions recommended by these teachings are based upon false thoughts.[27] By calling Confucius "the sage of the town" (*maeul seongin*), Seongcheol seems to disparage him.[28] Seongcheol literally interprets the parable of "the burning house of three worlds." For him the burning house cannot be the locus of true happiness and freedom. From the beginning of history, people have in various ways attempted to live more happily in the suffered life. But happiness cannot be found in the world of relativity, contradiction, and struggle. According to Seongcheol's belief, even a single person among so-called great men and heroes could not achieve the eternal happiness in the world of this [secular] reality.[29] In this world of sentient beings, one cannot find eternal happiness. Thus, there is no possibility for Seongcheol to develop a Confucian Buddhism or an engaged Buddhism. Instead, he would consider this type of Buddhism as the result or the cause of the corruption of Buddhism.

2.3. The Renunciation of the Secular Society (*Jeolsok*)

Seongcheol's view of the extreme sense of renunciation is clearly expressed in his spirit of "leaving home." His vows made in 1964 contain the following points: He should always stay at a saṅgha or a hermitage in a mountain, but never at a temple and a layman's house located in a city. He should practice the bequeathed doctrine to become a model for them; he should never talk of other matters; and he should never be engaged in all kinds of societies or meetings.[30] This extreme kind of total renunciation is also revealed in the first rule "Renunciation" in his "Eight Disciplinary Rules in Practicing the Way" (*sudo palgye*) given to Monks. It says: Since the secular world is the world of *saṁsāra*, and leaving home is the way to nirvana, one should renounce the secular society for the sake of nirvana. One should repay one's parental love through leaving home and practicing Dao. If one is drawn to the parental love, this is to make parents go into the hell, thus one should treat one's parents as passersby[31]. There named a monk Hyujeong (Seosan daesa, 1520-1604) in Joseon Dynasty, who was considered an original thinker who attempted to draw

---

[27] *Ibid.*, 138.

[28] *Ibid.*, 150.

[29] *Yeongwonhan jayu*, 25.

[30] *Baengnyeon Bulgyo nonjib* (Seul: Collected Articles of the White Lotus Association, 1994) 4: 20.

[31] *Jagileul baro bopshida*, 308.

together the various Buddhist traditions in Korea into a coherent whole. At the age of 72, Hyujeong rendered a great service to his country during the Hideyoshi invasion by organizing bands of warrior-monks who assisted the regular troops. However, Seongcheol's extremely strict attitude toward the renunciation makes him call Hyujeong "a monk hankering after fame and gain." Hyujeong was not seen as a true monk.[32]

Seongcheol shows his pride and contentment as a monk by describing himself as "a person living in a palace." When he was asked, "What are you doing in a mountain?" he replies that nourishing the mind of Dao by way of silence is a monk's life. And the aim of his life is to obtain the happiness of Dao.[33] Since Seongcheol places a great emphasis upon "sudden enlightenment" and gave an absolute value to it such words as people, politics and social justice are almost non-existent in his sermons.

2.4. The Rejection of the Skill-in-means *yāna* (*bangpyeon*) and the Bodhisattva Action

In examining a passage from the *Lotus sūtra*, "Since there is only *ekayāna*, the vehicle of oneness in Lands in all directions, all other ways of skill-in-means are excluded,"[34] he explains that as the fundamental perspective of Buddha there is only *ekayāna* (*ilseung*), the one Buddha-yāna (*ilbulseung*). This is "to realize immediately *Bhūtatathatā* Dharma-realm.[35]" "For Seongcheol there is only one "*ekayāna*" to attain the absolutely pure state of "Discovering Self-Nature." Every other way to attain Buddhahood except this *ekayāna*, including doctrinal teachings, skill-in-means, *Śrāvakayāna*, and the *Pretyakabuddhayāna*, is not right way to discover the self-nature. And he notes: "To attain the Buddhahood (*Seongbul*) through practicing six *pāramitās* and myriad activities is like crossing the ocean by means of a dead corpse."[36] Seongcheol further argues:

> The teaching of Sudden Enlightenment and Discovery of the Self-nature, which the preceding Buddhas and succeeding Patriarchs transmitted one another from mind to mind, is the pulse of Buddhas and Patriarchs and the marrow of the right teaching. All other various teachings are no more than skill-in-means for convenience and temporary expedients designed to guide people. Therefore when [we] take the standpoint of the fundamental right teaching, [we] should reject them as false teachings. If [a teacher] mistakes expedient explanations designed for skill-in-means as the true teaching and thus does not discard but attaches himself to them, sentient beings would be bound to those tentative expedient explanations and unable to

---

[32] *Baekil beommun,* 1:42.

[33] *Jagileul baro bopshida,* 208.

[34] *Baekil beommun,* 1:147.

[35] For details of the *ekayāna,* see *ibid.,* 149.

[36] *Ibid.,* 42.

return to the truth. Therefore [I] reject them ardently and advocate the fundamental right teaching.[37]

Among various false teachings, Seongcheol includes all kinds of Buddhist activities, or example, invocation of a Buddha, memorizing every *sūtra*, and building Buddhist temples. In comparison with the *Ekayāna*, that is, the true theory, as he argues, all of these activities are the life-death dharma (*saengsabeop*), which cannot be the right way to the salvation out of the life-death.[38] He even severely disparaged the Bodhisattvayāna as "a lie."[39] All other teachings took the gradualist approach, requiring indefinite length of time to discover the Self-nature.

What is wrong with the Bodhisattvayāna? This vehicle is a lower teaching, not even taught by the historical Sākyamuni Buddha himself. For a bodhisattva to become a Buddha needs the innumerable *kapla*s of time.[40] But the Buddha and his disciples in *sūtra*s were "now, immediately" enlightened ones. They did not need the infinite length of time. A bodhisattva is the being who neither gets rid of all kinds of false thoughts, nor discovered the Buddhahood.[41] In case of Avalokiteśvara Bodhisattva, six coarse thoughts were removed, but three fine thoughts still remain. For Seongcheol the Bodhisattvayāna is an incomplete, thus, false teaching which places a wrong emphasis upon incomplete activities.

Seongcheol, however, does not want his Buddhism to be perceived as a teaching of egoism (*kaein juui*). Once he was asked by a professor: "Since during harsh moments in our history, as that of the Korean War, after renouncing the family and the nation you were engaged in Seon practices in the mountain in order to discover the Self-nature. That is good for you. But you are an egoist, aren't you?" As a way of his reply, Seongcheol poses his own question to the professor: "Have you ever worked purely for other people except your family and parents?" Drawing the negative answer out of that professor, Seongcheol asserts to the effect that the motive to renounce the family to become a monk is to deliver all sentient beings, not to live for my own happy life. The motive of leaving home is to achieve a more precious and better thing by discarding a small matter.[42] As a purist and absolutist, Seongcheol gives a clear warning of and opposition to the secularization of Buddhism. He emphatically claims: "The secular society should become Buddhist. If Buddhism is secularized, then it will die." If a monk becomes secularized, he becomes drowned in his attempt to deliver sentient beings out of the ocean of suffering.

---

[37] *Seonmun jeongno*, 82.

[38] *Jagileul baro bopshida*, 233. Even when Seongcheol acknowledged bodhisattva activities, he qualifies them as the skill-in-means to see the true reality of oneself. *Ibid.*, 239.

[39] *Baekil beommun*, 1: 148.

[40] *Ibid.*,149.

[41] *Ibid.*, 43 and 66.

[42] See *Jagileul baro bopshida*, 94-5.

Elsewhere he called the ability not to be drowned in the secular society "the spirit of pure Buddhism."[43]

Seongcheol's spirit of pure Buddhism and his attempt to recover the lost ancient standard of "Discovering the Self nature," is also shown in his criticism on the reform (*hyeokshin*) of Buddhism and giving a new meaning to the word "reform." When he was asked his opinion of the reform of Korean Buddhism, he replied: "In case of religion, the 'reform' is not appropriate. It should be expressed a 'restoration' [to the original state] (*bokwon*).[44]" "When one talks of reform, this 'reform' should be based upon the fundamental thought of its founder. If the reform is contrary to Buddha's thought even a little bit, then it is not a reform but a counter-movement (*Yeokhaeng*). And cleaning up degenerated evils of Buddhism caused by the passage of years and going back to the fundamental thought of the founder, is the true way of reform."[45] In the Seongcheol's answer to the following question, "What should Korean Buddhism do in the 20th century?", is clearly exhibited his view that Buddhism is a teaching of eternity, transcending space and time. In Buddhism there is only One Truth which is not changeable regardless of ages and place.

Although Seongcheol has his own sense of history, his primary understanding of temporality is the standpoint of eternity expressed in the phrase "all ages (*mansae*) are now (*geum*)" and he shows a strong sense of returning to the original state. Naturally, he pays less attention to the political and social situation which people are facing during those historically and politically difficult moments in the 1970s and 1980s.

3. Comparative Perspective: Tears and Self-contentment

Now that among many expressions of the 20th century Korean Buddhism and its wide range of spectrum, this paper has discussed two extreme types, Manhae's and Seongcheol's views of Buddhism. We have witnessed that two traditional ideals, an *arhat* and a bodhisattva are vying with each other for the worthier ideal of a Buddhist.

Manhae placed a great emphasis upon the action of a bodhisattva and his Buddhism finally culminated in "Minjung Buddhism" (Buddhism of the People). Manhae's drive to deliver the world made him give a less attention to Seon practices in hermitages and to the establishment of the standard of the Discovering the Self-Nature. He did not perceive the hermitage as a suitable place for a monk. What mattered to him was the deliverance of beings, not the purity and height achieved through Discovering the Self-Nature. He praised a Confucian hero rather than a Seon master. He knew how to relate the vows of all Buddhas and all Bodhisattvas to save the sentient beings to the fate of the country and the Korean people, and gave positive meanings to such relative

---

[43] *Ibid.*, 221.

[44] *Ibid.*, 215.

[45] *Ibid.*, 227.

phenomena as institutions, laws, morals, revolutions, and isms. Manhae's engaged Buddhism gave a great influence to some of Korean intellectuals who fought against the Military regime to establish the democratic government during 1970s and 1980s. Only in 1980s and 1990s a certain number of monks belonging to Jogye Order began to pay a sincere attention to Manhae's Buddhist thought. In contrast to Manhae's Minjung Buddhism, Seon Master Seongcheol attempted to revive or return to the ideal of an *arhat*. He found his sole role in realizing "his own self-nature" by means of Seon practice, thus naturally showing less social and political concern.

To reveal differences, contrasts, and even inner criticisms in their views of Buddhism, this study has dealt with key words in both types of Buddhism. The author has confirmed the fact that the key words in Manhae's Buddhism were sudden enlightenment1gradual enlightenment, the action of a bodhisattva, a nation, a people, the Independence of the country, anger, parting, sadness and tears, whereas the key words in Seongchol's Buddhism are Discovering Buddha-nature, sudden enlightenment/sudden practice, Hwadu study in Seon practice, Old Buddhas and Old Patriarchs, the renunciation of the secular society, a monk of non-action, unengaged and rejoicing in Dao.

These two types seem to be incompatible to each other, in many respects. To reveal once more a sharp difference between these two views of Buddhism, I will try to answer to the thematic questions suggested by the sponsors of this seminar, all of which have often been debated in the 2500 years of Buddhist history. The questions are: In the context in which an *arhat* is pitted against a bodhisattva, chanting is contrasted with Seon, what does individual peace mean? Do the no-self doctrine imply the sublation of the individual to the society? Is inner peace possible only in a peaceful society? To the first question, "What does individual peace mean?" Seongcheol would answer that individual peace and happiness have absolute value. It is absolute in that it remains "ultimate" in spite of all kinds of social and political evils the Korean people have experienced. In the case of Manhae, individual peace and tranquility have no meaning at all, since no individual human being is immune to or independent of his social and political surroundings. The chanting mentioned by the sponsor, however, needs to be amended into political activities.

Concerning the second question, "Do the no-self doctrine imply the sublation of the individual to the society?" Manhae would give the affirmative answer. But Seongcheol the negative answer. Manhae could identify self with nation by way of expanding the realm where the causality is functioning, thus speaking of evils in politics. Seongcheol identifies "the realm of discovering self-nature" as the realm of the true self, which should be sought and preserved usually in the hermitage in the mountains. For Manhae the autonomy of his country was important, but for Seongcheol the autonomy of individual self was of paramount importance.

As to the last question, "Is inner peace possible only in a peaceful society? No, would answer Seongcheol. The inner peace or eternal happiness seems to be possible in spite of the non-peaceful society. It is not possible, however, for

Manhae to rejoice in the inner peace as long as the society is not peaceful because his "*nim*" is absent there. Furthermore, the difference between Manhae's view of Buddhism and that of Seongcheol may be seen in terms of the deliverance of the whole [world] and the deliverance of an individual being. "The Beloved" (*nim*) is the symbolic expression referring to something non-existent or lacked of, one of which is the Independence of the country. The non-existence or silence of the *Nim*, however, means the indefinitely delaying the deliverance of the country and the people. The tears which Manhae shed in parting *Nim*, were the result of pain, sadness, and agony which a bodhisattva is usually expected to suffer in the process of waiting or realizing *nim*. But "the Immediacy" (*don*) expresses the ultimate point of individual salvation.

The self-contentment of the ultimate happiness has been expressed in the Immediacy, which intrinsically refuses the lack of anything. Without any lack of something, there would be neither anger nor tears. For Manhae the happiness in Dao (*dorak*) is simply a skill-in-means. Seongcheol sees the compassionate action as merely a skill-in-means. Manhae's and Seongcheol's views of Buddhism seem to be theoretically and practically incompatible positions. There seem to be the different understandings of the essence of a human being. Are we ultimately doers or knowers? For Manhae the essence of being a Buddhist is to be agency. Only through the bodhisattvic action is human fulfillment possible. For him a life of full of action, that is real life. To perform the good works ordered by the compassionate love, that is the real way of renunciation. Those people are entitled to be called a Buddhist, who spends their life in works for the good of a nation or a people. On the other hand, Seongcheol seems to concern to find an ultimate self not subject to death and re-death. He evolves a different philosophy of self. Seeing action in a secular society as a source of bondage, Seongcheol rejected the agent self as ultimate. Indeed, from the top of the mountain Seongcheol upholds, like a torch-light, the ideal of "a man of Dao, action-less and disengaged" (*muwihan doin*). This ideal self is attainable in the state of No-mind with no traces of false thoughts. Seongcheol seems to believe that the essence of being a Buddhist is to realize Buddha-nature, which is fundamentally a state of knowledge in that the sudden enlightenment (of Sacred Knowledge of the Tathāgata) does not require gradual practices or performing moral obligations. Sudden enlightenment does not seem to enjoin Seongcheol to perform any moral action in order to make it more complete more perfect, which is already itself complete and perfect.

4. Concluding Remarks

Thus far, we have examined Manhae's view and Seongcheol's view of Buddhism by highlighting their differences, contrasts, and internal criticisms. Now, as a way of concluding this paper, let us begin with the question: Which type of Buddhism is a worthier Buddhism? In the light of Manhae's Buddhism, the happiness in Dao coming from Discovering the Self-Nature and the Great Quiescence is not the aim of a worthy Buddhism. For Seongcheol, the action of a bodhisattva and samādhis in sadness and tears would be seen as the result of false thoughts of not-yet-enlightened beings. Manhae's "non-existence" is the seed of tears, and Seongcheol's No-mind is the origin of the rejoicing in Dao. The Buddhism without the love and tears of a bodhisattva cannot be a compassionate religion. When the idea of compassion is not realized, the followers of that Buddhism are not seen as the worthy followers of the Buddha who is believed to be full of perfect knowledge and full compassion.

Although Manhae's Buddhism has its width but seemed to lack of the height; Seongcheol's Buddhism has shown the height to Korean Buddhists, but has lost the width of the compassion. Without the height, Buddhism tends to be degenerated, but without a sufficient width, it easily becomes the Buddhism of an *arhat*. Which Buddhism is a worthier type, the Buddhism of tears for *Nim*, or the Buddhism of purity and self-contentment without any false thoughts? What is the true skill-in-means in deliverance? The action of a bodhisattva with some traces of false thoughts? Or, the Sacred Knowledge of the Tathāgata? What constitutes a worthy Buddhist? Is a Buddhist worthy because of spiritual attainments-insight and enlightenment? Or because of strict observance of the disciplinary rules of the monastic community? Furthermore, is worthiness due to one's compassionate efforts to lead all beings out of suffering, or is it due to success in overcoming suffering in one's own life? Korean Buddhism is said to belong to the Mahāyāna tradition. Then, what are the meanings of an *arhat*, a bodhisattva and the small vehicle and the great vehicle in the context of Korean Buddhism? How would Śākyamuni Buddha with perfect knowledge and full compassion reply to all these and similar questions?

The controversy over who is a "worthy" follower of Śākyamuni Buddha that divided the early community in India into Sthaviras and Mahāsaṃghikas, the predecessors of the Theravādins and Mahāyānists, is being repeated here in Korea. Both Manhae and Seongcheol would argue that his type of Buddhism is a worthier one. If the Buddha were alive, he would answer to the question "Who is a worthier follower of his Way, Manhae and Seongcheol?" But here the historical Buddha exists only in the form of ideal type of personality who is supposed to realize both die height and width of Buddhism to their ultimate levels. Without his presence, the issues facing the Korean Buddhism in the final decade of the 20th century will remain as un-solvable. In the dialectical spirit, however, one may pose the following question: Is it possible for the Korean Buddhism in the future to realize both the height and the width? Or, is it possible to dialectically sublate the best portions represented separately by Manhae and Seongcheol? Is it possible for the pure self with no traces of all infinitesimal false thoughts to be extended to perform the bodhisattva action? Can the Korean Buddhism search for the Buddhist ideal to give a unity between the salvation of the entire world and the individual salvation? If possible, who or which group can realize that ideal in a concrete way? These questions will remain as questions unanswered until that person or that group appears in the future. One should constantly ask them as a special kind of Hwadus, because in asking these questions, the possibility will be impregnated.

CHAPTER 31

THE SHIN BUDDHIST APPROACH TO SPIRITUAL DISCIPLINE AND PEACE

Alfred Bloom

1. Introduction

A great paradox marks the world in which we live. One the one hand, we have developed a civilization and culture of great beauty and ease. Technological advancement has made the knowledge and wisdom of the ages virtually instantaneously available on a world-wide scale. Global networks of information, communication and travel bind all people in a common destiny, beyond race and political borders. On the other hand, ongoing violence, persistent tribalism, dehumanizing ethnic-cleansing, divisive religious conflict, environmental pollution, political corruption, proliferating nuclear development and unstable economic competition with widespread unemployment assault our senses and minds everyday through T.V., radio and newspapers.

As we approach the fiftieth anniversary of the first devastating nuclear holocaust in Japan, we must pause to contemplate the roots of this paradox within our own individual minds and spirits, as well as the spiritual resources we possess to heal the breach within ourselves and our world.

The modern world is a reflection of the distortion, delusion, and destructiveness arising from our ego-centric, selfish pursuits of personal advantage at the expense of our fellow human beings, whether in our daily, individual relations or in the global interactions of nations. It is a Hobbesian world of power-seeking and a Nietzschian world grasping for omnipotence. Our contemporary world is marked by various characteristics that lay at the basis of personal, social and national conflicts. There is increased alienation with resulting violence of all kinds. There is aloneness in which people feel isolated and cut off, despite the masses of population about them. Anomie appears in the decline in respect for law and order or justice. There is ambiguity concerning the worthwhile-ness of life resulting from the breakdown of authority of traditional values, and there is absurdity where we spend millions to explore space, but only a fraction to assist the needy; where we desire vengeance for crime, but give scant attention to prevention. We want small government to spend our tax money, but appeal to big government to save us from disasters or defend us against suspected enemies.

This is an age where rationalistic liberalism has been rejected, despite its positive contributions to modern life, because of its own built-in contradictions. Consequently, modern life has been left with no inspiring philosophy of life that can offer people meaning for their lives or a basis for strong commitments. There is lack of confidence that reason can solve problems. Many writers describe our age as the postindustrial, post-modern world, standing at the "end of history." There is no widely accepted ideology on a world scale. Theories of demythologization and deconstruction, which reveal the structures of power that control masses of people, have stripped our world of its easily assumed patterns of meaning. The New Science has widened our vista of the universe in the dimensions of time and space. It has created wondrous labor and life-saving instruments and procedures, yet decreasing the need for human participation. Science has brought convenience to modern life but neither fulfillment nor meaning. It could be argued that it has contributed to the dehumanization of life. Further, the growth of technology has reduced the significance of the individual, while increasing secularization of the culture has reduced religious faith to personal subjectivity and private opinion. Traditional certainties, derived from earlier ages, seem unreal, depriving life of the sense of mystery, awe and even fear that inspired our ancestors who, while sensing their smallness in the universe, had a lively awareness and faith in a higher order of things that embraced and cared for even the lowliest person. Modern people experience their smallness in a mass society and faceless world, appearing as pawns and toys of unknown forces. They do not have a deep faith in themselves, let alone in the universe which is silent to human suffering.

While expanding networks of information and communication are ushering us into a new age of possible global understanding and responsibility, the pace of change within our multi-faceted world has increased so rapidly that we are constantly forced to shift our attention from one concern to another, without being able to give serious consideration to the issues involved in these dilemmas. We have lost the sense of the connectedness of events and have become more fragmented persons, losing touch with the threads of the past that give texture to our lives. It is an age in which knowledge and its availability has increased a thousand-fold. However, people are manipulated by those who control the means to communicate information. The means of delivery make us more ignorant when important issues are reduced to thirty-second sound bytes. Modern knowledge has become so fragmented and specialized that it is difficult to get the big picture. Many people live totally in the present, as though in a vacuum. This raises the question of the meaning of human existence. How are we to deal with the anxieties, fears, and despair that infect our modern life and become the source of terror and violence?

There is widespread dissatisfaction with modern life, not only in America, but among other leading nations, because people feel that they are losing control over their lives. There is suspicion that leaders and government do not serve the people but have hidden agendas to gain or maintain their own power. Despite the great advances of modern science and thought, human life has not been made more secure and meaningful. Individual, personal life has declined in value because there is no unifying vision of life and reality that brings people together or enables them to rise above their differences in the realization of their common humanity and destiny. Our age resembles Humpty Dumpty who fell from the wall and not even the king's men could put Humpty Dumpty together again. We are confronted on every level of society with seemingly intractable social, economic and political problems.

With such conditions in the background of our lives, without a radical change in the understanding of human life and in the way that our religious faith expresses itself in the modern world, there is little hope that we can avoid the destruction and degradation of life that is amply represented and strikingly evident in the terrors of Hiroshima and Nagasaki or Auschwitz and Serbia.

It is more than ever the responsibility of religious people throughout the world, and certainly of Buddhists, to speak out against such horrors and to work to prevent their repetition. As it is stated in the Juseige, a gāthā or hymn from the *Larger Pure Land Sūtra*, we must open the treasury of the Dharma for all people universally and by being constantly in touch with the masses, declare the teaching with a lion's roar. Shinran's realism and his vision of sharing his faith with all others challenges modern people to the pursuit of justice and peace as the foundation of hope and meaning. Like a beacon light, his teaching makes clear the hope that sustained his life and that of his followers.

It is in this context that we undertake the quest for peace in its broadest dimensions. The issue is not only political or social peace, but a peace within the human psyche and mind that radiates to all areas of the society. It is a realistic peace that understands the unstable, erratic character of the human mind. It is a quest for peace that, without forgetting the exterior conditions of human suffering, focuses on the interior state of the human spirit. This has been the mission of Buddhism throughout its history until the present time. In this context, this paper will explore the perspective offered by Shinran Shōnin (1173-1263) as he confronted himself and his turbulent age.

Shinran Shōnin (1173-1263) would have understood this paradoxical world as it expressed itself within his own heart, as well as the general society and religious world of his time. He lamented that he did not have a pure mind or sincerity, that he was, as we all are, deceitful and given to flattery. He also recognized the unequal distribution of justice in his society, when he recalled Prince Shōtoku's observation that it is like throwing a stone into water, when a rich person goes to court, while for the poor, it is like throwing water into a stone. Shinran lamented his own egoism in posing as a teacher and leader, and he perceived the emptiness of the Buddhist Order of his day that had simply become an instrument of the state. He resembled the prophets of die Bible, when he described the Buddhist institutions as externally Buddhist but inwardly pagan.

Shinran was a realist as he faced himself and the world about him. Though he has been criticized as being negative and pessimistic about human nature, in actuality he was animated and inspired by the profound ideal and hope which he encountered and experienced in the Primal Vow of Amida Buddha and the path of *Nembutsu*, which is reflection on, and recitation of, the name of Amida Buddha, as the basis of everyday life. His life and teaching exemplify the compassion and wisdom of the Primal Vow in action within our world. He provides a model for our own understanding and approach to the modern world, despite the fact that he lived eight hundred years ago.

Shinran is important particularly for shifting the focus of religious attention from the traditional externalized, vocal practice of *Nembutsu*, regarded as a virtue and means of purification, to the inner character of the mind or spirit that motivates any practice. Thus he declares:

> The gist of this statement is that when we think good thoughts, we think we are good; and when we think evil thoughts, we think we are evil, not realizing fully that it is the inconceivable power of the Vow that makes our salvation possible. [1]

With respect to Shinran himself, his teaching was based on his personal religious experience of despair and uncertainty after twenty years of rigorous discipline as a monk in the Tendai monastery on Mount Hiei outside of Kyoto. He came to the conclusion that enlightenment, as traditionally pursued, was impossible to achieve through self-striving practices, because the ego still remains active. He himself confessed:

> I know truly how grievous it is that I, Gutoku Shinran, am sinking in an immense ocean of desires and attachments and am lost in vast mountains of fame and advantage; so that I rejoice not at all at entering the stage of the truly settled and feel no happiness at coming nearer the realization of true enlightenment. How ugly it is! How wretched! [2]

I. Shinran's Perspective on Religious Faith

For Shinran, religious practices such as the *Nembutsu* must arise through a two-fold inner awareness and movement of faith or trust. Traditionally, this has been termed: "Two types of deep faith." On the one hand, there must be a

---

[1] Taitetsu Unno, trans., *Tannishō: A Shin Buddhist Classic* (Honolulu: Buddhist Study Center Press, 1984), XIII, 23.

[2] Shin Buddhism Translation Series, the faith chapter, vol. 2, *The True teaching, Practice and Realization of the Pure Land Way* (Kyoto: Hongwanji International Center, 1985), 279.

realistic awareness of the pervasive egoism that infects even our religious efforts. He writes:

> All the ocean-like multitudinous beings, since the beginning-less past have been transmigrating in the sea of ignorance, drowning in the cycle of existences, bound to the cycle of sufferings, and having no pure, serene faith.... All the common and petty persons at all times constantly defile their good minds with greed and lust and their anger and hatred constantly bum the treasure of the Dharma. Even though they work and practice as busily as though they were sweeping fire off their heads, their practices are called poisoned and mixed good deeds and also called deluded and deceitful practices ... If one desires to be born in the Land of Infinite Light with these deluded and poisoned good (*sic*), he cannot possibly attain it.[3]

On the other hand, a lively, joyous awareness arises when we realize that our futile ego assertions are embraced by the universal compassion of Amida Buddha. Shinran declares:

> What a joy it is that I place my mind in the soil of the Buddha's Universal Vow and I let my thoughts flow into the sea of the Inconceivable Dharma.[4]

Within the awakened religious consciousness, there is a dialectic in which the negation of our externalized, individual and socially induced conscious persona opens us to the broader and deeper background and context of our true self. Therefore, Shinran writes:

> The diamond-like mind is the mind that aspires for Buddhahood. The mind that aspires for Buddhahood is the mind that saves sentient beings. The mind that saves sentient beings is the mind that grasps sentient beings and brings them to birth in the Pure Land of peace. This mind is the mind aspiring for great enlightenment. This mind is the mind of great compassion.[5]

In our tradition we symbolize the reality that embraces and sustains our lives as Amida Buddha. Amida Buddha is the symbol of the cosmic process of interdependence that sustains and supports our lives, in spite of our egoistic, aggressive pursuits and actions. Shinran describes as unconditional Boundless Compassion.

---

[3] Ryūkoku University Translation Series, vol. 5, *Kyōgyōshinshō* (Kyoto: Ryūkoku University, 1966), 107.

[4] *Ibid,* 211.

[5] *Op. cit.,* Shin Buddhism Translation Series, *The True Teaching,* etc., vol. 2, 259.

According to Shinran, the causes and conditions that lead to a life-transforming and deeply personal recognition of the truth of this dialectic of self-negation and emergent positive self-affirmation constitutes the experience of faith/trust. This process is interpreted as Amida's true-mind coming to manifestation or realization within the mind and heart of the existent person as that person's true selfhood. It is understood as Buddha-nature expressing itself within human consciousness Shinran writes:

> The Tathāgata (Buddha) with a pure and true mind perfected the complete, all-merging, unhindered, inconceivable, indescribable, and ineffable supreme virtue. The Tathāgata endows His Sincere Mind to the sea of all the multitudinous beings filled with evil passions, evil acts, and perverted knowledge.[6]

There is, therefore, a deeply religious basis for personal identity that redefines the meaning of religion and the significance of everyday life for that person. The bi-polar dialectic of religious subjectivity that Shinran discovered in his own life led him to declare that the *Nembutsu* is neither a practice nor a good deed (*Tannishō* IV). It is not a practice aimed at gaining enlightenment, nor is it a moralistic good deed, designed to purify the mind or accumulate merit for future reward. What he understood about the *Nembutsu* as a practice could be applied to all self-striving religious practices designed to achieve some degree of purity and perfection. From his perspective, these practices are inspired by the belief that one can attain perfection through one's own efforts, despite the fact that all our actions are tainted by egoistic self-interest. Within his own experience, Shinran saw this effort as self-defeating and ultimately impossible, just as it is impossible to lift ourselves by our own bootstraps.

2. Religious Practice and Peace

It is against the background of Shinran's experience and teaching that we must consider the issue of religious practices that contribute to peace. For Shinran, it is not the practice that makes for peace, but the inner motivation and understanding of the purpose of those practices. If practices are not viewed in a larger spiritual perspective as the background for all human action, they can lead to self-righteousness and spiritual competition through relative comparisons. One may do a practice longer, more frequently, or more correctly than someone else. We can frequently observe self-righteousness in those who claim they are working only for the benefit of humanity. It is most clear in those who resort to violence in the name of a good cause.

In order to transcend the relative character of practices, Shinran teaches that such endeavors are not means to an end, but an expression of a reality already

---

[6] *Op. cit.*, Ryūkoku University Translation Series, vol. 5, *Kyōgyōshinshō* (Kyoto: Ryūkoku University, 1966), 105.

experienced. He constantly reminds his followers that practices must not be undertaken with a conscious, deliberate intention or calculation. Naturally, he understands that we make conscious decisions to practice or act. He is not rejecting the phenomenal aspects of will and action. Rather, he is viewing the self and its actions against the background, and within the context of, the Boundless Compassion of the Primal Vow of Amida Buddha that expresses itself through our actions, exhibiting the true source of good. In the context of Mahāyāna Buddhist tradition, it is the dynamic manifestation of Buddha-nature whose essence is unconditional compassion and non-discriminating wisdom. From this standpoint, we cannot take any credit for good achieved. It was Shinran's intention to remove any basis for self-congratulation and self-complacency from our so-called "good deeds", and thereby to overcome the source of pride that creates conflict.

As life conditions open us to recognize our true natures as passion-ridden beings, unable to save ourselves, practice transforms to expressions of gratitude, dedication, openness and sharing. With the transformation of our ego-perspective, our actions are also transformed to channels by which the Boundless Compassion may reach our fellow human beings.

Through the *Nembutsu*/Faith in Shinran's sense, we establish the awareness that goes beyond the ordinary human wisdom and foolish-ness that create the struggles between individuals, within and without religious communities throughout the world. Through the *Nembutsu*, we recognize our connection and identity with all beings that are alike embraced in the Buddha's compassion. He writes:

> In reflecting on the ocean of great *shinjin*, I realize that there is no discrimination between noble and humble or black-robed monks and white-clothed laity, no differentiation between man and woman, old and young. The amount of evil one has committed is not considered and the duration of any performance of religious practices is of no concern…. It is simply *shinjin* (faith/trust) that is inconceivable, inexplicable and indescribable. It is like the medicine that eradicates all poisons. The medicine of the Tathāgata's Vow destroys the poisons of our wisdom and foolishness.[7]

Shinran shared the iconoclasm that permeates Buddhist teaching. According to Shinran, faith inspired by the Primal Vow challenges and breaks through our claims to wisdom and superiority similar to the Chan master Yixuan who exclaimed: "If you meet the Buddha, kill him," noting that the titles Buddha and Bodhisattva are words of honor, but also bondage. In both Shinran and Yixuan, egocentric, discriminating religious consciousness enslaves and deceives through the illusion of superiority. Such consciousness leads to the formation of religious elites and distinguishes people as saints and sinners, the good and evil.

---

[7] *Op. cit.,* Shin Buddhism Translation Series, *The True Teaching* etc., Faith chapter, vol. 2, 249-250.

Inspired by the inner meaning and spirit of the *Nembutsu*, Buddhists are to work for peace and human good, acutely aware of the deceptive pretensions and limitations of action implicit in our passion-ridden humanity. No one is to take credit for anything achieved. It all is due to the working of the wisdom and compassion of Amida Buddha. Further, there is to be humble recognition of the limits of ego-inspired action:

> There is a difference in compassion between the Path of Sages and the Path of Pure Land. The compassion in the Path of Sages is expressed through pity, sympathy, and care for all beings, but truly rare is it that one can help another as completely as one desires. The compassion in the Path of Pure Land is to quickly attain Buddhahood, saying the *nembutsu*, and with the true heart of compassion and love save all beings as we desire.
>
> In this life no matter how much pity and sympathy we may feel for others, it is impossible to help another as we truly wish; thus our compassion is inconsistent and limited. Only the saying of *nembutsu* manifests the complete and never ending compassion that is true, real, and sincere.[8]

3. Practice in Shin Buddhism

Traditionally, as we have noted throughout the paper, if there is any practice in Shin Buddhism, it is the *Nembutsu* as an expression of faith and gratitude. Consequently, the "practice" of Jōdo Shinshū is the recitation of the *Nembutsu* with self-reflection. It involves hearing the call of Amida Buddha, the Buddha of Eternal Life and Infinite Light, Compassion and Wisdom, within ours or others' recitation of the Name, which calls us to raise our spiritual perspectives beyond immediate ego interests to universal concerns for compassion, justice in the human community and concern for the life of Nature.

The *Nembutsu* for Shinran is not just a series of six syllables, mechanically recited. The whole of life is *Nembutsu*, a life lived in awareness, an awareness that we ourselves are the expressions, the manifestations, of interdependence and compassion and dedicated to bringing that reality to others as we have experienced it.

The *Nembutsu* is a spiritual shrine which can be transported and reverenced wherever one may be. Religious practice is not bound by time or space. Rather, from within the deep recesses of one's spirit the call of Amida Buddha can be heard, bringing our attention back to the very source of life itself and evidencing its presence in the very act of living itself.

Perhaps, some comparison can be made with Thomas a Kempis' practice of the presence of God, though for Shinran and his followers, attention is not directed to a specific, existent being, but to the whole fabric of life which declares to us the Boundless Compassion that is present in the very act of living

---

[8] *Op. cit.*, Taitetsu Unno, trans. *Tannishō: IV, 9.*

itself. When the spirit of Shinran permeates our religious understanding, any method of spiritual cultivation can be used to encourage and develop that awareness. In the West, through the influence of the Zen, Theravāda and Tibetan traditions of Buddhism, the practice of meditation has become popular a means of inner peace and tranquility.

Meditation can be used in the context of Shin Buddhism to allow the mind to settle and to focus the awareness of compassion in our lives. Likewise, the recitation and contemplation of the Name bring to clearer awareness the source of our spiritual life and meaning.

For some, the reading and chanting of *Sūtra* passages enlivens faith and strengthens commitment as the ideals of the text penetrate the consciousness. Though Shinran did not require or specify any practice other than the spontaneous recitation of the Name, if the mind is property motivated, any form of practice that would strengthen that faith could be used.

4. Shin Buddhism in Society

Shinran's interpretation of the nature of the ego and the limitations of religious practice forms the background of Shin Buddhist involvement in society. Though we cannot go into detail, there are two preliminary observations which we must make concerning the general understanding of Pure Land teaching. On the one hand, we should note that Shin Buddhism, as other forms of Buddhism and religion in general, is a pre-modern religion. As a consequence, we cannot expect direct responses to modern problem which were not envisaged in that age. While we cannot expect precise and uncompromising fixed answers to all problems, our spiritual traditions can assist in value formation and establishing priorities. Religious faith can offer perspectives and insight into the human condition which enables people to handle issues with compassion and commitment.

It is observable that Shinran does not advocate a repressive ethic-emphasizing abstention from any worldly activity simply because it is worldly. He is against calculating behavior that weighs odds and implies egocentrism. Rather, he seems to suggest an ethic of displacement in which contemplation of the Vow and the recitation of *Nembutsu* infuses an awareness of Amida's compassion within die consciousness. In this way the follower assimilates to the ideal of Amida, replacing negative forces by more positive ones within the personality. With proper associations within the community there would be positive reinforcement. Shinran recognizes that everyone has some aspiration to help others at some time. The problem in doing good is not so much in knowing the good, but in knowing how to do good. Shinran shows that when we act, as we must constantly do in the world, we must understand the true nature of those acts. Our human acts never measure up to the standard of Amida's perfect sincerity and truthfulness. However, we are not to give up doing good where we can, but recognize that the final outcome does not lie with us. Compassionate action joins with the compassionate heart of reality which we find in the depth of our own being.

The spiritual orientation of Shin Buddhism places a high value on the person. As the passage quoted earlier indicates, Shin Buddhism is fully egalitarian. Shinran constantly sought the welfare of die individual, as well as society as a whole. He also emphasized the responsibility of the person to make decisions based on the awareness that one is obligated to a higher order, symbolized by the compassion and wisdom of the Primal Vow. He rejected the arbitrary application of power, blind to both justice and compassion. Further, while Shinran is aware of the limitations of human actions to achieve ultimate resolution of problems, he does not advocate in-action or passivity. We must act, but act without egoistic expectations. In effect, we must live and act in the world with hopes but no expectations. We must have commitments but no demands that people merely conform to our desires.

In the context of faith emphasis is more on sharing insight rather than seeking domination or conformity to one's viewpoint. One will be more cognizant of the broad range of individual needs and circumstances. In effect all social issues would be approached with a sensitivity to the needs of all participants in the problem. Though problems may be complex with diverse contending constituencies, a compassionate search for truth and justice requires thoughtful-ness, openness, flexibility, and reciprocity.

On the other hand, within the modern context the Pure Land tradition with its apparent other-worldliness has frequently provided critics of religion with a good example of the irrelevance of Buddhism. Though Pure Land Buddhism has been frequently criticized as otherworldly or socially passive, its teachings have implications which can be applied socially. The foundational story of the creation of the Pure Land by Dharmākara Bodhisattva narrated in the Larger Pure Land Sūtra implies a judgment on the character of life in this world. The ancient king, surveying the mass of suffering in the world, renounces his throne to devote himself to the establishment of an ideal world where all forms of suffering would be abolished.

What is socially significant in this story is that the king abdicates his throne and recognizes that political power alone is not sufficient to bring meaning and salvation to all beings. Through this story, the self-sacrificing altruism of Mahāyāna Buddhism is clearly depicted, together with a social awareness that the highest endeavor is to establish ideal conditions for the happiness and welfare of all beings.

The Pure Land, though beyond this world, also recognizes the importance of the environment in fulfilling ideals. The Pure Land represents the ideal context for realizing enlightenment. The activities of the Bodhisattva in establishing ideal conditions for enlightenment provides a model for modern people to labor to improve the social environment so that all people may have opportunity to realize their potentials. It could also be applied to ecological thinking, motivating efforts for a more healthy physical environment.

When we survey the Pure Land tradition, we see that it is inspired by an ever-expanding vision of Amida's compassion. It embodies a humane idealism which neither discriminates nor rejects any person. It aims to motivate everyone to seek the highest good of others as the goal of their own progress toward Buddhahood. Shinran caught the spirit of Pure Land teaching, and it inspired him in his mission to communicate Amida's compassion to the masses in Eastern Japan where he settled after exile. Further, the struggles of later Shin Buddhism against the lords of medieval Japan show that such faith may not always be passive, weak in spirit, or incapable of taking a stand.

Shinran's thought is more oriented to living in this world rather than simply hoping to go to a better world beyond. He was deeply concerned with the actions of his followers and their attitudes toward others. In his own case, he deplored the lack of due process that brought about his exile. He exhorted his followers, however, to be good citizens. In spite of persecution, which Pure Land followers experienced, they were to have compassion on their enemies and to recite the *Nembutsu*, aspiring for the welfare of die country. Shinran states[9]:

> After all, not you alone, but all who live in the *Nembutsu* should say it be it not for your own good, but for the good of the general public and the nation: and this will be good. One not sure of one's own birth in the Pure Land may well say it first for that sake. But one firmly established in faith for birth in the Pure Land should think well of the great obligation one owes the Buddha and say the *Nembutsu*, as of thanksgiving, from the depths of heart praying for the peace of the world and for the dissemination of the teaching of the Buddha.

Further he wrote: "Those who live in the *Nembutsu* should have pity on and sympathy with those who work out troubles; they should say the *Nembutsu* all so truly and pray for the good of such persons."[10] We are not to harbor hatred and prejudice for those who oppose us. He indicated that recitation of the name with reflection transforms out heart/minds. Our attitudes become mild, overcoming hatred and prejudice. He writes:

> You should know that this *shinjin* is bestowed through the compassionate means of Śākyamuni , Amida and all the Buddhas in the quarters. Therefore you should not disparage the teachings of other Buddhas or the people who perform acts other than *nembutsu*. Neither should you despise those who scorn and slander people of *nembutsu*; rather you should have compassion and care for them. This was Honen's teaching.[11]

---

9 Yamamoto Kōshō, *The Private Letters of Shinran Shōnin* (Tokyo: Okazakiya Shoten, 1956), 59.

10 *Ibid.,* 65. Also, 68.

11 Ueda Yoshifumi, ed., *Letters of Shinran* (Kyoto: Hongwanji International Center, 1978), 25.

> Signs of long years of saying the *nembutsu* and aspiring for birth can be seen in the change in heart which had been bad and in deep warmth for friends and fellow-practitioners; this is the sign of rejecting the world....[12]

Also,

> When, upon hearing this (the Primal Vow, author), a person's trust in the Buddha has grown deep, he comes to abhor such a self and to lament his continued existence in birth-and death; and he then joyfully says the Name of Amida Buddha deeply entrusting himself to the Vow. That he seeks to stop doing wrong as his heart moves him....[13]

For Shinran rejection of the world did not mean to enter monastic life as taught in the traditional Buddhism of his age in the manner of renunciation. Rather, in his view it was to undergo a personal transformation in the normal course of life and manifesting itself in one's human relations.

Further, the Primal Vow is the reality of life, symbolizing the interdependence which makes life possible. The Vow pledges that when the Bodhisattva becomes Buddha, if all beings do not share in that attainment with him, he would not accept enlightenment for himself Salvation, like freedom, is indivisible.

Shinran's understanding of the unconditional, all-inclusive vision of Amida's compassion which illuminated his own passion-ridden ego provides a basis for the contribution of Shin Buddhism to contemporary social dialogue. Through a combination of deep awareness of the working of the Vow within our own lives and a competent, informed grasp of the problems of out world, we can join with others in common struggle to secure the welfare of all beings. Despite our limited and seemingly petty individual efforts, we may perceive the Great Compassion at work in our world and lives, thereby gaining a deeper sense of life-meaning in an otherwise absurd world of despair. In such a context religious faith enables us to retain our sense of human worth, despite the dehumanization that challenges and undermines our most cherished values.

5. Conclusion

Despite the distinctiveness of Shinran's approach to religious practice, he never condemned other religious paths. His teaching emerged from his own experience When people questioned him, he would state his position and declare that it is up to you to decide for yourself. Though he took a different approach to spiritual discipline, he was not dogmatic or combative. Such attitudes would be contradictory to his understanding that, in the ultimate sense,

---

[12] *Ibid.*, 58.
[13] *Ibid.*, 61.

all beings will realize the truth of Boundless Compassion in following their own life process. Shinran was not prescriptive for others, but simply professed what was true for his life.

Within Shinran's historical context though, he sharply distinguished his teaching and its implications from other forms of Buddhism, and, by extension, to all religion, our modern, pluralistic situation requires that we consider the teaching as broadly applicable to the wider religious world, sensitizing ourselves to the problems of the self and religion.

Shinran offers an insight into the distortions that afflict religion when it is used as a cloak for the ego, particularly in its institutional forms, or in the attempt to intimidate or exert total control over others. It is because of this problem that religion has very frequently been part of the problem of humanity rather than its solution. For Shinran and his followers when there is vigilance and insight into the ego, religion can become an instrument of peace.

With this awareness, Shinran's perspective is a healthy corrective to religious pretensions and assertions. I believe that Shinran would have agreed with the Bible that it is out of the heart that all issues emerge, with St. Francis who prayed for peace and that it should begin with oneself, as well as with the Great Learning text of Chinese Confucianism which teaches that peace in the world begins with oneself, extends through society to the world and then back to oneself. The foundation of peace lies in the human heart and mind of the person ultimately. Spiritual discipline for peace means, therefore, coming to grips with the self, seeing its connection to a greater reality, and its responsibility to others. Only in this way can future holocausts be avoided.

Photo 1: Group photo of contributors taken in front of the main hall at the Korean Buddhist Dae Won Sa Temple of Hawaii

Photo 2: Taken at the Residence of Governor Ben Kayetano of the State of Hawaii, who welcomed the participants of the 7th International Seminar on Buddhism and Leadership for Peace with dinner and his welcoming address.

INDEX

CONTRIBUTORS

Dr. **A. T. Ariyaratne**, President, Sarvodaya Sramadana Movement, Sri Lanka

Prof. **Nona R. Bolin**, Department of Art and Sciences, Memphis College of Art

Prof. **George Bond**, Department of Religion, Northwestern University

Professor Emeritus **Alfred Bloom**, Department of Religion, University of Hawaii – Manoa.

Prof. **Ronald Burr**, Department of Philosophy and Religion, University of Southern Mississippi

Prof. **David Chappell**, Department Religion, University of Hawaii – Manoa

Prof. **Byung-jo Chung**, Department of Ethics, College of Liberal Arts, Dongguk University, ROK

Dr. **Lance Cousins**, former Senior Lecturer in Comparative Religion, University of Mancaster, UK

Prof. **Lily de Silva**, Department of Buddhist Studies, University of Peradeniya, Sri Lanka

Prof. **Padmal de Silva**, Institute of Psychiatry, UK

Prof. **S. N. Dube**, Department of History and Indian Culture, University of Rajasthan, India

Prof. **Meenakshi Gopinath**, Principal, Lady Shri Ram College, University of Delhi, India

Dr. **Ronald S. Green**, Editor of Blue Pine, Honolulu, Hawaii

Dr. **Ian Charles Harris**, Senior Lecturer, S. Martin's College, UK

Dr. **Peter Harvey**, Reader in Buddhist Studies, School of Social and International Studies, University of Sunderland, UK

Prof. **Steve Heine**, Department of Religion, Pennsylvania State University

Prof. **Arthur Herman**, Department of Philosophy, University of Wisconsin – Stevens Point

Prof. **Woo-sung Huh**, Department of Philosophy, Kyung Hee University, ROK

Prof. **David Kalupahana**, Department of Philosophy, University of Hawaii – Manoa

Prof. **Leslie Kawamura**, Department of Religious Studies, University of Calgary, Canada

Prof. **Sallie B. King**, Department of Philosophy and Religion, James Madison University

Dr. **Stewart McFarlane**, Department of Religious Studies, Lancaster University, UK

Ven. Dr. **Chanju Mun** (Ordination Name: Seongwon), Department of Religious Studies, University of the West

Prof. **Sanath Nanayakkara**, Deputy Editor, Encyclopedia of Buddhism, Sri Lanka

Prof. **P. D. Premasiri**, Department of Philosophy, University of Peradeniya

Dr. **Daniel E. Ponce**, Department of Psychiatry, School of Medicine, University of Hawaii – Manoa

Dr. **Suwanna Satha-Anand**, Lecturer, Department of Philosophy, Chulalongkorn University, Thailand

Prof. **Jae-ryong Shim**, Department of Philosophy, Seoul National University, ROK

Prof. **Fumihiko Sueki**, Department of Indian Philosophy, University of Tokyo, Japan

Prof. **Donald Swearer**, Department of Religion, Swarthmore College

Prof. **K. N. Upadhyaya**, Forensic Science Laboratory, Government of Vihar, India

Dr. **Kwan Kah Yee**, Vice President, Singapore Buddha Yana Organization, Singapore

Prof. **Robert Zeuschner**, Department of Philosophy, Pasadena City College

Editor

Ven. **Chanju Mun** (Ordination Name: Seongwon) is the founder and chief editor of Blue Pine Books and is currently teaching East Asian Buddhist Studies at the University of the West in Los Angeles. He is also assigned to lead the International Seminar on Buddhism and Leadership for Peace, initiated in 1983 by Ven. Daewon Ki, founder of Dae Won Sa Buddhist Temple of Hawaii, the largest Korean temple in North America and Dr. Glenn D. Paige, founder of non-violence (non-killing) political science and professor emeritus of political science at the University of Hawaii – Manoa.

The editor received a Ph.D. in Buddhist Studies from the University of Wisconsin – Madison in 2002 and a Master's Degree in Philosophy from Seoul National University in 1991. He has been a researcher at exiled Tibetan Drepung Monastic University in South India and at the University of Tokyo.

His recent publications are as follows: *Buddhist Exploration of Peace and Justice* (Honolulu, Hawaii: Blue Pine, 2006), *The History of Doctrinal Classification in Chinese Buddhism: A Study of the* Panjiao *Systems* (Lanham, Maryland: University Press of America, 2006), "Tibetan Monastic Education Curriculum and its Theoretical Background" (*Buddhist Soteriology*, 2005), "Wonhyo (617-686): A Critic of Sectarian Doctrinal Classifications" (*Hsi Lai Journal of Humanistic Buddhism* 6, 2005), "Historical Introduction to Minjung Buddhism (Korean Liberation Buddhism)" (*Kankoku bukkyō semina* – 9, 2003) and others.

His forthcoming publications are as follows: "Korean Buddhism and the Formation of Japanese Buddhism" (*Journal of Korean Buddhist Research Institute* 44, 2006); "Imperialism and Temple Properties: A Case Study of Korean Buddhism during Japan's Occupation Period (1910-45)" (*Hsi Lai Journal of Humanistic Buddhism* 7, 2006); and "Dharmadhātuvāgīśvara-maṇḍala" (*Journal of Buddhist Textual Studies* 9, 2005; 10, 2006), *Peace-making in Buddhist Contexts* (Honolulu, Hawaii: Blue Pine, 2007) and others.